connect
College Reading

Ivan G. Dole
North Lake College

Leslie Taggart

WADSWORTH
CENGAGE Learning

Australia • Brazil • Japan • Korea • Mexico • Singapore • Spain • United Kingdom • United States

Connect: College Reading
Dole/Taggart

Publisher: Lyn Uhl

Director of Developmental English:
Annie Todd

Development Editor: Marita Sermolins

Assistant Editor: Janine Tangney

Editorial Assistant: Melanie Opacki

Associate Media Editor: Emily Ryan

Marketing Manager: Kirsten Stoller

Marketing Assistant: Ryan Ahern

Marketing Communications Manager:
Jean Thompson

Content Project Manager: Jessica Rasile

Art Director: Marissa Falco

Print Buyer: Sue Carroll

Text Permissions Manager: Roberta Broyer

Text Permissions Researcher: Sarah D'Stair

Production Service/Compositor: Lachina
Publishing Services, Inc.

Text Designer: Thompson Steele, Inc.

Photo Manager: Don Schlotman

Photo Researcher: Jill Engebretson

Cover Designer: Nancy Goulet

Cover Images: Beginning with stack of
magazines and continuing clockwise:
©Nancy Goulet, ©ArchMan
/Shutterstock, ©Shutterstock,
©Lorenzo Mondo/Shutterstock,
©Photos.com, ©Photos.com,
©Lim Yong Hian/Shutterstock

For product information and technology assistance, contact us at
Cengage Learning Academic Resource Center, 1-800-423-0563
For permission to use material from this text or product, submit all requests online at **www.cengage.com/permissions**.
Further permissions questions can be e-mailed to
permissionrequest@cengage.com.

Library of Congress Control Number: 2008943181

Student Edition:
ISBN-13: 978-1-4130-3316-8
ISBN-10: 1-4130-3316-4

Wadsworth
20 Channel Center Street
Boston, MA 02210
USA

Cengage Learning products are represented in Canada by Nelson Education, Ltd.

For your course and learning solutions, visit **www.cengage.com**.

Purchase any of our products at your local college store or at our preferred online store **www.ichapters.com**.

Printed in Canada
2 3 4 5 6 7 12 11 10 09

comprehension
is the destination

prior knowledge
is the vehicle

connect

will get you there

connect with college reading

Dear Student,

Welcome to *Connect: College Reading!* In this textbook, we provide you with everything we can to help you fulfill your goal, which is also our goal: We want you to succeed in this college-level reading course so that you will build the strong academic foundation you will need in all your future college courses.

So where can you begin to create success in your college reading course? The title of this book is our answer: The place to start to build your success is right where you are. If you **connect** with the inner strengths, abilities, and knowledge that you have developed over a lifetime of learning and experience, and if you **connect** that experience with the new ideas you are exposed to when you read, you have set out on the road to success.

Some students approaching the college reading course may think, "I really don't read much. I usually watch more TV." That is true of many students. We think that you have learned a lot more than you probably realize from watching TV. That's why in Chapter 1, we ask you to share your prior knowledge and to learn from your experiences of watching TV (or movies). In this first chapter, we ask you to connect what you have learned during the process of watching TV to the process of reading. Later, throughout the book, we continue to ask you to share your prior knowledge, even as you are building new knowledge.

Another thing to realize about becoming a successful college reader is that reading is an interaction between two people—the author and **you**. In *Connect*, we teach you effective reading strategies and then give you repeated opportunities to practice them. To become skilled at anything, **you must practice**—whether it is training to compete in the Olympics for a medal, learning to ride a unicycle for fun, or becoming a proficient reader so you can reach your academic and professional goals. **You** can ensure your progress by taking advantage of every reading opportunity. Also, check out "Plan for Success: A Course Preview" on pages xxv–xxxiv, especially the section on "Investigating What Makes Students Successful" on page xxxii.

On your road to successful college reading, you can think of the main purpose for reading as comprehension—that is, understanding what you read. If comprehension is your destination, then your prior knowledge (what you already know) is the vehicle. The more you read, the more you know. As on any journey, if you have a plan or a map, you'll reach your destination sooner. One plan for reading that you will find in *Connect* is called MAPPS. It's outlined in Chapter 4. Using MAPPS to structure your reading will aid your comprehension as you locate the topic, main idea, and supporting details. Understanding the key concepts of a reading will help you summarize those ideas in your own words, so you can do better on tests, papers, discussions, and projects.

Connect: College Reading is not just a book to read. You should also take advantage of the resources on the book Web site at **www.cengage.com/devenglish/ doleconnect**. Here are some of the resources you'll find there:

- **Video on related subjects.** For every major reading in the book—the Prep Reading at the beginning of each chapter and the two readings at the end—there is a video on a related topic, with a question that asks you to connect the video and the reading selection. A main purpose of a college education is to learn to connect information from diverse sources and thus create new ideas of your own. Here's your first chance!

- **Audio vocabulary.** Again for every major reading selection, there are audio files that include all the vocabulary words. Each word is spoken out loud so you can hear it being used. Take advantage of this feature so you can increase your speaking vocabulary. In the book's reading selections, the vocabulary words are in red and blue type.

- **Audio Prep readings.** For Prep Readings, which are the first selection in each chapter, you'll find an audio file of a person reading the selection out loud. You can use this audio as a reminder of what the reading says, as a way to hear the words spoken, or just as an additional method for making sure you understand the Prep Reading.

Reading is an amazingly powerful tool for learning about the world and opening up new opportunities—at school, at home, and at work. But we want to emphasize it is the beginning point. **You also need to think about what you read.** When you think about ideas you are reading, talk about ideas, hear other students' ideas, and explain your responses to questions about ideas, you will be able to fully participate in your other college courses. As philosopher George J. Seidel has written, "The ability to relate and to connect, . . . lies at the very heart of any creative use of the mind, no matter in what field or discipline."

We hope that after you have used this book, you will connect with us to tell us about your reading and thinking experiences and give us feedback about how well *Connect* worked for you. Please e-mail us at **Wadsworth.Connect@cengage.com**. We'd love to hear from you!

Ivan G. Dole   *Leslie Taggart*

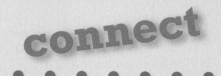
The reading class may be the first college course you take. **Connect** transitions you from high school or the work force by asking you to take stock of the skills you bring to class and by introducing you to strategies you can use to master college reading.

Connect builds confidence **by starting with what you know.** Chapter 1 starts with skills you have gained from the practice of watching TV and movies, putting core reading concepts and processes in terms that you already engage while watching TV or movies. Viewing and reading are both shown to be interactions that depend on the reader's (or viewer's) input as well as that of the text (or program).

Connect provides powerful vocabulary instruction **for academic and life success.** Chapter 3 introduces the four main context clues using the mnemonic "**EASY**"—**e**xamples, **a**ntonyms, **s**ynonyms, and **y**our logic (or inference). Readings extend this lesson by including marginal vocabulary prompts that draw your attention to specific context clues, helping you build strategies that practiced readers use all the time.

Interaction 3-1. Talking about Reading

For each sentence below, respond in writing to the following questi[ons.] [Compare] your answers with your classmates.

- What are the differences between the two words that are spelled [the same?]
- What clues help you decide what each word means?
- Can you identify the part of speech of each word?

1. We must *polish* the *Polish* furniture. _____

See page 101.

inextricable Use the "chicken and egg" example to decide what *inextricable* means.

[...] or vice versa is like asking which came fir[st.] Language and culture are **inextricable**. E[ither] to understand either, we must know som[ething] 1997; Hill and Mannheim 1992).

Vocabulary in Context

The following words were used in "Does Language Shape Culture?" Select the best word to complete the meaning of each sentence.

inextricable	determines	9 to 5	conceptualize	arbitrary

1. Many times, your effort in school _____ the grade you receive.

2. _____ your future and see yourself successful in your career and happy in your life.

See page 142 & 148.

- **Transfer new words to writing.** *Vocabulary in Context* gives you the opportunity to transfer a newly learned word into to practice.

- **Transfer written vocabulary to speaking vocabulary.** At the book Web site, you can find audio files of all the vocabulary words to move words into their speaking vocabularies and be sure you can pronounce new words correctly.

EMPOWERS YOU.

Connect gives you MAPPS to navigate text structure. Just as travelers consult maps to inform their journeys, readers can use **MAPPS** to:

→ **M**ark the reading as you decide what a reading is
→ **A**bout (its topic),
→ what its **P**oint is (main idea),
→ and what its **P**roof is (supporting details).

You can summarize readings by putting together these ideas in your own words. Chapter 4 on paragraph structure teaches MAPPS as an easy-to-remember strategy for navigating a paragraph or longer passage.

Figure 4.1
MAPPS, a Reading Strategy

Mark the answers to your questions = Mark what the reading is abou its point, and its proof.
About = Topic: What is the reading about?
Point = Main Idea: What is the point of the reading?
Proof = Supporting Detail: What is the proof? There are two kinds of proof or details: major and minor.
Summary = A synthesis of About (topic), Point (main idea), and Pr (supporting detail).

See page 155.

Connect gives you extensive help and practice with basic comprehension skills. All the end-of-chapter readings—24 in all—provide not only after-reading comprehension questions but also before- and during-reading questions to keep your attention focused on main ideas.

● **Reading Journal** *questions in the margins.* To get you to internalize the process of understanding the main points of each paragraph, *Reading Journal* prompts you to respond and annotate as you move through a reading.

◆ *Reading Journal*

◆Why does Mr. Paquette need Rainbow?
He lost his feet and legs in the war in Afghanistan.

● *Comprehension tested in five areas:* **main idea; supporting details; author's purpose; relationships; and fact, opinion, and inference.** To practice, you are given an explanation of each skill and an example question and answer as a model to follow in Chapter 1. You then answer a question on your own in each category to give you a means of checking your comprehension and be better prepared for future chapters.

● **Comprehension Questions**

Write the letter of the answer on the line. Then explain your thi

Main Idea

__c__ 1. What is the best statement of the main idea of paragraph
a. Mr. Paquette should be recognized for his service to hi

See page 77 & 80.

Connections between college reading and other college courses are made throughout the text so that you understand the importance of reading to your futures.

Connect builds cultural literacy. Readings, as well as paragraph-length examples, have been selected to introduce you to a wide range of ideas, disciplines, and current events. Many of these texts are excerpted from college textbooks in the fields of world history, biology, sociology, mathematics, anthropology, media studies, literature, art history, business, social work, American government, and so on. Many of the longer readings discuss important current events, such as the effects of the Iraq War on a veteran, the influence of television in Afghanistan and in the United States, and the danger of piracy on the high seas.

● **"Common Knowledge" boxes define concepts needed to understand readings.** "Common knowledge" can be defined as prior knowledge that many members of a culture share. Authors don't bother to define concepts they consider common knowledge, and yet you may not grasp the meaning of these terms clearly enough to understand what you read. Where needed, a few common knowledge terms are defined for you ahead of time so that you can understand the reading, but also be prepared to understand the concept before you reach your first-year composition courses.

Anthropology Textbook

...opology.
...nd in all
...ed.

...gage.com/devenglish/doleconnect and select Chapter 2 to hear
...rds from this selection and view a video about this topic.

Language and the Intellectual Abilities of Orangutans
Adapted from H. Lyn Miles

...urpose is

...n 1978, after researchers began to use American Sign Languag...
...he deaf to communicate with chimpanzees and gorillas, I bega...
...irst long-term study of the language ability of an orangutan na...

See page 85 & 86.

Common Knowledge

Conflict in Afghanistan (*paragraph 1*) The war initiated by the United Stat...
September 11, 2001, attacks in New York and Washington, D.C., intended...
ruling party in Afghanistan—the Taliban—from power.

Veterans Administration (*paragraph 4*) The U.S. government department r...
providing benefits (such as medical and educational benefits) to military p...
families.

See page 77.

is RELEVANT.

Connect teaches, practices, and requires critical thinking. Critical thinking, emphasized in every chapter, is required of you to succeed in your college courses, in your personal lives, and at work.

- **You will use a widely known system—Bloom's taxonomy—as a scaffold to understand what you read more deeply.** The levels of thinking are to remember, understand, apply, analyze, evaluate, and create.

- **You are asked to explain your thinking.** Every multiple-choice comprehension question is followed by the question "Why? What information in the selection leads you to give that answer?" You analyze the decisions you made and explain your reasoning. Used systematically, these questions can point to patterns of errors you are making, helping the instructor to gauge whether further instruction is needed.

- **Critical thinking questions lead you up the Bloom's taxonomy of thought processes.** Using a variety of verbs so you learn to link particular verbs with particular types of thinking, these questions help you in your other classes as you take essay exams that ask these questions.

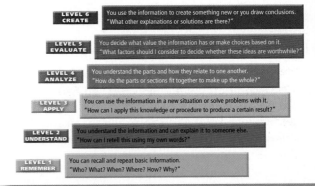

LEVEL 6 CREATE — You use the information to create something new or you draw conclusions. "What other explanations or solutions are there?"

LEVEL 5 EVALUATE — You decide what value the information has or make choices based on it. "What factors should I consider to decide whether these ideas are worthwhile?"

LEVEL 4 ANALYZE — You understand the parts and how they relate to one another. "How do the parts or sections fit together to make up the whole?"

LEVEL 3 APPLY — You can use the information in a new situation or solve problems with it. "How can I apply this knowledge or procedure to produce a certain result?"

LEVEL 2 UNDERSTAND — You understand the information and can explain it to someone else. "How can I retell this using my own words?"

LEVEL 1 REMEMBER — You can recall and repeat basic information. "Who? What? When? Where? How? Why?"

CRITICAL THINKING LEVEL 5 EVALUATE

Judge how much the opening quotation from the *Legally Blond* character Elle contributes to the main idea of this reading selection. Answers will vary, but may includ quotation includes an example of a fashion shift (pink to orange), and thus makes at least a modest contri

See page 66.

connect

You live in a stimulating multimedia world of movies, television, computer games, MP3 players, and Internet, and so it may be no wonder that a flat page of unmoving text seems unexciting. In addition, students all have marked differences in learning styles that may affect how they take in information most readily. The Web site that accompanies Connect (www.cengage.com/devreading/doleconnect) offers multimedia connections to the three main readings in each chapter, and the book itself includes numerous activities designed for auditory, visual, and kinesthetic learners.

Connect acknowledges students' diverse learning styles online at www.cengage.com/devreading/doleconnect:

- **Videos on related topics accompany readings.**

  Visit www.cengage.com/devenglish/doleconnect and select Chapter 6 to hear a reading of this selection and view a video about this topic.

  See page 272.

  Videos are presented on related topics and act as examples of ideas mentioned in readings or provide another perspective for you to consider. Each video is connected to the reading via a question you will find on the book Web site. Reading 1-2 is a sociology reading on popular culture and the media; the accompanying video is on comic book art. You are asked how the information on comic book art exemplifies the ideas in the reading selection.

- **Audio files of Prep Readings.** You can listen to Prep Readings as well as read them. These audio files benefit students who have auditory preferences and ESL students, but they can also be used by all students who want to give themselves another way to understand the readings that begin chapters.

MOTIVATES YOU.

● **Audio vocabulary files.** All the vocabulary words are pronounced in the related audio files online. This helps you feel comfortable making new words part of your spoken vocabulary, and it aids ESL students who will benefit from hearing words repeatedly to anchor them in memory.

Connect acknowledges students' diverse learning styles in the textbook.

● **Creative responses.** Although you get plenty of practice responding to readings by writing, occasionally you are asked for responses in other modalities.

Interaction 1-2 begins by asking for a written response but then asks you what tune you would set your words to, and what image you might pair with your words.

> ● **Interaction 1-2. Talking about Reading**
>
> Respond in writing to the questions below and then discuss classmates.
>
> 1. If you were asked to describe your week in three words, wha use?

See page 10.

● **Collaborative work.** Throughout the book are opportunities for you to work in groups or in whole-class settings. The questions after each Prep Reading can be used for a discussion with the entire class, or groups can talk about ideas based on the reading. Critical-thinking questions after the end-of-chapter readings—especially the highest-level "Create" questions—often call for or lend themselves to group work.

> **CRITICAL THINKING LEVEL 6 CREATE**
>
> Professor Miles notes in her 2004 update that Chantek co-creates songs with her band Animal Nation. Miles says elsewhere, "He plays notes on the keyboard, and we write songs around his efforts. He also keeps the beat" (Emily Sohn, "An Inspiring Home for Apes," *Science News for Kids*). *Compose* a song in a different way. Review the ways that Chantek puts words together, and the kinds of words he uses. Then create a short song using words in a similar way. Put your song to a beat.

See page 96.

Supplements

Instructor's Manual with Test Bank

Written by instructors who served on the advisory board that guided *Connect: College Reading* through development, this three-hole punched and perforated Instructor's Manual includes chapter summaries and various activities designed especially for every section of every chapter of the book, offering instructors a wealth of resources from which to choose, tutoring suggestions, lab activities and discussion, and multiple test banks for each chapter.

Online Resource Center

This Web Site offers an array of online resources for students, including downloadable Audio Prep Readings taken directly from the text, Web links to additional resources, vocabulary-building flashcards and audio pronunciations, reading quizzes, the Plagiarism Prevention Zone, exercises for practicing reading, a reading survey, videos related to the readings in each chapter, and discussion questions that integrate readings from the text. The videos give students the prior knowledge they might be lacking and increase their cultural literacy.

Aplia Developmental Reading

Aplia Developmental Reading, an online reading and learning solution, uses compelling material, interactive assignments, and detailed explanations to give students the structure and motivation to become better readers. With Aplia, students practice indentifying main points and supporting details, honing critical thinking skills, reviewing vocabulary, and improving comprehension.

Each chapter assignment begins with an engagement page that features an interactive multimedia application to spark students' interest. The engagement page also includes a quote, introduction to the chapter, and comprehension questions that correspond to the multimedia feature.

Core concepts covers the main objectives of the textbook, such as strategies to increase a student's reading comprehension, surveying and identifying the purpose, main idea and supporting details of a reading, and identifying word parts such as suffixes and prefixes. The material uses multiple choice, check box, scenario, identification, and comprehension questions.

Compelling readings provide questions of varying difficulty with detailed explanations that let students try a problem again if they get it wrong the first time. Students can also interact with the text by using built-in tools that allow them to annotate, underline, and highlight.

The in-text vocabulary review uses ten new and challenging words taken from the readings and reviews. The page also includes review of the synonyms and antonyms of each vocabulary word.

To learn more about Aplia Developmental Reading, visit **www.aplia.com/devreading**.

Acknowledgments

All textbooks represent the creativity and effort of many people working together, and this one is no exception. The outstanding team at Wadsworth has been a pleasure to work with, from Michael Rosenberg, who first suggested the project, to Marita Sermolins, who helped develop it. Thank you, Marita, for all the help you have given us. Annie Todd, Director of Developmental English, introduced us to each other and kept us going through two years of hard labor with her high energy and good-natured leadership. Marketing Manager Kirsten Stoller first had the idea for the cover, which we think is fantastic, and Emily Ryan, Associate Media Editor, made the book's Web site sing (all right, talk). Jessica Rasile, Content Project Manager, swiftly and ably directed the production process. Senior Publisher Lyn Uhl and Editor-in-Chief PJ Boardman have supported and encouraged us throughout the entire book-making process—thanks to you both for sharing your expertise and your confidence that the project will succeed.

We spent hours and hours talking with the members of the national Advisory Panel and hearing their ideas about developmental readers and reading. Each brings a rich history of teaching and mentoring developmental students. Thanks to you, Amy Garcia of Fullerton College, Lois Hassan of Henry Ford Community College, Yvette Myrick of the Community College of Baltimore County, and Jeffrey Siddall of the College of DuPage. Lyam Christopher of Palm Beach Community College and Suzette Schlapkohl of Scottsdale Community College also brought their expertise as, respectively, reading tutor and reading instructor to the table. To these remarkable educators: thank you. We couldn't possibly have done it without you.

As if these contributions weren't enough, Lyam Christopher and Yvette Myrick are also writing the Instructor's Manual to accompany the book. A more creative group we've never seen! We know their work is going to give instructors lots of new ideas for classroom activities, tutoring strategies, and additional commentary on teaching with the book. Thank you, Yvette and Lyam. We respect the many ways you help your students succeed.

We also enjoyed collaborating on paper with the following instructors from around the country who reviewed the manuscript and helped direct its evolution. Thank you for your careful reading, your critiques, and your honesty. We appreciate your time and your thoughts.

Cathryn Amdahl, Harrisburg Area Community College
Natalie Amiama, Interboro Institute
Andrea Berta, The University of Texas at El Paso
Diana Blauvelt, Passaic County Community College
Tim Brown, Riverside Community College
Helen Carr, San Antonio College
Nandan Choksi, American InterContinental University
Marlys Córdoba, College of the Siskiyous
Frank Crayton, Palo Alto College
David Elias, Eastern Kentucky University
Margaret Fox, Oregon State University
Maureen Fry, Riverside Community College

Richard Gair, Valencia Community College

Wendy Grace, Holmes Community College

Robin Greenberg, Central New Mexico Community College

Geri Gutwein, Harrisburg Area Community College

Karen Harrel, Tarrant County College, Northeast Campus

Valerie Hicks, Community College of Baltimore County, Essex

Patricia L. Hill-Miller, Central Piedmont Community College

Donna Johnson, Volunteer State Community College

Pete Kinnas, San Juan College

Amber Kinonen, Northern Michigan University

Evelyn Koperwas, Broward Community College

Jim Lambrinos, El Paso Community College, Valle Verde

Nora Lawson, Volunteer State Community College

Natalie McLellan, Holmes Community College

Gladys Montalvo, Palm Beach Community College

Sandy Nelson, San Juan College

Susan Nelson, Broward Community College

Lori Ogata-Keeler, Riverside Community College

Sandra Padilla, El Paso Community College, Valle Verde

Sandra L. Peck, El Paso Community College, Valle Verde

Sue Phillips, Rogue Community College

Hattie Pinckney, Florence-Darlington Technical College

Loretta Rodgers, Eastfield College

Jamie Sadler, Richmond Community College

Margaret J. Shaw, Nassau County Community College

Katie Smith, Riverside Community College

Shari Waldrop, Navarro College

In addition, Leslie would like to thank Ivan for his dedication to this project and for getting our collaboration off to a proper start by intoning those famous words of Albert-Laszlo Barabasi: "Everything is connected to everything else." Ivan's creative ideas and connection with his students have been constant sources of inspiration. And I'd like to thank my husband Chuck King for his love and his lasagna. To Sara, Harmony, and Phoenix—nothing would be worth doing if you weren't here. I'm glad you are.

Ivan would like to thank Leslie for her "constancy of purpose," which Benjamin Disraeli said is the secret of success. Leslie's insight, clarity, creativity, and enthusiasm are infectious. Ivan appreciates Leslie's willingness for working with this neophyte author. I would like to thank my wife, Denee' Dole, for her patience and grace under neglect. To my twin daughters—Bella and Lilli—double the trouble but quadruple the fun. And I would be remiss if I did not express my gratitude to my parents for instilling within me a love of words. I love you all. Thank you for loving me back.

Brief Contents

Contents

PART 2 Reading to Understand

Chapter 10 Analyzing the Author's Tone   475

Chapter 11 Evaluating the Author's Reasoning and Evidence   521

introduction

Plan for Success:
A Course Preview

> " *For success, attitude is equally as important as ability.* "
>
> —Harry F. Banks

To be successful in college, learn as much as you can at the beginning of each course.

- *Learn about the topics* that the class will cover, as well as the schedule of assignments and the rules of the class. This information can all be found in the course *syllabus* and perhaps the *class schedule* or *class calendar,* which your instructor will give you.
- *Preview your textbook.* As you will learn in this book, previewing is an important part of reading any complicated or lengthy reading material. Previewing your textbook gives you an overview of the material it covers and the features it has.
- *Investigate what it takes to be a successful student.* Being a successful student is like running a marathon: you need strategies that will help you keep going and keep learning. Later you will read ten tips that investigate what makes a successful student (page xxxii). As you read them, think about how you can use them so that you, too, will be a successful student.

Reading Your Syllabus and Class Schedule

Your instructor will hand out a syllabus for your course, typically during the first or second class meeting. When you get it, scan the headings to see what kinds of information it includes. *Scanning* means looking quickly down the page at only certain parts of the text, in this case, the headings.

Interaction 1. Scanning the Headings in Your Syllabus

What headings do you find?

- _____
- _____
- _____
- _____
- _____

Course Goals or Objectives

Your syllabus may include a list of the course goals—the general and specific ideas or skills that the course is designed to teach you. Sometimes goals are listed in broad groups, such as General Goals, Specific Goals, and Transferable Skills. Other times, they are listed more specifically by individual skills. For example, here is a partial list of reading comprehension skills you could expect to find on your college reading syllabus. (*Comprehension* means "understanding.")

Develop Reading Comprehension Skills

- Find, create, and summarize main ideas in paragraphs and passages.
- Identify major and minor supporting details.
- Recognize how paragraphs are organized.
- Understand the difference between a fact and an opinion.
- "Read between the lines" through logical inference and conclusion.

Interaction 2. Comprehending the Course Goals or Objectives

Read the course objectives or goals. Listen to what your instructor has to say about them. What are three important goals of the course?

- _____

- _____

- _____

Course Policies

Syllabi (the plural for *syllabus*) often include information about course policies. For example, there may be an attendance policy, a late-work policy, a plagiarism policy, and others.

Read the course policies, and listen to what your instructor has to say about them. Restate them using your own words. This is called paraphrasing. Then compare your paraphrase with a partner's. If you and your partner don't agree what a policy means, ask your instructor to explain it again.

Interaction 3. Paraphrasing Course Policies

Course policy on _____

Paraphrase:_____

_____

_____

Course policy on _____

Paraphrase: _____

_____

_____

_____

Grading or Evaluation

Your syllabus probably includes information about how your final score for the class will be calculated. In some classes, for example, class participation may count for a certain percentage of your final grade. Tests and quizzes may be counted as certain percentages. Read any information your syllabus gives about grading and make sure you understand it.

Interaction 4. Asking Questions about Grades

Write down a question you have about grades. Ask your instructor the question, and write down the answer. Also, listen carefully to the instructor's answers when other students ask their questions.

Question:

_____

_____

_____

Answer:

_____

_____

_____

Class Schedule

The schedule of classes and class assignments may be part of the syllabus or they may be in a separate document called something like "Class Schedule," "Class Assignments," or "Class Calendar." Examine the class schedule carefully to see what kinds of information are on it. Read your class schedule and respond to the checklist in Interaction 5.

Interaction 5. Checking Information on the Class Schedule

Circle "yes" or "no" to indicate whether a certain kind of information is on your class schedule.

1. The dates of each class   Yes   No

2. The date of the midterm examination   Yes   No

3. The date of the final examination   Yes   No

4. The reading assignment for each day or each week   Yes   No

5. The dates of holidays when class will not be held   Yes   No

Write down the other kinds of information your class schedule includes.

6. _____

7. _____

8. _____

9. _____

10. _____

Interaction 6. Transferring Important Dates to Your Planner

Get a planner (a scheduling book) if you don't already have one. You will need it to keep track of your school responsibilities and other commitments. Transfer the important dates from your class schedule into your planner. For example, write down "reading midterm" and "reading final exam" on the dates these important tests will be held. As you go through the term, make it a point to look ahead in your planner regularly to make sure you remember when assignments and projects are due, when tests will be held, and so on.

Surveying Your Textbook

Survey your textbook so you will know what it includes and where to find specific kinds of information.

The Table of Contents

The table of contents provides an outline of the entire book. Look at the table of contents to get an idea of all the areas you will be studying. Sometimes a brief table of contents precedes the detailed table of contents. A brief contents typically lists just the chapter titles and any larger divisions of material. The detailed contents includes these and the headings within chapters.

◑ Interaction 7. Surveying the Brief Table of Contents

Read the brief table of contents on page xv. List the four main parts of the textbook.

Part 1: _____

Part 2: _____

Part 3: _____

Part 4: _____

◑ Interaction 8. Surveying the Detailed Table of Contents

The detailed table of contents begins on page xvii. Read the chapter title and headings in Chapter 2. Then answer the following questions.

1. What two readings are listed as the "Prep Reading"? _____

   _____

2. What topic do the Prep Readings seem to be about? _____

   _____

3. What do the Chapter 2 headings suggest is the action to take if you want to establish your purpose for reading? _____

   _____

4. What is the process recommended for doing so?

   • _____

   • _____

   • _____

5. What is another use of asking questions, according to the headings? _____

_____

Chapter Features

Textbooks typically include features in each chapter that are designed to help students understand the material.

● Interaction 9. Considering the Purpose of Features

Look at the following chapter features in Chapter 4. For each one, write one way it might be helpful to you.

1. Feature: Interaction 4-2 on page 157

   Possible use: _____

2. Feature: Chapter Summary Activity on page 185

   Possible use: _____

3. Feature: Test Taking Tips box on page 187

   Possible use: _____

4. Feature: Reading 4-1 on page 188

   Possible use: _____

The Index

Like most textbooks, this book has an index that lists all the topics that the book covers. If you want to review a topic and don't recall where it is discussed, find the topic in the index.

● Interaction 10. Using the Index

Look at the index, which starts on page 655. Find each of the following topics and note the pages on which they are discussed.

MAPPS _____

Antonyms _____

Comparison and contrast _____

What is an antonym? _____

Interaction 11. Transferring Information to Your Planner

When your instructor assigns work in the textbook, write the assignment and its due date in your planner. Each weekend, review all your assignments and decide when during the week you are going to do them. Write this information in your planner.

Investigating What Makes Students Successful

Life as a student is nothing if not busy. You are trying to balance school with all its reading and homework. Many of you are working either part- or full-time jobs. Some of you have families, perhaps even young children. The demands on you are great. However, you have enrolled in college for a purpose. You have a goal in mind. You want to earn a degree, get a better job, or maybe make more money to provide a comfortable life for you and your family. Whatever your reason, it is yours and no one else's. You have chosen to be here to improve yourself through education, and that is a noble goal.

Understand that the main purpose of school is learning. No matter how many roles you are juggling, school will demand your attention. You will have to make choices in order to be successful in school—just enrolling will not be enough. Being in school is like running a marathon. Unlike a sprinter, who races all out for a short distance, marathon runners must pace themselves so they can go the whole distance. As a student, you are signing up for a whole semester, and you must pace yourself from beginning to end in order to be successful.

We assume that each of you wants to earn an A in this and in every course you take. To help you achieve that goal, here are some strategies that you should follow in order to be successful.

1. **Believe in yourself.** Belief in yourself is not a magic formula for automatic success. However, do not underestimate the power of belief. It affects your emotions, thoughts, assumptions, and behavior.

2. **Know what motivates you.** Remember why you are here. What is your goal? What are you striving for? Keep your long- and short-term goals in mind. Reward yourself for jobs well done. They can be small rewards—a piece of your favorite dessert after you complete your homework. Or it can be the big reward—buying yourself something after you earn a good grade on a test.

3. **Be organized.** Make sure you have a folder for important documents from each of your classes. Know when assignments are due. Turn them in following the format your instructor has requested. Buy a planner. Set study times in your planner so

that you have the time to do your work. Have an organized place where you do your homework.

4. **Prioritize.** Make "to-do" lists and order them by writing a "1" for the most important items that need to be done today, a "2" for items that are important but not as urgent as the number 1's, and a "3" for things that are least urgent but still need to be done soon.

5. **Be active.** Participate actively in class. Ask questions and be prepared to discuss ideas with classmates. If you do not understand something, ask your instructor. Chances are someone else has the same question. Also be present as you are studying. Do not passively read, but actively engage your mind so you do not waste your time or energy by just going through the motions.

6. **Don't procrastinate.** Do homework the day it is assigned rather than the night before it is due. You will be a much more effective student if you study a little each day rather than try to cram it all in at the last minute. Also, when you procrastinate, you tend to have emergencies. By planning, prioritizing, and organizing, you can avoid a lot of stress because you have a game plan and are following it.

7. **Network.** Who are the people you can use to your advantage to help you in your academic success? Are your parents a good resource? Are your friends encouraging you or distracting you from school? Are you utilizing your professors? Have you identified the good students in your classes with whom you can form study groups? Do you know what resources your school offers, such as labs, advising, counseling, career services, and so forth?

8. **Keep your health in mind.** Do not underestimate the power of a good night's sleep, a healthy diet, and exercise. All of these will help you manage stress, stay focused on your studies, and keep a positive attitude.

9. **Take the initiative.** Read ahead. Ask questions. Make connections. If you are absent, come to the next class with any missed work done. Review your material a few minutes each day in order to be better prepared for class discussions, quizzes, and tests. Make the effort to talk to your professor and develop a rapport with him or her.

10. **Always do your best.** If you always do your best, then you are a success, even if you do not get the highest grade. Be honest. Do not cheat, which actually leads to failure. Treat others the way you wish to be treated, and chances are they will return the gesture.

● Interaction 12. Being a Successful Student

Discuss each of the ten items from the preceding list with a partner. Talk about how you can be a successful student this semester. Write one action that you will take for each item on the list:

1. _____

2. _____

3. _____

4. _____

5. _____

6. _____

7. _____

8. _____

9. _____

10. _____

part 1

Reading to Succeed

chapter 1

© Julien Tromeur/Shutterstock

Exploring the Reading Process

" *I find television very educating. Every time someone turns on the set, I go into the other room and read a book.* "
—Groucho Marx

What do you think about Marx's joke? Is it funny? Why or why not?

www.cengage.com/devenglish/doleconnect

Videos Related to Readings **Vocab Words on Audio** **Prep Readings on Demand**

Share Your Prior Knowledge

Is there anything you have learned from watching television that might help you read more effectively at the college level?

Survey the Chapter

Leaf through pages 11 to 20, reading only the headings. Discuss any further thoughts with your classmates.

Getting Motivated to Read

Reading is the most important skill you can develop to help you succeed in college. You will do a tremendous amount of reading in your college classes. No matter what courses you take, you will read textbooks and other materials as a primary way to gain new knowledge and to give you new perspectives on knowledge you already have. Here are just a few examples.

- To earn a degree in business management, a student reads in the fields of accounting, finance, business law, human resources, management, and marketing.
- To become an elementary school teacher, a student reads in the areas of child growth and development, classroom management, the history of education, and methods of teaching particular subjects.
- To become an engineer, a student reads textbooks in calculus, physics, and of course, the different fields of engineering such as mechanical, electronic, and civil engineering.
- To get an associate's degree in nursing, a student reads textbooks in anatomy, physiology, pharmacology, microbiology, chemistry, nutrition, and psychology.

Taking one of these classes, or any other, will involve reading the course textbook and related books and articles. To complete your degree requirements, you'll need to learn to read and understand these materials. This book will help you do that.

Motivation to Complete Your Degree: Earning More Money

Learning to read better is going to help you complete your degree program. And completing your degree program is going to help you earn more money. Look at the comparison of earnings below. In 2005, the median earnings of workers aged 25 and older looked like this:

Full-time workers with this degree . . .	Earned this much per year . . .
Professional degree	$140,551
PhD	$107,808
Master's degree	$81,281
Bachelor's degree	$67,156
Associate degree	$47,159
High school	$38,344

*U.S. Census Bureau, Current Population Survey, 2006 Annual Social and Economic Supplement.

Does every person who holds a master's degree earn exactly $81,281 a year? No. Notice the word *median* in the preceding paragraph, as in "median earnings." The word *median* means that half the people who hold master's degrees make more than this, and half make less. But you can see the trend: The more schooling you complete, the more money you're likely to make.

1. Which degree will you be completing first? _____

_____

2. For workers 25 and above who hold this degree, what is the median annual earnings?_____

3. How much do you *want* to earn? (Don't be shy!)_____

4. What do you want the money for—what do you want that earning this amount of money will get you?_____

_____

Reading is an important part of a college education for another reason, too. The more you read, the better you become at understanding other people's points of view. In turn, this understanding will help enrich your connections to other people and enhance your life by showing you all the possibilities that are available to you in the worlds of work, community, family, and personal interests.

Seeing clearly what you want to achieve will help you stay motivated. The next section shows you how.

Fast Forward to Your Future

Scientists who study the brain have made some surprising discoveries about it. One fascinating piece of knowledge they have gained is that when a person fully imagines an activity, the brain responds as though that activity were actually occurring. Olympic athletes have taken advantage of this knowledge by adding visualization practices to their workouts. Now, in addition to actually swimming, skiing, or skating for five or six hours a day, many athletes also spend several periods of time each day visualizing themselves performing these activities exactly how they want to do them—in great detail, and in living color. You can use this Olympian strategy to fine-tune your present and future so that you can get what you want out of life.

◉ Interaction 1-1. Fine-tuning Your Present and Future

1. Imagine Yourself in the Future. Imagine that five years have passed and you are now living the future exactly as you want it to be at that time. Everything is going beautifully. You feel wonderful. Now feel that good feeling fully. Take your time with this—let the good feeling build. And for each of the next questions, take your time to fine-tune the details of your answer. Imagine the details as large as life, and in living color.

- How is your health?
- Where are you living?
- What is your dating, partnership, or family situation?
- What is your work life like? How's your financial situation?
- What is a typical day like?

Imagine your life as fully as you can, in as much detail as possible. Paint a rosy picture!

Now sit down and write a postcard to the self you are today. What do you want to tell yourself? Write your current self a postcard about what you want from that person *now*.

Now step back into your current self. Read the postcard. Be sure to act on any advice you have received. Your future self has only your best interests at heart!

TO MYSELF

2. Make That Future Happen. Now that you've developed a sense for where you want to be in five years, answer this question: What can you do to make that future happen? Only list things that you yourself can do—don't include any actions that other people would have to take.

I can make this future happen by . . .

- EXAMPLE: Take classes to get my nurse practitioner degree. _____
- _____
- _____
- _____
- _____

---

3. Consider the Value of Reading. Now use your imagination to consider the value of reading more effectively. How does reading at the college level fit into the picture you have just painted of your future? For each of the following life contexts, name at least one benefit of knowing how to read more effectively. If you can't think of one offhand, think again. After you have responded as well as you can on your own, get into small groups and discuss your answers together. Add any new ideas you gain to your list.

Life context	Reading benefits this context by . . .
Home and family (or attractiveness as a date or potential partner)	
Career and earning ability	

Life context	Reading benefits this context by . . .
Self-confidence and self-esteem	
Health and well-being	
Other contexts that matter to you: name them here	

As you work through this book, you may have other ideas about how reading more effectively will help you enjoy your life and understand more. If you do, we recommend that you add those new ideas to this chart. Then, if you ever get discouraged about the course, turn back and reread all your responses to Interaction 1-1. Reviewing your goals periodically will help you stay on course to the future you want to achieve.

Viewing Videos and Reading "Prep" Readings

Every chapter in this book starts with a suggestion about a video you can view and a "Prep" Reading you can read that will help to prepare your mind for the ideas to come in the reading selections at the end of the chapter. A second purpose is to give you something to talk about. When you read in your college classes, reading the material is just the beginning. After you read it, you, your instructor, and your classmates will often talk about the ideas that the assignment has raised.

Prep Reading . . . . Online Newspaper Article

In the summer of 2007, ABC News asked viewers to describe their week in three words. This article describes some of their responses.

Visit www.cengage.com/devenglish/doleconnect and select Chapter 1 to hear a reading of this selection and view a video about this topic.

"Three Little Words" on *Good Morning America*

Brian Stelter

1   A woman pans a video camera from her face to a computer screen, where a message says "It's not cancer."

2   Three little words can have quite an impact, as ABC News learned over the summer when it introduced a weekly segment on its **user-generated content** show *i-Caught*.

3   The segment, "Your 3 Words," is simple. "Describe your week in three words," anchor Bill Weir recalls asking viewers in August. "You can sing it, you can say it, you can write it, you can draw it. It can be funny or sad or poignant as long as it's honest."

4   Mr. Weir thought he'd be lucky to get five or six responses the first week. Instead, ABC received a few hundred — and by the time *i-Caught* ended its short summer run, a couple thousand had arrived via ABCNews.com. *i-Caught* was a low-rated and short-lived series, but "Your 3 Words" lived on; two weeks ago, the segment moved to *Good Morning America Weekend*, a program that Mr. Weir co-anchors.

5   It is perhaps the purest form of user-generated content. Most of the messages are written on hands, arms, or pieces of paper. "Accepting my loss," wrote a man who was missing a finger. "We can't wait!" a couple wrote, with an **ultrasound** in the background.

6   "It's rare that you can get such insight into your viewers' lives in such a simplistic, powerful, emotional way," said Andrew Morse, the executive producer of *Good Morning America Weekend*. "Gone are the days when you'd take a simple photograph and put it in an album for you to see," Mr. Morse said. "This allows you to share your most personal, precious moments with the whole world."

user-generated content Content such as stories, songs, or videos that readers, listeners, or viewers send for publication to a Web site, television show, or other media provider

ultrasound The use of ultrasonic waves to detect structures inside the body

● Interaction 1-2. Talking about Reading

Respond in writing to the questions below and then discuss your answers with your classmates.

1. If you were asked to describe your week in three words, what three words would you use? _____

2. If you set your words to a song, what tune would you use? Or, if you put your words with an image, what would the image be? Why? Explain your thinking. _____

_____

_____

3. Examine the words and images in the three photographs that follow. Next to each photo, write down a few words that indicate what you think the person who created the photo had in mind.

© clearviewstock/Shutterstock

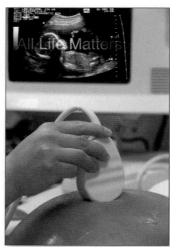

© Chad Ehlers/Alamy

© Andreas Gradin/Shutterstock

4. Imagine at least two different scenes in which the following three words might be spoken: "I'm so sorry." Write a brief description of each scene. _____

_____

_____

Reading Is an Interaction

What makes the same words mean different things? In the case of the photographs in question 3 from Interaction 1-2, it is the interaction between the words and the pictures that changes the meaning of the words. When the picture changed, suddenly the words took on a whole new meaning.

The same is true whether the picture is "out there" (as in a photo or a video), or "in here" (in your mind's eye): The picture affects the meaning. In the case of question 4, what made the words change meaning was the interaction between the writer's words "I'm so sorry" with your reader's imagination. Depending on what each reader's imagination supplied as a likely context for these words, "I'm so sorry" may have meant many different things. In the absence of images to supply the context, the meaning of written words depends on the interaction between the writer's words and the reader's imagination.

Using your imagination while you read is one way to be an active participant in the interaction of reading. **Interactivity** is the ability of two (or more) people or things to act on one another and affect one another. When you read, you have the best chance of understanding the text if you are interactive. Form a mental picture of what the author is saying. Use your imagination.

Another way to be interactive is to use your body. When you read, keep your pen in your hand. This automatically puts you in a different frame of mind than if you are just sitting there with limp muscles, moving only your eyes. And use the pen! When you get to a point in the text you don't understand, underline it, and scribble your question in the margin. When you disagree with the author, write "No way!" and then add your own explanation. When you read something completely new, try to figure out how it fits into what you already know.

Let's apply the principle of interactivity to something you probably do every day, or at least a couple of times a week—watch TV. Applying an interactive approach to watching TV will help you transfer this principle over to reading. (If you don't watch TV, you can take the exact same steps in relation to movies.) In both watching TV and reading, you can have different kinds of interactions *before* you view or read, *while* you view or read, and *after* you view or read.

Before You View or Read

Before you view or read, you can use several skills that dramatically improve comprehension (that is, understanding):

- Guess at the purpose of the program or reading selection.
- Survey it to get an overview of what will be coming.
- Predict what's going to happen.
- Think about your prior knowledge of the subject matter.

We will discuss each skill one at a time.

You and the Author Both Have Your Purposes

We will start with purpose, since we hope that you have reasons for what you do in life! People have all kinds of reasons for watching TV. Let's explore some of yours.

⬤ Interaction 1-3. Your Purposes for Viewing

1. Name five programs that you watch or have watched at least three or four times. Next to each program name, note what kind of program it is—for example, a talk show, a reality show, a sporting event, a cartoon, and so on.

Names of programs you watch	Types of programs
EXAMPLE: Grey's Anatomy	hospital drama
1.	
2.	
3.	
4.	
5.	

2. How many of these programs do you watch with the main purpose of

- being entertained? _____
- staying informed? _____
- being persuaded to believe or do something? _____

3. In question 2 you were thinking about your purpose for watching certain programs. What about the purpose of that particular *type* of program? Can types of programs also be divided into those meant to entertain, inform, and persuade? To answer this question, try to put different types of programs you've watched (not just those from above) into the three categories given at the top of page 13.

Types of programs meant to entertain viewers	Types of programs meant to inform or teach viewers	Types of programs meant to persuade viewers
EXAMPLE: Cartoons	News programs	Political commentary and debate programs (e.g., Real Time with Bill Maher)

4. Discuss your findings with the class or in a small group. What have you learned?

You can see that different types of programs, called **genres,** have different purposes. The same is true for different kinds of reading material. For example, news stories have the main purpose of informing readers about current events. College textbooks have the main purpose of teaching students—their purpose, too, is to inform. What about *People* magazine? The articles in *People* do inform readers about celebrities, but why? To entertain readers, and thus their main purpose is to entertain.

At times you can tell just from the title of a reading selection what its purpose is. For example, an article called "The President Should Be Ashamed" is a persuasive reading; the word *should* clearly shows that the writer wants readers to believe the president did something wrong. The article is not simply reporting information. (An informative title would state "The President Is Ashamed.")

Other times, you can make an educated guess based on where the reading selection appears—for example, if it's part of a newspaper, whether it is in the news section, on the opinion page, or part of the want ads. When an article is printed in the Letters to the Editor section, the writer's main purpose is to persuade readers. The publishing context can reveal a lot about the author's purpose.

🌑 Interaction 1-4. Purposes in Reading

For each of the following types of reading material, decide whether the main purpose is likely to be to persuade readers, to inform readers, or to entertain readers. Consider both the title and the publishing context. Be prepared to discuss your answer.

> **P** = persuade readers: cause them to change how they think or act.
> **I** = inform readers: teach them information.
> **E** = entertain readers: amuse them, often by using stories.

____ 1. A news article called "House Fire Kills Four in Fort Bend County" from the *Houston Chronicle*, a newspaper.

____ 2. A chapter in an American government textbook called "The President."

____ 3. An editorial by Anna Quindlen in *Newsweek* called "Getting Out of Iraq Isn't Rocket Science."

____ 4. A DC Comics title called "Shazam! The Monster Society of Evil" by Jeff Smith.

____ 5. An article called "What Happened in State Reproductive Health Law in 2006?" at the Guttmacher Institute's Web site.

____ 6. "Give Exxon a Break," an editorial in the *Los Angeles Times* online.

____ 7. A book by Michael Pollan entitled *In Defense of Food: An Eater's Manifesto*.

____ 8. A book by David McCullough called *The Great Bridge: The Epic Story of the Building of the Brooklyn Bridge*.

____ 9. A feature article in *Ebony* magazine called "Black Families and Heart Disease," by Adrienne P. Samuels.

____ 10. A feature article in *Outside* magazine called "50 Years on Everest: The Unsung Heroes of the World's Highest Mountain," by Jenny Dubin.

When you are preparing to read, spend a moment thinking about the likely purpose of the reading selection, based on the context in which the reading selection is printed and its title.

Interaction 1-5. Choose an Informative Article

Find an informative article whose subject interests you. The article should have at least ten paragraphs. To find it, look in your campus library's periodicals section; visit your local bookstore, newsstand, pharmacy, or grocery store; or go online. (Hint: Numerous special-interest magazines exist. You may want to think about subjects you care about and then see if you can find a magazine for people who share one of these interests.) You are going to use the article for five activities, so you need to save a copy of it. Don't read the article yet! We want to share a few strategies with you first.

1. What is the title of the article? _____

_____

2. What led you to believe the purpose of the article is informative? _____

_____

3. What is your purpose for choosing this article? _____

_____

4. Explain more about your answer to number 3. What exactly is your interest? _____

_____

Surveying a Reading Is Like Watching a Preview

When you go to a movie, often you have already seen the preview for it several times. The preview shows you some of the highlights of the movie. You often know who the main characters are (and which actors play them), you've viewed some of the scenery and settings, and you have a sense of the film's genre—whether the movie is going to be a fast-paced action adventure, a romantic comedy, or a horror flick.

Similarly, if you take a few moments to survey or preview a reading selection, you will tremendously improve your chances of comprehending the reading selection. When you preview, you do not read the whole selection, you only examine selected parts. Following are the parts to look at, shown on an article from *Newsweek* magazine.

Read These Parts Quickly When You Preview

Title: What do these words reveal about the subject?

Subtitle or sentence in large type: What do you learn from reading this sentence?

First sentences of paragraphs: Read the first sentence of each paragraph quickly.

CHINA 2008

GOING FOR GOLD

For Beijing, a smooth Games will take a lot of things—including winning more than anyone else.

Olympian Ambitions

By MARK STARR

ALL OLYMPIC GOLD SHINES BRIL-liantly, though not all equally so. Of China's 32 gold medals at the 2004 Athens Games, none was as lustrous as 20-year-old Liu Xiang's in the 110-meter hurdles, the first-ever gold for a Chinese man in Olympic track-and-field competition.

It wasn't that China didn't value its gold-medal athletes in sports at which it had long excelled—diving, table tennis and badminton among them. But those sports are of limited interest to much of the world and, crucially, to the companies that have transformed Chinese sports into a $5 billion industry. Liu's triumph was celebrated in China just like Yao Ming's selection as the No. 1 pick in the NBA draft two years earlier—a breakthrough in a sport in which Chinese athletes had been invisible.

Today Liu is arguably the most popular man in China and indisputably the most visible. His face is everywhere—on magazine covers, billboards and milk cartons. He cavorts on music videos with the hottest female stars and boasts an A-list of international sponsors, including Nike and Visa. Most important of all, Liu now stands as the symbol of China's hopes and dreams for its Beijing Olympics in August. "Everything here is about 2008," says Terry Rhoads, cofounder of Shanghai-based ZOU Marketing.

Although all host countries hope to excel in Olympic competition, far more is at stake in Beijing than athletic supremacy. Beijing is a target for a host of international grievances—human rights, environmental practices, food and manufacturing safety. The Games are its chance to sell the world on a more benevolent vision of China. "We will see an entire nation perform a carefully choreographed dance," says Jin Yuanpu, head of an Olympics study center at the People's University of China. "Each athlete knows that his individual struggle is unimportant when compared to the larger struggle of China to impress the world."

But athletics remains the centerpiece. Ever since the Games were awarded to China, the country has envisioned the Olympics as the stage on which it would establish its preeminence. China's goal: to rank as the top nation in gold medals, a spot the United States has held

OVER THE TOP: *Hurdler Liu Xiang's breakthrough was a big first for China*

since the breakup of the Soviet Union. Jim Scherr, CEO of the U.S. Olympic Committee, sees the Chinese challenge as both real and meaningful. "The world focuses on gold-medal count as the measure of the teams," says Scherr, "and we certainly think it's important to stay on top." At Athens 2004, China fielded a young team—80 percent of its athletes were Olympic rookies—and despite totaling 40 fewer medals than the U.S. team, it captured just three fewer golds.

But even as China seems poised to knock the United States off its Olympic perch—if not in Beijing, then in 2012 or 2016—this athletic rivalry hasn't engendered the passions that America vs. the Soviet Union once did. Political tensions and ideological animosity are nowhere near as heated. The two nations also excel in different sports. There are only a few Olympic events—diving, women's gymnastics and women's soccer—where an American gold medal might come at the expense of the Chinese or vice versa.

If history's a guide, China's "home-field" advantage should lift its medal count by at least 15 percent. Home crowds and home cooking will certainly help, but China is counting far more on dramatic increases in spending for its Olympic sports programs. Liu's upset victory over the U.S. champion in Athens was viewed as the first thrust for Project 119, a national program aimed at developing talent in Olympic sports that offer multiple medals—and in which Chinese athletes have had little success.

China's national sports program is, in many ways, the envy of its competitors, including the United States—and not simply because of its enormous talent pool. Elite athletes are identified as early as 6 years old and funneled through provincial and regional training schools up into the national teams. The once insular system is exhibiting some new worldliness. Not only are China's elite athletes competing outside the country's borders more frequently, but foreign coaches are being welcomed to fill the gaps in sports where China lacks expertise. Gymnastics coaching legend Bela Karolyi, who has faced Chinese teams for decades, says the changes make China even more formidable. "Their kids used to feel comfortable as long as they were hidden in their little hole," he says. "But as soon as they got out in the world, they fell apart. Being out there can only help them." Having seen its advances in track and field and swimming during the 1990s halted by drug scandals, China has repeatedly pledged to embrace Olympic ideals and international standards of fair play.

There's good reason to take China's commitment to reform seriously—at least for these particular Games. The whole world will be watching, and companies paid unprecedented sums to be associated with Beijing 2008. Any scandal involving the Chinese would be a disaster, viewed at home as an unacceptable loss of face. Chinese supremacy in Olympic athletics is inevitable, if not this time, then soon. What isn't inevitable for China is the world's warm embrace. "We want to see our athletes win," says Xing Yue, of the International Studies Institute at Tsinghua University. "But our country's success after the Olympics because of the Olympics is even more important to the Chinese people." That's the gold that will carry the most luster at these Games.

With QUINDLEN KROVATIN *and* JONATHAN ANSFIELD *in China*

MICHAEL STEELE—GETTY IMAGES FOR DAGOC

Photos and captions: What information can you gather from this photograph and its caption?

Headings: This brief article does not include headings, but many longer articles and textbook chapters certainly will. Read each heading and think about it for a moment.

Interaction 1-6. Survey Your Informative Article

1. You noted the title of your article in Interaction 1-5. What do the words in the title suggest about the subject? _____

_____

2. Does your article include any sentences in large type or a subtitle? If so, read them and then list additional pieces of information about the article that you learned from them.

   - _____

   - _____

   - _____

3. How many photos, illustrations, or other images appear throughout the article? _____ How many of these have captions? _____ What additional information about the article do you gain from viewing the images and reading the captions?

   - _____

   - _____

   - _____

4. How many headings do you find? _____ What content do they seem to indicate the article will discuss? (If there are no headings, answer the same question about the first sentences of paragraphs after you preview them.) _____

_____

_____

_____

When you survey or preview a reading, you become able to make predictions about it, as you have just done. Making predictions (an interactive process, as you have seen) allows you to access your prior knowledge about the material covered in the selection.

You Already Know Something about This

When you sit down to watch *Lost,* you already know from previous episodes that the whole saga started with a plane crash. When you've just surveyed a reading, you've learned something already from the title, the images, the captions, and the headings. Aside from these obvious pieces of information, though, it's quite likely you know more. For example, you have probably watched the Olympics on television before or read about the Games in a newspaper or magazine. You may have attended track and field events at your high school or college, and so have seen hurdlers like Liu Xiang competing. You may have watched a PBS special on Beijing, or news reports on what Beijing did to prepare to host the Olympics in 2008. All of this knowledge that you bring to your viewing or reading is called your **prior knowledge**. (*Prior* means "before.") You want to activate, or set in motion, your prior knowledge as much as you can before you start reading. Doing this takes advantage of a natural pattern of learning for people: fitting what they are learning about into what they already know.

Interaction 1-7. Activate Your Prior Knowledge

Reread what you wrote in Interaction 1-6 about the subjects that your informative article probably discusses. For each item you wrote, think of at least one piece of prior knowledge that you hold about that subject—even if the knowledge is somewhat vague. List five of these pieces of prior knowledge here.

- _____
- _____
- _____
- _____
- _____

While You Are Viewing or Reading

Have you ever gone to the movies with a movie buff, or watched a football game with someone who has watched every Monday night football game for the past fifteen years? (Or maybe you are one of these dedicated people!) If so, you'll understand when we say that there are the things a casual viewer sees and then there are the things a dedicated viewer sees. One of the differences is that the casual viewer gets caught up emotionally in the moment-by-moment movie scenes or football plays, but the dedicated viewer retains a broader, more critical perspective on what is happening. Due partly to their greater experience and partly to their intense curiosity, dedicated viewers know more about the wide range of choices a movie director or a football coach can make, and thus, they are in a better position to know why a particular choice was made this time and whether the choice made was a good one.

The same is true for casual and dedicated readers. While the casual reader may be reading one sentence at a time and thinking about its meaning, the dedicated reader is doing that, too, but is also staying interactive by asking the types of questions shown in **Table 1.1**.

Table 1.1 Learning Tasks to Accomplish While Reading

To accomplish these learning tasks while reading . . .	the interactive reader asks these questions.
The reader tries to understand what the author is saying.	• What does it mean when the author says this? • Can I explain this using my own words?
The reader monitors (tracks) whether he or she is comprehending the material and applies strategies to aid comprehension. (You may be losing comprehension if you have to slow your reading considerably, if you go back to reread a section several times, or if you can't tell what is important and what is not.)	• I don't understand. I'll keep reading to see if this becomes clearer. • I don't know this word. I wonder if I can figure it out from the surrounding words. If not, I'll use the dictionary. • I have read this same paragraph three times already and I don't get it. What is the main idea here?
The reader searches for the relevance of the reading to his or her own life and to other ideas and situations.	• How does this connect to what I already know? • What examples of this have I experienced or do I know about?
The reader is open to learning something new that doesn't necessarily fit easily into known information.	• How is this different from what I thought was true?
The reader searches for the significance of the ideas.	• Why is this important? • What effects do these ideas have? What are the consequences?

Interaction 1-8. Monitor Your Comprehension

Read the informative article you found in Interaction 1-5. As you read, jot down very brief notes in the margins of the article using the guidelines that follow.

1. Put a ✔ next to a paragraph when you understand most of it.

2. Put an ✘ next to a paragraph when you don't understand most of it.

3. Circle words you don't know *if* they seem important to know in order to understand the article.

4. After you read, compare the paragraphs that have ✔'s and those that have ✘'s. What makes some paragraphs easy to understand and other paragraphs hard to understand? List your ideas, and then share them with a classmate to get more ideas.

    • _____

    • _____

    • _____

5. Look up in a dictionary the meanings of the words you circled, and write the words and definitions here.

    • _____

    • _____

    • _____

6. Reread the parts of the article where the words appeared. Did looking up the definitions help you understand those parts? Why or why not? _____

   _____

   _____

Practice Learning While Reading

Refer back to Table 1.1 the next few times you read, and practice the strategies. Actively try to understand what the author is saying, monitor your own comprehension, search for the relevance and significance of the information you are reading, and remain open to learning something new. The rest of the chapters in this book will suggest strategies you can use to improve your comprehension, but the most important factor of all is your active participation.

After You View or Read

What you do after you watch a TV program, a movie, or a YouTube video depends partly on why you were watching it to begin with. If you were watching Ellen DeGeneres, you may just laugh a final laugh and turn the channel. But if you were watching local politicians debate whether or not to build a superhighway through your neighborhood next year, you would probably spend some time afterward thinking about what each person had said and whether you wanted to vote for them. Similarly, if you read a selection that was meant to be persuasive, you would probably ask yourself if the writer had convinced you of his or her point, and why. If you were reading a textbook or other informative reading material, it would make sense after you read to ask yourself what you had just learned—and why it mattered.

🌐 Interaction 1-9. Think about What You Learned, Its Relevance, and Its Significance

Review what you said in Interaction 1-5 on page 15 about your purpose for selecting your article, and then answer the following questions.

1. What did you learn from the article? List at least three ideas or pieces of information.

   • _____

   • _____

   • _____

2. What are the main points you want to remember? Why are these important?

   • _____

   • _____

   • _____

3. Was the article as relevant as you expected it to be when you selected it? Why or why not? _____

   _____

4. What did you find significant about the article? What was important about it to you? _____

   _____

5. Who else might find this article relevant, and why? _____

   _____

Beyond Skills: Knowledge

Much of this book is going to discuss skills to use while you are reading and after you read—skills that will improve your comprehension, help you understand text structure, and in general make reading college textbooks a more deliberate and interactive experience. There is another factor besides reading skills, however, that affects how well you read college-level material. That factor is prior knowledge, which we've already defined as being knowledge that you already have about a particular subject. Each person's prior knowledge is necessarily at least somewhat different from every other person's. Thus, readings that seem easy to you may be more difficult for your classmate, or vice versa.

When an author and readers share prior knowledge, reading becomes easier and comprehension improves. For example, often authors assume that members of a certain culture will share certain pieces of information. Former professor E. D. Hirsch has written several books in which he notes that literate Americans typically know what the phrase *Independence Day* refers to (July 4, the day America declared independence from the British back in 1776). They know what the term *civil rights movement* means. They know certain stories from the Bible, not necessarily because they are Jews or Christians who study the Bible, but because the Bible is a source of many stories that form part of the background of our culture. Hirsch calls this shared background knowledge *cultural literacy*.

We have no way of knowing which pieces of information you already have that might be considered cultural literacy. But a very important predictor of reading comprehension is prior knowledge. So whenever one of the readings in the book refers to a story, idea, or fact about our culture that seems especially important to know, a Common Knowledge box appears. Why would we consider certain ideas more important to know than others? If we find that many writers assume their readers will know a certain fact or understand a certain idea, then we think you should take the time to learn about it. That way, when you read a reference to it in another reading sometime in the future, you will hold that information as prior knowledge.

The more prior knowledge you bring to a reading, the more easily you will understand it. The more you read, the more knowledge you will hold in common with others.

● Interaction 1-10. Common Knowledge

Hirsch lists the following terms in his books as being ones that culturally literate Americans should know. If you don't know what they mean, use an encyclopedia, Web search, or college dictionary to find out.

Mortgage	Newton's laws of motion
Miranda decision	Johnny Appleseed
URL	Kilimanjaro

Do you agree that all these terms are important for everyone to know? Why or why not? _____

_____

_____

Chapter Summary Activity

This chapter has discussed tasks to do before, during, and after reading that will increase your reading comprehension and make reading an interactive experience. Construct a Reading Guide below by completing each idea on the left with information from the chapter on the right. You can keep returning to this guide later in the course as a reminder of how to use the reading process to your advantage.

Reading Guide to Using a Process

Complete this idea	with information from the chapter.
Before reading, make an educated guess about the author's purpose, which might be to	1. 2. 3.
Use three clues about the reading to make that educated guess about the author's purpose.	4. 5. 6.
Survey a reading before you read it. To survey, read only these parts of the reading selection:	7. 8. 9. 10. 11. 12.
Surveying the reading allows you to make predictions about what the reading will include. It also allows you to think about what you already know about the subject. This is called your	13.
The reason for activating your prior knowledge is that	14.

Complete this idea	with information from the chapter.
While you are reading, interact with the reading by doing five learning tasks.	15. 16. 17. 18. 19.
Three clues that you may not be comprehending what you read are	20. 21. 22.
For informative readings, you will probably ask yourself two questions after you read. They are:	23. 24.
For persuasive readings, a main question you might ask after reading is:	25.

Test Taking Tips

Using the Reading Process

Every chapter includes Test Taking Tips, which always follow the Chapter Summary Activity. Test Taking Tips serve two functions. First, we want to give you some general test taking tips you can use as you take a variety of tests across your academic career. These are in Chapters 1 and 2. Second, we want to give you specific tips for taking reading tests related to the skills discussed in Chapters 3–12. For example, in Chapter 4, you will get specific tips for answering main idea questions on your reading tests.

In this chapter we talked about the reading process—what to do before, during, and after reading. The same approach can be applied successfully to taking tests in any subject.

● **Before the Test**

Survey the test before you begin.

✔ How many questions are there? How much is each one worth?

✔ How much time do you have to complete each item? Use this information to plan how to take the test. For example, if you have thirty questions to finish in one hour, then you have two minutes to answer each question.

✔ Read and pay attention to all directions. It hurts when you miss a question due to carelessness rather than lack of skill.

● **During the Test**

✔ Start with what you already know. Work from what you know to what you don't know. If your survey of the test revealed that one type of question or one section will be significantly easier for you to respond to than others, answer that type or section first. Doing so may spark your memory of the course content and give you a better chance of answering more difficult questions well. It will also increase your confidence.

✔ Read each question on a reading test carefully. Understand key words so that you can identify which skill to use in that question, whether it is about finding the main idea, making an inference, defining a vocabulary word, and so on. Decide exactly what the question is asking for before you answer it.

✔ Read all the possible answers carefully before you choose one.

✔ Eliminate answers that you know are wrong first. If you can eliminate two out of four multiple-choice answers, for instance, you have doubled your chance of getting the right answer.

✔ Double-check the answer you think is correct.

✔ If you are unsure of an answer, mark the choice you think might be correct and then return to that question after you complete the test (assuming there is time).

✔ Change your answer if you have discovered a good reason that a different answer would be better.

● **After the Test**

✔ When you get the test back, if you have done well, celebrate! Make sure you repeat your successful strategies.

✔ If you have done poorly, ask questions. Ask yourself what you missed and how you could have done better. Ask your instructor for any suggestions about how you could do better on the next test. Ask students who did well on the test what they did, and ask if they would be willing to help you prepare for the next test.

Using the reading process before, during, and after tests will help you improve your test-taking ability and your ability to learn from taking tests.

Reading 1-1 . . . . Newspaper Article

● Pre-Reading the Selection

In August 2007, the article "Amid War, Passion for TV Chefs, Soaps and Idols" about the increasing popularity of television in Afghanistan appeared in the *New York Times*.

Guessing the Purpose

Based on the title of the article that begins on page 27 and the fact that it was published in a newspaper, what two main purposes do you suppose the author has: to persuade, inform, and/or entertain? _____

Surveying the Reading

What parts of the reading selection should you survey? _____

_____

Go ahead and survey the reading.

Predicting the Content

Based on your survey, what are three things you expect the reading selection to discuss?

- _____

- _____

- _____

Activating Your Knowledge

Search your memory for knowledge that you have on any of the following topics: Afghanistan, the Taliban, television in developing countries, or how democracy and television relate. Write down at least two of these pieces of prior knowledge.

- _____

- _____

- _____

Common Knowledge

Read these terms and their definitions to help you understand the reading selection.

Taliban (*paragraph 1*) A group of religious fundamentalists who ruled Afghanistan from 1994 to 2001, introducing very strict Sharia law (Islamic law), including many laws that negatively affected women's rights.

the call to prayer (*paragraph 9*) Muslims (people who follow Islam) pray five times each day; a man known as the *muezzin* calls the faithful to prayer each time.

taboos (*paragraph 21*) Actions, words, objects, and the like that are banned in a particular society. For example, cannibalism (eating human flesh) is a taboo in many cultures.

democracy (*paragraph 30*) A government led by the people, usually through voting periodically for political leaders.

Reading with Pen in Hand

Now read the selection. As you read, mark any ideas that seem important, and respond to the questions and vocabulary items in the margin. Monitor your comprehension by putting a ✔ next to a paragraph when you understand most of it. Place an ✘ next to a paragraph when you don't understand most of it.

Visit www.cengage.com/devenglish/doleconnect and select Chapter 1 to hear vocabulary words from this selection and view a video about this topic.

Amid War, Passion for TV Chefs, Soaps and Idols

Barry Bearak

◆ *Reading Journal*

1   KABUL, Afghanistan, July 25—Seven years ago, during a very different time in a very different Afghanistan, a medical student named Daoud Sediqi was bicycling from campus when he was stopped by the Taliban's whip-wielding religious police.

2   The young man immediately felt an avalanche of regret, for he was in violation of at least two laws. One obvious offense was the length of his hair. While the ruling Taliban insisted that men sprout untrimmed beards, they were otherwise opposed to scruffiness and the student had allowed his locks to grow shaggy. His other

◆ Paragraphs 1–3 focus on one person. Who? Why is he important?

transgression What synonym (word with similar meaning) is in the second sentence of this paragraph?

in fits and starts This phrase could be misunderstood as it is used in this sentence. So look it up online (try www.Bartleby.com), in a good dictionary (under *fit*), or in an idiom dictionary. What does it mean?

◆Paragraphs 4–8 suggest three reasons people in Afghanistan are watching TV. What are they?

transgression was more serious. If his captors searched his possessions, they would find a CD with an X-rated movie.

3   "Fortunately, they didn't look; my only punishment was to have my head shaved because of my long hair," recalled Mr. Sediqi, now at age 26 one of this nation's best-known men, someone sprung from a new wellspring of fame—not a warlord or a mullah, but a television celebrity, the host of "Afghan Star," this nation's "American Idol."

4   Since the fall of the Taliban in late 2001, Afghanistan has been developing in fits and starts. Among the unchanging circumstances that still leave people fitful: continuing war, inept leaders, corrupt police officers and woeful living conditions. According to the government's latest surveys, only 43 percent of all households have non-leaking windows and roofs, 31 percent have safe drinking water and 7 percent have sanitary toilets.

5   But television is off to a phenomenal start, with Afghans now engrossed, for better or worse, in much of the same escapist fare that seduces the rest of the world: soap operas that pit the unbearably conniving against the implausibly virtuous, chefs preparing meals that most people would never eat in kitchens they could never afford, talk show hosts wheedling secrets from those too shameless to keep their troubles to themselves.

6   The latest national survey, which dates from 2005, shows that 19 percent of Afghan households own a television, a remarkable total considering not only that owning a TV was a crime under the Taliban but that a mere 14 percent of the population has access to public electricity. In a study this year of Afghanistan's five most urban provinces, two-thirds of all people said they watched TV every day or almost every day.

7   "Maybe Afghanistan is not so different from other places," said Muhammad Qaseem Akhgar, a prominent social analyst and newspaper editor. "People watch television because there is nothing else to do."

8   Reading is certainly less an option; only 28 percent of the population is literate. "Where else can one find amusement?" Mr. Akhgar asked.

9   Each night, people in Kabul obey the beckoning of prime time much as they might otherwise answer the call to prayer. "As you can see, there is truth on the television, because all over the world the mother-in-law is always provoking a fight," said Muhammad Farid, a man sitting in a run-down restaurant beside the Pul-i-Khishti

Afghan children watching TV

© Joao Silva/The New York Times/Redux

Mosque, his attention fixed on an Indian soap opera that had been dubbed into Dari.

10 Women, whose public outings are constrained by custom, most often watch their favorite shows at home. Men, on the other hand, are free to make TV a **communal** ritual. In one restaurant after another, with deft fingers dipping into mounds of steaming rice, patrons sit cross-legged on carpeted platforms, their eyes fixed on a television set perched near the ceiling. Profound metaphysical questions hover in the dim light: Will Prerna find happiness with Mr. Bajaj, who is after all not the father of her child?

11 "These are problems that teach you about life," said Sayed Agha, who sells fresh vegetables from a pushcart by day and views warmed-over melodramas by night.

12 What to watch is rarely contested. At 7:30, the dial is turned to Tolo TV for "Prerna," a soap opera colloquially known by the name of its female protagonist. At 8, the channel is switched for "The Thief of Baghdad." At 8:30, it is back to Tolo for the **intrafamily** and **extramarital** warfare waged on "Tulsi," the nickname for a show whose title literally means "Because the Mother-in-Law Was Once the Daughter-in-Law."

13 Kabul has eight local television stations, including one feebly operated by the government. "The key time slots are from 6 to 9

◆Paragraphs 9–11 quote two Afghans. What point do the Afghans make?

communal Based on the contrast between women's and men's actions set up in the previous sentence and this one, what do you think *communal* might mean?

intrafamily Notice the two parts of this word: *intra-* + *family*. *Intra-* means "within." What does the whole word mean?

extramarital This word, too, has two parts: *extra-* + *marital*. *Extra-* means "outside of." *Marital* means "related to marriage." What does the whole word mean?

◆Paragraphs 12–19
discuss different genres
of TV shows that Afghans
watch. What are they?

p.m. because that's when people switch on their generators for electrical power," said Saad Mohseni, who runs Tolo, the channel that
dominates the market in most of the country. "People love the soap
operas."

14   "We've just bought the rights to '24,' the American show," he said.
"We had some concerns. Most of the bad guys are Muslims, but we
did focus groups and it turns out most people didn't care about that
so long as the villains weren't Afghans."

15   Mr. Mohseni, a former investment banker, and his three siblings
started Tolo TV (Tolo means "dawn" in Dari) in 2004, assisted by a
grant from the United States Agency for International Development.
After living most of their adult lives in exile in Australia, the Mohsenis
returned to post-Taliban Kabul looking for investment opportunities
and discovered a nearly prehistoric television wilderness ready for
settlement. A used color TV cost only $75.

gestate A human baby takes forty
to forty-one weeks to *gestate* inside
the mother's uterus. Look at the
context here. What is a general
definition of *gestate*?

16   But what did they want to watch? Afghan tastes had not been
allowed to **gestate** over decades, passing from Milton Berle to Johnny
Carson to Bart Simpson. Everything would be brand-new. "We let
ourselves be guided by what we liked," Mr. Mohseni said.

hackneyed What does this word
mean? Use a dictionary.

17   For the most part, that means that Tolo has harvested the **hackneyed** from television's vast international landscape. True-crime
shows introduce Afghans to the sensationalism of their own peder-
asts and serial killers. Reality shows pluck everyday people off the
streets and transform them with spiffed-up wardrobes. Quiz shows
reward the knowledgeable: How many pounds of mushrooms did
Afghanistan export last year? A contestant who answers correctly
earns a free gallon of cooking oil.

18   Some foreign shows, like those featuring disasters and police
chases, are so nonverbal that Tolo is able to rebroadcast them
without translation. Other formats require only slight retooling.

19   Mr. Sediqi is about to begin his third season with "Afghan Star."
He has never seen "American Idol" and said he had never heard of
his American counterpart, Ryan Seacrest. Nevertheless, he ably manages to introduce the competing vocalists and coax the audience to
vote for their favorites via cellphone.

◆What seems to be the
main point of this
paragraph?

20   "I must tell you that I am having very good fun," Mr. Sediqi said,
employing his limited English. He is one of several young stars at
Tolo whose hipness is exotic enough to seem almost extraterrestrial
to an average Afghan. Older men who prefer soap operas to singing
competitions are likely to want to give Mr. Sediqi a good thrashing.

"People in the countryside and the mosques say that the show is ruining society," Mr. Sediqi admitted.

21   Tolo has drawn a huge audience while testing the bounds of certain taboos. Zaid Mohseni, Saad's younger brother, said: "When we first put a man and woman on the air together, we had complaints: this isn't legal, this isn't Islamic, blah, blah, blah. Then the criticism softened. It was O.K. as long as they don't talk to each other. Finally, it softened more: O.K., they can talk as long as they don't laugh."

22   The bounds are pushed but not broken. A live talk show called "Woman" is co-moderated by a psychiatrist, Dr. Muhammad Yasin Babrak. While female callers are frank in their laments, the therapist limits himself to being Dear Abby to the lovelorn rather than Dr. Ruth to the sexually frustrated. "I won't talk about incest or homosexuality," he said.

◆What is the main point of paragraphs 21–25 ?

23   Music videos, primarily imports from India, are broadcast regularly. With a nod to Afghan tradition, the bare arms and midriffs of female dancers are obscured with a milky strip of electronic camouflage. And yet, sporting events are somehow deemed less erotic. Maria Sharapova was shown at Wimbledon with the full flesh of her limbs unconcealed.

24   Whatever the constraints, some observers consider TV a portal to promiscuity. "Forty million people are living with H.I.V.-AIDS, and television is finally helping Afghanistan contribute to those figures," the Ayatollah Asif Mohseni said with sarcasm.

25   He is an elderly white-bearded man, and while he is not related to the family who runs Tolo TV, he, too, has entered the television business, starting a station more inclined to showcase Islamic chanting. "We have an economy that is in ruins," Ayatollah Mohseni said. "Do you think rubbish Indian serials with half-naked people are the answer?"

26   But the strongest complaints against Tolo have come from politicians, including members of the government. Tolo's news coverage, while increasingly professional, is very often unflattering and even irreverent. Members of Parliament have been shown asleep at their desks or in overheated debate throwing water bottles. One lawmaker was photographed picking his nose and then guiltily cleaning his finger.

◆What is the main point of paragraphs 26–30?

27   In April, when Attorney General Abdul Jabar Sabet thought he had been quoted out of context, he sent policemen to Tolo's headquarters to arrest the news staff. The ensuing contretemps had to be mediated by the United Nations mission in Kabul.

28   "It has been quite odd," said Saad Mohseni, Tolo's chief. "This is Afghanistan, a young democracy, and we don't have problems with the drug dealers or the Taliban or even the local populace. Our problems are all with the government, either because of red tape or attempted censorship or someone with a vested interest trying to extract money."

29   He paused for effect.

30   "With democracy comes television. It's hard for some people to get used to."

Check Your Skills While Continuing to Learn

The questions that follow will check your understanding (comprehension) of the reading selection. They address all the skills you will learn throughout the book. Here in Chapter 1, each skill is first described briefly. Then a sample question, answer, and reason for the answer are given.

A Suggested Learning Process

- Read and think about the skill.
- Study all three parts of the example: the question, the answer, and the explanation.
- Look back at the reading selection so you can understand the example.
- Answer the second question as a check for yourself of how well you can already apply this skill.
- Note that you can keep track of your progress in applying the different skills by filling in the chart in the inside back cover of the book.

Comprehension Questions

Write the letter of the answer on the line. Then explain your thinking.

Main Idea

Skill

Think of the main idea as the "point" of the paragraph or passage. The main idea dominates the paragraph. To find the main idea, notice which sentence explains the author's most important point about the subject. The other sentences in the paragraph should offer explanations, examples, and details about the main idea. Sometimes a main idea may cover the supporting details from several paragraphs.

Example

__a__ 1. What is the best statement of the main idea of paragraph 12?

    a. What to watch is rarely contested.

    b. At 7:30, the dial is turned to Tolo TV for "Prerna."

    c. At 8, the channel is switched for "The Thief of Baghdad."

    d. At 8:30, it is back to Tolo for the intrafamily and extramarital warfare waged on "Tulsi."

WHY? What information in the selection leads you to give that answer? The first sentence is the point of the paragraph: Everyone in Kabul watches the same programs. The other sentences list the programs that everyone watches at different times.

Practice

_____ 2. What is the best statement of the main idea of the group of paragraphs 21–23?

    a. Tolo has drawn a huge audience while testing the bounds of certain taboos.

    b. They can talk as long as they don't laugh.

    c. The therapist limits himself to being Dear Abby for the lovelorn rather than Dr. Ruth to the sexually frustrated.

    d. Maria Sharapova was shown at Wimbledon with the full flesh of her limbs unconcealed.

WHY? What information in the selection leads you to give that answer? _____

_____

_____

Supporting Details

Skill

Think of the supporting details as the "proof" for the main idea. To locate the supporting details, find the main idea and then look for the information the author uses to explain it in more detail. Sometimes, if a main idea covers more than one paragraph, you will find the supporting details in several paragraphs.

Example

<u>b</u> 3. In paragraph 2, what are the two major supporting details?

    a. Men's untrimmed beards; his captors searched Sediqi's possessions.

    b. Sediqi's long, shaggy hair; his possession of an X-rated movie.

    c. The ruling Taliban; his possession of a CD.

    d. He felt an avalanche of regret; he was scruffy.

WHY? What information in the selection leads you to give that answer? <u>The main idea of paragraph</u> <u>2 is "The young man immediately felt an avalanche of regret, for he was in violation of at least two laws."</u> <u>Answer B gives the two major supporting details; it lists the two laws Sediqi broke. His hair was long and</u> <u>shaggy, and he had an X-rated movie with him.</u>

Practice

    4. Paragraph 5 has a single sentence. Nevertheless, it has a main idea and three supporting details. What are the supporting details?

    a. Television is off to a phenomenal start; Afghans are engrossed in television programs; soap operas pit evil against good.

    b. Afghans are engrossed in television programs; soap operas that pit evil against good; chefs who prepare too-expensive meals on TV.

    c. The same escapist shows seduce the rest of the world; soap operas that pit evil against good; chefs who prepare too-expensive meals on TV.

    d. Soap operas that pit evil against good; chefs who prepare too-expensive meals on TV; talk shows hosts who expose people's secrets.

WHY? What information in the selection leads you to give that answer? _____

_____

_____

Author's Purpose

Skill

The author's general purpose may be to persuade (change the reader's mind or behavior), inform (share information with the reader), or entertain (amuse the reader, often through stories); or it may be a combination of these purposes. At specific points in a text, an author may use a variety of methods to achieve the general purpose. You should always assume that the author has a particular reason for what he or she wrote.

Example

___d___   5. In the first sentence of paragraph 6, why does the author give the statistics (that is, facts stated as percentages)?

   a. To entertain readers by sharing how few Afghans have televisions.

   b. To inform readers that televisions are run using private rather than public electricity.

   c. To persuade readers that it was good for the Afghan people that the Taliban left power.

   d. To inform readers of how quickly watching television has become a major occupation, despite other shortages.

WHY? What information in the selection leads you to give that answer? The author says that 19% ownership of TVs is "remarkable" for two reasons: previously, owning a TV was a crime, and only 14% of the people have access to public electricity. Note that in paragraph 4, the author says the Taliban government fell in late 2001, and here in paragraph 6, he notes that the latest national survey was taken in 2005, only four years later.

Practice

_____   6. In paragraph 22, what is the author's purpose in saying that Dr. Babrak limits himself to being Dear Abby rather than Dr. Ruth?

   a. To inform readers how popular the live talk show "Woman" is.

   b. To persuade readers that Afghan women do not want to discuss their sexual needs on television.

   c. To inform readers to what extent Dr. Babrak pushes the bounds of Afghan custom but does not break them.

   d. To persuade readers that Dr. Babrak is one of the most conservative Muslims in Afghanistan.

WHY? What information in the selection leads you to give that answer? _____

_____

_____

Relationships

Skill

The ideas in a reading selection are related to one another in different ways. For instance, one sentence might discuss the causes of an event mentioned in a different sentence. Some relationships have to do with time, space, comparisons and contrasts, causes and effects, and so on. You may see the relationships between the ideas in different parts of one sentence, in different sentences, or even in different paragraphs. Many times, these relationships are indicated with signal words or transitions such as *but, and, however, for example*, and so on.

Example

_b_ 7. In paragraph 10, what signal word or words indicate a difference (a contrast) between how and where women and men watch television?

a. most often

b. on the other hand

c. after

d. not

WHY? What information in the selection leads you to give that answer? _On the other hand_ is used to say that while women usually have to watch TV at home alone, men can watch TV together in public. Sometimes, although not here, the first part of this expression is also used: _on the one hand._

Practice

____ 8. In the second sentence of paragraph 13, what is the relationship between the first part of the sentence—"The key time slots are from 6 to 9 p.m." and the second part—"because that's when people switch on their generators for electrical power"?

a. The first part is an example of the second part.

b. The second part is a contrast with the first part.

c. The second part is the cause of the first part.

d. The first part happened earlier in time than the second part.

WHY? What information in the selection leads you to give that answer? _____

_____

Fact, Opinion, and Inference

Skill

A fact is a true statement that can be verified by using another source of information: *It is 85 degrees outside.* An opinion is a person's personal reaction: *It's too hot to play baseball.* An inference is an idea the reader gets from the other ideas that the author has stated: *That person must be from up north.* To be valid, an inference must be a logical extension of what the author has written.

Example

__a__ 9. Which statement below is an opinion?
   a. All over the world, the mother-in-law is always provoking a fight.
   b. Seven years ago, Daoud Sediqi had his head shaved.
   c. Only 28% of the Afghan population is literate.
   d. Attorney General Abdul Jabar Sabet sent policemen to arrest the news staff at Tolo TV.

WHY? What leads you to give that answer? There are two overly broad ideas in answer A: *all over the world* and *always*. Often, such broad statements cannot be verified and thus cannot be considered facts. Also, very few things are always true all around the world. True statements tend to be more specific. Answers B, C, and D are facts that can be verified either by this newspaper article or the author's sources of information.

Practice

____ 10. Which of the following inferences is valid—that is, supported by the information in the article?
   a. Afghan society will remain as it is, despite the influence of television.
   b. Afghan society is changing due to the influence of television.
   c. People around the world use television mostly as a way to forget their troubles.
   d. Television contributes to the spread of HIV-AIDS.

WHY? What information in the selection leads you to give that answer? _____

_____

_____

_____

_____

_____

● Vocabulary in Context

The following words were used in "Amid War, Passion for TV Chefs, Soaps and Idols."
Choose the best word from the list to complete each sentence.

communal	gestated	in fits and starts	transgression
extramarital	hackneyed	intrafamily	

1. The hippies in the 1960s and 1970s made _____ living famous in America.

2. They tried to overcome the idea that people should live in nuclear families and have sexual relationships only with their husband or wife. Instead of considering _____ _____ sex a _____, they celebrated it as an expression of free love.

3. Although living in community was a fresh idea then, by now some of the hippies' notions of communes seem _____, even ridiculous. But the idea has _____, and now other kinds of communities have formed in the United States, such as cohousing, an idea that started in Denmark.

4. Forming an intentional community can be a process that happens _____ _____. So many difficult tasks are involved, such as finding land that the group can afford, that the effort can easily stop short of success.

5. In successful communities, however, the group can come to feel like a family. And as in all families, _____ tensions can skyrocket over matters like agreeing on how to make decisions.

Reading 1-2 . . . . **Sociology Textbook**

● Pre-Reading the Selection

The excerpt that begins on page 40 comes from a college sociology textbook. The excerpt is part of a section called "Popular Culture and the Media."

Guessing the Purpose

Based on the type of book this reading is from, do you suppose the authors' purpose is mostly to persuade, inform, or entertain? _____

Surveying the Reading

What parts of the reading selection should you survey? _____

_____

Go ahead and survey the reading.

Predicting the Content

Based on your survey, what are three things you expect the reading selection to discuss?

- _____

- _____

- _____

Activating Your Knowledge

Think about your daily life and the television programs, movies, radio programs, Web sites, newspapers, books, and magazines—the mass media—you pay attention to. How does the mass media affect your life? Write down two or three effects it has on your daily life.

- _____

- _____

- _____

Common Knowledge

Read this term and its definition to help you understand the reading selection.

Social issues (*paragraph 4*) Community problems that can't be explained by discussing only an individual's actions. Some examples are poverty, discrimination, violence, and crime.

Reading with Pen in Hand

Now read the selection. As you read, mark any ideas that seem important, and respond to the questions and vocabulary items in the margin. Monitor your comprehension by putting a ✔ next to a paragraph when you understand most of it. Place an ✘ next to a paragraph when you don't understand most of it.

Visit **www.cengage.com/devenglish/doleconnect** and select Chapter 1 to hear vocabulary words from this selection and view a video about this topic.

◆ *Reading Journal*

◆Think about your week. What forms of mass-produced culture did you consume?

consumed Based on the contrast with *produced*, what does *consumed* mean?

◆Read paragraphs 2–4. Where is the main idea for this whole group of paragraphs?

elite Based on the contrast with *"ordinary" citizens* and the general meaning, what does *elite* mean?

◆Does the information in Figure 1.1 surprise you? Why or why not?

Popular Culture and the Media

Margaret L. Andersen & Howard F. Taylor

1   Some aspects of culture pervade the whole society, such as common language, general patterns of dress, and dominant value systems. **Popular culture** includes the beliefs, practices, and objects that are part of everyday traditions. This includes mass-produced culture, such as popular music and films, mass-marketed books and magazines, large-circulation newspapers, and other parts of the culture that are shared by the general populace. Popular culture is distinct from elite culture, which is shared by only a select few but is highly valued. Unlike elite culture (sometimes referred to as "high culture"), popular culture is mass-produced and mass-**consumed** and has enormous significance in the formation of public attitudes and values. Popular culture is also supported by patterns of mass consumption, as the many objects associated with popular culture are promoted and sold to a consuming public.

2   Different groups partake of popular and elite culture in different ways. First, social class affects the ability of groups to participate in certain forms of culture (see **Figure 1.1**). The elite may derive

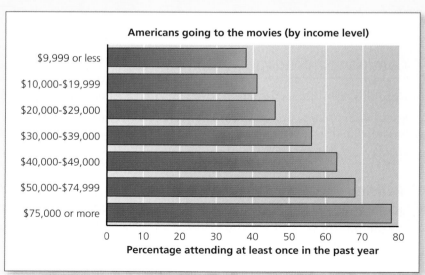

Americans going to the movies (by income level)

Percentage attending at least once in the past year

Figure 1.1 Who Goes to the Movies?

U.S. Census Bureau. 2005. *Statistical Abstract of the United States 2004.* Washington D.C.: U.S. Department of Commerce, p. 769.

their culture from expensive theater shows or opera performances where tickets can cost $100 each. Meanwhile, millions of "ordinary" citizens get their primary cultural experience from television, movie rentals, and increasingly, the Internet.

3   Second, familiarity with different cultural forms stems from patterns of **exclusion** throughout history, as well as integration into networks that provide information about the arts. As a result, African Americans are much more likely than White Americans to attend jazz concerts and listen to soul, blues, rhythm and blues, and other historically African American musical forms.

exclusion What verb (action word) does *exclusion* relate to?

◆How does the author label the three main points in paragraphs 2–4?

4   Third, popular culture is increasingly **disseminated** by the mass media, either through television, film, radio, or even the Internet; thus, it is buttressed by the interests of big entertainment and information industries that profit from the cultural forms they produce. Each of these factors reveals the social structure of popular and elite culture.

disseminated Based on the sentence's meaning, what does this word mean?

American Consumption of Popular Culture

5   Popular culture is characterized by mass distribution. **Mass media** are the channels of communication available to wide segments of the population—the print, film, and electronic media (radio and television), and increasingly, the Internet. The mass media have extraordinary power to shape information and public perceptions in an era when complex issues are reduced to "sound bites" and "photo opportunities."

◆Does the mass media increase or decrease the public's awareness of all the details of issues?

6   For most Americans, **leisure time** is dominated by television. 98 percent of all homes in the United States have at least one television—more than have telephone service. The average person consumes some form of media 73 hours per week—more time than they likely spend in school or at work; 34 of these hours are spent watching television. Watching television is also the most popular leisure activity of Americans; 26 percent say it is their favorite way to spend an evening, compared to 9 percent who would rather read and 1 percent whose favorite evening activity is listening to music.

leisure time Based on the meaning of the sentence, do these words mean *work time* or *play time*?

◆What type of media do Americans access most frequently in their free time?

The Influence of Mass Media

7   Television and other forms of mass media have enormous power to shape public opinion and behavior. If you doubt this, observe how familiar certain characters from television sitcoms and dramas are in everyday life. People at work may talk about last night's episode of a particular show or laugh about the antics of their favorite sitcom

◆Look at the details in paragraph 7 about how people talk about TV characters. Then look at the details about how TVs are everywhere. What more general idea in the paragraph do both of these groups of details support?

Figure 1.2
Percentage of Americans Who Say They Are Offended by the Content of Television (by age)

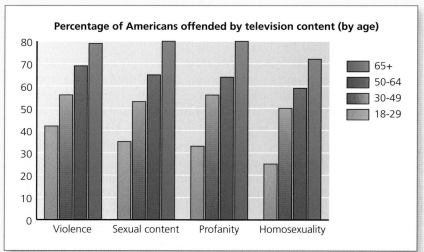

Percentage of Americans offended by television content (by age)

Legend:
- 65+
- 50-64
- 30-49
- 18-29

Categories: Violence, Sexual content, Profanity, Homosexuality

Data: Jones, Jeffrey M. 2004. "Most Americans Offended by Sex and Violence on Television." *The Gallup Poll*, Princeton, NJ. www.gallup.com

◆About what percentage of 18 to 29 year olds are offended by violent content on TV?

ubiquitous Based on the series of examples given in the sentence, does this word mean *everywhere* or *hardly anywhere*?

◆Does this paragraph support the idea that television has enormous power to shape public opinion and behavior?

◆How do the media shape our definition of social problems?

character. The media is also **ubiquitous**—present in airports, elevators, classrooms, bars and restaurants, and hospital waiting rooms. You may even be born to the sounds and images of television, since they are turned on in many hospital delivery rooms. Television is now so ever-present in our lives that 42 percent of all U.S. households are now called "constant television households"—that is, those households where television is on most of the time. Black children are more likely than White or Hispanic children to live in such households. For many families, TV is the "babysitter."

8   The mass media (and television, in particular) play a huge role in shaping people's perception and awareness of social issues. For example, even though crime has actually decreased, the amount of time spent reporting crime in the media has increased. Sociologists have found that people's fear of crime is directly related to the time they spend watching television or listening to the radio.

9   Although people tend to think of the news as authentic and true, news is actually manufactured in a complex social process. From a sociological perspective, it is not objective reality that determines what news is presented and how it is portrayed, but commercial interests, the values of news producers, and perceptions of what matters to the public. The media shape our definition of social problems by determining the range of opinion or information that is defined as legitimate and by deciding which experts will be called on to elaborate an issue.

● Comprehension Questions

Write the letter of the answer on the line. Then explain your thinking.

Main Idea

Skill

Think of the main idea as the "point" of the paragraph or passage. The main idea dominates the paragraph. To find the main idea, notice which sentence explains the author's most important point about the subject. The other sentences in the paragraph should offer explanations, examples, and details about the main idea. Sometimes a main idea may cover the supporting details from several paragraphs.

Example

  _d_   1. What is the best statement of the main idea of paragraph 7?

   a. You may even be born to the sounds and images of television, since they are turned on in many hospital delivery rooms.

   b. People at work may talk about last night's episode of a particular show or laugh about the antics of their favorite sitcom character.

   c. If you doubt this, observe how familiar certain characters from television sitcoms and dramas are in everyday life.

   d. Television and other forms of mass media have enormous power to shape public opinion and behavior.

WHY? What information in the selection leads you to give that answer? In paragraph 7, the other sentences all support the main idea, which is stated in answer D. Answers A, B, and C are some of these supporting details. Notice that they are more specific than the main idea. The main idea is more general.

Practice

   _____   2. What is the best statement of the main idea of paragraph 6?

   a. 34 of these hours are spent watching television.

   b. 26 percent of Americans say it is their favorite way to spend an evening.

   c. For most Americans, leisure time is dominated by television.

   d. 98 percent of all homes in the U.S. have at least one television.

WHY? What information in the selection leads you to give that answer? _____

_____

_____

Supporting Details

Skill

Think of the supporting details as the "proof" for the main idea. To locate the supporting details, find the main idea and then look for the information the author uses to explain it in more detail. Sometimes, if a main idea covers more than one paragraph, you will find the supporting details in several paragraphs.

Example

 b   3. In paragraph 6, what are the three major supporting details?

   a. Leisure time is dominated by TV; 98 percent of U.S. homes have at least one TV; 9 percent of Americans would rather read than watch TV.

   b. 98 percent of U.S. homes have at least one TV; the average American watches 34 hours of TV a week; 26 percent of Americans say watching TV is their favorite way to spend an evening.

   c. Leisure time is dominated by TV; 98 percent of U.S. homes have at least one TV; more homes have TV sets than have telephone service.

   d. 98 percent of U.S. homes have at least one TV; the average person consumes some form of media 73 hours a week; 1 percent of Americans prefer listening to music over watching TV.

WHY? What information in the selection leads you to give that answer? The main idea of paragraph 6 is "For most Americans, leisure time is dominated by television." (Thus answers A and C are not correct, since they include the main idea and not just supporting details.) Answer B gives the three major supporting details for the main idea. Each idea is a piece of evidence that Americans spend much of their leisure time watching television.

Practice

_____ 4. Which of the following statements do the two supporting details in paragraph 8 best support?

    a. The less people watch television or listen to the radio, the more they worry about crime.

    b. Television and radio cause people to believe that less crime is occurring.

    c. People's understanding of social issues is influenced by the media.

    d. Television, the Internet, and the radio are three forms of mass media.

WHY? What information in the selection leads you to give that answer? _____

_____

_____

_____

Author's Purpose

Skill

The author's general purpose may be to persuade (change the reader's mind or behavior), inform (share information with the reader), or entertain (amuse the reader, often through stories); or it may be a combination of these purposes. At specific points in a text, an author may use a variety of methods to achieve the general purpose. You should always assume that the author has a particular reason for what he or she wrote.

Example

 a 5. In paragraphs 1 and 5, what is the author's purpose for putting **popular culture** and **mass media** in bold type?

    a. To indicate that a definition of the term will follow.

    b. To indicate that these are the only two ideas in the selection that need to be memorized.

    c. To indicate that the two phrases mean the same thing.

    d. To indicate that these are the main ideas in the paragraph.

WHY? What information in the selection leads you to give that answer? In both paragraphs, first the term is given in bold, and then the definition follows immediately. There is no evidence in the selection for answer B or C. Answer D can't be right because the other paragraphs in the selection do not have any bold terms, yet they do have main ideas.

Practice

____   6. In paragraph 6, what is the author's purpose in noting that more U.S. homes have televisions than telephones?

   a. The reader would probably expect more homes to have phones than TVs, so this comparison strongly emphasizes the point about the domination of TV.

   b. The author wants readers to understand that people love their TVs as much as they love their phones.

   c. The author made the comparison in order to surprise readers and make them chuckle.

   d. The author is driving home the point that people now prefer to passively watch TV instead of actively talk on the phone with other people.

WHY? What information in the selection leads you to give that answer? _____

_____

_____

Relationships

Skill

The ideas in a reading selection are related to one another in different ways. For instance, one sentence might discuss the causes of an event mentioned in a different sentence. Some relationships have to do with time, space, comparisons and contrasts, causes and effects, and so on. You may see the relationships between the ideas in different parts of one sentence, in different sentences, or even in different paragraphs. Many times, these relationships are indicated with signal words or transitions such as *but, and, however, for example,* and so on.

Example

_c_   7. Paragraph 1 says, "Popular culture is distinct from elite culture. . . . Unlike elite culture, popular culture is mass-produced and mass-consumed." What is the relationship between popular culture and elite culture?

   a. They are both mass-produced.

   b. They are the same or similar.

   c. They are opposites or different.

   d. One is an example of the other.

WHY? What leads you to give that answer? The two words that show that the relationship is one of opposites, or at least difference, are *distinct* and *unlike*.

Practice

____   8. In paragraph 8, what is the relationship of the second sentence to the first sentence?

   a. It is a comparison.

   b. It is an example.

   c. It is an event that happened later in time.

   d. It is an event that happened at the same time.

WHY? What information in the selection leads you to give that answer? _____

_____

Fact, Opinion, and Inference

Skill

A fact is a true statement that can be verified by using another source of information: *It is 85 degrees outside*. An opinion is a person's personal reaction: *It's too hot to play baseball*. An inference is an idea the reader gets from the other ideas that the author has stated: *That person must be from up north*. To be valid, an inference must be a logical extension of what the author has written.

Example

<u>c</u>   9. Which statement below is an opinion?

    a. Tickets to opera performances can cost $100 each.

    b. Forty-two percent of U.S. households have TV on most of the time.

    c. People watch too much television.

    d. Older Americans are more offended by sexual content on TV than younger Americans.

WHY? What leads you to give that answer? The phrase *too much* indicates a value judgment that someone is making. Such statements can't be said to be accurate or inaccurate; they are simply the person's opinion. Answers A, B, and D can all be verified by the words and graphs in the textbook reading selection. Thus, they are facts.

Practice

_____   10. What valid inference can you draw from the information given in paragraph 2 and Figure 1.1?

    a. Elites are snobs.

    b. Social class is related to income.

    c. People with incomes under $75,000 never attend the opera.

    d. No one with an income of $9,999 or less can afford to go to the movies.

WHY? What information in the selection leads you to give that answer? _____

_____

_____

_____

● **Vocabulary in Context**

The following words were used in the reading selection "Popular Culture and the Media." Choose the best word from the list to complete each sentence.

| consumed | elite | exclusion | disseminated | leisure time | ubiquitous |

1. From 1876 to 1965, African Americans and other "black" residents were subject to _____ from public schools, overnight accommodations, restaurants, and public bathrooms used by whites.

2. The so-called Jim Crow laws were _____ in Southern and Western states. The laws were _____ in at least eighteen states.

3. _____ by a desire to maintain their _____ status as compared to black Americans, lawmakers in some states even made laws for maintaining separate phone booths, separate hospitals, and separate teachers' colleges.

4. Even _____ activities were affected: White and black amateur baseball teams in Georgia were not permitted within two blocks of one another, and in Oklahoma, fishing and boating were segregated activities.

chapter 2

Asking Questions

© Jack Hollingsworth/Blend Images/Jupiter Images

When I was in college, I was working for a savings-and-loan as a security guard at night. One evening, my identical twin brother stopped by, and one of my not-so-bright coworkers was amazed:

> COWORKER: Wow, are you guys twins?
> ME: Yeah.
> COWORKER: How do you tell each other apart?

Does the coworker ask good questions? Why or why not?

www.cengage.com/devenglish/doleconnect

Videos Related to Readings   **Vocab Words on Audio**   **Prep Readings on Demand**

Share Your Prior Knowledge

Have you used questions effectively to help you learn something? What kinds of questions did you ask?

Survey the Chapter

Survey pages 54 to 61. What kinds of questions might make reading and thinking more effective?

Prep Reading . . . . **Quiz and Magazine Article**

Take the Curiosity and Exploration Inventory, developed by Professor Todd Kashdan and his colleagues at George Mason University. Then read the article that follows, which discusses Kashdan's findings.

Visit **www.cengage.com/devenglish/doleconnect** and select Chapter 2 to hear a reading of this selection and view a video about this topic.

Curiosity and Exploration Inventory (CEI)

Using the scale shown below, please respond to each of the following statements according to how you would usually describe yourself. There are no right or wrong answers.

1	2	3	4	5	6	7
Strongly Disagree			Neither Agree nor Disagree			Strongly Agree

_____ 1. I would describe myself as someone who actively seeks as much information as I can in a new situation.

_____ 2. When I am participating in an activity, I tend to get so involved that I lose track of time.

_____ 3. I frequently find myself looking for new opportunities to grow as a person (e.g., information, people, resources).

_____ 4. I am *not* the type of person who probes deeply into new situations or things.

_____ 5. When I am actively interested in something, it takes a great deal to interrupt me.

_____ 6. My friends would describe me as someone who is "extremely intense" when in the middle of doing something.

_____ 7. Everywhere I go, I am out looking for new things or experiences.

Scoring: Total the scores you gave for items 1–3 and 5–7. For item 4, reverse the score. For example, if you scored yourself as 1, count it as a 7; if you scored yourself as 2, count it as a 6; if a 3, count it as a 5. If you scored 7, 6, or 5, count it as a 1, 2, or 3. A 4 remains a 4. Then add this number to your others. The highest possible score is 49; the lowest is 7. The higher the score, the more curious and exploratory you are. Of course, you can choose to become more curious—and the next reading selection will tell you how.

© Comstock Images/Jupiter Images

Cultivating Curiosity

Elizabeth Svoboda

1   Decades before Evan Schaeffer started practicing law, he developed an interest so all-consuming it verged on **obsession**: snakes. By the time he entered the fourth grade, he had so many reptile books that they took up an entire shelf, and he counted the gloves, golf putter and pillow-case he used for snake-hunting among his most prized possessions.

2   The snake fascination gradually faded, but Schaeffer's determination to learn as much as he could about everything that interested him remained. "I never have to try to have hobbies—they just seem to find me," he says. Outside of work, he plays the guitar, writes songs, is an amateur astronomer and photographer, and maintains a blog called Evan Schaeffer's Legal Underground. "I like that my mind gets to focus on things I've chosen on my own," he says. "It gives me a sense of freedom I wouldn't have otherwise."

3   Schaeffer is what psychologists call a "trait curious" person: someone with a tendency to delve deeply into subjects that grab his attention, learning more about himself and the world in the process.

4   Curious people are used to being joshed for their obsessions—**monikers** like "band geek" and "bookworm" are a way of saying "Just relax, already!" According to a new study by Todd Kashdan of George Mason University, however, the unusually curious often have the last laugh.

5   Kashdan asked students how much they agreed with statements such as, "When I am actively interested in something, it takes a great

obsession If an interest is *all-consuming*, and that interest is almost—but not quite—an *obsession*, what is the likely meaning of *obsession*?

monikers Two examples of this word follow the word *like*. What are the two examples? What is a *moniker*?

hedonistic Two examples of *hedonistic behavior* are given after the phrase *such as.* What are they? What does *hedonistic* probably mean?

deal to interrupt me." People who exhibit high levels of curiosity, he found, experience higher levels of satisfaction with life than their more disengaged peers. While the less curious derive more pleasure from **hedonistic** behaviors such as sex and drinking, curious people report finding a greater sense of meaning in life, which is a better predictor of sustainable, lasting happiness.

6   What accounts for the link between curiosity and well-being? Kashdan speculates that while dabbling in new activities or subject areas may be uncomfortable at first, curious people are likely to be rewarded for their efforts over the long run. These rewards can be social, like enjoying weekly lunches with friends you met in a beginning windsurfing class. Most of the time, though, the pleasure is **intrinsic** to the activity itself, as when you master the unicycle or a Mozart piano sonata. Because the sheer high of such an accomplishment is its own reward, the curious tend to be highly self-motivated.

intrinsic The previous sentence discusses a social reward of trying new activities, and then this sentence offers a contrast by starting with the words *Most of the time, though.* A third clue can be found in the sentence after that, which explains what *intrinsic* means. What words explain it?

7   "There's this paradoxical route to well-being," Kashdan says. "Maybe the real way to make yourself happy is by doing something that challenges you, makes you stretch." Self-reported curiosity, he adds, tends to build over time, which suggests that the knowledge and experience curious people gain give them satisfaction, motivating them to learn even more.

inquisitive Refer back to the first paragraph to remind yourself what Evan Shaeffer is like. What does *inquisitive* mean?

8   In Schaeffer's case, following his **inquisitive** mind led to new opportunities he'd never even considered. "Recently, a publisher got into contact with me through my blog and asked if I'd like to write a book about trial law," he says. "I'd always had a side career in writing, but I never expected it to turn into something like this." The lives of curious people may not always go according to plan, but their willingness to take a chance on improvisation pays big in dividends.

———— How to Flex Your Curiosity Muscle ————

9   **Reframe boring situations.** If you've got an inquiring mind, it's possible to turn even mundane events, like waiting in line at the DMV, into something meaningful. Look for details others might miss, and seek to learn more about them. For instance, try turning to another customer in line and saying, "I noticed the Purple Heart pinned to your jacket. What war did you serve in?"

10   **Don't let fear stop you from trying something new.** "If you're curious about something, it acts as a positive counterweight to anxiety and fear," Silvia says. Exercising your curiosity won't wipe out doubt, but it may help you focus on the likely positive consequences

of a new venture (learning to execute a perfect swan dive) rather than the negative ones (doing a belly flop and surfacing to the sound of laughter).

11   **Let your true passions shine.** A key component of curiosity is what Boston College psychologist Ellen Winner calls a "rage to master"—whether that involves accumulating rejection slips from *The New Yorker* or spending hours in the basement learning banjo fingerings. An intense focus on specific interests or goals invites the state of mental immersion called "flow," which in turn elicits feelings of accomplishment and well-being.

Interaction 2-1. Talking about Reading

Respond in writing to the questions below and then discuss your answers with your classmates.

1. What ideas, places, events, people, things, activities, or anything else have fascinated you in your lifetime? Name at least five. How did you go about investigating them? What did you do to learn more? _____

   _____

   _____

   _____

2. What does Professor Kashdan say are the reasons that curious people continue to be curious? _____

   _____

3. "How to Flex Your Curiosity Muscle" suggests three ways to develop curiosity. Think of a situation in which you typically experience boredom and would like to develop more curiosity. How could you apply each of these ideas to that situation?

   _____

   _____

4. How can you tell when someone is curious? What do they look like—their facial expressions, their body language? What do they sound like—their tone of voice, their words? What emotions do they seem to be feeling? Under what circumstances do *you* look, sound, and feel like this? _____

   _____

Asking Questions to Establish Your Purpose for Reading

When you genuinely want to know something, you ask a lot of questions about it. Asking questions leads to learning more. So when you need to learn from a reading selection, ask questions about it. Searching for the answers to your questions gives you a well-defined purpose for reading. Stating your purpose for reading will motivate you to read actively and clarify what information you are looking for.

Turn Headings or Titles into Questions

Start with the title or heading; turn it into a question and then look for the answer as you read. **Table 2.1** gives some titles of nonfiction trade books (non-textbooks) and some headings from college textbooks, along with questions that you might form from them.

Table 2.1 Questions Formed from Titles and Headings

Book title or textbook heading	Question
The Innocent Man: Murder and Injustice in a Small Town (book title)	Who is the innocent man, what was the injustice, and in what small town did this happen?
The Week that Changed the World (book title)	What week changed the world? How did it change the world?
"Material and Nonmaterial Culture" (sociology textbook heading)	How are material and nonmaterial culture different?
"Solving Equations Containing Fractions" (mathematics textbook heading)	How do you solve equations containing fractions?
"Why Hills Look Steeper Than They Are" (psychology textbook heading)	Why do hills look steeper than they are?
"The Fourteenth Century: A Time of Transition" (humanities textbook heading)	Why (or how) was the fourteenth century a time of transition?

Notice that to form the questions, we used the main words of the title or heading. These are the words that carry much of the meaning. For example, in the last heading, the subtitle is "A Time of Transition." The two main words, *Time* and *Transition,* are connected somehow to the main words of the title, *Fourteenth Century.* But how? That is the information to look for while you read.

We also tried to figure out what kind of information might be coming. For example, in the third heading, since the two kinds of culture, *material* and *nonmaterial,* seem to be opposites, we used the word *different* in forming the question about them. Sometimes asking more than one question seems necessary, especially when there is a title and a subtitle.

Interaction 2-2. Forming Questions and Activating Your Prior Knowledge

For each textbook heading, form a question that you think would be answered in the section that follows it. Take a moment to think about some possible answers to the question before moving on to the next item. In other words, activate your prior knowledge on the topic.

1. "The Causes of Obesity" (psychology). Question: <u>EXAMPLE: What are the causes of obesity?</u>

   _____

   Some possible answers: <u>EXAMPLE: eating too much, exercising too little, genetic influence.</u>

2. "The Process of Management" (business management). Question: _____

   _____

   Some possible answers: _____

   _____

3. "Comparing American and Metric Units of Measurements" (math). Question: _____

   _____

   Some possible answers: _____

   _____

4. "Muscles, Exercise, and Aging" (biology). Question: _____

   _____

   Some possible answers: _____

   _____

5. "The Great Balancing Act: The Rights of the Accused versus the Rights of Society" (American government). Question: _____

   _____

   Some possible answers: _____

   _____

   _____

● Interaction 2-3. Forming Questions and Stating a Purpose for Reading

The heading and four subheadings that follow are from one section of a chapter in a college biology textbook. Turn each one into a question and write the question next to the heading. You may need to form two questions if a heading has two ideas. Then make a statement about what will be your purpose for reading. Third, take a moment to call forth any prior knowledge you may have about the answer to each question.

1. Section heading: Overview of Life's Unity

   Question: EXAMPLE: What is included in an overview of life's unity?

   My purpose for reading: EXAMPLE: I want to get an overview of the unity of life.

2. First subheading: DNA, The Basis of Inheritance

   Question: _____

   My purpose for reading: _____

3. Second subheading: Energy, The Basis of Metabolism

   Question: _____

   My purpose for reading: _____

4. Third subheading: Energy and Life's Organization

   Question: _____

   My purpose for reading: _____

5. Fourth subheading: Life's Responsiveness to Change

   Question: _____

   My purpose for reading: _____

Read to Answer the Question, and Then Mark the Answer

When you have formed a question from the heading , stated a purpose for reading, and thought about any prior knowledge you may have, you are ready to read for the answer. The parts of the answer to the question are the main ideas of the section. When you reach an idea or fact that helps to answer the question you formed from the heading, mark it in some way: highlight it, underline it, or otherwise mark it as a main idea. Be careful to mark only the ideas that directly answer the question.

⬤ Interaction 2-4. Marking the Answer to the Question

Here is the first part of section 1.2 of *Biology: Today and Tomorrow,* which you just asked questions about in Interaction 2-3. The two questions we asked about the main heading and the first subheading are written in the margin.

The different parts of the answers to these questions are highlighted in the reading.

1.2 Overview of Life's Unity

What is included in an overview of life's unity?

1   "Life" is not easy to define. It is too big, and it has been changing for 3.9 billion years! Even so, you can frame a definition in terms of its unity and diversity. Here is the unity part: All living things grow and reproduce with the help of DNA, energy, and raw materials. They sense and respond to their environment. But details of their traits differ among many millions of kinds of organisms. That is the diversity part—variation in traits.

DNA, the Basis of Inheritance

What is DNA, and how is it the basis of inheritance?

2   You will never, ever find a rock made of nucleic acids, proteins, and complex carbohydrates and lipids. In the natural world, only living cells make these molecules. The signature molecule of life is the nucleic acid called DNA. No chunk of granite or quartz has it.

3   DNA holds information for building proteins from smaller molecules: the amino acids. By analogy, if you follow suitable instructions and invest enough energy in the task, you might organize a pile of a few kinds of ceramic tiles (representing amino acids) into diverse patterns (representing proteins), as in **Figure 2.1**.

4   Why are the proteins so important? Many kinds are structural materials, and others are enzymes. Enzymes are the main worker molecules in cells. They build, split, and rearrange the molecules of

Figure 2.1.
Examples of objects built from the same materials according to different assembly instructions.

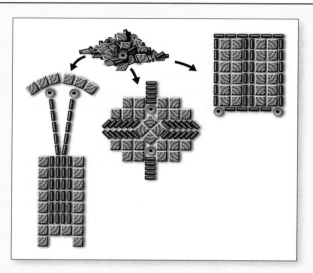

life in ways that keep a cell alive. Without enzymes, the information held in DNA could not be used. There would be no new organisms.

5   In nature, each organism inherits its DNA—and its traits—from parents. Inheritance means an acquisition of traits after parents transmit their DNA to offspring. Think about it. Why do baby storks look like storks and not like pelicans? Because storks inherit stork DNA, not pelican DNA.

6   *Reproduction* refers to actual mechanisms by which parents transmit DNA to offspring. For slugs, humans, trees, and other multicelled organisms, information in DNA guides *development*— the transformation of the first cell of a new individual into a multicelled adult, typically with many different tissues and organs.

—Starr, Evers, and Starr, *Biology: Today and Tomorrow,* 2nd Edition

Using the knowledge you gained from reading, answer these questions formed from the headings. The second question has been split into its two components (parts).

1. What is included in an overview of life's unity? _____

   _____

2. What is DNA? _____

   _____

3. How is DNA the basis of inheritance? _____

   _____

Mark Only the Most Important Ideas

Notice that answering the questions we posed about the headings did *not* require rewriting the whole reading selection. That's because most of the words a writer uses are details and examples that help readers understand the main ideas. It's the main ideas that you are searching for now. The only marking or highlighting you'll want to do to answer your questions is on the main ideas, which are the answers to the questions.

When you think about one of the purposes for highlighting, you will see why you should mark only the main ideas. Long after you have read a selection, you may need to review it as you study for a test on the material. If you highlight too much material, you will have to reread much of it, which is an inefficient way to study. Mark no more than 10-15% of a reading selection to make your highlighting the most effective.

● Interaction 2-5. Reading to Answer Your Question

The next subsection of "Overview of Life's Unity" is printed below. Review the heading and the question you formed from it, and mark the parts of the answer to the question. Then answer the questions that follow.

Energy, the Basis of Metabolism

1   DNA is only part of the picture. Becoming alive and maintaining life requires energy—the capacity to do work. Each normal living cell has ways to obtain and convert energy from its surroundings. By the process called metabolism, a cell acquires and uses energy to maintain itself, grow, and make more cells.

2   Where does the energy come from? Nearly all of it flows from the sun into the world of life, starting with **producers**. Producers are plants and other organisms that make their own food from simple raw materials. All other organisms are **consumers**. They cannot make their own food; they must eat other organisms.

3   When, say, zebras browse on plants, some energy stored in plant tissues is transferred to them. Later on, energy is transferred to a lion as it devours the zebra. It gets transferred again as decomposers go to work, acquiring energy from the remains of zebras, lions, and other organisms.

4   Decomposers are consumers, mostly bacteria and fungi that break down sugars and other molecules to simpler materials. Some of the breakdown products are cycled back to producers as raw materials. Over time, energy that plants originally captured from the sun returns to the environment.

—Starr, Evers, and Starr, Biology: *Today and Tomorrow*, 2nd Edition

1. What is energy? _____

2. How is energy the basis of metabolism? _____

   _____

3. What are paragraphs 2 to 4 mainly about? _____

   _____

4. What are two main kinds of organisms, grouped in terms of how they get energy?

   _____

5. What example does the author give of each kind of organism? _____

   _____

6. Since these paragraphs have been mostly about energy, what is the next topic you
   expect the author to cover? _____

Asking Questions to Improve Your Thinking

The questions you have been forming from headings are a natural way to start an inter-action with the author of the selection. The questions help you comprehend the main ideas, which you need to be able to do before you can work with them further. Once you have understood the author's ideas, using an organized method for asking ques-tions and thinking about them will allow you to compare and contrast these ideas with other ideas, follow the thoughts to their logical conclusions, or apply the ideas to other areas of your life. Critical thinking is the vehicle.

Critical Thinking Is a Learning Process

Critical thinking is a systematic process of thinking and learning that includes the fol-lowing kinds of activities:

- Gathering information about a subject and remembering it accurately.
- Gaining clarity about what the subject means or how it acts.
- Thinking about how ideas can be applied in different situations.
- Analyzing the parts of the subject to find out how they are related.
- Evaluating the usefulness or worth of the subject based on relevant criteria.
- Forming new ideas or creating something new based on this thinking process.

When you read textbooks, articles, and other materials in college and in your career, and when you listen to lectures in your courses or during work-related training, you will dramatically increase the amount you learn if you make it a habit to systematically apply these six thinking activities to the subject matter.

You won't learn nearly as much if you simply read the words the author has written, even if you remember the words well. You need to actively question the author's words, think about the ideas behind the words, and then make decisions or solve problems based on the understanding you have formed.

To help you form the habit of using this thinking process, after each chapter-end reading throughout *Connect,* you'll find a series of six critical thinking questions. The questions are arranged in six levels, according to a format of increasing complexity that Benjamin Bloom devised. (Bloom was a professor at the University of Chicago. His system has recently been revised by others, including Lorin W. Anderson and David R. Krathwohl.) Figure 2.2 describes the six levels.

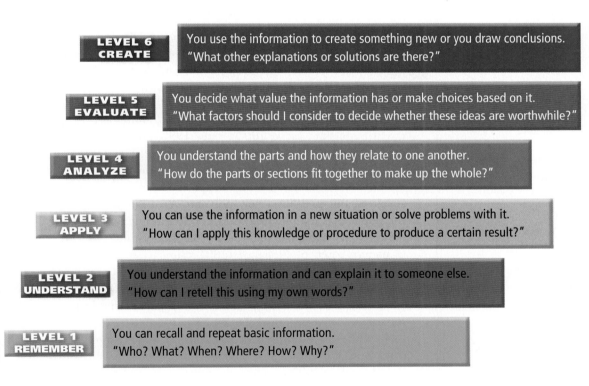

LEVEL 6 CREATE
You use the information to create something new or you draw conclusions. "What other explanations or solutions are there?"

LEVEL 5 EVALUATE
You decide what value the information has or make choices based on it. "What factors should I consider to decide whether these ideas are worthwhile?"

LEVEL 4 ANALYZE
You understand the parts and how they relate to one another. "How do the parts or sections fit together to make up the whole?"

LEVEL 3 APPLY
You can use the information in a new situation or solve problems with it. "How can I apply this knowledge or procedure to produce a certain result?"

LEVEL 2 UNDERSTAND
You understand the information and can explain it to someone else. "How can I retell this using my own words?"

LEVEL 1 REMEMBER
You can recall and repeat basic information. "Who? What? When? Where? How? Why?"

Figure 2.2 Bloom's Taxonomy with Questions. Each thinking action depends on mastering the steps below it. In order to draw conclusions from your reading, for example, you need to recall it, understand it, use it, grasp how its parts work together, and evaluate its worth.

You can use this thinking process to help you make decisions, solve problems, investigate majors or job offers, and read books, articles, and Web sites.

Interaction 2-6. Asking Reading and Thinking Questions

Use the reading process you summarized in the Chapter Summary Activity in Chapter 1 on page 23 to read the following selection from a sociology textbook. (The selection continues in Interaction 2-7.) Turn the headings into questions, and write them in the margin. Read for the answers, and then mark them. Finally, answer the critical thinking questions that follow.

Applying the Four Theories: The Problem of Fashion

Oh. Two weeks ago I saw Cameron Diaz at Fred Siegel and I talked her out of buying this truly heinous angora sweater. Whoever said orange is the new pink is seriously disturbed.
—Elle Woods (Actor Reese Witherspoon) in *Legally Blond* (2001)

Question:

1   In December 2002 the *Wall Street Journal* announced that Grunge might be back (Tkacik, 2002). Since 1998, one of the main fashion trends among white, middle-class, and preteen and young teenage girls was the Britney Spears look: bare midriffs, highlighted hair, wide belts, glitter purses, big wedge shoes, and Skechers "Energy" sneakers. But in 2002 a new pop star, Avril Lavigne, was rising on the pop charts. Nominated for a 2003 Grammy Award in the "Best New Artist" category, the 17-year-old skater-punk from the small Canadian town of Napanee (2001 population: 15,132), affects a shaggy, unkempt look (Statistics Canada, 2002). She sports worn-out T-shirts, 1970s-style plaid Western shirts with snaps, low-rise blue jeans, baggy pants, undershirts, ties, backpacks, chain wallets, and, for shoes, Converse Chuck Taylors. The style is similar to the Grunge look of the early 1990s, when Nirvana and Pearl Jam were the big stars on MTV and Kurt Cobain was king of the music world.

2   Why in late 2002 were the glamorous trends of the pop era giving way in one market segment to "neo-Grunge"? Why, in general, do fashion shifts take place? Sociological theory has interesting things to say on this subject (Davis, 1992).

The Functionalist Approach to Fashion Trends

Question:

3   Until the 1960s, the standard sociological approach to explaining the ebb and flow of fashion trends was functionalist. In the functionalist view, fashion trends worked like this: Every season, exclusive fashion houses in Paris and, to a lesser extent, Milan, New York, and London would show new styles. Some of the new styles would catch on among the exclusive clientele of Chanel, Dior, Givenchy, and other big-name designers. The main appeal of wearing expensive, new fashions was that wealthy clients could distinguish themselves from people who were less well off. Thus, fashion performed an important social function. By allowing people of different rank to distinguish themselves from one another, fashion helped preserve the ordered layering of society into classes. ("It is an interesting question," wrote 19th-century American writer Henry David Thoreau in *Walden*, "how far [people] would retain their relative rank if they were divested of their clothes.") By the 20th century, thanks to technological advances in clothes manufacturing, it didn't take long for inexpensive knockoffs to reach the market and trickle down to lower classes. New styles then had to be introduced frequently so that fashion could continue to perform its function of helping to maintain an orderly class system. Hence the ebb and flow of fashion.

4   The functionalist theory was a fairly accurate account of the way fashion trends worked until the 1960s. Then, fashion became more democratic. Paris, Milan, New York, and London are still hugely important fashion centers today. However, new fashion trends are increasingly initiated by lower classes, minority racial and ethnic groups, and people who spurn "high" fashion altogether. Napanee is, after all, pretty far from Paris, and today big-name designers are more likely to be influenced by the inner-city styles of hip-hop than vice versa. New fashions no longer just trickle down from upper classes and a few high-fashion centers. Upper classes are nearly as likely to adopt lower-class fashion trends that emanate from just about anywhere. As a result, the functionalist theory no longer provides a satisfying explanation of fashion cycles.

—Brym and Lie, *Sociology: Your Compass for a New World*, 3rd Edition

CRITICAL THINKING LEVEL 1 REMEMBER

Recall the ideas presented in the reading about the following topics. If you don't remember much about an item, skim the reading, quickly looking for the key phrase listed here. When you find it, reread that section to refresh your memory. Then return to recollecting (remembering). Jot down a few notes on separate paper if doing so will help you remember the points the authors are making.

- The functionalist view
- The main appeal of wearing expensive, new fashions
- The important social function that fashion performs
- The effect of technological advances in clothes manufacturing
- The change in the fashion industry that began in the 1960s

CRITICAL THINKING LEVEL 2 UNDERSTAND

Using the list of topics from Critical Thinking Level 1 to spark your memory and help you organize the ideas, *explain* the ideas in the selection to a classmate. Then turn to another classmate and listen to his or her explanation.

CRITICAL THINKING LEVEL 3 APPLY

Apply functionalism to Avril Lavigne's look as described in paragraph 1. Can functionalism explain the success of her look? _____

_____

CRITICAL THINKING LEVEL 4 ANALYZE

Analyze the quotation from Henry David Thoreau that is given in paragraph 3. Does it support a functionalist approach to fashion? Why or why not? _____

_____

CRITICAL THINKING LEVEL 5 EVALUATE

Judge how much the opening quotation from the *Legally Blond* character Elle Woods contributes to the main idea of this reading selection. _____

_____

CRITICAL THINKING LEVEL 6 CREATE

Construct an alternative explanation for the change in the fashion cycle that has taken place since the 1960s (since functionalism can't explain it very well). _____

_____

A Shift from the Author's Ideas to Your Ideas

You may have noticed that when you were answering questions on levels 1 and 2, you were merely recalling and restating material that came directly from the reading selection. At level 3, you had to take the knowledge and apply it to a new situation, a task that involved more of *you*. When you got to level 4, the balance really started to shift toward you, the reader, and away from the information in the reading. Now you had to think on your own, not just repeat or apply what the reading said. Your ability to think was stretched further in level 5, when the question became broader and more open-ended. By the time you reached level 6, you were on your own! You had to think up an entirely different explanation for the recent fashion cycle, perhaps by considering broader ideas about how things have changed since the 1960s.

You can use these ways of thinking as you study any reading selection (or any lecture) using the tasks in Table 2.1. Adapt the tasks as needed to fit the situation.

Table 2.2 General Critical Thinking Tasks

Critical thinking level	Tasks you can do to help you think about any reading or lecture
Level 1: Remember	Recall (remember) the ideas.
Level 2: Understand	Explain the ideas using your own words.
Level 3: Apply	Use the ideas in a new situation or think of problems you could solve with them.
Level 4: Analyze	Figure out how the parts relate to one another.
Level 5: Evaluate	Decide how valuable you find the ideas. Think about what choices you can make based on the ideas.
Level 6: Create	Draw conclusions from the ideas. Create something new from them.

Tasks are organized here in the order you should do them. For instance, be sure you know and understand the information before you apply it.

Interaction 2-7. Asking Reading and Thinking Questions

The rest of the sociology selection on fashion is printed here. Before you read it, turn the headings into questions and search for the answers as you read. When you find parts of the answer, mark them. Then answer the questions that follow.

Question:

Conflict Theory's View of the Fashion World

5   Some sociologists have turned to conflict theory as an alternative view of the fashion world. Conflict theorists typically view fashion cycles as a means by which industry owners make big profits. Owners introduce new styles and render old styles unfashionable because they make more money when many people are encouraged to buy new clothes often. At the same time, conflict theorists think fashion keeps people distracted from the many social, economic, and political problems that might otherwise incite them to express dissatisfaction with the existing social order and even rebel against it. Conflict theorists, like functionalists, thus believe that fashion helps maintain social stability. Unlike functionalists, however, they argue that social stability bestows advantages on industrial owners at the expense of nonowners.

6   Conflict theorists have a point. Fashion is a big and profitable business. Owners do introduce new styles to make more money. They have, for example, created The Color Marketing Group (known to insiders as the "Color Mafia"), a committee that meets regularly to help change the national palette of color preferences for consumer products. According to one committee member, the Color Mafia makes sure that "the mass media, fashion magazines and catalogs, home shopping shows, and big clothing chains all present the same options" (Mundell, 1993).

7   Yet the Color Mafia and other influential elements of the fashion industry are not all-powerful. Remember what Elle Woods said after she convinced Cameron Diaz not to buy that heinous angora sweater: "Whoever said orange is the new pink is seriously disturbed." Like many consumers, Elle Woods rejected the advice of the fashion industry. And in fact some of the fashion trends initiated by industry owners flop, one of the biggest being the introduction of the midi-dress with a hemline midway between knee and ankle) in the mid-1970s. Despite a huge ad campaign, most women simply would not buy it.

8   This points to one of the main problems with the conflict interpretation: It incorrectly makes it seem like fashion decisions are dictated from above. Reality is more complicated. Fashion decisions are made partly by consumers. This idea can best be understood by thinking of clothing as a form of symbolic interaction, a sort of wordless "language" that allows us to tell others who we are and learn who they are.

Clothing as a Form of Symbolic Interaction

Question:

9   If clothes speak, sociologist Fred Davis has perhaps done the most in recent years to help us see how we can decipher what they say (Davis, 1992). According to Davis, a person's identity is always a work in progress. True, we develop a sense of self as we mature. We come to think of ourselves as members of one or more families, occupations, communities, classes, ethnic and racial groups, and countries. We develop patterns of behavior and belief associated with each of these social categories. Nonetheless, social categories change over time, and so do we as we move through them and as we age. As a result, our identities are always in flux. We often become anxious or insecure about who we are. Clothes help us express our shifting identities. For example, clothes can convey whether you are "straight," sexually available, athletic, conservative, and much else, thus telling others how you want them to see you and indicating the kinds of people with whom you want to associate. At some point you may become less conservative, sexually available, and so forth. Your clothing style is likely to change accordingly. (Of course, the messages you try to send are subject to interpretation and may be misunderstood.) For its part, the fashion industry feeds on the ambiguities within us, investing much effort in trying to discern which new styles might capture current needs for self-expression.

10   For example, capitalizing on the need for self-expression among many young girls in the late 1990s, Britney Spears hit a chord. Feminist interpretations of the meaning and significance of Britney Spears are especially interesting in this respect because they focus on the gender aspects of fashion.

Feminist Interpretations of Britney Spears

Question:

11   Traditionally, feminists have thought of fashion as a form of patriarchy, a means by which male dominance is maintained. They have argued that fashion is mainly a female preoccupation. It takes a lot of time and money to choose, buy, and clean clothes. Fashionable clothing is often impractical and uncomfortable, and some of it is even unhealthy. Modern fashion's focus on youth, slenderness, and eroticism diminishes women by turning them into sexual objects, say some feminists. Britney Spears is of interest to traditional feminists because she supposedly helps lower the age at which girls fall under male domination.

12   In recent years, this traditional feminist view has given way to a feminist interpretation that is more compatible with symbolic interactionism ("Why Britney Spears Matters," 2001). Some feminists now applaud the "girl power" movement that crystallized in 1996 with the release of the Spice Girls' hit single, "Wannabe." They regard Britney Spears as part of that movement. In their judgment, Spears's music, dance routines, and dress style express a self-assuredness and assertiveness that resonate with the less submissive and more independent role that girls are now carving out for themselves. With her kicks, her shadow boxing, and songs like the 2000 single "Stronger," Spears speaks for the empowerment of young women. Quite apart from her musical and dancing talent, then, some feminists think that many young girls are wild about Britney Spears because she helps them express their own social and sexual power. Of course, not all young girls agree. Some, like Avril Lavigne, find Spears "phony" and too much of a "showgirl." They seek "more authentic" ways of asserting their identity through fashion (Pascual, 2002). Still, the symbolic interactionist and feminist interpretations of fashion help us see more clearly the ambiguities of identity that underlie the rise of new fashion trends.

Question:

The Usefulness of the Four Theoretical Perspectives

13   Our analysis of fashion shows that each of the four theoretical perspectives—functionalism, conflict theory, symbolic interactionism, and feminism—can clarify different aspects of a sociological problem. This does not mean that each perspective always has equal validity. Often, the interpretations that derive from different theoretical perspectives are incompatible. They offer competing interpretations of the same social reality. It is then necessary to do research to determine which perspective works best for the case at hand. Nonetheless, all four theoretical perspectives usefully illuminate some aspects of the social world.

—Brym and Lie, *Sociology: Your Compass for a New World,* 3rd Edition

CRITICAL THINKING LEVEL 1 REMEMBER

Including the material in Interaction 2-6 as well as this one, what four theories are applied to the fashion industry in this reading selection?

- _____
- _____
- _____
- _____

CRITICAL THINKING LEVEL 2 UNDERSTAND

What aspects of fashion does each of the four theories explain particularly well, according to the authors?

- _____
  _____
  _____
- _____
  _____
  _____
- _____
  _____
  _____
- _____
  _____
  _____

CRITICAL THINKING LEVEL 3 APPLY

Choose a character from a movie whose clothing seems like a statement of who they are. Using some of the categories of identity in the section on "Clothing as a Form of Symbolic Interaction," write a paragraph in which you describe the person's clothing and how it seems to identify them. What do you think their clothes say about their family, occupation, community, class, ethnic group, sexual orientation or availability, athleticism, political viewpoint, or anything else? Be sure to use plenty of details to describe their clothing and to support your points.

_____

_____

_____

_____

CRITICAL THINKING LEVEL 4 ANALYZE

What example is used to support the point that conflict theorists make about fashion? What counterexample (opposing example) is then given to show the limits of the first example?

• Example: _____

• Counterexample: _____

CRITICAL THINKING LEVEL 5 EVALUATE

Certain working situations seem to call for certain ways of dressing. For example, a day care provider might dress in roomy, comfortable clothes that won't be damaged by food or dirt. Consider three occupations you might want to have. Suggest appropriate dress for each one. How does dressing in that particular way help fulfill the needs of the job?

• _____

• _____

• _____

CRITICAL THINKING LEVEL 6 CREATE

Before you read this selection, what did you think about the fashion industry—its quickly changing trends, its origins in the upper or lower classes, its emphasis on profits, its usefulness in identifying yourself, or any other aspect? Write for ten minutes to explore your thoughts.

Now that you have read the selection, would you say that your earlier viewpoint was similar to any of the theories presented here? Different from one of them? Write for five more minutes to establish where among these theories your ideas fit.

Chapter Summary Activity

This chapter has discussed how asking questions can help you read and think more effectively. Construct a Reading Guide below by completing each idea on the left with information from the chapter on the right. You can use this guide later as you complete other reading assignments.

Reading Guide to Asking Questions

Complete this idea	with information from the chapter.
Before reading, ask questions about the reading selection by	1.
Asking questions in this way allows you to	2.
	3.
After you ask the questions, you should	4.
Once you are ready to read a section, you should do two tasks while reading:	5.
	6.
You should only mark the ideas that actually	7.
Why?	8.
Most of the words a writer uses are	9.
If you need to do more with a reading than just understand its basic meaning, you can	10.
What are the six levels of critical thinking, organized from easiest to most difficult?	11.
	12.
	13.
	14.
	15.
	16.

If you were asked to explain the information in this chapter to someone else, which critical thinking action would you be using?	17. _____
If you were asked to read a job description and determine whether you were interested in the job, which critical thinking task would you be doing?	18. _____
If you were reading an explanation about why something happened, and you thought of a different reason it could have happened, which critical thinking action are you engaged in?	19. _____
If you were asked to read a story and then discuss each aspect of its plot, which critical thinking task would you be doing?	20. _____

Test Taking Tips
Focusing on Critical Thinking Verbs

Tests in your college classes, such as literature, history, and even math, may include short answer and essay questions. Instead of choosing an answer from a list of possible answers, as you would on a multiple-choice test, you will be required to write out the answer yourself, either in a few sentences (short answer) or several paragraphs (essay).

A good strategy for approaching short answer and essay questions is to focus on the key **critical thinking verb** in the question and then make sure that your answer demonstrates the appropriate level of thinking. Earlier in the chapter, you learned about the six levels of critical thinking and verbs that are linked to each one. Following are some other verbs that may be used in questions to describe these thinking and writing tasks:

Level 6: Create, develop, design, adapt, imagine
Level 5: Evaluate, assess, rank, critique, justify
Level 4: Analyze, compare, examine, explain, investigate
Level 3: Apply, diagram, demonstrate, solve, illustrate
Level 2: Understand, paraphrase, conclude, match, exemplify
Level 1: Remember, identify, list, reproduce, define

When you read a question, identify the verb and decide what level of thinking is called for. For example, suppose you see this writing prompt on a history test:

● **Identify five factors that led to the American Revolution.**

Seeing the verb "identify," you know that this question is at the lowest level of thinking. You simply need to list the five factors to prove that you remember them.

In contrast, suppose you get this prompt:

● **Judge which of the five factors that led to the American Revolution was the most important one. Explain your thinking.**

Reading the verb "judge," you know that this task is more complex. You still need to write about the five factors, but you also need to decide which one was most important and support your judgment with convincing details. The question calls for you to form an opinion based on all the facts you can recall. The verb "explain" is a clue that you will need to analyze each factor in relation to the facts before you make a decision about which one is the most important.

The first question, at critical thinking level 1, is more likely to appear on a test as a question requiring a short answer than as an essay question. The second question, at level 5, is more probably an essay question. It's too complicated to be answered in just a few sentences; you might need five or six paragraphs to explain your evaluation. No matter which type of question you are being asked, be sure you understand

✔ how long your answer should be
✔ how many points it is worth
✔ in the case of short answers, whether you need to answer the question using complete sentences

Be sure you understand these criteria because your grade will reflect how well you fulfill them.

Reading 2-1 . . . . **Newspaper Article**

● Pre-Reading the Selection

The reading that follows appeared in the *New York Times* in October 2006, five years after the terrorist attacks of September 11, 2001. The attacks had many different effects on people around the United States, and this article outlines how one person's life has been affected by the choice he made after 9-11 to serve in the military in Afghanistan.

Guessing the Purpose

Based on the title (see page 77) and the place of publication, do you suppose the author's purpose is mostly to entertain, inform, or persuade? _____

Surveying the Reading

Survey the first sentence of each paragraph. Then fill in the basic information asked for in each question below.

- Who is discussed? _____

_____

- What is the topic? _____

_____

- When did the events mentioned in these first sentences happen? After you list them all, number them in the order they occurred.

_____

_____

_____

_____

_____

Predicting the Content

Based on your survey, predict three things that the selection will discuss.

- _____
- _____
- _____

Activating Your Knowledge

Think about what you have heard or read about dogs that help disabled people, veterans of recent wars, prison culture, or human-dog partnerships. Write down three items of prior knowledge.

- _____
- _____
- _____

Common Knowledge

Conflict in Afghanistan (*paragraph 1*) The war initiated by the United States after the September 11, 2001, attacks in New York and Washington, D.C., intended to remove the ruling party in Afghanistan—the Taliban—from power.

Veterans Administration (*paragraph 4*) The U.S. government department responsible for providing benefits (such as medical and educational benefits) to military personnel and their families.

Reading with Pen in Hand

Now read the selection. As you read, mark any ideas that seem important, and respond to the questions and vocabulary items in the margin. Monitor your comprehension by putting a ✔ next to a paragraph when you understand most of it. Place an ✘ next to a paragraph when you don't understand most of it.

Visit **www.cengage.com/devenglish/doleconnect** and select Chapter 2 to hear vocabulary words from this selection and view a video about this topic.

Trained by Inmates, New Best Friends for Disabled Veterans

Stephanie Strom

◆*Reading Journal*

1   Rainbow looks like any other Labrador retriever, but she is not a pet. Trained by a prison inmate, her mission is to help Roland Paquette, an injured veteran of the conflict in Afghanistan, stay on his new feet, the ones he got after an explosion destroyed his legs. While veterans who lose their sight or hearing or must use a wheelchair have long had "service" dogs as companions, Rainbow is one of the first dogs in the country trained to work with someone who uses both a wheelchair and **prosthetics** to get around.

◆Why does Mr. Paquette need Rainbow?

2   Mr. Paquette's hope is that eventually Rainbow will allow him to abandon his canes altogether and rely only on the metal handle attached to the harness she wears around her torso. "I'd much rather be able to walk with her at my side than with the canes," said Mr. Paquette, who is 28. "It makes me less obvious."

prosthetics Earlier in the paragraph, a type of *prosthetics* is mentioned: *his new feet.* What is the meaning of *prosthetics*?

◆What does Mr. Paquette want to do with his canes?

3   Rainbow is the first graduate of a new program, Canines for Combat Veterans, at a tiny nonprofit group here called NEADS, or New England Assistance Dog Services. The organization has been

◆Who runs the program that trained Rainbow?

Roland Paquette, who lost both legs in Afghanistan, and his new service dog, Rainbow, visiting Thomas Davison, right, who trained the dog.

© Andrea Mohin/The New York Times/Redux

training service dogs for the disabled since 1976. "I think we're going to have to double the number of dogs we train to meet the need," said Sheila O'Brien, NEADS's executive director. "Because of advances in medicine, a lot more veterans are surviving their injuries than ever before, and we want to be able to help as many of them as we can."

◆Does the Veterans Administration fund Canines for Combat Veterans?

4   In late 2001, President Bush signed a law authorizing the Veterans Administration to underwrite programs like Canines for Combat Veterans. But the Veterans Administration is still studying the matter, so NEADS must raise all the money for its program from private sources. It sells naming rights for its dogs—Rainbow got her name after a group of Rainbow Girls from Rhode Island, an organization **affiliated** with the Masons, held pancake breakfasts and other events to raise $500 for the right. That fund-raising has proved so successful that Ms. O'Brien has doubled the price to name a dog, but she said it costs up to $17,000 to buy and train a dog. Recipients of dogs are expected to raise about $9,500 for their animal with the help of the organization.

affiliated Based on the context of the sentence, what is a synonym (that is, a word that means the same thing) for *affiliated*?

◆Who completes the training that begins in the NEADS dog nursery?

5   Ms. O'Brien also hopes to double the size of a program in which service dogs are trained by prison inmates. Puppies begin their training in the NEADS "nursery," where they are housebroken and introduced to basic skills. Then about 80 percent of the dogs go to live in a prison cell with an inmate who completes their training. It

takes about half the time to train dogs in prison as it does in foster homes, Ms. O'Brien said, because of the more intensive training they get from inmates. Inmates are enthusiastic about the program. "It's great to do something that really helps someone else, especially a guy like him," said Thomas Davison, who trained Rainbow at the Northeast Correctional Center here. "I've never had a chance to do that, and I wasn't sure I could handle the responsibility."

6   Kathleen M. Dennehy, the state corrections commissioner, said the program had profound effects on the culture of a prison. "Officers stop by to pat the dogs, they smile, maybe they strike up a conversation with the inmate training the dog," Ms. Dennehy said. "It establishes a basic human connection." James J. Saba, superintendent at Northeast, is unsure, however, whether the program, already in six prisons in Massachusetts, can be expanded. "We have 268 inmates in this prison alone, which is already too many," Mr. Saba said. "And for every puppy, we lose a bed because the dogs take the place of an inmate in the cell."

◆What are two effects of having the puppies in prisons?

7   Mr. Paquette and Rainbow visited Mr. Davison and the four other inmate trainers at the prison on Thursday. Mr. Davison gave him a few pointers and handed over the toys he had bought the dog with the $28 a week he received for training her. "She was ready to do this at nine months," Mr. Davison said proudly. "She's a good dog." Mr. Paquette promised, "I'll take good care of her."

◆What did Mr. Davison do with the money he received for training Rainbow?

8   Mr. Paquette joined the military several months after the Sept. 11 attacks, leaving a job he had recently taken. "I felt like a **hypocrite** sitting around on the couch in front of the TV and saying, 'Go do it,' when I wasn't," he explained. He became a medical sergeant on a Special Forces team and headed for Afghanistan in the spring of 2004. He said he treated hundreds of soldiers and thousands of local residents for "everything from the common cold to gunshot wounds."

hypocrite Think about the words that Mr. Paquette is speaking. Guess what a *hypocrite* is:

◆What job did Mr. Paquette have in the military?

9   On Dec. 28, 2004, an explosion went off under the vehicle in which he was riding, severely injuring his legs. Yet he considers himself lucky that the impact was muted by the engine block, that an orthopedic surgeon happened to be on hand to perform the initial amputation and that new medical techniques have calmed the irritated nerves in his legs that threatened to keep him from walking. "At least I'm here, and I've got Rainey," he said, using his nickname for Rainbow.

◆What is the basic reason Mr. Paquette thinks he is lucky?

10   He said that he had been nervous about meeting her—"sometimes **chemistry** just doesn't work"—and that the first day of their partner-

chemistry The meaning here is different from the scientific one; it is similar to the meaning of *chemistry* in the phrase *the chemistry of love.* What does *chemistry* mean, roughly?

◆How many days does the paragraph discuss?

largely Based on this sentence and the one before it, what is a synonym for *largely*?

◆Where will Mr. Paquette and Rainbow be living?

◆Aside from Mr. Paquette's new job, what is in San Antonio?

ship had been difficult. He had expected to get a bigger dog who could support his weight, and Rainbow accidentally pulled him over when he was walking with her. The next day, however, Rainbow and Mr. Paquette clicked, taking turns outdoors using just a cane and her harness. The dog appeared to respond well to Mr. Paquette's commands and looked to him more and more for direction. He stayed in his wheelchair during his visit to Mr. Davison the next day because the NEADS trainers were worried that Rainbow would pull him down again in her excitement to see her prison trainer. She was indeed happy to see him but **largely** remained at Mr. Paquette's side.

11   The next challenge will be introducing her to Mr. Big, the German shepherd-Great Dane mix that is the Paquettes' pet. He has been sent to obedience school in preparation for her arrival. In about 10 days, Mr. Paquette and Rainbow will take off for their new life together, first in Albuquerque and then in San Antonio, where Mr. Paquette and his wife, Jennifer, and their daughter, Kristen, 17, and son, T. J., 11, are moving for his new job with an intelligence and security firm.

12   The Army has recently completed a new center in San Antonio specializing in amputation, the Intrepid Center, and Mr. Paquette expects to be an advertisement for service dogs. "I've got a feeling that lots of guys who see me with Rainbow are going to want a dog," he said.

● Comprehension Questions

Write the letter of the answer on the line. Then explain your thinking.

Main Idea

_____ 1. What is the best statement of the main idea of paragraph 2?

a. Mr. Paquette should be recognized for his service to his country.

b. Mr. Paquette fears that Rainbow will let him fall.

c. Mr. Paquette wants to appear to be the same as everyone else.

d. Mr. Paquette believes he is unlikely to ever walk again.

WHY? What information in the selection leads you to give that answer? _____

_____

____ 2. What is the best statement of the main idea of paragraph 4?
   a. NEADS raises all the money for its program from private sources.
   b. The Veterans Administration is studying the matter.
   c. Fund-raising has proved successful.
   d. It costs up to $17,000 to buy and train a dog.

WHY? What information in the selection leads you to give that answer? _____

_____

Supporting Details

____ 3. In paragraph 5, which detail supports Ms. O'Brien's desire to double the size of the program in which dogs are trained by inmates?
   a. Puppies begin their training in the NEADS "nursery."
   b. About 80% of the dogs live with a prisoner who completes the training.
   c. It takes about half the time to train dogs in prison as it does in foster homes.
   d. All of the above.

WHY? What leads you to give that answer? _____

_____

____ 4. Which details from paragraph 9 support the idea that Mr. Paquette is lucky?
   a. The engine block was between the explosion and Mr. Paquette.
   b. His feet were amputated by an orthopedic surgeon who was nearby.
   c. Irritated nerves in his legs have been soothed, allowing him to walk.
   d. All of the above.

WHY? What information in the selection leads you to give that answer? _____

_____

Author's Purpose

_____ 5. What is the writer's purpose for including the quotation from Thomas Davison at the end of paragraph 5?

  a. to suggest that every inmate needs a service animal

  b. to show that the Canines for Combat Veterans program has benefits for the inmates as well as the combat veterans

  c. to protest that inmates should not be allowed to participate in the Canines for Combat Veterans program

  d. to support Davison's request to train another puppy

WHY? What information in the selection leads you to give that answer? _____

_____

_____

_____ 6. What is the author's purpose for including paragraphs 10–12?

  a. to satisfy readers' curiosity about what lies ahead for Mr. Paquette and Rainbow

  b. to demonstrate how difficult Mr. Paquette's life is going to be in the future

  c. to point out that Mr. Paquette's family has suffered because of his choice

  d. to compare the training of Rainbow and Mr. Big

WHY? What information in the selection leads you to give that answer? _____

_____

_____

_____

Relationships

_____ 7. In paragraph 10, what is the relationship between the ideas in sentences 2 and 3?

  a. Sentence 3 offers an example of the idea in sentence 2.

  b. Sentence 3 offers a contrast to the idea in sentence 2.

  c. Sentence 3 offers the cause of an effect in sentence 2.

  d. Sentence 3 adds minor details to the ideas in sentence 2.

WHY? What information in the selection leads you to give that answer? _____

_____

____   8. In paragraph 11, how are the supporting details arranged?
   a. in chronological (time) order
   b. in order of importance
   c. in a contrasting pattern
   d. as cause and effect

WHY? What leads you to give that answer? _____

_____

_____

Fact, Opinion, and Inference

____   9. Choose the opinion.
   a. Rainbow is a Labrador retriever.
   b. NEADS has been training service dogs for the disabled since 1976.
   c. Rainbow is the first graduate of Canines for Combat Veterans.
   d. The Veterans Administration should be paying for Canines for Combat Veterans.

WHY? What leads you to make that selection? _____

____   10. Choose the fact.
   a. Mr. Big isn't going to like Rainbow.
   b. Mr. Paquette was nervous about meeting Rainbow.
   c. If Mr. Paquette hadn't been seated in a wheelchair, Rainbow would have knocked him over when they visited Mr. Davison.
   d. Dogs are easy to train.

WHY? What leads you to give that answer? _____

_____

_____

_____

● Critical Thinking Questions

CRITICAL THINKING LEVEL 1 REMEMBER

Specify how much NEADS now charges for naming rights to a dog for Canines for Combat Veterans. Why do you say so? _____

_____

CRITICAL THINKING LEVEL 2 UNDERSTAND

Describe five benefits an inmate who trains a dog likely receives. _____

_____

_____

CRITICAL THINKING LEVEL 3 APPLY

Working with others, *use* the information in the article to create a poster for NEADS that you can hang on campus. Before you begin, decide whether the purpose of the poster is to persuade people to donate money to NEADS or to share information about NEADS with people whose disabilities might make a service dog a good idea. You may want to consult the NEADS Web site for further information: **www.neads.org/**.

CRITICAL THINKING LEVEL 4 ANALYZE

In the article, *analyze* each group of paragraphs listed below. What is the main topic of each group? Be prepared to discuss how you know.

Main topic of paragraphs 1–2: _____

Main topic of paragraphs 3–4: _____

Main topic of paragraphs 5–7: _____

Main topic of paragraphs 8–9: _____

Main topic of paragraphs 10–12: _____

CRITICAL THINKING LEVEL 5 EVALUATE

Judge whether the Veterans Administration should be paying to train dogs to assist veterans who have become disabled because of combat. You might want to check to see what other kinds of assistance the VA gives veterans at the VA Web site: **www.va.gov**. Work with several other students to develop a list of reasons for your position.

CRITICAL THINKING LEVEL 6 CREATE

Imagine what the following kinds of service dogs can do, based on your understanding of different disabilities and dogs' capabilities: a hearing dog, a ministry dog, and a social dog.

● Vocabulary in Context

The following words were used in the reading selection "Trained by Inmates, New Best Friends for Disabled Veterans." Complete each sentence with the best word.

affiliated	chemistry	hypocrite	largely	prosthetics

1. Tatiana's passionate speech for greater independence seemed to go _____ unheard; she was discouraged by the blank looks on her grandparents' faces.

2. Mechanical heart valves are being replaced by valves made from human and animal tissue; these _____ cause fewer blood clotting problems.

3. Joanna and Max met at a local coffee house, and their _____ was immediately apparent to everyone present.

4. The Columbian Student Association (COLSA) at Florida International University is _____ with the Hispanic Organizations Council.

5. Politicians are often accused of being _____, but sometimes their lack of consistency is due to trying to please so many diverse groups of people.

Reading 2-2 . . . . **Anthropology Textbook**

● Pre-Reading the Selection

The reading that follows is from a college textbook called *The Essence of Anthropology*. Anthropology, according to the glossary of that text, is "the study of humankind in all times and places." Here, the language ability of a nonhuman primate is described.

Guessing the Purpose

Based on the type of book this reading is from, do you suppose the authors' purpose is mostly to entertain, inform, or persuade? _____

Surveying the Reading

Survey the headings. What topics do you expect the reading to cover? _____

_____

Predicting the Content

Survey the first sentence of each paragraph and predict three things that the selection will discuss.

- _____

- _____

- _____

Activating Your Knowledge

Think about any related knowledge you may have: Have you seen TV shows about the language abilities of other animals? Of other primates (gorillas, chimpanzees)? What about broad knowledge related to how humans view animals in general? For example, what abilities do humans like to think separate them from the other animals? List two or three things you know.

- _____

- _____

- _____

Reading with Pen in Hand

Now read the selection. As you read, mark any ideas that seem important, and respond to the questions and vocabulary items in the margin. Monitor your comprehension by putting a ✔ next to a paragraph when you understand most of it. Place an ✗ next to a paragraph when you don't understand most of it.

Visit **www.cengage.com/devenglish/doleconnect** and select Chapter 2 to hear vocabulary words from this selection and view a video about this topic.

◆*Reading Journal*

◆What abilities of Chantek was the researcher, Professor Lyn Miles, going to study?

Language and the Intellectual Abilities of Orangutans

Adapted from **H. Lyn Miles**

1   In 1978, after researchers began to use American Sign Language for the deaf to communicate with chimpanzees and gorillas, I began the first long-term study of the language ability of an orangutan named

Lyn Miles and Chantek

© AP Photo/Alan Mothner

Chantek. There was criticism that symbol-using apes might just be imitating their human caregivers, but there is now growing agreement that orangutans, gorillas, and both chimpanzee species can develop language skills at the level of a two- to three-year-old human child. The goal of Project Chantek was to investigate the mind of an orangutan through a developmental study of his cognitive and linguistic skills. It was a great ethical and emotional responsibility to engage an orangutan in what anthropologists call "**enculturation**," since I would not only be teaching a form of communication, I would be teaching aspects of the culture upon which that language was based. If my project succeeded, I would create a symbol-using creature that would be somewhere between an ape living under natural conditions and an adult human. This threatened to raise as many questions as I sought to answer.

enculturation The rest of the paragraph implies the meaning of this word. Notice, too, that the word itself is made up of *en-*, *culture*, and *−ation*. Guess at the meaning of this word.

Communicating with Sign Language

2   A small group of caregivers at the University of Tennessee, Chattanooga, began raising Chantek when he was 9 months old. They communicated with him by using gestural signs based on the American Sign Language for the deaf. After a month, Chantek produced his own first sign and eventually learned to use approximately

◆At what age did Chantek begin to sign?

150 different signs, forming a vocabulary similar to that of a very young child. Chantek learned names for people (Lyn, John), places (Yard, Brock-hall), things to eat (Yogurt, Chocolate), actions (Work, Hug), objects (Screwdriver, Money), animals (Dog, Ape), colors (Red, Black), pronouns (You, Me), location (Up, Point), attributes (Good, Hurt), and emphasis (More, Time-to-do).

spontaneous The next sentence suggests what *spontaneous* is not. What does spontaneous mean in this context?

3   We found that Chantek's signing was **spontaneous** and nonrepetitious. He did not merely imitate his caregivers, but rather he actively used signs to initiate communications and meet his needs. Almost immediately, he began using signs in combinations and modulated their meanings with slight changes in how he articulated and arranged his signs. He commented "Coke Drink" after drinking his Coke, "Pull Beard" while pulling a caregiver's hair through a fence, and "Time Hug" while locked in his cage as his caregiver looked at her watch. But, beyond using signs in this way, could he use them as symbols, that is, more abstractly to represent a person, thing, action, or idea, even apart from its context or when it was not present?

◆Did Chantek always use the signs in the way he was taught them?

◆Did Chantek point spontaneously?

4   One indication of the capacity of both deaf and hearing children to use symbolic language is the ability to point, which some researchers argued that apes could not do spontaneously. Chantek began to point to objects when he was 2 years old, somewhat later than human children. First, he showed and gave us objects, and then he began pointing where he wanted to be tickled and to where he wanted to be carried. Finally, he could answer questions like "where hat?" "which different?" and "what want?" by pointing to the correct object.

characteristics Another word that means the same thing is given: *attributes*. What do the examples previously given suggest is the meaning of these two words? (Examples were also given in paragraph 2.)

5   As Chantek's vocabulary increased, the ideas that he was expressing became more complex, such as when he signed "bad bird" at noisy birds giving alarm calls, and "white cheese food-eat" for cottage cheese. He understood that things had **characteristics** or attributes that could be described. He also created combinations of signs that we had never used before. In the way that a child learns language, Chantek began to over- or under-extend the meaning of his signs, which gave us insight into his emotions and how he was beginning to classify his world. For example, he used the sign "dog" for actual dogs, as well as for a picture of a dog in his Viewmaster, orangutans on television, barking noises on the radio, birds, horses, a tiger at the circus, a herd of cows, a picture of a cheetah, and a noisy helicopter that presumably sounded like it was barking. For Chantek, the sign "bug" included crickets, cockroaches, a picture of a cockroach, beetles, slugs, small moths, spiders, worms, flies, a

◆How did Professor Miles begin to understand how Chantek classified things in his world?

picture of a graph shaped like a butterfly, tiny brown pieces of cat food, and small bits of feces. He signed "break" before he broke and shared pieces of crackers, and after he broke his toilet. He signed "bad" to himself before he grabbed a cat, when he bit into a radish, and for a dead bird.

Missing Playmates and Telling Lies

6   We also discovered that Chantek could comprehend our spoken English (after the first couple of years we used speech as well as signing.) When he was 2 years old, Chantek began to sign for things that were not present. He frequently asked to go to places in his yard to look for animals, such as his pet squirrel and cat, who served as playmates. He also made requests for "ice cream," signing "car ride" and pulling us toward the parking lot for a trip to a local ice-cream shop.

◆What did Chantek learn to do by the time he was two?

7   We learned that an orangutan can tell lies. Deception is an important indicator of language abilities since it requires a deliberate and intentional misrepresentation of reality. In order to deceive, you must be able to see events from the other person's perspective and negate his or her perception. Chantek began to deceive from a relatively early age, and we caught him in lies about three times a week. He learned that he could sign "dirty" to get into the bathroom to play with the washing machine, dryer, soap, and so on, instead of using the toilet. He also used his signs deceptively to gain social advantage in games, to divert attention in social interactions, and to avoid testing situations and coming home after walks on campus. On one occasion, Chantek stole food from my pocket while he simultaneously pulled my hand away in the opposite direction. On another occasion, he stole a pencil eraser, pretended to swallow it, and "supported" his case by opening his mouth and signing "food-eat," as if to say that he had swallowed it. However, he really held the eraser in his cheek, and later it was found in his bedroom where he commonly hid objects.

perception Based on your own understanding of how to deceive someone, as well as the information in this sentence, what is *perception*?

◆Are orangutans similar to people in how they tell lies?

Measured by Human Standards

8   We carried out tests of Chantek's mental ability using measures developed for human children. Chantek reached a mental age equivalent to that of a two- to three-year-old child, with some skills of even older children. On some tasks done readily by children, such as using one object to represent another and pretend play, Chantek performed as well as children, but less frequently. He engaged in

◆What was Chantek's human mental age equivalent?

◆How did Chantek show that he has a sense that the future exists?

articulation Look at the sentence of which this phrase is part: *request that he improve the articulation of a sign,* and the clause that begins the next sentence: *When his articulation became careless.* What does *articulation* probably mean here?

◆What is an example of how Chantek became a creator of language?

◆What inventions besides language does Chantek create?

chase games in which he would look over his shoulder as he darted about, although no one was chasing him. He also signed to his toys and offered them food and drink.

9   By four and a half years of age, Chantek showed evidence of planning, creative simulation, and the use of objects in novel relations to one another to invent new meanings. For example, he simulated the context for food preparation by giving his caregiver two objects needed to prepare his milk formula and staring at the location of the remaining ingredient. A further indication that Chantek had mental images is found in his ability to respond to his caregiver's request that he improve the **articulation** of a sign. When his articulation became careless, we would ask him to "sign better." Looking closely at us, he would sign slowly and emphatically, taking one hand to put the other into the proper shape.

10   Chantek was extremely curious and inventive. When he wanted to know the name of something, he offered his hands to be molded into the shape of the proper sign. But language is a creative process, so we were pleased to see that Chantek began to invent his own signs. He invented: "no-teeth" (to show us that he would not use his teeth during rough play); "eye-drink" (for contact lens solution used by his caregivers); and "dave-missing-finger" (a name for a favorite university employee who had a hand injury). Like our ancestors, Chantek had become a creator of language.

11   **2004 update:** My relationship and research with Chantek continues, through the Chantek Foundation in Atlanta, Georgia. Chantek now uses several hundred signs and has invented new signs for "car water" (bottled water that I bring in my car), "catsup," and "annoyed." He makes stone tools, arts and crafts, necklaces, and other jewelry, and small percussion instruments used in my rock band Animal Nation. He even co-composes songs with the band. Plans are in the making for Chantek and other encultured apes to live in culture-based preserves where they have more range of choices and learning opportunities than zoos or research centers. An exciting new project under the auspices of ApeNet will give Chantek an opportunity to communicate with other apes via the Internet. It is of special note that based on great ape language skills, efforts will be underway in the next decade to obtain greater legal rights for these primates, as well as greater recognition of them as another type of "person."

⬤ Comprehension Questions

Write the letter of the answer on the line. Then explain your thinking.

Main Idea

_____ 1. What is the best statement of the main idea of paragraph 2?

    a. Chantek's caregivers communicated with him using gestures.

    b. Chantek eventually learned 150 signs.

    c. Chantek learned many signs and used them to get his needs met.

    d. Chantek's signing was spontaneous.

WHY? What information in the selection leads you to give that answer? _____

_____

_____

_____ 2. What is the best statement of the main idea of paragraph 5?

    a. As Chantek's vocabulary increased, the ideas that he was expressing became more complex.

    b. He understood things had characteristics or attributes that could be described.

    c. He created combinations of signs that his caregivers had never used before.

    d. Chantek began to over- or under-extend the meaning of his signs, which gave his caregivers insight into his emotions and how he was beginning to classify his world.

WHY? What information in the selection leads you to give that answer? _____

_____

_____

Supporting Details

_____ 3. What details support the idea that Chantek uses signs as symbols?

    a. Chantek uses 150 signs, steals food, and creates stone tools.

    b. Chantek points, classifies objects, and uses one object to represent another.

    c. Chantek is extremely curious and inventive.

    d. Chantek used signs in combination to communicate more precisely.

WHY? What information in the selection leads you to give that answer? _____

_____

_____

_____

_____

____   4. In paragraph 7, most of the supporting details about Chantek telling lies are
      a. definitions of problems created by lying.
      b. comparisons between telling the truth and telling lies.
      c. examples of lies and reasons Chantek told them.
      d. steps in a process of lying that Chantek always followed.

WHY? What information in the selection leads you to give that answer? _____

_____

_____

_____

Author's Purpose

____   5. Throughout the reading, Professor Miles compares Chantek's growing abilities to the abilities of a human child. What is her purpose in making that comparison?
      a. to demonstrate how limited an orangutan's language and cognitive abilities are
      b. to suggest that an orangutan should be treated exactly the same way as a child
      c. to provide a measure of his abilities in a way that readers are likely to understand
      d. to let readers know what a good mother figure Professor Miles was

WHY? What information in the selection leads you to give that answer? _____

_____

_____

_____

6. In paragraph 11, the 2004 update, the author states "My relationship and research with Chantek continues." Why might she put the words *relationship* and *research* in this order?

   a. to emphasize the personal bond she has formed with Chantek

   b. to pretend a level of empathy she doesn't feel

   c. to emphasize that she is Chantek's true adoptive mother

   d. no special reason

WHY? What information in the selection leads you to give that answer? _____

_____

_____

_____

_____

Relationships

7. In paragraph 2, what is the relationship between (a) "names for people" and (b) "(LYN, JOHN)"?

   a. (a) and (b) are two sets of examples of signs that Chantek learned.

   b. (a) and (b) are two sets of examples of signs that Chantek could not learn.

   c. (a) is a category of signs Chantek learned, and (b) are examples of that category.

   d. (a) is the cause of Chantek's learning signs, and (b) is the effect of this learning.

WHY? What information in the selection leads you to give that answer? _____

_____

_____

8. In paragraph 4, how are the supporting details arranged?

   a. in chronological (time) order

   b. in space order

   c. as comparison and contrast

   d. as cause-and-effect

WHY? What information in the selection leads you to give that answer? _____

_____

Fact, Opinion, and Inference

___ 9. Choose the idea that is best supported by the information in this selection.

a. Humans may not be the only creatures with language ability.

b. Humans should acknowledge that animals deserve careful attention.

c. Great apes that have been enculturated show distinct similarities to humans.

d. Treating apes like research animals is wrong.

WHY? What information in the selection leads you to give that answer? _____

_____

_____

___ 10. Choose the idea that is best supported by the information in this selection.

a. Chantek's thinking skills were based solely on memorization.

b. Language skills and thinking skills affect each other.

c. Without language, thought doesn't exist.

d. Further research needs to be done to discover what will happen when Chantek interacts with other, unenculturated orangutans.

WHY? What information in the selection leads you to give that answer? _____

_____

_____

_____

● Critical Thinking Questions

CRITICAL THINKING LEVEL 1 REMEMBER

Recall and fill in some of the events from Chantek's learning process in the following chart.

1978	
One month later	
Chantek 2 years old	
Chantek 4½ years old	
2004	

CRITICAL THINKING LEVEL 2 UNDERSTAND

Explain which of the following words are symbols: *ice cream, beard, hug, enculturation.*

CRITICAL THINKING LEVEL 3 APPLY

Chantek was asked on occasion to SIGN BETTER: to make a sign in a more precise way so that a person could understand what he was trying to say (paragraph 9). What words do people *use* to ask for this same thing when talking with other people?

CRITICAL THINKING LEVEL 4 ANALYZE

Look at the items for which Chantek used the signs DOG and BUG. For each term, *figure out* what all the items have in common, if possible, or at least what qualities many of them have in common. Try to account for every item. What common characteristics do you find?

DOG: _____

_____

BUG: _____

_____

_____

CRITICAL THINKING LEVEL 5 EVALUATE

Judge the ways enculturated apes like Chantek should be treated like humans. Make a list of situations in which enculturated apes should be treated like humans, and for each situation on the list, write down some of the possible benefits and disadvantages of doing so—to the apes and to people.

CRITICAL THINKING LEVEL 6 CREATE

Professor Miles notes in her 2004 update that Chantek co-creates songs with her band Animal Nation. Miles says elsewhere, "He plays notes on the keyboard, and we write songs around his efforts. He also keeps the beat" (Emily Sohn, "An Inspiring Home for Apes," *Science News for Kids*). *Compose* a song in a different way. Review the ways that Chantek puts words together, and the kinds of words he uses. Then create a short song using words in a similar way. Put your song to a beat.

● Vocabulary in Context

The following words were used in the reading selection "Language and the Intellectual Ability of Orangutans." Select the best word to complete the meaning of each sentence.

| enculturation | spontaneous | perception | articulation | characteristics |

1. Culture is shared; it is learned; it is taken for granted. These are some of culture's _____.

2. Children who are raised without being exposed to other people have not undergone the same process of _____ that other children raised socially do.

3. When speaking to children who haven't been listening well, some parents start to exaggerate the _____ of each word they speak.

4. The teacher's _____ of the difficulty of a task may not match the student's.

5. _____ outbursts of laughter characterized the audience's response to the comic.

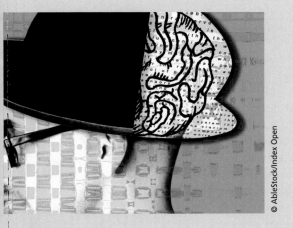

© AbleStock/Index Open

chapter 3

Developing Your Vocabulary

> 66 *The limits of my language are the limits of my mind. All I know is what I have words for.* 99
>
> —Ludwig Wittgenstein

Based on this quotation, what does Wittgenstein believe about vocabulary? Do you agree or disagree with Wittgenstein's opinion? Explain.

Share Your Prior Knowledge

How do you think having a good vocabulary will help you be successful in life?

Survey the Chapter

Take two minutes to skim Reading 3-1, "Vocabulary—A Treasure Chest for Success" on pages 132–134 to find some ways in which vocabulary might be beneficial. See if they are the same or different from your prior knowledge.

www.cengage.com/devenglish/doleconnect

Videos Related to Readings

Vocab Words on Audio

Prep Readings on Demand

Prep Reading . . . . English

The following selection is found frequently on the Web. It demonstrates some of the challenges that the English language presents. As you read through the sentences, think about what kinds of confusion are possible in English based on the "matching" words in each line.

Visit www.cengage.com/devenglish/doleconnect and select Chapter 3 to hear a reading of this selection and view a video about this topic.

Why English Is So Hard To Learn

1 We must polish the Polish furniture.
   He could lead if he would get the lead out.
   The farm was used to produce produce.

What does the second refuse mean? (It's a noun.)
   The dump was so full that it had to refuse more **refuse**.
5 The soldier decided to desert in the desert.
   This was a good time to present the present.
   A bass was painted on the head of the bass drum.
   When shot at, the dove dove into the bushes.

What does the first object mean? (It's a verb.)
   I did not **object** to the object.
10 The insurance was invalid for the invalid.
   The bandage was wound around the wound.
   There was a row among the oarsmen about how to row.
   They were too close to the door to close it.

What does the second does mean? (It's a noun.)
   The buck does funny things when the **does** are present.
15 They sent a sewer down to stitch the tear in the sewer line.
   To help with planting, the farmer taught his sow to sow.
   The wind was too strong to wind the sail.

What does the second number mean? (It's an adjective.)
   After a number of injections my jaw got **number**.
   Upon seeing the tear in my clothes I shed a tear.
20 I had to subject the subject to a series of tests.
   How can I intimate this to my most intimate friend?
   I read it once and will read it again.
   I learned much from this learned treatise.

What does the first content mean ? (It's an adjective.)
   I was **content** to note the content of the message.
25 The Blessed Virgin blessed her. Blessed her richly.
   It's a bit wicked to over-trim a short wicked candle.
   If he will absent himself we mark him absent.
   I incline toward bypassing the incline.

⬤ Interaction 3-1. Talking about Reading

For each sentence below, respond in writing to the following questions. Then discuss your answers with your classmates.

- What are the differences between the two words that are spelled the same?
- What clues help you decide what each word means?
- Can you identify the part of speech of each word?

1. We must *polish* the *Polish* furniture. _____

_____

2. The farm was used to *produce produce*. _____

_____

3. The soldier decided to *desert* in the *desert*. _____

_____

4. When shot at, the *dove dove* into the bushes. _____

_____

5. I was *content* to note the *content* of the message. _____

_____

Vocabulary Strategies

As you work through this chapter, you will learn strategies to help you determine the meanings of words you do not know based on the context in which they are used. But before you are introduced to these strategies, we want to talk about what to do with the new words you are exposed to. How can you learn them? How can you remember them? This is important to know now so that as you work through this chapter (and this book), you can practice the strategies you need to make new words your own.

Learning words in their naturally occurring context is more effective than learning them from, say, a list of vocabulary words. We learn words better when we see them in an article or a book or hear them in a conversation because in those contexts, we understand their connections with other ideas. Learning words in context also helps us connect them to our own prior knowledge. So how is it that you will most effectively learn new words? You have to read!

The next step is to incorporate new words into your daily life. You could *read* twenty new words a day and never *learn* one of them. The only way to truly learn a new word is to actively make it a part of your writing and speech. As you write in your college courses, use the vocabulary you are learning. You can also use new words in a vocabulary notebook, journal, letters, e-mails, blogs, and IMs—anywhere you write. And you can transfer new words into your speaking vocabulary by learning how they are pronounced. The audio files that accompany this book online at **www.cengage.com/ devenglish/doleconnect** can help. Listen to the words, practice them on your own, and then introduce them into your conversation.

Organize Your Vocabulary Words Using VAN

To remember all the new words you are going to learn in college, you need to have an approach to learning new words and organizing them. Here is a strategy called VAN.

Visual Aid. *Visualize an example of the word, and if you like, draw it on paper.* Take the word *aerobic*, for example. Imagine you are taking a physical education course and you read about aerobic activity being good for the heart. To help you remember what *aerobic* means, you can visualize an aerobic activity—such as running—in your head. However, the sillier or funnier the visual is, the easier it will be to remember. So you could take your visualization a step further by visualizing a muscular, healthy heart running down the road. This image helps you connect the meaning of aerobic exercise with its effect: a healthy heart.

© Cengage Learning

Do not worry if you cannot draw very well; a stick figure or doodle works just fine. However, you do not have to draw anything at all if you do not want to. The mental image alone will typically be enough to help you remember the definition of a new term. Drawing the image just helps reinforce the learning process.

Now let's read an example from a biology textbook to see how creating a visual aid can be helpful.

Modern **bryophytes** include 24, 000 species of mosses, liverworts, and hornworts. None of these nonvascular plants is taller than twenty centimeters (eight inches). Despite their small size, they have leaflike, stemlike, and usually rootlike parts.

—Starr, Evers, and Starr, *Biology: Today and Tomorrow*, 2nd Edition

The word you have to learn and remember is **bryophytes**. The word sounds like bry-o-fights. You know a moss is a bryophyte from the reading, so you imagine (or draw) two mosses dressed in boxing shorts with gloves on. One of the mosses is named Bryan, but his nickname is "Bry-o." You imagine a caption under the two fighting mosses that says, "Bry-o fights!" Now you will remember that a moss nicknamed "Bryo" fights. And what is a moss? A bryophyte! This is much more fun than writing the definition twenty times on a piece of paper. It is also more helpful than simply telling yourself that you will remember the definition. This strategy helps you move words from short-term memory into long-term memory.

Association. *Connect a word picture with something or someone you already know.* Associations are similar to visual aids, except they are usually connected to something or someone you know. Take the word *obstinate*. You might know that this word means "stubborn." Think of someone you know who is stubborn or obstinate. Maybe it is a brother or sister, mother or father . . . or you yourself! Now the next time you come across the word *obstinate*, you will associate it with the person who shows that quality.

Let's look at a word from a business textbook to show how you can connect the new with the old to remember a vocabulary word:

> Some of a firm's plans may not be finalized until specific business conditions are known. For this reason, firms use **contingency planning**; that is, they develop alternate plans for various possible conditions. The plan to be implemented is contingent on the business conditions that occur.
>
> —Madura, *Introduction to Business*, 4th Edition

When you first see the word *contingency*, you might realize that it sounds a lot like *emergency*. Once you understand that a **contingency plan** is an alternate plan, you know you have a good association. A contingency plan is like preparing for an emergency. If things do not work out the way you want them to, you need to have an alternative plan. So companies have contingency plans, just like buildings have emergency escape plans if they catch fire. In simplest terms, contingency plan = emergency plan.

Note Card Creation. *Make a vocabulary file using 3 × 5 cards.* These cards can be purchased with rings already punched through them at most stores that carry school supplies, or you can hole-punch a corner and put them on your own ring. Make sure you include your visualization and association.

Your vocabulary learning strategy is VAN (**v**isual aid, **a**ssociation, **n**ote card creation). It may sound silly, but silliness is often easy to remember. Imagine your brain is driving around in a van. You are constantly loading the van with vocabulary knowledge. As it fills up, you are storing this knowledge in your vocabulary warehouse until it is needed. When the need arises, you will have your VAN deliver the right word.

Be prepared to use your VAN as you work through the rest of this chapter and book. And remember, there is no wrong visual aid or association. If it helps you remember the definition of a new word, it's a help.

Figure 3.1 Make a Vocabulary File Using 3 × 5 Cards

FRONT

The word on one side

Identify the part of speech: you need to know how a word is used

(noun, verb, adjective, adverb)

BACK

a. Definition: Write it in your own words to make it easier to remember.

b. Visual: Use a picture, or use an example that triggers a visual.

c. Association: Use the word in a familiar context. Connect it to a person or other words (like synonyms or antonyms) you already know by writing an original sentence based on the association.

d. Find or create fun quotations that use the word you are trying to learn (optional).

FRONT

Obstinate

(adjective)

BACK

a. Definition: stubborn

b. Visual: my miniature Schnauzer

c. Association: My miniature Schnauzer is obstinate about getting on the couch. He knows it is against the rules, but he does it anyway!

d. "I am firm. You are obstinate. He is a pig-headed fool." —Katherine Whitehorn

Figure 3.2 VAN (Visual aid, Association, Note Card Creation)

© Cengage Learning

Context Clues

What do you do when you are reading and don't know the meaning of a word? One option is to stop reading and find your dictionary, which is probably in the other room. By the time you make it back to the room where you were reading, you have forgotten the word you went to look up. So now you have to find the word in your reading again. You look it up, read the definition, and close the dictionary. Now you have to reread because you have forgotten what the paragraph was about. You finally get back to the word, and you have already forgotten what it meant!

Don't throw your hands up in despair. There is an easier option. You can use **context clues**. Let's unpack the meaning of "context clue," starting with the easy word. What is a synonym for **clue**? How about *sign, hint,* or *evidence*? What does **context** mean? It means *environment* or *setting*. In other words, a context clue is a hint (clue) about the meaning of a word that is located in the surrounding words or sentences (context).

When you are trying to figure out what a word means, look in the sentences surrounding the word. Clues to your word's meaning can be found anywhere within a paragraph, but they are often found in one or more of the following three places:

1. The actual sentence in which the unknown word appears.

2. The sentence before the one in which the word appears.

3. The sentence after the one in which the word appears.

Students often pressure themselves by thinking they have to come up with a specific definition for a word they do not know. But when you use context clues, you are not looking for the exact meaning of a word; you are simply looking for an approximate meaning that will give you enough of an understanding to keep reading. That way you won't have to stop and get distracted every time you come across a word you do not know.

There are several types of context clues. The most common ones are examples, antonyms, synonyms, and your own logic interacting with the words on the page. Context clues are *easy*. Literally—**EASY as 1, 2, 3.** Check out the following **mnemonic.** (Can you guess the meaning of **mnemonic** based on the *example* context clue?)

Example

Antonym

Synonym

Your Logic

as

1. Look for signal words, or "transitions."

2. Focus on what you know.

3. Pay attention to punctuation.

Examples

Examples are probably the most straightforward kind of context clue. First the author uses a word and then gives an example that describes or explains it, using signal words like these.

> **Words that signal examples:**
>
> *for example, for instance, such as, to illustrate*

Felix is convinced Jessica is clairvoyant. **For example**, she has saved him from getting a ticket three times by telling him she had a feeling there was a police officer ahead.

As you can see, the word *clairvoyant* has something to do with being able to see things that haven't happened yet. You can tell because of the example given: *she had a feeling there was a police officer ahead.*

Interaction 3-2. Using Example Context Clues with Signal Words

Each sentence includes a **boldfaced** vocabulary word. Underline the example that provides a clue to its meaning. Circle the signal word. Then guess the meaning of the vocabulary word and write it on the line.

1. Roy's friends tell him he will never get a date because he is too **reticent**. For example, he almost never talks to anyone other than his closest friends. _____

2. Many pregnant women are convinced that they will not **exhibit** basic maternal behaviors, such as holding their baby correctly, nursing them, or even keeping them safe. _____

3. One classic example of **integrity** is Abraham Lincoln, who is said to have walked several miles to return a few cents he had overcharged a customer. _____
   _____

4. Depending on one's preference, the **grandeur** of nature can be illustrated by sunrises and sunsets, mountain vistas, or beach scenery. _____

5. Actions like stabbing a friend in the back or cheating on a partner often cause the victim to become **incensed**. _____

Now follow the VAN strategy (on pp. 102–105) for the words you did not know. Bring your note card(s) to class to share your ideas.

Signal Words May Not Be Present. One important thing to know about context clues is that signal words are optional. Suppose you read a sentence that does not include any signal words. You can figure out if there are examples by adding example signal words to different places to see if they make sense. If they do, that's an example context clue. See how it works here:

> Felix is convinced Jessica is clairvoyant. [**for example**] She has saved him from getting a ticket three times by telling him she had a feeling there was a police officer ahead.

So remember, you can still have an example context clue without a transition.

Interaction 3-3. Using Example Context Clues without Signal Words

Each item includes a **boldfaced** vocabulary word. First, add example signal words where they fit best in the sentence. Then underline the example that provides a clue to its meaning. Finally, guess the meaning of the vocabulary word and write it on the line.

1. **Ageism** predisposes us to discriminate against old people by avoiding them or in some way victimizing them primarily because of their age. For example, We might think all elderly are senile, or they cannot contribute to society, or they are not open to change.

—Corey and Corey, *I Never Knew I Had a Choice*, 8ᵗʰ Edition

2. **Checkbook journalism** is alive and well. In 2004, CBS paid singer Michael Jackson $1 million for an entertainment special and an interview on *60 Minutes* during a time when Jackson was under investigation for child molestation. In 2006, *People* magazine paid actress Angelina Jolie $400, 000 for exclusive use of photos that confirmed she was pregnant with Brad Pitt's child.

—Adapted from Biagi, *Media/Impact*, 8ᵗʰ Edition

Now follow the VAN strategy (on pp. 102–105) for the words you did not know. Bring your note card(s) to class to share your ideas.

Antonyms

Antonyms are words that have opposite meanings, such as *light* and *dark*. Sometimes you can figure out the meaning of a word by finding its antonym in a context that shows the author means to contrast (show the difference between) the two words.

Words that signal antonyms:

on the other hand, in contrast, however, but,
yet, instead, even though, although, unlike

Although the lawyer's question seemed innocuous enough, its true intent was to harm the character of the witness.

The word *although* signals a contrast between the two parts of the sentence that are divided by the comma. To figure out the meaning of *innocuous*, you can use that signal word as a clue. You might also notice that the sentence shows contrast in its wording: *seemed* innocuous . . ., its *true* intent was to harm . . . The word with an opposing meaning is *harm*. So *innocuous* means "not harmful." Once you determine the opposite word, you can put *not* or *doesn't* in front of it; this will often help you form a working definition.

Interaction 3-4. Using Antonym Context Clues

Each sentence includes a **boldfaced** vocabulary word. Underline the antonym that provides a clue to its meaning. If there are signal words that indicate contrast, circle them. Then guess the meaning of the vocabulary word and write it on the line.

1. Looking for a new car can be quite frustrating. There are so many choices. The sporty model I like loses its value quickly. However, the model that looks like every other car on the road **retains** its value.

   A. What is your "working definition" for **retains**? _____

   B. What does **retains** mean? _____

2. To become an efficient reader, you must practice active reading strategies. On the other hand, **passive** reading requires nothing more than running your eyes over a page.

   A. What is your "working definition" for **passive**? _____

   B. What does **passive** mean? _____

3. John bought a rental property thinking that collecting a monthly rental would make it a nice investment, but it has turned into an enormous **liability** because there have been no tenants and tons of repairs.

   A. What is your "working definition" for **liability**? _____

   B. What does **liability** mean? _____

4. It is a myth to say that to get ahead in society, education is **sufficient**. The truth is that education is not enough. Success depends significantly on one's class origins; the formal education of one's parent or parents; and one's race, ethnicity, and gender.

   —Andersen and Taylor, *Sociology*, 4th Edition

   A. What is your "working definition" for **sufficient**? _____

   B. What does **sufficient** mean? _____

5. Despite the impressive collection of research findings for personality **stability** using the five-factor model, there is growing evidence for personality change.

   —Kail and Cavanaugh, *Human Development*, 4th Edition

   A. What is your "working definition" for **stability**? _____

   B. What does **stability** mean? _____

Now follow the VAN strategy (on pp. 102–105) for the words you did not know. Bring your note card(s) to class to share your ideas.

Synonyms

Synonyms are words that have a similar meaning or the same meaning, such as *small* and *little*. Sometimes you can figure out the meaning of a word by finding its synonym in a context that shows the author means to compare (show the similarities between) the two words. Other times the author actually defines the word, so be on the lookout for phrases that mean the same thing as the word.

> **Words that signal synonyms:**
>
> *like, as, also, as well, or, in other words,*
> *that is, in the same way*

Hominids were bipedal—**that is**, two-legged, a trait that enabled them to move over long distances and make use of their arms and legs for different purposes.

—Adapted from Duiker and Spielvogel, *World History,* 5th Edition

The words *that is* signal that the author is going to repeat the same idea using different words. The word *bipedal* means the same thing as "two-legged." These words are synonyms.

Interaction 3-5. Using Synonym Context Clues

Each sentence includes a **boldfaced** vocabulary word. Underline the synonym (or definition) that provides a clue to its meaning. If there is a transition to signal the synonym, circle it. Then guess the meaning of the vocabulary word and write it on the line.

1. Many young children think their parents know everything. In the same way, people who have faith in God believe that God is **omniscient**. _____

    _____

2. The amount of light that enters a camera is determined by the size of the **aperture**, or opening, in the shutter.

    —Adapted from Fichner-Rathus, *Understanding Art,* 8th Edition

    _____

    _____

3. Banks today try to convince consumers that their ATMs are **ubiquitous**, that is, that they can find one on every corner. _____

    _____

© William R. Hutchison Jr./Shutterstock

4. Glass is usually made from molten sand, or **silica**, mixed with minerals such as lead, copper, cobalt, cadmium, lime, soda, or potash. Certain combinations of minerals afford the glass a rich quality as found in stained-glass windows of the great cathedrals and in the more recent stained-glassworks of Henri Matisse and Marc Chagall.

—Fichner-Rathus, *Understanding Art*, 8th Edition

5. President Theodore Roosevelt once made the following statement: "People used to say to me that I was an astonishingly good politician and **divined** what the people are going to think. . . . I did not [predict] how the people were going to think; I simply made my mind up what they ought to think and then did my best to get them to think it."

—Schmidt, Shelley, and Bardes, *American Government and Politics Today, 2007-2008*, 13th Edition

Now follow the VAN strategy (on pp. 102–105) for the words you did not know. Bring your note card(s) to class to share your ideas.

Your Logic

We said earlier that context clues for the meaning of a word are found in the surrounding words or sentences—that is, in the context of the reading selection. However, the reader's context plays a role, too, especially the context of how you think—your logic. Your ability to understand logical connections as you interact with the words on the page will help you make meaning as you read. Starting with what you already understand, actively try to figure out what you don't yet know. This process of making inferences is one you should always be using as you read.

> Despite his **valiant** effort, the young boxer was no match for the defending champion.

Here, you can assume that the young boxer tried his best to beat the champion. The sentence also says the young boxer was "no match" for the champion. Trying hard even when losing marks a person as brave, which is the meaning of *valiant*.

Interaction 3-6. Using Your Logic

Each sentence includes a **boldfaced** vocabulary word. Underline the part of the sentence that provides a clue to the word's meaning. Then use your logic and any prior knowledge you may have to guess the meaning of the word and write it on the line.

1. Janice and Renee are both Pilates instructors who work at the YMCA. They have decided that if they **collaborate**, they might be able to open their own studio.

   A. What does **collaborate** mean? _____

   B. How did your logic help? _____

   _____

2. The artist had created an interesting display of black-and-white photos of homeless men and women **juxtaposed** with color images of celebrities.

   A. What does **juxtaposed** mean? _____

   B. How did your logic help? _____

   _____

3. Remember that you will almost never memorize a speech or read it from a manuscript. Most often, you will choose the exact words of your speech as you are speaking it. Therefore, you need a **speaking outline** to help remember specific information that you plan to include in your speech.

   —Griffin, *Invitation to Public Speaking,* 2nd Edition

   A. What is a **speaking outline**? _____

   B. How did your logic help? _____

   _____

4. Hurricane Katrina created **havoc** in the north central Gulf coast region when it struck in the summer of 2005.

   A. What does **havoc** mean? _____

   B. How did your logic help? _____

   _____

5. A **lackadaisical** defense in the first half of the game left the defending Super Bowl champs in a weakened position.

   A. What does **lackadaisical** mean? _____

   B. How did your logic help? _____

   Now follow the VAN strategy (on pp. 102–105) for the words you did not know. Bring your note card(s) to class to share your ideas.

EASY as 1, 2, 3

Regardless of whether you are using an example, antonym, synonym, or your logic, you should follow these three steps:

1. Look for signal words (leads to *example, antonym, synonym* context clues).

2. Focus on what you know (leads to *your logic*).

3. Pay attention to punctuation (turns grade school rules into college assets).

1. Look for signal words

Signal words or "transitions" that help you find context clues are a good place to start determining the meanings of words. Remember that signal words often lead to example, synonym, and antonym context clues.

Interaction 3-7. Look for Signal Words

Each sentence includes a **boldfaced** vocabulary word. Underline the word or words that provide a clue to its meaning. Then guess the meaning of the word and write it on the line.

1. Humans have an aptitude for acting out of love, but we also have a **capacity** for evil.

   A. What does **capacity** mean? _____

   B. What kind of context clue was used? _____

2. Despite the serious **allegations** against him, Mr. Smith's only crime was being in the wrong place at the wrong time.

   A. What does **allegations** mean? _____

   B. What kind of context clue was used? _____

3. Meenu's big sister often **patronized** her; Meenu looked down on their little brother as well.

   A. What does **patronized** mean? _____

   B. What kind of context clue was used? _____

4. In his book *The Prophet*, Kahlil Gibran points out that love is two-sided: as it can give you great **ecstasy**, so it can cause you great pain.

   A. What does ecstasy mean? _____

   B. What was the context clue? _____

5. **Secularization** is one of the dominant trends influencing religion throughout the world. We can detect **secularization** in survey data that track religious attitudes and practices over time. For example, between 1972 and 2000, the percentage of Americans expressing no religious preference increased from 5 to 14 percent, while the percentage of people attending religious services once a month or more fell from 57 to 45 percent.

   —National Opinion Research Center, 2002

   A. What does **secularization** mean? _____

   B. What kind of context clue was used? _____

   Now follow the VAN strategy (on pp. 102–105) for the words you did not know. Bring your note card(s) to class to share your ideas.

2. Focus on what you know

Readers often pay attention to what they *do not* know rather than what they *do* know. Your knowledge connects to many fields of study and types of information. Start training yourself to look for the connections between your prior knowledge and the new information you read. By focusing on what you know, you will be able to understand more of what you read than if you focus on what you do not know.

◉ Interaction 3-8. Focus on What You Know

Each sentence includes a **boldfaced** vocabulary word. Underline the word or words that provide a clue to its meaning. Then guess the meaning of the word and write it on the line.

1. While one late credit card payment is not usually a problem, a habitual pattern can lead not only to your card being **revoked** but also to long-term damage to your credit report._____

2. Traditional Western doctors are now more frequently **advocating** the use of acupuncture, a Chinese medical practice of puncturing the body with needles at particular pressure points to relieve pain or treat disease.

—Adapted from Hales, *An Invitation to Health*, 12ᵗʰ Edition

_____

3. During my first years in college, Martin Luther King's message of love as the path to ending racism and healing the wounds of racial domination had been replaced by a black power movement stressing militant resistance. While King had called for nonviolence and compassion, this new movement called on us to harden our hearts, to wage war against our enemies. Loving our enemies, militant leaders told us, made us weak and easy to **subjugate**, and many turned their backs on King's message.

—Hooks and Nhat, "Building a Community of Love"

_____

4. Having two or more wives in a **polygynous** society is usually seen as a mark of prestige or high status. In highly stratified kingdoms, **polygyny** is one of the privileges of royalty and aristocrats, as was the case with the late King Sobhuza of Swaziland, who, it was estimated, had well over a hundred wives.

—Ferraro, *Cultural Anthropology*, 6ᵗʰ Edition

A. What is a **polygynous society**? _____

B. What does **polygyny** mean? _____

5. At least 260,000 species of flowering plants live in **diverse** habitats. They bloom in **spacious** meadows and **aromatic** forests, in **parched** deserts and on **craggy** mountaintops.

—Starr, *Biology: Concepts and Applications*, 6ᵗʰ Edition

A. What does **diverse** mean? _____

B. What does **spacious** mean? _____

C. What does **aromatic** mean? _____

D. What does **parched** mean? _____

E. What does **craggy** mean? _____

F. What prior knowledge helped you determine the meaning of **diverse**, **spacious**, **aromatic**, **parched**, and **craggy**? _____

Now follow the VAN strategy (on pp. 102–105) for the words you did not know. Bring your note card(s) to class to share your ideas.

3. Pay attention to punctuation

Punctuation may not be the most exciting topic you'll ever read about, but punctuation is important. Here's a humorous example that shows how punctuation alone can change the meaning of the same words:

> An English professor wrote the words, "Woman without her man is nothing" on the blackboard and directed his students to punctuate it correctly. The men wrote: "Woman, without her man, is nothing." The women wrote: "Woman! Without her, man is nothing."
>
> —Author unknown

Both sentences are correctly punctuated, but because of their punctuation, they have very different meanings. However, when it comes to context clues, punctuation does not have to be this tricky. Look at the following pairs of punctuation marks for extra information on a word you do not know.

1. **dashes**—Material within dashes may be a definition of the word that came before. Or a dash may introduce or follow an example.

   Triathlons—races that include biking, swimming, and running—have become popular in recent years.

   Iron, bronze, wood, ivory, terra-cotta—sculptors from the kingdom of Benin used all these materials with great skill.

   > —Adapted from Fichner-Rathus, *Understanding Art,* 8th Edition)

2. **(parentheses)** Parentheses may enclose definitions.

   Trans fat (hydrogenated or partially-hydrogenated oil) is called "trans" because it is a process that "transfers" fat from a non-saturated to a saturated state.

3. **, commas,** The words enclosed by commas may restate the meaning of the previous word.

   Mariel is a chatty, even garrulous, person.

4. **colons (:)** Words after a colon often are examples or illustrations of the words before it.

   The most important skill for college graduates entering the work force is effective oral communication: listening, following instructions, conversing, and giving feedback.

   > —Adapted from Williams, *Management,* 4th Edition

● Interaction 3-9. Pay Attention to Punctuation

Each sentence includes a **boldfaced** vocabulary word. Underline the word or words that provide a clue to its meaning. Circle any punctuation marks that act as clues. Then guess the meaning of the word and write it on the line.

1. To have a championship team requires the perfection of certain **tactics:** speed, skill, effective execution of plays, and, most of all, teamwork.

   What are **tactics?** _____

2. To be an **advocate,** or supporter, for the rights of an unpopular group of people requires courage, determination, and grace.

   What does **advocate** mean (other than supporter)? _____

3. Devin's little brother Cameron creates such a **disruption**—whenever Devin tries to study, Cameron sneaks up behind him and shouts in his ear.

   What does **disruption** mean? _____

4. The growing use of technology has created a **bifurcated workforce,** two tiers of workers whose different skills with technology have resulted in two distinct levels of income, even at the entry level.

   —Adapted from Segal, Gerdes, and Steiner, *An Introduction to the Profession of Social Work,* 2nd Edition

   What is a **bifurcated workforce?** _____

   _____

5. One of the earliest, and perhaps the most primitive, methods of enhancing sound is **onomatopoeia,** which occurs when the sound of a word echoes its meaning, as it does in common words (*bang, crash,* and *hiss*).

   —Kirszner and Mandell, *Literature,* 6th Edition

   What does **onomatopoeia** mean? _____

Now follow the VAN strategy (on pp. 102–105) for the words you did not know. Bring your note card(s) to class to share your ideas.

Word Parts

There are three basic words parts: roots, prefixes, and suffixes. All words are made up of one or more of these pieces.

1. **Root.** The core or essence of a word, the root can be a stand-alone word or a building block for other words.

2. **Prefix.** Attached at the beginning of a word, a prefix changes the word's meaning.

3. **Suffix.** Attached at the end of a word, a suffix changes the word's meaning and/or its part of speech.

Example

> **Root = form**—the shape of something (noun); to create something (verb)
>
> **Root + prefix = inform**—to give facts or information; to tell (verb). Notice that this prefix changes the meaning of the root "form."
>
> **Root + prefix + suffix = informer**—a person who gives information or facts about another person (often to the authorities). Notice that adding the suffix **–er** changes this word from a verb to a noun (person). However, the basic definition of *inform* did not change.

The benefit of learning word parts is that by knowing a single piece, you have a clue to the meaning of multiple words. Look at the example of the common prefix *un-*, which means *not* or *the opposite of*. Did you know that *un-* is used in more than 2,000 words? Just by knowing one two-letter prefix, you have partial knowledge of thousands of words. List as many words as you can think of that use the prefix *un-*.

_____	_____	_____	_____
_____	_____	_____	_____
_____	_____	_____	_____
_____	_____	_____	_____

You can use note cards as you learn word parts, just as you did in the VAN vocabulary strategy, but the layout on the cards will be a bit different since you are learning one part rather than a whole word.

Figure 3.3a Note Card for Word Parts

FRONT

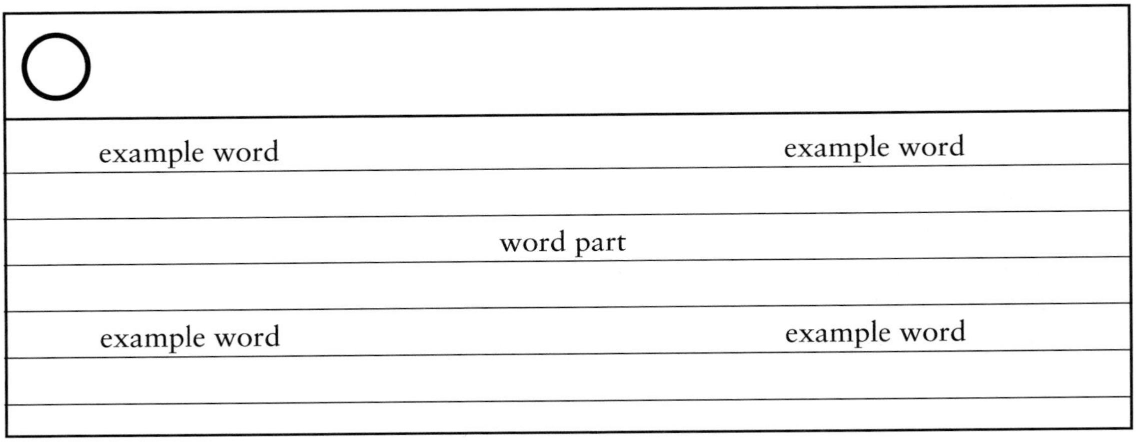

Figure 3.3b

BACK

◯
Define the word part in the middle.
Define each of the words that use the word part.
Visualize: Use a picture or an example that triggers a visual.
Associate: Use the words in a familiar context: connect them to people or other words (like synonyms or antonyms) you already know by writing an original sentence.

Roots

English is sort of a "mutt" language—many of its words come from several other languages, including Latin and Greek. **Table 3.1** displays ten common Latin roots.

Table 3.1 Common Latin Roots

Latin root	Basic meaning	Example words
-dict-	to say	contradict, dictate, diction, edict, predict
-duc-	to lead, bring, take	conduct, deduce, produce, reduce
-gress-	to walk	digress, progress, transgress
-ject-	to throw	eject, inject, interject, project, reject, subject
-pel-	to drive	compel, dispel, impel, repel
-pend-	to hang	append, depend, impend, pendant, pendulum
-port-	to carry	comport, deport, export, import, report, support
-scrib-, -script-	to write	describe, description, prescribe, prescription, subscribe, subscription, transcribe, transcription
-tract-	to pull, drag, draw	attract, contract, detract, extract, protract, retract, traction
-vert-	to turn	convert, divert, invert, revert

From the sample words in the Latin roots table, it is easy to see how roots combine with prefixes to form new words. For example, the root *-tract-*, meaning "to pull," can be combined with a number of prefixes, including *de-* and *re-*. Detract means "to pull away" (*de-* means "away, off") and *retract* means "to pull back" (*re-* means "again, back").

Table 3.2 Common Greek Roots

Greek root	Basic meaning	Example words
-anthrop-	human	misanthrope, philanthropy, anthropomorphic
-bio-	life	biology, biological, biography, autobiography
-chron-	time	anachronism, chronic, chronicle, synchronize, chronometer
-dem-	people	democracy, demography, demagogue, endemic, pandemic
-log-, -logue-	word, thought or speech	dialogue, monologue, epilogue, logic
-morph-	form	amorphous, metamorphic, morphology
-path-	feeling, suffering	empathy, sympathy, sympathetic, apathy, apathetic, psychopathic
-pedo-, -ped-	child, children	pediatrician, pedagogue
-philo-, -phil-	having a strong affinity or love for	philanthropy, philharmonic, philosophy
-phon-	sound	polyphonic, cacophony, phonetics

From the sample words in the Greek roots table, you can see how roots combine with suffixes to form words that are a different part of speech (such as a noun, verb, adjective, or adverb). For example, the root *-path-*, meaning "feeling," can be combined with a number of suffixes that change its part of speech. For example, *sympathy* is a noun; *sympathetic* is an adjective; and *sympathetically* is an adverb. The basic meaning does not change, but the suffix changes how the word is used.

Prefixes

One key way to improving your vocabulary is to know the most common prefixes. In fact, by knowing just the five most common prefixes in English (*un-*, *re-*, *in-*, *dis-*, and *en-*), you will have a partial understanding of more than 60 percent of all English words that have prefixes (see **Figure 3.4**).

Figure 3.4 Prefixes

Rank	Prefix	%	Rank	Prefix	%
1.	un- (not, opposite of)	26	11.	pre- (before)	3
2.	re- (again)	14	12.	inter- (between, among)	3
3.	in-, im-, ir-, il- (not)	11	13.	fore- (before)	3
4.	dis- (not, opposite of)	7	14.	de- (opposite of)	2
5.	en-, em- (cause to)	4	15.	trans- (across)	2
6.	non- (not)	4	16.	super- (above)	1
7.	in-, im- (in or into)	4	17.	semi- (half)	1
8.	over- (too much)	3	18.	anti- (against)	1
9.	mis- (wrongly)	3	19.	mid- (middle)	1
10.	sub- (under)	3	20.	under- (too little)	1

Available at http://teacher.scholastic.com/reading/bestpractices/phonics/prefixes.pdf

Suffixes

Figure 3.5 is a list of the twenty most frequent suffixes appearing in words found in the *Word Frequency Book* (Carroll, Davies, and Richman, 1971). The suffixes *-s*, *-es*, *-ed*, and -ing account for almost two-thirds of the words. The suffixes *-s* and *-es* are used to form the plurals of most nouns. The suffixes *-ed* and *-ing* are added to verbs to change their tense.

The list of the most common suffixes includes some suffixes that change the part of speech of a word. For example, if you add *–ful* to a noun, the noun becomes an adjective: *helpful, wishful, graceful*. There are many other suffixes that indicate the part of speech of a word. Here are some of them.

Noun suffixes: *-age, -al, -ance, -ant, -ate, -ee, -ence, -ent, -er, -or, -ar, -ese, -ess, -hood, -ice, -ism, -ist, -ment, -ness, -sion, -tain, -tion, -ure*

Suffixes that form adjectives: *-able, -al, -er, -est, -ette, -let, -ful, -fully, -ible, -ic, -ical, -ish, -ive, -less, -ous, -some, -worthy*

Suffixes that form adverbs: *-ly, -wards, -ways, -wide, -wise*

Suffixes that create a verb form: *-ate, -ed, -en, -ing, -ise, -ize, -yze*

(Available at http://teacher.scholastic.com/reading/bestpractices/phonics/suffixes.pdf)

Figure 3.5 Suffixes

Rank	Suffix	%	Rank	Suffix	%
1.	-s, -es (plurals)	31	11.	-ity, -ty (state of)	1
2.	-ed (past-tense verbs)	20	12.	-ment (action or process)	1
3.	-ing (verb form/ present participle)	14	13.	-ic (having characteristics of)	1
4.	-ly (characteristic of)	7	14.	-ous, -eous, -ious (possessing the qualities of)	1
5.	-er, -or (person connected with)	4	15.	-en (made of)	1
6.	-ion, -tion, -ation, -ition (act, process)	4	16.	-er (comparative)	1
7.	-ible, -able (can be done)	2	17.	-ive, -ative, -itive (adjective form of a noun)	1
8.	-al, -ial (having characteristics of)	1	18.	-ful (full of)	1
9.	-y (characterized by)	1	19.	-less (without)	1
10.	-ness (state of, condition of)	1	20.	-est (comparative)	1

Interaction 3-10. Roots, Prefixes, and Suffixes

Load up your vocabulary VAN by creating a note card for each of the roots, prefixes, and suffixes you do not know. Use the note card style modeled in the example on pages 119–120. Make sure the sample words you use on your note cards are words you know.

Sometimes students have trouble keeping the meanings of "root," "prefix," and "suffix" straight. Keep in mind that in the alphabet, P comes before R, and S comes after R (p, q, r, s . . .). Therefore, prefixes come at the beginning of a word (first in the alphabet order), suffixes come at the end of a word (last in the alphabet order), and roots are what prefixes and suffixes attach to (in the middle of R and S in the alphabet order).

Denotation and Connotation

Denotation is the literal meaning of a word. It is straightforward. When you see denotation, think "d"—denotation is the dictionary definition. When you look up a word in the dictionary, the definition is the denotation of that word.

ret·i·cent [ret-*uh*-s*uh*nt] *–adjective* 1. disposed to be silent or not to speak freely; reserved. 2. reluctant or restrained.

Connotation, on the other hand, is the emotional meaning of a word. When you see connotation, think "conn": connotation is the emotional **conn**ection of a word. Connotation is the feeling associated with a word. Some words have positive connotations, and others have negative connotations.

Take the words *slender, thin,* and *skinny*. They have similar denotative meanings, and they are considered synonyms. But their connotations are quite different. *Slender* implies a generally attractive thinness. *Thin* can suggest a reduced state, for example, from being sick. *Skinny* connotes "too thin" or even "emaciated." Of the three words, then, *slender* is the most complimentary, and skinny the least.

Imagine that you go over to your friend's grandmother's house for dinner. When she opens the door, she is a large, rosy woman with a double chin and an infectious smile. She grabs you in a warm hug and enthusiastically welcomes you into her home. Then she looks at you and says, "You are a twig! You are such a tiny bird! You need to eat something!" Do you think the grandmother would describe you as *slender, thin,* or *skinny*? Which term best fits the connotation of this scenario? Hint: What do the words "twig" and "tiny bird" suggest?

Interaction 3-11. Understanding Denotation and Connotation in a Quotation

Read the words of comic strip creator Jules Feiffer, and answer the questions that follow.

> I used to think I was poor. Then they told me I wasn't poor—I was needy. Then they told me it was self-defeating to think of myself as needy. I was deprived. (Oh not deprived but rather underprivileged.) Then they told me that *underprivileged* was overused. I was disadvantaged. I still don't have a dime. But I have a great vocabulary.

1. Are there any differences in the denotations of *poor, needy, deprived, underprivileged,* and *disadvantaged*? Use a dictionary to answer this question. _____

   _____

2. Are there any differences in the connotations of *poor, needy, deprived, underprivileged,* and *disadvantaged*? _____

3. Form a group with two or three other students. Each of you should have your dictionary handy. Using your dictionaries and discussing prior knowledge that you each may have about the words listed in number 2, arrange the words from the one with the most negative connotation to the word with the most positive connotation.

   _____

   _____

● Interaction 3-12. Determining Denotation and Connotation While You Read

Read the following paragraphs from a sociology textbook and answer the questions that follow.

Paragraph A

Language reflects the assumptions of a culture. This can be seen and exemplified in several ways:

Language affects people's perceptions of reality.
Example: Researchers have found that men tend to think that women are not included when terms such as "man" are used to refer to all people. Studies find that when college students look at job descriptions written in masculine pronouns, they assume that women are not qualified for the job.

A quote by Alma Graham illustrates this gender bias created by language: If a woman is swept off a ship into the water, the cry is 'Man overboard!' If she is killed by a hit-and-run driver, the charge is 'manslaughter.' If she is injured on the job, the coverage is 'workmen's compensation.' But if she arrives at a threshold marked 'Men Only,' she knows the admonition is not intended to bar animals or plants or inanimate objects. It is meant for her.

—Andersen and Taylor, *Sociology*, 4ᵗʰ Edition

Can you think of any other examples of how the words we use connote a gender bias?

_____

_____

Paragraph B

Language reflects the social and political status of different groups in society.
Example: a term such as "woman doctor" suggests that the gender of the doctor is something exceptional and noteworthy. The term "working woman" (used to refer to women who are employed outside the home) also suggests that women who do not work for wages are not working.

—Andersen and Taylor, *Sociology*, 4ᵗʰ Edition

Ask yourself what the term "working man" connotes and how this differs from "working woman." Discuss with your class. _____

_____

Paragraph C

Groups may advocate changing language referring to them as a way of asserting a positive group identity.
Example: Some advocates for the "disabled" challenge the term "handicapped," arguing that it stigmatizes people who may have many abilities, even if they are physically distinctive. Also, though someone may have one disabling condition, they may be perfectly able in other regards.

—Andersen and Taylor, *Sociology*, 4th Edition

Which word has a more positive connotation, "disabled" or "handicapped"? Support

your opinion. Can you think of any terms that would have a more positive connotation

than either of the words used above? _____

_____

Paragraph D

The implications of language emerge from specific historical and cultural contexts.
Example: The naming of so-called races comes from the social and historical processes that define different groups as inferior or superior. Racial labels do not just come from physical, natural, or cultural differences. The term "Caucasian," for example, was coined in the seventeenth century when racist thinkers developed alleged scientific classification systems to rank different societal groups. Alfred Blumenthal used the label Caucasian to refer to people from the Caucuses of Russia, who he thought were more beautiful and intelligent than any group in the world.

—Andersen and Taylor, *Sociology*, 4th Edition

Is the term *Caucasian* used accurately today? _____

_____

Paragraph E

Language shapes people's perception of groups and events in society.
Example: Native American victories during the nineteenth century are typically described as "massacres"; comparable victories by White settlers are described in heroic terms. The statement that Columbus "discovered" America implies that Native American societies did not exist before Columbus "found" the Americas.

—Andersen and Taylor, *Sociology*, 4th Edition

Discuss the connotation of *massacre*. _____

What are some words that connote the actions or people associated with the word *heroism*?

_____

Discuss how describing Columbus as *discovering* America creates a negative connotation of the Native American societies. _____

_____

Chapter Summary Activity

This chapter has discussed how asking questions can help you read and think more effectively. Construct a Reading Guide to Developing Your Vocabulary below by completing each idea on the left with information from the chapter on the right. You can use this guide later as you complete other reading assignments.

Reading Guide to Developing Your Vocabulary

Complete this idea	with information from the chapter.
You can use three methods for remembering new vocabulary words; you can create	1. _____ 2. _____ 3. _____
Using VAN helps you incorporate new words into your vocabulary because	4. _____
To figure out a word's meaning while you are reading, you can search the surrounding sentences for	5. _____
A mnemonic, or memory device, for how to use these clues is	6. _____
What four types of clues does the first word of the mnemonic summarize?	7. _____ 8. _____ 9. _____ 10. _____
Two signal words or phrases that indicate an example is coming next are	11. _____
An antonym is	12. _____
A synonym is	13. _____
The signal words *although* and *however* indicate contrasts, which may lead to finding which kind of context clue?	14. _____
The transitions *that is* and *like* indicate comparisons, which may lead to finding which kind of context clue?	15. _____

The fourth type of context clue depends on you, the reader, to use your logic to make	16.
Three steps to focus on when using context clues are	17. 18. 19.
List and define three word parts that can help you figure out a word's meaning.	20. 21. 22.
Words have two kinds of meaning. One kind is denotation, which is	23.
The second kind is connotation, which is	24.
Decide which of these two words has a positive connotation: *aromatic, smelly.*	25.

Test Taking Tips
Using Vocabulary Strategies

Reading tests often include questions about vocabulary. The first action you should take to determine the meaning of a vocabulary word is the one we have recommended throughout this chapter—look for context clues. Keep in mind "EASY as 1, 2, 3" when you approach these vocabulary items, and use examples, antonyms, synonyms, and your logic to figure them out.

Many items will require you to use your logic. Here are three types.

1. Literal or Figurative Use.

At times you will have to decide if a word or phrase is being used literally (it means exactly what it says) or figuratively (the author is using one thing to represent something else).

For example, you might encounter a question like this:

What did the author mean when she said, "The memory of what had happened so long ago still haunted her"?
   a. Something awful happened to the author at a haunted mansion.
   b. The author is afraid of ghosts.
   c. The author is still affected by a memory.
   d. The author has buried her past and rarely thinks about it.

When you read the word "haunted," you may be tempted to take this literally—perhaps the author has been visited by a ghost. If so, you might pick answer A or B, since these refer to ghosts. If you look at the context of the sentence, however, you can see that the author is equating "a ghost" with "a memory." She doesn't say a ghost haunts her, she says a memory haunts her. So the meaning is figurative. C is the only answer that shows her memories still affect or haunt her "like a ghost." (D is easily eliminated because it doesn't fit the context.)

2. Vocabulary and the Author's Purpose

Some questions ask you to decide why the author used a certain word, phrase or sentence—what purpose it serves. In order to determine the purpose, you first have to understand both its meaning and its context. Here is an example of a sentence from a reading in Chapter 10 entitled "Attila the Honey I'm Home," by Kristin van Ogtrop:

> Any minute now <u>my head is going to blast off my body, burst through the screen door, and buzz around my little town, eventually losing steam before landing with a thud somewhere near the train station, where it will be run over by one of my smiling neighbors </u>being picked up by what I imagine are calm spouses who will drive them calmly home to houses calm and collected where the children are already bathed and ready for bed. As for me, it's time to start yelling.

A reading comprehension question might ask:

The author uses the sentence "<u>my head is going to blast off my body, burst through the screen door, and buzz around my little town, eventually losing steam before landing with a thud somewhere near the train station, where it will be run over by one of my smiling neighbors</u>" for what purpose?
   a. To emphasize the author's ability to have out-of-body experiences.
   b. To explain how bad the author's headaches can be when she is stressed by life's daily trials.
   c. To teach readers how important it is to stay calm and collected.
   d. To express how frustrated the author feels when she compares her stressful life to the orderly lives of her neighbors.

Now it should be obvious that the author's head is not *literally* blasting off her body, buzzing around town, and being run over. Nor is she having "out-of-body experiences," so A can be eliminated. While B does refer to the stress the author seems to be expressing, the author does not seem to be describing a headache—she doesn't say anything about pain, for example. So B doesn't fit the context. C doesn't seem to fit the tone of the passage, which from the words used seems to be more about entertaining readers than teaching them anything. D mentions the author's frustration and stress, as well as the comparison she makes between her life and her neighbors' lives. In the excerpt, she uses a dramatic figure of speech about her head blasting off that plays off the cliché "steam was coming out of my ears," which is used to express stress or anger. (When the steam builds up enough, the head pops off!) She continues the contrast between her and her neighbors in the last sentence when she says, "As for me, it's time to start yelling." So D is the correct answer. To fully understand the sentence, you have to make the logical connection between the meaning and of its purpose in the paragraph.

3. Positive or Negative Tone

A third way to apply your logic is to ask whether the vocabulary word has a positive or negative tone. You can then eliminate any answer choices that do not match the tone. If the word or phrase in the passage has a positive tone, for example, then you can eliminate any answers that are negative or neutral.

Here is a specific example in Ken Olan's "Vocabulary—A Treasure Chest for Success":

> A large vocabulary is a common characteristic among all successful individuals, regardless of their occupation. That's because it <u>enhances</u> your ability to think and understand things more clearly. With the ability to make greater distinctions comes the capacity for greater understanding and knowledge.

Suppose the vocabulary question is as follows:

Choose the best definition for *enhances*:
    a. decreases
    b. improves
    c. diminishes
    d. complicates

You can eliminate answers A, B, and D since they all have a negative tone and the reading has a positive tone, which matches answer B. Sometimes tone can help you find a correct answer or eliminate a wrong one.

Finally, if you find yourself at an utter loss as to what a word means and cannot seem to find any context clues, replace the unknown word or phrase in the passage with each answer. Choose the one that seems to fit best. This is not an ideal way to answer a question, but at least it is better than blindly guessing.

Reading 3-1 . . . . **Web Article**

● Pre-Reading the Selection

The size of your vocabulary affects your professional success. Read the following article by Ken Olan, who is an executive with Every Advantage Business Solutions in Houston, Texas.

Guessing the Purpose

Judging from the title of this article (page 132), what do you suppose are Ken Olan's purposes for writing? _____

Surveying the Reading

Survey the title of the selection and the first sentence of each paragraph. What is the general topic of the reading selection? _____

Predicting the Content

Predict three things this selection will discuss.

- _____

- _____

- _____

Activating Your Knowledge

Think about several people you know who have a large vocabulary. What kind of jobs do they have?

- _____

- _____

- _____

Common Knowledge

Reader's Digest (*paragraph 2*) a general-interest family magazine published monthly by the Reader's Digest Association.

Americans with Disabilities Act (*paragraph 8*) often referred to with the acronym ADA, it is a 1990 federal law that prohibits discrimination against persons with a disability.

Reading with Pen in Hand

Now read the selection. As you read, mark any ideas that seem important, and respond to the questions and vocabulary items in the margin. Monitor your comprehension by putting a ✔ next to a paragraph when you understand most of it. Place an ✘ next to a paragraph when you don't understand most of it.

Visit **www.cengage.com/devenglish/doleconnect** and select Chapter 3 to hear vocabulary words from this selection and view a video about this topic.

◆ *Reading Journal*

◆What point does the author want to make?

perspective Consider the meaning of the sentence *perspective* is in to decide what the word means.

persons from all walks of life What does *all walks of life* suggest?

◆What does Blake Clark's article say?

◆What does the author suggest about prisoners and vocabulary?

distinctions The sentence before this one mentions that a person who knows fewer words has *fewer choices* and *fewer ideas*. A person who knows more words would be able to notice more distinctions. What are *distinctions*?

Vocabulary—A Treasure Chest for Success

Ken Olan

1   In my years of studying success I've learned some fascinating facts about the relationship between the size of one's vocabulary and how successful a person is in life. I think these insights may provide you with some new **perspective** on just how important it is to develop your personal vocabulary. At least I hope they will.

2   *Readers Digest* published an article by Blake Clark some years ago entitled, "Words Can Do Wonders for You." In the article he wrote, "Tests of more than 350,000 **persons from all walks of life** show that, more often than any other measurable characteristic, knowledge of the exact meanings of a large number of words accompanies outstanding success."

3   The same dynamic can also be seen at the other end of the socio-economic spectrum. Several years ago there was a study done on penitentiary prisoners to see what impact their vocabulary had on their actions. The study found that the more limited the person's vocabulary, the more limited their behavior was likely to be. In other words, they had fewer choices they could understand and therefore fewer ideas about what their potential actions could be. Vocabulary is a way of seeing things, of making **distinctions**, of understanding the world we live in. We use vocabulary to interpret and express ourselves. The prisoners, who had a limited vocabulary, were unable

to make the distinctions needed to acquire personal success. They just didn't understand. In fact, some of these prisoners may have even resorted to violence because it was their only effective way of expressing their feelings.

4   Legendary success expert Earl Nightingale wrote of a 20-year study of college graduates. The study concluded, "Without a single exception, those who had scored highest on the vocabulary test given in college were in the top income group, while those who had scored the lowest were in the bottom income group."

◆ What is the point of the twenty-year study that Earl Nightingale reported on?

5   Work done by scientist Johnson O'Connor involved tests that were given to executive and supervisory personnel in 39 large manufacturing companies. Every person who was tested scored high in basic aptitudes that go along with leadership. The differences in their vocabulary ratings, however, were dramatic and distinct. Here's how it turned out:

◆ What did the work by scientist Johnson O'Connor show?

- Presidents and vice presidents averaged 236 out of a possible 272 points.
- Managers averaged 168 points.
- Superintendents, 140 points.
- Foremen, 86 points.

In virtually every case, the size of each person's vocabulary **correlated** with the career level they had achieved. Could it be a coincidence? Absolutely not.

correlated Based on what the previous list shown, what does *correlated* mean?

6   When I was in high school I remember taking weekly vocabulary tests. Although I enjoyed learning new words I didn't think I'd ever use a lot of the words very often. You know what? I was right. I don't speak a lot of those words on a daily basis. But when I hear someone else using them I know what they mean. I don't have to sit there and wonder what in the world the other person is talking about. So developing a great vocabulary isn't really all about how important or how intelligent you sound when you speak. The biggest benefit of having an understanding of what different words mean is how intelligently you can listen to and understand what others are saying. A large vocabulary is a common characteristic among all successful individuals, regardless of their occupation. That's because it **enhances** your ability to think and understand things more clearly. With the ability to make greater distinctions comes the capacity for greater understanding and knowledge.

◆ What is the biggest benefit of having an understanding of what different words mean?

enhances Look in the previous sentence and the sentence *enhances* is in. Note that *enhances* is a verb— an action word. What does it mean?

7   Many people don't appreciate the phenomenal importance of understanding the meaning of a lot of different words until they start running into other people using words they don't comprehend. Here's

◆What example does the author give about the importance of knowing a lot of words?

an extreme example I often use to drive this point across. Imagine you had to move to a different country with a different language you didn't know. Would you be at a disadvantage to the people who did speak the language? Of course you would. Would you be able to understand everything that was going on around you? Definitely not. But what if you knew just some of the language? Would you be better off? Absolutely, and the more of that language you learned the better off you'd be. So then, I hope we can agree that if you went somewhere and didn't understand the language, you'd quickly realize the importance of knowing the meaning of different words . . . as many words as you could learn. For the exact same reason we can agree that it is just as important to understand as many words as possible in your native language. Without that advantage you can become almost as ignorant as if you didn't understand it at all.

◆What is the effect of a small vocabulary?

8 Certainly those who have a better grasp on the language will have an advantage over you. By having a smaller vocabulary, you become handicapped, meaning that you can't do, or won't understand, things that others with a larger vocabulary can. You are at a competitive disadvantage, and the Americans with Disabilities Act does nothing to help people who are handicapped with a poor vocabulary. So grab yourself a dictionary or thesaurus and commit to learning just one new word a week, or more, and watch how your ability to operate in this place we call the "real world" gets easier and more rewarding for you.

● Comprehension Questions

Write the letter of the answer on the line. Then explain your thinking.

Main Idea

_____ 1. Which of the following best states the main idea of this passage?

a. Those who have a better grasp of a language have an advantage.

b. There is a relationship between one's vocabulary knowledge and a person's ability to function and succeed in the "real world."

c. Many people don't appreciate the phenomenal importance of understanding the meaning of a lot of different words.

d. Vocabulary is a way of seeing things, of making distinctions, of understanding the world we live in.

WHY? What information in the selection leads you to give that answer? _____

_____

_____

_____ 2. Which of the following statements best summarizes this passage?

   a. Work done by scientist Johnson O'Connor tells us that vocabulary knowledge is an important key to getting a good job. In fact, his research indicated that a good vocabulary was the number one factor for being successful.

   b. Vocabulary is important.

   c. There is a direct relationship between the size of one's vocabulary and success in life.

   d. The biggest benefit of having an understanding of what different words mean is how intelligently you can listen to and understand what others are saying.

WHY? What information in the selection leads you to give that answer? _____

_____

Supporting Details

_____ 3. According to the passage, what is the biggest benefit of having an understanding of what different words mean?

   a. Success in life

   b. The ability to communicate in a foreign language

   c. Improved listening and comprehension skills

   d. A greater ability to understand what others are saying

WHY? What information in the selection leads you to give that answer? _____

_____

_____ 4. Based on the reading selection, which of the following does not support the idea that there is a direct relationship between the size of one's vocabulary and success in life?

   a. Johnson O'Connor's research

   b. Blake Clark's article

   c. Taking weekly vocabulary tests in high school

   d. Earl Nightingale's study

WHY? What information in the selection leads you to give that answer? _____

_____

_____

Author's Purpose

____   5 What is the purpose or purposes of the passage?
   a. To entertain
   b. To inform and persuade
   c. To persuade
   d. To inform

WHY? What information in the selection leads you to give that answer? _____

_____

_____

____   6. Why does the author refer to Johnson O'Connor's study?
   a. To persuade the reader to obtain a position of leadership
   b. To entertain the reader
   c. To illustrate the relationship between success at work and having a large vocabulary
   d. To persuade the reader to avoid violence as a means of self-expression

WHY? What information in the selection leads you to give that answer? _____

_____

_____

Relationships

____   7. What is the overall pattern of organization of the reading selection?
   a. Comparison and contrast
   b. Cause-and-effect
   c. Time order
   d. Process

WHY? What information in the selection leads you to give that answer? _____

_____

_____   8. What organizational pattern do you find in the first sentence of paragraph 6?
   a. Cause-and-effect
   b. Classification
   c. Process
   d. Time order

WHY? What information in the selection leads you to give that answer? _____

_____

Fact, Opinion, and Inference

_____   9. Which of the following statements is a fact?
   a. The Americans with Disabilities Act does nothing to help people who are handicapped with a poor vocabulary.
   b. Some of these prisoners may have even resorted to violence because it was their only effective way of expressing their feelings.
   c. I think these insights may provide you with some new perspective on just how important it is to develop your personal vocabulary.
   d. I hope we can agree that if you went somewhere and didn't understand the language, you'd quickly realize the importance of knowing the meaning of different words.

WHY? What leads you to give that answer? _____

_____

_____   10. Which of the following inferences would the author be likely to agree with?
   a. Prisoners are in jail because they have a bad vocabulary.
   b. It's better to learn the language of a culture before you visit it so you can avoid being taken advantage of.
   c. The author did not enjoy high school.
   d. Vocabulary is a contributing factor to failure.

WHY? What information in the selection leads you to give that answer? _____

_____

_____

Critical Thinking Questions

CRITICAL THINKING LEVEL 1 REMEMBER

Identify three studies the author mentions to illustrate the idea that there is a direct relationship between the size of one's vocabulary and success in life.

1. _____

2. _____

3. _____

CRITICAL THINKING LEVEL 2 UNDERSTAND

Describe how these studies support the idea of a relationship between person's vocabulary knowledge and his or her ability to function and succeed in the "real world."

1. _____

_____

2. _____

_____

3. _____

_____

CRITICAL THINKING LEVEL 3 APPLY

Ken Olan gives an example of traveling to a country where you don't know the language. Have you ever traveled to a country where you did not speak the language? *Discuss* your experience. If you have not had an experience like this, *imagine* what it would be like. What kind of problems did (or might) you experience?

CRITICAL THINKING LEVEL 4 ANALYZE

"Those who prefer their English sloppy have only themselves to thank if the advertisement writer uses his mastery of the vocabulary and syntax to mislead their weak minds."

—Dorothy L. Sayers (British writer, 1893–1957)

First, restate this quotation in your own words. _____

_____

Second, *analyze* this quotation according to the information given in Ken Olan's article. Would Olan agree with Dorothy Sayers? Explain your answer. _____

_____

_____

_____

CRITICAL THINKING LEVEL 5 EVALUATE

Having a large vocabulary allows you to vary your use of language according to the situation. In each of the following pairs of sentences, *evaluate* whether the language is informal or formal. Write "informal" next to the sentence that would be appropriate in an informal conversation between friends. Write "formal" next to the sentence that could be used in a context such as an article in a magazine or newspaper or in a college essay.

Pair A

1. Knowing lots of words makes you rich. _____

2. Having a large vocabulary leads to wealth. _____

Pair B

3. The overweight Siamese lay on the lawn. _____

4. The fat cat sat on the grass. _____

Pair C

5. The man is talkative. _____

6. The dude talks a lot. _____

CRITICAL THINKING LEVEL 6 CREATE

Make a plan for a personal "Vocabulary Learning Plan." Include the following information:
- How increasing your vocabulary will personally benefit you
- In general, your strategy for learning and incorporating new vocabulary words into your conversation and writing
- Specific, practical daily or weekly goals for learning new vocabulary. How many words will you commit to learning? What actions will you take to make that happen? How will you ensure that you actually learn the vocabulary words and not just do busy work?

● Vocabulary in Context

The following words were used in "Vocabulary—A Treasure Chest for Success." Select the best word to complete the meaning of each sentence.

| correlated | distinctions | enhance | perspective | people from all walks of life |

1. Historically, the _____ that divide people have to do with ethnicity, class, and gender.

2. A more inclusive _____ allows us to find the human qualities we all share.

3. Even though steroids are illegal, many athletes take them because the drugs _____ their performances.

4. However, men's overuse of steroids is _____ with developing a sometimes frightening aggressiveness.

5. Drug abuse of any kind can negatively affect _____, of course, not just athletes taking steroids but also businesspeople drinking too much alcohol and young people smoking cigarettes.

Reading 3-2 . . . . Sociology Textbook

● Pre-Reading the Selection

The reading that begins on page 142 comes from a sociology textbook. The title of the reading is a question: Does language shape culture? What do you think? Poll the class to see who says "yes" and who says "no."

Guessing the Purpose

Judging from the title of this article, what do you suppose the purpose of this article is?

_____

Surveying the Reading

Survey the title of the selection and the first sentence of each paragraph. What is the general topic of the reading selection? _____

_____

Predicting the Content

Predict three things this selection will discuss.

- _____
- _____
- _____

Activating Your Knowledge

Think about your culture and the language you use. Does it impact how you view the world? Can you give three examples?

- _____
- _____
- _____

Common Knowledge

Read this term and its definition to help you understand the reading selection.

work ethic (*paragraph 5*) What a person, company, or culture finds acceptable within the work arena. The American work ethic suggests that a person who works hard and diligently is morally superior to people who do not. Other desired qualities are timeliness, responsibility, and honesty. Usually, an employee or student with a good "work ethic" can expect to find favor with a manager or instructor.

Reading with Pen in Hand

Now read the selection. As you read, mark any ideas that seem important, and respond to the questions and vocabulary items in the margin. Monitor your comprehension by putting a ✔ next to a paragraph when you understand most of it. Place an ✘ next to a paragraph when you don't understand most of it.

Visit www.cengage.com/devenglish/doleconnect and select Chapter 2 to hear vocabulary words from this selection and view a video about this topic.

◆ Reading Journal

◆What is the Sapir-Whorf hypothesis?

determines In the three uses of this word in the paragraph, the author says that language determines thought or aspects of culture. What does *determine* mean?

◆What is the difference between how Hopi and English-speaking people see time?

conceptualize What is the synonym of *conceptualize* given in the second part of the sentence? What do these two words mean?

◆What is the relationship between language and culture?

inextricable Use the "chicken and egg" example to decide what *inextricable* means.

◆What example supports the idea that language and culture shape each other?

Does Language Shape Culture?

Margaret L. Andersen and Howard F. Taylor

1   Edward Sapir (writing in the 1920s) and his student Benjamin Whorf (writing in the 1950s) thought that language was central in determining social thought. Their theory, the Sapir-Whorf hypothesis, states that language determines other aspects of culture because language provides the categories through which social reality is understood. In other words, Sapir and Whorf thought that language **determines** what people think because language forces people to perceive the world in certain terms (Sapir 1921; Whorf 1956). It is not that you perceive something first and then think of how to express it, but that language itself determines what you think and perceive.

2   If the Sapir-Whorf hypothesis is correct, then people who speak different languages have different perceptions of reality. Whorf used the example of the construction of time to illustrate cultural differences in how language shapes perceptions of reality. He noted that the Hopi Indians **conceptualize** time as a slowly turning cylinder, whereas English-speaking people conceive of time as running forward in one direction at a uniform pace. European languages place great importance on verb tense, and things are located unambiguously in the past, present, or future.

3   Sapir and Whorf did not think that language single-handedly dictates the perception of reality, but it undoubtedly has a strong influence on culture. Scholars now see two-way causality between language and culture. Asking whether language determines culture or vice versa is like asking which came first, the chicken or the egg. Language and culture are **inextricable**. Each shapes the other, and to understand either, we must know something of both (Aitchison 1997; Hill and Mannheim 1992).

4   Consider again the example of time. Contemporary Americans think of the week as divided into two parts: weekdays and weekends. The words *weekday* and *weekend* reflect the way Americans think about time. When does a week end? Language that defines the weekend encourages people to think about the weekend in specific ways. It is a time for rest, play, and chores. In this sense, language shapes thoughts about the passage of time (looking forward to the weekend, preparing for the work week), but the language itself (the

very concept of the weekend) stems from patterns in the culture, specifically, the work patterns of advanced capitalism. Language and culture shape each other.

5   The work ethic in American culture also shapes our language since the rhythm of life in the United States is the rhythm of the workplace. The phrase "9 to 5" defines an entire lifestyle. The capitalist work ethic makes it morally offensive to merely "pass the time"; instead, time is to be managed for maximum productivity. Concepts of time in preindustrial, agricultural societies involve time and calendars that follow a seasonal rhythm. The year proceeds according to the change of seasons, not **arbitrary** units of time such as weeks and months.

◆What example supports the idea that America's work ethic affects Americans' language?

"9 to 5" What happens between the hours of 9:00 a.m. and 5:00 p.m. in the United States? The previous sentence gives a clue.

arbitrary What phrase in the sentence suggests a meaning that contrasts with *arbitrary*?

What does *arbitrary* mean?

● Comprehension Questions

Write the letter of the answer on the line. Then explain your thinking.

Main Idea

_____   1. Which of the following sentences states the main idea of paragraph 2?

    a. If the Sapir-Whorf hypothesis is correct, then people who speak different languages have different perceptions of reality.

    b. Whorf used the example of the construction of time to illustrate cultural differences in how language shapes perceptions of reality.

    c. He noted that the Hopi Indians conceptualize time as a slowly turning cylinder, whereas English-speaking people conceive of time as running forward in one direction at a uniform pace.

    d. European languages place great importance on verb tense, and things are located unambiguously in the past, present, or future.

WHY? What information in the selection leads you to give that answer? _____

_____

_____   2. Which of the following sentences best summarizes this reading selection?

    a. People who speak different languages have different perceptions of time.

    b. Language determines culture.

    c. Language and culture shape each other.

    d. The work ethic in American culture shapes our language.

WHY? What information in the selection leads you to give that answer? _____

_____

_____

Supporting Details

_____   3. According to paragraph 5, what two things impact American language?

    a. A time for rest and a time for chores

    b. Time and the work ethic

    c. Weekdays and weekends

    d. The rhythm of the workplace and "9 to 5"

WHY? What information in the selection leads you to give that answer? _____

_____

_____

_____   4. Based on the reading selection, which of the following is true?

    a. Sapir and Whorf think that language alone determines reality.

    b. Many different cultures have the same view of time.

    c. The Hopi Indians view time as running forward in one direction at a uniform pace.

    d. Agricultural societies follow a seasonal rhythm rather than a rhythm of the workplace.

WHY? What information in the selection leads you to give that answer? _____

_____

_____

Author's Purpose

_____   5. What is the main purpose of the passage?

    a. to entertain

    b. to inform

    c. to persuade

    d. to inform and entertain

WHY? What information in the selection leads you to give that answer? _____

_____

_____ 6. Why does the author use the example of time in paragraphs 2 and 4?
   a. To persuade the reader to improve their language skills
   b. To entertain the reader with anecdotal information
   c. To give examples of how different languages construct versions of reality
   d. To illustrate how time is important in every culture

WHY? What information in the selection leads you to give that answer? _____

_____

_____

Relationships

_____ 7. What pattern of organization is used in the following sentence from paragraph 2? *If the Sapir-Whorf hypothesis is correct, then people who speak different languages have different perceptions of reality.*
   a. comparison and contrast
   b. process
   c. time order
   d. cause-and-effect

WHY? What leads you to give that answer? _____

_____ 8. What pattern of organization is used in paragraph 5 to discuss the idea of time in preindustrial societies and the idea of time in America today?
   a. contrast
   b. narrative
   c. process
   d. definition

WHY? What information in the selection leads you to give that answer? _____

_____

_____

Fact, Opinion, and Inference

____ 9. Which of the following statements is an opinion?

    a. Edward Sapir (writing in the 1920s) and his student Benjamin Whorf (writing in the 1950s) thought that language was central in determining social thought.

    b. Contemporary Americans think of the week as divided into two parts: weekdays and weekends.

    c. English-speaking people conceive of time as running forward in one direction at a uniform pace, which is probably the most accurate view of time.

    d. Concepts of time in preindustrial, agricultural societies involve time and calendars that follow a seasonal rhythm.

WHY? What leads you to give that answer? _____

_____

____ 10. With which of the following inferences would Sapir and Whorf likely agree?

    a. The Hopi idea of time as a slowly turning cylinder causes Hopis to think differently than English speakers about when events occur.

    b. America's work ethic is one reason many working-age Americans are so stressed.

    c. A seasonal rhythm is an arbitrary unit of time.

    d. Language does not shape culture as much as culture shapes language.

WHY? What information in the selection leads you to give that answer? _____

_____

_____

_____

● Critical Thinking Questions

CRITICAL THINKING LEVEL 1 REMEMBER

Define the Whorf-Sapir Hypothesis and give an example to illustrate it. _____

_____

CRITICAL THINKING LEVEL 2 UNDERSTAND

After reading this passage, how would you *answer* the question that was asked in the title: Does language shape culture? _____

_____

CRITICAL THINKING LEVEL 3 APPLY

Apply the Sapir-Wharf hypothesis to the smaller "culture" of your family. How does the way your family uses certain kinds of language affect their experience of how the world works? You might want to think about just one narrow area, such as how your family talks about romantic relationships, athletic events, or animals.

CRITICAL THINKING LEVEL 4 ANALYZE

Suppose the Sapir-Whorf hypothesis applies to individuals as well as to cultures. How would you *see* a person whom you think of in the following terms? What images come to mind?

A. thrifty _____ versus

   stingy _____

B. pretty _____ versus

   cute _____

CRITICAL THINKING LEVEL 5 EVALUATE

Decide whether Ludwig Wittgenstein (page 99) would agree with the Sapir-Whorf hypothesis. Why or why not? Support your answer. _____

_____

_____

CRITICAL THINKING LEVEL 6 CREATE

Working with classmates, *create* a list of phrases you have heard that reflect your various cultures' attitudes toward food. _____

_____

_____

● Vocabulary in Context

The following words were used in "Does Language Shape Culture?" Select the best word to complete the meaning of each sentence.

inextricable	determines	9 to 5	conceptualize	arbitrary

1. Many times, your effort in school _____ the grade you receive.

2. _____ your future and see yourself successful in your career and happy in your life.

3. Before caller ID was invented, kids used to dial _____ phone numbers and talk to whoever answered.

4. Don and Donna have been married for more than 50 years. Their memories are _____.

5. People who get tired of the _____ may feel differently when they see their friends getting laid off from their jobs.

part 2

Reading to Understand

© prism_68/shutterstock

chapter 4

Understanding Paragraph Structure

66 *The main thing is to keep the main thing the main thing.* 99
—Stephen Covey

Well, that seems pretty straightforward. Keep the main thing the main thing . . . okay, great! "So . . . um . . . what is the main thing?" Discuss ideas with a classmate about what "the main thing" could be.

Share Your Prior Knowledge
What do you think "the main thing" could refer to when it comes to reading?

Videos Related to Readings

Vocab Words on Audio

Prep Readings on Demand

www.cengage.com/devenglish/doleconnect

Survey the Chapter
Take two minutes to skim this chapter to find some of the ideas this chapter will discuss. What do you already know about what you find?

Prep Reading . . . . Nonfiction Book

This reading comes from the beginning of chapter five of *First Things First* by Stephen Covey. The following excerpt is one suggestion Mr. Covey gives for keeping "the main thing the main thing" in life. As you read through this passage, keep the title in mind, and ask yourself what is the main thing Mr. Covey is trying to say to you, the reader.

Visit **www.cengage.com/devenglish/doleconnect** and select Chapter 4 to hear a reading of this selection and view a video about this topic.

The Passion of Vision

Stephen Covey

capacity Think about the meaning of the sentence. What is a synonym for *capacity*?

1   Viktor Frankl, an Austrian psychologist who survived the death camps of Nazi Germany, made a significant discovery. As he found within himself the **capacity** to rise above his humiliating circumstances, he became an observer as well as a participant in the experience. He watched others who shared in the ordeal. He was intrigued with the question of what made it possible for some people to survive when most died.

2   He looked at several factors—health, vitality, family structure, intelligence, survival skills. Finally, he concluded that none of these factors was primarily responsible. The single most significant factor, he realized, was a sense of future vision—the **impelling** conviction of those who were to survive that they had a mission to perform, some important work left to do.

impelling Use your logic. If you believe you are on a mission, does your belief urge you forward or caution you to hold back? What does *impelling* mean?

3   Survivors of POW camps in Vietnam and elsewhere have reported similar experiences: a compelling, future-oriented vision is the primary force that kept many of them alive. The power of vision is incredible! Research indicates that children with "future-focused role images" perform far better scholastically and are significantly more competent in handling the challenges of life. Teams and organizations with a strong sense of mission significantly outperform those without the strength of vision. According to Dutch sociologist Fred Polak, a primary factor influencing the success of civilizations is the "collective vision" people have of their future.

manifestation This noun is related to the verb *manifest*. Another way to state the first part of this sentence is "Creative imagination manifests itself best in vision." Also examine the next sentence to figure out this word's meaning.

4   Vision is the best **manifestation** of creative imagination and the primary motivation of human action. It's the ability to see beyond our present reality, to create, to invent what does not yet exist, to become what we not yet are. It gives us capacity to live out of our imagination instead of our memory. We all have some vision of ourselves and our future. And that vision creates consequences. More than any other factor, vision affects the choices we make and the way we spend our time.

5   If our vision is limited—if it doesn't extend beyond the Friday night ball game or the next TV show—we tend to make choices based on what's right in front of us. We react to whatever's urgent, the impulse of the moment, our feelings or moods, our limited awareness of our options, other people's priorities. We **vacillate** and fluctuate. How we feel about our decisions—even the way we make them—changes from day to day.

> **vacillate** Look for a synonym and a definition in this sentence and the next. What does *vacillate* mean?

6   If our vision is based on illusion, we make choices that aren't based on "true north" principles. In time, these choices fail to create the quality-of-life results we expect. Our vision becomes no more than platitudes. We become disillusioned, perhaps cynical. Our creative imagination withers, and we don't trust our dreams anymore.

7   If our vision is partial—if we focus only on our economic and social needs and ignore our mental and spiritual needs, for example—we make choices that lead to imbalance. If our vision is based on the social mirror, we make choices based on expectations of others. It's been said that "when man discovered the mirror, he began to lose his soul." If our self-vision is no more than a reflection of the social mirror, we have no connection with our inner selves, with our own uniqueness and capacity to contribute. We're living out of scripts handed to us by others—family, associates, friends, enemies, the media.

8   And what are those scripts? Some may seem **constructive**: "You're so talented!" "You're a natural ball player!" "I always said you should be a doctor!" Some may be destructive: "You're so slow!" "You can't do anything right!" "Why can't you be more like your sister?" Good or bad, these scripts can keep us from connecting with who we are and what we're about.

> **constructive** Look at the examples that follow *constructive* and find an antonym in a later sentence to uncover this word's meaning.

9   And consider the images the media project—cynicism, skepticism, violence, indulgence, fatalism, materialism, "that important news" is bad news. If these images are the source of our personal vision, is it any wonder that many of us feel disconnected and at odds with ourselves?

🔵 Interaction 4-1. Talking about Reading

Respond in writing to the questions that follow and then discuss your answers with your classmates.

1. Can you define *vision* using your own words? _____

_____

_____

2. Why is vision so powerful? List some of the results of having vision that Covey mentioned and then add any of your own. _____

_____

_____

3. Based on what you read, what factors weaken the power of vision? _____

_____

_____

4. What vision do you hold for your education? What will your education open up for you to do, have, or be? What is the "main thing" you are seeking from your college experience? Do you have a plan for manifesting your vision? _____

_____

_____

MAPPS: A Reading Plan

How many of you have ever just gotten into the car and taken a long trip or vacation without any plans—you had no idea where you were going or how long you were going to be gone? Probably not many of you. Maybe you have thought about doing this or are thinking it sounds romantic or cool. It might be spontaneous, but it is not very practical. Even spontaneous people have maps or navigation systems in their car or use AAA, GoogleMaps, Mapquest or some other source to help them figure out where they are going.

Just as it is important to have a road map in driving, the same is true for reading. Reading without a plan is about the same as driving without a clue about where you are going. You end up driving in circles, retracing your steps, wasting time, or worse, never arriving where you want to go. Similarly, if you read without a plan, you often end up "reading in circles"—rereading the same information again and again and becoming frustrated that you don't understand what you want to read. Or worse, maybe you just give up and never even complete the reading.

To successfully navigate when you are driving, there are always at least three things you need to know:

A. Where you are

B. Where you are going

   AND . . .

C. How to get from point A to point B (a map)!

Figure 4.1
MAPPS, a Reading Strategy

Mark the answers to your questions = Mark what the reading is about, its point, and its proof.

About = Topic: What is the reading about?

Point = Main Idea: What is the point of the reading?

Proof = Supporting Detail: What is the proof? There are two kinds of proof or details: major and minor.

Summary = A synthesis of About (topic), Point (main idea), and Proof (supporting detail).

It's the same with reading. To successfully navigate a reading, you need to know:

1. What you are reading

2. What your purpose is for reading

3. A reading strategy: MAPPS (See **Figure 4.1**)

MAPPS is the mnemonic for a visual outline that can help you organize what you are reading and lead you to better comprehension. It is based on surveying a reading, asking "wh" questions (who, what, when, where, why, how, to what extent), and then marking the answers to your questions while you read, which encourages active reading. After you read, filling in the MAPPS outline will allow you to check your understanding as well as give you a convenient way to review important content for tests.

Marking the Answers to Your Questions

Reading actively means reading with questions in mind and searching for the answers. In Chapter 2 you learned to use headings in this way. You changed the headings into questions and then marked the answers. Do the same with the APP in MAPPS as you learn about each one. The A, P, and P each represent a level of information in a reading. To help you distinguish (tell apart) the three main information levels, mark each level in some way. You'll see examples of how to do this throughout the chapter.

What Is the Reading About? The Topic

Asking the simple question "What is the reading about?" will lead you to the **topic**. The topic is *who* or *what* a reading is about. In longer passages, you will often find the topic stated in the title, but even in single paragraphs, words related to the topic are usually repeated throughout the paragraph in different ways. Topics are normally stated in a single word or a phrase. If your reading has a title, start by reading it to figure out what the topic is. However, if there is no title, you can still look for people, places, things, or concepts repeated throughout the reading. Look at the following example from a history book:

In 1930, <u>Mohandas Gandhi</u>, the sixty-one-year-old leader of the nonviolent movement for Indian independence from British rule, <u>began a march to the sea</u> with seventy-eight followers. Their destination was Dandi, a little coastal town some 240 miles away. <u>The group covered about 12 miles a day</u>. As they went, <u>Gandhi</u> preached his doctrine of nonviolent resistance to British rule in every village <u>he</u> passed through: "Civil disobedience is the inherent right of a citizen. He dare not give it up without ceasing to be a man." <u>By the time he reached Dandi, twenty-four days later, his small group had become a nonviolent army of thousands</u>. When they arrived at Dandi, <u>Gandhi</u> picked up a pinch of <u>salt</u> from the sand. All along the coast, thousands did likewise, openly breaking British laws that prohibited Indians from making their own <u>salt</u>. The British had long profited from their monopoly and sale of <u>salt</u>, an item much in demand in a tropical country. By their simple acts of disobedience, <u>Gandhi</u> and the Indian people had taken a bold step on <u>their long march</u> to independence. <u>The salt march</u> was but one of many nonviolent activities that <u>Mohandas Gandhi</u> undertook between World War I and World War II to win India's goal of national independence from British rule.

—Duiker/Spielvogel, *World History*, 5th Edition

Gandhi's name is mentioned several times in this paragraph, and thus, it should be evident that the paragraph has something to do with him. You can also see that the passage is about a "salt march." Almost every sentence describes something about this march. Combining the *who* with the *what,* you might guess that the topic is "Gandhi's salt march." If you are marking the text as you read, you might write that phrase in the margin to spark your memory when you come back to review for a test. The marginal note acts as a title—it focuses your attention on the topic. Or you could use a highlighter to mark the words in the paragraph itself.

Determining the topic is a good starting point for comprehending a reading selection. Follow these steps to keep it simple:

1. If there is a title, consider it first.

2. Look for **bold** or *italicized* terms.

3. Look for repeated words, phrases, or concepts.

Once you figure out what the reading is about, you can begin to predict what kinds of information and ideas you might find in it.

⚫ Interaction 4-2. Identifying the Topic of a Paragraph

Read each paragraph and decide what the topic is. Start with the question "What is this about?" Remember to look for repeated words, and mark them as you read. When you are finished reading, create a title for the paragraph based on your findings.

Paragraph 1   **Mass Media Textbook**

The term *wiki* derives from the Hawaiian word *wiki*, which means fast. This technology allows many users to collaborate to create and update an Internet page. A wiki Web site allows registered users to add and edit content on a specific topic. The best known wiki is Wikipedia.com, an online encyclopedia where registered contributors may post additions to any entry. Wiki technology records the original material, plus the material that contributors add over time. Wikis have great potential to gather in one place contributions worldwide from all the specialists on one subject, for example, but there are not necessarily any safeguards that the material placed on the site is accurate or reliable.

—Biagi, *Media/Impact*, 8th Edition

What is a good title? _____

Paragraph 2   **Anthropology Textbook**

As with other forms of artistic expression, the functions of dance are culturally variable. Dance is likely to function in a number of different ways both between and within societies. Dance often performs several functions simultaneously within a society, but some functions are more prominent than others. To illustrate, dance can function psychologically by helping people cope more effectively with tensions and aggressive feelings; politically by expressing political values and attitudes, showing allegiance to political leaders, and controlling behavior; religiously by various methods of communicating with supernatural forces; socially by articulating and reinforcing relationships between members of the society; and educationally by passing on the cultural traditions, values, and beliefs from one generation to the next.

—Ferraro, *Cultural Anthropology*, 6th Edition

What is a good title? _____

Paragraph 3   Sociology Textbook

School districts rely primarily on property taxes for revenue. As a result, schools in low-income communities generally have more students and receive less revenue than do schools in higher-income communities. Students in the poorer schools, therefore, often must learn from old textbooks and poorly paid teachers in overcrowded classrooms within substandard buildings. The result is inadequate preparation for higher educational opportunities for low-income children and youth, who disproportionately are people of color. Social workers need to be interested in improving the opportunities of all children and youth, and so must identify and advocate for strategies that provide equal educational opportunities for all.

—Segal/Gerdes/Steiner, *An Introduction to the Profession of Social Work*, 2nd Edition

What is a good title? _____

Paragraph 4   Anthropology Textbook

The varied diet available to arboreal primates—shoots, leaves, insects, and fruits—required relatively unspecialized teeth, compared to those found in other mammals. The evolutionary trend for primate dentition has been toward a reduction in the number

and size of the teeth. The earliest mammals as well as many living species of mammals today possess more incisors, premolars, and molar teeth than primates. The canines of most of the primates, especially males, are dagger like and useful for ripping into tough foods. Canine teeth also serve well in social communication. All an adult male gorilla or baboon needs to do to get a youngster to be submissive is to raise his upper lip to display his sharp canines.

—Haviland/Prins/Walrath/McBride,
The Essence of Anthropology

© T-Design/Shutterstock

What is a good title? _____

Paragraph 5   Psychology Textbook

Participating in sports has many benefits for youth. In addition to improved physical fitness, sports can enhance participants' self-esteem and can help them to learn initiative. Athletes also learn about teamwork and competitiveness. At the same time, there are some potential costs. About 15% of high school athletes will be injured and require some medical treatment. Boys are most likely to be injured while playing football or wrestling; girls are injured while participating in cross-country or soccer. Fortunately, most of these injuries are not serious ones but are more likely to involve bruises or strained muscles.

—Kail/Cavanaugh, *Human Development*, 4th Edition

What is a good title? _____

What Is the Point of the Reading? The Main Idea

Asking what the point of a reading is will lead you to the **main idea.** The main idea is, of course, the main thing that the author is trying to get across to you. The main idea limits the topic to what the author wants to discuss. For example, suppose the topic is love. Love is a very broad topic. An author could explore any number of main ideas in regard to love. Here are a few examples.

There are several health benefits associated with [being in love.]

[Love] is viewed differently in different cultures.

[Love] is more complicated than many people realize.

In these sentences, the topic is in brackets and the main idea is underlined. When the topic and the main idea appear in a single sentence, that sentence is called the *topic sentence.* Use this formula as a memory aid:

$$T + MI = TS$$
topic plus main idea equals topic sentence

Notice that in these examples, the topic is always *love.* The main idea, however, is different in each topic sentence. Each main idea is about different aspects of love. As a result, each topic sentence would lead to a paragraph with different supporting details.

● Interaction 4-3. Finding the Main Idea of a Paragraph

What is the main idea of each paragraph? First, look for repeated ideas to help you find the topic. Second, to figure out the main idea, think about how the author is limiting the topic to just the point he or she wants to discuss. Third, look for a sentence in which T + MI = TS. In the topic sentence, put brackets around the topic and underline the main idea.

Paragraph 1   Public Speaking Textbook

Even though we usually think of our audience as the listeners in a speech, speakers are also listeners. When you give a speech, listen to your audience for signs of disinterest, hostility, or opposition. Also listen to make sure your style and mannerisms aren't confusing or distracting. Finally, listen for signs that your audience is confused by the information in your speech. Each of these signals helps you adapt your message so your speech is a listenable one.

—Adapted from Griffin, *Invitation to Public Speaking*, 2nd Edition

A. What is the paragraph about? Topic: _____

B. What is the point of this paragraph? Main idea: _____

C. What is the topic sentence? T + MI = TS: _____

_____

Paragraph 2   Health Textbook

The major threat to the lives of college students isn't illness but injury. Almost 75 percent of deaths among Americans 15 to 24 years old are caused by "unintentional injuries" (a term public health officials prefer), suicides, and homicides. The odds of dying from an injury in any given year are about 1 in 765; over a lifetime they rise to 1 in 23. In all, injuries—intentional and unintentional—claim almost 150,000 lives a year. Accidents, especially motor vehicle crashes, kill more college-age men and women than all other causes combined; the greatest number of lives lost to accidents is among those 25 years of age.

—Hales, *An Invitation to Health*, 12th Edition

A. What is the paragraph about? Topic: _____

B. What is the point of this paragraph? Main idea: _____

_____

C. What is the topic sentence? T + MI = TS: _____

_____

Paragraph 3   Mass Media Textbook

The image of women portrayed by the media has been the subject of significant contemporary studies by many media researchers. Observers of the stereotyping of women point to past and current media portrayals showing very few women in professional roles or as strong, major characters. The media's overall portrayal of women in mass culture is slowly improving, but in her book *Loving with a Vengeance: Mass-Produced Fantasies for Women*, Tania Modleski says that the portrayal in popular fiction of women in submissive roles began in 1740, with the British novel *Pamela*, which was then published in America by Benjamin Franklin in 1744.

—Adapted from Biagi, *Media/Impact*, 8th Edition

A. What is the paragraph about? Topic: _____

B. What is the point of this paragraph? Main idea: _____

_____

C. What is the topic sentence? T + MI = TS: _____

_____

Paragraph 4   Sociology Textbook

Teen pregnancy is integrally linked to gender expectations of men and women in society. Some teen men consciously avoid birth control, thinking it takes away from their manhood. Teen women often romanticize motherhood, thinking that becoming a mother will give them social value they do not otherwise have. For teens in disadvantaged groups, motherhood confers a legitimate social identity on those otherwise devalued by society.

—Andersen/Taylor, *Sociology*, 4th Edition

A. What is the passage about? Topic: _____

B. What is the point of this paragraph? Main idea: _____

_____

C. What is the topic sentence? T + MI = TS: _____

_____

Paragraph 5   Government Textbook

It is difficult to estimate how many people are homeless because the number depends on how the homeless are defined. There are *street people*—those who sleep in bus stations, parks, and other areas. Many of these people are youthful runaways. There are the so-called *sheltered homeless*—those who sleep in government-supported or privately-funded shelters. Many of these individuals used to live with their families or friends. Whereas street people are almost always single, the term *sheltered homeless* includes many families with children. Homeless families are the fastest-growing subgroup of the homeless population. There are also the *hard-core homeless*—which are those who have been on the streets a year or more.

—Schmidt/Shelley/Bardes, *American Government and Politics Today 2007-2008*, 13ᵗʰ Edition

A. What is the paragraph about? Topic: _____

B. What is the point of this paragraph? Main idea: _____

_____

C. What is the topic sentence? T + MI = TS: _____

_____

Interaction 4-4. More on Finding the Main Idea of a Paragraph

This interaction gives you more opportunity to practice finding the main idea of a paragraph. Your process will be the same as in Interaction 4-3 or anytime you need to find the main idea. First, look for repeated ideas to help you find the topic. Second, think about how the author is limiting the topic to just the point he or she wants to discuss to figure out the main idea. Third, look for a sentence in which T + MI = TS. In the topic sentence, put brackets around the topic and underline the main idea.

Paragraph 1   **Public Speaking Textbook**

Invitational speeches are usually given in two contexts. In the first context, we give invitational speeches when there are two sides to an issue and we want to be sure we explore and understand them as fully as possible. In the second context, we give invitational speeches when an audience is polarized about an issue and we know we can't persuade them to change.

—Adapted from Griffin, *Invitation to Public Speaking*, 2ⁿᵈ Edition

A. What is the paragraph about? Topic: _____

B. What is the point of this paragraph? Main idea: _____

C. What is the topic sentence? T + MI = TS: _____

_____

Paragraph 2   Health Textbook

Whenever you work out, you don't want to risk becoming sore or injured. Starting slowly when you begin any new fitness activity is the smartest strategy. Keep a simple diary to record the time and duration of each workout. Get accustomed to an activity first and then begin to work harder or longer. In this way, you strengthen your musculo-skeletal system so you're less likely to be injured, you lower the cardiovascular risk, and you build the exercise habit into your schedule.

—Hales, *An Invitation to Health*, 12th Edition

A. What is the paragraph about? Topic: _____

B. What is the point of this paragraph? Main idea: _____

_____

C. What is the topic sentence? T + MI = TS: _____

_____

Paragraph 3   American History Textbook

A spirit of *Chicanismo*—a pride in a heritage that could be traced back to the ancient civilizations of Middle America—emerged among Mexican Americans in the late 1960s. Young activists made *Chicano* and *Chicana*, terms that older Mexican Americans had generally avoided in the past, into positive symbols of their heritage. "Crusade for Justice," an organization that first took root in Denver, Colorado, provided a model for other local movements that emphasized getting young people through school and training them for careers in business, education, and social activism. At the same time, many of these groups favored a view of the distant past that stressed how the ancestors of *chicanos* and *chicanas* of the 1960s had once controlled vast amounts of land and determined their own destiny. Some activists even began to talk about regaining control of parts of this territory, which they called *Atzlan*.

—Adapted from Murrin et al., *Liberty, Equality, Power*, 5th Edition

A. What is the paragraph about? Topic: _____

B. What is the point of this paragraph? Main idea: _____

_____

C. What is the topic sentence? T + MI = TS: _____

_____

_____

Passage 4   Business Textbook

Sole proprietors must be willing to accept full responsibility for the firm's performance. The pressure of this responsibility can be much greater than any employee's responsibility. Sole proprietors must also be willing to work flexible hours. They are on call at all times and may even have to substitute for a sick employee. Their responsibility for the success of the business encourages them to continually monitor business operations. They must exhibit strong leadership skills, be well organized, and communicate well with employees.

Many successful sole proprietors have had previous work experience in the market in which they are competing, perhaps as an employee in a competitor's firm. For example, restaurant managers commonly establish their own restaurants. Experience is critical to understanding the competition and the behavior of customers in a particular market. In short, sole proprietors need certain characteristics to be successful.

—Madura, *Introduction to Business*, 4th Edition

A. What is the passage about? Topic: _____

B. What is the point of this passage? Main idea: _____

C. What is the topic sentence? T + MI = TS: _____

_____

Paragraph 5   Anthropology Textbook

Like so many other words we think we understand, the term *language* is far more complex than we might imagine. Language, which is found in all cultures of the world, is a symbolic system of sounds that, when put together according to a certain set of rules, conveys meanings to its speakers. The meanings attached to any given word in all languages are totally arbitrary. That is, the word *cow* has no particular connection to the large bovine animal that the English language refers to as a *cow*. The word *cow* is no more or less reasonable a word for that animal than would be *kaflumpha*, *sporge*, or *four-pronged squirter*. The word *cow* does not look like a cow, sound like a cow, or have any particular physical connection to a cow. The only explanation for the use of the word is that somewhere during the evolution of the English language the word *cow* came to be used to refer to a large, milk-giving, domesticated animal. Other languages use different, and equally arbitrary, words to describe the very same animal.

—Ferraro, *Cultural Anthropology*, 6th Edition

A. What is the paragraph about? Topic: _____

B. What is the point of this paragraph? Main idea: _____

C. What is the topic sentence? T + MI = TS: _____

_____

Location of the Topic Sentence: Anywhere

You may have noticed in Interaction 4-4 that the topic sentence appeared in different places in each paragraph. In one paragraph the topic sentence was the first sentence. In another paragraph it came last. And you can find a topic sentence anywhere in between. The rule about topic sentences is that they can be anywhere in a paragraph. It is not the location of the topic sentence that is important, it is the relationships between the ideas in the paragraph that matter.

Think about this analogy. Some of you may live in cities, states, or even countries far away from the rest of your family. Let's say, just for example, that you live in Dallas, Texas, and your parents live in Villahermosa, Mexico. Are you still their child? Are they still your parents? Of course! It is the relationship between you and your parents that matters, not your respective locations.

In a paragraph, it is the same for the topic, main idea, and supporting details. It does not matter where they are located; their relationship is always the same:

- The topic is a broad, general idea.
- The main idea narrows the topic to the specific point the author wants to discuss.
- The major and minor details support the main idea with even narrower, more specific ideas.

Let's look at an example. The topic sentence has been underlined for you. Notice that it is in the middle of the paragraph.

Women and the Monastic Life

We tend to think of monasticism as a masculine enterprise, but it should be remembered that the vowed religious life was open to both men and women. The entire early history of Christianity records a flourishing monastic life for women. <u>In the late Roman period, groups of religious women flourished all over the Roman Empire.</u> Saint Benedict's sister, Scholastica, was head of a monastery. Her contemporary, Brigid of Ireland, was such a powerful figure in the Irish church that legends grew up around her. In England, Hilda, abbess of Whitbey, not only ruled over a prominent monastery that was a learning center, but she also held a famous Episcopal gathering to determine church policy.

—Adapted from Cunningham/Reich, *Culture and Values, Volume 1,* 6th Edition

Let's put this paragraph into the diagram we've been using to visualize these relationships (see **Figure 4.2**).

What about the first two sentences in the paragraph? They are not in our diagram. When the topic sentence falls in the middle of a paragraph, sometimes the sentences

Figure 4.2
Three Levels of Information

broad About = Topic: _____

narrower Point = Main Idea: _____

narrowest 1. **Proof** = **Supporting Detail:** Saint Benedict's sister, Scholastica, was head of a monastery.

2. **Proof** = **Supporting Detail:** Her contemporary, Brigid of Ireland, was such a powerful figure in the Irish church that legends grew up around her.

3. **Proof** = **Supporting Detail:** In England, Hilda, abbess of Whitbey, not only ruled over a prominent monastery that was a learning center, but she also held a famous Episcopal gathering to determine church policy.

that come before it introduce the idea even more broadly than the topic sentence does. They act as a funnel, giving readers a very broad context that quickly narrows down to the main idea. Often, sentences like these introduce the main idea for a whole group of paragraphs. (And when a main idea introduces a group of paragraphs, it's often called a *thesis statement* rather than a main idea.)

Note that if you were to rewrite the paragraph, putting the supporting details first and then ending with the main idea, the relationships between the ideas would be exactly the same as shown in the diagram above.

Saint Benedict's sister, Scholastica, was head of a monastery. Her contemporary, Brigid of Ireland, was such a powerful figure in the Irish church that legends grew up around her. In England, Hilda, abbess of Whitbey, not only ruled over a prominent monastery that was a learning center, but she also held a famous Episcopal gathering to determine church policy. <u>In the late Roman period, groups of religious women flourished all over the Roman Empire.</u>

—Adapted from Cunningham/Reich, *Culture and Values, Volume 1*, 6th Edition

So when you are searching for the topic sentence of a paragraph, look for the relationships among the ideas—which ideas are the broadest, narrower, and narrowest—rather than expecting to find the topic sentence in a particular location.

Interaction 4-5. Finding the Topic Sentence

Remember that T + MI = TS. Locate the topic sentence of each paragraph. Then mark the parts of the topic sentence: put brackets around the topic, and underline the main idea.

Paragraph 1   Biology Textbook

Ecstasy is a drug that makes you feel socially accepted, relieves anxiety, and sharpens the senses while giving you a mild high. It can also leave you dying in a hospital bed, foaming at the mouth and bleeding from every orifice as your temperature skyrockets. It can send your family and friends spiraling into horror and disbelief as they watch you stop breathing. Lorna Spinks ended life that way. She was nineteen years old. Her family wants you to know what Lorna did not: Ecstasy can kill.

—Adapted from Starr/Evers/Starr, *Biology Today and Tomorrow*, 2nd Edition

A. What is the topic? _____

B. What is the main idea? _____

C. What is the topic sentence? _____

Paragraph 2   Management Textbook

Communication cost is the cost of transmitting information from one place to another. The most important information that an electric utility company collects each month is the information from the electric meter attached to the side of your house. Traditionally, electric companies employed meter readers to walk from house to house to gather information that would then be entered in to company computers. Now, however, meter readers are losing their jobs to water, gas, and electric meters built with radio frequency (RF) transmitters. The transmitters turn on when a meter reader drives by the house in a utility company van that has a laptop computer specially equipped to receive RF signals. Such vans, traveling at legal speeds, can read 12,000 to 13,000 meters in an eight-hour day. By contrast, a meter reader on foot can record data from 500 meters per day.

—Adapted from Williams, *Management*, 5th Edition

A. What is the topic? _____

B. What is the main idea? _____

C. What is the topic sentence? _____

Paragraph 3   Humanities Textbook

The Islamic statement of faith begins: "There is but one God, Allah. . . ." To grasp this belief in monotheism is to understand a whole variety of issues connected to Islam. The word Islam means "submission" to God. Because God is almighty, his divinity is hidden from humanity; as a consequence Allah may not be depicted in artistic form. Because the revelation of Allah is final and definitive, Islam sees the reality of God beyond the revelation of the God of the Jewish Scriptures and is explicitly resistant to the Trinitarian faith of Christianity. The fundamental monotheism of Islam also helps explain why Islam has a tradition of missionary expansion. The omnipotent will of God is for all humanity to submit to God.

—Adapted from Cunningham/Reich, *Culture and Values, Volume 1,* 6th Edition

A. What is the topic? _____

B. What is the main idea? _____

_____

C. What is the topic sentence? _____

_____

Paragraph 4   Psychology Textbook

When confronted with stress, people sometimes simply give up and withdraw from the battle. Some people routinely respond to stress with fatalism and resignation, passively accepting setbacks that might be dealt with effectively. This syndrome is referred to as *learned helplessness.* Learned helplessness is passive behavior produced by exposure to unavoidable aversive events.

—Weiten, *Psychology,* 7th Edition

A. What is the topic? _____

B. What is the main idea? _____

C. What is the topic sentence? _____

_____

What Is the Proof? The Supporting Details

Asking "What is the proof?" leads you to the author's *supporting details.* The details are called "supporting" because they give support—evidence or proof for the author's point. The support might consist of examples, statistics, facts, anecdotes, or expert opinion. To find the supporting details in a paragraph, turn the topic sentence into a question and look for the answers. Each one should be a supporting detail. Let's look at an example from a finance textbook. The topic sentence is underlined.

Small Savings Mean Big Bucks!

It should be obvious: spend less than you earn, so you'll have money to invest. Yet so many people don't recognize this simple fact. They run up large credit card bills and take out loans instead of building a nest egg for the future. Where to start? How about with the little stuff? <u>You'd be amazed at how reducing even your smallest expenses can lead to big savings!</u> Here are some examples of how reducing your discretionary spending now will yield big payoffs later, thanks to the large impact of compound interest:

- Instead of buying 40 $5 lottery tickets a year, invest the $200 at the end of each year at 8 percent. If you start at age 18, you'll have $106,068 by the time you reach age 67!
- Buy a used car instead of a new one, and invest the amount you saved at 8 percent for 40 years. If you saved $9,000 buying a used car, you'd have more than $195,000 available for your retirement fund!
- Stop the money drain into vending machines, espresso stands, and restaurant or fast food lunches. Buy a regular cup of coffee rather than a latte or espresso, avoid the vending machines, and take a brown-bag lunch to work several days a week. If you save $22 a week for 50 weeks a year at 8 percent for 40 years, your savings will grow by more than $284,000!
- Use less of things like shampoo, detergent, and toothpaste. Try cutting the amount you use in half. Then look for other areas where you can do this.
- Pay attention to how you spend your loose change. Limit the amount of cash and coins you carry, and you'll plug one of the biggest financial leaks in most Americans' pockets.

—Gitman/Joehnk, *Personal Financial Planning*, 11th Edition

If you were to fill in the APP in MAPPS, it would look like this:

About: reducing even your smallest expenses

Point: can lead to big savings
To find the proof, form a question from the topic sentence: How can reducing even your smallest expenses lead to big savings? Look for each answer the author gives.

Proof: 1. Don't buy lottery tickets; invest instead.
2. Buy a used car instead of a new one, and invest the difference.
3. Pack lunch and avoid expensive drinks and snacks.
4. Reduce consumption of household products.
5. Carry smaller amounts of cash and save change.

Thinking about the supporting details will help you decide whether you understand or agree with an author's point.

Interaction 4-6. Mapping the Details

Reread each of the following paragraphs. **Mark** the topic and the main idea in the paragraph itself if you haven't already done so. Then form a question from the topic sentence and complete the outline with the supporting details.

1. Paragraph 2 on page 157

   About: the functions of dance

      Point: vary within a society, but some are more prominent than others

      Form a question from the topic sentence: _____

   _____

       Proof: 1. _____

             2. _____

             3. _____

             4. _____

             5. _____

2. Paragraph 5 on page 164

   About: the meanings attached to given words

      Point: are totally arbitrary

      Form a question from the topic sentence: _____

   _____

       Proof: 1. _____

             2. _____

             3. _____

   _____

             4. _____

3. Paragraph 4 on page 168

   About: learned helplessness

      Point: is passive behavior produced by exposure to unavoidable aversive events.

      Form a question from the topic sentence: _____

   _____

       Proof: 1. _____

             2. _____

Major Versus Minor Details

There are two types of supporting details: major and minor. Let's look at the difference between major and minor details by examining the details from the passage on page 169 about spending less to make more money. The major details are in **bold**; the minor details are in regular type.

- **Instead of buying 40 $5 lottery tickets a year, invest the $200 at the end of each year at 8 percent.** If you start at age 18, you'll have $106,068 by the time you reach age 67!
- **Buy a used car instead of a new one and invest the amount you saved at 8 percent for 40 years.** If you saved $9,000 buying a used car, you'd have more than $195,000 available for your retirement fund!
- **Stop the money drain into vending machines, espresso stands, and restaurant or fast food lunches. Buy a regular cup of coffee rather than a latte or espresso, avoid the vending machines, and take a brown-bag lunch to work several days a week.** If you save $22 a week for 50 weeks a year at 8 percent for 40 years, your savings will grow by more than $284,000!
- **Use less of things like shampoo, detergent, and toothpaste.** Try cutting the amount you use in half. Then look for other areas where you can do this.
- Pay attention to how you spend your loose change. **Limit the amount of cash and coins you carry,** and you'll plug one of the biggest financial leaks in most Americans' pockets.

—Gitman/Joehnk, *Personal Financial Planning,* 11th Edition

Notice how the major details capture the direct support for the main idea. They are all ways you can reduce your discretionary spending. The minor details give extra information about the major details. In this passage, they describe how much money each type of savings could yield.

In general, *proof* refers to both major and minor supporting details. However, it is the major details that show the direct proof for the main idea and give organizational structure to the paragraph. The minor details give extra information about the major details.

◉ Interaction 4-7. Mapping the Minor Details

Reread each paragraph listed below. Mark any parts of the APP in the paragraph itself that you didn't mark the first time you read it. Then complete each of the following outlines.

1. Paragraph 2 on page 167

   About: The most important information that an electric utility company collects each month

   Point: is the information from the electric meter attached to the side of your house.

Proof: 1. Traditionally, meter readers walked from house to house.

2. Now, meters are built with RF transmitters.

a. _____

_____

b. _____

_____

c. _____

2. Paragraph 2 on page 160: *Hint*: Two different parts of the main idea are in different sentences. Look for antonyms to find them.

About: youths' participation in sports

Point: _____

Proof: 1. _____

a. _____

b. _____

c. _____

d. _____

2. _____

a. _____

_____

b. _____

_____

c. _____

Interaction 4-8. Identifying the Proof of Paragraphs

In each paragraph, mark the APP. Bracket the topic, underline the main idea, and use numbers or parentheses to indicate the major supporting details. Then fill in the MAPP that follows. Put only the major supporting details under "Proof."

Paragraph 1   **Finance Textbook**

You'll soon find many other ways to "save small," such as taking public transportation, comparing prices before you buy, reading books and magazines from the library instead of buying them, and using coupons to buy groceries. Then, make saving a given, not something you do when you have money left over. Pay yourself first. Have your employer deposit the maximum amount in your 401(k) plan each pay period. It will grow even faster if your employer matches your contributions. You can also authorize withdrawals from your checking account to an investment account or to a mutual fund.

—Gitman/Joehnk, *Personal Financial Planning*, 11ᵗʰ Edition

About: _____

Point: _____

Proof: 1. _____

2. _____

3. _____

4. _____

5. _____

Paragraph 2   Psychology Textbook

True wine lovers go through an elaborate series of steps when they are served a good bottle of wine. Typically, they begin by drinking a little water to cleanse their palate. Then they sniff the cork from the wine bottle, swirl a small amount of the wine around in a glass, and sniff the odor emerging from the glass. Finally, they take a sip of the wine, rolling it around in their mouth for a short time before swallowing it. At last they are ready to confer their approval or disapproval.

—Weiten, *Psychology*, 7ᵗʰ Edition

About: _____

Point: _____

Proof: 1. _____

2. _____

_____

3. _____

_____

4. _____

Paragraph 3   Speech Textbook

Communication apprehension, or nervousness, can take two forms. People who are apprehensive about communicating with others in any situation are said to have *trait anxiety*. People who are apprehensive about communicating with others in a particular situation are said to have *state*, or *situational*, anxiety. Take a moment to consider whether you are trait anxious or state anxious in communication situations. Do you fear all kinds of interactions or only certain kinds? Most of us experience some level of state anxiety about some communication events, such as asking a boss for a raise, verbally evaluating another's performance, or introducing ourselves to a group of strangers.

—Griffin, *Invitation to Public Speaking*, 2nd Edition

About: _____

Point: _____

Proof: 1. _____

2. _____

Paragraph 4   Human Development Textbook

The notion that love will endure forever without any change is unrealistic. Although love can last over a period of time, love takes on different forms as the relationship matures. Love is complex and involves both joyful experiences and difficulties. The intensity of your love changes as you change. You may experience several stages of love with one person, deepening your love and finding new levels of richness. Conversely, you and your partner may become stagnant and the love you once shared fades.

—Corey/Corey, *I Never Knew I Had a Choice*, 8th Edition

About: _____

Point: _____

Proof: 1. _____

2. _____

3. _____

Interaction 4-9. More Practice Mapping Paragraphs

For each of the first two paragraphs in this passage, mark the APP. Bracket the topic, underline the main idea, and use numbers or parentheses to indicate the major supporting details. Then fill in the MAPP that follows. Put only the major supporting details under "Proof."

Orlan's Art

For centuries, artists have offered their full resources, their lives, to their work. Orlan has also offered a pound of flesh—to the surgeon's scalpel. Orlan is a French multimedia performance artist who has been undergoing a series of cosmetic operations

© AP Photo/Joe Kohen

© The Art Archive/Galleria degli Uffizi Florence/ Alfredo Dagli Orti

to create, in herself, a composite sketch of what Western art has long set forth as the pinnacle of human beauty: the facial features that we find in classic works such as Botticelli's *The Birth of Venus*, Leonardo's *Mona Lisa* and *Boucher Europa*, or, more specifically, Venus's chin, the Mona Lisa's forehead, and Europa's mouth.

Most people undergo cosmetic surgery in private, but not Orlan. Several of her operations have been performances or media events. Her first series of operations were carried out in France and Belgium. The operating rooms were filled with symbols of flowering womanhood in a form compatible with medicine: sterilized plastic fruit. There were huge photos of Orlan, and the surgeons and their assistants were decked out not in surgical greens but in costumes created by celebrated couturiers. A recent operation was performed in the New York office of a cosmetic surgeon and transmitted via satellite to the Sandra Gering Gallery in the city's famed SoHo district. Orlan did not lie unconscious in a hospital gown. Rather, she lay awake in a long black dress and read from a work on psychoanalysis while the surgeon implanted silicone in her face to imitate the protruding forehead of Mona Lisa.

When will it all end? Orlan says that "I will stop my work when it is as close as possible to the computer composite," as the lips of Europa split into a smile.

—Fichner/Rathus, *Understanding Art*, 8th Edition

About: _____

  Point: _____

    Proof: _____

_____

_____

About: _____

  Point: _____

    Proof: 1. _____

          2. _____

_____

_____

Using the Proof (Details) to Double-Check the Point (Main Idea)

So far we have taken what we might call a "forest-to-the-trees" approach to finding the main idea. Starting with the broad question, "What is the topic?" we then moved to the narrower question, "What is the main idea?" and finally to the narrowest question, "What are the supporting details?" But suppose you find it easier to see the individual trees than the forest.

You can start with the details and use them to find the main idea. (In Chapter 6, you will use a very similar approach to find implied main ideas, so follow this discussion closely.) Here are the steps you can follow.

1. Identify the topic. Ask the question, "What is the paragraph about?"

2. Find the supporting details.

3. Use the supporting details to find the main idea. Ask the question, "What do these details support?" or "What do all these details add up to?" The answer to the question should be the main idea.

4. Double-check that the main idea both supports the topic and is supported by the details.

Here is an example from a sociology textbook.

In the 1980s and early 1990s most observers believed that social interaction by means of computer would involve only the exchange of information between individuals. It turns out they were wrong. Computer-assisted social interaction can profoundly affect how people think of themselves.

Internet users interact socially by exchanging text, images, and sound via e-mail, messaging services and online dating services. In the process, they form **virtual communities.** Virtual communities are associations of people, scattered across the country or the planet, who communicate via computer and modem about subjects of common interest. Because virtual communities allow interaction using concealed identities, people are free to assume new identities and are encouraged to discover parts of themselves they were formerly unaware of. In virtual communities, shy people can become bold, normally assertive people can become voyeurs, old people can become young, straight people can become gay, and women can become men (Turlde, 1995).

—Brym/Lie, *Sociology: Your Compass for a New World,* Brief Edition

1. Identify the topic. What is the passage about?

> We have a bold term, **virtual community,** and that seems to be what this passage is about.

2. Find the details. What is the proof?

> The details from the paragraph are as follows:
> There is a definition of what a virtual community is:
> *Virtual communities are associations of people, scattered across the country or the planet, who communicate via computer and modem about subjects of common interest.*
>
> This next detail talks about how people can discover new sides of themselves:
> *Because virtual communities allow interaction using concealed identities, people are free to assume new identities and are encouraged to discover parts of themselves they were formerly unaware of.*
>
> The next details are examples of how in virtual communities people can act contrary to how they behave in person.
> *In virtual communities, shy people can become bold, normally assertive people can become voyeurs, old people can become young, straight people can become gay, and women can become men.*

3. Use the supporting details to find the main idea. Ask the question, "What do these details support?" or "What do all these details have in common?" The answer to these questions should be the main idea.

> You know that two of these details talk about how people alter who they really are or act like they are afraid to act face-to-face. As you go back and look at the passage, you ask, "What do these details support?" You see the following sentence: *Computer-assisted social interaction can profoundly affect how people think of themselves.* The details support this sentence.

4. Double-check that the main idea both supports the topic and is supported by the details.

> Virtual communities are a type of computer-assisted social interaction. You have already identified this idea as the topic. And "can profoundly affect how people think of themselves" is directly supported by the details: *people are free to assume new identities and are encouraged to discover parts of themselves they were formerly unaware of. In virtual communities, shy people can become bold, normally assertive people can become voyeurs, old people can become young, straight people can become gay, and women can become men.*

◉ Interaction 4-10. Practice the Trees-to-Forest Approach

With a partner, apply the approach you just read about to the following paragraph from a psychology textbook by talking through the four steps. Mark the three levels of information in the paragraph: bracket the topic, underline the main idea, and use numbers or parentheses to indicate the supporting details. Note that the paragraph includes both major and minor supporting details; mark only the major ones. Then fill out the APP in the outline.

The age-related changes in vision we have considered can significantly affect people's ability to function in their environment. Similarly, age-related changes in hearing can also have this effect and interfere with people's ability to communicate with others. Experiencing hearing loss is one of the well-known normative changes with age. A visit to any housing complex for older adults will easily verify this point; you will quickly notice that television sets and radios are turned on fairly loud in most of the apartments. Yet you don't have to be old to experience significant hearing problems. When it became difficult to hear what was being said to him, President Bill Clinton obtained two hearing aids. He was 51 years old at the time, and he attributed his hearing loss to too many high school bands and rock concerts when he was young. His situation is far from unique. Loud noise is the enemy of hearing at any age. You probably have seen people working in noisy environments wearing protective gear on their ears so they are not exposed to loud noise over extended periods of time.

—Kail/Cavanaugh, *Human Development*, 4th Edition

Topic: _____

    Main idea: _____

      Supporting details: 1. _____

                               _____

                            2. _____

                                 _____

                            3. _____

Other Outlines and Visual Maps

In this chapter you have been using a visual outline—a MAPP—to show the relationships among the ideas in a paragraph. But there are other kinds of outlines and visual maps that perform the same function. Formal and informal outlines are similar to MAPPs in that they also use a system of indentation to show how broad or narrow an idea is. Concept maps use a different method of organization that puts each idea into a bubble and connects the bubbles with arrows to show the connections between them. All of these are strategies intended to help you note the relationships among ideas in a reading selection. All are equally valid. The one you use will depend on your preference and the organization of the material. (We will talk more about this in Chapter 5.)

Formal and Informal Outlines

An outline is a hierarchical organization from the broadest idea (topic) to the narrowest (minor detail). You are probably familiar with the formal outline:

> I. Topic + Main Idea
>   A. Major Detail
>   1. minor detail
>   2. minor detail
>   B. Major Detail
>   1. minor detail
>   2. minor detail

Notice the hierarchical nature of the outline. Broader ideas are supported by the narrower details. Working from bottom to top, the minor details support the major details, and the major details support the main idea.

You are probably also familiar with informal outlines. In fact, we have been using one kind of informal outline throughout the chapter: the "A-P-P" of MAPPS.

About = Topic: What is the reading about?

Point = Main Idea: What is the point of the reading?

Proof = Supporting Detail: What is the proof? There are two kinds of proof or details: major and minor.

The informal outline has the same hierarchical structure as the formal outline. The difference is that the informal outline does not use Roman numerals, letters, and/or numbers. Instead, the informal outline uses bullets, dashes, indentations, or in our case, an A-P-P.

Interaction 4-11. Using a Formal Outline

Mark the following reading selection from a math textbook: Bracket the topic, underline the main idea, and use numbers or parentheses to indicate the major supporting details. Then fill in the formal outline to show the relationships among the ideas.

> Sometimes students who have had difficulty learning math in the past think that their problem is not being born with the ability to "do math." This isn't true! Learning math is a skill and, much like learning to play a musical instrument, takes daily, organized practice. Below are some strategies that will get you off to a good start.

Attend Class. Attending class every meeting is one of the most important things you can do to succeed. Your instructor explains material, gives examples to support the text, and information about topics that are not in your book, or may make announcements regarding homework assignments and test dates. Getting to know at least a few of your classmates is also important to your success. Find a classmate or two on whom you can depend for information, who can help with homework, or with whom you can form a study group.

Make a Calendar. Because daily practice is so important in learning math, it is a good idea to set up a calendar that lists all of your time commitments and time for studying and doing your homework. A general rule for how much study time to budget is to allot two hours outside of class for every lecture hour. If your class meets for three hours per week, plan on six hours per week for homework and study.

Gather Needed Materials. All math classes require textbooks, notebooks, pencils (with big erasers!), and usually as much scrap paper as you can gather. If you are not sure that you have everything you need, check with your instructor. Ideally, you should have your materials by your second class meeting and bring them to every class meeting after that. Additional materials that may be of use outside of class are the online tutorial program iLrn (www.iLrn.com) and the Video Skillbuilder CD-ROM that is packaged with your textbook.

What Does Your Instructor Expect From You? Your instructor's syllabus is documentation of his or her expectations. Many times your instructor will detail in the syllabus how your grade is determined, when office hours are held, and where you can get help outside of class. Read the syllabus thoroughly and make sure you understand all that is required.

—Tussy/Gustafson, *PreAlgebra*, 3rd Edition

I. Strategies for getting off to a good start learning math

    A. _____

        1. _____

        2. _____

    B. _____

        1. _____

        2. _____

    C. _____

        1. _____

        2. _____

    D. _____

        1. _____

        2. _____

Concept Maps

You may know several terms to describe this strategy: mind map, visual, bubble, or cluster. We like to use the term *concept map* because it describes very precisely what you are doing—mapping out the important concepts (that is, ideas) from a reading or lecture and showing their relationships to one another.

Figure 4.3 "Top to Bottom" Concept Map

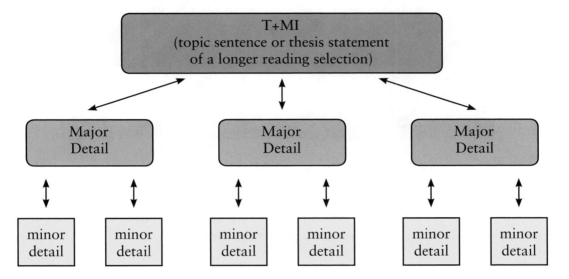

Figure 4.4 "Suns and Rays" Concept Map

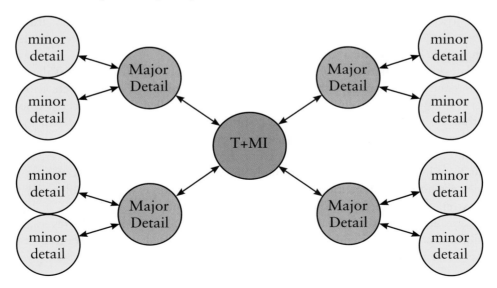

© Radius Images/Jupiter Images

Interaction 4-12. Using a Concept Map

Mark the following reading selection: Bracket the topic, underline the main idea, and use numbers or parentheses to indicate the major supporting details. Then fill in the concept map to show the relationships among the ideas.

Pilates for Strength and Flexibility

Used by dancers for deep-body conditioning and injury rehabilitation, Pilates (pronounced puh-LAH-teez), was developed more than seven decades ago by German immigrant Joseph Pilates. Increasingly used to complement aerobics and weight training, Pilates exercises improve flexibility and joint mobility and strengthen the core by developing pelvic stability and abdominal control.

Pilates-trained instructors offer "mat" or "floor" classes—classes that stress the stabilization and strengthening of the back and abdominal muscles. Fitness centers also may offer training on Pilates equipment, primarily a device called the Reformer, a wooden contraption with various cables, pulleys, springs, and sliding boards attached that is used for a series of progressive, range-of-motion exercises. Instructors typically work one-on-one or with small groups of two or three participants and tailor exercise sessions to individual flexibility and strength limitations. Unlike exercise techniques that emphasize numerous repetitions in a single direction, Pilates exercises involve very few, but extremely precise, repetitions in several planes of motion.

According to research from the American College of Sports Medicine, Pilates enhances flexibility and muscular endurance, particularly for intermediate and advanced practitioners, but its potential to increase cardiorespiratory fitness and reduce body weight is limited. The intensity of a Pilates workout increases from basic to intermediate to advanced levels, as does the number of calories burned. For intermediate practitioners, a 30-minute session burns 180 calories, with each additional quarter-hour burning another 90 calories. A single weekly session enhances flexibility but has little impact on body composition.

—Hales, *An Invitation to Health*, 12th Edition

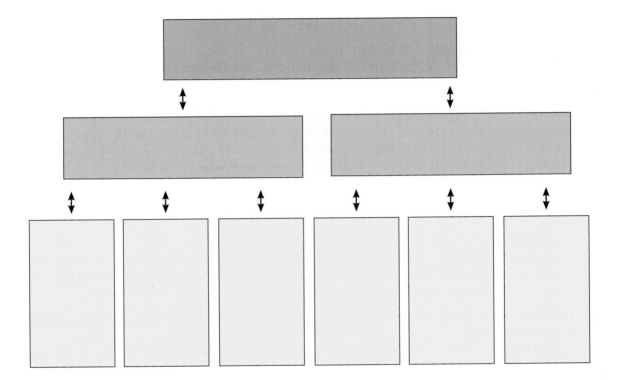

Writing a Summary

All the outlines and maps we have discussed can help you understand how the ideas in a reading selection are related to one another. Whether you use outlines, concept maps, or MAPPS to help you find the topic, main idea, and supporting details, having a way to organize the author's ideas as you are reading is an invaluable aid to comprehension. One more strategy you can use to help you understand and remember what you read is writing a summary.

The *S* in MAPPS stands for "summary." A *summary* is a brief restatement of the main idea and most important supporting details of a reading. Adding the S on MAPPS gives you a way to think about how the important pieces of information you have gathered fit together.

You can write a summary by capturing the key points of a reading or a lecture in your own words. You already have the pieces you need to write a summary: the topic (T) and the main idea (MI)—in other words, the topic sentence (TS). However, if the topic sentence is all you include, the summary won't be very helpful as a study aid. To be effective for study, a summary should also include the major details (MDs):

$$\textbf{Summary} = \textbf{[T]} + \underline{\textbf{MI}} + \textbf{(MDs).}$$

Sometimes you might find that you also need to include the minor details. This will depend upon the complexity of the material you are summarizing and your prior knowledge. The more complex the material, usually the more information you need to include to make sense of it. On the other hand, the more prior knowledge you have on a subject, the less information you need because your understanding is more complete. Regardless of the material's complexity or your prior knowledge, the thing to keep in mind is that you want to condense the information and put it in your own words. Do not just copy. Putting the author's ideas into your own words is a good way to be sure you understand them.

Here is an example based on the reading selection that you outlined in Interaction 4-11 on page 179. First reread your outline, and then read the following summary.

Summary: [T] + <u>MI</u> + (MDs).
To do well in math, you should go to class, organize your schedule to be sure you can put in two hours of study for every hour you spend in class, bring all needed materials to each class, and read your syllabus to be sure you understand it.

Notice that this summary includes the main idea and all four major supporting details from the outline.

Summaries are not normally written for very short pieces like single paragraphs. They are more helpful when they condense a longer reading selection into fewer words.

Interaction 4-13. Writing Summaries

Write a summary that includes the main idea and major supporting details for each of the following reading selections. Be sure to use your own words. Note that a summary can be more than one sentence.

1. "Small Savings Mean Big Bucks!" on page 169

_____

_____

_____

_____

2. "Pilates for Strength and Flexibility" on page 182

_____

_____

3. "Orlan's Art" on page 174

_____

_____

_____

Chapter Summary Activity

This chapter has discussed how using MAPPS and other strategies can help you understand the relationships between ideas in a paragraph. Construct a Reading Guide below by completing each idea on the left with information from the chapter on the right. You can use this guide later as you complete other reading assignments.

Reading Guide to Paragraph Structure

Complete this idea	with information from the chapter.
To understand paragraph structure, you can use a reading plan called	1.
The different letters in the reading plan mean	2.
	3.
	4.
	5.
	6.
MAPPS is written in an outline format to show that the different ideas in a paragraph are	7.
Of the topic, the main idea, and the supporting details, the broadest idea is the	8.
The narrowest ideas are the	9.
To find the topic while you are reading, ask "wh-" questions such as	10.

Another clue to finding the topic is to look for ideas and words that the author	11.
The part of a paragraph that limits the subject to what the author wants to discuss is called the	12.
When the topic and main idea are in the same sentence, that sentence is called the	13.
You can remember this with the mnemonic	14.
Supporting details can be two different kinds:	15. 16.
The supporting details that directly support the author's main idea are the	17.
When you write a summary, you include	18.
To find the major supporting details, you can change the topic sentence into	19.
If you can't figure out the main idea, you can always find the supporting details first and then ask yourself	20.
Two kinds of outlines that can be used instead of MAPPS are	21. 22.
A visual strategy that performs a similar function is a	23.
If you had to say that one sentence in a paragraph was the most important one, which one would you choose?	24.
Why did you give that answer?	25.

Test Taking Tips
Understanding Paragraph Structure

Reading tests often include questions about main ideas. That's because your comprehension of a reading passage depends on your ability to sort out which ideas are more important than others. Which ideas are the main points the author wants to make about a topic? If you can answer this question about the material on a reading test, you can probably also understand the material you will need to read in your other college courses. Here are some reminders from this chapter to help you locate the main idea, as well as other test-taking tips you may find helpful.

✔ Remember that the main idea is the point that the author is trying to make.

✔ To help you identify the main idea, first make sure you know what the topic is. Once you determine the topic, ask yourself, "What is the most important idea the author wants me to understand about this topic?" A simpler way to ask this question is, "What's the point?" See if any of the possible answers are similar to your answer.

✔ Realize that on multiple-choice reading tests, the possible answers to main idea questions generally fall into three categories:

1. Too broad—the topic or an idea falls outside the scope of the passage.
2. Too narrow—these are often the supporting details of the passage. A too-narrow answer will actually support the correct answer choice.
3. Just right—this is an answer that both supports the topic and is supported by the details.

✔ Double-check your answer once you narrow it down to the one you think is correct. Do this by turning the answer into a question. If it is the main idea, the details of the passage should answer the question.

COMMON MAIN IDEA STEMS

When you see items that use the following language on reading tests, you should answer with the main idea.

The author's main point is . . .

What is the main idea of . . . ?

Which of the following best summarizes . . . ?

The principal idea of this article is . . .

Reading 4-1 . . . . **American Government Textbook**

● Pre-Reading the Selection

Despite the American dream of liberty and justice for all, it took concerted efforts by many people to extend voting and other rights to African Americans. In this reading you will learn about how many people's actions, including Martin Luther King Jr.'s, impacted the fight for equal rights in America.

Guessing the Purpose

Judging from the title of the reading as well as the title of the book from which this selection is taken, *American Government and Politics Today*, what do you suppose the purpose for writing is? _____

Surveying the Reading

Survey the title of the selection, the headings, and the first sentence of each paragraph. What is the general topic of the reading selection? _____

Predicting the Content

Predict three things this selection will discuss.

- _____

- _____

- _____

Activating Your Knowledge

What do you already know about the Civil Rights Movement, Martin Luther King, Jr., sit-ins, and other related topics? Note two or three things you know.

- _____

- _____

- _____

Common Knowledge

Freedom Rides (*paragraph 3*) African American and white volunteers, many of them college students, riding public buses into segregated Southern states to test a 1960 United States Supreme Court decision outlawing racial segregation in interstate transportation facilities like bus and train stations.

Jim Crow laws (*paragraph 5*) Laws that mandated "separate but equal" status for African Americans in Southern states between 1876 and 1965. The laws allowed for inferior treatment of African Americans by segregating them from whites in many public places like restaurants, stores, schools, and public restrooms.

The Civil Rights Act of 1964 (*paragraph 5*) A bill prohibiting discrimination based on race and color in public places, schools, and government, among other things.

Reading with Pen in Hand

Now read the selection. As you read, mark any ideas that seem important, and respond to the questions and vocabulary items in the margin. Monitor your comprehension by putting a ✔ next to a paragraph when you understand most of it. Place an ✘ next to a paragraph when you don't understand most of it.

Visit www.cengage.com/devenglish/doleconnect and select Chapter 4 to hear vocabulary words from this selection and view a video about this topic.

The Civil Rights Movement

Steffen W. Schmidt, Mack C. Shelley II. and Barbara A. Bardes

◆ *Reading Journal*

◆What started the civil rights movement?

1   In December 1955, a forty-three-year-old African American woman, Rosa Parks, boarded a public bus in Montgomery, Alabama. When the bus became crowded and several white people stepped aboard, Parks was asked to move to the rear of the bus (the "colored" section). She refused, was arrested, and was fined $10 but that "was not the end of the matter." For an entire year, African Americans boycotted the Montgomery bus line. The protest was headed by a twenty-seven-year-old Baptist minister, Dr. Martin Luther King, Jr. During the protest period, he went to jail, and his house was bombed. In the face of overwhelming odds, King won. In 1956, a federal district court issued an injunction prohibiting the segregation of buses in Montgomery. The era of civil rights protests had begun.

boycotted Think about how African Americans might have protested the treatment of Rosa Parks. Then guess at the meaning of this word, or use your dictionary.

King's Philosophy of Nonviolence

2 The following year, in 1957, King formed the Southern Christian Leadership Conference (SCLC). King **advocated** nonviolent civil disobedience as a means to achieve racial justice. King's philosophy of civil disobedience was influenced, in part, by the life and teachings of Mahatma Gandhi (1869–1948). Gandhi had led resistance to the British colonial system in India from 1919 to 1947. He used **tactics** such as demonstrations and marches, as well as nonviolent, public disobedience to unjust laws. King's followers successfully used these methods to gain wider public acceptance of their cause.

Nonviolent Demonstrations

3 For the next decade, African Americans and sympathetic whites engaged in sit-ins, freedom rides, and freedom marches. In the beginning, such demonstrations were often met with violence, and the contrasting image of nonviolent African Americans and violent, hostile whites created strong public support for the civil rights movement. When African Americans in Greensboro, North Carolina, were refused service at a Woolworth's lunch counter, they organized a sit-in that was aided day after day by sympathetic whites and other African Americans. **Enraged** customers threw ketchup on the protesters. Some spat in their faces. The sit-in movement continued to grow, however. Within six months of the first sit-in at the Greensboro Woolworth's, hundreds of lunch counters throughout the South were serving African Americans.

4 The sit-in technique also was successfully used to integrate interstate buses and their terminals, as well as railroads engaged in interstate transportation. Although buses and railroads engaged in interstate transportation were prohibited by law from segregating African Americans from whites, they stopped doing so only after the sit-in protests.

Marches and Demonstrations

5 One of the most famous of the violence-plagued protests occurred in Birmingham, Alabama, in 1963, when Police Commissioner Eugene "Bull" Connor unleashed police dogs and used electric cattle prods against the protesters. People throughout the country viewed the event on television with **indignation** and horror. King himself was thrown in jail. The media coverage of the Birmingham protest and the violent response by the city government played a key role in the

---

advocated Reread the heading above this paragraph. What does it suggest is the meaning of *advocated*?

tactics Three examples of tactics are given in this sentence, and the next sentence includes a synonym. What are *tactics*?

◆ What are some examples of King's use of non-violence?

◆ What did the Woolworth's sit-in achieve?

enraged Use your logic. How does a person probably feel if they throw ketchup and spit at people?

◆ What else did the sit-ins achieve?

◆ What effect on Americans did the media coverage of the violence used on the protesters have?

indignation Use your logic to consider how people felt when they saw others being poked with electric cattle prods. What does *indignation* mean?

Dr. Martin Luther King, Jr. acknowledges the crowd of nearly a quarter-million African Americans and sympathetic whites at the August 1963 March on Washington for Jobs and Freedom, for which King is best remembered for his "I Have a Dream" speech.

© Bettmann/CORBIS

process of ending Jim Crow in the United States. The ultimate result was the most important civil rights act in the nation's history, the Civil Rights Act of 1964.

6   In August 1963, African American leaders A. Philip Randolph and Bayard Rustin organized a massive March on Washington for Jobs and Freedom. Before nearly a quarter-million white and African American spectators and millions watching on television, King told the world his dream: "I have a dream that my four little children will one day live in a nation where they will not be judged by the color of their skin but by the content of their character."

What was Martin Luther King, Jr.'s dream?

● Comprehension Questions

Write the letter of the answer on the line. Then explain your thinking.

Main Idea

____ 1. Which of these sentences from paragraph 3 is the statement of its main idea?

a. For the next decade, African Americans and sympathetic whites engaged in sit-ins, freedom rides, and freedom marches.

b. In the beginning, such demonstrations were often met with violence, and the contrasting image of nonviolent African Americans and violent, hostile whites created strong public support for the civil rights movement.

c. When African Americans in Greensboro, North Carolina, were refused service at a Woolworth's lunch counter, they organized a sit-in that was aided day after day by sympathetic whites and other African Americans.

d. Enraged customers threw ketchup on the protesters.

WHY? What information in the selection leads you to give that answer? _____

_____

_____

____ 2. What is the main idea of paragraph 2?

a. King advocated nonviolent civil disobedience as a means to achieve racial justice.

b. King's philosophy of civil disobedience was influenced, in part, by the life and teachings of Mahatma Gandhi (1869–1948).

c. Gandhi used tactics such as demonstrations and marches, as well as nonviolent, public disobedience to unjust laws.

d. King's followers successfully used these methods to gain wider public acceptance of their cause.

WHY? What information in the selection leads you to give that answer? _____

_____

_____

Supporting Details

____ 3. According to the passage, what was the most important achievement of the Civil Rights movement?

a. Rosa Parks' boycott of the Montgomery bus line

b. the formation of the Southern Christian Leadership Conference (SCLC)

c. the March on Washington for Jobs and Freedom

d. the Civil Rights Act of 1964

WHY? What information in the selection leads you to give that answer? _____

_____

____ 4. Based on the reading, which of the following was *not* a response to the Woolworth's sit-in participants in Greensboro?

a. The customers were enraged.

b. The customers threw ketchup on the protesters.

c. The protesters were fined $10.

d. Some customers spat in the protesters' faces.

WHY? What information in the selection leads you to give that answer? _____

_____

Author's Purpose

____ 5. What is the overall purpose of this passage?

a. to inform

b. to entertain

c. to persuade

d. to inform and entertain

WHY? What information in the selection leads you to give that answer? _____

_____

_____ 6. Why did the author mention Gandhi in paragraph 2?

    a. to inform readers that Gandhi led resistance to the British colonial system in India from 1919 to 1947

    b. to explain how King's philosophy of civil disobedience was influenced, in part, by the life and teachings of Mahatma Gandhi

    c. to persuade readers that the use of nonviolence is the most convenient and successful way to lead a social revolution

    d. to entertain readers with amusing anecdotes from the Civil Rights movement era

WHY? What information in the selection leads you to give that answer? _____

_____

_____

Relationships

_____ 7. What is the overall pattern of organization of this passage?

    a. narration in time order

    b. definition

    c. comparison and contrast

    d. cause-and-effect

WHY? What information in the selection leads you to give that answer? _____

_____

_____

_____ 8. What is the relationship between the two main parts of the following sentence? *When African Americans in Greensboro, North Carolina, were refused service at a Woolworth's lunch counter, they organized a sit-in that was aided day after day by sympathetic whites and other African Americans.*

    a. classification

    b. comparison and contrast

    c. cause-and-effect

    d. definition

WHY? What leads you to give that answer? _____

_____

_____

Fact, Opinion, and Inference

____ 9. Which of the following statements is an opinion?
   a. Within six months of the first sit-in at the Greensboro Woolworth's, hundreds of lunch counters throughout the South were serving African Americans.
   b. "I have a dream that my four little children will one day live in a nation where they will not be judged by the color of their skin but by the content of their character."
   c. King's followers successfully used these methods to gain wider public acceptance of their cause.
   d. For an entire year, African Americans boycotted the Montgomery bus line.

WHY? What leads you to give that answer? _____

_____

_____

____ 10. What does the following sentence imply (suggest) about Gandhi?
   King's philosophy of civil disobedience was influenced, in part, by the life and teachings of Mahatma Gandhi (1869–1948).
   a. Gandhi had not been successful in his civil disobedience efforts.
   b. Gandhi had been successful in his civil disobedience efforts.
   c. Gandhi was an African American pioneer who inspired King.
   d. Gandhi and King were friends, who though they had never met, corresponded with each other frequently.

WHY? What leads you to give that answer? _____

_____

_____

_____

◉ Critical Thinking Questions

CRITICAL THINKING LEVEL 1 REMEMBER

Review the annotations you made on the "The Civil Rights Movement," and jot down a few things you learned that you found interesting.

_____

_____

_____

CRITICAL THINKING LEVEL 2 UNDERSTAND

Fill in the topic sentence in the "top to bottom" concept map for paragraph 5. You can use the "trees-to-forest" method (page 176) if needed to figure out the main idea.

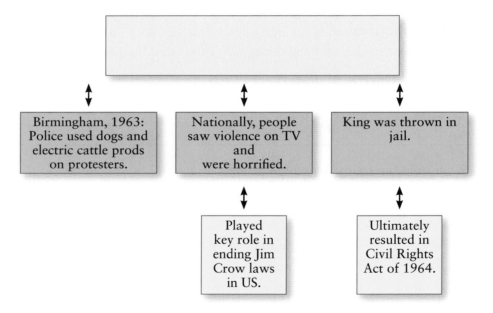

CRITICAL THINKING LEVEL 3 APPLY

Suppose that the food choices at your school are awful. You have complained, but no one seems to be listening. Following Martin Luther King Jr.'s lead, what are some steps you could take to change the quality of the food at your school? *Develop a plan of action* with a partner or small group in your class.

_____

_____

_____

CRITICAL THINKING LEVEL 4 ANALYZE

What *connections* can you make between Gandhi (from the reading excerpt on page 156) and King (from Reading 4-1)? How are they similar?

Gandhi	**King**
_____	_____
_____	_____
_____	_____

What differences can you list about the two men and their situations? Stay away from the obvious distinctions like, "One was in India and one was in the United States."

Gandhi	**King**
_____	_____
_____	_____
_____	_____
_____	_____

CRITICAL THINKING LEVEL 5 EVALUATE

Not all African Americans agreed with Martin Luther King Jr.'s philosophy of nonviolence. For example, in the early 1960s Malcolm X urged African Americans to "fight back" against white supremacy. Some people have argued that such a militant approach is always counterproductive. Others believe that a militant alternative may have made King's peaceful approach more attractive. *Evaluate* these statements. Does one make more sense to you than the other? Why or why not?

_____

_____

_____

CRITICAL THINKING LEVEL 6 CREATE

One of the best-known songs from the Civil Rights Movement is "We Shall Overcome." What can you tell about the topic of the song based on this title? Use your prior knowledge to expand your prediction. What do you think this song is about? Give some specific predictions.

_____

_____

_____

● Vocabulary in Context

The following words were used in "The Civil Rights Movement." Select the best word to complete the meaning of each sentence.

boycott	advocate	tactics	enraged	indignation

1. In the debate over abortion, some people _____ for the rights of the unborn child over the rights of the mother; others believe it is the woman's right to choose.

2. If you were wrongly charged with committing a crime you did not commit, you would be _____.

3. Gandhi _____ British goods in order to achieve independence for his country.

4. Seeing the strong use their power to abuse the weak stirs my _____.

5. The toddler's _____ for getting attention was simple yet ingenious; he cried.

Reading 4-2 . . . . **Newspaper Article**

● Pre-Reading the Selection

The article that follows, "Wiping Out TB and AIDS," appeared in *U.S. News and World Report*. It discusses the vision and accomplishments of the founders of Partners In Health (PIH), Paul Farmer and Jim Yong Kim.

Guessing the Purpose

Judging from the title of the reading, what do you suppose the purpose is?

_____

Surveying the Reading

Survey the title of the reading selection and the first sentence of each paragraph. What is the general topic of the reading? _____

_____

Predicting the Content

Predict three things this selection will discuss.

- _____

- _____

- _____

Activating Your Knowledge

This reading shows how one person's passion and beliefs have had a global impact. Talk with your classmates about how you have made an impact in your world with a cause that you have taken up or talk about a cause you are passionate about and hope to make a difference in someday.

Common Knowledge

TB (*in title*) Tuberculosis, a disease that people and animals spread, often attacks the lungs. It causes infected people to cough up blood-tinged mucus and causes fever, chest pain, and weight loss. People who live in crowded conditions are particularly susceptible to TB, and before the invention of antibiotics, many died from it.

AIDS (*in title*) Auto immune deficiency syndrome, symptoms caused by the HIV virus. The virus causes the immune system to lose its ability to fight off infections such as TB.

drug protocol (*paragraph* 6) The plan for a course of medical treatment.

Reading with Pen in Hand

Now read the selection. As you read, mark any ideas that seem important, and respond to the questions and vocabulary items in the margin. Monitor your comprehension by putting a ✔ next to a paragraph when you understand most of it. Place an ✘ next to a paragraph when you don't understand most of it.

Visit **www.cengage.com/devenglish/doleconnect** and select Chapter 4 to hear vocabulary words for this selection and view a video about this topic.

◆ *Reading Journal*

◆What does paragraph 1 suggest this passage will cover?

born with a plastic spoon in his mouth This phrase is a play on words. The original phrase is "born with a silver spoon in his mouth," which means that someone was born into money. In contrast, what do you think the "plastic spoon" is referring to?

stymied Use the clue in the next sentence that contrasts what Paul did with what other young people do. What does *stymied* mean, roughly?

◆How was Farmer different from other young people?

◆What caused Farmer to choose Haiti as a location for his work?

◆What does *Zanmi Lasante* mean?

Wiping out TB and AIDS

Michael Satchell

1   As one of six kids who spent part of his boyhood without running water in a converted passenger bus in a Florida trailer park, Paul Farmer has come a lot further than his untraditional beginnings might have predicted. Farmer may have been **born with a plastic spoon in his mouth**, but his hardscrabble childhood forged a quicksilver intellect and unstoppable drive. Exposed to the miseries of the world's poor, he turned his formidable focus, coupled with a genius for innovation, to solving their health problems.

2   "What set him apart as a young man was his ability to envision things that no one else could. A lot of young people go to places like Haiti and see the desperate conditions, but they feel **stymied** when it comes to doing something. Paul saw an opportunity, drew up a plan, and saw it through," says Ophelia Dahl, who went to Haiti with Farmer in 1983 and is now president and executive director of Partners in Health.

3   The son of a rootless, restless father who bounced from salesman to fruit picker to would-be commercial fisherman, Farmer is a physician and medical anthropologist with a MacArthur "genius" grant on his resume and two Harvard doctorates simultaneously earned. The seeds for his life's work, however, were planted when he was an undergraduate at Duke University, volunteering at Duke's hospital and in local migrant labor camps where Haitians worked the tobacco and vegetable fields. After graduation, he enrolled in Harvard Medical School and headed to central Haiti, volunteering to work in Cange on the central plateau, a collection of tin-roofed hovels in the poorest region of the poorest country in the West.

Global Model

4   In Cange, he studied medicine at Harvard long distance, applying what he was learning to his Haitian patients. To support his work, he founded a small, Boston-based charity called Partners in Health in 1987 with fellow Harvard medical student Jim Yong Kim. PIH set up a clinic called Zanmi Lasante, Creole for "partners in health," which became the settlement's first community-based healthcare delivery system.

5   Today, the well-equipped facility, with its operating rooms, blood bank, satellite communications, laptops, and other components of modern medicine, is a global model for delivering public-health services. PIH fights tuberculosis, AIDS, malaria, and other infectious diseases afflicting millions of the poor in Haiti, Peru, Russia, Mexico, Guatemala, Rwanda, and Boston's inner city. And its approach is unique. Patients receive not only lifesaving medicines and surgical care but also food, clean water, housing, education, and other social services, all delivered by locals trained in nursing skills and paid as community health workers.

◆What is the effect of the success of the holistic approach used by PIH?

6   This holistic approach by PIH, coupled with revolutionary drug protocols Farmer and Kim developed, proved that patients with drug-resistant tuberculosis could be cured rather than die by the hundreds of thousands each year. PIH's success in this and in treating AIDS patients has been so impressive that the World Health Organization has reversed long-held policies and now uses PIH treatment models in more than 30 countries. To the **self-deprecating**, 46-year-old Farmer, it's only a modest start. "A small group of British abolitionists in the [19th] century began a movement that said, 'Slavery is wrong, and we're going to change it.' And they did," he says. "I believe we can convince people that it's wrong for the destitute sick of the world to die unattended. We can change that, too."

self-deprecating Contrast the impressive things Farmer has done with his attitude about them. Guess what *self-deprecating* means.

The Bus to Duke

7   Farmer considers it a privilege, not a deprivation, that when he was 12 his family took up a **peripatetic** residence in an old school bus. When the bus was wrecked in an accident, the family moved into a campground tent and then into a jury-rigged houseboat moored in the Gulf of Mexico. Still, says Farmer, his family bonds were loving and strong, and the high school senior class president won a full scholarship to Duke.

peripatetic Use your logic of where he was living to help you.

◆How was Farmer's attitude toward the conditions of his childhood different from what you might expect?

8   Inspired by the writings of Rudolf Virchow, a 19th-century German medical pioneer whom he discovered at Duke, and pushed by his own Roman Catholicism to help the poor, Farmer went to Haiti in 1983, planning to spend a year there. He stayed much longer. When he received his Harvard M.D. and Ph.D. degrees in 1990, the 31-year-old had treated more types of illness and injury than many doctors see over a career.

◆What motivated Farmer to help the poor?

9   By the early 1990s, his Haitian clinic had become a well-equipped center, with trained community health agents serving 100,000 people around Cange. Farmer and his staff enjoyed mounting

◆What had Farmer accomplished in Haiti by the early 1990s?

burgeoning What was happening to his program?

◆What was Jim Yong Kim's role in the founding of PIH?

badgering What was Jim Yong Kim doing to the pharmaceutical companies?

◆What is Farmer and Kim's larger goal?

◆How much money has PIH been given charge of?

◆Who are Farmer's heroes and why?

success in treating infectious diseases, spending $150 to $200 to cure TB patients in their homes compared with $15,000 to $20,000 in a U.S. hospital setting. In 1993, the MacArthur Foundation recognized his work with a $220,000 grant that he plowed into his **burgeoning** program.

10   Several people shared credit for PIH's growing success, none more than co-founder Jim Yong Kim, who was born in South Korea and grew up in one of the only two Asian families in Muscatine, Iowa. Like his friend and fellow Harvard student, Kim was a physician and medical anthropologist with M.D. and Ph.D. degrees. Kim focused his energy on helping Farmer design better treatment protocols and **badgering** U.S. and foreign pharmaceutical companies to cut deals for cheaper and more effective drugs.

11   In 1996, PIH faced an outbreak of patients with drug-resistant TB in a Lima, Peru, shantytown. Instead of trying the usual front-line antibiotics, which didn't work, PIH administered a carefully calibrated regimen of as many as seven other drugs to patients in their homes, along with needed social services. Cure rates exceeded a stunning 80 percent—better than in U.S. hospitals. Now Farmer and Kim—who later received his own MacArthur genius award—had a larger goal: to wipe out TB throughout Peru and in other developing countries. And they saw no reason that their successful PIH treatment model couldn't be applied to other catastrophic infectious diseases like HIV/AIDS and malaria.

12   That required serious money. Kim had been building a relationship with the Bill and Melinda Gates Foundation, and in 2000, the foundation gave PIH $45 million. That was enough to allow PIH not only to launch a nationwide TB offensive in Peru but to establish a pilot project in Russia as well. More funding soon followed. In 2002, PIH received a $13 million grant from the Global Fund for new facilities and equipment for improvements at the Cange medical complex. Last April, the William J. Clinton Presidential Foundation launched a $10 million HIV/AIDS initiative, and PIH is responsible for establishing the first phase in Rwanda. And in September, PIH was awarded the 2005 Conrad N. Hilton Humanitarian Prize of $1.5 million for significantly alleviating human suffering.

13   Farmer's heroes are not towering figures; they are "the mothers of families in Haiti or wherever who get up in the morning without any food or water or wood for the fire and somehow feed their kids, plant a garden, go to the market."

14   "We've proven that people in poor settings with very complex diseases can be treated and cured," Farmer says, but he is far from satisfied. "We've had some victories," he says. "But if I were truly influential, everyone in the world would have the right to healthcare, food, clean water, other basics. That's the goal."

◆What is Farmer's ultimate goal?

● Comprehension Questions

Write the letter of the answer on the line. Then explain your thinking.

Main Idea

_____ 1. What is the thesis statement that includes the main idea of this reading selection?

    a. Exposed to the miseries of the world's poor, he [Farmer] turned his formidable focus, coupled with a genius for innovation, to solving their health problems.

    b. Farmer deserves all the credit for establishing Partners in Health in Haiti.

    c. Even though Farmer had an odd childhood, he grew up to have a quicksilver intellect and unstoppable drive.

    d. As one of six kids who spent part of his boyhood without running water in a converted passenger bus in a Florida trailer park, Paul Farmer has come a lot further than his untraditional beginnings might have predicted.

WHY? What information in the selection leads you to give that answer? _____

_____

_____

_____ 2. What sentence best states the main idea of paragraph 5?

    a. Today, the well-equipped facility, with its operating rooms, blood bank, satellite communications, laptops, and other components of modern medicine, is a global model for delivering public-health services.

    b. PIH fights tuberculosis, AIDS, malaria, and other infectious diseases afflicting millions of the poor in Haiti, Peru, Russia, Mexico, Guatemala, Rwanda, and Boston's inner city.

    c. And its approach is unique.

    d. Patients receive not only lifesaving medicines and surgical care but also food, clean water, housing, education, and other social services, all delivered by locals trained in nursing skills and paid as community health workers.

WHY? What information in the selection leads you to give that answer? _____

_____

_____

Supporting Details

_____ 3. Which paragraphs include direct support for the part of the thesis statement that says Farmer was "exposed to the miseries of the world's poor"? Underline the details in the selection and then see which answer matches your underlines.

a. Paragraphs 1, 3, 5, 8, 11, 13

b. Paragraphs 2, 4, 6, 7, 9, 10

c. Paragraphs 1, 2, 9, 10, 12

d. Paragraphs 3, 4, 8, 10, 12, 13

WHY? What information in the selection leads you to give that answer? _____

_____

_____ 4. Which of the following details best supports the main idea of this passage?

a. Still, says Farmer, his family bonds were loving and strong, and the high school senior class president won a full scholarship to Duke.

b. Several people shared credit for PIH's growing success, none more than co-founder Jim Yong Kim, who was born in South Korea and grew up in one of the only two Asian families in Muscatine, Iowa.

c. But his hardscrabble childhood forged a quicksilver intellect and unstoppable drive.

d. This holistic approach by PIH, coupled with revolutionary drug protocols Farmer and Kim developed, proved that patients with drug-resistant tuberculosis could be cured rather than die by the hundreds of thousands each year.

WHY? What information in the selection leads you to give that answer? _____

_____

_____

Author's Purpose

____ 5. What is the main purpose of this passage?

a. to inform readers about the progress and success of Paul Farmer and PIH

b. to acknowledge some of the major issues in the world today and present them to enlightened readers

c. to persuade readers about ways in which they should become involved in global health

d. to inform and entertain with anecdotes about the struggles Farmer has had in creating PIH

WHY? What information in the selection leads you to give that answer? _____

_____

_____

____ 6. What is the purpose of paragraph 8?

a. to persuade the reader that they should be concerned with the welfare of the world's poor

b. to inform the reader of where Farmer's inspiration came from

c. to inform the reader of Farmer's bias toward Roman Catholicism

d. to entertain the reader with the inspirational story of a man from humble beginnings

WHY? What information in the selection leads you to give that answer? _____

_____

_____

_____

Relationships

____ 7. What is the pattern of organization in paragraph 12?

a. chronological order (time)

b. cause-and-effect

c. definition

d. comparison and contrast

WHY? What information in the selection leads you to give that answer? _____

_____

_____ 8. What pattern of relationship do you find in the following sentence?
If I were truly influential, everyone in the world would have the right to health-care, food, clean water, other basics.
   a. Comparison and contrast
   b. Narration
   c. Cause-and-effect
   d. Listing

WHY? What leads you to give that answer? _____

_____

Fact, Opinion, and Inference

_____ 9. Which of the following inferences is supported by the passage?
   a. Even though Paul Farmer has done a lot of good, at heart he is just a spoiled rich kid.
   b. The Bill and Melinda Gates Foundation gave PIH $13 million.
   c. Paul Farmer feels it is morally wrong to neglect the poor of the world.
   d. Paul Farmer is better at raising funds for PIH than Jim Yong Kim.

WHY? What information in the selection leads you to give that answer? _____

_____

_____ 10. Which of the following assumptions would Farmer agree with?
   a. That poor people in Haiti have stronger immune systems than poor people from other countries and are a better investment of time, effort, and money
   b. That the more money he can raise, then more money he will have to lobby the World Health Organization to change their policies
   c. That the poor of the world are entitled to the same treatment as people with resources
   d. That PIH is the best non-profit in the world, and they deserve to be at the forefront of the battlefield for global healthcare

WHY? What information in the selection leads you to give that answer? _____

_____

● **Critical Thinking Questions**

CRITICAL THINKING LEVEL 1 REMEMBER

Recall (or reread the selection to find) how many grants, awards, and prizes PIH has received for their work according to this article, and who gave each one:

1. _____

2. _____

3. _____

4. _____

5. _____

CRITICAL THINKING LEVEL 2 UNDERSTAND

Fill in the APP of MAPPS for this reading selection. For the proof, summarize the main support for each phrase in the main idea.

    About: _____

       Point: _____

           _____

       Proof: _____

        1. Exposed to the miseries of the world's poor

           ○ _____

             _____

        2. Paul Farmer turned his formidable focus

           ○ _____

             _____

        3. coupled with a genius for innovation

           ○ _____

             _____

           ○ _____

        4. to solving the poor's health problems

           ○ _____

           ○ _____

             _____

CRITICAL THINKING LEVEL 3 APPLY

Contrast the ideas in the following quotation to your own life:

> Farmer's heroes are not towering figures; they are "the mothers of families in Haiti or wherever who get up in the morning without any food or water or wood for the fire and somehow feed their kids, plant a garden, go to the market."

1. Who are your heroes? Why? How do they compare with Farmer's heroes?

_____

_____

2. Compare the lives of the families Farmer is referring to with your own life. Discuss what you might take for granted.

_____

_____

CRITICAL THINKING LEVEL 4 ANALYZE

Analyze this quotation by Mother Teresa:

> Do not wait for leaders; do it alone, person to person.

How have Paul Farmer and Jim Yong Kim put this idea into practice? _____

_____

CRITICAL THINKING LEVEL 5 EVALUATE

With a classmate, *evaluate* the current PIH vision statement from their Web site (**http://www.pih.org/who/vision.html**), and determine how each sentence is supported by the details of this reading. Find at least one piece of support for each sentence:

Whatever it takes

At its root, our mission is both medical and moral. It is based on solidarity, rather than charity alone. When a person in Peru, or Siberia, or rural Haiti falls ill, PIH uses all of the means at our disposal to make them well—from pressuring drug manufacturers, to lobbying policy makers, to providing medical care and social services. Whatever it takes. Just as we would do if a member of our own family—or we ourselves—were ill.

At its root, our mission is both medical and moral.

• _____

_____

- _____
_____

It is based on solidarity, rather than charity alone.

- _____

- _____

When a person in Peru, or Siberia, or rural Haiti falls ill, PIH uses all of the means at our disposal to make them well—from pressuring drug manufacturers, to lobbying policy makers, to providing medical care and social services.

- _____
_____

- _____
_____

Whatever it takes. Just as we would do if a member of our own family—or we ourselves—were ill.

- _____
_____

- _____
_____

CRITICAL THINKING LEVEL 6 CREATE

In the "Activating Your Knowledge" section before the reading, you were given the following task:

> Talk with your classmates about how you have made an impact in your world with a cause that you have taken up or talk about a cause you are passionate about and hope to make a difference in someday.

Now that you have talked about it, _create_ a plan of action. What can you realistically do in the next six months to a year to take your ideas from discussion to action?

_____

_____

● Vocabulary in Context

The following words were used in "Wiping Out TB and AIDS." Select the best word to complete the meaning of each sentence.

born with a silver spoon in his mouth	stymied
self-deprecating peripatetic burgeoning badgering	

Even though Paolo was _____ and has had many opportunities that most people do not, he is surprisingly _____. In fact, he often feels _____ by the pressure his family puts on him to follow in his father's footsteps. He especially feels that his mother is always _____ him to become a businessman like his father. He often feels that his life would be a lot simpler if he had the courage to run off with the circus and live a _____ life.

chapter 5

Recognizing Patterns of Organization

© Daniel B. Wood/The Christian Science Monitor/ Getty Images

Design is not just what it looks like and feels like. Design is how it works.

—Steve Jobs

Think about Jobs's idea about design in relation to a couple of objects that you use every day. How does design matter in "how it works"?

Share Your Prior Knowledge

Consider a piece of writing that you've read. What can you say about its design?

www.cengage.com/devenglish/doleconnect

Videos Related to Readings **Vocab Words on Audio** **Prep Readings on Demand**

Survey the Chapter

Survey the box on page 217. Are these paragraph patterns only designs for writing, or also for thinking? Discuss your ideas.

Prep Reading . . . . **Newspaper Article**

Each September, fashion designers show their new creations for the following spring during Fashion Week in New York. Now others are using photos of these designs on the Internet to make quick, less expensive copies of the clothing and accessories. Should clothing designs be copyrighted like music? Eric Wilson lays out the issues.

Visit www.cengage.com/devenglish/doleconnect and select Chapter 5 to hear a reading of this selection and view a video about this topic.

Fashion Industry Grapples with Designer Knockoffs

Eric Wilson

1   Buyers from leading U.S. department stores began sifting through the work of hundreds of designers as another Fashion Week started Tuesday in New York, seeking the looks that shoppers will want to wear next spring. Seema Anand will be looking for the ones they want right now.

2   Anand, who will be following the catwalk shows through photographs posted instantly on the Web, is a designer few would recognize, even though she has dressed more people than most of the famous designers exhibiting a few blocks from her Garment District studio. Her company, Simonia Fashions, is one of hundreds that make inexpensive clothes inspired by other designers' runway looks, for trendy stores like Forever 21 and retail behemoths like Macy's and Bloomingdale's.

3   "If I see something on Style.com, all I have to do is e-mail the picture to my factory and say, 'I want something similar, or a silhouette made just like this,'" Anand said. The factory, in Jaipur, India, can deliver stores a knockoff months before the designer version. Anand compared a gold sequined tunic she created with a nearly identical one by the designer Tory Burch. Bloomingdale's had asked her to make several hundred of the dresses for its private label Aqua, she said. The Tory Burch dress sells for $750; Anand's is $260.

4   A debate is raging in the American fashion industry over designs like those by Anand. Copying, which has always existed in fashion, has become so pervasive in the Internet era it is now the No. 1 priority of the Council of Fashion Designers of America, which since last year has been lobbying Congress to extend copyright protec-

behemoths Two examples of *retail behemoths* are given. What are they?

Does *behemoth* more likely mean "enormous" or "tiny"?

pervasive Based on the meaning of the sentence, does *pervasive* mean "limited" or "widespread"?

© Joe Fornabaio/The New York Times/Redux

tion to clothing. Charles Schumer, a Democratic senator from New York, is co-sponsoring a bill and held a news conference in August to rally sympathy for designers. An expert working with the designers' council estimates that knockoffs represent a minimum of 5 percent of the $181 billion American apparel market.

5   Outlawing them is certainly an uphill battle, since many shoppers see nothing wrong with knockoffs, especially as prices for designer goods skyrocket. Critics of the designers' group even argue that copies are good for fashion, because they encourage designers to continuously invent new wares to stay ahead. Designers say that is pre-Internet thinking. "For me, this is not simply about copying," said Anna Sui, one of more than 20 designers who have filed lawsuits against Forever 21, one of the country's fastest growing clothing chains, for selling what they claim are copies of their apparel. "The issue is also timing," Sui said. "These copies are hitting the market before the original versions do."

6   At the factory in Jaipur that Simonia Fashions contracts with, 2,000 workers specialize in pattern making, design and tailoring and are equipped with computer programs that recreate the design

Simonia Fashions is one of many companies that makes less expensive clothes inspired by other designers' runway looks, for trendy stores like Forever 21 and retail behemoths like Macy's and Bloomingdales.

of a garment from a Web image without the need to pull apart the seams. The factory can return finished samples within 14 days. Sometimes the results are awful, "and sometimes it looks so great you're just shocked," Anand said. "They've done a better job than the designer."

7   The collections for spring shown this week will not arrive in stores until February, typical of the decades-old industry cycle developed when Fashion Week was a trade event. But now that the news media and the Internet **disseminate** runway looks instantly, fashion followers seek them out earlier. Anand's factory can deliver stores copies of runway styles four to six weeks after an order.

8   The cut or details of a garment cannot be **copyrighted** under existing law, although logos and original prints can be protected. Anna Sui's lawsuit against Forever 21, which has 400 stores and sales estimated at more than $1 billion, claims it has infringed against her prints on 26 occasions. "It seems to be their business model to find things that are popular in the marketplace by other designers and copy them," said Marya Lenn Yee, an attorney for Sui. A spokeswoman for Forever 21, Meghan Bryan, had no comment on the lawsuit. "In working with our enormous vendor base, regularly buying items from hundreds of vendors, it is extremely difficult to be certain of the origin of each item, on each and every occasion," she said in an e-mail message.

9   Designers say that if the knockoffs continue **unabated**, their businesses will be in jeopardy. Anand maintains that her reproductions of designer styles have been changed enough that they do not violate a designer's intellectual property. "We don't copy anything," she said. "We tweak it. We get inspired before we create it."

10   Anand sees her work meeting the needs of the vast majority of consumers who cannot afford designer prices. "Especially the younger girls do not have so much money," she said, "but they want to wear fashionable clothes. They want to look fabulous," she said. "It's their right to look fabulous."

---

disseminate Use context clues to decide what *disseminate* means.

copyrighted Write down the meaning of *copyrighted*. If you need to, use your dictionary.

unabated What prefix, root, and suffix is this word composed of?

Look up the root in the dictionary; what does it mean?

What does *unabated* mean?

Interaction 5-1. Talking about Reading

Respond in writing to the questions below and then discuss your answers with your classmates.

1. What conflict does the article describe, and who is involved in it? _____

_____

_____

_____

2. What is the difference between the amount of time it takes a runway designer to get his or her designs into stores and the amount of time it takes Simonia Fashions? ___

_____

3. What aspects of a design can and cannot be copyrighted? _____

_____

4. Do you think knockoffs should be illegal? If so, how should the courts determine the difference between clothing that has been inspired by previous designs and those that should be considered outright copies? _____

_____

_____

_____

Predicting Paragraph Patterns

In Chapter 2 we talked about turning titles and headings into questions in order to predict what a reading selection is going to be about. For example, you might read the heading "Characteristics of a Good Nursing Home" in a psychology book and form the question, "What are the characteristics of a good nursing home?" This allows you to reflect on what you already know about a subject before reading and prepares you to search for the parts of the answer to the question, which are the main ideas.

In addition to predicting content, you may also be able to predict the structure of the information that you will be reading. Predicting the structure is helpful because it gives you a chance to form a *schema,* that is, a structure that you can use to format the material mentally.

For example, suppose you read the sentence "The first signs of civilization in Mesoamerica appeared with the emergence of what is called Olmec culture." First, you can apply to this sentence the same questioning strategy you've been using for titles and headings: What signs of civilization appeared in Mesoamerica with the emergence of Olmec culture? Second, you can mentally prepare a structure for the answers to this question, which you are about to learn. Your mental schema might look like this:

Sign: ?

Sign: ?

Sign: ?

Sign: ?

In other words, you don't know yet what the signs of civilization are, and you don't know how many signs there are, but you have prepared yourself to pick them out from all the other details in the passage. As you are reading, you will mentally be filling in the schema with the first sign, the second sign, and so on.

● Interaction 5-2. Fill in the Schema with Information

Read the following paragraph to find out what the first signs of civilization in Mesoamerica were. After you read, fill in the schema with the signs.

Early Civilizations in Central America

The first signs of civilization in Mesoamerica appeared in the first millenium B.C.E., with the emergence of what is called Olmec culture in the hot and swampy lowlands along the coast of the Gulf of Mexico south of Veracruz. Olmec civilization was characterized by intensive agriculture along the muddy riverbanks in the area and by the carving of stone ornaments, tools, and monuments at sites such as San Lorenzo and La Venta. The Olmec peoples organized a widespread trading network, carried out religious rituals, and devised a system of hieroglyphics that is similar in some respects to later Mayan writing and may be the ancestor of the first true writing systems in the New World.

—Duiker/Spielvogel, *World History,* 5th Edition

First signs of civilization in Mesoamerica

Sign: _____

Sign: _____

Sign: _____

Sign: _____

Sign: _____

As you can see from Interaction 5-2, if you mentally form a blank schema before you read, then as you read you can be actively searching for the information to fill it. Taking the time to form schema as you read is an important part of improving your reading comprehension. Noticing the paragraph pattern will help you grasp which details are more important than others to the author's main idea.

Examining Paragraph Patterns

The MAPPS format you studied in Chapter 4 gives you a way to visualize the relationships between the general and specific ideas in paragraphs. Once you see in outline form what the paragraph is **A**bout and what the author's **P**oint about the subject is, you can examine what **P**roof the author offers to support the point. In this chapter we will discuss eight different patterns in which supporting details may be organized.

Patterns of Support

- **Description** shows readers what something looks, sounds, feels, tastes, or smells like. Descriptions are often arranged in space order.

- **Narration** tells readers how something happened. Narratives use time order.

- **Process** reveals to readers what steps need to occur for something to happen, and in what order.

- **Cause-and-effect** lets readers know what made something happen (causes), or what an event leads to (effects).

- **Examples** are used to support general ideas and make them come alive for readers. Sometimes examples are organized in lists.

- **Comparison and contrast** describe how things are the same (comparison) and/or how they are different (contrast).

- **Definition** tells readers what something means.

- **Classification** tells readers what kinds of an event or thing exist.

Description: What Does This Look, Sound, Feel, Taste, and Smell Like?

People learn about the world through their senses of sight, hearing, feeling, smelling, and tasting. No matter where you are right now, you can use your senses to orient yourself. If you look up from this book, you can move your eyes around the room or landscape and say things like, "The small blue desk is to the left of the CD player" or "The tires of the trucks are squealing, and I can smell the exhaust of all the traffic." What you are sensing may remind you of something else that seems similar: "The clock's ticking sounds like a child's heartbeat." This use of the word *like* to link two very different thoughts is called a *simile*. When a writer emphasizes sensory details, the writing pattern is called *description*.

Description answers questions such as "What does this look like?" "What does it sound like?" and "What does it feel like?" Description sometimes relies on spatial order to organize details.

Reading Strategy for Description

As you read, mentally use your senses of sight, hearing, feeling, smelling, tasting, and your sense of movement to re-create the scene the author is describing.

Description Paragraphs   ## Nonfiction Book

Using the reading strategy for description, read the passage. Then go back and read the highlighted words and the annotations that explain their function in the description pattern. More explanation follows the paragraph.

From the Wild

Spatial arrangement	He came out of the night, appearing suddenly in my headlights, a big, golden dog, panting, his front paws tapping the ground in an anxious little dance. Behind him, tall cottonwoods in their April bloom. Behind the grove, the San Juan River, moving quickly, dark and swollen with spring melt.
Signal words (transitions) for space order, for example *behind* and *next to*	It was nearly midnight, and we were looking for a place to throw down our sleeping bags before starting our river trip in the morning. Next to me in the cab of the pickup sat Benj Sinclair, at his feet a midden of road-food wrappers, smeared with the scent of corn dogs, onion rings, and burritos. Round-cheeked, Buddha-bellied, thirty-nine years old, Benj had spent his early years in the Peace Corps, in West Africa, and had developed a stomach that could digest anything. Behind him in the jump seat was Kim Reynolds, an Outward Bound instructor from Colorado known for her grace in a kayak and her long braid of brunette hair, which held the odor of a healthy, thirty-two-year-old woman who had sweated in the desert and hadn't used deodorant. Like Benj and me, she had eaten a dinner of pizza in Moab, Utah, a hundred miles up the road where we'd met her. Like us, she gave off the scents of garlic, onions, tomato sauce, basil, oregano, and anchovies.
Sensory details	

—Kerasote, *Merle's Door: Lessons from a Freethinking Dog*

Spatial arrangement. Placement in space often is an important method for organizing sensory details. When you are reading, look for words that signal how the elements of the scene are arranged.

Signal Words (Transitions) for Space Order

- in the foreground, in the background
- on the left, in the middle, on the right
- in front of, behind, in back of
- north, south, east, west
- above, below, underneath, behind, forward, in front of
- off in the distance, beyond, up close
- farther away, near, nearby, closer, through
- at, in, on (as in *at the store*, *in the wilderness*, *on the table*)
- here, there
- inward, outward

Sensory details. Words that describe sights, sounds, smells, feelings, tastes, and movements help descriptive writing come alive: *a big, golden dog; dark and swollen with spring melt; gave off the scents of garlic, onions, tomato sauce.* Combinations of sensory details create word-pictures with emotional overtones. For example, *his front paws tapping the ground in an anxious little dance* includes sights, sounds, and the writer's interpretation of the dog's emotional state (*anxious*).

Interaction 5-3. Recognizing Words That Signal Space Order

In the following sentences, underline words that signal space order. (Consult the list above as needed.)

1. In the Verkhoyansk Mountains of northeast Siberia, Eveny nomads are on the move.

2. Teams of reindeer pull caravans of sledges down the steep slide of a frozen mountain river.

3. Bells tinkle on the lead reindeer while dogs on short leashes dive closely alongside through the snow like dolphins beside a boat.

4. One man sits on the lead sledge of each caravan, his right foot stretched out in front of him and his left foot resting on the runner ready to fend off hidden rocks and snagging roots. Passengers or cargo sit on the sledges behind.

5. The passage of each caravan is visible from afar by a cloud of frozen reindeer breath.

—Vitebsky, *The Reindeer People*

Narration: How Did That Happen?

For all of human history, people have been telling stories. When stories are made up, we call them *fiction*, and the pattern of events in the story or novel is called the *plot*. But any time people recount events, whether the events actually occurred or not, we call the pattern *narration*.

Narration answers the questions: "How did that happen?" or "How is that happening now?" or even "How will that happen in the future?" Narration relies on time order. Time order indicates which events happened first, second, third, and so on. Writers who use time order use various kinds of words and phrases to indicate what happened when.

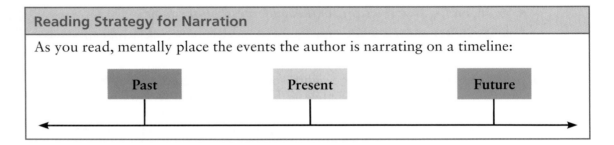

Reading Strategy for Narration

As you read, mentally place the events the author is narrating on a timeline:

Past — Present — Future

A Narration Paragraph   Magazine Article

Using the reading strategy for narration, read the paragraph. Then go back and read the highlighted words and the annotations that explain their function in the narration pattern. More explanation follows the paragraph.

Specific time words and dates

Signal words (transitions) for time order, such as *ago* and *before*

Verbs and verb phrases

Fire in the Hole

This hellish landscape constitutes about all that remains of the once-thriving town of Centralia, Pennsylvania. Forty-three years ago, a vast honeycomb of coal mines at the edge of the town caught fire. An underground inferno has been spreading ever since, burning at depths of up to 300 feet, baking surface layers, venting poisonous gases and opening holes large enough to swallow people or cars. The conflagration may burn for another 250 years, along an eight-mile stretch encompassing 3,777 acres, before it runs out of the coal that fuels it.

–Krajick, *Smithsonian* (May 2005)

Specific time words and dates. Time is a crucial element in narration. When you are reading, look for phrases that will help you figure out when things have occurred.

Signal Words (Transitions) for Time Order

- Monday through Friday
- during that time
- before, during, after
- first, second, third
- first, next, then, later
- since [a date]: since 1976
- on Wednesday; on March 17, 2007
- in the period from 1865 to 1877
- ever since [something happened]: ever since she graduated
- as, meantime, meanwhile
- preceding, immediately, following, afterward
- as soon as, when, until
- still
- subsequently, eventually

Verbs and verb phrases: Verbs are a major indicator of when things happened in relation to other events. Here, coal mines *caught* fire. The verb *caught* is in the simple past tense. That means that the event already occurred. In the next sentence, *has been spreading* is a verb phrase that shows duration in time—a raging fire started spreading and it is *still* spreading, forty-three years later. In general, *-ing* verbs (such as *burning, baking, venting,* and *opening*) describe continuing actions. They are happening over a period of time.

● Interaction 5-4. Recognizing Time Words and Verb Tenses

In the following sentences, underline words that signal time order. (Consult the list above as needed.) Circle the verbs, and on the line after each sentence, write the time period indicated by the verb: past, present, or future.

> *Examples of verbs*
> Past tense: was, did, had, baked, filmed, hoped, burnt, spoken
> Present tense: is, does, has, bakes, film, hope, burn, speaks
> Future tense: will be, will do, will have, will bake, will hope

1. In 1999, Ken Burns made a documentary film, *Not for Ourselves Alone,* on the women's rights movement. _____

2. Part One tells the story from about 1840 through the Civil War. _____

3. The film focuses on the collaboration between Susan B. Anthony and Elizabeth Cady Stanton. _____

4. In 1848, after a visit with her friend and fellow activist Lucretia Mott, Stanton helped organize the first Women's Rights Convention in Seneca Falls. _____

5. Stanton demanded civil and legal equality for women, including the right to vote.

_____

—Adapted from Murrin et al., *Liberty, Equality, Power,* 5th Edition

Process: What Steps Need to Occur, and in What Order?

In science courses and other technical contexts, you will often find a special version of narration called *process writing.* The point of process writing is to tell readers what steps to follow to achieve a certain result or to describe the stages that lead to a certain event or result. For example, a biology book may describe the process of how a cell divides. Process writing answers the question: "What steps need to occur, and in what order, to make something else happen?" To make sure that readers understand a process thoroughly, a writer makes it plain what has to happen first, second, and third. So just like narration, process writing relies on time order. Sometimes the writer also needs to outline general conditions that need to be true before the process can occur.

Reading Strategy for Process Writing

To keep the order of events clear as you read, mentally fill in the events on a generalized timeline:

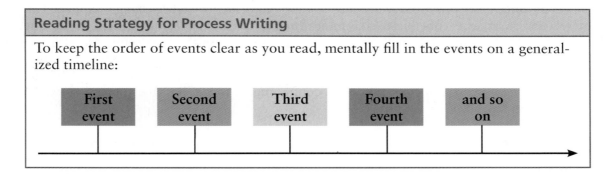

Process Paragraphs   ## Sociology Textbook

Using the reading strategy for process writing, read the paragraph. Then go back and read the highlighted words and the annotations that explain their function in the process pattern. More explanation follows the paragraph.

Ecological Theory

Nearly a century ago, Robert Park proposed an influential theory of how race and ethnic relations change over time (Park, 1914; 1950). His **ecological theory** focuses on the struggle for territory.

It distinguishes five stages in the process by which conflict between ethnic and racial groups emerges and is resolved:

Ordering devices. Numbers help readers keep track of the stages, and labels summarize each stage.

1. *Invasion.* The territory may be as large as a country or as small as a neighborhood in a city.
2. *Resistance.* The established group tries to defend its territory and institutions against the intruding group. It may use legal means, violence, or both.
3. *Competition.* If the established group does not drive out the newcomers, the two groups begin to compete for scarce resources. These resources include housing, jobs, public park space, and political positions.

Narrative elements. After some labels is a narrative explaining what usually happens.

4. *Accommodation and Cooperation.* Over time, the two groups work out an understanding of what they should segregate, divide, and share. **Segregation** involves the spatial and institutional separation of racial or ethnic groups. For example, the two groups may segregate churches, divide political positions in proportion to the size of the groups, and share public parks equally.
5. *Assimilation.* **Assimilation** is the process by which a minority group blends into the majority population and eventually disappears as a distinct group. Park argued that assimilation is bound to occur as accommodation and cooperation allow trust and understanding to develop. Eventually, goodwill allows ethnic groups to fuse socially and culturally. Where two or more groups formerly existed, only one remains.

Conditions. Sometimes processes work only under certain conditions.

Park's theory stimulated important and insightful research. However, it is more relevant to some ethnic groups than others.

—Brym/Lie, *Sociology,* 3rd Edition

Ordering devices. Authors Brym and Lie use two main ordering devices in this passage to clearly distinguish the five stages of the process they are describing: numbers, which help readers understand the order of the stages; and labels, which act as a summary of what each stage consists of. In process writing that is printed as a paragraph instead of as a numbered list, the stages or steps might be ordered with letters such as (a), (b), and (c), or with words such as the following:

Signal Words (Transitions) for Process Writing

- first step, second step, third step
- first stage, second stage, third stage

- phases
- that (that, these, those) stages or steps
- first, then, eventually, last
- start, continue, end
- as [one things happens, another thing happens], during, meanwhile, while
- any of the words from the narration list on page 221

Narrative elements. If you don't read the numbers and the labels, and instead just read the rest of each stage of the ecological theory, you will see that it is a kind of narration. In this particular piece of writing, the events are described at a level of generality that is higher than in the narratives you read in the narration section. The highlighted sentence in number 4, for instance, does not refer specifically to how particular groups decide to segregate, divide, and share. Instead it generalizes about any such interaction between two ethnic groups.

Conditions. Sometimes processes only work under certain conditions—for instance, water changes to ice only at 32°F. Here, the theory is outlined in the textbook before the conditions under which it proves true are given. We haven't reprinted the next section here, but Brym and Lie go on to say that ecological theory is an accurate description of what happened when white Europeans immigrated to America, but it has not proved to be accurate regarding other ethnic groups who have come here.

Interaction 5-5. Recognizing Words that Signal a Process

Underline words that signal the stages of a process. (See pages 223–224 for a list.) One sentence doesn't include any.

1. The theory of *assortative mating* states that people find partners based on their similarity to each other along many dimensions, such as age and intelligence.

2. When people meet, according to Murstein's (1987) classic theory, they apply three filters, representing discrete stages.

3. The first stage is represented by the idea of *stimulus.* The question asked about a potential mate in this step is "Do the person's physical appearance, social class, and manners match your own?"

4. Second, people want to know about possible mates' *values:* "Do the person's values regarding sex, religion, politics, and so on match your own?"

5. The third stage or filter is *role:* "Do the person's ideas about the relationship, communication style, gender roles, and so on match your own?"

—Adapted from Kail/Cavanaugh, *Human Development,* 4th Edition

Cause-and-Effect: What Made This Happen?
What Does This Lead To?

Cause-and-effect paragraphs may focus on the causes of an event, in which case they answer a question such as "What made this happen?" or "What's the reason this occurred?" When they focus on the effects that came about because of something else that happened, a cause-and-effect paragraph answers a question like "What does this lead to?" or "What is the result of this action?" Another kind of variation is that a cause-and-effect paragraph may describe how a single cause leads to multiple effects, or how multiple causes create a single effect. A piece of writing may even describe how one cause leads to an effect, which then becomes the cause of a second effect, which then becomes the cause of yet another effect, and so on. This last type is called a *causal chain*.

Reading Strategy for Cause-and-Effect

As you read, visualize the causes that lead to effects as arrows:

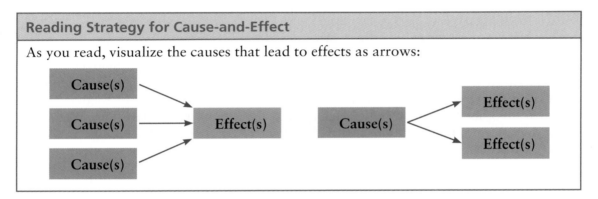

A Cause-and-Effect Paragraph   Anthropology Textbook

Using the reading strategy for cause and effect, read the paragraph. Then go back and read the highlighted words and the annotations that explain their function in the cause-and-effect pattern. More explanation follows the paragraph.

Time order is not necessarily followed. A writer may choose to discuss an effect before a cause, as in the first sentence.

Cell Phones and Pedestrian Behavior

[1]In some U.S. cities there has been a dramatic rise in automobile accidents caused by inattentive pedestrians crossing the street while talking on their phones. [2]In addition to the dangers involved, the sidewalks of cities like New York are losing some of their civility. [3]In pre-cell phone days, crowded rush-hour sidewalks were reasonably easy to navigate because most people were looking where they were going. . . . [4]Today, however, with their minds elsewhere, phone-using pedestrians bump into other walkers, confuse others with their

Words that express de-
grees of uncertainty

Signal words indicating
that one thing causes
another

public conversations, and accidentally hit other pedestrians with their unrestrained hand gestures. ⁵The widespread use of cell phones, in other words, is making normal pedestrian traffic flow increasingly more difficult. ⁶Moreover, the rise of personal isolation caused by extensive cell phone use makes it less likely that pedestrians will help strangers in need or exchange pleasantries in a chance encounter—two occurrences that make urban living invigorating. ⁷These developments raise an important question: just how aware are we of the negative social consequences of our signing a one-year contract with a cell-phone company offering us 5,000 "anytime" minutes per month?

—Adapted from Ferraro, *Cultural Anthropology*, 6ᵗʰ Edition

Words indicating that one thing leads to another. In sentence 1, the words *caused by* point to a cause-and-effect relationship between people talking on cell phones crossing the street and car accidents: The first causes the second. In sentences 5, 6, and 7 are other words that indicate cause-and-effect: *is making, makes, caused by,* and *consequences* (which is another words for *effects*). Words that indicate cause and effect include the following. The lines tell you where you will find the cause or effect.

Signal Words (Transitions) for Causes:

_____ causes
_____ creates
_____ allows for
_____ leads to
because _____
are due to ___
_____ makes
reason is _____
is/are shaped by a number of factors: ___, ___, ___
brought about by ___

Signal Words (Transitions) for Effects:

_____ depends on
causes _____
_____ were the effects
_____ is the result
leads to _____
makes (or made) _____
consequences are _____

Words that express degrees of uncertainty. It's hard to be sure what causes what, and the writer here is careful to say that personal isolation makes it *less likely* that walkers will help a stranger or strike up a conversation—not that personal isolation makes it *impossible*. Here are some words that express degrees of uncertainty:

- may [cause, affect]
- might, could [be a reason, lead to, be an effect]
- tends to

- possibly
- to a degree, to some degree

Time order is not necessarily followed. Even though logically, causes must precede (come before) effects in time, writers may choose to discuss the effect first, as Ferraro does in the first sentence. The accidents come after people talking on their cells cross the street without noticing what's going on, but the sentence puts the accidents first.

Interaction 5-6. Recognizing Cause-and-Effect Words

Underline the transitions that signal cause and effect in the following sentences.

1. When Hernan Cortes and his fellow conquistadors arrived in Mesoamerica in 1519, the local inhabitants were frightened of the horses and the firearms that accompanied the Spaniards.

2. But the most lethal effects were caused by invisible disease-bearing microbes brought by these strange new arrivals. Diseases have made the lives of human beings, in the words of the English philosopher Thomas Hobbes, "nasty, brutish, and short."

3. Illnesses such as malaria and tuberculosis caused our immediate ancestors to sicken and die.

4. With the explosive growth of the human population brought about by the agricultural revolution, the problems posed by the presence of disease intensified.

5. People started living in close quarters in villages and cities, and this allowed bacteria to settle in their piles of refuse. Lice also carried bacteria around in people's clothing.

—Adapted from Duiker/Spielvogel, *World History*, 5th Edition

Interaction 5-7. Applying Your Knowledge of Patterns

Circle the signal words in each selection. If the signal words relate to the major details, use this information to determine which paragraph pattern is being used. However, for two selections, signal words won't help much. You will also need to think about the APP of each selection (What's it **A**bout, what's the **P**oint, what's the **P**roof?).

Choose from these paragraph patterns:

description	narration	process	cause-and-effect

Selection A   Anthropology Textbook

Pattern: _____

Chomsky believes that language is more than the accumulation of words, sounds, and rules; rather, all languages share a limited set of organizing principles. All humans are born with a blueprint or basic linguistic plan, which Chomsky calls universal grammar. When children from any part of the world are learning a language, they are not starting as completely blank slates but rather have an outline of a limited set of grammatical rules. Children listen to the language around them in order to determine which rules apply and which do not. They then add this grammatical rule to their growing number of rules. To illustrate, a child from an English-speaking family will observe that to change a word from the present to the past one adds *–ed*. The rule certainly works when dealing with such verbs as *talk, walk,* and *climb.* This then becomes the child's general rule for past tense. As children are confronted with other verbs that do not conform to this rule (for instance, *eat/ate, hold/held, run/ran),* they must alter the rule or make an additional rule that accounts for the variations. The learning process, then, involves a constant editing of the grammatical rules until they eventually conform to that of adult speech. Along the way children have rejected the various principles or rules useful for other languages because they do not apply to their own language. Thus, as children learn to speak, they master a specific grammar system that has been embedded in a universal grammar.

—Ferraro, *Cultural Anthropology,* 6ᵗʰ Edition

Selection B   Health Textbook

Pattern: _____

Two-thirds of American adults, up from fewer than half 20 years ago, are overweight. About one in every three Americans is obese. Since the 1970s, the obesity rate has doubled for teens and tripled for children between the ages of 6 and 11. How did we get so fat? A variety of factors played a role. Here are some of them.

1. **More calories.** Bombarded by nonstop commercials for taste treats, tempted by foods in every form to munch and crunch, Americans are eating more—some 200 to 400 calories more a day than they did several decades ago.
2. **Bigger portions.** The size of many popular restaurant and packaged foods has increased two to five times during the past 20 years. According to studies of appetite and satiety, people presented with larger portions eat up to 30 percent more than they otherwise would.
3. **Fast food.** Young adults who eat frequently at fast-food restaurants gain more weight and develop metabolic abnormalities that increase their risk of diabetes

in early middle age. In a recent study, those who ate fast food at least twice a week gained an extra 10 pounds and had a two-fold increase in insulin.

4. **Physical inactivity.** As Americans eat more, they exercise less. Experts estimate that most adults expend 200 to 300 fewer calories a day than people did 25 years ago. The most dramatic drop in physical activity often occurs during the college years.

5. **Passive entertainment.** Television is a culprit in an estimated 30 percent of new cases of obesity. TV viewing may increase weight in several ways: It takes up time that otherwise might be spent in physical activities. It increases food intake since people tend to eat more while watching TV. And compared with sewing, reading, driving, or other relatively sedentary pursuits, television watching lowers metabolic rate so viewers burn fewer calories.

—Adapted from Hales, *An Invitation to Health,* 12th Edition

Selection C   Magazine Article

Pattern: _____

"Not many people can say a guitar saved their life—me and B. B. King, maybe," says musician and legendary long-distance hiker "Walkin'" Jim Stolz. In June 1982, Stolz was trekking the length of Utah (about 700 miles from Arizona to Idaho) when he scaled snowy Mt. Timpanogos near Provo and spent the night looking down on the twinkling city lights. Downclimbing the next morning proved dicier: Lacking an ice axe and crampons, Stolz slipped and started sliding on his belly toward a sheer cliff. He kicked and clawed at the ice, but to no avail. "In a way, I gave up," Stolz recalls. "I rolled onto my back, thinking at least I'd see what I was about to hit, and that's when I was jerked to a halt." The neck of his guitar—which he had lashed to his backpack upside down, without a case—had plowed into the ice like an axe, stopping him just short of certain death. The guitar still played, too.

—*Backpacker* Magazine (October 2006)

Selection D   World History Textbook

Pattern: _____

Three hundred years later, a new power, the kingdom of Chimor, with its capital at Chan Chan, at the mouth of the Moche River, emerged in the area. Built almost entirely of adobe, Chan Chan housed an estimated thirty thousand residents in an area of over 12 square miles that included a number of palace compounds surrounded by walls nearly 30 feet high. One compound contained an intricate labyrinth that wound its way progressively inward until it ended in a central chamber, probably occupied by the ruler.

Like the Moche before them, the people of Chimor relied on irrigation to funnel the water from the river into their fields. An elaborate system of canals brought the water through hundreds of miles of hilly terrain to the fields near the coast.

—Duiker/Spielvogel, *World History,* 5th Edition

Examples: What Are Examples of This General Idea?

Examples give the specific, down-to-earth details that help readers understand the general statements a writer is making. For example, if you tell a friend that you had a fabulous Caribbean vacation, you might use as examples the warm sun, which was always shining; the food, all freshly caught fish and local fruits and vegetables; the snorkeling, where you met a new romantic interest; and your hotel, which was right on the beach. Examples help make general statements come alive.

Reading Strategy for Examples

As you read, create a mental list of examples the author is providing.

> General statement
>> Example
>> Example
>> Example

An Example Paragraph   Health Textbook

Using the reading strategy for examples, read the paragraph. Then go back and read the highlighted words and the annotations that explain their function in the example pattern. More explanation follows the paragraph.

Stress on Campus

General idea that examples will support

Signal words such as *For example* may introduce examples

You've probably heard that these are the best years of your life, but being a student—full-time or part-time, in your teens, early twenties, or later in life—can be extremely stressful. For example, you may feel pressure to perform well to qualify for a good job or graduate

Examples

school. To meet steep tuition payments, you may have to juggle part-time work and coursework. You may feel stressed about choosing a major, getting along with a difficult roommate, passing a particularly hard course, or living up to your parents' and teachers' expectations. If you're an older student, you may have children, housework, and homework to balance. Your days may seem so busy and your life so full that you worry about coming apart at the seams. One thing is for certain: you're not alone.

—Adapted from Hales, *An Invitation to Health*, 12th Edition

General idea. This first sentence offers the general statement that the rest of the passage will support; in other words, this is the topic sentence. The last part of the sentence leads into the examples: being a student can be extremely stressful.

The examples. The author lists seven different examples of how students may feel stressed. Some sentences describe a single example; one of them describes four different stressors.

Signal words for examples and lists. In example paragraphs, examples are often given in a list: here is one example, here is the second example, and here is the third example. In this paragraph, the repeated use of the word *may* is an indication that each sentence is performing a similar function. Transitions are sometimes used to let the reader know an example is coming.

Signal Words (Transitions) for Examples

- for instance,
- to illustrate,
- namely,
- for example,

Notice that example phrases are often followed by a comma.

Listing words may be used to list the examples, although they are not used in this paragraph.

Signal Words (Transitions) for Lists

- in addition, also, add to this
- first, second, third
- first, and, then

◐ Interaction 5-8. Recognizing Words That Signal Examples

In the following sentences, underline words and phrases that signal an example has just been given or will follow. (See page 231 for a list.)

1. Gender-specific interaction styles have serious implications for who is heard and who gets credit at work. For instance, a female office manager doesn't want to seem bossy or arrogant, so she spends a good deal of time soliciting coworkers' opinions before making an important decision. But her boss considers her approach indecisive and selects an assertive man for a senior job.

2. As another example, male managers tend to say "I" in situations where female managers tend to say "we"—as in "I'm hiring a new manager." The male phrasing emphasizes personal accomplishments.

3. The contrasting interaction styles illustrated previously often result in female managers not getting credit for competent performance.

4. As background to this issue, the gender roles that children learn in their families, at school, and through the mass media form the basis for their social interaction as adults. For instance, by playing team sports, boys tend to learn that social interaction is often about competition, conflict, self-sufficiency, and hierarchical relationships. Girls play with dolls and tend to learn that socialization is about maintaining cordial relationships, avoiding conflict, and resolving differences of opinion through negotiation.

5. Based on these patterns, misunderstandings between men and women are common. A stereotypical example: Harold is driving around lost. However, he refuses to ask for directions because doing so would amount to an admission of inadequacy. Meanwhile, it seems perfectly "natural" to Sybil to want to share information, so she urges Harold to ask for directions. Conflict results.

—Adapted from Brym/Lie, *Sociology*, 3rd Edition

Comparison and Contrast: How Are These the Same? How Do They Differ?

Comparisons show how two things are similar. Contrasts show how they are different. Sometimes the word *comparison* is used more generally to indicate both of these moves. Comparison and contrast are two of the most important patterns of thought that we have. The formation of words and the use of language, and therefore thought itself, depends on comparison and contrast. Comparison and contrast is the basis for several other patterns covered in this chapter. It is used to show what is and is not part of a term's definition, and it is used as a basis for organizing ideas or items into categories for classification.

Reading Strategy for Comparison and Contrast

Mentally or on paper, form two lists, one for each item being compared or contrasted. As the author gives each piece of information for an item, place it in the appropriate list.

Item 1	Item 2
A. Similarity or difference	A. Similarity or difference
B. Similarity or difference	B. Similarity or difference

A Comparison Paragraph   Government Web Site

Using the reading strategy for comparison, read the paragraph. Then go back and read the highlighted words and the annotations that explain their function in the comparison pattern. More explanation follows the paragraph.

Heart-Healthy Diets

Words that indicate sameness

Similar phrasing may be used to indicate similarity, such as *Both of these diets* and *The diets both*

Minor differences may be noted.

Heart disease is the No. 1 killer of adult Americans. To improve heart health, the U.S. Department of Health and Human Services recommends following a heart-healthy diet. Two such diets are the Heart Healthy Diet and the Therapeutic Lifestyle Changes (TLC) Diet; they are nearly identical. Both of these diets are designed to maintain healthy levels of cholesterol or reduce unhealthy levels of cholesterol. Cholesterol, a waxy substance, comes in two versions: LDL, or "bad" cholesterol, which causes arteries to narrow and become blocked; and HDL, or "good" cholesterol, which does the opposite. The diets both call for choosing foods that are low in saturated fat, which raises LDL more than any other food. The Heart Healthy Diet calls for getting only 8 to 10 percent of total daily calories from saturated fat, and the TLC, less than 7 percent. The two diets also recommend the same daily amounts of fat, dietary cholesterol, and sodium (salt): roughly 30 percent or less of total calories from fat, less than 300 milligrams (mg) of dietary cholesterol, and no more than 2400 mg of sodium. Not surprisingly, given the fact that people who are overweight have higher blood cholesterol than people who are not overweight, another similarity of the diets is that they call for eating just enough calories to achieve or maintain a healthy weight.

—Adapted from "Heart Healthy Eating," WomensHealth.gov

Words that indicate sameness. Comparison shows how things are alike, and thus writing organized in this pattern often includes words such as the following:

Signal Words (Transitions) for Comparisons

- the same, identical
- similar, similarly, a similarity
- alike, like, likewise
- both
- share
- agree
- not only . . . but also

Similar phrasing. At times, similar ideas are stated in sentences that have similar patterns. Here, look for the sentences that begin *Both of these diets, These diets both, The two diets, similarity of the diets.* The sentence patterns are not exactly the same, but they are similar enough to point out that the ideas in the sentences may be similar as well.

Minor differences may be noted. Two things are never exactly the same—think about it. If they were, would they be two things, or one? So even in a paragraph that's mainly about similarities, you will often find information about differences, too.

Interaction 5-9. Recognizing Words That Indicate Sameness

In the following sentences, underline words and phrases that indicate sameness. (Consult the list above as needed.)

1. Kluckhorn and Murray summarized personality quite well when they noted that to some extent a person's personality is like all other people's, like some other people's, and like no other people's.

2. Individual personality varies tremendously, but we also know that many people share similar personality traits.

3. Most personality scholars agree that the sources of personality are the interaction of heredity, environment, maturity, and learning.

4. We are born with a predisposition to a common set of personality traits.

5. Most scholars today support the concept of an interactive approach to personality.

—Adapted from Dumler/Skinner, *A Primer for Management,* 2nd Edition

Contrast Paragraphs   Nonfiction Book

Using the reading strategy for contrast, read the passage. Then go back and read the highlighted words and the annotations that explain their function in the contrast pattern. More explanation follows the paragraph.

Words that indicate differences

Sentence patterns that point out differences, such as the ones highlighted here and in the next paragraph

Video Games versus Traditional Games

Most video games differ from traditional games like chess or Monopoly in the way they withhold information about the underlying rules of the system. When you play chess at anything beyond a beginner's level, the rules of the game contain no ambiguity; you know exactly the moves allowed for each piece, the procedures that allow one piece to capture another. The question that confronts you sitting down at the chessboard is not: What are the rules here? The question is: What kind of strategy can I concoct that will best exploit those rules to my advantage?

In the video game world, on the other hand, the rules are rarely established in their entirety before you sit down to play. You're given a few basic instructions about how to manipulate objects or characters on the screen, and a sense of some kind of immediate objective. But many of the rules—the identity of your ultimate goal and the techniques available for reaching that goal—become apparent only through exploring the world. You literally learn by playing.

—Johnson, *Everything Bad Is Good for You*

Words that indicate differences. Contrast is a pattern that emphasizes differences, so you will often see words like these in writing that contrasts:

Signal Words (Transitions) for Contrast
- differs from, differs by, a difference
- contrasts with, in contrast, to the contrary
- on one hand . . . on the other hand
- however, although, but, while
- instead, rather

Sentence patterns that point out differences. These patterns may take obvious forms such as "On the one hand, …" and "On the other hand, …" but they may also be more subtle. Here, notice first that the first paragraph is about traditional games and the second paragraph is about video games. If you compare some of the sentences from each paragraph, you can see that Johnson used similar phrasing in order to make the differences stand out.

From first paragraph	From second paragraph
The rules of the game contain no ambiguity.	The rules are rarely established in their entirety.
You know exactly the moves allowed for each piece.	You're given a few basic instructions about how to manipulate objects.

Notice also the two sentences at the end of the first paragraph that suggest a contrast through the use of the pairing *is not . . . is.*

Interaction 5-10. Recognizing Words That Indicate Difference

In the following sentences, underline words that indicate difference. If necessary, refer to the list on page 235. Some sentences may not have any such words.

1. Harvard University professor Jeffrey Frankel points out that budget deficits rose during the administrations of Republicans Ronald Reagan (1981–1989) and George W. Bush, but fell under Bill Clinton.

2. Other observers have noted a contrast in Democratic and Republican budgets.

3. Reagan faced a Congress controlled by the Democrats; Clinton in turn faced a Republican Congress for most of his administration.

4. Reagan regularly submitted budgets larger than the ones that the Democratic Congress eventually passed, however, while Clinton's budgets were typically smaller than those approved by the Republican Congress.

5. The perception is that the Democrats still tend to favor the less well-off, while the Republicans tend to favor the prosperous.

—Adapted from Schmidt/Shelley/Bardes, *American Government
and Politics Today 2007–2008*, 13th Edition

Definition: What Does This Mean?

Definition answers the question: "What does this mean?" Definitions include the term being taught and a description of its meaning. Examples are often given to illustrate the meaning of the term. Sometimes, illustrations of what the term does *not* include are also provided.

Reading Strategy for Definition

As you read a definition, mentally slot the various parts of the definition into these categories:

General category

Specific type

Particular example

A Definition Paragraph

Mathematics Textbook

Using the reading strategy for definition, read the paragraph. Then go back and read the highlighted words and the annotations that explain their function in the definition pattern.

The Fair-Division Problem

Examples that readers can relate to

Often you must share something you want with other people. As a child, you probably shared toys, space in a room, and parents' attention. Adults might share living space, inherited property, vacation homes, and valuables from a divorce settlement. In this chapter we study the **fair-division problem,** that is, the problem of finding ways in which two or more people can fairly divide something among themselves without the aid of an outside arbitrator. By tradition, the people who are trying to share the desirable object or objects are called players.

A definition that includes a general term and then the specifics

Words that signal a definition or a term is coming, such as *that is* and *are called*

—Parks/Musser/Trimpe/Maurer/Maurer,
A Mathematical View of Our World

Examples that readers can relate to. Writers usually try to help readers understand new ideas by showing how they relate to familiar ideas. Here, the writer gives seven different examples of when the fair-division problem might come up in everyday life, for children and for adults. And although this paragraph doesn't include them, sometimes the following phrases are used to indicate that the writer is providing examples in support of a definition:

for example, for instance
to illustrate, to exemplify
as an illustration, as an example

Words that signal a definition or a term is coming. Sometimes a term is simply followed by the word *is* and the definition: *A fair-division problem **is** a problem of finding . . .* Here, the authors have given readers a clue that a definition is coming by using the phrase *that is* after the term being defined. In the next sentence, the words are called indicate that a definition has just been given and that the term being defined will follow.

Signal Words (Transitions) for Definitions

- is
- that is
- are called
- means, has come to mean
- can be understood as

A definition that includes a general term and then the specifics. The fair-division problem is called, first, a problem, which is a general term, and then is described very specifically as a certain type of problem: *a problem of finding ways in which two or more people can fairly divide something among themselves without the aid of an outside arbitrator.* If any part of the definition were not matched by the real-life scenario, for example, if an outside arbitrator were to be called in to help solve the problem, it would no longer be considered *a fair-division problem.*

⦿ Interaction 5-11. Recognizing the Words That Signal Terms, Definitions, and Examples

In the following sentences, underline words and phrases that signal a term, definition, or example. (Consult the list above as needed.)

1. A *business entity* is an individual, association, or organization that engages in economic activities and controls specific economic resources. For instance, General Motors is a business entity.

2. Three basic accounting elements exist for every business entity: assets, liabilities, and owner's equity. These elements are defined below.

3. *Assets* are items that are owned by a business and will provide future benefits. Examples include cash, merchandise, buildings, and land.

4. *Liabilities* represent something owed to another business entity. One kind of liability are formal written promises to pay suppliers or lenders specified sums of money at definite future times, known as *notes payable*.

5. *Owner's equity* is the amount by which the business assets exceed the business liabilities. An owner's personal assets, such as a house and clothing, are not considered in the business entity's accounting records.

—Adapted from Heintz/Parry, *College Accounting*, 19th Edition

Classification: What Kinds Are There?

Classification answers the question "What kinds are there?" Suppose someone asked you, "What kinds of movies do you like?" You might answer, "I like romantic comedies, psychological thrillers, and espionage movies." These are categories, or kinds, of movies. In other words, a general topic, movies, has been divided up into different types.

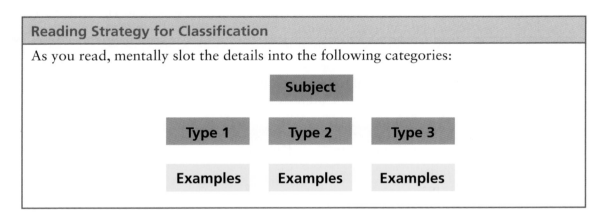

Reading Strategy for Classification

As you read, mentally slot the details into the following categories:

Subject

Type 1   Type 2   Type 3

Examples   Examples   Examples

A Classification Paragraph   Mass Media Textbook

Before you read this paragraph, survey the title and first sentence, and note the words and parts of words that are in *italics*. Then read the paragraph, using the reading strategy for classification. Finally, go back and read the highlighted words and the annotations that explain their function in the classification pattern.

Ways People Communicate

Words that indicate divisions into kinds, such as Three ways

Information on the principle behind the classification

Definitions of the types according to the principle of classification

Three ways to describe how people communicate are intrapersonal, interpersonal, and mass communications. Each form of communication involves different numbers of people in specific ways. If you are in a market and you silently debate with yourself whether to buy a package of double-chunk chocolate chip cookies, you are using what scholars call *intra*personal communication—communication within one person. To communicate with each other, people rely on their five senses—sight, hearing, touch, smell and taste. Scholars call this direct sharing of experience between two people *inter*personal communication. **Mass communication** is communication from one person or group of persons through a transmitting device (a medium) to large audiences or markets. In *Media/Impact* you will study *mass* communication.

—Biagi, *Media/Impact*, 8th Edition

Words that indicate division into kinds. The first words of this paragraph immediately tell us that it will offer classification when it says *Three* ways. Many classification paragraphs have this combination of a number and a word indicating kinds, such as the following:

Signal Words (Transitions) for Classification
- several kinds
- certain forms
- three patterns
- four types
- different groups

Other kinds of words that indicate classification are verbs that show the action of dividing up:
- divided into
- classified by
- split up

Information on the principle behind the classification. The second sentence tells us that this classification is going to be based on the number of people involved.

Definitions of the types according to the principle of classification. Often, definitions of each type are provided. Notice that these definitions are based on the principle of classification. If the intended readers already know what the types are, the writer might just give some examples instead of definitions. But in textbooks, you'll usually find definitions of each type.

Interaction 5-12. Recognizing Words That Signal Division into Kinds

Underline words in the following sentences that indicate division into kinds. Consult the list on page 240 needed.

1. Cultural anthropologists have identified three major types of marriage based on the number of spouses permitted.

2. *Monogamy,* the practice of having only one spouse at a time, is the kind of marriage one finds in the United States and Canada.

3. A second form of marriage is *polygamy*: the practice of one man having more than a single wife. Approximately 70 percent of the world's cultures prefer polygamy; however, within those cultures, only about a third of men will actually have more than one wife.

4. The third kind of marriage, which is much rarer than polygamy, is *polyandry.* Polyandry involves the marriage of a woman to two or more men at a time.

—Adapted from Ferraro, *Cultural Anthropology,* 6th Edition

Interaction 5-13. Applying Your Knowledge of Patterns

Circle the signal words in each selection. If the signal words relate to the major details, use this information to determine which paragraph pattern is being used. However, for two selections, signal words won't help much. You will also need to think about the APP of each selection (What's it **A**bout, what's the **P**oint, what's the **P**roof?).

Choose from these paragraph patterns:

examples	comparison	contrast	definition	classification

Selection A   Psychology Textbook

Pattern: _____

Prosocial behavior is any behavior that benefits another person. Cooperation—that is, working together toward a common goal—is one form of prosocial behavior. Of course, cooperation often "works" because individuals gain more than they would by not cooperating. In contrast, altruism is behavior that is driven by feelings of responsibility toward other people, such as helping and sharing, in which individuals do not benefit directly from their actions. If two youngsters pool their funds to buy a candy bar to share, this is cooperative behavior. If one youngster gives half of her lunch to a peer who forgot his own, this is altruism.

—Kail/Cavanaugh, *Human Development*, 4th Edition

Selection B   Public Speaking Textbook

Pattern: _____

The power to influence others through opposition and even anger seems quite common and almost normal. But there are other ways to influence people when you give speeches. As you've watched and listened to combative exchanges, you may have heard critics of this approach call for more civility in public exchanges. The word *civility* comes from a root word meaning "to be a member of a household." In ancient Greece, *civility* referred to displays of temperance, justice, wisdom, and courage. Over time, the definition has changed only slightly, and in public speaking, **civility** has come to mean care and concern for others, the thoughtful use of words and language, and the flexibility to see the many sides of an issue. To be civil is to listen to the ideas and reasons of others and to give "the world a chance to explain itself."

—Adapted from Griffin, *Invitation to Public Speaking*, 2nd Edition

Selection C   Health textbook

Pattern: _____

Two depressants of the central nervous system that are commonly abused are Xanax and Halcion. Prescribed for people who are experiencing anxiety, tension, panic attacks, acute stress reactions, and sleep disorders, Xanax and Halcion both have the effect of slowing brain activity, which produces a sense of calm. In the short term, using these depressants causes people to feel sleepy and uncoordinated; after a few days, the body becomes used to the effects and these feelings diminish. In the long term, these drugs may cause physical dependence and addiction.

—Adapted from Hales, *An Invitation to Health*, 12th Edition

Selection D   Biology Textbook

Pattern: _____

Most plants and animals have cells, tissues, organs, and organ systems that split up the task of survival. . . . In other words, the plant or animal body shows a division of labor. A **tissue** is a community of cells and intercellular substances that are interacting in one or more tasks. For example, wood and bone are tissues that function in structural support. An **organ** has at least two tissues that are organized in certain proportions and patterns and that perform one or more common tasks. A leaf adapted for photosynthesis and an eye that responds to light in the surroundings are examples. An **organ system** has two or more organs interacting physically, chemically, or both in the performance of one or more common tasks. A plant's shoot system, with organs of photosynthesis and reproduction, is like this. So is an animal's digestive system, which takes in food, breaks it up into bits of nutrients, absorbs the bits, and expels the unabsorbed leftovers.

—Starr/Evers/Starr, *Biology,* 2nd Edition

Selection E   Mass Media Textbook

Pattern: _____

Today's media markets are increasingly global. U.S. media companies are looking for markets overseas at the same time that overseas media companies are purchasing pieces of media industries in the United States and other countries. MTV, for example, is available 24 hours a day in St. Petersburg, Russia. In the U.S., Yahoo Inc. paid $1 billion to buy a 40 percent interest in China's biggest online commerce firm, alibaba.com. The U.S. TV network ABC and the British Broadcasting Corporation have formed a news-gathering partnership to share television and radio news coverage worldwide. This service will compete with CNN to deliver news by satellite. Jim Murai, who has been called "the father of Japan's Internet," created a non-profit network to connect all of Japan's universities to the Internet, without government approval. Ultimately, he says, he "wants to connect all the computers in this world."

—Adapted from Biagi, *Media/Impact,* 8th Edition

Transition Words and the Patterns They Signal

The following chart lists signal words that point to different patterns of organization. You may want to consult the chart when you are trying to figure out how a reading is organized.

Organizational Pattern	Some Transitions That Signal This Pattern
causes	___ causes, ___ creates, ___ leads to; because ___, is due to ___, reason is ___
classification	certain forms, different classes, x number of patterns, several types, some kinds; classified by, divided into, split up
comparisons (to show similarities)	agree, alike, both, identical, not only . . . but also, share
contrasts (to show differences)	although, but, contrasts with, differs by, differs from, however, on the one hand . . . on the other hand, rather, while
definition	are called, can be understood as, has come to mean, is, means, that is
effects	causes ___, consequences are ___, leads to ___, makes ___, ___ depends on
examples	for example, for instance, namely, to illustrate
listing	add to this, also, first, furthermore, in addition
process	first (second, third, etc.) stage, first (second, third, etc.) step, x number of phases + all time order words
space order (used to describe things)	above, behind, below, closer, farther away, here, in front of, left, near, nearby, north, right, south, there, through, under
time order (used to narrate events)	after, as soon as, before, during, first, meanwhile, next, on (a day), second, since, subsequently, until, when

Chapter Summary Activity

This chapter has discussed how preparing your mind to receive information in certain patterns and then recognizing those patterns in writing leads to better comprehension. Construct a Reading Guide below by completing each idea on the left with information from the chapter on the right. You can use this guide later as you complete other reading assignments.

Reading Guide to Patterns of Organization

Predicting Paragraph Patterns

Complete this idea	with information from the chapter.
The purpose of predicting paragraph patterns is	1.
The mental preparation that you do to predict paragraph patterns is called	2.
The way you form a schema from the topic sentence is	3.

Noticing Paragraph Patterns

For each question given, identify which paragraph pattern an author may use to answer it.

* How are these the same?	4.
* What does this mean?	5.
* How did this happen?	6.
* What does this lead to?	7.
* What steps need to occur, and in what order?	8.
*What kinds are there?	9.
* How do these differ?	10.
* What made this happen?	11.

For each set of signal words, decide which pattern of organization an author may be using.

several kinds, four types, divided into, dividing up	12.
during that time, before, during, after, since, meantime	13.

alike, agree, similarity, share, in common	14. _____
___ creates, ___ allows for, are due to ___, reason is ___	15. _____
is, means, that is, can be understood as	16. _____
first step, the next stage, last, meanwhile, during	17. _____
to the contrary, differs from, however, although, but	18. _____
consequences are ___, ___were the effects, leads to ___, ___ depends on	19. _____
behind, below, near, in front of, inside	20. _____

Test Taking Tips
Examining Questions about Patterns of Organization

On reading tests, understanding how patterns of organization reveal the relationship between two or more ideas may be useful in several different contexts. You might need to understand the pattern in order to figure out the meaning of a vocabulary word in context, to answer a reading comprehension question, or to answer a question specifically about the organizational pattern. The relationship of ideas you need to uncover may occur within a sentence, between sentences, or between paragraphs. (Note that throughout this text you can practice answering questions about patterns in the "Relationships" questions after each reading at the ends of chapters, such as those on pages 254.)

Here are two practice items that show you the kinds of questions you can expect to see on the reading sections of some major reading tests such as the ACCUPLACER and COMPASS, which are both given nationally; the College Level Academic Skills Test (CLAST) in Florida; and the Texas Higher Education Assessment (THEA). Notice that the multiple-choice answers are not always stated using the same terms we have used to describe each pattern.

⬤ **Sample Test Questions**

1. Two sentences are followed by a question or statement. Read the sentences, and then choose the best answer to the question or the best completion of the statement.

> Although there is much legitimate cultural variation in the routines that parents establish for their children, certain routines are so advantageous for all children that parents everywhere would be wise to follow them.
>
> Breakfast for school-age children is critical to their academic performance.
>
> —Damon, *The Youth Charter*

What does the second sentence do?
  A. It repeats the idea in the the first sentence.
  B. It offers an exception to the information given in the first sentence.
  C. It cancels the meaning of the first.
  D. It provides an example of the first sentence.

You can see that the first sentence is about how parents would be wise to do certain things for their children's advantage. The second sentence then talks about how feeding children breakfast helps them in school. Helping your children do well in school (sentence 2) is a specific example of the more general idea of giving children an advantage (sentence 1). Feeding them breakfast (sentence 2) is a specific example of "certain routines" (sentence 1). So answer D is correct.

Try this: For an answer you think may be correct, think about what signal word you could try out in the second sentence as a test. To test answer D, you could insert the words "For example" at the beginning of the second sentence. Do the two sentences still make sense? Yes.

Be sure to focus on the relationship that the question is about—here, it's the relationship between the two sentences. Even though the first sentence begins with the signal word *although*, the relationship it reveals is within the first sentence only. So it does not directly affect the relationship you should focus on.

2. How are these sentences related?

> Games are more organized than play, usually with formal, or at least agreed-upon rules, with some goal and usually some scoring mechanism. As a result, games tend to be competitive, with winners and losers.
>
> —Norman, *Emotional Design*

  A. They state a cause and an effect.
  B. They present a problem and a solution.
  C. They contradict one another.
  D. They compare two forms of activity.

This item is easier than item 1 because signal words appear in the sentences. The signal words that show the relationship between the sentences are *as a result.* So the second sentence is a result or an effect of the first sentence. That means the first sentence must be the cause.

Use your logic to double-check the possible answer. Does it make sense that because games have rules, goals, and scoring, they are competitions with winners and losers? Yes. So the answer is A.

● **Common Pattern Of Organization Stems**

You have just seen two ways that relationship questions may be worded on reading tests. Here are some others. When you see items on reading tests that use the following language, your task is to figure out the relationship between the ideas presented.

✔ How are the two passages related?
✔ Which statement below best describes the organizational method used in this passage?
✔ How is the information in this paragraph organized?
✔ What does the second sentence do?

Reading 5-1. . . . . **Nonfiction Book**

● Pre-Reading the Selection

The following selection is taken from a book called *The Wal-Mart Effect*, by Charles Fishman. Fishman is a senior editor for the business magazine *Fast Company*, and he wrote many articles about Wal-Mart for the magazine that he later turned into *The Wal-Mart Effect*.

Guessing the Purpose

Based on the title of the book and the information about the author, do you suppose the book's purpose is to entertain, inform, persuade, or a combination of these purposes?

_____

Surveying the Reading

Survey the title and the first sentence of each paragraph, reading quickly. What is the general topic of the reading selection? _____

_____

_____

Predicting the Content

Predict three things this selection will discuss.

- _____

- _____

- _____

Activating Your Knowledge

What experiences with Wal-Mart have you had? What have you seen on TV or read about Wal-Mart? What do you know about factory conditions around the world? List two or three things you know.

- _____

- _____

- _____

Common Knowledge

global economy (*paragraph 1*) Businesses manufacturing (making) and selling their goods and services around the world, that is, not being limited to any one country

sweatshop (*paragraph 3*) A place of work where employees work long hours for little money under poor working conditions (for example, in a place without windows, or in a smoky room)

developing country (*paragraph 4*) A country with a relatively low standard of living and not much industrial development

Reading with Pen in Hand

Now read the selection. As you read, mark any ideas that seem important, and respond to the questions and vocabulary items in the margin. Monitor your comprehension by putting a ✔ next to a paragraph when you understand most of it. Place an ✘ next to a paragraph when you don't understand most of it.

Visit www.cengage.com/devenglish/doleconnect and select Chapter 5 to hear vocabulary words for this selection and view a video about this topic.

Reading Journal

◆ Where do you assume these factories are? Why?

◆ What is Sethi saying about Wal-Mart?

a world long gone What two words could you substitute for this phrase? Hint: Contrast this with the opening of the next sentence.

◆ What can't we do anymore that we could do before?

◆ What is meant by "the view is unsettling"?

allegations Based on the example that follows, what does this word mean?

◆ Why did the two women come to the United States in fall 2004?

Dark Bargains of the Global Economy

Charles Fishman

1 One of the dark bargains of the global economy is that while the familiar stuff, like clothes, toys, and food, continues to arrive at the local Wal-Mart without interruption, and often with prices steadily dropping, the way that stuff is made is less and less familiar, more and more remote, and perhaps less and less acceptable, all the time. The factories themselves would be illegal in the United States because of the way those factories treat their workers and their communities; but the products of those factories are perfectly legal; indeed, the very unappealing manner in which they are produced makes them cheaper all the time, and so more appealing all the time.

2 "Because of the pressure of cost," says S. Prakash Sethi, an expert on global factory conditions, "factories do everything possible to save on the third decimal of a penny. Wal-Mart is one of the primary, if not the most important, engines that pushes those costs down."

3 In a world long gone, we could step onto the fishing wharf, we could step into the dress shop, we could stop at the roadside vegetable stand and have some sense, however modest, of the conditions under which the food and products we bought were created. Today we rely on the laws, and on the companies themselves, sometimes to our disappointment and disgust. Nike, the Gap, Reebok, Disney, and Wal-Mart have all had to face, explain, and recover from sweatshop problems in the last twenty years.

4 And every time the door of a factory in a developing country that makes stuff for Americans is cracked open, the view inside is unsettling. The prices suddenly make sense, and not in a reassuring way. Both Kathie Lee Gifford and Wal-Mart denied the allegations that a Honduran factory using children was making clothing for the Kathie Lee Gifford line. The denials were both true and a lie. By the time of the congressional hearing, the clothes were no longer being made by children. But they had been.

5 In the fall of 2004, two women from Bangladesh spent a month touring college campuses, talking about their experiences working in clothing factories in Dhaka, the capital of Bangladesh. They were brought to the United States by a labor rights group, the National Labor Committee (NLC), which works to uncover and publicize inhumane factory conditions around the world. It was the NLC's

executive director, Charles Kernaghan, who told Congress about the child labor that had been making Kathie Lee Gifford clothing. The two factory workers from Bangladesh spoke no English; their translator for the tour was an NLC staffer who came over with the women from the NLC's Dhaka office. The details of the women's lives as Bangladeshi garment workers—lives they described over and over again, at Yale, at Harvard, at the University of Iowa, at the University of Wisconsin—are like something not just from around the world, but from a different century.

6   As a sixteen-year-old junior sewing operator at the Western Dresses factory in Dhaka, Robina Akther's job was to sew pocket flaps on the back pockets of pants that Western Dresses was making for Wal-Mart. She says she earned 13 cents an hour—fourteen hours of work a day, $26.98 a month. If she didn't sew to the **mandated** pace, 120 pairs of pants an hour, here is what Akther said would happen: A supervisor would slap her across the face with the pants she was sewing. "If you made any mistakes or fell behind on your goal, they beat you," says Akther's translated account, which is posted on the NLC's Web site. "They slapped you and lashed you hard on the face with the pants. This happens very often. They hit you hard. It is no joke."

> **mandated** Based on the detail that follows, what does this word mean?
>
> ◆Are the rewards and demands of Akther's job well balanced? Why or why not?

7   If what Akther says is true—Wal-Mart did not challenge the account as it was published in college newspapers, nor have they challenged the account that is posted on the NLC's Web site—then it is possible that Wal-Mart's customers were buying pants off the display racks that might literally have been used to beat the people who made them. Who is wearing those pants now?

> ◆Does the writer imply (suggest) here that Akther is telling the truth? If so, how?

8   As Akther describes it, life in the Western Dress factory was an **unending** series of days making clothes, starting before 8:00 A.M., lasting until 10:00 P.M. or 11:00 P.M., seven days a week. Ten days off in a year—not even one a month. No talking at the sewing tables, no drinking water at the sewing tables. No going to the bathroom except at the moment when permission is given, and then, "the bathrooms are filthy with no toilet paper or soap."

> **unending** Based on its use here, what does the prefix *un-* mean?
>
> ◆What one word would you use to describe the work conditions related here?

9   Despite the **relentless** work, Akther told college audiences, "I clean my teeth with my finger, using ash. I can't afford a toothbrush or toothpaste." Do Americans need clothing to be so inexpensive that the people making it cannot afford a toothbrush?

> **relentless** Based on the details in paragraph 8, what does this word mean?
>
> ◆How would you answer the last question here? Why?

10   At the wages she described—typical for garment workers in Bangladesh—if Robina Akther were to have worked for fifty years as she did for those twenty months at the Western Dresses factory, if she

◆What conclusion does the writer want us to come to by providing these sets of numbers?

alleging What word earlier in the reading passage relates to this word? What part of speech is each word?

◆What is the new forum mentioned in the first sentence of paragraph 11?

◆What are the workers who are suing Wal-Mart trying to achieve?

systematic The suffix *–ic* makes nouns into adjectives. What noun is part of this word?

Based on this noun, what does *systematic* mean?

could have survived fifty years, her total wages for the half century would have been $16,200. Wal-Mart's profit in 2004—profit, not sales—is $19,597 per minute.

11   Robina Akther's account now appears in a new forum: In September 2005, she sued Wal-Mart in court in the United States, **alleging** that in a factory making clothing for Wal-Mart, she was not even provided with the basic wages, overtime pay, and protection from physical abuse that Bangladeshi law provides. Actually, in the lawsuit, Akther is identified only as Jane Doe II—she is anonymous, along with fourteen other workers from five countries who are plaintiffs against Wal-Mart. The fifteen factory workers—from China, Indonesia, Swaziland, and Nicaragua, as well as Bangladesh—all make or made merchandise for Wal-Mart, and all have nearly identical claims of sweatshop mistreatment. In the suit, Jane Doe II—Robina Akther—is arguing that Wal-Mart didn't just have a contract to buy clothes from the Western Dresses factory; Wal-Mart had a contract with her and her fellow factory workers, and that their **systematic** mistreatment is Wal-Mart's responsibility. Not Wal-Mart's ethical responsibility, Wal-Mart's legal responsibility. It is possible that Robina Akther is going to reach out from Dhaka and turn the Wal-Mart effect on its head.

● Comprehension Questions

Write the letter of the answer on the line. Then explain your thinking.

Main Idea

_____   1. Which of the following statements best describes the main idea of this passage?

    a. Foreign factories should operate the way U.S. factories do.

    b. The low prices of goods in stores such as Wal-Mart are only possible because of the low wages and poor working conditions of factory workers around the world.

    c. Robina Akther worked for 13 cents an hour, fourteen hours a day, and in a month's time, all she made was $26.98.

    d. Fifteen factory workers are suing Wal-Mart in U.S. courts for the mistreatment of workers in factories in China, Indonesia, Swaziland, and Nicaragua.

WHY? What information in the selection leads you to give that answer? _____

_____

_____

_____ 2. What is the main idea of paragraph 4?

   a. Clothing for the Kathie Lee Gifford line was made by children in Honduras.

   b. Kathie Lee Gifford and Wal-Mart lied about the use of child labor.

   c. Child labor stopped once investigations by Congress began.

   d. Prices in the United States depend on what happens inside factories in developing countries.

WHY? What information in the selection leads you to give that answer? _____

_____

_____

Supporting Details

_____ 3. The main idea of paragraph 6 is stated in the last sentence of paragraph 5. What are the major supporting details in paragraph 6?

   a. Akther earned 13 cents an hour; she worked fourteen hours a day; she had to sew 120 pairs of pants an hour; if she didn't reach that goal, she got beaten.

   b. The two women spent a month touring college campuses; Akther earned 13 cents an hour; Akther's job was to sew pocket flaps on pants.

   c. Akther's remarks had to be translated by an NLC staff member; Charles Kernaghan told Congress about children making Kathie Lee Gifford clothing; the women seemed to be working in a different century.

   d. Akther worked at the Western Dresses factory in Dhaka; her job was to sew pocket flaps on the back pocket of pants being made for Wal-Mart; she made $26.98 a month.

WHY? What information in the selection leads you to give that answer? _____

_____

_____

_____ 4. Where does the information about Kathie Lee Gifford in paragraph 4 fit into the APPS of a MAPPS structure?

    a. A: what the reading selection is about

    b. P: the author's point about the subject

    c. P: proof that supports the author's point

    d. S: summarize the reading

WHY? What information in the selection leads you to give that answer? _____

_____

_____

_____

Relationships

_____ 5. In paragraph 3, what is the relationship between the first two sentences?

    a. The two sentences offer a contrast.

    b. The second sentence is an example of the first sentence.

    c. The two sentences are in a cause-and-effect relationship.

    d. The first sentence is a major detail and the second sentence is a minor detail.

WHY? What information in the selection leads you to give that answer? _____

_____

_____ 6. What pattern of organization provides structure for the supporting details in paragraph 5?

    a. Narration

    b. Comparison

    c. Classification

    d. Cause-and-effect

WHY? What information in the selection leads you to give that answer? _____

_____

_____

Author's Purpose

____ 7. What is one possible reason Fishman includes paragraph 7?

   a. To give an example of his main point that Wal-Mart didn't challenge Akther's account

   b. To make readers feel emotionally involved

   c. To cast doubt on Akther's story

   d. To laugh at the person who is wearing the pants now

WHY? What information in the selection leads you to give that answer? _____

_____

____ 8. What is one way the author makes sure that we feel, not just think about, the role of sweatshops in the global economy?

   a. He describes the National Labor Committee's work.

   b. He contrasts the way things used to be with the way they are now.

   c. He recounts Robina Akther's experiences in a sweatshop.

   d. He gives the facts about the factory workers suing Wal-Mart.

WHY? What information in the selection leads you to give that answer? _____

_____

_____

Fact, Opinion, and Inference

____ 9. In paragraph 6, Akther's wages are said to be 13 cents an hour. Given that she works for fourteen hours a day and in a typical month has only one day off, how much money should she be making in a month?

   a. $26.98

   b. $73.25

   c. $12.33

   d. $54.60

WHY? What leads you to give that answer? _____

_____

_____ 10. In paragraph 11 the author notes that workers from several developing countries are suing Wal-Mart in U.S. court for the "systematic mistreatment" they have suffered. What does their action imply (suggest without stating outright)?

a. Wal-Mart cannot be held responsible for the actions of another company.

b. They hope to leave their jobs once they collect the financial settlements they want the court to award them.

c. They believe a U.S. court has the right to rule on what happens in other countries.

d. Wal-Mart should win because their contracts are with the companies who own those factories, not with the workers at the factories.

WHY? What information in the selection leads you to give that answer? _____

_____

_____

● Critical Thinking Questions

CRITICAL THINKING LEVEL 1 REMEMBER

Recount (tell) the details of the conditions of the factory in which Robina Akther worked.

_____   _____

_____   _____

_____   _____

_____   _____

_____   _____

CRITICAL THINKING LEVEL 2 UNDERSTAND

Four kinds of organizations in the United States are mentioned in this reading selection as having an interest in the dark bargain of the global economy. Name them, and _identify_ their interests in the chart that follows.

U.S. Organizations and Their Interests

Group 1: _____	Their interests: _____
Group 2: _____	Their interests: _____

Group 3:	Their interests:
Group 4:	Their interests:

CRITICAL THINKING LEVEL 3 APPLY

Fishman mentions in paragraph 4 that Honduran children were making Kathie Lee Gifford clothing to be sold at Wal-Mart. An article that the *New York Times* published about that case noted that in the Honduran factory, Global Fashions, "15-year-old girls earn 31 cents an hour and work 75-hour weeks." Do those pieces of information indicate that Global Fashions is a sweatshop? *Examine* each fact in the quotation and discuss how it relates to sweatshop conditions, as you understand them.

What Constitutes Sweatshop Conditions?

Fact	A sweatshop condition? Why or why not?
15-year-old girls	
earn 31 cents an hour	
work 75-hour weeks	

CRITICAL THINKING LEVEL 4 ANALYZE

Consider a product that you use every day. Name the product: _____

1. Look on the label. Where was it made? _____

2. Is this a developing country? If you don't know, go online to **www.worldbank.org** and

    a. Select "Data and Research."

    b. Select "Country Classification."

    c. Select the link in the text for View All Groups.

3. If you found out that the people making this product were paid less than the U. S. minimum wage, would you still use the product? Why or why not? _____

_____

4. If they were paid so little they themselves couldn't afford to buy the same product, would you still use it? Why or why not? _____

_____

5. If they were paid so little they couldn't feed their children well, would you still use it? Why or why not? _____

_____

CRITICAL THINKING LEVEL 5 EVALUATE

Fishman uses Robina Akther's story to show readers the working conditions in sweatshops. He gives other bits of evidence that sweatshops exist, which are listed in the left column below. Some kinds of evidence can be considered stronger than other kinds. Which piece of evidence most strongly supports the idea that sweatshops exist? Give the strongest piece of evidence an A, the second strongest a B, and the third strongest a C. Then explain your ratings. Why is one piece of evidence more convincing than another?

Evidence That Sweatshops Exist

Evidence that sweatshops exist (with paragraph number)	Rating (A, B, and C) and explanation of rating
Nike, the Gap, Reebok, Disney, Wal-Mart have all faced sweatshop problems in the last 20 years. (para. 3)	
Kathie Lee Gifford example (para. 4)	
Factory workers from China, Indonesia, Swaziland, and Nicaragua involved in the suit against Wal-Mart (para. 11)	

CRITICAL THINKING LEVEL 6 CREATE

Suppose you were on a committee set up to monitor sweatshop conditions in factories around the world. With a group of classmates, *develop* a method that could be used by inspectors sent in to monitor the factories. Think about how an inspector going into a factory could find out about the workers' pay, hours, and working conditions, without putting workers in danger, and perhaps without the cooperation of the factory owners or managers.

● Vocabulary in Context

The following words were used in "Dark Bargains of the Global Economy." Choose the best word to complete each sentence below.

| a world long ago | mandated | systematically | allegations | unending |

1. Amid _____ that the chief of police was involved in a burglary ring, he was caught trying to remove a kilo of cocaine from the evidence room.

2. The court _____ that he stay in the county while his bank records were searched.

3. Then a seemingly _____ series of discoveries came to light.

4. The chief and five other senior officers had been _____ shaking down local drug dealers in exchange for letting them operate in the city.

5. It reminded a newspaper reporter of another police scandal two decades earlier, which by now seems from _____.

Reading 5-2. . . . . **Sociology Textbook**

● Pre-Reading the Selection

The following selection is taken from a college sociology textbook. It's from a chapter called "Globalization, Inequality, and Development."

Guessing the Purpose

Based on the title of the chapter and the type of book it's from, do you suppose the reading selection's purpose is to entertain, inform, persuade, or a combination of these purposes? _____

Surveying the Reading

Survey the reading. What is the general topic? _____

_____

Predicting the Content

Predict three things this selection will discuss.

- _____

- _____

- _____

Activating Your Knowledge

Think about what you know about any of the following topics: globalization, including what causes it or contributes to it; transnational corporations; and the size and influence of the U.S. economy. List two or three things you know.

- _____

- _____

- _____

- _____

Common Knowledge

Globalization (*paragraph 1*) The process by which formerly separate economies, states, and cultures are being tied together and people are becoming increasingly aware of their growing interdependence

GDP (*Figure 5.1*): Abbreviation for "gross domestic product," which is the total market value of all the goods and services produced within a country during a particular period of time

Reading with Pen in Hand

Now read the selection. As you read, mark any ideas that seem important, and respond to the questions and vocabulary items in the margin. Monitor your comprehension by putting a ✔ next to a paragraph when you understand most of it. Place an ✘ next to a paragraph when you don't understand most of it.

Visit www.cengage.com/devenglish/doleconnect and select Chapter 5 to hear vocabulary words from this selection and view a video about this topic.

The Sources of Globalization

Robert J. Brym and John Lie

1   Few people doubt the impact of globalization. Although social scientists disagree on its exact causes, most of them stress the importance of technology, politics, and economics.

Technology

2   Technological progress has made it possible to move objects and information over long distances quickly and inexpensively. The introduction of commercial jets radically shortened the time necessary for international travel and the cost of such travel dropped dramatically after the 1950s. Similarly, various means of communication, such as telephone, fax, and e-mail, allow us to reach people around the globe inexpensively and almost instantly. Whether we think of international trade or international travel, technological progress is an important part of the story of globalization. Without modern technology, it is hard to imagine how globalization would be possible.

Politics

3   Globalization could not occur without advanced technology, but advanced technology by itself could never bring globalization about. Think of the contrast between North Korea and South Korea. Both countries are about the same distance from the United States. You have probably heard of major South Korean companies like Hyundai and Samsung and may have met people from South Korea or their descendants, Korean Americans. Yet, unless you are an expert on North Korea, you will have had no contact with North Korea and its people. We have the same technological means to reach the two Koreas. Yet, although we enjoy strong relations and intense interaction with South Korea, we lack ties to North Korea. The reason is political. The South Korean government has been a close ally of the United States since the Korean War in the early 1950s and has sought greater political, economic, and cultural integration with the outside world. North Korea, in an effort to preserve its authoritarian political system and socialist economic system, has remained isolated from the rest of the world. As this example shows, politics is important in determining the level of globalization.

Reading Journal

◆What pattern of organization do you predict the author will use?

◆What has technology made possible?

◆How does politics impact globalization?

ally Reread the two sentences before this one. What does *ally* mean?

authoritarian What root does this word begin with?

Guess at the meaning of *authoritarian*.

◆What is an important
cause of globalization?

capitalism What root do you find
at the beginning of this word?

Look in a dictionary for the meaning
of *capitalism*.

◆What pattern does the
author use to describe
transnational corpora-
tions?

autonomous Look at the phrase
in the previous sentence *work with
or under national governments.*
Contrast this with *autonomous from
national governments.* What does
autonomous mean?

◆What is the point of the
example used in this paragraph and the next?

Economics

4   Finally, economics is an important source of globalization. As we saw in our discussion of global commodity chains and the new international division of labor, industrial **capitalism** is always seeking new markets, higher profits, and lower labor costs. Put differently, capitalist competition has been a major spur to international integration (Gilpin, 2001; Stopford and Strange, 1991).

5   Transnational corporations—also called multinational or international corporations—are the most important agents of globalization in the world today. They are different from traditional corporations in five ways (Gilpin, 2001; LaFeber, 1999):

1. Traditional corporations rely on domestic labor and domestic production. Transnational corporations depend increasingly on foreign labor and foreign production.
2. Traditional corporations extract natural resources or manufacture industrial goods. Transnational corporations increasingly emphasize skills and advances in design, technology, and management.
3. Traditional corporations sell to domestic markets. Transnational corporations depend increasingly on world markets.
4. Traditional corporations rely on established marketing and sales outlets. Transnational corporations depend increasingly on massive advertising campaigns.
5. Traditional corporations work with or under national governments. Transnational corporations are increasingly autonomous from national governments.

6   Technological, political, and economic factors do not work independently in leading to globalization. For example, governments often promote economic competition to help transnational corporations win global markets. Consider Philip Morris, the company that makes Marlboro cigarettes (Barnet and Cavanagh, 1994). Philip Morris introduced the Marlboro brand in 1954. It soon became the country's best-selling cigarette, partly because of the success of an advertising campaign featuring the Marlboro Man. The Marlboro Man symbolized the rugged individualism of the American frontier, and he became one of the most widely recognized icons in American advertising. Philip Morris was the smallest of the country's six largest tobacco companies in 1954, but it rode on the popularity of the Marlboro Man to become the country's biggest tobacco company by the 1970s.

© John Van Hasselt/CORBIS SYGMA

"I want to emphasize that the embassy and the various U.S. government agencies in Washington will keep the interests of Philip Morris and the other American cigarette manufacturers in the forefront of our daily concerns" [Commercial counselor, U.S. embassy, Seoul, South Korea, in a 1986 memo to the public affairs manager of Philip Morris Asia].

◆Why is this photograph used in the selection?

7   In the 1970s, the antismoking campaign began to have an impact, leading to slumping domestic sales. Philip Morris and other tobacco companies decided to pursue globalization as a way out of the **doldrums.** Economic competition and slick advertising alone did not win global markets for American cigarette makers, however. The tobacco companies needed political influence to make cigarettes one of the country's biggest and most profitable exports. To that end, the U.S. trade representative in the Reagan administration, Clayton Yeutter, worked energetically to dismantle trade barriers in Japan, Taiwan, South Korea, and other countries. He threatened legal action for breaking international trade law and said the United States would restrict Asian exports unless these countries allowed the sale of American cigarettes. Such actions were critically important in globalizing world trade in cigarettes. As the commercial counselor at the U.S. Embassy in Seoul, South Korea, wrote to the public affairs manager of Philip Morris Asia in a 1986 memo: "I want to emphasize that the embassy and the various U.S. government agencies in Washington will keep the interests of Philip Morris and the other American cigarette manufacturers in the forefront of our daily concerns" (quoted in Frankel, 1996). As the case of Philip Morris illustrates, then, economics and politics typically work hand in hand to globalize the world.

doldrums Based on the meaning of the whole sentence, does *doldrums* mean "a period of brisk activity" or "a period of stagnation"?

Figure 5.1 The Size and Influence of the U.S. Economy, 2000
This map will help you gauge the enormous importance of the United States in globalization because it emphasizes just how large the U.S. economy is. The economy of each U.S. state is as big as that of a whole country. Specifically, this map shows how the GDP of various countries compares to that of each state. For example, the GDP of California is equal to that of France, the GDP of New Jersey is equal to that of Russia, and the GDP of Texas is equal to that of Canada.

John Van Hasselt/Corbis Sygma. Reprinted with permission from the *The Globe and Mail*. "The United States of the World," *Globe and Mail*, March 8, 2003, p. Fl.

◆Find your state. What country has the same size of economy?

● Comprehension Questions

Write the letter of the answer on the line. Then explain your thinking.

Main Idea

_____ 1. Which of the following statements best describes the main idea of this passage?

a. Three main sources of globalization are technology, politics, and economics.

b. Of the three main sources of globalization, technology is clearly the most important one.

c. There are five major differences between traditional and transnational corporations.

d. The United States has an enormous economy.

WHY? What information in the selection leads you to give that answer? _____

_____

_____

_____ 2. Which sentence states the main idea of paragraph 3?

  a. The first sentence

  b. The last sentence

  c. Sentence 3

  d. Sentence 2

WHY? What information in the selection leads you to give that answer? _____

_____

_____

Supporting Details

_____ 3. What examples are given in paragraph 2 to support the main idea?

  a. Objects, information, commercial jets, international travel

  b. Travel, time, inexpensively, instantly

  c. Information, telephone, fax, e-mail

  d. Commercial jets, telephone, fax, e-mail

WHY? What information in the selection leads you to give that answer? _____

_____

_____

_____ 4. Where does the information about transnational corporations in paragraph 5 fit into the APPS of the MAPPS structure for the reading as a whole?

  a. A: what the paragraph is about

  b. P: the author's point about the subject

  c. P: proof that supports the author's point

  d. S: summarize the reading

WHY? What information in the selection leads you to give that answer? _____

_____

_____

Relationships

_____ 5. In paragraph 3, how is the major supporting information organized?
   a. Effects
   b. Comparisons
   c. Processes
   d. Contrasts

WHY? What information in the selection leads you to give that answer? _____

_____

_____

_____ 6. What pattern of organization provides structure for the supporting details in paragraph 7?
   a. Cause-and-effect
   b. Narration
   c. Comparison
   d. Classification

WHY? What information in the selection leads you to give that answer? _____

_____

_____

Author's Purpose

_____ 7. Why do the authors use one paragraph to discuss technology, one paragraph to discuss politics, and then two paragraphs to discuss economics?
   a. Technology is the least important source of globalization.
   b. The authors want the discussion of politics to stay focused.
   c. Economics is the most important factor in globalization.
   d. None of the above.

WHY? What information in the selection leads you to give that answer? _____

_____

_____

____ 8. What is one possible reason the authors chose the tobacco company example of globalization?

   a. To show that globalization can be beneficial

   b. To show that globalization can be harmful

   c. To express their admiration for the power of the United States

   d. To express their surprise that the American government would uphold a company's profits over people's health

WHY? What information in the selection leads you to give that answer? _____

_____

_____

Fact, Opinion, and Inference

____ 9. Which of the following statements is an accurate portrayal of facts shown in Figure 5-1?

   a. New York and the Netherlands have the same number of people.

   b. The economies of Washington and Turkey are linked.

   c. Canada and Texas have economies that are dissimilar in size.

   d. Indiana has the same size economy as Denmark.

WHY? What information in the selection leads you to give that answer? _____

_____

_____

____ 10. Which of the following states an opinion?

   a. South Korea and North Korea are the same distance from the United States.

   b. Marlboros were the best-selling cigarette in America for a time.

   c. North Korea should open its borders to trade with the United States.

   d. Social scientists disagree on the exact causes of globalization.

WHY? What information in the selection leads you to give that answer? _____

_____

_____

● Critical Thinking Questions

Recall and list the comparisons between the U.S. relationships with North and South Korea that the authors discuss.

U.S. Relationships with North and South Korea

North Korea	South Korea
Similarity:	
Similarity:	
Difference:	Difference:
Difference:	Difference:
Difference:	Difference:

Give an example of a transnational corporation. How do you know it's a transnational? _____

_____

_____

_____

_____

Using your vocabulary knowledge, divide the word *globalization* into its root and suffix. _____ What does the root mean? _____ What does its suffix mean? (Use a dictionary as needed.) _____

CRITICAL THINKING LEVEL 4 ANALYZE

Use the APP of MAPPS to outline the selection. The **p**roof should consist of all the topic sentences of the paragraphs. Remember that they may appear anywhere in the paragraph.

About: _____

   Point: _____

_____

     Proof (para. 2): _____

     Proof (para. 3): _____

     Proof (para. 4): _____
     Proof (para. 5): _____

_____

     Proof (para. 6): _____

_____

     Proof (para. 7): _____

_____

CRITICAL THINKING LEVEL 5 EVALUATE

Research to *evaluate* the accuracy of Figure 5.1 beyond the year 2000.

1. Use the information online at **http://www.StateMaster.com** to check the most recent Gross State Product for your state. What is your state's GSP (similar to the GDP for countries)? _____

   Look at the "Sources" section and note the most likely year this data was gathered:

   _____

2. Then check it against the GDP for the country that Figure 5.1 says is the same as that for your state by going to the CIA World Factbook online at **https://www.cia. gov/library/publications/the-world-factbook/index.html**. Select your country and scroll

down to the "Economy" section to find the GDP. What does the Factbook list as the GDP of the country? _____

What year was this data gathered or estimated? _____

3. Were you able to confirm the accuracy of Figure 5.1 as it pertains to your state? Why or why not? _____

_____

CRITICAL THINKING LEVEL 6 CREATE

With a small group, a partner, or on your own, *plan* or actually *design* a presentation for a small group of thirteen-year-olds based on *one* of the paragraphs in this selection. Your purpose is to convey the information given in the paragraph. Consider the knowledge that you can expect thirteen-year-olds to have already, and consider how to make the information interesting to them. If you are to plan the presentation, use a comic strip format to detail step by step how you would give each kind of information—for example, one square might say "show photo of jet and discuss how jets make the world smaller." If you are to actually design the presentation, then find visuals, newsclips, audio files, graphs, and so on, and create your own text for the presentation. You do not need to give the information in the same order as it was given in the paragraph.

Vocabulary in Context

The following words (or forms of them) were used in "The Sources of Globalization." Choose the best word to complete each sentence below.

ally	authoritarian	autonomous	capitalist	doldrums

1. By 1991 the formerly monolithic Soviet Union had split into 15 _____ countries, including Russia.

2. Unlike its _____ enemy the United States, the Soviet Union had been a socialist state.

3. Today, Russia's _____ Kremlin has taken power into its own hands once again.

4. Once in the economic _____, Russia now boasts 60 billionaires among its citizens, according to *Forbes* magazine.

5. Russian president Vladimir Putin's 2007 trip to Iran led some Iranians to call Russia its _____, but the *New York Post* preferred the term "frenemies."

© Ismael Montero Verdu/Shutterstock

chapter 6

Identifying Implied Main Ideas

66 *Write the bad things that are done to you in sand, but write the good things that happen to you on a piece of marble.* 99

—Arabic saying

Explain what idea or principle this quotation implies (suggests without saying). Noticing the pattern of organization may help you come to a conclusion. Do you think this advice is good? Why or why not?

Share Your Prior Knowledge

Share one of your favorite memories—something you have written on a piece of marble—with the class or a classmate. Also, if you want to, share a memory that you have written in sand—that is, if you can remember it!

Survey the Chapter

Take two minutes to skim Reading 6-2, "The Global Epidemic," on pages 306–311 and see what the global epidemic is. See how much prior knowledge you have about this topic. Then keep this knowledge in mind as you start the Prep Reading.

www.cengage.com/devenglish/doleconnect

Videos Related to Readings

Vocab Words on Audio

Prep Readings on Demand

Prep Reading . . . . Newspaper Article

Do you choose what you eat and how much of it you consume? Read the following article from the *New York Times* and find out.

Visit **www.cengage.com/devenglish/doleconnect** and select Chapter 6 to hear a reading of this selection and view a video about this topic.

Seduced by Snacks? No, Not You

Kim Severson

1   People almost always think they are too smart for Prof. Brian Wansink's quirky experiments in the psychology of overindulgence. When it comes to the slippery issues of snacking and portion control, no one thinks he or she is the schmo who digs deep into the snack bowl without thinking, or orders dessert just because a restaurant plays a certain kind of music. "To a person, people will swear they aren't influenced by the size of a package or how much variety there is on a buffet or the fancy name on a can of beans, but they are," Dr. Wansink said. "Every time."

2   He has the data to prove it. Dr. Wansink, who holds a doctorate in marketing from Stanford University and directs the Cornell University Food and Brand Lab, probably knows more about why we put things in our mouths than anybody else. His experiments

© AP Photo/David Duprey

examine the cues that make us eat the way we do. The size of an ice cream scoop, the way something is packaged and whom we sit next to all influence how much we eat. His research doesn't pave a clear path out of the obesity **epidemic**, but it does show the significant effect one's eating environment has on slow and steady weight gain.

3   Dr. Wansink's research on how package size accelerates **consumption** led, in a roundabout way, to the popular 100-calorie bags of versions of Wheat Thins and Oreos, which are promoted for weight management. Although food companies have long used packaging and marketing techniques to get people to buy more food, Dr. Wansink predicts companies will increasingly use some of his research to help people eat less or eat better, even if it means not selling as much food. He reasons that companies will make up the difference by charging more for new packaging that might slow down consumption or that put seemingly healthful twists on existing brands. And they get to wear a halo for appearing to do their part to prevent obesity.

4   To his mind, the 65 percent of Americans who are overweight or obese got that way, in part, because they didn't realize how much they were eating. "We don't have any idea what the normal amount to eat is, so we look around for clues or signals," Wansink said. "When all you see is that big portions of food cost less than small ones, it can be confusing." Although people think they make 15 food decisions a day on average, his research shows the number is well over 200. Some are obvious, some are **subtle**. The bigger the plate, the larger the spoon, the deeper the bag, the more we eat. But sometimes we decide how much to eat based on how much the person next to us is eating, sometimes moderating our intake by more than 20 percent up or down to match our dining companion.

5   Much of Wansink's work is outlined in the book *Mindless Eating: Why We Eat More Than We Think* (Bantam). The most fascinating material is directly from his studies on university campuses and in test kitchens for institutions like the United States Army.

6   An **appalling** example of our mindless approach to eating involved an experiment with tubs of five-day-old popcorn. Moviegoers in a Chicago suburb were given free stale popcorn, some in medium-size buckets, some in large buckets. What was left in the buckets was weighed at the end of the movie. The people with larger buckets ate 53 percent more than people with smaller buckets. And people didn't eat the popcorn because they liked it, he said. They were driven by hidden persuaders: the distraction of the movie, the sound of other

---

epidemic Use your prior knowledge. What do you know about obesity in the United States? See if you can connect your prior knowledge to the word *epidemic*.

consumption Use the context. To what did Wansink's research lead? So what does *consumption* mean?

subtle Look for an antonym clue and an example clue.

appalling Read the rest of the paragraph, which offers an example of *appalling*.

people eating popcorn and the Pavlovian popcorn trigger that is activated when we step into a movie theater.

devised This word is a verb; what did Wansink and his students do?

7   Dr. Wansink is particularly proud of his bottomless soup bowl, which he and some undergraduates devised with insulated tubing, plastic dinnerware, and a pot of hot tomato soup rigged to keep the bowl about half full. The idea was to test which would make people stop eating: visual cues, or a feeling of fullness. People using normal soup bowls ate about nine ounces. The typical bottomless soup bowl diner ate 15 ounces. Some of those ate more than a quart, and didn't stop until the 20-minute experiment was over. When asked to estimate how many calories they had consumed, both groups thought they had eaten about the same amount, and 113 fewer calories on average than they actually had.

8   In *Mindless Eating,* Dr. Wansink outlines an eating plan based on simple awareness. Employ a few tricks and you can take in 100 to 300 fewer calories a day. At the end of a year you could be 10 to 30 pounds lighter. For example, sit next to the person you think will be the slowest eater when you go to a restaurant, and be the last one to start eating. Plate high-calorie foods in the kitchen but serve vegetables family style. Never eat directly from a package. Wrap tempting food in foil so you don't see it. At a buffet put only two items on your plate at a time.

9   "Will being more mindful about how we eat make everyone 100 pounds lighter next year?" he said. "No, but it might make them 10 pounds lighter." And the best part, he promises, is that you won't even notice.

🌑 Interaction 6-1. Talking about Reading

Respond in writing to the questions below and then discuss your answers with your classmates.

1. Do you think you are "influenced by the size of a package or how much variety there is on a buffet or the fancy name on a can of beans?" Why or why not? _____

_____

_____

2. Do you ever eat when you're not hungry just because you are with a friend who is eating? Do you ever eat more or less based on whom you are eating with? _____

   _____

   _____

3. Have you ever used any of the tricks that Wansink describes in paragraph 8? Do you have any similar tricks of your own? Explain. _____

   _____

   _____

4. What does Wansink imply (suggest without actually saying) when he says in paragraph 3 "companies will make up the difference by new packaging . . . that put[s] seemingly healthful twists on existing brands. And they get to wear a halo for appearing to do their part to prevent obesity"? What words in this excerpt are clues to his meaning? _____

   _____

What Is an Implied Main Idea?

Many paragraphs and longer passages have a stated main idea; the author tells readers directly what the point is. This is especially true in certain genres, or kinds, of writing. For example, in college textbooks, the main idea is usually stated. However, even in textbooks authors don't always state the point. Sometimes the main idea is only implied. In the genre of narrative writing, the main idea is frequently implied by which events the author has chosen to recount.

An implied main idea is not stated directly; rather, it is suggested. To suggest the main idea, the author carefully selects which details to share. Readers then infer the main idea from the details. In a sense, it becomes your job to create a topic sentence. Another way to say this is that you summarize the details of the passage in one sentence in order to draw a conclusion about the author's meaning.

Cartoons are a good beginning point for figuring out implied main ideas since cartoonists rarely state their ideas directly. Instead, they expect viewers to look at the details and supply the main idea themselves. The following cartoon is from the Cornell University Food and Brand Lab, where Brian Wansink, whom you read about in the Prep Reading, is the director. What details do you notice? What is the implied main idea of the cartoon?

Illustration by Brian Wansink, Ph.D., author of *Mindless Eating: Why We Eat More than We Think* (Bantam, 2006). Used by permission of Dr. Brian Wansink.

One important detail of the cartoon is the words the two men are exchanging. The first man asks "Aren't you through yet?" Notice that the second man does not respond by saying, "I'm still hungry." He says instead that the popcorn isn't gone yet. What does that imply about why he is eating?

The relative size of the men's buckets seems to be another important detail. The title at the bottom, "Beware of Big Buckets," also seems prominent. The implied main idea of the cartoon seems to be something like "When popcorn comes in a bigger bucket, people will eat more of it." Or "Give people larger servings to make them eat more."

Interaction 6-2. Identifying the Implied Main Idea of Cartoons

Notice the important details of the following cartoons. What is the implied main idea?

1. Cartoon by Roz Chast (*The New Yorker*)

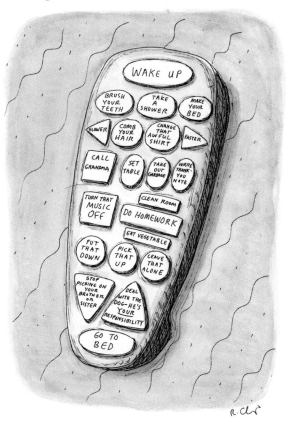

Important details: _____

_____

Implied main idea: _____

_____

2. Cartoon by Daryl Cagle (caglepost.com)

Important details: _____

_____

Implied main idea: _____

_____

Making Generalizations

When you start with details and then make an umbrella statement about them, you are making a generalization. Working with the cartoon "Beware of Big Buckets," we casually stated that the implied main idea was about "people" eating more food. Since there is only one person in the cartoon who is eating more, it's a bit of a leap to say it's about people in general. However, since we have also read "Seduced by Snacks? No, Not You" we have more information to go on than just the cartoon itself.

When it comes to the reading you're doing in college, you'll need to be careful about the size of the generalization you infer from the details. In fact, a typical problem when trying to formulate an implied main idea about reading materials is making a statement that is too broad for the details shared by the author, or too narrow. The generalization you make needs to be the right size. It should fit the details as closely as possible.

Interaction 6-3. Generalizing from Details

On the line, write a generalization about each set of details by naming the smallest category into which all the details fit.

1. keyboard, mouse, CPU, monitor _____

2. *Survivor, The Bachelor, House Arrest* _____

3. Netflix, Apple, Blockbuster _____

4. Erie, Ontario, Superior _____

5. Ghana, Nigeria, Cameroon, Guinea _____

6. Gisele Bundchen, Kate Moss, Tyra Banks _____

7. tongue, eyes, nose, chin, cheeks _____

8. maples, sumacs, birches, oaks _____

9. Porsche Spyder, BMW Z4, Mercedes-Benz McLaren _____

10. *The Sorcerer's Stone, The Chamber of Secrets, The Prisoner of Azkaban* _____

Understanding the Breadth of Information

One way to visualize information is by how broad or narrow it is—that is, how many other pieces of information it encompasses. In fact, back in Chapter 4 that is how we talked about the topic, main idea, and supporting details.

You can see from **Figure 6.1** that the topic takes the largest area. That's because it is the most general idea. Within the broader topic, the main idea is the area that the

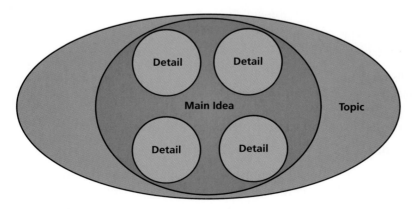

Figure 6.1 Different Breadths of Information.
The broadest information is the most general.

author has staked out as the idea he or she wishes to discuss. Finally, the main idea is broader than the specific supporting details. All the details are more specific than the main idea. They are all part of the main idea's territory.

When you are trying to formulate a main idea (or an entire topic sentence or thesis statement), you need to pay close attention to how broad or narrow your statement is. Take this set of details as an example.

- Managers can be insensitive to others, or even intimidating.
- They may betray their employees' trust.
- Managers may be unable to delegate or build a team.
- Managers may be unable to think strategically.

—Williams, *Management*, 4th Edition

What is the topic of these details? Managers. What point is the author trying to make about managers? In other words, what do all these details have in common? Would the following sentence make the point well?

Managers may not be able to manage people well.

No. While this sentence does fit the first three details, it can't be the point because it doesn't take into account the fourth detail about strategic thinking. The sentence is too narrow. A diagram of the ideas would look like **Figure 6.2.**

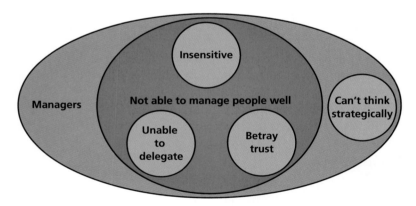

Figure 6.2 A Main Idea That Is Too Narrow.
The main idea is not general enough. It doesn't encompass all the details.

Would this next sentence make a good topic sentence for the details?

Managers are incompetent.

No. This statement goes well beyond the details, which suggest only that managers *may* have certain difficulties. This statement has three problems: (1) having difficulty doesn't make a person incompetent; (2) in the details, the words *can be* and *may* don't imply that something always *is;* and (3) in the statement, the use of the word *managers* implies the idea of all: *all managers.* Clearly, that idea is not supported by these details. It is too broad. (See **Figure 6.3.**)

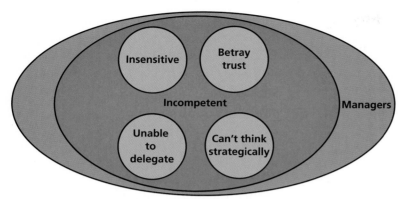

Figure 6.3 A Main Idea That Is Too Broad.
The main idea is not specific enough. It encompasses far more territory than the details suggest. Put another way, the author would have to supply far more evidence to support this topic sentence adequately.

Let's try a third time to identify a topic sentence. Is this one effective?

Managers sometimes make mistakes.

Yes, this statement is more accurate than the previous two tries. Because it uses the word *sometimes,* it takes into account the fact that each detail says *can be* or *may.* Because it focuses on actions—*mistakes*—it is more accurate than the sentence that called managers *incompetent.* If you check each detail against the statement, you will see that it takes each one into account. (See **Figure 6.4.**)

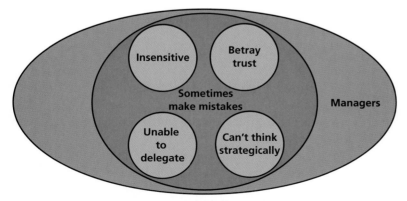

Figure 6.4 A Main Idea That Is the Right Size.
The topic sentence covers the right amount of territory to include the supporting details.

Don't lose sight of the need for the topic sentence to be more general than the details themselves, but less general than the topic. The generalization you make needs to cover the right amount of territory.

Interaction 6-4. Deciding Whether a Topic Sentence Covers the Right Amount of Information

For each set of details, choose the topic sentence that covers the right amount of information by putting a C for "correct" on the line. For each other possible topic sentence, put a B beside statements that are too broad, and an N beside statements that are too narrow. For sentences that are too broad or too narrow, underline the part of the sentence that makes them unworkable.

1. • Roman Catholic Christians go to Rome and Lourdes.
    • Jewish pilgrims go to Jerusalem.
    • Muslims travel to Mecca.
    • Such places have religious significance.
    • They might be the birthplace of a prophet, the final resting place of a saint, or the site of a miracle.

_____ A. People from various religions make pilgrimages to different holy places.

_____ B. Religious fanatics make pilgrimages to different holy places.

_____ C. The world seems to be traveling to the places those of its religions consider holy.

2. • Some people use the Internet to find a particular fact for a specific reason.
    • Others perform transactions, such as buying, selling, or trading.
    • Some users spend their time online talking with others at social networking sites.
    • And at times, people go online in order to learn something new.

_____ A. People use the Internet to gather information.

_____ B. There is nothing a person can do in real life that he or she can't also do online.

_____ C. Some of the things people used to get done by talking with others in person can now be accomplished online.

3. • In prehistoric America, in what is now central Illinois, natives built a city or town now known as Cahokia.
    • Cahokians built a huge mound of earth now called Monk's Mound, each side of which aligns with the directions of north, south, east, and west.
    • The North Plaza of Cahokia has a mound on each side that also lines up with north, south, east, and west.

- Seven mounds line up north-south with the west edge of Monk's Mound.
- Eight mounds align with the east edge.
- Nine mounds are on an east-west line across the site and line up with Monk's Mound.

—Chappell, *Cahokia: Mirror of the Cosmos*

____ A. Cahokia was a prehistoric city in what is now central Illinois.

____ B. Cahokia's mounds are oriented to the four directions and to one another.

____ C. Prehistoric American cities included systems of mounds aligned with the cardinal directions.

4.
- When pain messages are sent from damaged tissue through the nervous system, they pass through several "gates," starting in the spinal cord, before they get to the brain.
- But these messages travel only if the brain gives them "permission," after determining they are important enough to be let through.
- If permission is granted, a gate will open and increase the feeling of pain by allowing certain neurons to turn on and transmit their signals.
- The brain can also close a gate and block the pain signal by releasing endorphins, the narcotics made by the brain to quell pain.

—Doigne, *The Brain That Changes Itself*

____ A. The nervous system controls the passage of pain and pleasure to the brain through a series of "gates."

____ B. When a person experiences tissue damage to their hands or feet, they only feel pain if the brain decides the damage is extensive enough.

____ C. The "gate control theory of pain" proposed a series of controls, or "gates," between the site of injury and the brain.

5.
- If a person drinks quickly, the alcohol will have a more significant effect on him or her than if the same amount was taken in over a longer period of time.
- How much a person drinks matters.
- Food in the stomach slows the rate at which alcohol is absorbed, and so decreases the effects of the alcohol.
- The more the drinker weighs, the less the same amount of alcohol will affect him or her.

_____ A. The amount and the timing of drinks, as well as the condition of the drinker, help determine how alcohol will affect the drinker.

_____ B. The way a person drinks determines how drunk he or she will get.

_____ C. A wide array of factors determines how alcohol will affect a drinker.

When you are trying to decide what main idea the author is implying, be sure to consider whether your idea is too broad or too narrow by checking it against each detail. If you find that it is, decide which part of the sentence is the problem and make that part either more general or more specific. Adjust it until it fits the details.

Using MAPPS to Identify the Implied Main Idea

Recall from Chapter 4 that MAPPS is a visual outline to help you organize and understand what you are reading.

A Quick Review of MAPPS

Mark: Mark the answers to the questions you ask while reading.

   About: What is the reading about? = Topic

         Point: What is the point of the reading? = Main Idea

               Proof: What is the proof? = Major Supporting Detail

Summary: Synthesize the About (topic), Point (main idea), and Proof (major supporting detail)

Following is the APP of MAPPS that includes only the supporting details of a paragraph from a business management textbook. In other words, there is no topic sentence. Read the details and see if you can figure out the following.

- The topic: What is the paragraph about? To figure out what the topic is, look for repeated ideas.

- The main idea: What is the author's point about the topic? To determine the author's main idea, two helpful questions to ask yourself are:

  1. What do all these details have in common?
  2. What pattern of organization is used to organize the details? To create a topic sentence, remember that T + MI = TS. That is, put the topic and the main idea together in one sentence to create a topic sentence.

About (topic): _____

    Point (main idea): _____

        Proof (supporting details):

        1. Background questions: Interviewers ask applicants about their work experience and education.

        2. Job-knowledge questions: Interviewers ask applicants to demonstrate job knowledge.

        3. Situational questions: Interviewers ask applicants how they would respond in a hypothetical situation.

        4. Behavioral questions: Interviewers ask applicants what they did in previous jobs that were similar to the job for which they are applying.

           —Adapted from Williams, *Management*, 4th Edition

Combine the topic and the main idea. (Remember that T + MI = TS.) What would make a good topic sentence for a paragraph with this APP?

_____

_____

Interaction 6-5. Identifying Implied Main Ideas from Lists of Details

Read each set of supporting details. Then put the topic and main idea into the APP. Finally, write a topic sentence for the details.

    1. About: _____

       Point: _____

          Proof: 1. In the United States, we show our agreement by nodding.

               2. In Ethiopia, the same message is sent by throwing the head back.

               3. The Semang of Malaya sharply thrust the head forward.

               4. The Dyaks of Borneo raise the eyebrows.

                 —Adapted from Ferraro, *Cultural Anthropology*, 6th Edition

    Topic sentence: _____

2. About: _____

   Point: _____

      Proof: 1. Spending for health care is estimated to account for about 15 percent of the total U.S. economy.

           2. In 1965, about 6 percent of our income was spent on health care.

           3. That percentage has been increasing ever since.

           4. Measured by the percentage of the gross domestic product devoted to health care, America spends almost twice as much as Australia or Canada.

                —Adapted from Schmidt/Shelley/Bardes, *American Government and Politics Today 2007-2008*, 13th Edition

Topic sentence: _____

3. About: _____

   Point: _____

      Proof: 1. Children in the primary grades learn about their country mostly in patriotic ways: They learn about the Pilgrims, the flag, and some of the presidents.

           2. Later, in the middle grades, children learn more historical facts and come to understand the structure of the government.

           3. By high school, students have a more complex understanding of the political system, may identify with a political party, and may take positions on issues.

                —Adapted from Schmidt/Shelley/Bardes, *American Government and Politics Today 2007-2008*, 13th Edition

Topic sentence: _____

_____

4. About: _____

     Point: _____

          Proof: 1. First, because of the widespread use of Spanish on signs in cities like Los Angeles and Miami, many people assume that Latinos do not speak English or have no desire to learn it.

2. But the rate of learning English for Latinos is about the same as for other immigrant groups.

3. Second, Latinos are sometimes viewed (wrongly) as not fully participating in the economy.

4. However, Mexicans and Central Americans have a labor force participation rate of 62 percent, which exceeds the Anglo rate.

5. Third, many mainstream Americans view recent immigrants as "short-timers" who are interested only in making enough money to return home.

6. But when asked in a national survey if they planned to stay permanently in the United States, more than 90 percent of the legal immigrants said yes.

—Adapted from Ferraro, *Cultural Anthropology,* 6th Edition

Topic sentence: _____

Applying the Strategy to Paragraphs

You can add a step to this same process to identify the implied main ideas of paragraphs. You will need to find the details after you find the topic.

1. Find the topic by looking for repeated ideas.

2. Search the paragraph for the details. Often, these will be specific facts, reasons, and examples. You may find it helpful to put parentheses ( ) around the major supporting details or to number them.

3. Figure out the main idea by asking what all the details have in common and what the pattern of organization is. You can review the list of **box on "Patterns of Support"** on page 217 to help you remember the patterns.

◉ Interaction 6-6. Identifying the Implied Main Ideas of Paragraphs

Put parentheses around (or number) each major supporting detail. For each paragraph, write a topic sentence that fits the details.

Paragraph 1   Literature Textbook

In ancient China and Japan, poetry was prized above all else. One story tells of a samurai warrior who, when defeated, asked for a pen and paper. Thinking that he wanted to write a will before being executed, his captor granted his wish. Instead of writing a will, however, the warrior wrote a farewell poem that so moved his captor that he immediately released him. To the ancient Greeks and Romans, poetry was the medium of spiritual and philosophical expression. Today, throughout the world, poetry continues to delight and inspire.

—Kirszner/Mandell, *Literature*, 6th Edition

Topic: _____

Main idea: _____

Topic sentence: _____

Paragraph 2   Nonfiction Book

The largest redwoods, which are called redwood giants or redwood titans, are usually not the very tallest ones. In this way, they are rather like people. A football player is often bigger than a basketball player—more massive, that is. The basketball player is taller and more slender. So it is with redwoods. The tallest redwoods are often slender, and so they aren't the largest ones. Even so, most massive redwoods (the redwood titans) are among the world's tallest trees anyway, and are more than thirty stories tall. Today, almost no trees of any species, anywhere, reach more than three hundred feet tall, except for redwoods. The main trunk of a redwood titan can be as much as thirty feet in diameter near its base.

—Preston, *Wild Trees*

Topic: _____

Main idea: _____

Topic sentence: _____

Paragraph 3   World History Textbook

It is a very frequent thing at Mr. Marshall's [at Shrewsbury] where the least children were employed (for there were plenty working at six years of age,) for Mr. Horseman to start the mill earlier in the morning than he formerly did; and provided a child should be drowsy, the overlooker walks around the room with a stick in his hand, and he touches that child on the shoulder, and says, "Come here." In a corner of the room there is an iron cistern; it is filled with water; he takes the boy, and takes him up by the legs, and dips him over the head in the cistern, and sends him to work for the remainder of the day . . . sometimes they would tap them over the head, or nip them over the nose, or give them a pinch of snuff, or throw water in their faces, or pull them off where they were, and job them about to keep them waking.

—Duiker/Spielvogel, *World History,* 5th Edition

Topic (hint: you will need to supply your own term for the repeated idea): _____

_____

Main idea: _____

Topic sentence: _____

_____

Applying the Strategy to Longer Passages

To identify the implied main idea of a longer passage, use the same strategy. Just keep in mind that when you are making a generalization that will be broad enough to cover several paragraphs or more, the major supporting details you are looking for will be the topic sentences of the individual paragraphs. And the generalization that covers several paragraphs is not called a topic sentence; instead, it's called a *thesis statement.*

Interaction 6-7. Identifying the Implied Main Idea of a Longer Passage

Identify the topic of the passage and its main idea. Then write a thesis statement.

Rather than pay cash for large purchases such as houses and cars, most people borrow part of the purchase price and then repay the loan on some scheduled basis. Spreading payments over time makes big-ticket items more affordable, and consumers get the use of an expensive asset right away. Most people consider the cost of such borrowing a small price to pay for the immediate satisfaction they get from owning the house, car, or whatever it happens to be. In their minds, at least, the benefits of current consumption outweigh the interest costs on the loan. Unfortunately, while the initial euphoria of the purchase may wear off over time, the loan payments remain—perhaps for many more years to come.

Some borrow to meet a financial emergency. For example, people may need to borrow to cover living expenses during a period of unemployment, or to purchase plane tickets to visit a sick relative.

Others borrow for convenience. Merchants as well as banks offer a variety of charge accounts and credit cards that allow consumers to charge just about anything—from gas and oil or clothes and stereos to doctor and dental bills and even college tuition. Further, in many places—restaurants, for instance—using a credit card is far easier than writing a check. Although such transactions usually incur no interest (at least initially), these credit card purchases are still a form of borrowing, because payment is not made at the time of the transaction.

Finally, others borrow for investment purposes. It's relatively easy for an investor to partially finance the purchase of many different kinds of investment vehicles with borrowed funds. In fact, margin loans, as they're called, amounted to nearly $220 billion in late 2005—a tidy sum, but down substantially from the $280 billion reached when the stock market peaked in March 2000.

—Gitman/Joehnk, *Personal Financial Planning,* 11th Edition

Topic: _____

Main idea: _____

Topic sentence: _____

_____

Interaction 6-8. Identifying the Implied Main Idea of a Longer Passage

Identify the topic of the passage and its main idea. Then write a thesis statement.

Leaders begin with the question, "What should we be doing?" while managers start with "How can we do what we're already doing better?" Leaders focus on vision, mission, goals, and objectives, while managers focus on productivity and efficiency. Managers see themselves as preservers of the status quo, while leaders see themselves as promoters of change and challengers of the status quo in that they encourage creativity and risk taking. One of the reasons for Dell, Inc.'s long-term success and profitability is that founder and chairman Michael Dell never accepts the status quo. He fervently believes that everything the company does can be changed and improved. Says Dell, "Celebrate for a nanosecond. Then move on."

Another difference is that managers have a relatively short-term perspective, while leaders take a long-term view. When Dell opened its first factory in Asia, Michael Dell congratulated the plant manager by sending him one of his old running shoes to stress that opening that plant was just the first step in the company's strategy of opening manufacturing plants in that part of the world. Managers are also more concerned with means, how to get things done, while leaders are more concerned with ends, what gets done. Managers are concerned with control and limiting the choices of others, while leaders are more concerned with expanding people's choices and options. Finally, managers solve problems so that others can do their work, while leaders inspire and motivate others to find their own solutions.

—Williams, *Management,* 4th Edition

Topic: _____

Main idea: _____

Topic sentence: _____

● Interaction 6-9. Identifying the Implied Main Idea of a Longer Passage

Identify the topic of the passage and its main idea. Then write a thesis statement.

Subsistence agriculture, in which each family produces enough food to feed itself, accounts for more than half of tropical rainforest loss. Subsistence farmers often practice slash-and-burn agriculture in which they first cut down the forest and allow it to dry, then burn the area and immediately plant crops. The yield from the first crop is often quite high, because the minerals that were in the trees are available in the soil after the trees are burned. However, soil productivity declines rapidly so the subsequent crops are poor. In a very short time, the people farming the land must move to new forest and repeat the process.

More than 20 percent of tropical deforestation is the result of commercial logging. Vast tracts of tropical trees are being removed for export abroad, including to the United States. Most tropical countries are allowing commercial logging to proceed at a much higher rate than is sustainable.

More than 10 percent of destruction of rain forests occurs to provide open rangeland for cattle. Much of the beef raised on ranches cleared from forests is exported to fast-food chains. After the forests are cleared, cattle can be grazed on the land for 6 to 10 years, after which time shrubby plants, known as scrub savanna, take over the range.

—Berg, *Introductory Botany*

Topic: _____

Main idea: _____

Topic sentence: _____

Chapter Summary Activity

This chapter has discussed how to find the implied main idea of paragraphs and longer passages. Construct a Reading Guide here by completing each idea on the left with information from the chapter on the right. You can use this guide later if you need to figure out an implied main idea.

Reading Guide to Implied Main Ideas

Complete this idea	with information from the chapter.
The difference between a stated main idea and an implied main idea is that	1.
The clues for figuring out the implied main idea of a cartoon are	2. 3.
When you make an umbrella statement about the details, you are making a	4.
To make sure that general statements are the right size to fit the supporting details, the general statement should be	5.
If you are supplying a topic sentence for a group of details, make sure it is _____ than the supporting details.	6.
However, it should be _____ than the topic.	7.
To make sure it's the right size, you should check your topic sentence against	8.
The parts of MAPPS that you use to help you figure out the implied main idea are	9.
To find what the details are about (the topic), you	10.
To figure out what point the author is making about the topic (that is, the implied main idea), you can ask two questions, which are	11. 12.
You can locate the supporting details in a paragraph by looking for	13.
When you are figuring out the implied main idea of a longer passage, the major supporting details you are looking for will be the	14.
Thus, the implied main idea of a longer passage will not be called a topic sentence but a	15.

Test Taking Tips 293

Test Taking Tips
Implied Main Ideas

Figuring out an implied main idea involves using your higher-level critical thinking skills. You use **analysis** to distinguish the topic and select the major details. Then you **evaluate** the topic and details to determine what main idea could cover the details at the right level of generality, while remaining more specific than the topic. Finally, in order to state the main idea that the author implied, you must **create** a sentence that fits those specifications.

On reading tests, you may be choosing from a multiple-choice list of possible main ideas, but it would still be smart to create a sentence of your own first and then see which multiple-choice answer matches it best. The same process we have recommended throughout the chapter can be used on a reading test:

1. Look for the topic of the passage by noticing repeated words, phrases, and ideas.

2. Find the details. Pay attention to how they are organized (the pattern of organization).

3. Think about what all the details have in common and then create a sentence around this idea. See if one of the answers closely matches the answer you came up with.

Here is a sample implied main idea question. Instead of choosing among multiple-choice answers, however, write out a sentence of your own that is the implied main idea.

Read the following passage adapted from an anthropology textbook. Then write a statement that accurately expresses its main idea.

The Ju / 'hoansi are a people of the Kalahari Desert in South Africa. Their equivalent of "retirement" comes somewhere around the age of 60, which is many years beyond their average life expectancy. Elderly people, while they will usually do some foraging for themselves, are not expected to contribute much food. However, older men and women alike play an essential role in spiritual matters. Freed from food taboos and other restrictions that apply to younger adults, they may handle ritual substances considered dangerous to those still involved with hunting or having children. By virtue of their old age, they have recollections of things that happened far in the past. Thus, they are repositories of accumulated wisdom—the "libraries" of a nonliterature people—and are able to suggest solutions to problems younger adults have never before had to face.

—Haviland/Prins/Walruth/McBride, *The Essence of Anthropology*

Topic: _____

Major Details: 1. _____

            2. _____

Statement of Main Idea: _____

_____

Now compare your statement to each of the following statements. Which statement is the best expression of the main idea?

A. Elderly Ju / 'hoansi people are given additional responsibilities as they age.
B. Elderly Ju / 'hoansi people are far from being unproductive members of society.
C. It is only when a Ju / 'hoansi person has reached the age of 60 that his or her spiritual life begins.
D. Unlike in American society, older people among the Ju / 'hoansi are highly valued.

Answer A? The word "additional" implies that older people are given more responsibilities—not different ones. The paragraph specifically stated that they are no longer responsible for providing much food. So this answer is incorrect.

Answer B? The way this sentence is expressed is a bit tricky. It says they are "far from being unproductive." That means they are productive. Answer B is correct.

Answer C? The paragraph doesn't say that their spiritual life is just beginning. In fact, it implies the opposite when it says that younger people can't handle certain ritual substances. Answer C is incorrect.

Answer D? The first part of this sentence goes too far beyond what the author has stated in the paragraph. While it may be true, the author never mentions another culture. Therefore, this answer is incorrect.

Common Implied Main Idea Questions

Here are some forms that implied main idea questions can take on reading tests:

✔ Which of the following does the author imply?
✔ This passage indicates that:
✔ Which of the following can be concluded from the passage?
✔ What implication can be drawn from paragraph 1?
✔ What can you infer from this reading?

Reading 6-1 . . . . Web Article

● Pre-Reading the Selection

This reading comes from MSN.com's Health and Fitness section. Think about the portions you eat on a daily basis as you read through this passage.

Guessing the Purpose

Judging from the title of the reading, what do you suppose is the author's purpose? __

_____

Surveying the Reading

Survey the title of the selection and the first sentence of each paragraph. What is the general topic of the reading selection? _____

_____

Predicting the Content

Predict three things this selection will discuss.

- _____

- _____

- _____

Activating Your Knowledge

Share what you know about correct portion sizes. For example, how much meat, vegetables, or bread should a person eat at dinner? If you are not sure of the correct amount, then just share what you typically eat for dinner. _____

_____

Common Knowledge

"Clean Plate Club" (*paragraph 3*) National campaigns started during wartimes to encourage schoolchildren to eat all the food on their plates in order to conserve limited resources. Parents even now still sometimes demand that children eat all they are served.

Reading with Pen in Hand

Now read the selection. As you read, mark any ideas that seem important, and respond to the questions and vocabulary items in the margin. Monitor your comprehension by putting a ✔ next to a paragraph when you understand most of it. Place an ✘ next to a paragraph when you don't understand most of it.

Visit www.cengage.com/devenglish/doleconnect and select Chapter 6 to hear vocabulary words from this selection and view a video about this topic.

◆ *Reading Journal*

accustomed Look at the cause-and-effect relationship between the first and last part of the sentence to guess the meaning of this word.

◆Which sentence states the conclusion that Brian Wansink reached?

◆What did the research from Cornell University and Penn State show?

phenomenon Use your prior knowledge to think about what this word might mean.

◆What does the author say about our ability to recognize portion sizes?

◆What are "units" and what is deceiving about them?

Portion Control: Change Your Thinking or Your Plate?

Karen Collins

1   According to experts, we have become so accustomed to over-sized portions of food and extra-large serving dishes that we can no longer tell how much we are overeating. We may have more success at reducing our excessive portions by reducing the size of our food packages and serving pieces than by trying to figure out a healthy portion size. That's essentially the conclusion Cornell University professor Brian Wansink reaches in a recent analysis published in the Journal of the American Dietetic Association on the problem of Americans' extra-large portions.

2   Research from Cornell University and Penn State has repeatedly shown that the larger the amount of food we are faced with—whether on our plates or in serving bowls—the more we will eat. We might not eat everything, but we still eat more than if we started with less. This has been demonstrated in single meals, such as comparing the amount eaten of different size sub sandwiches, and in totals over a period of several days.

3   For many people, eating more when presented with large amounts of food may be tied to the "Clean Plate Club" phenomenon. We have been taught to view not eating all we are given as wasteful. However, researchers suggest that we may often be unable to even recognize extra-large portions. Studies show that when an equal amount of food is presented on a relatively large and small plate, we see the large plate as having less food than the smaller plate, which seems more full.

4   Studies also show that we tend to eat in "units." If we buy a package of six cookies or crackers, we usually eat them all rather than leaving part of a package. If a "unit" or package of candy, French fries or soft drinks gets larger, we are more likely to eat the whole container

anyway. And food units in the United States—packages in stores and portions in restaurants—have grown **dramatically** in the last 20 years. For example, a bottle of soda 20 years ago was 6.5 ounces and had 85 calories; today's soda comes in 20 ounce bottles that can contain about 250 calories. Along with calorie consumption, extra large portions can significantly increase the amount of fat and sodium we get.

dramatically Use the example clue in the following sentence to decide what *dramatically* means.

Portion Size Management

5   One way to improve your portion size management is to learn to better judge the amount of food in front of you. Studies have shown that if people practice measuring out different portion sizes, their accuracy can improve. The American Institute for Cancer Research and the United States Department of Agriculture have both developed educational materials to help people learn to recognize serving sizes by comparing food amounts to common objects. For example, three ounces of meat, poultry or fish look like a deck of cards or a checkbook. A half-cup of pasta or rice looks like a tennis ball or a cupped handful.

◆What suggestion is given for recognizing correct portion sizes?

6   Because of how our **perception** of portion size changes depending on the size and shape of the container, Wansink argues that we should pay more attention to our packages, plates, and serving bowls. Market research shows that single-serving packages are booming in popularity, which may be one step in this direction. Look around your kitchen at the different size plates, bowls and glasses you have available. Instead of serving ice cream in two- or three-cup cereal bowls, make half- or one-cup custard cups the official ice cream bowl. With 200 calories per cup in even many healthful cereal choices, our tendency to simply fill a bowl and then eat it all could turn that bowl of cereal into a higher-calorie breakfast than you realize if you use large bowls. You don't have to get rid of those big bowls; large portion sizes are one way to increase the amount of nutrients we get. If you want people to eat more salad, they will do so automatically with bigger salad bowls.

perception Look at the cause-and-effect relationship in this sentence to guess what *perception* means.

◆What suggestion is given for using the dishes you have?

7   Finally, Wansink's research shows that the more food we have on hand, the more we will eat. So ignore the "common sense" of grocery store marketing **urging** you to buy two packages of cookies or chips for the price of one; you may just eat twice as much. If you find it's easier or less expensive to buy large quantities of snack foods (such as nuts or trail mix), you can separate the food into several healthful portions, or take some out and tuck the big package out of sight.

urging The word *urging* is a verb. Based on the context, what does it mean?

◆What should you do when you buy larger-portion items at the grocery store?

● Comprehension Questions

Write the letter of the answer on the line. Then explain your thinking.

Main Idea

_____ 1. What is the topic sentence of paragraph 3?

    a. For many people, eating more when presented with large amounts of food may be tied to the "Clean Plate Club" phenomenon.

    b. We have been taught to view not eating all we are given as wasteful.

    c. However, researchers suggest that we may often be unable to even recognize extra-large portions.

    d. Studies show that when an equal amount of food is presented on a relatively large and small plate, we see the large plate as having less food than the smaller plate, which seems more full.

WHY? What information in the selection leads you to give that answer? _____

_____

_____ 2. What is the implied main idea of this reading passage?

    a. The more food the average person is given, the more calories he or she will consume.

    b. Training ourselves to perceive more accurately how much food we are eating will help us stop overeating.

    c. Following the example of the American Institute for Cancer Research and the United States Department of Agriculture, people should learn to recognize serving sizes by comparing food amounts to common objects.

    d. Most of us overeat due to eating strategies instilled in us while we were children, such as the "Clean Plate Club."

WHY? What information in the selection leads you to give that answer? _____

_____

_____

_____

_____

Supporting Details

_____ 3. According to the reading passage, why do many people eat portions that are too large?

a. People have become desensitized to proper portion size.

b. Many people know when they should stop eating, but they have trouble because food is so delicious.

c. Food today has more calories in it than it did 20 years ago.

d. The dishes that we serve our food on are too small and need to be larger.

WHY? What information in the selection leads you to give that answer? _____

_____

_____ 4. Which of the following is *not* a suggestion given for controlling portion size?

a. Use smaller dishes.

b. Compare correct portions to common items as an easy guideline.

c. Only buy food that is an appropriately sized package.

d. Do not buy two-for-one deals.

WHY? What information in the selection leads you to give that answer? _____

_____

_____

Author's Purpose

_____ 5. What is the main purpose of this reading passage?

a. To inform

b. To entertain

c. To persuade

d. To persuade and inform

WHY? What information in the selection leads you to give that answer? _____

_____

_____

_____ 6. What is the purpose of the section entitled "Portion Size Management"?

  a. To persuade readers to manage their portion size by informing them of some basic strategies

  b. To entertain the reader with anecdotal information of successful portion size management

  c. To inform the reader of the best strategies for managing portion size

  d. To inform readers of the latest portion size management research by The American Institute for Cancer Research and the United States Department of Agriculture

WHY? What information in the selection leads you to give that answer? _____

_____

_____

_____

Relationships

_____ 7. What is the pattern of organization of this sentence?
According to experts, we have become so accustomed to oversized portions of food and extra-large serving dishes that we can no longer tell how much we are overeating.

  a. Time order

  b. Cause-and-effect

  c. Comparison

  d. Classification

WHY? What leads you to give that answer? _____

_____

_____ 8. What is the main pattern of organization in the section entitled "Portion Size Management"?

  a. Classification

  b. Comparison and contrast

  c. Cause-and-effect

  d. Examples

WHY? What information in the selection leads you to give that answer? _____

_____

_____

Fact, Opinion, and Inference

_____ 9. Which of the following statements is an opinion?

　　a. Wansink's research shows that the more food we have on hand, the more we will eat.

　　b. It's easier and less expensive to buy large quantities of snack foods, such as nuts or trail mix.

　　c. Market research shows that single serving packages are booming in popularity.

　　d. According to research, if we buy a package of six cookies or crackers, we usually eat them all rather than leaving part of a package.

WHY? What leads you to give that answer? _____

_____

_____

_____ 10. With which of the following statements would Wansink probably agree?

　　a. Consumers should leave packaging decisions to product developers, grocery stores, and marketing companies.

　　b. With slick marketing and the large portions served at restaurants, correct portion size is impossible to decipher.

　　c. By using common sense, most consumers are successfully eating properly sized portions.

　　d. We will eat more if we have large portions of food piled on a small plate than if we have the correct portion size on a larger plate.

WHY? What information in the selection leads you to give that answer? _____

_____

_____

● Critical Thinking Questions

CRITICAL THINKING LEVEL 1 REMEMBER

List three suggestions given in the passage to improve your portion size management.

1. _____

2. _____

3. _____

CRITICAL THINKING LEVEL 2 UNDERSTAND

Summarize the reading in several sentences. Include the major details.

_____

_____

_____

_____

_____

CRITICAL THINKING LEVEL 3 APPLY

Think of restaurants at which you have eaten. *Apply* your knowledge of their menus to the problem of oversized portions. Do you think their portion sizes are appropriate? How big are they? List the name of each restaurant and a few menu items served there, along with a description of the portion size. Discuss your list with a classmate. What size would be appropriate for the menu items? If you mentioned the same restaurants, see if you measured their portions in the same way.

_____

_____

_____

CRITICAL THINKING LEVEL 4 ANALYZE

Analyze how much you eat for dinner tonight. Write down each item that you eat, and *compare* it to the size of a common object, such as a baseball, a deck of cards, or a fist. Then compare each item on your list to the following portion size guidelines provided by the Missouri Diabetes Prevention and Control Program (**Table 6.2**).

Table 6.2 Portion Size Guidelines

Below are ways you can picture a serving or portion size using everyday objects.
(Note: hands and finger sizes vary from person to person! These are GUIDES only).

Food Portion	Looks Like
Grains, Beans, and Starchy Vegetables Group	
½ cup cooked rice or pasta	half of a baseball
½ cup cooked dry beans, lentils, or peas	cupcake wrapper full
½ cup potatoes, corn, green peas	level ice cream scoop
corn on the cob	4-inch corn cob
Vegetable	
1 cup green salad	baseball or a fist
¾ cup tomato juice	small styrofoam cup
½ cup cooked broccoli	half baseball or light bulb
½ cup serving	6 asparagus spears, 7 or 8 baby carrots
Fruit	
½ cup of fresh fruit	custard cup
1 medium size fruit	fist or baseball
¼ cup raisins	large egg
Meat and Protein Foods	
3 ounces cooked meat, fish, poultry	deck of cards
3 ounces cooked chicken	leg plus thigh or ½ whole breast
1 ounce of cheese	4 stacked dice
2 tablespoons peanut butter	ping-pong ball
1 teaspoon peanut butter	fingertip
1 tablespoon peanut butter	thumb tip
Fats, Oils and Nuts	
1 teaspoon butter, margarine	fingertip
2 tablespoons salad dressing	ping-pong ball

Did you know that. . .

- 1 cupped hand holds 2 tablespoons of liquid.

- 1 slice of bread is one ounce or 1 serving; some rolls or bagels weigh 3 to 5 ounces or more making them equal to 3 to 5 servings of bread

For each item, decide whether your portion was smaller than the guideline (such as 50 percent), 100 percent (that is, the same as the guideline), 200 percent (twice as much as the guideline), and so on. When you have compared each item, write a few sentences about what you learned.

_____

_____

_____

CRITICAL THINKING LEVEL 5 EVALUATE

Go to My Pyramid.gov at **www.mypyramid.gov/mypyramid/index.aspx** and enter in your information to see what amount of each food group you need daily. Bring your results to class and _evaluate_ them with a classmate to determine how you should change your diet to better match your results.

CRITICAL THINKING LEVEL 6 CREATE

Create a strategy list with a partner or group of classmates that helps you plan how you will control your portions based on information from the readings in this chapter. Brainstorm together two lists of portion control strategies: one list for eating at home, and the other list for eating out. Share the list you create with your class.

_____

_____

_____

_____

◉ Vocabulary in Context

The following words (or forms of them) were used in "Portion Control: Change Your Thinking or Your Plate?" Choose the best word to complete each of the following sentences.

accustomed	phenomenon	dramatically	perceive	urging

1. In the U.S., the collapse of the major financial institutions in 2008 was a _____ unmatched since the 1920s and 1930s.

2. Researchers have confirmed that men and women _____ pain differently, talk about pain differently, and even are prescribed different amounts of medication to treat pain by doctors.

3. Given enough time, a person can become _____ to almost anything.

4. Claudia never gave up on her dream of finishing school, due in part to the constant _____ of her parents.

5. The importance of computer skills in the workplace has increased _____ over the past decade.

Reading 6-2 . . . . **Health Textbook**

● Pre-Reading the Selection

This reading comes from a textbook entitled *An Invitation to Health*. Think about your health as you read through this passage and do the exercises associated with it.

Guessing the Purpose

Judging from the title of the reading and the book from which it was taken, what do you suppose is the purpose for writing? _____

Surveying the Reading

Survey the title of the selection and the first sentence of each paragraph. What is the general topic of the reading selection? _____

Predicting the Content

Predict three things this selection will discuss.

- _____

- _____

- _____

Activating Your Knowledge

Share what you know about the epidemic of obesity in America and the world. Do you know its causes and effects? On separate paper, create a list with a partner.

Common Knowledge

The World Health Organization (*paragraph 2*) An agency of the United Nations responsible for coordinating health efforts around the world

Reading with Pen in Hand

Now read the selection. As you read, mark any ideas that seem important, and respond to the questions and vocabulary items in the margin. Monitor your comprehension by putting a ✔ next to a paragraph when you understand most of it. Place an ✘ next to a paragraph when you don't understand most of it.

Visit www.cengage.com/devenglish/doleconnect and select Chapter 6 to hear vocabulary words from this selection and view a video about this topic.

◆ *Reading Journal*

◆How many people around the world are overweight or obese?

malnourished The prefix *mal-* means "bad or badly." What does *malnourished* mean?

◆What does the World Health Organization recommend governments do to fight obesity?

The Global Epidemic

Dianne Hales

1   For the first time in history, more than half of the people on the planet are overweight. Obesity, as headlines blare and health experts warn, is emerging as the number-one public health problem of the twenty-first century. An estimated 1.1 billion people around the world—seven in ten of the Dutch and Spanish, two in three Americans and Canadians, and one in two Britons, Germans, and Italians—are overweight or obese. In Europe, excess weight ranks as the most common childhood disorder. Since 1980, obesity rates have tripled in parts of Eastern Europe, the Middle East, China, and the Pacific Islands. In many poor countries, obesity is common among city dwellers, while people in rural areas remain underweight and **malnourished**.

2   The World Health Organization, in its first global diet, exercise, and health program to combat obesity, recommends that governments promote public knowledge about diet, exercise, and health; offer information that makes healthy choices easier for consumers to make; and require accurate, comprehensible food labels. Although ultimately each individual decides what and how much to eat, policy makers agree that governments also must act to reverse the obesity epidemic.

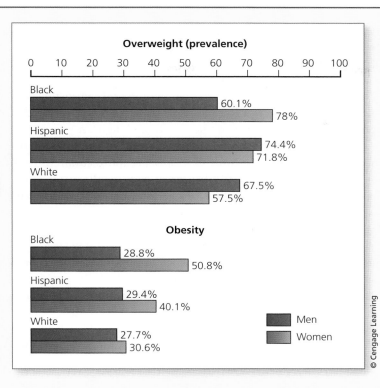

Figure 6.5
Weight Problems by Race/Ethnic Group and Gender

3   Exposure to a Western lifestyle seems to bring out **susceptibility** to excess weight. Obesity is much more common among the Pima Indians of Arizona compared to Pimas living in Mexico, who have maintained a more traditional lifestyle, with more physical activity and a diet lower in fat and richer in complex carbohydrates. Native Hawaiians who follow a more traditional diet and lifestyle also have lower rates of obesity and cardiovascular disease. Simply moving to America increases the risk of obesity. In a study of immigrants, the rate of obesity more than doubled within 15 years—from 8 percent among recent immigrants to 19 percent.

susceptibility The clue for this word hinges on the cause-and-effect relationship between *susceptibility* and *Western lifestyle.*

◆What factor significantly impacts obesity?

Supersized Nation

4   Two-thirds of American adults, up from fewer than half 20 years ago, are overweight. About one in every three Americans is obese. Since the 1970s, the obesity rate has doubled for teens and tripled for children between the ages of 6 and 11. Although more men than women are overweight, more adult women (38 percent) are obese than men (28 percent). Non-Hispanic black women have the highest

◆How many American adults are overweight?

obesity rate (50 percent), compared with 40 percent of Hispanic women and 30 percent of white women (Figure 6-5). In some Native American communities, up to 70 percent of all adults are dangerously overweight. Differences in metabolic rates may be one factor.

◆How many children face potential health problems because they are overweight?

5   Weight problems are starting earlier than ever. One in ten preschoolers and one in five grade schoolers are seriously overweight. According to federal estimates, some 6 million American youngsters are so heavy that their health is in jeopardy. Another 5 million are on the threshold of this danger zone. Not only are more children overweight today, but they're 30 to 50 percent heavier than "fat" kids were a decade ago. The percentage of obese teenagers has tripled in the last 20 years.

◆Which region of the United States has the most obese residents?

6   Not all Americans are equally likely to be overweight or obese. As Figure 6-6 shows, the southern states have the highest concentration of obese residents. Mississippi is home to the county with the highest percentage of people with a body mass index (BMI) between 30 and 40. (BMI is defined as the ratio between weight and height that correlates with percentage of body fat.)

7   States also vary in their efforts to control obesity. According to an ongoing evaluation program at the University of Baltimore, no

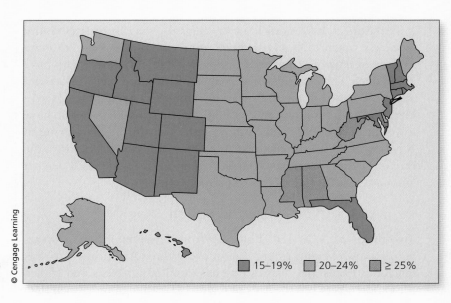

Figure 6.6 Obesity in the United States

© Cengage Learning

15–19%   20–24%   ≥ 25%

states deserve an A overall. Only one state—California—earned an A in the report card. For the high grade, the researchers credited the state's legislative package targeted at the nutrition and diets of schoolchildren at risk of becoming obese. Overall, California earned a B for its anti-obesity work for all populations. Five states—Idaho, Nevada, South Dakota, Utah, and Wyoming—received an F on the report card for failing to take any action in combating obesity.

◆Why did California receive an A from the University of Baltimore's evaluation program?

How Did We Get So Fat?

8   A variety of factors, ranging from heredity to environment to behavior, played a role in the increase in overweight and obesity. They include:

◆What three general factors influence obesity?

A. More calories. Bombarded by nonstop commercials for taste treats, tempted by foods in every form to munch and crunch, Americans are eating more—some 200 to 400 calories more a day than they did several decades ago. Many of these extra calories come from refined carbohydrates, which can raise levels of heart-damaging blood fats called triglycerides and increase the risk of diabetes as well as obesity.

bombarded If Americans are eating more calories than they used to and the commercials are nonstop, what do you think *bombarded* means?

B. Bigger portions. The size of many popular restaurant and packaged foods has increased two to five times during the past 20 years. Some foods, like chocolate bars, have grown more than ten times since they were first introduced. Popular 64-ounce sodas can pack a

Food/Beverage	Original Size (year introduced)	Today (largest available)
Budweiser (bottle)	7 oz. (1976)	40 oz.
Nestle's Crunch	1.6 oz. (1938)	5 oz.
Soda (Coca Cola)	6.5 oz. (1916)	34 oz.
French fries (Burger King)	2.6 oz. (1954)	6.9 oz.
Hamburger (McDonald's) (beef only)	1.6 oz. (1955)	8 oz.

Matthew Farruggio (both)

**Figure 6-7
Supersized Portions**

satiety *Satiety* is presented here with its antonym, *appetite.* What does it mean?

whopping 800 calories. According to studies of appetite and satiety, people presented with larger portions eat up to 30 percent more than they otherwise would.

C. Fast food. Young adults who eat frequently at fast-food restaurants gain more weight and develop metabolic abnormalities that increase their risk of diabetes in early middle age. In a recent study, those who ate fast food at least twice a week gained an extra 10 pounds and had a two-fold greater increase in insulin resistance, a risk factor for diabetes. The men in the study visited fast-food restaurants more often than the women; blacks did so more frequently than whites.

D. Physical inactivity. As Americans eat more, they exercise less. Experts estimate that most adults expend 200 to 300 fewer calories than people did 25 years ago. The most dramatic drop in physical activity often occurs during the college years.

culprit This noun is part of a cause-and-effect relationship. Determine what effect television viewing has on obesity to predict the meaning of *culprit.*

E. Passive entertainment. Television is a culprit in an estimated 30 percent of new cases of obesity. TV viewing may increase weight in several ways: It takes up time that otherwise might be spent in physical activities. It increases food intake since people tend to eat more while watching TV. And compared with sewing, reading, driving, or other relatively sedentary pursuits, television watching lowers metabolic rate so viewers burn fewer calories. The combination of watching television (at least two and one-half hours a day) and eating fast food more than twice a week triples the risk of obesity, according to a 15-year study of more than 3,700 white and black young adults.

F. Modernization. The growth of industry and technology has led to an abundance of food, less need for physical activity, urbanization, labor-saving devices, and a more sedentary lifestyle. Suburban sprawl directly contributes to obesity, according to a recent study. People who live in neighborhoods where they must drive to get anywhere are significantly more likely to be obese than those who can easily walk to their destinations. Each hour spent in a car was associated with a 6 percent increase in the likelihood of obesity and each half-mile walked per day reduced those odds by nearly 5 percent.

G. Socioeconomics. The less money you make, the more likely you are to be overweight. One in four adults below the poverty level is obese, compared with one in six in households earning $67,000 or more. Minorities are at even greater risk. One in three poor African Americans is obese.

H. Prenatal factors. A woman's weight before conception and weight gain during pregnancy influence her child's weight. A substantial number of children are prone to gaining weight because their mothers developed gestational diabetes during their pregnancies. Children born to obese women are more than twice as likely to be overweight by age four.

I. Childhood development. Today's children don't necessarily eat more food than in the past, but they eat more high-fat, high-calorie foods and they exercise much, much less. On days when they eat fast food, youngsters consume an average of 187 more calories per day. Fewer than half of grade schoolers participate in daily physical education classes. Many spend five hours or more a day in front of a computer or television screen.

J. Genetics. Although scientists have identified genes involved in appetite and metabolism, they have not found a genetic cause for obesity. It may be that various genes contribute a small increase in risk or that rare abnormalities in many genes create a predisposition to weight gain and obesity.

K. Emotional influences. Obese people are neither more nor less psychologically troubled than others. Psychological problems, such as irritability, depression, and anxiety, are more likely to be the result of obesity than the cause. Emotions do play a role in weight problems. Just as some people reach for a drink or a drug when they're upset, others cope by overeating, bingeing, or purging.

Comprehension Questions

Write the letter of the answer on the line. Then explain your thinking.

Main Idea

_____   1. What is the topic sentence of paragraph 6?

   a. Not all Americans are equally likely to be overweight or obese.

   b. As Figure 6-6 shows, the southern states have the highest concentration of obese residents.

   c. Mississippi is home to the county with the highest percentage of people with a body mass index (BMI) between 30 and 40.

   d. (BMI is defined as the ratio between weight and height that correlates with percentage of body fat.)

WHY? What information in the selection leads you to give that answer? _____

_____

_____

____ 2. Which of the following sentences states the main idea of this reading passage?

   a. For the first time in history, more than half of the people on the planet are overweight.

   b. The World Health Organization, in its first global diet, exercise, and health program to combat obesity, recommends that governments promote public knowledge about diet, exercise, and health.

   c. A variety of factors, ranging from heredity to environment to behavior, played a role in the increase in overweight and obesity.

   d. Although scientists have identified genes involved in appetite and metabolism, they have not found a genetic cause for obesity.

WHY? What information in the selection leads you to give that answer? _____

_____

_____

Supporting Details

____ 3. According to the reading passage, which of the following is not a confirmed cause of obesity?

   a. Sedentary pursuits

   b. Suburban sprawl

   c. High-fat, high-calorie foods

   d. Genetics

WHY? What information in the selection leads you to give that answer? _____

_____

_____

____ 4. Based on Figure 6-5 on page 307, which of the following details is accurate?

   a. White males have a higher rate of obesity than black males.

   b. Hispanic women have the highest obesity rate among female minorities.

c. White and Hispanic males have a higher prevalence of being overweight and obese than their female counterparts.

d. Black, white, and Hispanic women all have a higher obesity rate than their male counterparts.

WHY? What information in the selection leads you to give that answer? _____

_____

_____

_____

Author's Purpose

_____ 5. What is the main purpose of this reading passage?

a. To inform

b. To entertain

c. To persuade

d. To inform and entertain

WHY? What information in the selection leads you to give that answer? _____

_____

_____ 6. What is the purpose of Figure 6-7 on page 309?

a. To persuade the reader to eat original portion sizes

b. To inform the reader why he or she is getting fat

c. To inform the reader of how the available sizes of popular food products have increased since they were first introduced

d. To entertain students with fun facts about the benefits of eating larger portion sizes

WHY? What information in the selection leads you to give that answer? _____

_____

_____

Relationships

_____ 7. What is the overall pattern of organization of this reading passage?

   a. Time order

   b. Listing

   c. Comparison and contrast

   d. Cause-and-effect

WHY? What information in the selection leads you to give that answer? _____

_____

_____ 8. What relationship is found in the following sentence?
   Obese people are neither more nor less psychologically troubled than others.

   a. Classification

   b. Comparison and contrast

   c. Cause-and-effect

   d. Narration

WHY? What leads you to give that answer? _____

_____

Fact, Opinion, and Inference

_____ 9. Which of the following information is stated as a fact in the reading passage?

   a. Less than 50 percent of the earth's human population is obese.

   b. The percentage of obese women has tripled in the last 20 years.

   c. Native Americans may have different metabolic rates than other Americans, causing their communities to have very high percentages of overweight adults.

   d. Wyoming has the lowest obesity rate among adults in the United States.

WHY? What leads you to give that answer? _____

_____

_____

____ 10. Which of the following can be inferred from this reading passage?

    a. The government is ultimately responsible for the obesity rates in the United States because it allows people the choice of what they eat.

    b. Obesity may be caused partly by cheap food.

    c. This author is overweight, if not obese. That is why she knows so much about obesity.

    d. The World Health Organization is winning the war against obesity.

WHY? What information in the selection leads you to give that answer? _____

_____

_____

_____

_____

● Critical Thinking Questions

CRITICAL THINKING LEVEL 1 REMEMBER

Recall two examples of how exposure to a Western lifestyle influenced groups to become overweight.

    1. _____

    _____

    2. _____

CRITICAL THINKING LEVEL 2 UNDERSTAND

Summarize the reading. First fill in the APP of MAPPS, and then write out a summary. In your summary, note examples of each important point in the main idea.

About (topic): _____

    Point (main idea): A variety of factors, ranging from heredity to environment to behavior, played a role in the increase in overweight and obesity.

      Proof (supporting details):

        1. _____

        _____

        2. _____

        _____

3. _____

_____

4. _____

_____

_____

_____

Summary: _____

_____

_____

_____

_____

CRITICAL THINKING LEVEL 3 APPLY

Apply what you have been reading about to you and your family. What kind of choices that affect your weight do you and your family make? Explain your thoughts. _____

_____

_____

_____

CRITICAL THINKING LEVEL 4 ANALYZE

Compare and contrast this idea from the passage with the idea about guns that follows: *Although ultimately each individual decides what and how much to eat, policy makers agree that governments also must act to reverse the obesity epidemic.*

People who shoot and kill others would never be able to do that if they couldn't purchase a gun. And they couldn't buy guns if gun manufacturers didn't make them. So gun manufacturers should be held legally responsible for the deaths of shooting victims.

List all the similarities and differences you can find between these two ideas.

_____

_____

_____

_____

CRITICAL THINKING LEVEL 5 EVALUATE

With classmates, *evaluate* who is responsible for obesity. Is it the government, the individual, fast food restaurants, or someone or something else? If you can't agree on an answer, try to rank the various answers in terms of who is most responsible, next most responsible, and so on. _____

_____

_____

CRITICAL THINKING LEVEL 6 CREATE

Imagine you are on the World Health Organization task force to create a global diet, exercise, and health program to combat obesity. Work with a group of classmates to create a list of suggestions you would include in this plan. _____

_____

_____

● Vocabulary in Context

The following words (or forms of them) were used in "The Global Epidemic." Choose the best word to complete each sentence below.

satiated	malnourished	susceptibility	bombarded	culprit

1. The commercials on television that show _____ children always prick my conscience, and I have sponsored two of them.

2. A person with HIV/AIDS has a much higher _____ to infection than most other people without the virus.

3. I thought my sister had eaten the last cookie, but then she pointed out a trail of crumbs that led to the real _____—our dog!

4. Sometimes I wish I could go back to a quieter time. I get tired of being constantly _____ by noise from all the technology in modern life.

5. My husband and I were completely _____ after the amazing meal we had for our first anniversary.

© Jeffrey M. Horler/Shutterstock

chapter 7

Reading and Taking Notes on Textbook Chapters

> ❝ *A book is a version of the world. If you do not like it, ignore it; or offer your own version in return.* ❞
> —Salman Rushdie,
> *O Magazine,* April 2003

Like individual books, every academic discipline offers a different version of the world. For example, what are some differences between an artist's and a scientist's versions of the world?

Share Your Prior Knowledge

Have you thought yet about the versions of the world you want to explore? What draws you to these?

Survey the Chapter

Look ahead at some of the topics covered in this chapter. What can you say about how textbooks organize the "world" within their pages?

www.cengage.com/devenglish/doleconnect

Videos Related to Readings

Vocab Words on Audio

Prep Readings on Demand

Prep Reading . . . . Sociology Textbook

The following excerpt comes from a college sociology textbook. It is in a chapter called "Social Interaction."

Visit www.cengage.com/devenglish/doleconnect and select Chapter 7 to hear a reading of this selection and view a video about this topic.

Emotion Management

Robert J. Brym and John Lie

1 *My marriage ceremony was chaos, unreal, completely different than I imagined it would be. . . . My sister didn't help me get dressed or flatter me, and no one in the dressing room helped until I asked. I was depressed. I wanted to be so happy on our wedding day. I never ever dreamed how anyone could cry at their wedding. [Then] from down the long aisle we looked at each other's eyes. His love for me changed my whole being from that point. When we joined arms I was relieved. The tension was gone. From then on, it was beautiful.*

2 *I was in the sixth grade at the time my grandfather died. I remember being called to the office of the school where my mother was on the phone from New York (I was in California). She told me what had happened and all I said was, "Oh." I went back to class and a friend asked me what had happened and I said, "Nothing." I remember wanting very much just to cry and tell everyone what had happened. But a boy doesn't cry in the sixth grade for fear of being called a sissy. So I just went along as if nothing happened while deep down inside I was very sad and full of tears.*

—In Hochschild (1983: 59–60, 67)

3 Some scholars think that emotions are like the common cold. In both cases, an external disturbance causes a reaction that we experience involuntarily. The external disturbance may involve exposure to a particular virus that causes us to catch cold, or exposure to a grizzly bear attack that causes us to experience fear. In either case, we cannot control our body's patterned response. Emotions, like colds, just happen to us (Thoits, 1989: 319).

4 The trouble with this argument is that we can and often do control our emotions. Emotions do not just happen to us; we manage them. If a grizzly bear attacks you in the woods, you can run as fast as your legs will carry you or you can calm yourself, lie down, play dead, and silently pray for the best. You are more likely to survive the grizzly bear attack if you control your emotions and follow the second strategy. You will also temper your fear with a new emotion: hope (**Figure 7.1**).

involuntarily Use context clues from the entire paragraph and/or word parts to decide what this word means.

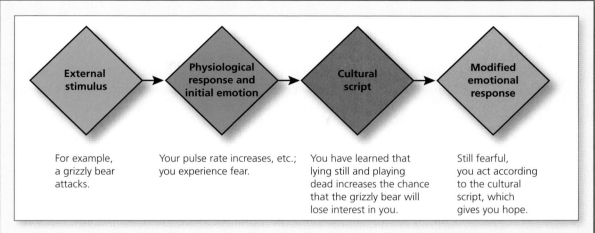

For example,
a grizzly bear
attacks.

Your pulse rate increases, etc.;
you experience fear.

You have learned that
lying still and playing
dead increases the chance
that the grizzly bear will
lose interest in you.

Still fearful,
you act according
to the cultural
script, which
gives you hope.

Figure 7.1 How We Get Emotional

5   When we manage our emotions, we tend to follow certain cultural "scripts," like the culturally transmitted knowledge that lying down and playing dead gives you a better chance of surviving a grizzly bear attack. That is, we usually know the culturally designated emotional response to a particular external stimulus and we try to respond appropriately. If we don't succeed in achieving the culturally appropriate emotional response, we are likely to feel guilty, disappointed, or (as in the case of the grizzly bear attack) something much worse.

designated Based on the context, decide what a good synonym (word with similar meaning) would be for *designated*.

6   The reminiscences quoted at the beginning of this section illustrate typical emotional response processes. In the first case, the bride knew she was not experiencing her wedding day the way she was supposed to, that is, the way her culture defined as appropriate. So by an act of will she locked eyes with the groom and pulled herself out of her depression. In the second case, the schoolboy entirely repressed his grief over his grandfather's death so as not to appear a "sissy" in front of his classmates. As these examples suggest, emotions pervade all social interaction, but they are not, as we commonly believe, spontaneous and uncontrollable reactions to external stimuli. Rather, the norms of our culture and the expectations of the people around us pattern our emotions.

reminiscences This sentence provides its own clue about the meaning of the word.

7   Sociologist Arlie Russell Hochschild is one of the leading figures in the study of emotion management. In fact, she coined the term. She argues that emotion management involves people obeying "feeling rules" and responding appropriately to the situations in which they find themselves (Hochschild, 1979; 1983). So, for example, people talk about the "right" to feel angry, and they acknowledge that they "should" have mourned a relative's death more deeply. We have

suppressing A form of this word (suppress) is a synonym with *repress*, which appears in paragraph 6. A form of its antonym (*expression*) is also used in this paragraph. What does *suppressing* mean?

8   conventional expectations not only about what we should feel but also about how much we should feel, how long we should feel it, and with whom we should share our feelings.

Moreover, feeling rules vary from one category of the population to the next. For example, Hochschild claims that "women, Protestants, and middle-class people cultivate the habit of suppressing their own feelings more than men, Catholics, and lower-class people do" (Hochschild, 1983: 57). This variation exists because our culture invites women to focus more on feeling than action and men to focus more on action than feeling. Similarly, Protestantism invites people to participate in an inner dialogue with God, whereas the Catholic Church offers sacrament and confession, which allow and even encourage the expression of feeling. Finally, more middle-class than lower-class people are employed in service occupations in which the management of emotions is an important part of the job. Hence they are more adept at suppressing their own feelings.

⬤ Interaction 7-1. Talking about Reading

Respond in writing to the questions below and then discuss your answers with your classmates.

1. Can you recall moments in which you managed your emotions? Name two or three times. _____

_____

_____

2. What do you think are the appropriate emotions to feel in these situations?

    a. You tell your friend's secret to someone else. _____

    b. Someone at the dinner table burps. _____

    c. You realize you've been monopolizing the conversation. _____

3. With whom should you share your feeling of anger that you didn't receive the promotion at work you were told you would get? _____

4. Do other people's expectations, or more generally, cultural expectations, affect how you feel about attending college? Give an example. _____

_____

_____

Applying the Reading Process to Textbooks

You're expected to do a lot of reading in college, and much of what you read will not be discussed in class. You will still be responsible for knowing the material, however. Three things will help make reading your textbooks a more efficient and productive activity:

1. Use the reading process to your advantage. Refer back to the Reading Guide you created in Chapter 1 (pages 23–24) to remind yourself of the activities you can use before, during, and after reading.

2. Use the learning aids in your textbooks during each stage of the reading process. Textbooks are deliberately constructed to help make your reading process, and learning, easier. The second part of this chapter will discuss textbook learning aids in detail and suggest how you can use them when you study.

3. Take notes when you read, making brief annotations in the margins of your textbooks and taking longer notes in a notebook.

Taking Useful Notes from Textbook Chapters

As you've learned, when reading in college you should focus your attention on the main idea of the reading selection, along with the major details that support it.

- In Chapter 2 you learned one strategy for picking out the main ideas: they are the ideas that answer the question you formed from the heading. Once you find these ideas, you highlight or mark them in some way. When you study for a test, you review the marked ideas.

- In Chapter 4 you learned to MAPP a paragraph or longer passage as an aid to sorting out the more important ideas from the less important. You also learned how to outline ideas and make concept maps to show the relationships among ideas. Finally, as a study aid, you learned how to summarize ideas in order to remember the main idea and most important supporting details—you added the S to make MAPPS.

- In Chapter 5 you learned to look for the pattern that organizes the major details so you can remember how the ideas relate to one another. You learned to visualize each pattern in a certain way to improve your ability to comprehend and remember the material.

Other writing strategies to improve reading comprehension and remember what you have read are:

- annotating—that is, writing in the margin of the text.
- using a double-column system in your notebook.
- paraphrasing.

In the first part of this chapter we will discuss how to refine some of those earlier strategies and also show you how to use the strategies we haven't yet discussed.

Forming Questions from Headings and Reading for the Answers

You have been using a reading strategy in which you read a heading, turn it into a question, and then read to find the answer to the question. Once you find parts of the answer, then you mark them in some way—highlight them or underline them. This method helps you identify main ideas. You can use it for each major section of a chapter that you read.

But what can you do if there are no headings and thus, no questions to answer? In this case, read one paragraph or one section at a time and then pause to think about what the main idea was. Then go back and highlight the main idea and most important supporting details. Read first, and then return to mark the text once you are sure which ideas should be highlighted. Be selective: highlight only the most important ideas.

Another helpful strategy is to create your own heading for a section. You can write it in the margin. When you return to study for a test, you can use the headings you wrote as a guide to the most important ideas.

Interaction 7-2. Refining the Strategy: Highlighting *after* You Read

Read the following excerpt from a college history text. We have kept the section title but removed the other headings. However, note that paragraphs 2–4 are related to one another, and paragraphs 5 and 6 are related to each other. Consider each of these as separate groups of text.

- Before you read, turn the title into a question and write it in the margin.
- As you read, look for the answers to the question. Read all the paragraphs in a group before marking any of their main ideas.
- When you mark the main ideas, highlight just a few key words—enough so that if you were reading only the highlights later, they would remind you of the main ideas.
- Write your own heading for each group of paragraphs on the lines given.

The Road to World War I

Question:

1 On June 28, 1914, the heir to the Austrian throne, the Archduke Francis Ferdinand, was assassinated in the Bosnian city of Sarajevo. Although this event precipitated the confrontation between Austria and Serbia that led to World War I, underlying forces had been propelling Europeans toward armed conflict for a long time.

2 The system of nation-states that had emerged in Europe in the second half of the nineteenth century had led to severe competition. Rivalries over colonies and trade intensified during a frenzied imperialist expansion, while the division of Europe's great powers into two loose alliances (Germany, Austria, and Italy; France, Great Britain, and Russia) only added to the tensions. The series of crises that tested those alliances in the 1900s and early 1910s had left European states embittered, eager for revenge, and willing to revert to war as an acceptable way to preserve the power of their national states.

Heading for paragraphs 2-4:

3 The growth of nationalism in the nineteenth century had yet another serious consequence. Not all ethnic groups had achieved the goal of nationhood. Slavic minorities in the Balkans and the polyglot Habsburg Empire, for example, still dreamed of creating their own national states. So did the Irish in the British Empire and the Poles in the Russian Empire.

4 National aspirations, however, were not the only source of internal strife at the beginning of the twentieth century. Socialist labor movements had grown more powerful and were increasingly inclined to use strikes, even violent ones, to achieve their goals. Some conservative leaders, alarmed at the increase in labor strife and class division, even feared that European nations were on the verge of revolution. Did these statesmen opt for war in 1914 because they believed that "prosecuting an active foreign policy" as some Austrian leaders expressed it, would smother "internal troubles"? Some historians have argued that the desire to suppress internal disorder may have encouraged some leaders to take the plunge into war in 1914.

5 The growth of large mass armies after 1900 not only heightened the existing tensions in Europe but also made it inevitable that if war did come, it would be extremely destructive. **Conscription**—obligatory military service—had been established as a regular practice in most Western countries before 1914 (the United States and Britain were major exceptions). European military machines had doubled in

Heading for paragraphs 5-6:

size between 1890 and 1914. With its 1.3 million men, the Russian army had grown to be the largest, but the French and Germans were not far behind, with 900,000 each. The British, Italian, and Austrian armies numbered between 250,000 and 500,000 soldiers.

6   **Militarism,** however, involved more than just large armies. As armies grew, so did the influence of military leaders, who drew up vast and complex plans for quickly mobilizing millions of men and enormous quantities of supplies in the event of war. Fearful that changing these plans would cause chaos in the armed forces, military leaders insisted that the plans could not be altered. In the crises during the summer of 1914, the generals' lack of flexibility forced European political leaders to make decisions for military instead of political reasons.

—Duiker/Spielvogel, *World History,* 5th Edition

1. Discuss the questions you and your classmates formed from the title. Which question seems most helpful? Why?

2. Compare the headings you created for each of the two blocks of paragraphs. Which headings seem most helpful? How do these differ from less helpful headings?

3. Discuss the ideas you marked in the first paragraph. What are the two main points?

4. What is the one main idea discussed in both paragraphs 2 and 3?

5. What is the main idea of paragraph 4?

6. What two main ideas are discussed in paragraphs 5 and 6?

Taking Marginal Notes (Annotating) As You Read

While you are reading, you can annotate the text. That is, you can write brief notes, symbols, and abbreviations in the margin to point out important ideas that you want to review the next time you look at the chapter. For instance, you might {bracket} all the definitions of important terms, or note the most important examples of main ideas with stars ✲. Develop your own personal list of symbols and abbreviations. The actual abbreviations are not important, as long as you can remember them and use them consistently. Some possibilities are presented in **Table 7.1**.

Table 7.1 Use Symbols and Abbreviations to Point Out Important Ideas

Use this symbol or abbreviation	to indicate . . .
main (or) *key* (or) *	A main idea or important point
① ② ③	List of details or steps in a sequence
def	Definition of a key term
imp ex	An important example
! (or) *?*	Personal reactions to the material
Exam	Possible exam question

You can also write short responses to the author's ideas, engaging in a dialogue to keep your mind working actively while you read. The following example from a sociology textbook chapter on aging includes symbols, abbreviations, and short responses combined with highlighting.

Age Prejudice and Discrimination

def. [Age prejudice refers to a negative attitude about an age group that is generalized to all people in that group. Prejudice against the elderly is prominent. As an example, people may talk "baby talk" to the elderly. Doing so defines the elderly as childlike and incompetent. Prejudice relegates people to a perceived lower status in society and stems from the stereotypes associated with different age groups.

ex.

language use important!
Remember Aunt Donna
and the nurse

—Andersen/Taylor, *Sociology*, 4th Edition

◕ Interaction 7-3. Taking Marginal Notes

Annotate the next paragraph from the chapter on aging.

> Age discrimination is the different and unequal treatment of people based solely on their age. While age prejudice is an attitude, age discrimination involves actual behavior. Some forms of age discrimination are illegal. The Age Discrimination Employment Act, first passed in 1967 but amended several times since, protects people from age discrimination in employment. An employer can neither hire nor fire someone based solely on age, nor segregate or classify workers based on age. Age discrimination cases have become one of the most frequently filed cases through the Equal Employment Opportunity Commission (EEOC), the federal agency set up to monitor violations of civil rights in employment.
>
> —Andersen/Taylor, *Sociology*, 4th Edition

Organizing Information with Timelines and Other Maps

In Chapter 5, we suggested a visual reading strategy for each pattern of organization. For example, the narration strategy is to visualize a timeline of the events being described. You can create these maps in your notebook as aids to comprehension and memory. They can be used to organize information from longer texts as well as from paragraphs.

1. Mapping events on a timeline

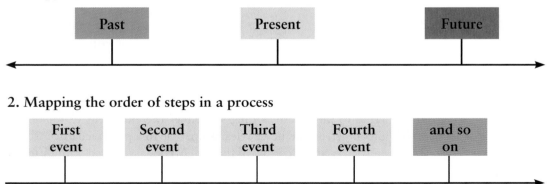

2. Mapping the order of steps in a process

3. Mapping causes and effects

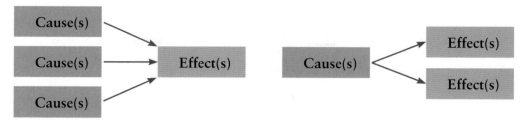

4. Mapping examples using two methods

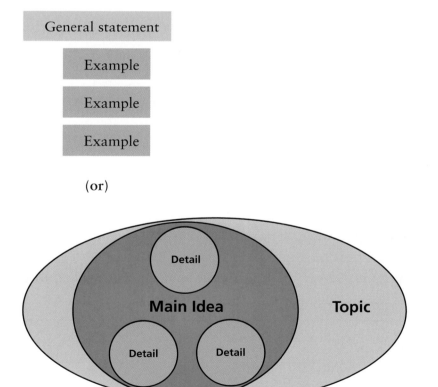

5. Mapping comparisons and/or contrasts

Item 1

A. Similarity or difference
B. Similarity or difference

Item 2

A. Similarity or difference
B. Similarity or difference

6. Mapping definitions

General category

Specific type

Particular example

It is helpful to use a format that visually reminds you of the relationships among the different pieces of information you are mapping.

⬤ Interaction 7-4. Using Organizational Maps

Discuss which kind of map you might use to remember the most important points of each of the following passages. How do you know to use that kind of map?

1. Paragraph 3 from the Prep Reading on page 320. _____
   _____

2. Reading 7-1 on page 354. Survey the title and headings in this reading to decide which map to use. _____
   _____

3. The paragraph on "Age Prejudice and Discrimination" on page 327. _____
   _____

Taking Notes in Your Notebook

Once you have asked the questions and marked the answers, you can use a notebook to record the main points you want to remember. A popular and helpful system for doing so is called the Cornell note-taking system (named for the university at which Walter Pauk, the creator of the system, taught). You can use this system by making two columns in your notebook, as in the following example. In the left column, write a heading or a few key words that summarize a main idea. In the right column, take more detailed notes. You can use the mapping formats described on pages 328–330, short outlines, or lists to write down the major supporting details. Hints:

- **Use words or images** that will help you remember the pattern of relationship between the ideas. In the example below based on the reading "The Road To World War I" found on page 325, the pattern words are "immediate event" and "underlying forces." These words set up a contrast between the two ideas. Ideas are easier to remember when you understand their relationship.
- **Number lists.** After you have reviewed your notes several times, you will remember how many points there are in a particular answer. You can use that knowledge as a check to see whether you are remembering all the points.
- **Abbreviate as you like.** In the example, we have not abbreviated to make sure you will understand the notes, but in your own notes, develop a system of abbreviations you can use in all your classes to make note-taking more efficient.

Partial Page from a Notebook

Immediate event: assassination of the Archduke Ferdinand, heir to Austrian throne
Underlying forces had been leading Europeans toward war for a long time:

1. nationalism

2. internal dissent

3. militarism

Interaction 7-5. Practicing the Strategy: Noting the Supporting Details

Refer back to the selection, "The Road to World War I" (pages 325-326) for this interaction. In the left column of the notebook page that follows, write answers to the other two questions you formed from the headings. For each answer, consider whether it would be helpful to briefly note a couple of examples of the idea. If it would, include them in the right column using just a word or phrase for each one.

	Nationalism:
_____	_____
_____	_____
_____	Internal dissent:
_____	1. _____
	_____
	2. _____
	_____
	_____
_____	1. _____
_____	2. _____
_____	3. _____
_____	4. _____
	_____

When you are reviewing for a test, cover the right column with a sheet of paper and read the key phrases on the left. See if you can say or write all the major examples from the right column. Then check your answer by reviewing the right column.

Paraphrasing to Improve Comprehension

A paraphrase is a restatement of someone else's ideas using your own words. Paraphrasing an author's thoughts is a good way to improve your comprehension of text. Because paraphrasing takes some time, you should use it particularly when there is a rather short section of text you don't understand but believe is important to know in detail.

Two methods of paraphrasing will be covered here:

1. Reducing the text to an outline, map, or list and then rewriting.

2. Using synonyms for key ideas and rewriting sentences around them.

Paraphrasing Method 1

Here we will discuss an appropriate method of paraphrasing for taking notes for your own use in a class. If you were paraphrasing a passage in order to write a research paper, you would follow a somewhat different procedure.

Original passage from a biology textbook

Early practitioners of photosynthesis filled the atmosphere with oxygen. Before then, the iron and other metals abundant on all surfaces both above and below the seas were in reduced form. All of the oxygen released by the early autotrophs immediately became bound to (oxidized) these metals. Over time, all of the exposed iron rusted, as evidenced by global bands of red iron deposits below the seafloor. Eventually, there was little exposed metal that was not oxidized. Oxygen, bubbling from the now tremendous populations of photoautotrophs, gushed unimpeded into the atmosphere.

—Starr/Evers/Starr, *Biology,* 2nd Edition

Steps to a Paraphrase

1. Carefully read the passage. Use your prior knowledge to understand as much as you can. Then reread to see if you can understand even more the second time. Actively try to remember related information. For instance, do you remember what photosynthesis is?

2. If there are technical terms you don't know, use the textbook glossary to find out what they mean. Here are excerpts from this biology textbook's glossary:

> **autotroph:** organism that uses energy captured from sunlight or inorganic chemicals to make its own food from inorganic compounds

> **photosynthesis:** The chemical process by which photoautotrophs capture and use light energy to make sugars from CO_2 and water.

3. Use your vocabulary development strategies to figure out the meanings of other words you may not know. Here are some examples.

> **oxidized:** Based on the context, this means "bound to."

> **photoautotrophs:** Look at the meaning above for *autotrophs*. *Photo-* means "light." This kind of autotroph is the one that uses sunlight to make its own food from inorganic compounds.

> **unimpeded:** *Un-* means "not," and *impeded* means "obstructed." So *unimpeded* means free flowing.

4. Since this paragraph organizes details by a process that occurred, you might want to take notes in first, second, third order. If you like, you could put the details on a timeline as shown on page 322.

> 1st: Metals, including iron, appeared everywhere, under water and on land, in reduced form.

> 2nd: Photosynthesizers used sunlight and carbon dioxide to make oxygen, which filled the atmosphere.

> 3rd: The oxygen bound itself to all the metals, and eventually they rusted.

> 4th: Scientists know the metals rusted because all over the world there is a band of red iron under the seafloor.

> 5th: Pretty much all of the metal rusted.

> 6th: As more and more photosynthesizers appeared, an enormous amount of oxygen was released into the atmosphere.

5. Using your notes as a guide, write out the meaning of the paragraph. Here is one example.

> Under water and on land, metals, including iron, were everywhere. Organisms that used photosynthesis made oxygen, which filled the atmosphere. When the oxygen touched the metals, the metal became oxidized, and eventually, the oxidized metal rusted. In fact, pretty much all the metal rusted. As more photosynthesizers appeared, even more oxygen—an enormous amount—was released into the atmosphere.

6. If you are going to turn in your paraphrase or use it in a research paper, you need to add this step: check your paraphrase against the original to make sure you haven't copied any ideas directly. If you did, you should change your paraphrase to avoid committing the academic offense of plagiarism. (Other requirements also apply.)

● Interaction 7-6. Paraphrasing Using Method 1

Using method 1, paraphrase the following material about arthropods from a biology textbook.

> *Respiratory structures.* Many freshwater and marine arthropods use gills as respiratory organs. Among the insects and other arthropods on land, air-conducting tubes called tracheae evolved. The tubes start at pores on the body surface. Their extensive branching ends in fluid near tissues. Diffusion of oxygen into this fluid supports the high rates of aerobic respiration essential for flight and other energy-demanding activities.
>
> —Starr/Evers/Starr, *Biology,* 2nd Edition

1. What can you understand by reading the passage carefully twice?

   _____

   _____

   _____

2. Since you don't have access to the textbook's glossary, use your dictionary to look up the meanings of these scientific terms.

   arthropod: _____

   _____

   aerobic: _____

3. Use your vocabulary strategies or your dictionary to figure out the meanings of the following words:

   respiratory: _____

   marine: _____

   tracheae: _____

   diffusion: _____

4. Take notes, make a diagram, or perhaps do both to trace the meaning of the paragraph.

   _____

   _____

   _____

   _____

_____

_____

_____

5. Using your notes as a guide, write out the meaning of the passage.

_____

_____

_____

_____

Paraphrasing Method 2

Another method of paraphrasing is to find synonyms for some of the key words the author uses, and rewrite the sentence using them. Even if you use this method, don't paraphrase technical terms such as *photosynthesis;* proper nouns such as the names of states, countries, and people; or statistics such as *12 percent of the U. S. population.*

Original sentence from an art history textbook

The lush land that lays between the Tigris and Euphrates rivers, providing sustenance for the Mesopotamian civilization, is called the Fertile Crescent.

—Fichner-Rathus, *Understanding Art,* 8th Edition

Paraphrase based on synonyms, with rearranged order of ideas

The Fertile Crescent, which is the rich ground between the Tigris and Euphrates rivers, feeds the people of the Mesopotamian civilization.

Interaction 7-7. Paraphrasing Sentences

In each sentence adapted from Dumler and Skinner's *A Primer for Management,* 2nd Edition, underline at least two words for which you can find synonyms. Write the synonyms above the words. Then rewrite the sentence using your own words.

1. Before objectives can be established, the current state of the organization must be assessed.

   Paraphrase: _____

2. Not all plans are created equal.

   Paraphrase: _____

3. Difficult objectives sometimes result in better employee performance than easier objectives.

Paraphrase: _____

_____

Interaction 7-8. Paraphrasing Definitions

Paraphrase the following definitions, which are adapted from the glossary of Ferraro, *Cultural Anthropology*, 6th Edition. _____

1. **affinal relatives** kinship ties formed through marriage

Paraphrased definition: _____

2. **ancestor worship** the worshipping of deceased relatives

Paraphrased definition: _____

3. **barter** the direct exchange of commodities between people that does not involve a standardized currency

Paraphrased definition: _____

_____

4. **displacement** the ability to talk about things that are remote in time and space

Paraphrased definition: _____

_____

Interaction 7-9. Paraphrasing a Paragraph Using Method 2

Paraphrase the following paragraph about a manager's authority. Do not paraphrase the word *authority*, however, since that is the term being discussed. First, underline words for which you can think of or find synonyms, and write the synonyms above the words. Then try to paraphrase sentences or phrases based on their meaning rather than paraphrasing word by word.

Authority. Authority accompanies the position, not the person. In an organization, those in authority have the right to make decisions and to expect that subordinates will comply with those decisions. A manager with authority can expect employees to carry out a plan as long as it does not require illegal or unethical behavior. Authority is often sufficient to implement simple plans, but a complex plan can seldom be implemented through authority alone.

—Dumler/Skinner, *A Primer for Management*, 2nd Edition

Paraphrase: _____

_____

_____

_____

Use paraphrasing to unpack complicated ideas and to understand fairly brief sections of text in detail.

Learning Aids in Textbook Chapters

Textbooks differ from other kinds of nonfiction books in that they provide many aids to help you learn the most that you can. In the introductory textbooks that you will read for your general education courses, each chapter typically has a wide variety of features to help you learn the material. These features help textbooks fulfill their almost purely informative purpose.

Chapter Outlines, Objectives, Focus Questions, or FAQs

Chapters often start with an outline or a series of questions designed for you to use as a chapter preview. These learning aids give you an overview of the chapter's scope (breadth of coverage) and sequence (order). Here is a combined chapter outline and set of focus questions from a world history textbook.

**CHAPTER OUTLINE
AND FOCUS QUESTIONS**

tenets Guess the meaning of the word here based on its context.

Look up the word in a dictionary. What does it mean?

successors Break this word down into three parts, a root and two suffixes.

What does each suffix mean?

The word means:

The Rise of Islam

▫ What were the main tenets of Islam, and how does the religion compare with Judaism and Christianity?

The Arab Empire and Its Successors

▫ Why did the Arabs undergo such a rapid expansion in the seventh and eighth centuries, and why were they so successful in creating an empire?

Islamic Civilization

▫ What were the main features of Islamic society and culture during its era of early growth?

continued

The Byzantine Empire

▣ What were the main features of Byzantine civilization, and why did it follow a separate path from that taken by Christian societies in the West?

CRITICAL THINKING

▣ In what ways did Byzantine and Islamic civilizations resemble and differ from each other? Was their relationship overall based on cooperation or conflict?

—Duiker/Spielvogel, *World History,* 5th Edition

● Interaction 7-10. Integrating Your Knowledge of Patterns

For each focus question on page 338-339, name the pattern(s) of organization or level of critical thinking that is (are) suggested. Refer to Chapters 2 and 5 as needed.

1–2. The two patterns in the question under "Rise of Islam" are _____.

3.   The pattern in the question under "Arab Empire" is _____.

4.   The pattern in the question under "Islamic Civilization" is _____.

5–6. The two patterns in the question under "Byzantine Empire" are _____.

7–8. The pattern in the first critical thinking question asks for _____.

9.   The type of critical thinking that is asked for in the second critical thinking question

   is _____.

10.   Overall, what pattern of organization do you expect to find in the chapter?

   _____

● Interaction 7-11. Reading for Content

1. What three religions are going to be discussed in this chapter? _____

   _____

2. When did the Arabs expand rapidly into neighboring territories? _____

   _____

3. Was the Byzantine Empire in the East or the West? _____

Using the Chapter Outline and Focus Questions to Learn

You can see that the chapter outline and focus questions give you a wealth of information about what is coming in the chapter. You can use the chapter outline or similar features in several different ways:

1. **Survey and Predict.** When you are getting ready to read the chapter, take about five minutes to read and study the chapter outline. Use the strategies you've learned for turning headings into questions, searching for patterns of organization, and figuring out what content is to come. Reflect on anything you've seen in the movies or on television (which, you realize, may or may not be accurate), and anything you've heard or read about the topics.

2. **Read One Section at a Time.** Textbook chapters can be long and complex, so it's wise to break up a chapter into its parts and read one at a time. For instance, in the world history chapter, you would read the section "The Rise of Islam" as if it were a separate reading selection, using the full reading process on it and taking notes. Only then would you proceed to the next section, "The Arab Empire and Its Successors."

3. **Put the Pieces of the Puzzle Together.** After you read a section of the chapter, refer back to the chapter outline so that you can see once again how that piece fits into the larger puzzle. Learn to move back and forth from specific details to big picture to specific details to big picture. You need to understand both.

4. **Use the Outline to Structure a Study Session for a Test.** After you have studied your notes in preparation for a test, use the chapter outline and any focus questions as a way to test yourself. One way to do this is to write the heading or question and then list all the information you can about it. If you like to study with other people, take turns asking the questions and answering them. Do take the step of writing them down, however, if your test will be written.

Headings

Most college textbooks include several levels of headings. Major headings show the most important chapter divisions. A second level of headings divides the content within each major section. There may be a third and even a fourth level of headings in a chapter, depending on the complexity of the topic. Here are the three levels of headings from one part of a chapter from a public speaking textbook.

TYPES OF PUBLIC SPEAKING	This is the major heading.
Informative Speeches	
Invitational Speeches	These three headings are the main divisions of the topic, "Types of Public Speaking."
Persuasive Speeches	
Speaking on Special Occasions	This section is divided into three subsections.
Introductory speeches. When you present information about...	
Commemorative speeches. When you give a commemorative...	
Acceptance speeches. Speeches of acceptance are delivered...	
—Griffin, *Invitation to Public Speaking,* 2nd Edition	

Notice that the headings are designed to make it clear which ones represent the broadest ideas in the chapter. In this public speaking book, the major headings are signaled by the use of all capital letters in a large type size. The second-level headings include both capital and lower-case letters; they are a smaller size; they are a different color; and they are underlined. The third-level headings are not set off above the text like the first- and second-level headings; they are part of the paragraph that follows them, even though they are distinguished from the text by color and type style.

Using the Headings to Stay Oriented

1. Remember to form questions from the headings before you read each section, and to quickly survey the section before you read it.

2. **Stay aware of where you are in a section and in a chapter.** The headings provide you with valuable information about how experts in a field of study think about their topic and classify its subtopics. The headings act as an outline for the ideas you are learning about, and thus you can use them as an aid while you study, just as we suggested for the chapter outlines on page 340.

Interaction 7-12. Learning from Textbook Headings

The following headings come from a chapter of a sociology textbook. Study them and answer the questions that follow.

THE IMPORTANCE OF GROUPS

CHARACTERISTICS OF SOCIAL GROUPS

Group Size and Structure

PRIMARY AND SECONDARY GROUPS

GROUP SIZE AND RELATIONSHIPS

DYADS AND TRIADS

Communities

Networks

IN-GROUPS AND OUT-GROUPS

REFERENCE GROUPS

SOCIAL NETWORK ANALYSIS

INTERACTION IN GROUPS
Principles of Interaction

THE PLEASURE PRINCIPLE

THE RATIONALITY PRINCIPLE

THE RECIPROCITY PRINCIPLE

THE FAIRNESS PRINCIPLE

The Economic Person Versus the Social Person
Communication and Behavior in Groups

—Kornblum, *Sociology in a Changing World,* 7ᵗʰ Edition

1–3. What are the three main topics this chapter covers?

- _____
- _____
- _____

4–5. For the first main topic, what question would you form as a guide to reading that section? What does the question reveal about the pattern of organization you can expect to find in the section? (Refer to Chapter 5 if needed.)

Question: _____

Pattern: _____

6–8. What are three considerations about group size and structure that this chapter covers?

- _____
- _____
- _____

9. How many principles of group interaction are listed? _____

10. Based on this information, would you say that people always act fairly in groups? What information in the headings makes you say so? _____

_____

Boxed Material or Sidebars

Many textbooks include special-interest material in boxes or sidebars. These may be stories that illustrate the chapter concepts, summaries of research studies that relate to the chapter topic, interesting "real-world" applications of the chapter ideas, or material to help students learn to think more critically. Some may include questions; others may be cases in which you are asked to apply the chapter concepts in particular ways. Don't skip this material! The information is featured for a reason: it's important to know.

Here is an example of an illustrative anecdote from a cultural anthropology textbook.

CROSS-CULTURAL MISCUE

Tony Manza, a high-level sales executive with a Canadian office furniture company, was in Kuwait trying to land a large contract with the Kuwaiti government. Having received an introduction from a mutual friend, Manza made an appointment with Mr. Mansour, the chief purchasing agent for the government. In his preparation for the trip, Manza had been told to expect to engage in a good deal of small talk before actually getting down to business. So Manza and Mansour chatted about the weather, golf, and Tony's flight from Toronto. Then, quite surprisingly, Mansour inquired about Manza's 70-year-old father. Without giving it much thought, Manza responded by saying that his father was doing fine but that the last time he had seen him four months ago in the nursing home, he had lost some weight. From that point onward, Mansour's attitude changed abruptly from warm and gracious to cool and aloof. Manza never did get the contract he was after.

Although Manza thought he was giving Mansour a straightforward answer, his response from Mansour's perspective made Manza an undesirable business partner. Coming from a society that places very high value on family relationships, Mansour considered putting one's own father into a nursing home (to be cared for by total strangers) to be inhumane. If Manza could not be relied upon to take care of his own father, he surely could not be trusted to fulfill his obligations in a business relationship.

—Ferraro, *Cultural Anthropology*, 6th Edition

This feature appeared in a chapter on marriage and the family. The chapter compares family life in different countries, and this feature gives one example of how cultural differences regarding family can influence people even when they are outside the family environment.

⬤ Interaction 7-13. Thinking about the Feature

1–2. What country is Tony Manza from? _____ Mr. Mansour? _____

3. What did Manza understand about doing business in Kuwait before he arrived?

    _____

4–5. What are two things Manza did not understand about Kuwaiti culture that led to his not getting a contract?

    • _____

    • _____

Using Boxed Features to Learn

When you read a boxed feature or sidebar, don't just read it and move on. First read the information carefully, and then ask and answer questions about it:

- How does this information relate to the chapter topic?

- Which chapter concepts does this information illustrate?

- Does the feature provide leads to other interesting information about this topic?

Review Questions or Self-Quiz

Review questions, sometimes including multiple-choice answers, can often be found at the end of a textbook chapter. These questions are designed to help you decide whether or not you have learned the material. If you find that you cannot answer some questions or have answered them incorrectly, then go back to the section of the chapter where the material was covered and review it. Later, answer the review questions again to see if you now remember the material.

Another way to use such questions is to read them before you read the chapter; in other words, use them to check your prior knowledge. As you read the chapter, refer back to your answers and correct any that you answered incorrectly.

⬤ Interaction 7-14. Checking Prior Knowledge with a Self-Quiz

Here are five of the ten questions from a chapter on alcohol use, misuse, and abuse from a college health textbook. As you read them, suppose you are using the questions as a check of your prior knowledge. Circle the letter of the answers you think are correct.

Making This Chapter Work for You

Review Questions

1. An individual's response to alcohol depends on all of the following *except*
   a. the rate at which the drink is absorbed into the body's tissues.
   b. the blood alcohol concentration.
   c. socioeconomic status.
   d. gender and race.

2. Responsible drinking includes which of the following behaviors?
   a. Avoiding eating while drinking because eating speeds up absorption of alcohol
   b. Limiting alcohol intake to no more than four drinks in an hour
   c. Taking aspirin while drinking to lower your risk of a heart attack
   d. Socializing with individuals who limit their alcohol intake

3. Which of the following statements about drinking on college campuses is true?
   a. The percentage of students who abstain from alcohol has increased.
   b. The number of women who binge drink has decreased.
   c. Because of peer pressure, students in fraternities and sororities tend to drink less than students in dormitories.
   d. Students who live in substance-free dormitories tend to binge-drink when alcohol is available.

4. Which of the following statements about the effects of alcohol on the body systems is true?
   a. In most individuals, alcohol sharpens the responses of the brain and nervous system, enhancing sensation and perception.
   b. Moderate drinking may have a positive effect on the cardiovascular system.
   c. French researchers have found that drinking red wine with meals may have a positive effect on the digestive system.
   d. The leading alcohol-related cause of death is liver damage.

5. Health risks of alcoholism include all of the following *except*
   a. hypertension.   c. peptic ulcers.
   b. lung cancer.   d. hepatitis.

—Hales, *An Invitation to Health*, 12th Edition

The answers to the questions from the health textbook as follows: (1) c, (2) d, (3) a, (4) b, and (5) b. Once you discovered which questions you answered correctly and incorrectly, you would focus carefully on the sections that explained the information you didn't know.

Chapter Summary

Sometimes when reading a lot of information, a person can get bogged down in details. So often a chapter summary is included to help you remember the big picture of the chapter topics. The chapter summary may be a bulleted list of key points, or one or more paragraphs that pull together the main ideas of the chapter. Sometimes the summary is a list of questions and answers. The chapter summaries in one introductory biology textbook summarize each chapter section by section. Here is the summary of the first of one chapter's seven sections.

Summary

Section 1.1 Life shows many levels of organization. All things, living and nonliving, are made of atoms. Atoms join to form molecules, and molecules of life assemble into cells. Cells are the smallest living units. An organism may be a single cell or multicellular. In most multicelled species, cells are organized as tissues and organs.

A population consists of individuals of the same species in a specified area. A community consists of all populations occupying the same area. An ecosystem is a community and its environment. The biosphere includes all regions of Earth's atmosphere, waters, and land where we find living organisms.

—Starr/Evers/Starr, *Biology*, 2nd Edition

These two short paragraphs summarize two whole pages of the chapter. Notice that each statement in the summary is quite general.

Using the Chapter Summary to Review and to Survey

Review. If you are reading the summary after you have read the chapter, read each sentence and then pause. Can you fill in the details that explain the general statement? If not, review that section of the chapter again and search for the explanation. After you have explained each general statement with the proof that supports it, check your understanding by skimming through the chapter again. Have you missed anything major? Once you can explain the general statements in the chapter summary using details, you can feel assured that you understand much of the chapter content.

Survey. You can read the chapter summary before you read the chapter itself as part of your survey of the material. This will help you form a structure, or schema, in which to place information as you come to it in the reading. It will also help you immediately see the similarities and differences between your prior knowledge and the ideas you will be reading about.

⬤ Interaction 7-15. Surveying Using a Chapter Summary

Read the Review of Key Points on page 361. What ideas are similar to what you already know or believe? _____

_____

_____

What ideas are different from or contradict what you know and believe?

_____

_____

Key Terms

Key terms, or key concepts, may be listed at the beginning or end of a chapter. In some books, the term and its definition are provided in that section. In other books, a list of key terms is given with the numbers of the pages on which you will find their definitions. Any terms that are called *key* or *important* are terms that you should be able to define and provide examples for.

Using Key Terms to Review

Use the list of key terms to be sure you understand the important concepts in a chapter. Four instances in particular can cue you that the term is important to know:

- The term is in **boldface.**
- It is called an *Important Term* or a *Key Term.*
- The term is included in a major heading.
- The author spends a paragraph or more explaining a term.

When the chapter emphasizes a certain concept, then in addition to knowing the definition of the term, be sure you can discuss specific examples of it.

Chapter Summary Activity

This chapter has discussed note-taking strategies you can use when you read college textbooks, as well as a number of learning aids that textbook chapters include to help students learn. Create a Reading Guide below by completing each idea on the left with information from the chapter on the right. Return to this guide anytime you need a refresher on how to read and study textbook chapters.

Reading Guide to Reading and Taking Notes on Textbook Chapters

Complete this idea	with information from the chapter.
When reading a textbook chapter, you should follow the general reading process given in Chapter 1, which includes three stages of reading activities. The stages and their related activities are:	1. _____ 2. _____ 3. _____

Before you read, you can survey the contents of the chapter by studying	4.
You can use the headings in a chapter to establish your purpose for reading, as discussed in Chapter 2, by	5.
In general, you should read how much of a chapter at a time?	6.
If there are no headings, create your own by	7.
Highlight the main ideas after you read to make sure you	8.
Annotate in the margins of your text to mark these kinds of information:	9.
Take notes in your notebook using the Cornell system, in which you	10.
The purpose of creating headings, highlighting, annotating, and taking notes in your notebook is to	11.
Paraphrasing to improve comprehension takes some time and thus is best done	12.
Two methods of paraphrasing are	13. 14.
Aside from using it to survey the chapter, two other uses for the chapter outline are	15. 16.
For a more detailed chapter survey, you could also read either of these two learning aids:	17. 18.

The headings in a chapter reveal how experts in the field	19.
To help you figure out the everyday relevance or applications of the chapter topics, be sure to read the	20.
To get the most out of reading this kind of material,	21.
After you read, use these two learning aids to help you decide whether you have learned the chapter material well.	22. 23.
When a chapter emphasizes a certain concept, you should be able to	24. 25.

Test Taking Tips
Predicting Exam Questions

You can prepare for a test by creating possible test questions as you read and think about the chapter material. In addition to answering questions that your textbook author may have provided and your instructor may have emphasized in class, you might want to develop questions based on the six critical thinking levels you have been working with throughout this book. (See page 63 for a diagram of them.)

Also, depending on the information your instuctor gives you about the format of the test, you might choose to focus on just one or two of the levels. For instance, if you know that the entire test will be short identification items, you might focus your efforts on questions that ask you to remember. Most tests will not be written at this low level, however, so if you have not taken an instructor's tests before, cover all your bases by preparing questions at all six levels.

● **Constructing Test Questions Using Bloom's Taxonomy**

1. **Questions that ask you to remember:** These questions include specific details, such as dates, names, and important terms.

    ✔ When did the Battle of Gettysburg happen and who won?

✔ What is the name of the person who invented Silly Putty and when was it invented?

✔ Define the First Law of Thermodynamics.

2. **Questions that ask you to understand:** These questions focus on the relationships between ideas. Do you understand processes, steps, requirements, the timeline of events, and so on?

✔ Why was the battle at Gettysburg important in the Civil War?

✔ Explain the events surrounding the invention of Silly Putty.

✔ Explain how the First Law of Thermodynamics works.

3. **Questions that ask you to apply what you have learned:** These questions focus on your ability to understand a process and apply it to a familiar or new situation.

✔ Show the strategy used in the Battle of Gettysburg.

✔ Physically work through the formula for Silly Putty.

✔ What are situations that would be affected by the First Law of Thermodynamics?

4. **Questions that ask you to analyze:** These questions deal with breaking up events, materials, or processes into parts to figure out how the parts relate to one another and to the overall topic.

✔ What are three significant missteps General Lee made that made it difficult for the South to win the Civil War?

✔ Silly Putty has decreased in popularity since the 1980s. How did trends in toy use, manufacturing processes, and regulatory costs from 1980 to the present affect the sales of Silly Putty?

✔ How do two objects reach equilibrium of heat? Analyze and explain this process.

5. **Questions that ask you to evaluate:** These questions ask you to decide on the criteria that should be used to judge the value of something and then judge it based on these criteria.

✔ Was the Civil War successful? Were its objectives achieved? Could it have been done in a different or better way? How or why?

✔ Evaluate the impact that Silly Putty has had in the toy industry.

✔ You are a member of group A. You are evaluating Group B's experiment. Determine if their experiment correctly follows and illustrates the First Law of Thermodynamics.

⬭ **Creating Questions That Work for You**

You can create your questions and answers in any number of formats—and which ones you choose may depend on how you learn best. Do you prefer to write out questions and answers, or type them? Do you want to create a PowerPoint slide show that you review each night before you go to sleep? Or would you rather create a visual map or outline? Should you draw an illustration? Might you create a study guide (like the reading guide at the end of each chapter in this book)?

Create a format that helps you remember best based on your learning style. If you aren't sure which way is best, experiment. And if you like to study with others, talk over with your study group what may be the most effective ways to study for a particular test or to learn particular content.

Reading 7-1 . . . . **Psychology Textbook**

⬤ Pre-Reading the Selection

People tend to be very interested in the question, "What will make me happy?" The following reading from a psychology textbook, *Psychology: Themes and Variations,* addresses some of the research into this question.

Guessing the Purpose

Judging from the title of the selection and the publication context, what do you suppose is the purpose of this selection? _____

Surveying the Reading

Survey the title, the headings, the sentence printed in blue, and the Review of Key Points. Then answer the following questions.

What factors . . .
- do not seem to predict happiness? _____

  _____

- seem to be moderately good predictors of happiness? _____

  _____

- seem to be strong predictors of happiness? _____

  _____

Surveying the Graphics and Photos in the Reading

Survey the graphics, cartoon, and photo, and their captions, and then answer the following questions.

Are people generally more happy or more unhappy? _____

Are people generally happier when they are married or unmarried? _____

Are some people just more likely to be happy than other people, no matter what happens to them? _____

Predicting the Content

Predict two things besides those covered above that this selection will discuss.

- _____
- _____

Activating Your Knowledge

Think about a person you know who seems happy. Of the predictors of happiness covered in this reading, which do you think most apply to them?

- _____
- _____
- _____

Entries from the Glossary of *Psychology*

Refer to these entries as you read.

correlation the extent to which two variables are related to each other.

empiricism the premise that knowledge should be acquired through observation.

hypothesis a tentative statement about the relationship between two or more variables.

Reading with Pen in Hand

Now read the selection. As you read, mark any ideas that seem important, and respond to the questions and vocabulary items in the margin. Monitor your comprehension by putting a ✔ next to a paragraph when you understand most of it. Place an ✘ next to a paragraph when you don't understand most of it.

Visit www.cengage.com/devenglish/doleconnect and select Chapter 7 to hear vocabulary words from this selection and view a video about this topic.

◆ *Reading Journal*

Exploring the Ingredients of Happiness

Wayne Weiten

1   Answer the following "true" or "false."

____   1. The empirical evidence indicates that most people are relatively unhappy.

____   2. Although wealth doesn't guarantee happiness, wealthy people are much more likely to be happy than the rest of the population.

____   3. People who have children are happier than people without children.

____   4. Good health is an essential requirement for happiness.

____   5. Good-looking people are happier than those who are unattractive.

◆ **What seems to be the main idea of the reading selection?**

subjective well-being This expression is defined in the same sentence. What does it mean?

2   The answer to all these questions is "false." These assertions are all reasonable and widely believed hypotheses about the correlates of happiness, but they have not been supported by empirical research. Recent years have brought a surge of interest in the correlates of **subjective well-being**—individuals' personal perceptions of their overall happiness and life satisfaction. The findings of these studies are quite interesting. As you have already seen from our true-false questions, many commonsense notions about happiness appear to be inaccurate.

How Happy Are People?

◆ **How would you answer the question that the heading poses?**

3   One of these inaccuracies is the apparently widespread assumption that most people are relatively unhappy. Writers, social scientists, and the general public seem to believe that people around the world are predominantly dissatisfied and unhappy, yet empirical surveys consistently find that the vast majority of respondents—even those who are poor or disabled—characterize themselves as fairly happy (Diener & Diener, 1996; Myers & Diener, 1995). When people are asked to rate their happiness, only a small minority place themselves below the neutral point on the various scales used (see **Figure 7.2**). When the average subjective well-being of entire nations is computed, based on almost 1000 surveys, the means cluster toward the

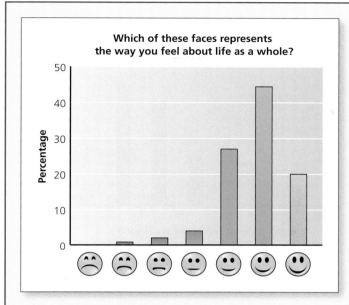

Which of these faces represents the way you feel about life as a whole?

Percentage

Figure 7.2 Measuring Happiness with a Nonverbal Scale
Researchers have used a variety of methods to estimate the distribution of happiness. For example, in one study in the United States, respondents were asked to examine the seven facial expressions shown and select the one that "comes closest to expressing how you feel about your life as a whole." As you can see, the vast majority of participants chose happy faces. (Data adapted from Myers, 1992.)

positive end of the scale, as shown in **Figure 7.3** (Veenhoven, 1993). That's not to say that everyone is equally happy. Researchers find substantial and thought-provoking disparities among people in subjective well-being, which we will analyze momentarily, but the overall **picture seems rosier** than anticipated.

picture seems rosier A person who looks out of "rose-colored glasses" is an optimist. What does this phrase mean in this sentence?

Factors That Do Not Predict Happiness

4   Let us begin our discussion of individual differences in happiness by highlighting those things that turn out to be relatively unimportant determinants of subjective well-being. Quite a number of factors that you might expect to be influential appear to bear little or no relationship to general happiness.

◆What pattern of organization is implied throughout this reading selection?

5   **Money.** There is a positive correlation between income and subjective feelings of happiness, but the association is surprisingly weak (Diener & Seligman, 2004). For example, one study found a correlation of just .13 between income and happiness in the United States (Diener et al., 1993). Admittedly, being very poor can make people unhappy, but once people ascend above the poverty level, little relation is seen between income and happiness. On the average, wealthy people are only marginally happier than those in the middle classes. The problem with money is that in this era of voracious consumption, pervasive advertising and rising income fuel escalating material desires (Frey & Stutzer, 2002; Kasser et al., 2004). When these

◆Give examples of what makes people happier and less happy.

ascend Given the immediate context, what does *ascend* mean?

What is the antonym of *ascend*?

Figure 7.3 The Subjective Well-Being of Nations
Veenhoven (1993) combined the results of almost 1000 surveys to calculate the average subjective well-being reported by representative samples from 43 nations. The mean happiness scores clearly pile up at the positive end of the distribution, with only two scores falling below the neutral point of 5. (Data adapted from Diener and Diener, 1996)

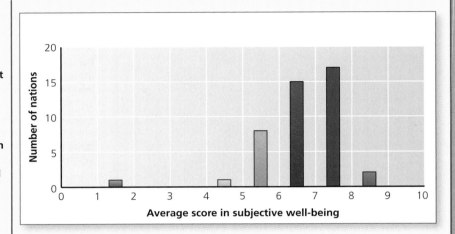

materialistic Break this word into a root and two suffixes—*material + ist + ic.* What does it probably mean?

◆Does age have a big impact on happiness?

◆Does parenthood have an impact on happiness?

◆Do intelligence and attractiveness have an impact on happiness?

growing material desires outstrip what people can afford, dissatisfaction is likely (Solberg et al., 2002). Thus, complaints about not having enough money are routine even among people who earn hefty six-figure incomes. Interestingly, there is some evidence that people who place an especially strong emphasis on the pursuit of wealth and materialistic goals tend to be somewhat less happy than others (Kasser, 2002; Ryan & Deci, 2001), perhaps in large part because they are so focused on financial success that they don't derive much satisfaction from their family life (Nickerson et al, 2003).

6   **Age.** Age and happiness are consistently found to be unrelated. Age accounts for less than 1 percent of the variation in people's happiness (Inglehart, 1990; Myers & Diener, 1997). The key factors influencing subjective well-being may shift some as people grow older—work becomes less important, health more so—but people's average level of happiness tends to remain remarkably stable over the life span.

7   **Parenthood.** Children can be a tremendous source of joy and fulfillment, but they can also be a tremendous source of headaches and hassles. Compared to childless couples, parents worry more and experience more marital problems (Argyle, 1987). Apparently, the good and bad aspects of parenthood balance each other out, because the evidence indicates that people who have children are neither more nor less happy than people without children (Argyle, 2001).

8   **Intelligence and Attractiveness.** Intelligence and physical attractiveness are highly valued traits in modern society, but researchers have not found an association between either characteristic and happiness (Diener, 1984; Diener, Wolsic, & Fujita, 1995).

Moderately Good Predictors of Happiness

9   Research has identified three facets of life that appear to have a moderate association with subjective well-being: health, social activity, and religious belief.

10   **Health.** Good physical health would seem to be an essential requirement for happiness, but people adapt to health problems. Research reveals that individuals who develop serious, disabling health conditions aren't as unhappy as one might guess (Myers, 1992; Riis et al., 2005). Good health may not, by itself, produce happiness, because people tend to take good health for granted. Considerations such as these may help explain why researchers find only a moderate positive correlation (average = .32) between health status and subjective well-being (Argyle, 1999).

11   **Social Activity.** Humans are social animals, and interpersonal relations do appear to contribute to people's happiness. Those who are satisfied with their social support and friendship networks and those who are socially active report above-average levels of happiness (Diener & Seligman, 2004; Myers, 1999). Furthermore, people who are exceptionally happy tend to report greater satisfaction with their social relations than those who are average or low in subjective well-being (Diener & Seligman, 2002).

12   **Religion.** The link between religiosity and subjective well-being is modest, but a number of large-scale surveys suggest that people with heartfelt religious convictions are more likely to be happy than people who characterize themselves as nonreligious (Argyle, 1999; Ferriss, 2002). Researchers aren't sure how religious faith fosters happiness, but Myers (1992) offers some interesting conjectures. Among other things, he discusses how religion can give people a sense of purpose and meaning in their lives, help them accept their setbacks gracefully, connect them to a caring, supportive community, and comfort them by putting their ultimate mortality in perspective.

Strong Predictors of Happiness

13   The list of factors that turn out to have fairly strong associations with happiness is surprisingly short. The key ingredients of happiness appear to involve love, work, and personality.

14   **Love and Marriage.** Romantic relationships can be stressful, but people consistently rate being in love as one of the most critical ingredients of happiness (Myers, 1999). Furthermore, although people complain a lot about their marriages, the evidence indicates

◆Does this paragraph include a thesis statement?

◆Are the next three predictors stronger or weaker than the ones discussed in the previous section?

interpersonal Break this word into a prefix, a root, and a suffix— *inter + person + al.* Based on the meaning of these words—*international, interweave, interoffice*—what does *inter-* mean?

What does *interpersonal* mean?

◆When people are isolated, are they less happy than others?

◆How many possible reasons does Myers give for how having heartfelt religious convictions makes people somewhat happier?

conjectures Based on the meaning of the sentence it is in, what does *conjectures* mean?

mortality Although this word consists of more than two word parts, consider it as *mortal + ity.* What does *mortal* mean?

What do you guess is the purpose for the *–ity* ending?

◆Does this paragraph include a topic sentence?

Figure 7.4 Happiness and Marital Status

This graph shows the percentage of adults characterizing themselves as "very happy" as a function of marital status (Myers, 1999). Among both women and men, happiness shows up more in those who are married as opposed to those who are separated, are divorced, or have never married. These data and many others suggest that marital satisfaction is a key ingredient of happiness.

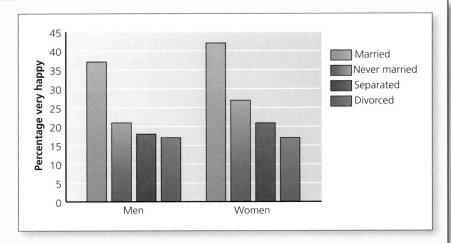

Source: Myers, 0. C. (1999). Close relationships and quality of life. In 0. Kahneman, F. Diener, & N. Schwarz (Eds.), *Well-being: The foundations of hedonic psychology*. New York: Russell Sage Foundation. Copyright © 1999. Reprinted by permission of the Russell Sage Foundation.

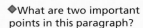◆What are two important points in this paragraph?

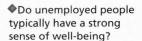◆Do unemployed people typically have a strong sense of well-being?

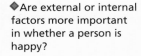◆Are external or internal factors more important in whether a person is happy?

that marital status is a key correlate of happiness. Among both men and women, married people are happier than people who are single or divorced (see **Figure 7.4;** Myers & Diener, 1995), and this relationship holds around the world in widely different cultures (Diener et al., 2000). However, the causal relations underlying this correlation are unclear. It may be that happiness causes marital satisfaction more than marital satisfaction promotes happiness. Perhaps people who are happy tend to have better intimate relationships and more stable marriages, while people who are unhappy have more difficulty finding and keeping mates.

15   **Work.** Given the way people often complain about their jobs, one might not expect work to be a key source of happiness, but it is. Although less critical than love and marriage, job satisfaction has a substantial association with general happiness (Warr, 1999). Studies also show that unemployment has strong negative effects on subjective well-being (Lucas et al., 2004). It is difficult to sort out whether job satisfaction causes happiness or vice versa, but evidence suggests that causation flows both ways (Argyle, 2001).

16   **Personality.** The best predictor of individuals' future happiness is their past happiness (Diener & Lucas, 1999). Some people seem destined to be happy and others unhappy, regardless of their triumphs or setbacks. The limited influence of life events was apparent in a stunning study that found only marginal differences in overall happiness between recent lottery winners and recent accident victims who became quadriplegics (Brickman, Coates, & Janoff-Bulman,

1978). Investigators were amazed that such extremely fortuitous and horrible events didn't have a dramatic impact on happiness. Several lines of evidence suggest that happiness does not depend on external circumstances—buying a nice house, getting promoted—so much as internal factors, such as one's outlook on life (Lykken & Tellegen, 1996). With this fact in mind, researchers have begun to look for links between personality and subjective well-being, and they have found some intriguing correlations. For example, extraversion is one of the better predictors of happiness. People who are outgoing, upbeat, and sociable tend to be happier than others (Fleeson, Malanos, & Achille, 2002). Additional positive correlates of happiness include self-esteem and optimism (Lucas, Diener, & Suh, 1996).

Conclusions about Subjective Well-Being

17 We must be cautious in drawing inferences about the causes of happiness, because the available data are correlational (see **Figure 7.5**). Nonetheless, the empirical evidence suggests that many popular beliefs about the sources of happiness are unfounded. The data also demonstrate that happiness is shaped by a complex constellation of variables. In spite of this complexity, however, a number of worthwhile insights about the ingredients of happiness can be gleaned from the recent flurry of research.

◆Does this paragraph include a topic sentence?

18   First, research on happiness demonstrates that the determinants of subjective well-being are precisely that: subjective. Objective realities are not as important as subjective feelings. In other words, your

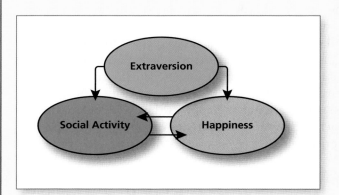

Figure 7.5 Possible Causal Relations Among the Correlates of Happiness
Although we have considerable data on the correlates of happiness, it is difficult to untangle the possible causal relationships. For example, we know that a moderate positive correlation exists between social activity and happiness, but we can't say for sure whether high social activity causes happiness or whether happiness causes people to be more socially active. Moreover, in light of the research showing that a third variable—extraversion—correlates with both variables, we have to consider the possibility that extraversion causes both greater social activity and greater happiness.

◆What is the main idea of this paragraph?

◆How do people decide if they have enough?

◆What is the main message of this paragraph?

health, your wealth, and your job are not as influential as how you feel about your health, wealth, and job (Schwarz & Strack, 1999). These feelings are likely to be influenced by what your expectations were. Research suggests that bad outcomes feel worse when unexpected than when expected and good outcomes feel better when unexpected than when expected (Shepperd & McNulty, 2002). Thus, the same objective event, such as a pay raise of $2000 annually, may generate positive feelings in someone who wasn't expecting a raise and negative feelings in someone expecting a much larger increase in salary.

19   Second, when it comes to happiness, everything is relative (Argyle, 1999; Hagerty, 2000). In other words, you evaluate what you have relative to what the people around you have. Generally, we compare ourselves with others who are similar to us. Thus, people who are wealthy assess what they have by comparing themselves with their wealthy friends and neighbors. This is one reason for the low correlation between wealth and happiness. You might have a lovely home, but if it sits next door to a neighbor's palatial mansion, it might be a source of more dissatisfaction than happiness.

20   Third, research on subjective well-being indicates that people often adapt to their circumstances. This adaptation effect is one reason that increases in income don't necessarily bring increases in happiness. Thus hedonic adaptation occurs when the mental scale that people use to judge the pleasantness/unpleasantness of their experiences shifts so that their neutral point, or baseline for comparison, changes. Unfortunately, when people's experiences improve; hedonic adaptation may sometimes put them on a hedonic treadmill—their neutral point moves upward, so that the improvements yield no real benefits (Kahneman, 1999). However, when people have to grapple with major setbacks, hedonic adaptation probably helps protect their mental and physical health. For example, people who are sent to prison and people who develop debilitating diseases are not as unhappy as one might assume, because they adapt to their changed situations and evaluate events from a new perspective (Frederick & Loewenstein, 1999). That's not to say that hedonic adaptation in the face of life's difficulties is inevitable or complete (Lucas et al., 2003). People who suffer major setbacks, such as the death of a spouse or serious illness, often are not as happy as they were before the setback, but generally they are not nearly as unhappy as they or others would have predicted.

> **REVIEW OF KEY POINTS**
>
> - Research on happiness reveals that many commonsense notions about the roots of happiness appear to be incorrect, including the notion that most people are unhappy. Factors such as income, age, parenthood, intelligence, and attractiveness are largely uncorrelated with subjective well-being.
> - Physical health, good social relationships, and religious faith appear to have a modest impact on feelings of happiness. The only factors that are good predictors of happiness are love and marriage, work satisfaction, and personality.
> - Research on happiness indicates that objective realities are not as important as subjective feelings and that subjective well-being is a relative concept. The evidence also indicates that people adapt to their circumstances.

● Comprehension Questions

Write the letter of the answer on the line. Then explain your thinking.

Main Idea

____ 1. The four statements that follow are a main idea and three supporting details. Select the letter of the main idea.

a. Wonderful and horrible life events don't necessarily affect happiness much.

b. Extraversion, self-esteem, and optimism are linked to happiness.

c. People's happiness seems to depend on internal factors, not external factors.

d. Buying a nice house and getting promoted don't necessarily lead to happiness.

WHY? What information in the selection leads you to give that answer? _____

_____

____ 2. Myers (1992) speculates that having a sense of purpose and meaning, the ability to accept setbacks gracefully, and connections to community may foster happiness. Which of the factors discussed provides these three traits?

a. parenthood

b. social activity

c. religion

d. work

WHY? What information in the selection leads you to give that answer? _____

_____

Supporting Details

_____ 3. What is the single most important factor in predicting someone's future happiness?

a. marriage

b. work

c. religious beliefs

d. past happiness "

WHY? What information in the selection leads you to give that answer? _____

_____

_____ 4. Of the following, which is the most important determinant of happiness?

a. subjective feelings

b. intelligence

c. money

d. objective realities

WHY? What information in the selection leads you to give that answer? _____

_____

_____

Author's Purpose

_____ 5. What is the author's purpose in beginning this feature with the true/false quiz?

a. to make students realize they must read this section

b. to demonstrate that commonsense ideas about happiness are often incorrect

c. to show how unhappy most people around the world are

d. to help students understand they should have children if they want to be happy

WHY? What information in the selection leads you to give that answer? _____

_____

_____   6. What seems to be the general purpose of Figures 7.2 to 7.5?

      a. to support the conclusions of the text with more specific details

      b. to demonstrate times when the conclusions of the text do not hold true

      c. to provide an overall framework for the more specific words in the text

      d. to suggest the conditions under which the conclusions of the text are true

WHY? What information in the selection leads you to give that answer? _____

_____

_____

Relationships

_____   7. In the third conclusion about subjective well-being, the author notes that "when people's experiences improve, hedonic adaptation may *sometimes* put them on a *hedonic treadmill*—their neutral point moves upward, so that the improvements yield no real benefits (Kahneman, 1999)." What is the relationship of the next sentence, which begins with "However, when . . ." to this one?

      a. cause

      b. definition

      c. contrast

      d. exemplification

WHY? What information in the selection leads you to give that answer? _____

_____

_____   8. In the next sentence, which begins "For example, people who . . .," what relationship is established between the two parts of the sentence with the word *because*?

      a. definitions-term

      b. effect-cause

      c. cause-effect

      d. definition-examples

WHY? What information in the selection leads you to give that answer? _____

_____

Fact, Opinion, and Inference

_____ 9. Which of the following statements is the author's opinion?

    a. The findings of these studies are quite interesting.

    b. Recent years have brought a surge of interest in the correlates of subjective well-being.

    c. One study found a correlation of just .13 between income and happiness in the United States (Diener et al., 1993).

    d. The key ingredients of happiness appear to involve love, work, and personality.

WHY? What leads you to give that answer? _____

_____

_____ 10. The author writes, "Some people seem destined to be happy and others unhappy, regardless of their triumphs or setbacks." What does the verb _destined_ imply?

    a. that personality is not or cannot be shaped by the individual

    b. that happiness is temporary

    c. that setbacks lead to unhappiness in general

    d. that environment is more important than heredity

WHY? What leads you to give that answer? _____

_____

● Critical Thinking Questions

CRITICAL THINKING LEVEL 1 REMEMBER

If I am happy that I bought a new house, but later, find that I am not as happy as I expected to be, what are three possible explanations? _____

_____

CRITICAL THINKING LEVEL 2 UNDERSTAND

Fill in the APP of MAPPS to show the relationship among the ideas in the reading selection.

    About: _____

      Point: _____

        Proof:

1. _____

   _____

2. _____

   _____

3. _____

   _____

4. _____

5. _____

6. _____

7. _____

CRITICAL THINKING LEVEL 3 APPLY

If you knew that having more money wasn't going to make you any happier, but that job satisfaction would be an important factor, what job would you seek? _____

_____

_____

CRITICAL THINKING LEVEL 4 ANALYZE

Choose two time periods in your life: one period in which you were generally happy and another in which you were generally unhappy. Use the moderately good predictors of happiness and the strong predictors of happiness to take notes on each period of your life. You might want to set up your notes in a table format as shown here. Do your individual results support the research results that love, work, and personality strongly predict happiness and that health, social activity, and religion moderately predict happiness?

Moderate and Strong Predictors of Happiness

Predictors	Generally happy time	Generally unhappy time
Health		
Social activity		
Religion		
Love and marriage		
Work		
Personality		

CRITICAL THINKING LEVEL 5 EVALUATE

Rate the usefulness of the information on happiness to you, personally, on a scale of 1 to 10, with 10 being "very useful." Write a paragraph on a separate sheet of paper to explain your rating.

CRITICAL THINKING LEVEL 6 CREATE

Based on the three conclusions about subjective well-being, *create* a list of at least three suggestions to give to a friend about how to be happy. Make sure that each suggestion is something that your friend can do, not something that another person would have to do, or a way the world would have to change.

1. _____

   _____

   _____

2. _____

   _____

   _____

3. _____

   _____

   _____

● Vocabulary in Context

The following words (or forms of them) were used in "Exploring the Ingredients of Happiness." Fill in the blank in each sentence with one of the following words or phrases.

ascend	conjecture	rosy picture	materialistic
	subjective well-being	mortality	

1. One field of psychology prefers not to judge the interests of different people have as being either positive or negative; practitioners call people who are _____ "thing-oriented."

2. The princess will soon _____ to the throne and become queen.

3. Sherlock Holmes's _____ about who murdered the man in the robe was based on his knowledge of the soil types in the region and the sole patterns of the various manufacturers of men's footwear.

4. The saying "Disappointment requires adequate planning" reflects the impact of a person's expectations on his or her _____

5. The name of a character from a book by Eleanor H. Porter, Pollyanna, has become synonymous with painting a _____; Pollyanna is an incurable optimist.

6. The _____ rate in the United States in 2005 was 825.9 deaths per 100,000 people.

Reading 7-2 . . . . **Management Textbook**

⬤ Pre-Reading the Selection

The next reading comes from a college business management textbook, *Management*. The chapter it comes from is called "Managing Individuals and a Diverse Work Force."

Guessing the Purpose

Judging from the title of the chapter, the title of the selection, and the publication context in a textbook on business management, what do you suppose is the main purpose of this selection? _____

Surveying the Reading

Survey the title, the first sentence of each paragraph, and the marginal definitions. What does the reading discuss? _____

_____

Predicting the Content

Predict two things that this selection will probably discuss.

• _____

• _____

Activating Your Knowledge

Read the first paragraph and answer the questions about a boss you have or used to have. If you've never had a boss, answer the questions about a teacher you've had.

_____

_____

_____

Reading with Pen in Hand

Now read the selection. As you read, mark any ideas that seem important, and respond to the questions and vocabulary items in the margin. Monitor your comprehension by putting a ✔ next to a paragraph when you understand most of it. Place an ✗ next to a paragraph when you don't understand most of it.

Visit www.cengage.com/devenglish/doleconnect and select Chapter 7 to hear vocabulary words from this selection and view a video about this topic.

◆*Reading Journal*

◆Why does the author start with this paragraph?

◆Why are the Big Five called that?

gregarious Notice that a list of traits is given, and then their antonyms, in the same order. There are three antonyms for *gregarious*. What does *gregarious* mean?

Big Five Dimensions of Personality

Chuck Williams

1   Stop for a second and think about your boss (or the boss you had in your last job). What words you use to describe him or her? Is your boss introverted or extraverted? Emotionally stable or unstable? Agreeable or disagreeable? Organized or disorganized? Open or closed to new experiences? When you describe your boss or others in this way, what you're really doing is describing dispositions and personality.

2   A **disposition** is the tendency to respond to situations and events in a predetermined manner. **Personality** is the relatively stable set of behaviors, attitudes, and emotions displayed over time that makes people different from each other. For example, which of your aunts or uncles is a little offbeat, a little out of the ordinary? What was that aunt or uncle like when you were small? What is she or he like now? Chances are she or he is pretty much the same wacky person. In other words, the person's core personality hasn't changed. For years, personality researchers studied thousands of different ways to describe people's personalities. In the last decade, however, personality research conducted in different cultures, different settings, and different languages has shown five basic dimensions of personality account for most of the differences in people's behaviors, attitudes, and emotions (or for why your boss is the way he or she is!). The Big Five Personality Dimensions are extraversion, emotional stability, agreeableness, conscientiousness, and openness to experience.

3   **Extraversion** is the degree to which someone is active, assertive, **gregarious**, sociable, talkative, and energized by others. In contrast to extraverts, introverts are less active, prefer to be alone, and are shy, quiet, and reserved. For the best results in the workplace, introverts and extroverts should be correctly matched to their jobs. For example, the Peabody Hotel in Memphis, Tennessee, solved one of its problems by having job applicants complete an introversion/extraversion per-

sonality measure. Ken Hamko, a manager at the hotel, explained how this worked: "We had hostesses who wouldn't stay by the door or greet guests or smile. When we gave them the personality profile, we found they didn't like being in front of people. So we moved them into other positions and replaced them with extraverts."

4   **Emotional stability** is the degree to which someone is not angry, depressed, **anxious**, emotional, insecure, or excitable. People who are emotionally stable respond well to stress. In other words, they can maintain a calm, problem-solving attitude in even the toughest situations (e.g., conflict, hostility, dangerous conditions, or extreme time pressure). By contract, under only moderately stressful situations, emotionally unstable people find it difficult to handle the most basic demands of their jobs and become distraught, tearful, self-doubting, and anxious. Emotional stability is particularly important for high-stress jobs, such as police work, fire fighting, emergency medical treatment, or piloting planes. John S. Blonsick, a captain with Delta Air Lines, said:

5   *From the first day of flight training, pilot aspirants are tested for their ability to separate their emotions from their operational environment. The process allows a pilot to erect psychological barriers to avoid distractions in an environment which the decision-making process is conducted at slightly under the speed of sound…. Abnormal and emergency situations are handled in a cool and professional manner. Voice-recorder transcripts of accidents invariably read like training manuals, despite the life-threatening situations they depict. Crew members are focused and actively working to correct the situation as they have been trained to do right up to the very last moment before impact.*

6   **Agreeableness** is the degree to which someone is cooperative, polite, flexible, forgiving, good-natured, tolerant, and trusting. Basically, agreeable people are easy to work with and be around, whereas disagreeable people are distrusting and difficult to work with and be around. A number of companies have made general attitude or agreeableness the most important factor in their hiring decisions. Small business owner Roger Cook says, "Hire nice people. I'm looking for personal—not professional—traits. I want a good or nice person. I can teach the skills. I call their references and ask, 'Is he or she a nice person?' I take a close look at how applicants answer questions and carry themselves. Why nice people? Because they're trustworthy; they get along with other crew members: they are good with customers and they are usually hard workers."

◆ To what kinds of jobs are extraverts well suited?

anxious Use an antonym clue to decide what *anxious* means.

◆ In what general conditions is it important to have emotional stability?

◆ Does the information here suggest that emotional stability can be learned?

◆ Why would a manager want to hire an agreeable person?

persevering Use a dictionary to define this word.

◆ Define a conscientious person.

ambiguity Use a dictionary to define this word.

◆ Is openness to experience an important trait for a job that requires a person to follow rules all day long?

stringent Use a dictionary to define this word.

◆ In terms of job performance, which of the Big Five is most important?

7   **Conscientiousness** is the degree to which someone is organized, hardworking, responsible, **persevering**, thorough, and achievement oriented. One management consultant wrote about his experiences with a conscientious employee:

8   *He arrived at our first meeting with a typed copy of his daily schedule, a sheet bearing his home and office phone numbers, addresses, and his email address. At his request, we established a timetable for meetings for the next four months. He showed up on time every time, day planner in hand, and carefully listed tasks and due dates. He questioned me exhaustively if he didn't understand an assignment and returned on schedule with the completed work or with a clear explanation as to why it wasn't done.*

9   **Openness to experience** is the degree to which someone is curious, broad-minded, and open to new ideas, things, and experiences; is spontaneous, and has a high tolerance for **ambiguity**. Most companies need people who are strong in terms of openness to experience to fill certain positions, but for other positions, this dimension is less important. People in marketing, advertising, research, or other creative jobs need to be curious, open to new ideas, and spontaneous. By contrast, openness to experience is not particularly important to accountants, who need to consistently apply **stringent** rules and formulas to make sense out of complex financial information.

10   Which of the Big Five Personality Dimensions has the largest impact on behavior in organizations? The cumulative results indicate that conscientiousness is related to job performance across five different occupational groups (professional, police, managers, sales, and skilled or semiskilled jobs). In short, people "who are dependable, persistent, goal directed, and organized tend to be higher performers on virtually any job; viewed negatively, those who are careless, irresponsible, low-achievement striving, and impulsive tend to be lower performers on virtually any job. See the What Really Works feature in this chapter for further explanation. The results also indicate that extraversion is related to performance in jobs, such as sales and management, which involve significant interaction with others. In people-intensive jobs like these, it helps to be sociable, assertive, and talkative and to have energy and be able to energize others. Finally, people who are extraverted and open to experience seem to do much better in training. Being curious and open to new experiences, as well as sociable, assertive, talkative, and full of energy, helps people perform better in learning situations.

⬤ Comprehension Questions

Write the letter of the answer on the line. Then explain your thinking.

Main Idea

_____ 1. Which of the following is the main idea of the entire reading selection?

     a. Stop for a second and think about your boss (or the boss you had in your last job.)

     b. The Big Five Personality Dimensions are extraversion, emotional stability, agreeableness, conscientiousness, and openness to experience.

     c. A disposition is the tendency to respond to situations and events in a predetermined manner.

     d. In other words, the person's core personality hasn't changed.

WHY? What information in the selection leads you to give that answer? _____

_____

_____ 2. What is the implied main idea of the last paragraph?

     a. Conscientiousness has the largest impact on behavior in organizations, and extraversion also plays a large role in certain situations.

     b. See the What Really Works feature in this chapter for further explanation.

     c. The results also indicate that extraversion is related to performance in jobs, such as sales and management, which involve significant interaction with others.

     d. Finally, people who are extraverted and open to experience seem to do much better in training.

WHY? What information in the selection leads you to give that answer? _____

_____

_____

Supporting Details

____ 3. The paragraphs on extraversion, emotional stability, agreeableness, and conscientiousness all have the same kind of supporting details. What kind?

    a. statistics

    b. process writing

    c. classification

    d. examples

WHY? What information in the selection leads you to give that answer? _____

_____

_____

____ 4. What are some situations in which emotional stability is especially important?

    a. police work, fire fighting, and emergency medical treatment

    b. filing, interviewing prospective employees, and warehouse work

    c. acting, dancing, and singing

    d. selling insurance, owning a small business, and managing others

WHY? What information in the selection leads you to give that answer? _____

_____

Author's Purpose

____ 5. What is the author's general purpose?

    a. to highlight the importance of hiring mostly extraverts in sales positions

    b. to ensure that future managers don't hire emotionally unstable people

    c. to emphasize that creative positions require people who are open to new experiences

    d. to share information with students that they can use in hiring decisions later, when they are managers

WHY? What information in the selection leads you to give that answer? _____

_____

_____

_____ 6. Why does the author emphasize conscientiousness in the What Really Works feature?

   a. because conscientiousness has been studied so much

   b. because the conscientious person is complex

   c. because the author wants to emphasize that conscientious people tend to make good employees

   d. because the author wants to emphasize that conscientious workers have less than a 71 percent chance of success in jobs requiring motivational effort

WHY? What information in the selection leads you to give that answer? _____

_____

_____

Relationships

_____ 7. What relationship does the word *whereas* establish in this sentence: "Basically, agreeable people are easy to work with and be around, whereas disagreeable people are distrusting and difficult to work with and be around."

   a. effect

   b. definition

   c. comparison

   d. contrast

WHY? What information in the selection leads you to give that answer? _____

_____

_____ 8. Two paragraphs in this reading are in *italic* type. What relationship to the paragraph that precedes each one does the italic type represent?

   a. example

   b. cause

   c. process writing

   d. classification

WHY? What information in the selection leads you to give that answer? _____

_____

Fact, Opinion, and Inference

____ 9. Which of the following statements is a fact?

    a. Ken Hamko said the hostesses who wouldn't greet customers were extraverts.

    b. In stressful job situations, openness to experience is the most important quality.

    c. Small business owner Roger Cook likes to hire nice people.

    d. Accountants should be curious and spontaneous.

WHY? What information in the selection leads you to give that answer? _____

_____

____ 10. Which of the following statements is a good summary of the selection?

    a. A person's disposition doesn't matter as much as their personality.

    b. When hiring employees, try to find conscientious people. Also, match the needs of the position with the personality traits of the potential employee.

    c. Bosses should be extraverted, stable, agreeable, conscientious, and open to experience.

    d. When a worker is conscientious, he or she will also be extraverted and open to experience.

WHY? What information in the selection leads you to give that answer? _____

_____

● Critical Thinking Questions

CRITICAL THINKING LEVEL 1 REMEMBER

Think about a person you have enjoyed working or studying with. Which of the Big Five personality traits did he or she have? _____

_____

CRITICAL THINKING LEVEL 2 UNDERSTAND

Fill in the APP of MAPPS for this passage.

    About: _____

      Point: _____

Proof:

1. _____

_____

2. _____

3. _____

4. _____

_____

5. _____

_____

6. _____

_____

CRITICAL THINKING LEVEL 3 APPLY

Based on this passage, what traits should you cultivate to do well in college? _____

_____

CRITICAL THINKING LEVEL 4 ANALYZE

Determine which two of the Big Five personality traits would be very important for a door-to-door salesperson to have. Give your reasons for saying so.

• _____

• _____

CRITICAL THINKING LEVEL 5 EVALUATE

Rate yourself from 1 to 10 on each of the following characteristics..

Where Are You on the "Big Five"?

Extravert									Introvert
10	9	8	7	6	5	4	3	2	1

Emotionally stable									Unstable
10	9	8	7	6	5	4	3	2	1

Agreeable									Disagreeable
10	9	8	7	6	5	4	3	2	1

Conscientious									Not conscientious
10	9	8	7	6	5	4	3	2	1

Open to experience									Not open to experience
10	9	8	7	6	5	4	3	2	1

Based on your responses, write down three jobs you might be (or are) good at, and explain why. If you can't think of particular jobs, then discuss the types of jobs you might be good at.

- _____

- _____

- _____

CRITICAL THINKING LEVEL 6 CREATE

Create a job description for a job that would be a good fit for a person who is introverted, conscientious, and open to experience. _____

_____

● Vocabulary in Context

The following words (or forms of them) were used in "Big Five Dimensions of Personality." Choose the word that best fills the blank in each sentence.

gregarious	anxious	perseverance	ambiguity	stringent

1. The _____ of the scientist's laboratory results may have been due to a faulty experimental design, but at least she knew what her next steps had to be.

2. At the Web page "Birds Online—No Solitary Keeping," I learned that budgies are _____ birds.

3. From the 1960s to the 1980s, when many state hospitals for the mentally ill were being closed, the families of patients were _____ about what would happen to their institutionalized relatives. As it turned out, they were right to be worried.

4. The motto printed on the New York Post Office building is all about _____ _____: "Neither snow nor rain not heat nor gloom of night stays these couriers from the swift completion of their appointed rounds."

5. _____ laws intended to stop people from drinking and driving have been implemented in many states.

© Andrey Plis/Shutterstock

chapter 8

Using and Integrating Visual Information

● ● ● ● ● ● ● ● ● ● ● ● ● ● ● ● ● ●

❝ *The ultimate freedom is the right and power to decide how anybody or anything outside ourselves will affect us.* ❞
—Stephen Covey

Do you agree with Covey?
What other kinds of freedom
do you find important?

Share Your Prior Knowledge

How do personal friends, images in magazines, and ideas that people in your culture share affect the way you act, the things you believe, and how you view yourself? How can you tell?

Survey the Chapter

Survey Reading 8-1 on pages 399-403. What do you think the reading will discuss about "The Mass Media and Body Image"? Discuss your own ideas as well.

www.cengage.com/devenglish/doleconnect

**Videos Related
to Readings**

**Vocab Words
on Audio**

**Prep Readings
on Demand**

Prep Reading . . . . Anthropology Textbook

Suppose someone from another culture visited you and your family at home. What would they see that would allow them to make some guesses about what is important in your culture?

Visit **www.cengage.com/devenglish/doleconnect** and select Chapter 8 to hear a reading of this selection and view a video about this topic.

Our Bodies and Culture

Gary Ferraro

appreciable The next sentence gives a general example. Does *appreciable* mean "unnoticeable" or "noticeable"?

1   The nonmaterial aspects of our culture, such as ideas, values, and attitudes, can have an **appreciable** effect on the human body. Culturally defined attitudes concerning male and female attractiveness, for example, have resulted in some dramatic effects on the body. Burmese women give the appearance of elongating their necks by depressing their clavicles and scapulas with heavy brass rings, Chinese women traditionally had their feet bound, men in New Guinea put bones through their noses, and **scarification** and tattooing are practiced in various parts of the world for the same reasons that women and men in the United States pierce their ear lobes (that is, because their cultures tell them that it looks good). People intolerant of different cultural practices often fail to realize that had they been raised in one of those other cultures, they would be practicing those **allegedly** disgusting or irrational customs.

scarification If the root word here is *scar*, what do you suppose this word means?

allegedly In courtrooms, defendants are often described as having *allegedly* committed the crime for which they are being tried. Does this word mean "supposedly" or "definitely"?

2   Even our body stature is related to a large extent to our cultural ideas. In the Western world, people go to considerable lengths to become as slender as possible. They spend millions of dollars each year on running shoes, diet plans, appetite suppressants, and health spa memberships to help them take off "ugly pounds." However, our Western notion of equating slimness with physical beauty is hardly universally accepted. In large parts of Africa, for example, Western women are perceived as **emaciated** and considered to be singularly unattractive. This point was made painfully obvious to me when I was conducting fieldwork in Kenya during the 1970s. After months of living in Kenya, I learned that many of my male Kikuyu friends pitied me for having such an unattractive wife (5 feet 5 inches tall and 114 pounds). Kikuyu friends often came by my house with a bowl of food or a chicken and discreetly whispered, "This is for your wife." Even though I considered my wife to be beautifully propor-

emaciated From the context before and after this word, what does it mean?

tioned, my African friends thought she needed to be fattened up in order to be beautiful.

3   Altering the body for **aesthetic** purposes (what is known euphemistically as "plastic surgery") has become increasingly widespread in U.S. culture over the last decade. To illustrate, 1.8 million Americans submitted to plastic surgery in 2003, a 12 percent increase from the previous year, while 6.4 million Americans opted for non-surgical procedures such as Botox injections, an increase of 22 percent from the previous year. In fact, surgical and non-surgical altering of our physical appearance is becoming so widespread and routine that it has become a wildly popular form of entertainment. Such reality TV shows as ABC's *Extreme Makeover* and Fox network's *The Swan* feature seemingly unattractive people who voluntarily submit to a **host of** cosmetic surgical procedures and emerge at the end of the show transformed to enjoy rave reviews from friends, family members, and the sizable viewing audience. After liposuction, nose jobs, forehead lifts, lip and breast augmentation, tooth veneering, and chin implants, the women begin to look like Barbie dolls or Pamela Anderson, while the men take on a number of physical traits of action heroes (Kuczynski, 2004).

aesthetic Based on the information that follows in parentheses, what does this word mean?

a host of Looking ahead to the next sentence will give you an idea about the meaning of this phrase. What does it mean?

© Lindsey Hebberd/Woodfin Camp & Associates

This man from Irian Jaya in Indonesia illustrates the concept that cultural ideas of beauty can affect our bodies.

◉ Interaction 8-1. Talking about Reading

Respond in writing to the questions below and then discuss your answers with your classmates.

1. Have you ever watched *Extreme Makeover* (about changing your body) or *What Not to Wear* (about changing your "look")? What was your reaction? Would you ever submit to such public procedures? _____

   _____

2. What are some various attitudes or assumptions in the United States toward people who have a lot of tattoos? _____

   _____

   _____

3. What do you think are some of the purposes people might have for getting piercings?

   _____

   _____

4. What was your first response when you saw the photograph of the Indonesian man in this selection? Did your response change after you read the selection? _____

   _____

   _____

The Power of Visuals

Visuals such as photographs, cartoons, charts, and graphs can present readers with information in a way that affects them powerfully. For example, you may read or hear that there is a decreasing supply of fresh water in the world. But the cartoon on page 381 makes the point more personal and immediate.

Because we are not used to thinking about water as a resource that we have to pay for, the cartoon's surprising equation of gas and water speaks to our emotions as well as our minds.

Even when visuals don't affect us emotionally, they are still a powerful means of communicating a large amount of information in a small amount of space. Examine the following bar graph (**Figure 8.1**) about computer ownership.

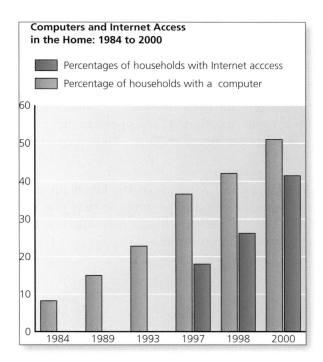

Figure 8.1 Computers and Internet Access in the Home: 1984 to 2000

Kendall, *Sociology in Our Times*, 6th Edition

Even if you didn't consider the exact numbers of households with a computer, you would still be left with the accurate impression that each year from 1984 to 2000, the number of households with computers was rising.

If you do examine the graph closely, as you certainly should if you find it in your reading material for a college course, you might be left with the question of why no Internet access figures are reported for the years before 1997. The reason is that the Internet was not available for public use until 1995.

Reading and Thinking about Visuals

Visuals in textbooks, magazines, and on the Web perform different functions. They may

- provide examples of the concepts being discussed.

- give specific numerical information to support the generalizations in the running text.

- make large amounts of information easier to compare.

In college textbooks, sometimes visuals include information that you must understand in order to comprehend the chapter completely, and other times the visuals are less crucial but still visually pleasing. In the Prep Reading, the photograph of the Indonesian man provides an eye-catching illustration of the main idea of the selection.

In this chapter we will discuss several major types of visual material, such as tables, pie charts, line graphs, bar graphs, and photographs. The following points, with some adaptations, apply to reading most of these different kinds of visuals.

1. **Read the title of the table or graphic carefully.** The title often provides a summary of important information you need in order to understand the graphic. The title may function as the topic. Captions that appear under photographs are similarly important. Often, the caption functions as the main idea or the topic sentence of the graphic.

2. **Read the headings of rows and columns or the labels on *x* and *y* axes carefully.** In a table, you should read the column headings so that you will know which groups are being compared. The information in the rows often is the point of comparison between the groups listed in the columns.

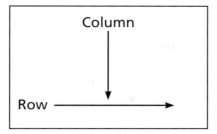

When you are reading graphics, the y axis is the vertical line and the x axis is the horizontal line along the bottom of the figure. Read the labels carefully to make sure you understand how the information is set up.

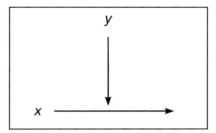

3. **Notice the meaning of each color used.** In some figures, the colors that different parts are printed in have specific meanings. Look for a key to tell you what the colors mean.

4. **Think critically about the implications of the headings, the numbers, and the way the information is presented.** Remember that graphics and tables summarize large amounts of data. In the process of reading so much information, sometimes it's easy to lose track of potential problems or questions that should be asked. Throughout the chapter we'll draw your attention to questions you might want to ask about specific graphics.

Interpreting Tables

A table is an arrangement of information in rows and columns. Tables condense a lot of information into a small space, and they make pieces of information easy to compare. Tables may be composed of information reported in words or in numbers.

Example 1: Table from a Human Development Textbook

Before you read a table, preview the title and column headings.

Table 8.1 Characteristics of Adolescents' Thinking

Feature	Definition	Example
Adolescent egocentrism	Adolescents are overly concerned with their own thoughts and feelings.	When Levi's grandmother died unexpectedly, Levi was preoccupied with how the funeral would affect his weekend plans and ignored how upset his mother was by her own mother's death.
Imaginary audience	Adolescents believe that others are watching them constantly.	Tom had to ride his bike to football practice because his dad wouldn't let him have the car; he was sure that all his car-driving friends would see and make fun of him.
Personal fable	Adolescents believe that their experiences and feelings are unique.	When Rosa's boyfriend decided to date another girl, Rosa cried and cried. She couldn't believe how sad she was, and she was sure her mom had never felt this way.
Illusion of invulnerability	Adolescents think that misfortune only happens to others.	Kumares and his girlfriend had been having sex for about 6 months. Although she thought it would be a good idea to use birth control, he thought it was unnecessary. There was no way his girlfriend would get pregnant.

Kail/Cavanaugh, *Human Development: A Life-Span View*, 4th Edition

Notice the following kinds of information when you read a table:

- **What is the title of the table?** Here, it is "Characteristics of Adolescents' Thinking."

- **What kind of information is given in each column (vertical line)?** In this table, the columns each have a heading that describes the type of information in them: "feature," "definition," and "example."

- **What kind of information is given in each row (horizontal line)?** If you read the first row of this table from left to right, you'll see that "adolescent egocentrism" is defined and then exemplified. Each succeeding feature is similarly defined and exemplified.

Tables often summarize information that the author has been discussing in greater detail over the previous pages of the chapter. When you are reviewing for a test, it's a good idea to use this kind of table as a study aid.

Example 2: Table from an American Government and Politics Textbook

This table is more complicated than the first one you read. First preview the title and column headings.

Table 8.2 Characteristics of the 110th Congress, 2007-2009

Characteristic	U.S. Population (2000)*	House	Senate
Age (median)	35.3	56.0	61.9
Percentage minority	24.9	15.9	5
Religion			
Percentage church members	61.0	90.6	99
Percentage Roman Catholic	39.0	29.4	24
Percentage Protestant	56.0	55.6	56
Percentage Jewish	4.0	6.7	13
Percentage female	50.9	16.1	16
Percentage with advanced degrees	5.0	66.7	78
Occupation			
Percentage lawyers	0.4	38.4	58
Percentage blue-collar workers	20.1	1.6	3
Family Income			
Percentage of families earning over $50,000 annually	22.0	100.0	100
Personal wealth			
Percentage with assets over $1 million†	0.7	16.0	33

*Estimates based on 2000 census.
†108th Congress.

Schmidt/Shelley/Bardes, *American Government and Politics Today, 2007-2008*, 13th Edition

Notice these features as you study the table:

- In the "characteristic" column, notice that for most items, percentages of populations are being compared. For example, under "religion," the different groups to be compared are the percentage of the population who are church members; who are Roman Catholics; who are Protestants; and who are Jewish. Age, however, cannot be stated as a percentage of the population. The ages given in the remaining three columns are median ages. (You may recall from Chapter 1 that *median* means that half the people are younger than this age and half are older than this age.)

- The second, third, and fourth columns compare the U.S. population as a whole, the members of the House of Representatives, and the members of the Senate on the basis of the characteristics listed in the first column.

- To use the table, start with a characteristic you want to examine—let's say "percentage minority." Reading across the second row of the table, you can see in the United States, minorities make up 24.9 percent of the population. In the House, they make up 15.9 percent of the members. In the Senate, minorities are 5 percent of the members.

● Interaction 8-2. Reading and Thinking about a Table

Use the table from the American government textbook (**Table 8.2**) to answer the following questions.

1. What is the median age of the U.S. population? _____ Of the House of Representatives? _____ Of the Senate? _____

2. What is the percentage of church members in the U.S. population? _____ In the House? _____ In the Senate? _____

3. Compare the three populations on the basis of the percentage of people holding advanced degrees. United States: _____ House: _____ Senate: _____

4. Which of the three populations has the highest percentage of lawyers? What is the percentage? _____

5. Which of the three populations has the highest percentage of blue-collar workers? What is the percentage? _____

Take a Moment to Think about . . . The Congress as a Reflection of the American People

Based on the characteristics included in this table, are the members of Congress (that is, the House and Senate combined) more similar to or more different from the general U.S. population? Does this seem important to you? Why or why not? _____

_____

_____

⬗ Interaction 8-3. Reading the Explanation That Goes with the Table

A table in a textbook is normally introduced or explained by the author. Here is how the authors introduce **Table 8.2**.

Congresspersons and the Citizenry: A Comparison

Members of the U.S Senate and the U.S. House of Representatives are not typical American citizens. Members of Congress are older than most Americans, partly because of constitutional age requirements and partly because a good deal of political experience normally is an advantage in running for national office. Members of Congress are also **disproportionately** white, male, and trained in high-status occupations. Lawyers are by far the largest occupational group among congresspersons, although the proportion of lawyers in the House is lower now than it was in the past. Compared with the average American citizen, members of Congress are well paid. In 2006, annual congressional salaries were $165,200. Increasingly, members of Congress are also much wealthier than the average citizen. Whereas fewer than 1 percent of Americans have **assets** exceeding $1 million, about one-third of the members of Congress are millionaires. Table 8.2 summarizes selected characteristics of the members of Congress.

> **disproportionately** Use your knowledge of word parts to figure out the meaning of this word: *dis-* + *proportion* + *ate* + *ly*. What does it mean?

> **assets** Use context to figure out the likely meaning of this word.

—Schmidt/Shelley/Bardes, *American Government and Politics Today, 2007-2008*, 13ᵗʰ Edition

1. What does this paragraph explain that the table does not about the age of congresspersons? _____

2. What does the paragraph explain that the table does not about why the family income of every single congressperson is more than $50,000? _____
   _____

3–5. A sentence in this paragraph makes the following generalization: "Members of Congress are also disproportionately white, male, and trained in high-status occupations." In the table, what three characteristics from the first column will lead a reader to the exact percentages involved for each part of that general statement?

• White: _____

• Male: _____

• High-status occupation: _____

Interaction 8-4. Reading a Table from a Media Textbook

Examine the following table and answer the questions that follow.

Table 8.3 What Consumers Spend for Wireless Content

Year	Instant Messaging	E-mail & Information Alerts	Ringtones	Wireless Games	Picture & Video Downloads	Mobile Advertising & Marketing	Total Wireless Content Spending
2004	$1.8 B	$433 M	$307 M	$82 M	$70 M	$105 M	$2.8 B
2005	$2.4 B	$683 M	$681 M	$224 M	$151 M	$201 M	$4.3 B
2006*	$2.9 B	$945 M	$1 B	$430 M	$250 M	$318 M	$5.9 B
2007*	$3.3 B	$1.2 B	$1.4 B	$634 M	$371 M	$425 M	$7.3 B
2008*	$3.8 B	$1.3 B	$1.7 B	$791 M	$449 M	$516 M	$8.5 B

*projected   B=Billion, M=Million

Biagi, *MediaImpact*, 8th Edition

1. What is this table **About**; what is its topic? _____

2. What is the **P**oint of the table; what is the main idea? _____
   _____

3. How many different types of wireless content did the author of this table examine?
   _____

4. Which years include actual data, and which years include projected data?
   Actual: _____   Projected: _____

5. In what year do you suppose this table was created? _____

6. What does the abbreviation *B* stand for? _____ What does *M* stand for? _____

7. How much more does this table predict that consumers will spend in 2008 on instant messaging than they spent in 2004? _____

8. How much more does the table predict that consumers will spend overall on wireless content in 2007 than in 2005? _____

9. In 2004, on which type of wireless content did consumers spend the least amount of money? _____

10. In 2008, on which type of wireless content does the table predict that consumers will spend the most amount of money? _____

11. Does the table suggest that in any category, spending on wireless content will decrease from 2004 to 2008? _____

12. To prove the point that consumers pay the most for instant messaging, which parts of the table should be compared? _____
    _____

13. To prove the point that spending on ringtones is growing quickly, which parts of the table should be compared? _____
    _____

14. What true statement can you make about how spending on picture and video downloads changed from 2004 to 2008? _____

_____

15. What true statement can you make about how overall spending on wireless content changed from 2004 to 2008? _____

Interpreting Pie Charts

A pie chart shows how a whole pie—100 percent of something—is divided up. Pie charts help readers compare the percentages or proportions of different components of a whole.

Example: Pie Charts from an American History Textbook

Figure 8.2 Sources of Immigration

Source: Data from *Historical Statistics of the United States, Colonial Times to 1970* (White Plains, NY: Kraus International, 1989), pp. 105-109.

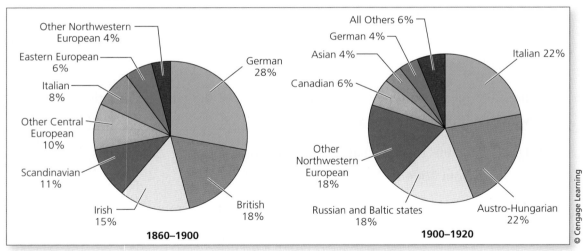

Adapted from Murrin et al., *Liberty, Equality, Power*, 5th Edition

© Cengage Learning

Notice the following kinds of information when you read a pie chart:

- **What is the title?** The title of the figure overall is "Sources of Immigration." Based on the information that follows the title, you can tell that this information is about the United States.

- **What are the titles of the individual pie charts?** The chart on the left is called "1860–1900." The one on the right is titled "1900–1920." So from the titles alone, you can see that the purpose of the pie charts is to compare the sources of immigration during two different time periods.

- **How is the pie divided?** Let's look at the information for 1860–1900. Because the largest piece of the pie is so obvious, you can see right away that more immigrants to the United States were German than any other nationality. This pie chart includes the actual percentage, 28 percent. Notice that the largest slice begins at 12:00 (if this circle were a clock face). Continuing around to the right you will find that each slice of the pie gets smaller. Thus, the second largest group of immigrants during that period was British, the next largest group was Irish, and so on.

- **What conclusions can you draw by thinking critically?** Think about all the groups represented on the pie chart for 1860–1900. What generalization can you make about where these immigrants came from? Notice that they are all from Europe, and mostly Western Europe.

Interaction 8-5. Reading and Thinking about a Pie Chart

Use the pie charts in Figure 8.2 to answer the following questions.

1. What are the nationalities of the two largest groups of immigrants during the period from 1900 to 1920? _____

2. Did the percentage of Italians arriving in the United States increase or decrease from the period from 1860 to 1900 to the period from 1900 to 1920? By what percentage?

   _____

3. Was Asian immigration to the United States a significant factor from 1860 to 1920? Explain your answer. _____

   _____

4. Compare the immigrants' nationalities on the two pie charts. Are there more similarities or more differences in where the immigrants came from? _____

5. What further information would help you understand the information in these pie charts more precisely? Where might you look for it? _____

_____

_____

_____

_____

● Interaction 8-6. Reading a Pie Chart

Read the pie chart and answer the questions that follow.

Figure 8.3 What Type of Music Do People Buy?

Data from Recording Industry Association of America, 2004

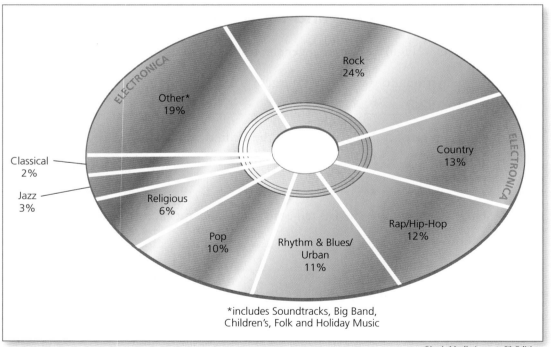

*includes Soundtracks, Big Band, Children's, Folk and Holiday Music

Biagi, *Media Impact*, 8th Edition

1. What is the topic of this pie chart? _____

2. What is the main idea? _____

3. How much of music that people buy is rock music? _____

4. What type of music was purchased the least? _____

5. Do people purchase your favorite type of music much? _____

Interpreting Line and Bar Graphs

A graph shows the relationship between two sets of numbers, such as the number of people doing something over a certain number of years. Line graphs and bar graphs are often used in college textbooks.

Line Graphs

Line graphs are used to show how a condition or behavior changes over time. The number of people engaging in a behavior is often plotted on the *y* axis (the vertical line). The units of time, such as years, are plotted on the *x* axis, or horizontal line. Line graphs, like the example from a health textbook that you see in **Figure 8.4**, make it easy to see trends in data.

Figure 8.4 Number of Cohabiting, Unmarried, Adult Couples of the Opposite Sex (United States)

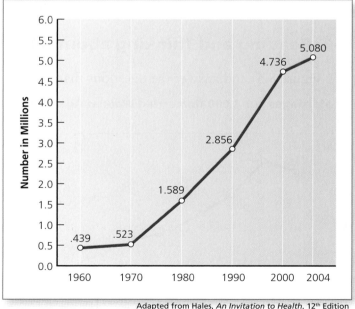

Adapted from Hales, *An Invitation to Health*, 12ᵗʰ Edition

Notice the following points about the preceding line graph:

- **What is the title?** It is "Number of Cohabiting, Unmarried, Adult Couples of the Opposite Sex (United States)." Notice that the title tells us that the graph does *not* include information about couples who were not living together (cohabiting), who were married, who were not adults, who were living with same-sex partners, or who were not in the United States.

- **What are the headings on the *x* axis and *y* axis?** The *y* axis is labeled "Number in Millions" and the *x* axis is not labeled. The *x* axis gives a series of years starting at 1960 and ending at 2004. Notice that all the years are ten years apart except for the last two.

- **Think about the trend that this line graph shows.** First, notice that for each point at a particular year, the actual number is given. For instance, in 1960 less than half a million unmarried heterosexual couples were cohabiting in the United States (since the numbers are given in millions, 1 = 1 million, so the .439 means 439,000 people). Between 1960 and 1970, the number didn't change dramatically. From 1970 to 1980, however, the number tripled, approximately, and it nearly doubled in the next decade, from 1980 to 1990. In the next decade the number rose from about 2.8 million (2,800,000) to 4.7 million (4,700,000), again almost doubling. The last time period, remember, is only four years. So the small rise in numbers may be due to the fact that the time period is less than half that of the other time periods on the line graph, or it may be an indication that the numbers are increasing less rapidly than before.

Interaction 8-7. Reading and Thinking about a Line Graph

Read the line graph (**Figure 8.5**) and answer the questions that follow.

Figure 8.5 Number of Marriages per 1,000 Unmarried Women Age 15 and Older (United States)

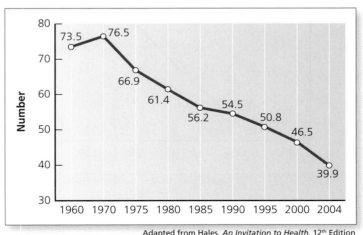

Adapted from Hales, *An Invitation to Health*, 12th Edition

1. Based on the title, whose behavior does this line graph describe? _____

_____

2. What do the numbers on the *y* axis represent? _____

_____

3. What spread of years does the data cover? _____

4. How many years are the intervals between the dates? _____

_____

5. How many marriages per 1,000 unmarried women 15 and older were there in 1960? _____

6. In what year did the highest number of marriages occur, and how many marriages were there? _____

7. When did the smallest number occur, and how many were there? _____

8. Is the number of marriages among this group of women rising or falling? _____

9. Using the years and numbers from the highest and lowest points, write a sentence that describes the trend that this graph describes. _____

_____

10. Think about the intervals between the years on the *x* axis. Do you think we can use the steepness of the lines to judge accurately the differences in the numbers of marriages in the first three dates given? Why or why not? _____

_____

Bar Graphs

Bar graphs help readers compare differences between groups, or as seen in **Figure 8.6**, the differences between groups over time.

Example: A Bar Graph from a Business Management Textbook

Figure 8.6 % of Married Women (with Children) Who Work

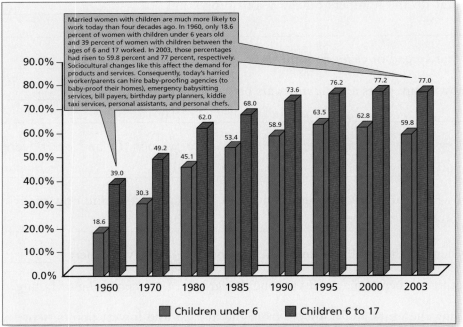

Adapted from Williams, *Management*, 4th Edition

Let's examine the bar graph based on the general questions.

- **What is the title of the bar graph?** It is "Percentage of Married Women (with Children) Who Work." Notice that unmarried mothers are not included in this data.

- **What information does the *y* axis provide?** Since there is no label, we can look at the numbers, which are percentages ranging from 0 percent at the bottom to 90 percent at the top. The title of the graph suggests that these are the percentages who work.

- **What information does the *x* axis provide?** These are years, but with variable intervals between the years. The range is from 1960 to 2003.

- **What do the colors mean?** Notice that for each year there is a pair of bars, one blue and the other red. The key at the bottom notes that blue represents children under six, and red represents children aged six to seventeen.

- **What do you notice overall about the trend over time?** Has the number of married mothers who work increased or decreased over time? How about for those with young children? How about for those with older children? These have all increased over time.

◆ Interaction 8-8. Reading and Thinking about a Bar Graph

Answer the following questions about the bar graph (**Figure 8.6**).

1. In what year was there the greatest difference in the number of married mothers working between those with young children and those with older children? Write a sentence or two that describes this difference. _____

_____

_____

2. What was the time period in which the number of married mothers who worked was larger than the number who did not? _____

_____

_____

3. Using general phrases like "more than half" or "about a quarter," describe in a sentence the data for the year 2003. _____

_____

_____

4. Suppose unmarried mothers *were* included in this data. Do you think the percentages for each year would go up or down? Why? _____

_____

_____

Interpreting Flow Charts

Flow charts, also called *process charts*, show how different stages in a process are connected. You should read flow charts from left to right and from top to bottom. Flow charts can become quite technical, with different box colors representing different aspects of the process.

Example: A Flow Chart from a Business Textbook

Figure 8.7 How Planning Functions Are Related

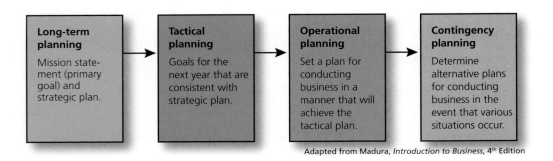

Adapted from Madura, *Introduction to Business*, 4th Edition

Let's examine this simple flow chart from an introduction to a business textbook:

- **What is the title?** The title is "How Planning Functions Are Related."

- **What do the headings indicate?** There are four headings, one in each box, and they are four different stages of planning: long-term, tactical, operational, and contingency.

- **What is the direction of flow?** The planning processes start at the left box, long-term planning, and flow through each box one by one, with contingency planning as the last box.

- **What does the flow chart mean?** In a business there are four stages of planning, each with a different goal. The one that all the others depend on is long-term planning. You can see that this consists of developing a mission statement and a strategic plan. These guide the other business plans. Tactical planning emphasizes shorter-term plans that will help make the long-term plans come into being. Then operational planning takes place to work out the "how" to make those shorter-term goals happen. Finally, after all the goal-directed planning has been done, the downside is examined in contingency planning. If things don't work out as planned, what should the company do?

Take a Moment to Think about . . . Planning to Achieve Your Goals

When you study tables and graphs, you will focus mostly on the meaning of the data for the course you are taking. But it's also smart to think how you personally might be able to make use of any and all information that you come across in your studies. Consider the flow chart in Figure 8.7 with your own goals in mind. Do you start your planning processes with your long-term goals? How will you move forward on them in the next year? Consider at least one long-term goal that you have and fill in the following chart (**Figure 8.8**) with the stages of your planning as you think through how to make your goal a reality.

Figure 8.8 Planning to Achieve Your Goals

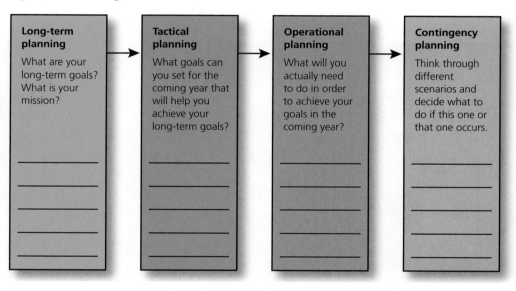

Long-term planning

What are your long-term goals? What is your mission?

Tactical planning

What goals can you set for the coming year that will help you achieve your long-term goals?

Operational planning

What will you actually need to do in order to achieve your goals in the coming year?

Contingency planning

Think through different scenarios and decide what to do if this one or that one occurs.

Interpreting Photographs

Photographs are used in textbooks to illustrate the concepts under discussion. Just as you should carefully read the title of a pie chart or bar graph, you should carefully read the caption of a photograph. The caption will tell you why the photo has been included.

Example: A Photograph from an Anthropology Textbook

This photograph appears in a chapter on political organization and social control. It is in a section titled "Changing State Systems of Government." In order to get the most out of the photograph, you would need to know these terms from the caption: *participatory democracy* and *post-apartheid*.

© David Turnley/CORBIS

The worldwide trend during the last several decades has been toward greater participatory democracy. Here a South African woman casts her vote in the nation's first post-apartheid election, in 1994.

Ferraro, *Cultural Anthropology,* 6th Edition

🔘 Interaction 8-9. Reading and Thinking about a Photograph

1. Where in the text might you look for the definitions of *participatory democracy* and *post-apartheid* ? _____

   _____

2. Define *participatory democracy*. Use your knowledge of word parts and a dictionary if necessary. _____

   _____

3. Define *apartheid*. Use a dictionary if necessary._____

   _____

4. What does the prefix *post-* mean? _____Thus, what does *post-apartheid* mean?

   _____

5. Notice the two people in the photo. What is one possible reason these people in particular were photographed? _____

   _____

   _____

Chapter Summary Activity

This chapter has discussed the purposes of visuals and tables, general points about reading them, and specific information about different types of visuals. Create a Reading Guide on page 402 by completing each idea on the left with information from the chapter on the right. Return to this guide any time you need a refresher on how to read and study textbook chapter visuals.

Reading Guide to Reading Visuals

Complete this idea	with information from the chapter.
Textbook authors let you know when you should examine a figure by	1.
Visuals perform different functions in a text. They may	2. 3. 4.
Four general guidelines for reading visual material are to	5. 6. 7. 8.
A table can be defined as	9.
Before you read a table, you should	10.
Information in tables may be given in	11.
A pie chart shows	12.
The size of each piece of the pie shows	13.
Line graphs are used to show	14.
The number of people exhibiting a behavior is often plotted on the	15.
The units of time are plotted on the	16.
Line graphs make it easy to see	17.
Bar graphs help readers compare	18.
Flow charts show how	19.
Photographs are used in textbooks	20.

Test Taking Tips
Interpreting Visuals

If you need to interpret a visual such as a table, chart, or graph on a test, use the APP of MAPPS to your advantage. Ask yourself what the visual is about, what the point of the visual is, and what proof you find in the visual to support the point. Often, you will also have to use your skill at finding an implied main idea since many visuals don't have a caption that states the main idea.

Turn to Figure 1.2 on page 42 as an example. Examine the title, the numbers and what they mean, the key to the use of colors, and the headings under each set of bars. Refer to this figure as you read the filled-in topic and proof points in the APP outline. Can you fill in the implied main idea based on the topic and the supporting details?

About (the topic): percentage of Americans who say they are offended by content on TV

Point (implied): _____

_____

Proof: 1. Concerning violence on TV, almost 80 percent of people 65 and older are offended, and the percentage decreases as age goes down.
2. Regarding sexual content, the same progression can be seen, with the youngest viewers (18–29 years old) being the least offended.
3. Similarly, in the area of profanity on TV, about 30% of people aged 18–29 are offended; about 55% of people aged 30–49 are offended; about 65% of those 50–64 are offended; and a whopping 80% of those 65 and older are offended.
4. The same basic results also pertain to homosexuality on TV.

As you can see from the combination of skills needed to figure out the main point of this figure, reading is a complex process composed of many different kinds of activities. The more you practice combining the different activities, the more effective you will become as a college reader.

Reading 8-1 . . . . Sociology Textbook

⬤ Pre-Reading the Selection

The reading that follows, "Mass Media and Body Image," is part of a sociology textbook chapter on sexuality and gender.

Guessing the Purpose

Judging from the genre of the book from which this selection is taken, what do you suppose is the purpose of the selection? _____

Surveying the Reading

In addition to surveying the title and first sentences of paragraphs, be sure to survey the caption of the photo and the titles of the tables and the figure. What is the topic of the reading selection? _____

_____

Predicting the Content

Predict three things this selection will discuss.

- _____

- _____

- _____

Activating Your Knowledge

Think of two friends or relatives who have been influenced by the media to see their bodies in a certain way. Briefly note the kinds of influence the media has had on them.

- _____

- _____

Common Knowledge

Read these terms and their definitions to help you understand the reading selection.

revenue (*paragraph 4*) Income produced from a particular source

industry (*paragraph 4*) A specific type of manufacture

Reading with Pen in Hand

Now read the selection. As you read, mark any ideas that seem important, and respond to the questions and vocabulary items in the margin. Monitor your comprehension by putting a ✔ next to a paragraph when you understand most of it. Place an ✘ next to a paragraph when you don't understand most of it.

Visit www.cengage.com/devenglish/doleconnect and select Chapter 8 to hear vocabulary words from this selection and view a video about this topic.

The Mass Media and Body Image

Robert J. Brym and John Lie

1   The social construction of **gender** does not stop at the school steps. Outside school, children, adolescents, and adults continue to negotiate gender roles as they interact with the mass media. If you systematically observe the roles played by women and men in TV programs and ads one evening, you will probably discover a pattern noted by sociologists since the 1970s. Women will more frequently be seen cleaning house, taking care of children, modeling clothes, and acting as objects of male desire. Men will more frequently be seen in aggressive, action-oriented, and authoritative roles. They reinforce the normality of traditional gender roles. As you will now see, many people even try to shape their bodies after the body images portrayed in the mass media.

2   The human body has always served as a sort of personal billboard that advertises gender. However, historian Joan Jacobs Brumberg (1997) makes a good case for the view that the importance of body image to our self-definition has grown over the past century. Just listen to the difference in emphasis on the body in the diary resolutions of two typical white, middle-class American girls, separated by a mere 90 years. From 1892: "Resolved, not to talk about myself or feelings. To think before speaking. To work seriously. To be self

◆ *Reading Journal*

gender Notice that the authors didn't use the word *sex*. Also notice they say the *social construction of gender*. Take a guess at the meaning of *gender*, or use a dictionary to find the meaning.

◆ On TV, what roles do women and men fill?

◆ In what difference in the two girls' diaries is Joan Jacobs Brumberg interested?

restrained in conversation and actions. Not to let my thoughts wander. To be dignified. Interest myself more in others." From 1982: "I will try to make myself better in any way I possibly can with the help of my budget and baby-sitting money. I will lose weight, get new lenses, already got new haircut, good makeup, new clothes and accessories" (quoted in Brumberg, 1997: xxi).

◆ **What do the examples of the Gibson Girl and the White Rock Girl show about the changing definition of the ideal female body?**

3   As body image became more important for one's self-definition in the course of the twentieth century, the ideal body image became thinner, especially for women. Thus, the first American "glamour girl" was Mrs. Charles Dana Gibson, who was famous in advertising and society cartoons in the 1890s and 1900s as the "Gibson Girl." According to the Metropolitan Museum of Art's Costume Institute, "[e]very man in America wanted to win her" and "every woman in America wanted to be her. Women stood straight as poplars and tightened their corset strings to show off tiny waists" (Metropolitan Museum of Art, 2000). As featured in the *Ladies Home Journal* in 1905, the Gibson Girl measured 38-27-45—certainly not slim by today's standards. During the twentieth century, however, the ideal female body type thinned out. The "White Rock Girl" featured on the logo of the White Rock beverage company, was 5'4" and weighed 140 pounds in 1894. In 1947 she had slimmed down to 125 pounds. By 1970 she was 5'8" and 118 pounds (Peacock, 2000).

◆ **What are two reasons that a slimmer body image became the ideal in the twentieth century?**

4   Why did body image become more important to people's self-definition during the twentieth century? Why was slimness stressed? Part of the answer to both questions is that more Americans grew overweight as their lifestyles became more **sedentary**. As they became better educated, they also grew increasingly aware of the health problems associated with being overweight. The desire to slim down was, then, partly a reaction to bulking up. But that is not the whole story. The rake-thin models that populate modern ads are not promoting good health. They are promoting an extreme body shape that is virtually **unattainable** for most people. They do so because it is good business. In 1990 the United States diet and low-calorie frozen entrée industry alone enjoyed revenues of nearly $700 million. Some 65 million Americans spent upward of $30 billion in the diet and self-help industry in the pursuit of losing weight. The fitness industry generated $43 billion in revenue, and the cosmetic surgery industry another $5 billion (Hesse-Biber, 1996: 35, 39, 51, 53). Bankrolled by these industries, advertising in the mass media blankets us with images of slim bodies and makes these body types appealing. Once people become convinced that they need to develop bodies like the

sedentary Look at the context. What is the meaning?

unattainable Both word parts and context can provide clues here. What does *unattainable* mean?

Lou Chardonnay/CORBIS

The low-calorie and diet food industry promotes an idea of slimness that is often impossible to attain and that generates widespread body dissatisfaction.

ones they see in ads, many of them are really in trouble because these body images are very difficult for most people to attain.

5   Survey data show just how widespread dissatisfaction with our bodies is and how important a role the mass media play in generating our discomfort. For example, a 1997 survey of North American college graduates showed that 56 percent of women and 43 percent of men were dissatisfied with their overall appearance (Garner, 1997). Only 3 percent of the dissatisfied women, but 22 percent of the dissatisfied men, wanted to gain weight. This reflects the greater desire of men for muscular, stereotypically male **physiques**. Most of the dissatisfied men, and even more of the dissatisfied women (89 percent), wanted to lose weight. This reflects the general societal push toward slimness and its greater effect on women.

6   **Figure 8.9** reveals gender differences in body ideals in a different way. It compares women's and men's attitudes toward the appearance of their stomachs. It also compares women's attitudes toward their breasts with men's attitudes toward their chests. It shows, first, that women are more concerned about their stomachs than men are. Second, it shows that by 1997 men were more concerned about their

◆ Did Gardner's 1997 study indicate that a majority of women and a majority of men were dissatisfied with their appearance?

physiques Use the context to determine the meaning of *physiques*.

◆ How does Figure 8.9 reveal gender differences in body ideals?

Figure 8.9 Body Dissatisfaction, United States, 1972–1997 (in percentage, *N*=4000)
Note: The *N* of 4000 refers only to the 1997 survey. The number of respondents in the earlier surveys was not given.

◆What is the main idea of this figure?

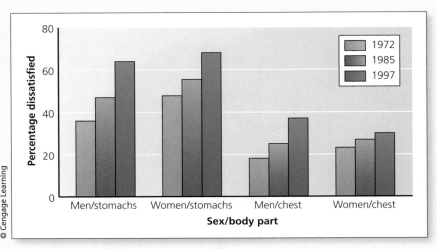

◆How do fashion models stimulate body dissatisfaction among North American women?

7

◆What percentage of North American women and men have dieted, according to the 1997 study?

8

chests than women were about their breasts. Clearly, then, people's body ideals are influenced by their gender. Note also that Figure 8.9 shows trends over time. North Americans' anxiety about their bodies increased substantially between 1972 and 1997.

Table 8.5 suggests that advertising is highly influential in creating anxiety and insecurity about appearance, particularly about body weight. Here we see that in 1997 nearly 30 percent of North American women compared themselves with the fashion models they saw in advertisements, felt insecure about their own appearance, and wanted to lose weight as a result. Among women who were dissatisfied with their appearance, the percentages were much larger, with about 45 percent making comparisons with fashion models and two-thirds feeling insecure and wanting to lose weight. It seems safe to conclude that fashion models stimulate body dissatisfaction among many North American women.

Body dissatisfaction, in turn, motivates many women to diet. Because of anxiety about their weight, 84 percent of North American women said they had dieted in the 1997 survey. The comparable figure for men was 54 percent. Just how important is it for people to achieve their weight goals? According to the survey, it's a life or weight issue: 24 percent of women and 17 percent of men said they would trade more than three years of their lives to achieve their weight goals.

Table 8.5 The Influence of Fashion Models on Feelings about Appearance, North America (in percent, *N*=4000)

	Men	Women	Extremely Dissatisfied Women
I always or often:			
Compare myself to models in magazines	12	27	43
Carefully study the shape of models	19	28	47
Very thin or muscular models make me:			
Feel insecure about my weight	15	29	67
Want to lose weight	18	30	67

9   Body dissatisfaction prompts some people to take dangerous and even life-threatening measures to reduce. In the 1997 survey, 50 percent of female smokers and 30 percent of male smokers said they smoked to control their weight. Other surveys suggest that between 1 percent and 5 percent of American women suffer from anorexia, or refusal to eat enough to remain healthy. About the same percentage of American female college students suffer from bulimia, or regular self-induced vomiting. For college men, the prevalence of bulimia is between 0.2 percent and 1.5 percent (Averett and Korenman, 1996: 305–6). In the United Kingdom, eating disorders are just as common, and the British Medical Association warned that celebrities such as *Ally McBeal* star Calista Flockhart were contributing to a rise in anorexia and bulimia. However, U.K. magazine editors are taking some responsibility for the problem. They recognize that waif-thin models are likely influencing young women to feel anxious about their weight and shape. As a result, the editors recently drew up a **voluntary** code of conduct that urges them to monitor the body images they portray, impose a minimum size for models, and use models of varying shapes and sizes ("British Magazines": 2000). Whether similar measures are adopted in the United States remains to be seen.

◆What is the percentage difference between men's and women's insecure feelings when they compare themselves to models?

◆What are two dangerous methods people use to lose weight?

voluntary This adjective relates to the noun *volunteer*. What does it mean?

● Comprehension Questions

Write the letter of the answer on the line. Then explain your thinking.

Main Idea

____   1. What is the main idea of this selection?
   a. TV actors reinforce gender roles.
   b. Self-improvement is a North American trait.
   c. Many people try to shape their bodies to look like bodies portrayed in the media.
   d. Slimness has been stressed as an ideal body image in the twentieth century.

WHY? What information in the selection leads you to give that answer? _____

_____

_____

____   2. What is the main idea of paragraphs 2–4, taken together?
   a. Body image has become more important to our self-definition during the twentieth century.
   b. The Gibson Girl and the White Rock Girl demonstrate how body image has changed.
   c. As people became more sedentary, they gained weight.
   d. The diet food and fitness industries make billions of dollars from women dissatisfied with their bodies.

WHY? What information in the selection leads you to give that answer? _____

_____

_____

Supporting Details

____   3. From 1972 to 1997, what was the increase in the percentage of men who were dissatisfied with their stomachs?
   a. about 10%
   b. about 15%
   c. about 20%
   d. about 25%

WHY? What information in the selection leads you to give that answer? _____

_____

_____

      4. What proportion of men compare themselves to models in magazines always or often?

         a. 12%

         b. 19%

         c. 15%

         d. 18%

WHY? What information in the selection leads you to give that answer? _____

_____

Relationships

      5. What is the relationship between the first two sentences of paragraph 2?

         a. similarity

         b. cause

         c. example

         d. difference

WHY? What information in the selection leads you to give that answer? _____

_____

      6. What is the relationship of Table 8.5 to paragraph 7?

         a. Table 8.5 is the main idea and paragraph 7 gives the details.

         b. Paragraph 7 states the main ideas and Table 8.5 gives the details.

         c. Paragraph 7 gives the causes and Table 8.5 gives the effects.

         d. Table 8.5 gives the causes and paragraph 7 gives the effects.

WHY? What information in the selection leads you to give that answer? _____

_____

_____

Author's Purpose

____   7. What is the author's purpose for discussing the Gibson Girl and the White Rock Girl in paragraph 3?

a. They show how advertising images promote glamour in harmful ways.

b. They are media images that illustrate the change in the ideal body type of women over time.

c. They promote extreme body shapes that are virtually unattainable for most people.

d. They demonstrate the impact of media on women's self-esteem.

WHY? What information in the selection leads you to give that answer? _____

_____

_____

____   8. Which general statement is the author supporting by listing the amounts of money that the diet, low-calorie frozen entrée, self-help, fitness, and cosmetic surgery industries make?

a. Slimness is stressed in the twentieth century because it is good business.

b. These industries are supporting an extreme body shape that few people can attain.

c. Overweight people will do anything to lose weight.

d. People in general are not satisfied with their bodies.

WHY? What information in the selection leads you to give that answer? _____

_____

_____

Fact, Opinion, and Inference

____   9. Which of the following statements expresses an opinion?

a. Advertising in the mass media blankets us with images of slim bodies.

b. About the White Rock girl: By 1970 she was 5'8" and 118 pounds (Peacock, 2000).

c. About the Gibson girl: "Every man in America wanted to win her."

d. Body dissatisfaction motivates many women to diet.

WHY? What leads you to give that answer? _____

_____

____ 10. According to the information in this reading selection, which of the following statements is true?

    a. Seventeen percent of women would exchange at least three years of their lives to become their ideal weight.

    b. Only women compare themselves to fashion models in magazines.

    c. About 75% of women would not give up three years of their lives to achieve their weight goals.

    d. Nearly one-tenth of college women are in danger of becoming bulimic.

WHY? What information in the selection leads you to give that answer? _____

_____

● Critical Thinking Questions

CRITICAL THINKING LEVEL 1 REMEMBER

Define *anorexia* and *bulimia*. Then *identify* the percentages of college students affected by bulimia. Display the percentages in a simple table (**Table 8.6**). (Unlike most tables, it will have only one row of data.) Include a table title and source information where indicated.

- Anorexia: _____

- Bulimia: _____

Table 8.6 _____

	Women	Men
Bulimia	_____	_____

Source: _____

CRITICAL THINKING LEVEL 2 UNDERSTAND

Describe the woman in the photograph on page 407: What does she look like? What is she doing? In light of the ideas in the reading selection, does anything about the photo seem odd? Explain your response. _____

_____

_____

CRITICAL THINKING LEVEL 3 APPLY

In pairs or groups, *use* one idea from each paragraph in the reading selection to form questions you can ask your classmates about how the mass media has affected their body image. You should have nine questions in all. You can ask open-ended questions, in which the person can respond freely, or you can offer a range of choices and let them choose one.

Example of an open-ended question: How much do you think your body image has been affected by the mass media? (Let them answer however they choose.)

Example of a closed question: How much do you think your body image has been affected by the mass media? Choose the statement that best reflects your belief.
—It's been affected tremendously.
—It's been affected a fair amount.
—It's been somewhat affected.
—It hasn't been affected very much.
—It hasn't been affected at all.

Follow-up question if needed: You say that your body image has been affected by the mass media a fair amount. What are some examples of that?

After you have written your questions as a group, make a copy for each group member. Each person can then ask three other people in the class the questions and write down the answers. Get back with your group to compare the answers. Depending on what you've asked, you may want to display your findings in graphic form.

CRITICAL THINKING LEVEL 4 ANALYZE

In Figure 8.9, read the note to the left of the table about N. Then answer the following questions.

1. What does N mean? _____

2. What possible problems do you see in the comparison of the three studies? _____

_____

_____

3. When you consider the x axis, what has been left out that might be relevant information? _____

CRITICAL THINKING LEVEL 5 EVALUATE

Assess whether the reading selection has convinced you that the mass media affects body image. If it has, which evidence was the most convincing to you? Why? If it has not, what further evidence would you need to be convinced? Why? _____

_____

_____

CRITICAL THINKING LEVEL 6 CREATE

Refer back to the notes you took about friends or relatives in the "Activating Your Knowledge" section on page 398. Using at least three specific pieces of information from the reading selection, *expand* your notes to explain further exactly how their body images have been affected by media. Feel free to include anecdotes (brief stories) about your friends as well as material from the reading.

_____

_____

_____

_____

_____

● Vocabulary in Context

The following words were used in "The Mass Media and Body Image." Fill in the blank in each sentence with one of the following words.

gender	sedentary	voluntary	physique	unattainable

1. Boxing is a sport that demands a well-developed _____.

2. Sometimes families sign a _____ commitment agreement so their mentally ill child or spouse or sibling can get help in a hospital without a court order.

3. However, good mental health care is nearly _____ for poor Americans.

4. African _____ roles cause women to do the vast majority of the farming.

5. As you will find out if you read "A Day in the Life of a Woman Farmer" at the Web site of The Hunger Project at www.thp.org, the African woman food farmer must be about the least _____ person on the planet!

Reading 8-2 . . . . .Psychology Textbook

● Pre-Reading the Selection

The psychology textbook reading that follows includes information that can help you think critically about thinking. This process is sometimes called "metacognition."

Guessing the Purpose

Judging from the genre of the book from which this selection is taken, what do you suppose is the purpose of the selection? _____

Surveying the Reading

In addition to surveying the title and first sentences of paragraphs, be sure to survey the titles of the figures and table. What is the topic of the reading selection? _____

Predicting the Content

Predict three things this selection will discuss.

- _____

- _____

- _____

Activating Your Knowledge

Have you ever noticed that a person you know in one context seems very different when they are in another context? Or been in a situation in which something suddenly looked very different from the way it had before? Jot down a few notes about the situation and why you think your perception changed. _____

Common Knowledge

Read these terms and their definitions to help you understand the reading selection.

principle (*paragraph 3*) A basic truth or law (such as a scientific law)

relative (*paragraph 3*) Not absolute; dependent on something else

stimuli (*paragraph 4*) Plural for *stimulus*; things that cause responses

---

Reading with Pen in Hand

Now read the selection. As you read, mark any ideas that seem important, and respond to the questions and vocabulary items in the margin. Monitor your comprehension by putting a ✔ next to a paragraph when you understand most of it. Place an ✘ next to a paragraph when you don't understand most of it.

Visit **www.cengage.com/devenglish/doleconnect** and select Chapter 8 to hear vocabulary words from this selection and view a video about this topic.

Recognizing Contrast Effects: It's All Relative

Wayne Weiten

◆ *Reading Journal*

1   You're sitting at home one night when the phone rings. It's Simone, an acquaintance from school who needs help with a recreational program for youngsters that she runs for the local park district. She tries to persuade you to volunteer four hours of your time every Friday night throughout the school year to supervise the volleyball program. The thought of giving up your Friday nights and adding this sizable obligation to your already busy schedule makes you cringe with horror. You politely explain to Simone that you can't possibly afford to give up that much time and you won't be able to help her. She accepts your **rebuff** graciously, but the next night she calls again. This time she wants to know whether you would be willing to supervise volleyball every third Friday. You still feel like it's a big obligation that you really don't want to take on, but the new request seems

◆What is the difference between the two calls from Simone?

rebuff Based on the context of the previous sentence, what does this word mean?

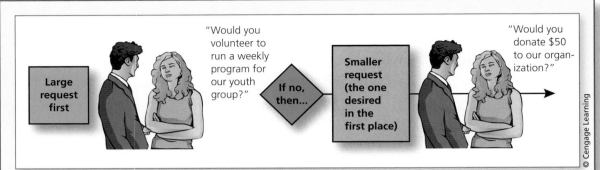

© Cengage Learning

Figure 8.10 Door-in-the-Face Technique

---

succumbed Look this word up in the dictionary. What does it mean?

◆What is the door-in-the-face technique?

manipulative Based on the explanation that precedes it and the example that follows, what does *manipulative* mean?

◆Why is the door-in-the-face technique a highly effective persuasive strategy?

---

much more reasonable than the original one. So, with a sigh of resignation, you agree to Simone's request.

2   What's wrong with this picture? Well, there's nothing wrong with volunteering your time for a good cause, but you just **succumbed** to a social influence strategy called the *door-in-the face technique*. The door-in-the-face technique involves making a large request that is likely to be turned down as a way to increase the chances that people will agree to a smaller request later (see **Figure 8.10**). The name for this strategy is derived from the expectation that the initial request will be quickly rejected (the "door" is slammed in the "salesperson's" face). Although they may not be familiar with the strategy's name, many people use this manipulative tactic. For example, a husband who wants to coax his frugal wife into agreeing to buy a $30,000 SUV might begin by proposing that they purchase a $50,000 sports car. By the time the wife talks her husband out of the $50,000 car, the $30,000 price tag may look quite reasonable to her—which is what the husband wanted all along.

3   Research has demonstrated that the door-in-the-face technique is a highly effective persuasive strategy (Cialdini, 2001). One of the reasons it works so well is that it depends on a simple and pervasive perceptual principle. In the domain of perceptual experience, everything is relative. This relativity means that people are easily swayed by contrast effects. For example, lighting a match or a small candle in a dark room will produce a burst of light that seems quite bright, but if you light the same match or candle in a well-lit room, you may not even detect the additional illumination. The relativity of perception is apparent in the painting by Josef Albers shown in **Figure 8.11**. The two Xs are exactly the same color, but the X in the top half looks yellow, whereas the X in the bottom half looks brown. These varied perceptions occur because of contrast effects—the two X's are contrasted against different background colors.

Figure 8.11 Contrast Effects in Visual Perception
This composition by Joseph Albers shows how one color can be perceived differently when contrasted against different backgrounds. The top X looks yellow and the bottom X looks brown, but they're really the same color.

© Cengage Learning

4   The same principles of relativity and contrast that operate when we are making judgments about the intensity or color of visual stimuli also affect the way we make judgments in a wide variety of domains. For example, a 6'3" basketball player, who is really quite tall, can look downright small when surrounded by teammates who are all over 6'8". And a salary of $36,000 per year for your first full-time job may seem like a princely sum, until a close friend gets an offer of $65,000 a year. The assertion that everything is relative raises the issue of relative to what? *Comparitors* are people, objects, events, and other standards used as a baseline for comparison in making judgments. It is fairly easy to manipulate many types of judgments by selecting extreme comparitors that may be unrepresentative.

5   The influence of extreme comparitors was demonstrated in a couple of interesting studies of judgments of physical attractiveness. In one study, undergraduate males were asked to rate the attractiveness of an average-looking female (who was described as a potential date for another male in the dorm) presented in a photo either just before or just after the participants watched a TV show dominated by strikingly beautiful women (Kenrick & Gutierres, 1980). The female was viewed as less attractive when the ratings were obtained just

◆What are comparitors?

assertion In paragraph 3, the author said "everything is relative." Now he is referring back to that. What is an assertion?

◆How did the introduction of extreme comparitors influence the participants in Kenrick and Guiterres' 1980 study?

Figure 8.12 Contrast effects in judgments of physical attractiveness. Participants rated their own physical attractiveness under two conditions. In the experimental condition, the ratings occurred after subjects were exposed to a series of photos depicting very attractive models. The resulting contrast effects led to lower self-ratings in this condition. (Data based on Thornton & Moore, 1993)

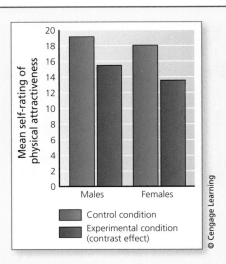

© Cengage Learning

◆In general, how can people use extreme comparitors to influence your judgment?

transgression This word is defined by example before it is used. What does it mean?

◆How can you protect yourself from others manipulating you by using these techniques?

after the men had seen gorgeous women cavorting on TV as opposed to when they hadn't. In another investigation (Thornton and Moore, 1993), both male and female participants rated themselves as less attractive after being exposed to many pictures of extremely attractive models (see **Figure 8.12**). Thus, contrast effects can influence important social judgments that are likely to affect how people feel about themselves and others.

6   Anyone who understands how easily judgments can be manipulated by a careful choice of comparitors could influence your thinking. For example, a politician who is caught in some illegal or immoral act could sway public opinion by bringing to mind (perhaps subtly) the fact that many other politicians have committed acts that were much worse. When considered against a backdrop of more extreme comparitors, the politician's transgression will probably seem less offensive. A defense attorney could use a similar strategy in an attempt to obtain a lighter sentence for a client by comparing the client's offense to much more serious crimes. And a realtor who

Table 8.6 Critical Thinking Skills Discussed in This Application

Skill	Description
Understanding how contrast effects can influence judgments and decisions	The critical thinker appreciates how striking contrasts can be manipulated to influence many types of judgments.
Recognizing when extreme comparitors are being used	The critical thinker is on the lookout for extreme comparitors that distort judgments.

wants to sell you an expensive house that will require huge mortgage payments will be quick to mention other homeowners who have taken on even larger mortgages.

7   In summary, critical thinking is facilitated by conscious aware-ness of the way comparitors can influence and perhaps distort a wide range of judgments. In particular, it pays to be vigilant about the possibility that others may manipulate contrast effects in their per-suasive efforts. One way to reduce the influence of contrast effects is to consciously consider comparitors that are both worse and better than the event you are judging, as a way of balancing the effects of the two extremes.

facilitated If you speak some Spanish, you probably know the meaning of *facil*. Even if you don't, however, context can lead you to a guess about the meaning of this word.

vigilant Look this word up in a dictionary if you need to.

● Comprehension Questions

Write the letter of the answer on the line. Then explain your thinking.

Main Idea

_____   1. What is the main idea of this selection?

    a. You're sitting at home one night, when the phone rings.

    b. The door-in-the-face technique is a highly persuasive social influence strategy.

    c. The influence of extreme comparitors was demonstrated in a couple of inter-esting studies of judgments of physical attractiveness.

    d. Due to the relativity of contrast effects, a person's perceptions can be manipu-lated by using extreme comparitors.

WHY? What information in the selection leads you to give that answer? _____

_____

_____

_____   2. What is the main idea of Figure 8.12?

    a. The difference between how men and women rated their physical attractive-ness was significantly different.

    b. Both men and women rated their own physical attractiveness lower after viewing attractive models, thus showing the consequences of contrast effects.

    c. In the experimental condition, the ratings occurred after subjects were exposed to a series of photos depicting very attractive models.

    d. This data was based on a 1993 study by Thornton and Moore.

WHY? What information in the selection leads you to give that answer? _____

_____

_____

Supporting Details

____ 3. What kinds of supporting details are used in paragraph 6?
 a. classification
 b. causes
 c. steps in a process
 d. examples

WHY? What information in the selection leads you to give that answer? _____

_____

_____

____ 4. Figure 8.11 is a supporting detail for which of the following ideas in the selection?
 a. Physical attractiveness is relative.
 b. Selection of extreme comparitors is relative.
 c. Perception is relative.
 d. Balancing the effects of two extremes is relative.

WHY? What information in the selection leads you to give that answer? _____

_____

_____

Relationships

____ 5. What is the relation of paragraph 1 to paragraph 2?
 a. Paragraph 1 demonstrates the causes of the effects described in paragraph 2.
 b. Paragraph 1 lists the three main features of the object discussed in paragraph 2.
 c. Paragraph 1 provides a narrative example of the concept defined in paragraph 2.
 d. Paragraph 1 classifies the four criteria that need to be satisfied to achieve the technique outlined in paragraph 2.

WHY? What information in the selection leads you to give that answer? _____

_____

_____

_____ 6. What word in paragraph 3 signals a contrast within a sentence?
     a. for example
     b. but
     c. apparent
     d. the same

WHY? What information in the selection leads you to give that answer? _____

_____

_____

Author's Purpose

_____ 7. Why did the author include Table 8.6 in this selection?
     a. to inform students how to develop critical thinking skills related to the information in the selection
     b. to summarize the main ideas of the reading selection as a reminder
     c. to entertain students with humorous descriptions of critical thinking skills
     d. to teach students how to manipulate others

WHY? What information in the selection leads you to give that answer? _____

_____

_____

_____ 8. Why does the author include the information about the candle and the Albers painting in paragraph 3?
     a. They support by example the idea that people's perceptions are easily influenced by contrast effects.
     b. They introduce Figures 8.11 and 8.12.
     c. They categorize perception into the real and the artistic.
     d. They demonstrate the same principles of relativity and contrast that affect judgment-making more widely.

WHY? What information in the selection leads you to give that answer? _____

_____

Fact, Opinion, and Inference

____ 9. Which of the following statements is a fact?

    a. What's wrong with this picture?

    b. Well, there's nothing wrong with volunteering for a good cause.

    c. But you've just succumbed to a social influence strategy called the *door-in-the-face technique*.

    d. Social influence strategies are unethical.

WHY? What information in the possible answer choices leads you to give that answer? _____

_____

_____

____ 10. Based on what you have read in the selection, which of the following inferences is probably correct?

    a. When she stood next to Oprah, she felt unsuccessful.

    b. When she repaired her car engine with her daughter, she felt stupid.

    c. When she decided to go to the library, she felt disciplined.

    d. When she was introduced to Brad Pitt, she felt uncomfortable.

WHY? What information in the selection leads you to give that answer? _____

_____

_____

_____

⬤ Critical Thinking Questions

CRITICAL THINKING LEVEL 1 REMEMBER

List five of the eleven examples of contrast effects given in the selection. Write the paragraph number in which the example appears.

- _____   Paragraph number: _____

- _____   Paragraph number: _____

- _____   Paragraph number: _____
- _____   Paragraph number: _____
- _____   Paragraph number: _____

CRITICAL THINKING LEVEL 2 UNDERSTAND

Suppose that Andrea and Kurt have a two-bedroom, one-bath house in a neighborhood where most houses are considerably smaller. They move into a larger house with four bedrooms and two baths in a very nice suburb; their house is one of the smallest ones. Which comparitor can the couple use to feel good in their new home? Which comparitor may make them feel dissatisfied, if used? _____

_____

_____

CRITICAL THINKING LEVEL 3 APPLY

Briefly describe a situation from your life in which contrast effects played or now play a major role. Be sure to name the comparitor(s) and decide whether or not the comparitor was or is extreme. _____

_____

_____

CRITICAL THINKING LEVEL 4 ANALYZE

The author of the Prep Reading says on page 378 (last sentence of the first paragraph), "People intolerant of different cultural practices often fail to realize that had they been raised in one of those other cultures, they would be practicing those allegedly disgusting or irrational customs." Using the main idea from the current reading, provide one possible reason such intolerance arises. _____

_____

CRITICAL THINKING LEVEL 5 EVALUATE

Suppose that suddenly, every commercial you saw on television was showing happy muscular women mowing their lawns, building houses, fixing their cars, and downing icy cold beers, while very thin men were cooking dinner, folding laundry, smiling at children, and wearing provocative clothing while being watched by the happy women. *Predict* what effect this change would have on you, in the short term and in the long term. Explain your answer by referring specifically to ideas in any of the main readings in the chapter: the Prep reading (page 378), Reading 8-1 (page 405), or Reading 8-2 (page 417). _____

_____

_____

_____

CRITICAL THINKING LEVEL 6 CREATE

Using the information from the last paragraph of the reading selection, *invent* a strategy you can use on yourself the next time you find you are comparing some aspect of who you are, what you have, or what you do with an unrepresentative or extreme comparitor. _____

_____

● Vocabulary in Context

The following words (or words related to them) were used in "Recognizing Contrast Effects." Fill in the blank in each sentence with a form of one of the following verbs. In other words, you may need to use the verb in the past tense or change the basic form in some other way to make it fit the context of the sentence. One verb will not be used.

assert	manipulate	succumb	facilitate	rebuff	transgress

1. The earth on the side of the steep mountain _____ to gravity and started sliding.

2. The backcountry in the 13,000-foot Sierra Nevadas _____ the casual day hiker.

3. Signs at every trailhead _____ that hikers need to tell a ranger where they intend to go and for how long.

4. Having hikers' plans _____ the rangers' ability to search among the granite mountains for lost or injured hikers.

5. Few hikers are so confident, or so stupid, that they _____ this requirement.

part 4

Reading Critically

chapter 9

Distinguishing Fact and Opinion

© Thomas Röpke/CORBIS

> ❝ *The fact that an opinion has been widely held is no evidence whatever that it is not utterly absurd.* ❞
> —Bertrand Russell

What does the quotation from Russell mean? Restate it using your own words. Discuss the quotation and your opinion of it with your classmates.

Share Your Prior Knowledge

How can you tell the difference between fact and opinion?

Survey the Chapter

Think about what you "know" about pirate life. Then survey Readings 9-1 on page 453 and 9-2 on page 464. Was your knowledge correct? Did you know the facts?

www.cengage.com/devenglish/doleconnect

Videos Related to Readings

Vocab Words on Audio

Prep Readings on Demand

Prep Reading . . . . Newspaper Article

Do you think it is all right to download media you did not pay for? Free file-sharing is a pretty hot topic on the Internet. Many consumers, and even some companies, fight for the right to file-share for free. On the other side, recording companies and musicians are fighting to protect their musical property.

 Visit **www.cengage.com/devenglish/doleconnect** and select Chapter 9 to hear a reading of this selection and view a video about this topic.

Britney to Rent, Lease, or Buy

David Pogue

1   The Internet has been described by enthusiasts as a global conversation, a giant encyclopedia or a 24-hour news service—and by **detractors** as the world's most technologically advanced time waster. What peeves record-company executives, however, is how many people see it as a free music store.

2   A Supreme Court decision at the end of June [2005], however, may eventually put an "Out of Business" sign on that store…. Using Grokster, or similar services like Kazaa, always **entailed** a degree of risk, from PC virus and spyware infections. Getting sued—a frequent record-industry tactic—is never a highlight of anyone's day, either. And now the courts are getting involved. What's a music download fan to do—actually pay for music?

3   If it comes to that, they'll find that a lot has changed in the online music business since Apple opened its wildly successful iTunes Music Store in 2003. In that time, Apple's catalog has grown from 200,000 songs to nearly 1.5 million. Apple has sold half a billion songs, and it has been joined by similar stores run by Microsoft, Yahoo, Sony, Real Networks, MusicMatch, Dell, and even Wal-Mart.

4   The essentials are the same for all: each song costs about $1, each album $10. Each song is **encrypted** in such a way that you can copy it onto five computers, burn it onto several blank CDs and copy it to pocket music players—but not distribute it on the Internet.

5   The insanely popular iPod music player and the iTunes Music Store, for Mac and Windows, still work only with each other. Most of the other stores' songs come in a Microsoft format that works on much less popular music players….

6   But "a dollar a song" is no longer the only game in town. In an effort to **exploit** the popularity of music downloads and still make money, the music stores have begun to tinker with the formula.

---

detractors Use the antonym clue found earlier in the sentence.

entailed Use your logic to figure out what this verb means.

encrypted See the examples that follow.

exploit This verb sometimes has a negative connotation, but not here.

3:55	Pedro the Lion
4:07	Guided By Voices
4:25	The Rolling Stones
5:42	Blind Faith
2:08	Rocket from The Cry
4:00	Yeah Yeah Yeahs
4:33	Massive Attack
2:35	Yeah Yeah Yeahs
7:02	Trans Am
4:02	Shuggie Otis
4:39	Air
4:24	The Undisputed Trut

In 2003, entrepreneur Steve Jobs of Apple introduced iTunes, a Web site that offers a way for consumers to legally download music directly from the Internet. Other pay music services soon followed after the U.S. Supreme Court ruled in 2005 that free file-sharing services, such as Kazaa and Grokster, were illegal.

© Jim Watson/AFP/Getty Images

7   One **intriguing** alternative is the subscription plan allowing unlimited downloads that is currently offered by Napster, Yahoo, and Rhapsody. (Each also maintains a traditional $1-a-song service.) Microsoft, Target, MTV, and AOL have also announced plans to get into this subscription business, and even Apple is rumored to be interested....

intriguing Look up this adjective in a dictionary if you can't guess its meaning from the example that follows.

SOURCE: "Britney to Rent, Lease, or Buy." *The New York Times*, August 7, 2005, page 2-1. Copyright © 2005 by The New York Times Co. Reprinted with permission.

—Biagi, *Media Impact*: An Introduction to Mass Media.

● Interaction 9-1. Talking about Reading

Respond in writing to the questions below and then discuss your answers with your classmates.

1. Have you ever downloaded music using Grokster or Kazaa? Have any of your friends? How often? If not, are there any sites you do use for free music downloads?

_____

_____

2. What are the economic consequences of file-sharing for the recording industry and for the recording artists?

_____

_____

3. If you knew you were going to be caught and fined for file-sharing would you still do it? Explain.

_____

_____

4. Do you think the U.S. government should be able to limit file-sharing? Explain.

_____

_____

Fact and Opinion

The sentence that begins the last paragraph of the Prep Reading is a good example of how writers mix fact and opinion all the time. David Pogue, the writer, explains Napster's subscription plan that allows unlimited music downloads (a fact) but also calls the plan "intriguing" (his opinion). It is often difficult to figure out whether a statement is based on an individual's opinion or on a widely accepted fact. For this reason, you should always read with a questioning mind. And it is not only in reading that this blurring of fact and opinion occurs. When you talk with others, watch television, and even when you get second opinions at the doctor's office, stay alert for opinions pretending to be facts.

Facts

Fact = **object,** as in **object**ive. *Objective* means not influenced by personal judgments or feelings. Facts exist externally. They are physical, observable things (like any object in the physical world). They exist separately from you and outside of you. They are independent of you. They can be verified—you can check to see if they are true. No matter what you do, believe, or feel, facts will still be facts. Facts are objective reality.

The list of films in **Table 9.1** on page 433 and the money they made is factual. Each item on it can be proven true (or false). You can verify this information from many different sources, such as Worldwide Box Office online or the *World Almanac and Book of Facts* in the library. Or the list—or items on it—could be proven false. Say, for example, that the numbers for the movies in positions 4 and 5 were reversed. That error would not make the information an opinion; it would just make it wrong. Once corrected, the information would be factual. Information that is proven correct is fact. Information that is proven wrong is fiction, false, make-believe, an assumption, or even a lie. A fact must be verifiable.

Table 9.1 List of Highest-Grossing Films (Unadjusted)

Rank	Movie Name	Worldwide Gross
1	*Titanic* (1997)–20th Century Fox / Paramount	$1,845,034,188
2	*The Lord of the Rings: The Return of the King* (2003)–New Line Cinema	$1,118,888,979
3	*Pirates of the Caribbean: Dead Man's Chest* (2006)–Buena Vista/Walt Disney Pictures	$1,065,659,812
4	*Harry Potter and the Sorcerer's Stone* (2001)–Warner Bros.	$976,475,550
5	*The Lord of the Rings: The Two Towers* (2002)–New Line Cinema	$926,267,400

Interaction 9-2. Identifying Information That Can Be Verified

Put a check mark beside each sentence that contains information that could be verified by research, such as reading encyclopedias, other reference works, or Web sites.

_____ 1. In 2008, Jimmy Buffett played at Jazzfest in New Orleans.

_____ 2. Jimmy Buffett's voice is whiny.

_____ 3. The U.S. market for brain fitness software, or neurosoftware, is worth more than $225 million.

_____ 4. The interior department is considering whether polar bears should be considered an endangered species.

_____ 5. Hunting polar bears is an act of cruelty that should be banned.

Sentence Stems That Introduce Facts

The following sentence beginnings typically introduce facts that should be verifiable—that is, they can be shown to be true or false.

- *According* to a study by . . .
- The research *demonstrated* . . .
- The results of the test *showed* . . .
- Scientists *confirmed* . . .
- The poll *discovered* . . .

Even when you see these kinds of sentence stems, be sure to think critically about what you are reading. Remember that the writer could be mistaken. If you're in a situation where big decisions are resting on the facts, always verify that they are, in fact, true.

Opinions

Opinion = **subject**, as in **subject**ive. *Subjective* means based on or influenced by personal beliefs, feelings, or tastes. Opinions are internal. They exist inside you (or me, or someone else). They depend upon the person who holds the opinion. So where does "subject" come in? Think of your self as the "subject" of your life. Just like the subject of a sentence controls the action of a sentence, you control your opinions. Think of the ways you express your beliefs, feelings, preferences, or desires: those are all opinions. Without you, they do not exist. Opinions are subjective reality. There is a difference between reality and "your reality." Reality is fact. "Your reality" is opinion.

Read this excerpt from a review of the movie *Titanic*:

Excerpt from Roger Ebert's Review of *Titanic*

Movies like this are not merely difficult to make at all, but almost impossible to make well. The technical difficulties are so daunting that it's a wonder when the filmmakers are also able to bring the drama and history into proportion. I found myself convinced by both the story and the saga. The setup of the love story is fairly routine, but the payoff—how everyone behaves as the ship is sinking—is wonderfully written, as passengers are forced to make impossible choices. Even the villain, played by Zane, reveals a human element at a crucial moment (despite everything, damn it all, he does love the girl).

What words in this part of Ebert's review tell you that he is giving you his opinion of the movie *Titanic*? Here are the opinion words from the first two sentences: *not merely difficult, almost impossible, well, so daunting, it's a wonder,* and *proportion.* Underline the opinion words in the rest of the paragraph.

Unlike facts, opinions can't be verified by looking in dictionaries, encyclopedias, or newspapers. Because opinions are personal, they may be held by only one person, several people, or many people. A person can give reasons for holding a certain opinion, and another person might still disagree.

⬤ Interaction 9-3. Comparing Facts and Opinions

For each pair of sentences, decide which one is the opinion. Underline the opinion word or words, and write O on the line.

© AP Photo/General Motors, Blake J. Discher

1. The Chevy SSR looks awesome in yellow, but it's a bit cramped inside. _____

   The Chevrolet SSR is a two-passenger convertible truck. _____

2. California is the best state to live in _____.

   California is the most populous state in the United States. _____

3. You should stop using jackhammers when you're working on the road. _____

   Repeated exposure to loud noise can lead to permanent hearing loss. _____

4. On March 31, 2008, 1.35 billion people were logged onto the Internet. _____

   A lot of Internet users have a serious addiction to online games. _____

5. You are going to get sunburned! _____

   Ultraviolet rays of the sun can cause sunburn. _____

Sentence Stems That Introduce Opinions

The following words introduce opinions that may be held by one person or by a group of people.

- The defendant *claims* . . .
- The author *argues* that . . .
- My *point of view* is . . .
- Police *suspect* . . .
- Many *believe* . . .

A good habit to get into when you read a sentence that expresses the author's opinion is to pause and ask yourself whether the author has given you enough facts so you can decide whether or not you agree with the opinion. If there are enough facts, do you agree? If there aren't enough facts, what else would you need to know before you could decide?

Interaction 9-4. Creating Fact and Opinion Sentences

For each topic, create one factual sentence and one opinion sentence. Then exchange sentences with a classmate and circle all the opinion words you find. Do you agree on which sentences state facts and opinions?

1. Children

    a. Fact: _____

    b. Opinion: _____

2. A balanced budget

    a. Fact: _____

    b. Opinion: _____

3. Cats

    a. Fact: _____

    b. Opinion: _____

4. Voting

    a. Fact: _____

    b. Opinion: _____

5. Music

    a. Fact: _____

    b. Opinion: _____

Words That Can Express Opinions

Fact and opinion are not always easy to distinguish. In this section you'll read about some kinds of words to pay close attention to. When you come to them in your reading, be very careful to think about whether you would be able to verify the information in other sources of information. If you could verify the information, you are reading facts. If you could not, you are reading opinions.

Adjectives

Many words that tell you an opinion is being expressed are adjectives. Adjectives describe nouns. (You may recall that nouns are people, places, things, and ideas.) In the following sentence, the adjective refers to the writer's opinion.

    The death penalty is immoral.

The word *immoral* is an adjective. It describes the noun phrase *death penalty*. Since you could not look in a reference book to find out whether the death penalty is, indeed, immoral, this is the opinion of the writer. One person might think the death penalty is immoral because no one should ever kill another, but a second person might believe it is moral because it prevents more serious crimes from occurring. Other people might think it's moral sometimes and immoral other times. Since an absolute answer is not definitive and many people may disagree, it's an opinion.

Here are some adjectives.

abnormal	classical	implicit	prime
abstract	compatible	incompatible	professional
academic	conservative	inherent	radical
accurate	considerable	irrational	random
adequate	consistent	isolated	rational
advocate	constant	liberal	relevant
afraid	contrary	modern	reluctant
aggressive	cooperative	mature	restricted
alternative	definite	maximum	short
ambiguous	different	minimum	stable
appropriate	dramatic	marginal	subjective
arbitrary	dynamic	modified	sufficient
attached	enhanced	normal	sustainable
attractive	enormous	objective	symbolic
bad	expert	passive	unique
beautiful	explicit	persistent	visible
big	finite	precise	voluntary
capable	immature	primary	widespread

Not all adjectives point to opinions, however. Sometimes they merely describe facts. For example, read this sentence.

When the world population gets larger, there is increased demand for oil.

There are two adjectives here, *larger* and *increased*. But they both refer to facts that can be verified by checking an encyclopedia or other reference book. You could look in an almanac and find out when the population has grown larger, and by how much. You could also look in reference books to find out whether during those times, more oil was sold around the world. So these adjectives do not point to opinions.

When you see adjectives, think carefully about whether they point to facts or opinions.

◉ Interaction 9-5. Identifying Adjectives

A. Underline the adjectives in the following sentences. Remember that adjectives describe nouns.

1. Economic growth in China, India, and elsewhere has led to increased demand for food.

2. That's a good thing because it means people are able to eat more.

3. However, soaring food prices mean the poorest people can't even afford food.

4. It's ridiculous that some people are becoming obese while others are starving.

5. In Egypt, people are calling for the army to step in and distribute wheat in a fair manner.

B. Write down the adjectives from each sentence that point to opinions rather than facts. Write "none" if there aren't any.

6. Sentence 1 _____

7. Sentence 2 _____

8. Sentence 3 _____

9. Sentence 4 _____

10. Sentence 5 _____

◉ Interaction 9-6. Working with Adjectives

Think about your favorite adjectives and write five of them below.

_____   _____   _____

_____   _____

Now use each adjective in an original sentence.

1. _____

2. _____

3. _____

4. _____

5. _____

Which adjectives point to your opinion? Circle them.

Interaction 9-7. Fun with Fact and Opinion

Create three sentences. Write one sentence that includes a fact, and one that is not true (but is also not an opinion). Do not reveal which factual sentence is true—make your classmates guess. The third sentence should be an opinion. Have your classmates pick the words that make it an opinion. Here are three examples from one of your book authors, Ivan Dole.

1. One time I went scuba diving in Florida with an 18-foot whale shark and held on to its dorsal fin while it swam around.

2. I am a certified yoga instructor.

Which one is true? _____

3. I have a smart dog that does extraordinary tricks, like playing dead, rolling over, and catching Frisbees in mid-air.

Which words indicate opinions? _____

Now it's your turn.

1. _____
2. _____
3. _____

Opinion words:

_____

Qualifiers

Some statements are qualified. That is, the writer describes how often something happens or how many of a group are being discussed. *Qualifiers* may be used to express an opinion or a fact. Often, they are used to limit the extent of whatever the writer is describing.

- She *rarely* cries at the movies. (The sentence carefully qualifies how often she cries there.)
- *Some* police officers are corrupt. (The number isn't definite, but it's fewer than all the police officers.)
- You ate *all* the ice cream! I didn't get *any*! (Facts that were verified at the time.)

Here are some qualifiers that tell how often or how many.

a few	all	always	any	every	frequently	often
never	none	normally	rarely	some	sometimes	usually

Another group of qualifiers modify, or change, the meanings of the verbs following them:

can	could	may	might	must	have to	shall	will	should	would

These qualifiers indicate degrees of certainty, permission, and necessity. Notice how none of the following statements could really be called a "fact."

- I might do the laundry. (It's not too certain that I will.)
- I must do the laundry. (I really have to do it.)
- I will do the laundry. (I'm going to do it.)

These statements are all opinions. The last one is considered an opinion because the event has not yet occurred. Future events can't be considered facts—not yet.

- The war *will be* over by September.
- You *are going to be* sorry you said that!

Some qualifiers, such as *all, always, never, none, must,* and *have to,* are absolute. In conversation, people often use absolute qualifiers when they are exaggerating.

- He is *always* late. (Has he never been on time, even once?)
- She *never* cleans her room. (Has she ever cleaned her room, even one time?)
- You *must* do it this way! (Is there any other way to do it?)

Statements using absolute qualifiers are often not true. So if you see a statement with an absolute qualifier on a test, the statement is usually false (unless the facts of the passage prove it is true). The more extreme the qualifier (*all* or *none*), the more likely it is to be an opinion or simply incorrect.

⬤ Interaction 9-8. Thinking about Qualifiers

The qualifiers in the following sentences are in bold type. If the sentence is true, write *T* on the line. If it is false, write *F*. If a statement is false, rewrite it using a different qualifier to make it true.

Example:

___F___ I am **always** tired.

Often is a less extreme word and more likely to be true.

_____ 1. **Every** person in the world needs water to survive.

_____

_____ 2. It is **always** warm in Hawaii.

_____

_____ 3. Children are **always** brats.

_____

_____ 4. Parents are **often** mean.

_____

_____ 5. **All** turtles are green.

_____

_____ 6. Laughter is **frequently** an effective medicine.

_____

____ 7. Gasoline **sometimes** makes a good ingredient for a smoothie.

_____

____ 8. In golf, the person with the highest score **never** wins.

_____

____ 9. In the United States, wedding rings are **usually** made from gold.

_____

____ 10. Dessert is **normally** served at the end of a meal.

_____

Comparatives and Superlatives

Comparatives and superlatives are words you should think about carefully as you decide what is fact and what is opinion. A *superlative* compares one thing to all the other things of the same kind. Superlatives usually end with *–est* or have *most* before a word, as in *most intelligent*. Some examples of superlatives are *best, greatest, strongest, most clearly,* and *most often.* The *comparative* is typically used to compare two items: *better, greater, stronger, more helpful* or *more beautifully.* (As you may have noticed, comparatives and superlatives can be adjectives or adverbs.)

Now, as always, the question is whether we can find proof for a comparison so that we can consider it a fact. If a child says, *My dad is stronger than your dad,* we can verify whether this is a true statement simply by having a weight-lifting contest. But what about the next statement? *My dad is better than your dad.* How do we prove this? Can we? No. The statement is just too broad and general. So sometimes, superlatives and comparatives are opinions, and other times they are verifiable as fact (or just plain wrong). You always have to come back to the question: Can I verify this statement?

Interaction 9-9. Thinking about Comparisons

Write *Y* in the blank if the sentence can be proven. Write *N* if it cannot be proven. If you aren't sure, discuss the sentence with classmates to see if you can agree on an answer. Explain your answer.

____ 1. Exxon/Mobil is the **largest** publicly traded oil and gas company in the world. Your explanation: _____

____ 2. Michael Jordan is a **better** basketball player than Magic Johnson. Your explanation:

_____

_____

____ 3. George W. Bush was a **more influential** president than his father, George Bush Sr.
Your explanation: _____

_____

____ 4. The habanero pepper is the **hottest** pepper in the world. Your explanation: ____

_____

_____

____ 5. The Inland Taipan or Fierce Snake is the world's **deadliest** snake.

© blickwinkel/Alamy

Your explanation:

_____

_____

_____

____ 6. Go Fish is the **best** card game to play with children. Your explanation: _____

_____

_____

____ 7. Mobile, Alabama, is the **rainiest** city in the contiguous forty-eight states. Your
explanation: _____

_____

_____

_____ 8. Grandparenthood is **tougher** today than it used to be. Your explanation: _____

_____

_____

Interaction 9-10. Identifying Fact and Opinion in Movie Reviews

Below are two reviews of *Pirates of the Caribbean: At World's End*. Read each review with careful attention to which parts are fact and which are opinion. As you read, underline any words (adjectives, qualifiers, comparatives, and superlatives) you think suggest an opinion. Then summarize the reviewer's evaluation.

Review #1

I cannot put into words how disappointed I am with this movie. The series has sunk. The first one was incredible, the second was ridiculous and this third installment is ludicrous. *World's End* has no plot and is boring and flat. Even the characters, who were so fresh in the first one, are stale now. A dozen Jack Sparrows could not save this film. Keira Knightley looks horrible and acts horribly! All of the fight scenes are recycled. The only saving grace is Keith Richards' cameo as Jack's pirate daddy. Haven't we learned by now that trilogies never live up to the fans' expectations?

Summarize the author's opinion in your own words:

_____

_____

Review #2

Why do critics generally seem to tear down the *Pirates of the Caribbean* franchise? Of course they are not perfect films, few are. But what is it audiences see that critics don't? Credit Johnny Depp for creating one of the most endearing characters ever to grace the screen as Jack Sparrow. Credit some wonderful chemistry from Orlando Bloom and Keira Knightley. And credit the magnificent score by Hans Zimmer, some eye-popping direction by Gore Verbinski, and a mass of talented character actors having a blast. And don't forget what may be the best visual effects in the series, from an angry Calypso to an imaginative and fierce battle at sea. With that, you get the final (for now) installment of one of the most popular franchises ever to invade the screen, critics be damned. And with *At World's End*, the best of the series, you will find a darker, more complex, action-packed adventure that will please most of the fans by bringing the best of the earlier installments to a thrillingly death-defying journey to the end of the world.

Summarize the author's opinion in your own words:

_____

_____

If you have seen the movie *Pirates of the Caribbean: At World's End*, with which critic do you agree and why? On separate paper, express your opinion and support it with facts about the movie.

Sources of Information

Suppose someone says "That's not what I heard. I heard that *she* left *him*!" While the speaker might have heard that "she left him," if you want to decide whether you believe the statement is true, you first have to determine if the speaker is trustworthy. Does this person usually speak honestly, often exaggerate, or have a reason to lie? Even if you trust the speaker, ultimately you would need to go to the people involved to determine what was true.

There are many sources for information. Generally they fall into two categories: trustworthy and not trustworthy. But there are shades of trust in between. Also keep in mind that mistakes and errors are always possible. Regardless, it is the author's *ethos*, or credibility, that makes them believable. In order to decide whether you trust someone's facts or should consider their opinion carefully, you should think about how credible the source is likely to be.

To simplify sources, we will break them into three categories: experts, people with informed opinions, and people on the street.

Expert Opinion

An *expert* is someone who earns our trust because he or she has gained extensive education and/or experience in a particular field of study. Or the expert may hold a position of authority or respect in the field. It is important to note that people are experts only in their own fields. Just because Kym Rock is an expert in karate does not mean we should follow her advice about rock climbing or parasailing.

Examples of experts

- Bill Phillips, author of *Body for Life*, is an expert on exercise and nutrition for body building.
- Deborah L. Smith, member of the international executive board of Amnesty International, is an expert on human rights.
- Natalie Goldberg, novelist, poet, and writing instructor, is an expert on teaching fiction writing.

- Basil Davidson, a historian who has written extensively about Africa, is an expert on African history.
- Dale Earnhardt Jr., NASCAR racer, is an expert on stock car racing.

Experts get their information from other experts and from direct study or experience with the facts of their field of study. Experts usually build their opinions upon facts that they have studied intently. However, experts are not infallible: at times, they can be wrong. Also, sometimes experts build opposing opinions or interpretations from the same factual information.

Informed Opinion

People who are informed have researched or experienced something we have not and are sharing what they have learned. Included in this category are news journalists, TV news anchors, and other media people who gather and relay the news to the public. We expect them to know more than we do, but we don't necessarily accept their opinions.

Examples of informed people

- a student who researches a local environmental issue online and at local meetings
- a person who shares first-hand travel tips for a place they have been recently
- a newspaper reporter who interviews people in order to write a story
- a person who is concerned about an issue and who has read several books and articles on the topic
- a journalist or news anchor who has discussed a topic with several experts

People who are informed get their information directly from experts, from the media, and/or from personal experience. Informed opinions are often based on fact mixed with emotional experience. In terms of credibility, informed people are often credible, but they don't have the extensive knowledge of the expert. More of their knowledge comes from other people's descriptions and interpretations of events.

People on the Street

People on the street are just ordinary people whose expertise is unknown. If you have ever seen interviews with sports fans after a big game, you know that every person has an opinion, but you may or may not care what it is. Is the opinion based on the most important and relevant facts? It's often impossible to know.

Examples of people on the street

- a celebrity sharing his or her personal views on a political position or candidate
- regular people who are interviewed about any recent event as they walk down the street
- people who write blogs to give their opinions on a wide variety of topics
- "reporters" for newspapers that publish stories about alien babies and virgin pregnancies

People on the street are not necessarily uninformed; it's just difficult to know whether they are informed or not—sometimes. The alien babies aren't real!

◉ Interaction 9-11. Identifying the Credibility of Sources

Write *E* for expert sources, *I* for informed sources, and *S* for people on the street.

_____ 1. Madonna talking about the music industry

_____ 2. Madonna on the topic of Kabbalah, a Jewish mystical tradition she studies

_____ 3. Madonna on the unemployment rate in Fort Wayne, Indiana

_____ 4. Mitch Albom's weekly newspaper column in the *Detroit Free Press*

_____ 5. Mitch Albom conducting a writing workshop

_____ 6. Mitch Albom's neighbor discussing the New York Knicks

_____ 7. Al Gore's book *An Inconvenient Truth*

_____ 8. A college student's research paper on Al Gore's political career

_____ 9. Dennis Bushnell, NASA Chief Scientist, on global warming

_____ 10. Secretary of State Condoleezza Rice on politics

_____ 11. Secretary of State Condoleezza Rice on ice-skating (she skated competitively as a child)

_____ 12. A doctor on Secretary of State Condoleezza Rice's Middle East policies

Interaction 9-12. Distinguishing Fact and Opinion

Analyze the use of fact and opinion in the following paragraphs. As you read, underline any words that you think express opinions. Then in the space provided, note whether each sentence contains fact or opinion. Some sentences include both fact and opinion.

Zapping

The image has lost all intensity. It produces no surprise or intrigue; in the end, it is not especially mysterious or especially transparent. It is there for but a moment, filling up the time it takes to wait for the next image that follows. Likewise this subsequent image fails to surprise or intrigue; it too turns out to lack mystery or even much in the way of transparency. It stays there only a fraction of a second before being replaced by a third image, one that is again unsurprising and unintriguing, as indifferent as the previous two images. This third image lasts an infinitesimal fraction of a second, then dissolves as the screen turns bluish gray. You've intervened by using the remote control.

—Beatriz Sarlo

We will get you started on the first few:

The image has lost <u>all</u> intensity.   <u>opinion</u>

It produces <u>no</u> surprise or intrigue; in the end, it is <u>not especially mysterious or especially transparent</u>.   <u>opinion</u>

You finish the rest:

1. It is there for but a moment, filling up the time it takes to wait for the next image that follows. _____

2. Likewise this subsequent image fails to surprise or intrigue; it too turns out to lack mystery or even much in the way of transparency. _____

3. It stays there only a fraction of a second before being replaced by a third image, one that is again unsurprising and unintriguing, as indifferent as the previous two images. _____

4. This third image lasts an infinitesimal fraction of a second, then dissolves as the screen turns bluish gray. _____

5. You've intervened by using the remote control. _____

The Power of Marriage

Anybody who has several sexual partners in a year is committing spiritual suicide. He or she is ripping the veil from all that is private and delicate in oneself, and pulverizing it in an assembly line of selfish sensations.

But marriage is the opposite. Marriage joins two people in a sacred bond. It demands that they make an exclusive commitment to each other and thereby takes two discrete individuals and turns them into kin.

Few of us work as hard at the vocation of marriage as we should.

—David Brooks

Analysis

6. Anybody who has several sexual partners in a year is committing spiritual suicide.

   _____

7. He or she is ripping the veil from all that is private and delicate in oneself, and pulverizing it in an assembly line of selfish sensations. _____

8. But marriage is the opposite. _____

9. Marriage joins two people in a sacred bond. _____

10. It demands that they make an exclusive commitment to each other and thereby takes two discrete individuals and turns them into kin. _____

    _____

11. Few of us work as hard at the vocation of marriage as we should. _____

About The Word "Theory"

So what exactly constitutes the truth? Or proof or it? Most scientists carefully avoid the word "truth" when discussing science, preferring instead to use "accurate" in reference to data. In science, there is only evidence that supports a hypothesis.

For example, the hypothesis that the sun comes up every day has been supported by observable evidence for all of recorded history. Scientists no longer attempt to disprove that hypothesis, for the simple reason that after thousands of years of observation, no one has yet seen otherwise. The hypothesis is consistent with all of the data that has been collected, and it is now used to make different predictions. When a hypothesis meets these criteria, it has become a scientific theory.

—Starr/Evers/Starr, _Biology Today and Tomorrow,_ 2nd Edition

Analysis

We will skip the first two sentences, which are questions and can't be fact or opinion. They make no statement at all.

12. Most scientists carefully avoid the word "truth" when discussing science, preferring instead to use "accurate" in reference to data. _____

13. In science, there is only evidence that supports a hypothesis. _____

14. For example, the hypothesis that the sun comes up every day has been supported by observable evidence for all of recorded history. _____

15. Scientists no longer attempt to disprove that hypothesis, for the simple reason that after thousands of years of observation, no one has yet seen otherwise. _____

16. The hypothesis is consistent with all of the data that has been collected, and it is now used to make different predictions. _____

17. When a hypothesis meets these criteria, it has become a scientific theory. _____

Chapter Summary Activity

This chapter has discussed fact and opinion and some of the factors that you should consider as you determine which is which as you read. Construct a Reading Guide below by completing each idea on the left with information from the chapter on the right. You can use this guide as a reminder for how to distinguish fact from opinion.

Reading Guide to Fact and Opinion

Complete this idea	with information from the chapter.
Facts are different from opinions. For one thing, facts exist _____ of the self.	1.
In contrast, opinions exist _____ the self.	2.
Objective reality is represented by	3.
Subjective reality is represented by	4.
Opinions are neither true nor false, but facts can be	5.
You can find out whether facts are true or not by	6.
For example, you could check these two sources of information:	7. 8.
Several different kinds of words can be used to express opinions although they may also express facts. They are	9. 10. 11. 12.
The words that describe nouns are called	13.

Three examples of words that show how often or how much something happens are	14. 15. 16.
Two examples of absolute qualifiers are	17. 18.
Two examples of words that qualify the meaning of the verb that follows are:	19. 20.
To decide whether comparatives and super-latives are expressing facts or opinions, determine if	21.
You might need to think about how cred-ible a source is in order to	22.
Three types of sources and brief descrip-tions of them are:	23. 24. 25.

Test Taking Tips

Fact and Opinion

Multiple-choice tests often use absolute qualifiers such as *all* and *none* in some of the answer choices. Usually, choices that include absolute qualifiers are wrong. The only time such statements can be considered true is if the qualifier statement is fully supported by details in the passage. For example, suppose an answer to a test question said,

All organisms on earth grow at a similar rate.

We know this cannot be true because it says ALL are similar. A synonym for *organism* is *living being*. Is it true that all living beings on earth grow at the same rate? Do flies, humans, and turnips all grow at similar rates? No. Such an answer choice can't be correct.

However, suppose an answer said:

All subjects in study group A showed signs of improvement.

The statement would be true if all the details of the material on which the test is based supported it, even though it says "all." You must decide what the details support.

Here is another common example of a multiple-choice answer. It uses a superlative:

The greatest medical advances have been made in the realm of cancer research.

You need to ask yourself, "Is there a way to measure *greatest medical advances*?" While cancer is a serious illness, can you really measure the *greatest medical advances* without drifting into opinion? How could you prove such a statement as fact? Unless evidence has been presented in the class that directly states this is true, then you do not have enough information to choose this answer as being correct.

Reading 9-1 . . . . **Web Article**

● Pre-Reading the Selection

The reading that follows, "Grim Life Cursed Real Pirates of Caribbean," may be an eye-opener about what pirate life was really like.

Guessing the Purpose

Judging from the title of the reading, what do you suppose is the purpose for writing?

_____

Surveying the Reading

Survey the title of the selection and the first sentence of each paragraph. What is the general topic of the reading selection? _____

Predicting the Content

Predict three things this selection will discuss.

• _____

- _____
- _____

Activating Your Knowledge

Make a list of three or four things that you know (or think you know) about the life of pirates.

- _____
- _____
- _____
- _____

Common Knowledge

Robinson Crusoe (paragraph 8) A famous English novel about a man, Robinson Crusoe, who is shipwrecked on an island for many years before being rescued. He endures many adventures on the island, including rescuing a native from cannibals.

Reading with Pen in Hand

Now read the selection. As you read, mark any ideas that seem important, and respond to the questions and vocabulary items in the margin. Monitor your comprehension by putting a ✔ next to a paragraph when you understand most of it. Place an ✘ next to a paragraph when you don't understand most of it.

Visit **www.cengage.com/devenglish/doleconnect** and select Chapter 9 to hear vocabulary words from this selection and view a video about this topic.

Grim Life Cursed Real Pirates of Caribbean

Stefan Lovgren

1   Pirates have been figures of fascination and fear for centuries. The most famous buccaneers have been shrouded in legend and folklore for so long that it's almost impossible to distinguish between myth and reality. Hollywood movies—filled with buried treasures, eye patches, and the Jolly Roger—depict pirate life as a swashbuckling adventure. In Disney's *Pirates of the Caribbean: The Curse of the Black Pearl*, the pirate hero, played by Johnny Depp, is a lovable

◆ *Reading Journal*

◆ Describe what real pirate life was like.

grim Look at the examples in the next sentence to guess the meaning of *grim*.

rogue. But what was life really like for an early 18th-century pirate? The answer: pretty grim. It was a world of staggering violence and poverty, constant danger, and almost inevitable death. The life of a pirate was never as glorious and exciting as depicted in the movies, said David Moore, curator of nautical archaeology at the North Carolina Maritime Museum in Beaufort. "Life at sea was hard and dangerous, and interspersed with life-threatening storms or battles. There was no air conditioning, ice for cocktails, or clean sheets aboard the typical pirate ship."

◆When was the "Golden Age of Piracy"?

2   While the period from the late 1600s to the early 1700s is usually referred to as the "Golden Age of Piracy," the practice existed long before Blackbeard and other famous pirates struck terror in the hearts of merchant seamen along the Eastern Seaboard and Caribbean. And it exists today, primarily in the South China Sea and along the African coast.

Valuable Loot

◆What did Julius Caesar do to the pirates who captured him?

3   One of the earliest and most high profile incidents of piracy occurred when a band of pirates captured Julius Caesar, the Roman emperor-to-be, in the Greek islands. Instead of throwing him overboard, as they did with most victims, the pirates held Caesar for ransom for 38 days. When the money finally arrived, Caesar was let go. When he returned to port, Caesar immediately fitted a squadron of ships and set sail in pursuit of the pirates. The criminals were quickly caught and brought back to the mainland, where they were hanged.

flourish Look at the rest of the paragraph for a logical clue to figure out what *flourish* means.

◆Why did piracy flourish in the Caribbean and along America's Eastern Seaboard?

4   It's no coincidence that piracy came to **flourish** in the Caribbean and along America's Eastern Seaboard during piracy's heyday. Traffic was busy and merchant ships were easy pickings. Although pirates would search the ship's cabins for gold and silver, the main loot consisted of cargo such as grain, molasses, and kegs of rum. Sometimes pirates stole the ships as well as the cargo.

◆Who was Captain Edward Teach or Thatch?

5   Neither Long John Silver nor Captain Hook actually existed, but the era produced many other infamous pirates, including William Kidd, Charles Vane, Sam Bellamy, and two female pirates, Anne Bonny and Mary Read. The worst and perhaps cruelest pirate of them all was Captain Edward Teach or Thatch, better known as "Blackbeard." Born in Britain before 1690, he first served on a British privateer based in Jamaica. Privateers were privately owned, armed ships hired by the British government to attack and plunder French and Spanish ships during the war.

6   After the war, Blackbeard simply continued the job. He soon became captain of one of the ships he had stolen, *Queen Anne's Revenge*, and set up base in North Carolina, then a British colony, from where he preyed on ships traveling the American coast. Tales of his cruelty are legendary. Women who didn't relinquish their diamond rings simply had their fingers hacked off. Blackbeard even shot one of his lieutenants so that "he wouldn't forget who he was." Still, the local townspeople tolerated Blackbeard because they liked to buy the goods he stole, which were cheaper than imported English goods. The colony's ruling officials turned a blind eye to Blackbeard's violent business. It wasn't until Alexander Spotswood, governor of neighboring Virginia, sent one of his navy commanders to kill Blackbeard that his reign finally came to an end in 1718.

◆In what ways was Blackbeard cruel?

True or False

7   The most famous pirates may not have been the most successful. "The reason many of them became famous was because they were captured and tried before an Admiralty court," said Moore. "Many of these court proceedings were published, and these pirates' exploits became legendary. But it's the ones who did not get caught who were the most successful in my book."

◆Who does Moore think are the best pirates?

exploits Ask yourself, "What became legendary?"

8   *Treasure Island*, by Robert Louis Stevenson, may be the most famous pirate story. But the most important real-life account of pirate life is probably a 1724 book called *A General History of the Robberies and Murders of the Most Notorious Pyrates*, by Captain Charles Johnson. The tome depicts in gruesome detail the lives and exploits of the most famous pirates of that time. Much of it reads as a first-hand account by someone who sailed with the pirates, and many experts believe Johnson was actually Daniel Defoe, the author of *Robinson Crusoe*, which was published in 1719. What is not in doubt is the book's commercial success at the time and the influence it had on generations of writers and filmmakers who adopted elements of his stories in creating the familiar pirate image.

◆Who do some people think Captain Charles Johnson was?

tome Look in the previous sentence for a clue.

9   So what part of the movie pirate is true and what is merely Hollywood fiction? What about, for example, the common practice of forcing victims to "walk the plank"? "Not true," said Cori Convertito, assistant curator of education at the Mel Fisher Maritime Museum in Key West, Florida. The pirates' favorite form of punishment was to tie their victims to the boat with a length of rope, toss them overboard, and drag them under the ship, a practice known

◆What myths about pirate life do movies spread?

ubiquitous Look at the sentence where you find the word *ubiquitous* for a general context clue.

◆Which characteristics of piracy that we know from movies are true?

marooned Think about where a person was *marooned*, and guess at the word's meaning.

stipulates Look for examples and punctuation context clues in the sentence where you find *stipulates*.

◆How accurate is the character Jack Sparrow?

◆What earned respect among pirates in the pirate world?

notorious Use two context clues in this sentence to help guide you to its meaning.

as "keel hauling." Sadly, buried treasures—and the ubiquitous treasure maps—are also largely a myth. "Pirates took their loot to notorious pirate hang-outs in Port Royal and Tortuga," said Convertito. "Pirates didn't bury their money. They blew it as soon they could on women and booze."

Eye Patches, Peg Legs, and Parrots

10　　On the other hand, pirate flags, commonly referred to as Jolly Rogers, were indeed present during the Golden Age. And victims were often **marooned** on small islands by pirates. Eye patches and peg legs were also undoubtedly worn by pirates, and some kept parrots as pets. Some pirates even wore earrings, not as a fashion statement, but because they believed they prevented sea sickness by applying pressure on the earlobes.

11　　In the movie *Pirates of the Caribbean*, prisoners facing execution can invoke a special code, which stipulates that the pirate cannot kill him or her without first consulting the pirate captain. Indeed pirates did follow codes. These varied from ship to ship, often laying out how plundered loot should be divided or what punishment should be meted out for bad behavior. But Jack Sparrow, Johnny Depp's hero, probably wouldn't have lasted very long among real pirates. In the movie, he will do anything possible to avoid a fight, something real-life pirates rarely did.

12　　The endless sword duels, a big part of all pirate movies, probably happened on occasion. But real-life encounters were often far more bloody and brutal, with men hacking at each other with axes and cutlasses. In one legendary account, a notorious pirate, trying to find out where a village had hidden its gold, tied two villagers to trees, facing each other, and then cut out one person's heart and fed it to the other. As Captain Johnson wrote in his book:

In the commonwealth of pirates, he who goes to the greatest length of wickedness is looked upon with a kind of envy amongst them, as a person of a more extraordinary gallantry, and is thereby entitled to be distinguished by some post, and if such a one has but courage, he must certainly be a great man.

● Comprehension Questions

Write the letter of the answer on the line. Then explain your thinking.

Main Idea

____ 1. Which sentence best summarizes the main idea for the section entitled "Eye Patches, Peg Legs, and Parrots"?

a. Pirates were a bloody lot who enjoyed fighting more than eating, which is why Jack Sparrow would not have lasted very long.

b. Several characteristics of movie pirates are true of real pirates.

c. Pirates wore eye patches and peg legs.

d. Although some pirate lore is true, most is fictitious.

WHY? What information in the selection leads you to give that answer? _____

_____

_____

____ 2. Which sentence is the topic sentence of paragraph 3?

a. One of the earliest and most high-profile incidents of piracy occurred when a band of pirates captured Julius Caesar, the Roman emperor-to-be, in the Greek islands.

b. Instead of throwing him overboard, as they did with most victims, the pirates held Caesar for ransom for thirty-eight days.

c. When he returned to port, Caesar immediately fitted a squadron of ships and set sail in pursuit of the pirates.

d. The criminals were quickly caught and brought back to the mainland, where they were hanged.

WHY? What information in the selection leads you to give that answer? _____

_____

Supporting Details

____ 3. Which of the following statements about pirates is not true?

a. Pirates wore earrings because they believed it prevented seasickness.

b. Pirates probably did have peg legs and eye patches.

c. The battles of pirates were often bloody and brutal.

d. The "Jolly Roger" was the common nickname of the ship that pirates sailed.

WHY? What information in the selection leads you to give that answer? _____

_____

_____ 4. Which of the following is least relevant to the main idea of this passage?

    a. It was a world of staggering violence and poverty, constant danger, and almost inevitable death.

    b. *Treasure Island*, by Robert Louis Stevenson, is probably the most famous pirate story.

    c. There was no air conditioning, ice for cocktails, or clean sheets aboard the typical pirate ship.

    d. The life of a pirate was never as glorious and exciting as depicted in the movies.

WHY? What information in the selection leads you to give that answer? _____

_____

_____

Author's Purpose

_____ 5. What is the purpose of the section titled "Valuable Loot"?

    a. to focus the reader's attention on Julius Caesar's plight

    b. to entertain the reader with true stories from history about piracy

    c. to persuade readers that piracy was a lucrative business

    d. to inform the reader that obtaining valuables was one of the main reasons for piracy

WHY? What information in the selection leads you to give that answer? _____

_____

_____ 6. What is the overall purpose of this passage?

    a. to entertain the reader with true stories about the life of pirates

    b. to inform readers about the reality of pirate life based on true accounts of pirate life

    c. to persuade the reader that he or she should not watch movies about pirates because they are mostly untrue

    d. to emphasize the brutality of pirate battles

WHY? What information in the selection leads you to give that answer? _____

_____

_____

Relationships

____ 7. Identify the pattern of organization found in the following two sentences:
The endless sword duels, a big part of all pirate movies, probably happened on occasion. But real-life encounters were often far more bloody and brutal, with men hacking at each other with axes and cutlasses.

a. time order

b. listing

c. contrast

d. cause-and-effect

WHY? What leads you to give that answer? _____

_____

____ 8. What is the pattern of organization of paragraph 6?

a. definition

b. narration

c. cause-and-effect

d. example

WHY? What information in the selection leads you to give that answer? _____

_____

Fact, Opinion, and Inference

____ 9. Which of the following statements is an opinion?

a. Pirates believed earrings prevented seasickness by applying pressure on the earlobes.

b. Traffic was busy and merchant ships were easy pickings.

c. The worst and perhaps cruelest pirate of them all was Captain Edward Teach or Thatch, better known as "Blackbeard."

d. The pirates' favorite form of punishment was to tie their victims to the boat with a length of rope, toss them overboard, and drag them under the ship, a practice known as "keel hauling."

WHY? What leads you to give that answer? _____

_____

_____

____ 10. Which of the following can be inferred from information found in this passage?
   a. Alexander Spotswood was responsible for Blackbeard's death.
   b. Pirates living in the 1600s were crueler than those who lived in the 1700s.
   c. *Pirates of the Caribbean* is a movie filled with more pirate fact than myth.
   d. Julius Caesar became a dedicated pirate hunter after his abduction in Greece, practically eradicating piracy in his day.

WHY? What information in the selection leads you to give that answer? _____

_____

_____

● Critical Thinking Questions

CRITICAL THINKING LEVEL 1 REMEMBER

Write as many details as you *remember* about the book *A General History of the Robberies and Murders of the Most Notorious Pyrates.*

_____

_____

_____

CRITICAL THINKING LEVEL 2 UNDERSTAND

Fill in the APP of the MAPPS for this reading selection.

About: _____

Point: _____

_____

Proof:

1. _____

_____

2. _____

_____

3. _____

_____

4. _____

_____

_____

5. _____

_____

CRITICAL THINKING LEVEL 3 APPLY

Using your prior knowledge and logic, see if you can come up with some other popular movie characters that are stereotyped and different from reality. For example, you might think of a Western you may have seen, or another type of movie. Are the cowboys or Indians portrayed realistically? Brainstorm with one or more classmates and use the chart here to come up with a list of myths versus facts.

Myths Versus Reality

Myth	Reality

CRITICAL THINKING LEVEL 4 ANALYZE

Read the following web article from National Public Radio:

A federal judge ordered a Minnesota woman to ante up thousands of dollars for violating copyright laws by sharing music illegally downloaded, marking the first time such a suit against an individual had gone to trial. Jammie Thomas has to pay $222,000 for the dozens of songs she pulled from the Internet.

"This does send a message, I hope, that downloading and distributing our recordings is not OK," said Richard Gabriel, the lead attorney for the music companies that sued Thomas. He made the comments late Thursday when the three-day civil trial in Duluth, Minnesota, ended. In closing arguments he had told the jury: "I only ask that you consider that the need for deterrence here is great."

Thomas, 30, was ordered to pay the six record companies that sued her $9,250 for each of 24 songs they focused on in the case. They had alleged she shared 1,702 songs in all. Copyright law sets a damage range of $750 to $30,000 per infringement, or up to $150,000 if the violation was "willful." Jurors ruled that Thomas' infringement was willful but awarded damages in a middle range. The record companies accused Thomas of downloading the songs without permission and offering them online through a Kazaa file-sharing account.

Why has computer file-sharing been called "piracy"? Discuss your thoughts on this article with your class or group.

CRITICAL THINKING LEVEL 5 EVALUATE

In the *Activating Your Knowledge* question on page 453 you were asked to share what you know (or what you think you know) about the life of pirates. Using the table here, *evaluate* whether your knowledge was correct and what you learned from the reading passage.

Evaluating Your Knowledge

What you knew	Were you right?	Something new you learned
1.		
2.		
3.		
4.		

CRITICAL THINKING LEVEL 6 CREATE

In small groups, imagine you are pirates and *create* your own "code of honor." What are the rules by which you will abide? Once you have created your rules, compare them with the other groups' rules to see how they are similar and different. _____

_____

_____

● Vocabulary in Context

The following words were used in "Grim Life Cursed Real Pirates of Caribbean." Choose the best word to complete each sentence.

| grim | flourish | ubiquitous | stipulates | notorious |

1. In today's media-driven world, there is no shortage of _____ celebrities.

2. It is common knowledge that children usually _____ in a loving environment.

3. Unfortunately, many people living in poverty around the world face a _____ existence.

4. You cannot go too many places in this world where you will not find someone talking on a cell phone; they are _____.

5. The divorce lawyer created a document that _____ rules the husband and wife must follow to have an orderly meeting.

Reading 9-2 . . . . **Newspaper Article**

● Pre-Reading the Selection

The pirate theme continues in the next reading passage "Danger Adrift: Modern-Day Pirates Threaten More Than the High Seas," which discusses modern-day pirates.

Guessing the Purpose

Judging from the title of this passage and the headings, what do you suppose is the purpose of the selection? _____

_____

Surveying the Reading

Survey the title, headings, and the first sentence of each paragraph. What is the topic of the reading passage? _____

Predicting the Content

Predict three things this selection will discuss.

- _____

- _____

- _____

Activating Your Knowledge

Many of you have probably seen at least one (if not all) of the *Pirates of the Caribbean* trilogy. Take a moment to write out who you think a modern-day pirate would be as well as what their life would be like.

Common Knowledge

Skull and crossbones (*paragraph 1*) A symbol consisting of a human skull and two crossed bones under the skull

"Terminator"-style (*paragraph 1*) As is done in the *Terminator* movie series with Arnold Schwarzenegger

Band-Aid stuff (*paragraph 6*) An attempt to fix a major problem with minimal effort, like putting a Band-Aid on a gunshot wound. It might briefly slow the blood flow but not do much good (if any) in the long run

Herculean (*paragraph 7*) Having the superhuman strength and abilities of Hercules, a mythical Greek hero

Reading with Pen in Hand

Now read the selection. As you read, mark any ideas that seem important, and respond to the questions and vocabulary items in the margin. Monitor your comprehension by putting a ✔ next to a paragraph when you understand most of it. Place an ✘ next to a paragraph when you don't understand most of it.

Visit **www.cengage.com/devenglish/doleconnect** and select Chapter 9 to hear vocabulary words from this selection and view a video about this topic.

◆ *Reading Journal*

audacity Look for the punctuation clue and the examples given of audacity.

Danger Adrift: Modern-Day Pirates Threaten More Than the High Seas

Charlotte Sector

1   Skull and crossbones buccaneers have resurfaced with "Terminator"-style tactics, shining a spotlight on an age-old crime that some experts warn could inspire terrorists. The Carnival-owned cruise liner *Seabourn Spirit* recently fended off a pirate attack along Africa's eastern coast, with one person sustaining injuries. The attempt to hijack a cruise ship highlights the pirates' growing audacity—

© Sarah Nicholl/Shutterstock

wielding rocket-propelled grenades and machine guns, the pirates off of Somalia's coast have stolen some of the fairy-tale glamour of yesteryear's high sea thieves.

2   "Modern-day piracy is not Johnny Depp-inspired characters with an eye patch," said John Burnett, author of *Dangerous Waters: Modern Piracy and Terror on the High Seas*. Referring to the popular swashbuckling, charcoal-eyed Captain Jack Sparrow of *Pirates of the Caribbean*, Burnett warns that twenty-first-century pirates plague many parts of the world and are better armed, and more brutal. Forget about muggings at sea, pirates want the full loot, regardless of casualties, he said.

◆What does paragraph 2 suggest about modern-day pirates?

Modern-Day Buccaneers

3   From March to November of 2005, 29 attacks have occurred off the coast of Somalia, according to the International Maritime Bureau (IMB). Although this was the first attack on a cruise ship in more than a decade, pirates attacked 205 ships in the first nine months of 2005 compared with 251 in the same period a year ago, according to the IMB's Piracy and Armed Robbery Against Ships Report. "Although the decline in the number of attacks has decreased, some key hot spots have **deteriorated**, like off the coast of Somalia," said Jayant Abhyankar, deputy director of the IMB, explaining that since the early '90s, crime on the high seas has resurfaced.

◆Is the rate of pirate attacks increasing or decreasing?

deteriorated Consider the first sentence of this paragraph. Does *deteriorated* mean improved or worsened?

4   Indonesian waters pose the greatest danger with 61 incidents in the first nine months of 2005 and a total of 93 attacks reported in

◆What are some of the pirate hot spots around the world? (Do you know where these places are located on a map?)

loot Look for several example clues for this word. What does it mean?

◆What concern does Burnett express about piracy and terrorists?

vessels Look at the general context of the sentence where you find *vessels*.

◆Burnett says that there are probably 2,000 pirate attacks yearly versus IMB's estimate of 205. What reason does he give for this difference?

◆What two possible solutions are given?

2004, according to the IMB. Hot spots around the world include the Malacca Straits (between Malaysia and the Indonesian island of Sumatra) followed by Nigeria, Bangladesh, Iraq, and the northeastern coast of South America. And despite the falling numbers, the attacks have been more fatal. Pirates killed 30 crew members in 2004, up from 21 a year earlier. Pirates usually work in bands but go after different targets, said Abhyankar. Some will go after any boat—a yacht, a cruise liner or a barge—hoping to find some good loot, like the sea-faring guerrillas in Somalia. Some will hijack ships simply for the cargo while others will attack a boat to kidnap the crew in the hopes of a hefty ransom. Boats represent "easy pickings," especially off the coast of lawless countries like Somalia or in places where maritime security is weak, he said.

Terrorism on the High Seas?

5   Burnett commends the *Seabourn*'s brilliant seamanship and the cruise lines' long track record of safety at sea but fears that piracy will become a terrorist tool. "When terrorists learn to hijack, kidnap passengers and crew, they will probably get involved," he said. Merchant vessels represent an even easier target since they chug along slowly, lugging more than 95 percent of the world's goods. "The global economy could come to a screeching halt if you close off the world's choke points like the Malacca Strait," Burnett said. The strait connects the Pacific and Indian oceans and is the shortest sea route to Asian countries.

6   Shipping experts agree that the *Seabourn* incident is a wake-up call to all sailors and non-sailors. "Most efforts to control piracy are Band-Aid stuff," said Burnett. He and others hope that the IMB, along with the United Nations' International Maritime Organization, can convince the United Nations Security Council to take action. Despite the global decline in reported pirate attacks, he believes the number of attacks probably stands more in the ballpark of 2,000 a year versus IMB's number of 205. "It's not just about bad press or about keeping insurance premiums low, it's mostly about cost," Burnett said. It costs $20,000 to $50,000 a day to run a ship, making all stops—even for an investigation—expensive, lost time, he said.

7   That's why Unitel, a maritime security firm, recommends that all ships have armed security personnel on board or have an armed escort in power boats. "A bank doesn't transport money without armed guards or an armored car, why should boats not be able to protect themselves?" said Unitel security adviser William Callahan.

The IMB says armed guards pose more of a risk than a safeguard. In addition, countries don't want to have foreigners impeding on their sovereign territory. And if ships are transporting volatile cargo like oil, a gunshot could lead to an explosive situation. Armed escorts might be the better solution, but Burnett points out that securing every ship is a Herculean feat that would blow shipping costs out of the water.

volatile Look for an example clue that follows the word.

Still Safe to Cruise?

8   So does that mean you shouldn't book a "Love Boat" cruise? "I would take a cruise, but just not in pirate territory," Burnett said. He recommends Hawaii, Alaska and yes, the Caribbean. "Cruising is the safest way to travel and there is no reason why that is not the case today," said Michael Crye, president of the International Council of Cruise Lines. He stressed that cruise ships screen all of their passengers and their belongings. In addition, all ships have up to 20 trained security officers on board at all times and boats have surveillance cameras and high-tech communication as well as non-lethal weapons to thwart attacks.

◆Is cruising still safe? Why or why not?

9   "The fact that this ship [*Seabourn Spirit*] was able to safely deliver its passengers to a safe port demonstrates the effectiveness of the security plans and countermeasures," Crye said. In *Seabourn's* case, the captain out-navigated the pirates and used a parabolic audio device, a "boom box" that emits an ear-splitting sound, to ward off the attackers. Regardless, the captain was about 100 miles offshore despite IMB's warning to stay 200 miles away from the coast. Crye said the cruise ship industry heeds the IMB's sea warnings and meets every two months with different intelligence agencies to review its security plans, and map out new cruise itineraries.

◆With what does Crye credit the *Seabourn Spirit's* ability to escape?

● Comprehension Questions

Write the letter of the answer on the line. Then explain your thinking.

Main Idea

_____ 1. What is the main idea of the section entitled "Terrorism on the High Seas?"

    a. When terrorists learn to hijack and kidnap passengers and crew, they will probably get involved in piracy.

    b. Shipping experts agree that the *Seabourn* incident is a wake-up call to all sailors and non-sailors.

    c. Unitel recommends that all ships have armed security personnel on board or have an armed escort in power boats.

    d. Merchant vessels represent an even easier target since they chug along slowly, lugging more than 95 percent of the world's goods.

WHY? What information in the selection leads you to give that answer? _____

_____

_____

_____ 2. Which sentence is the topic sentence of paragraph 4?

    a. Pirates usually work in bands but go after different targets, said Abhyankar.

    b. Some will go after any boat—a yacht, a cruise liner or a barge—hoping to find some good loot like the sea-faring guerrillas in Somalia.

    c. Some will hijack ships simply for the cargo while others will attack a boat to kidnap the crew in the hopes of a hefty ransom.

    d. Boats represent "easy pickings," especially off the coast of lawless countries like Somalia or in places where maritime security is weak, he said.

WHY? What information in the selection leads you to give that answer? _____

_____

_____

Supporting Details

_____ 3. Which of the following does *not* support the idea that cruise ships are safe?

    a. Ships screen all of their passengers and their belongings.

    b. All ships have up to 20 trained security officers on board at all times.

    c. Boats have surveillance cameras and high-tech communication.

    d. The captain of the *Seabourn Spirit* was 100 miles off the coast of Somalia.

WHY? What leads you to give that answer? _____

_____

_____ 4. Which of the following is not mentioned as a target of modern pirates in this reading?

    a. loot

    b. political prisoners

    c. cargo

    d. ransoms

WHY? What information in the selection leads you to give that answer? _____

_____

Author's Purpose

_____ 5. What is the purpose of the section entitled "Still Safe to Cruise?"

    a. to inform that it is still safe to cruise

    b. to entertain with stories about close calls

    c. to encourage passengers to only cruise to Alaska, Hawaii, or the Caribbean

    d. to persuade people that it is still safe to cruise

WHY? What information in the selection leads you to give that answer? _____

_____

_____

_____ 6. What is the author's overall purpose in this passage?

a. to update the status of piracy from mythical to methodical

b. to inform readers about the dangers of modern piracy

c. to persuade readers that they should take a cruise because they will be safe from pirates

d. to persuade ship owners to strengthen their maritime security

WHY? What information in the selection leads you to give that answer? _____

_____

_____

Relationships

_____ 7. Identify the pattern of organization in the following sentence:
Armed escorts might be the better solution, but Burnett points out that securing every ship is a Herculean feat that would blow shipping costs out of the water.

a. time order

b. listing

c. contrast

d. cause-and-effect

WHY? What leads you to give that answer? _____

_____

_____ 8. What is the pattern of organization in paragraph 3?

a. chronological

b. comparison and contrast

c. cause-and-effect

d. example

WHY? What information in the selection leads you to give that answer? _____

_____

Fact, Opinion, and Inference

_____ 9. What word or words best describe the following sentence?
The global economy could come to a screeching halt if you close off the world's choke points like the Malacca Strait.

   a. fact

   b. opinion

   c. fact and opinion

   d. subjective

WHY? What leads you to give that answer? _____

_____

_____

_____ 10. What can be inferred from the section entitled "Still Safe to Cruise?"

   a. It is not safe to cruise because of the increase in modern-day piracy.

   b. It will only be safe to cruise again when ships are outfitted with more efficient counter-terrorism strategies.

   c. Yes, taking a cruise is safe; you just need to be careful to stay in safe areas.

   d. Yes, you can choose to cruise, but remember you are taking your life into your own hands because a pirate can strike anytime, anywhere.

WHY? What information in the selection leads you to give that answer? _____

_____

_____

⬤ Critical Thinking Questions

CRITICAL THINKING LEVEL 1 REMEMBER

State two of John Burnett's worries concerning modern-day piracy. _____

_____

_____

CRITICAL THINKING LEVEL 2 UNDERSTAND

Fill in the APP of the MAPPS for this reading selection.

About: _____

    Point: _____

_____

        Proof:

- _____

_____

- _____

_____

- _____

_____

_____

- _____

_____

CRITICAL THINKING LEVEL 3 APPLY

Apply what you have learned in this chapter about types of sources by labeling each of the following sources of information quoted in the reading passage as an *expert source*, an *informed source*, or a *person on the street*. Give a piece of information about each source to explain your label.

John Burnett   _____

_____

Jayant Abhyankar   _____

_____

Michael Crye   _____

_____

William Callahan   _____

_____

Piracy and Armed
Robbery Against Ships Report   _____

Write down which source made each of the following statements, and then write whether it is fact or opinion.

1. "Most efforts to control piracy are Band-Aid stuff." _____

2. "Cruising is the safest way to travel and there is no reason why that is not the case today." _____

3. "Although this was the first attack on a cruise ship in more than a decade, pirates attacked 205 ships in the first nine months of 2005 compared with 251 in the same period a year ago, according to the IMB's Piracy and Armed Robbery Against Ships Report." _____

_____

4. "Indonesian waters pose the greatest danger, with 61 incidents in the first nine months of 2005 and a total of 93 attacks reported in 2004, according to the IMB." _____

_____

5. "Burnett commends the *Seabourn*'s brilliant seamanship and the cruise lines' long track record of safety at sea but fears that piracy will become a terrorist tool." _____

_____

_____

CRITICAL THINKING LEVEL 4 ANALYZE

If you have also read Reading 9-1, *compare and contrast* modern pirates with pirates from the past. _____

_____

_____

CRITICAL THINKING LEVEL 5 EVALUATE

Read the following statement and then answer the questions that follow:

Unitel, a maritime security firm, recommends that all ships have armed security personnel on board or have an armed escort in power boats.

Why do you think Unitel takes this position? _____

_____

_____

_____

What would be the position of the shipping companies concerning guards? Why?

_____

_____

_____

CRITICAL THINKING LEVEL 6 CREATE

Imagine you are with the International Maritime Bureau. Based on the information found in this article, your answers from the previous questions, and your logic, come up with some ideas on how to address this increase in piracy. Once you have come up with several ideas on your own, get together with several classmates to discuss your ideas.

_____

_____

_____

Vocabulary in Context

The following words were used in "Danger Adrift: Modern-Day Pirates Threaten More Than the High Seas." Choose the best word to complete each sentence below.

audacity	vessel	deteriorated	loot	volatile

1. Oil, gas, nitrate, and my uncle's temper are all examples of things that are _____.

2. According to many pirate movies, the pirate's main objective is to steal some _____.

3. I guess on the ocean, you would ask someone what kind of _____ they drive.

4. It is sad when relationships _____ to the point where people who used to profess undying love are no longer even friends.

5. Aaron, who is normally shy, spoke with an _____ that surprised even him.

chapter 10

Analyzing the Author's Tone

© Guy Erwood/Shutterstock

One could always point to a time, a choice, an act that set the tone for a life and changed a personal destiny.

—Carol O'Connell

Do you agree with O'Connell? Can a single choice set the tone for a life?

Share Your Prior Knowledge

Discuss a time when you misunderstood a friend's or family member's tone of voice and it caused a problem.

Survey the Chapter

Take two minutes to skim Reading 10-2, "Attila the Honey I'm Home" on pages 509–513. What is the author's tone of voice concerning managing her home and work life?

www.cengage.com/devenglish/doleconnect

Videos Related to Readings

Vocab Words on Audio

Prep Readings on Demand

Prep Reading . . . . Web Video

The following text comes from a video at the Web site of *The Onion*. As you read it, decide how you would describe its tone (as in "tone of voice").

Visit www.cengage.com/devenglish/doleconnect and select Chapter 10 to hear a reading of this selection and view a video about this topic.

The Next Frontier of Outsourcing

The Onion Web Site

1   Increasingly, American parents are spending more time at work and less time at home. With the cost of nannies on the rise, many are turning to a new solution to their child care dilemma.

2   Susan and Mark Andelman of Portland, Oregon, started sending their son Timothy to a daycare facility in India four months ago. "It used to be quite a hassle in the morning," says Mark. "Yes, now sometimes I'm able to get him right into the box without waking him up," agrees Susan. "So it's a lot easier." Outsourcing Timothy works so well, they decided to send their three-week-old daughter Britney to infant care in Sri Lanka.

3   Though the wages earned by overseas child care workers would seem low to Americans, in countries like India they are over a billion times the average salary. As Kendra Trilson notes, "It's only twelve cents an hour in India, which is a lot cheaper than the $300 I was paying a week here in the United States."

4   "It's a big improvement," say the Andelmans, sitting on their couch and nodding their heads in unison. "Before, he was acting out, a lot of yelling and screaming," says Susan as she puts Timothy into a cardboard box and covers him with plastic peanuts. "Now, when we uncrate him, he's completely quiet." Mark nods: "Yeah, for like two or three days."

● Interaction 10-1. Talking about Reading

1. What word would you use to describe the tone of this text?_____

2. List four specific bits of text that let you know that the tone of the piece was not serious.

   • _____

   • _____

- _____
- _____

3. Were you surprised when you read these bits of text? Why?_____

_____

_____

4. Is surprise a necessary part of humor, do you think? Why or why not?_____

_____

_____

What Is Tone?

You are probably familiar with the term "tone of voice." Even if you are not, you still know how it works. You can tell if someone is mad or sad or happy or serious or playful just by how his or her voice sounds. We also "read" body language such as facial expressions to determine the tone of a speaker. We become good at this at a very young age. We all know when a parent calls our name whether or not we are in trouble!

In written language, tone has the same meaning. The difference is, of course, that you are reading words, not listening to and seeing a person. So instead of the quality of the speaker's voice and the meaning of his or her body language, you have to use certain qualities of the text to figure out the tone.

Why does tone matter? If you can understand the tone, you can realize much more clearly what the author is trying to accomplish and how you will choose to respond. Let's say for a moment that you were fooled into believing that parents actually are packing their children into cardboard boxes each day to ship them off to day care in another country. You might have gotten upset, written a letter to the editor, or even started a campaign to make the practice illegal. Or you might have done nothing, but felt really bad. But if you realized that the piece was supposed to be funny, you could just make faces and laugh about it in a horrified kind of way. Your reaction would be totally different.

You have already studied some of the aspects of tone in previous chapters. First, tone is influenced by an author's purpose. Second, the author often hints at the tone by using words that have certain denotations and connotations. Two other aspects of tone that you haven't yet studied are the author's point of view and any figures of speech that an author uses. Figuring out the tone is somewhat complicated, but it's worth the effort since you can't really evaluate what an author is saying unless you can grasp whether the piece is playful or serious, arrogant or humble, optimistic or cynical.

The Author's Purpose

Throughout this book you have been identifying the author's general purpose in various reading selections. The purpose might be to entertain readers, to inform readers, or to persuade readers. The author's tone of voice supports the purpose. (See **Table 10.1**)

Table 10.1 Tone Supports Purpose

General Purpose	General Tone
to inform (teach) readers	objective: focusing on facts and not on the author's feelings about the facts, matter-of-fact, impersonal
to entertain readers or to express the feelings or thoughts of the writer	subjective: emotional (sad, happy, funny, exciting, and every other possible emotion), personal
to persuade readers to believe or do something	subjective, personal

Remember that looking at the language of the topic sentence (or thesis statement of longer selections) can help you figure out the author's purpose and so can looking at the kinds of details used to support it. If you see the word *should* in the topic sentence, you can decide whether the author is trying to persuade readers. If you see that the details list different types of diseases, the purpose is probably informative. Always use what you know to help you figure out what you need to know.

Here are some examples of the connection between purpose and tone.

Informative purpose and objective tone

A company that makes surfboards recently started a wellness program in which employees must participate.

This sentence merely tells readers that something happened. It doesn't give the writer's thoughts or feelings about the wellness program. It just reports the facts. So it has an objective tone.

Entertainment/expressive purpose and subjective tone

When I was on that elliptical trainer, I felt like my legs were going to fall off.

The writer is expressing personal feelings about his or her own experience. The tone is subjective.

Persuasive purpose and subjective tone

All employees should achieve their ideal weight, stop smoking, and exercise every day.

This sentence tells readers what the writer thinks the employees should do. Others might not agree. The tone is subjective.

Interaction 10-2. Determining an Author's Purpose and Tone

Determine the purpose and tone of the following passages. Circle or underline any words that help you make your decision.

1. The word **statistics** is actually used to mean two different things. The better-known definition is that statistics are numbers measured for some purpose. A more appropriate, complete definition is the following:

   Statistics is a collection of procedures and principles for gaining and analyzing information in order to help people make decisions when faced with uncertainty.

   Using this definition, you have undoubtedly used statistics in your own life. For example, if you were faced with a choice of routes to get to school or work, or to get between one classroom building and the next, how would you decide which one to take? You would probably try each of them a number of times (thus gaining information) and then choose the best one according to some criterion important to you, such as speed, fewer red lights, more interesting scenery, and so on. You might even use different criteria on different days—such as when the weather is pleasant versus when it is not. In any case, by sampling the various routes and comparing them, you would have gained and analyzed useful information to help you make a decision.

   —Utts, *Seeing Through Statistics,* 3rd Edition

   A. What is the purpose of this paragraph? _____

   B. Circle the tone words that you think best describe the tone of the passage.

objective	or	subjective
factual	or	emotional
impersonal	or	personal

2. Two statisticians were traveling in an airplane from Los Angeles to New York City. About an hour into the flight, the pilot announced that although they had lost an engine, there was no need for worry as the plane had three engines left. However, instead of 5 hours travel time it would now take them 7 hours to get to New York. A short while later, the pilot announced that a second engine failed. They still had two left, but it would take 10 hours to get to New York. Somewhat later, the pilot announced that a third engine had died. Never fear, he announced, because the plane could fly on a single engine. However, it would now take 18 hours to get to New York. At this point, one

statistician turned to the other and said, "Gee, I hope we don't lose that last engine, or we'll be up here forever!"

—*http://davidmlane.com/hyperstat/humorf.html*

A. What is the purpose of this paragraph? _____

B. How do you know? _____

_____

3. When you hear the word *statistics,* you probably either get an attack of math anxiety or think about lifeless numbers, such as the population of the city or town where you live, as measured by the latest census, or the per capita income in Japan. The goal of this book is to open a whole new world of understanding to the term *statistics.* By the time you finish reading this book, you will realize that the invention of statistical methods is one of the most important developments of modern times. These methods influence everything from life-saving medical advances to which television shows remain on the air.

—Utts, *Seeing Through Statistics,* 3rd Edition

A. What is the purpose of this paragraph? _____

B. Circle the tone words that you think best describe the tone of the passage.

objective	or	subjective
factual	or	emotional
impersonal	or	personal

The Author's Point of View

Do you have any friends who are always talking about themselves—*I did this, I think that, I want, I, I, I?* Their focus on themselves may be funny or irritating, but in any case, they like to express themselves. How about friends who are always talking about you—*What did you do then? Why are you acting that way? What are you doing tonight?* You may be glad they care or wish they would go away, but you can tell that they are interested in you. What about friends who like to talk about other people (that's all of us, right?)—*Fabio and Jill are going out on Friday. Zoe is going to be a starter on the soccer team. Mr. Broderbund gave their section a five-page paper that's due on Friday.* Most of us are interested in what other people are doing and saying and what is happening in the world around us.

Point of view in an article, book, or other reading material is the same—it's how the author positions himself or herself in relation to the readers and the topic.

- **When an author uses the pronoun *I* or *we* as the point of view, we call it first-person point of view.**

  When <u>I</u> was fifteen years old, <u>my</u> mother died of alcoholism.

By sharing her personal experience with readers, the author makes the tone personal. First person often sounds informal. However, depending on the context, first person can also be formal:

> I asked the accused if he had ever owned a gun.

This sentence sounds formal because of the context, or circumstances, in which it is used. There is only one circumstance in which a person is called "the accused." This is when he or she has been accused of a crime but has not yet been convicted of it. This legal context has a lot of rules that must be followed, and thus it is a formal context.

- **When a writer directly addresses the readers as *you*, we call the point of view second person.**

> As soon as the body senses cold, it constricts the thin web of capillaries in <u>your</u> extremities, first <u>your</u> fingers and toes, then farther up <u>your</u> arms and legs.
> —From Moalem/Prince, *Survival of the Sickest*

The second-person point of view sets up a text as a conversation between the author and the reader, and so it may feel somewhat personal. This point of view is often used when giving directions about how to do something. Second person sounds informal.

- **When an author refers to the topic using the pronouns *he, she, it,* and *they* as the point of view, we call it third-person point of view.** Even if the words *he, she, it,* and *they* aren't present, you'll find nouns (people, places, things, ideas) that could be replaced with *he, she, it,* and *they*. For example, *the house* could be replaced by the pronoun *it, Ms. Macgiver* by the pronoun *she,* and *freedom* by the pronoun *it.*

> <u>Scientists</u> used to believe that "<u>junk DNA</u>" served no purpose, but now many of <u>them</u> think <u>it</u> may play a role in evolution.
> —Adapted from Moalem/Prince, *Survival of the Sickest*

The third-person point of view tends to make the tone impersonal. The writer acts as a reporter who keeps personal experience out of the writing. Also, it often sounds formal.

Now, many times all these different pronouns—*I, he, she, it, you,* and *they*—will be in one article or book. You will need to decide which one is most important overall. One clue may be how you feel after you read the piece. Do you feel you understand the writer at a personal level? This feeling may be the result of first-person point of view. Do you feel as if the author was talking directly to you? It might be because of second-person point of view. Do you think you understand a situation better, even if neither the author nor you is involved in it? That might be because the writer used third person.

But you should check the text after you consider your feelings and thoughts and see if you are right. Sometimes you may need to take into account other aspects of the text, such as the purpose or the particular words the author chose, to decide on the point of view.

Interaction 10-3. Identifying the Author's Point of View and Tone

Underline all the pronouns. If there aren't any, decide which pronouns would replace the nouns (people, places, things, ideas) you do find. Decide whether each item is written in first-, second-, or third-person point of view. Then characterize each item as formal or informal, personal or impersonal. Circle your choices after each item.

1. The psychologist Alice Isen and her colleagues have shown that being happy broadens the thought processes and facilitates creative thinking. Isen discovered that when people were asked to solve difficult problems, ones that required unusual "out of the box" thinking, they did much better when they had just been given a small gift—not much of a gift, but enough to make them feel good.

   —From Norman, *Emotional Design*

first person	or	second person	or	third person
personal	or	impersonal		
informal	or	formal		

2. Dad once told me he withheld his support so I would learn to fend for myself. He wanted me to make it on my own, to become strong. And I did. . . . I became, as my father hoped, strong. But I also became hard, never easy to befriend or to date; never able to accept anything from anyone—not dinner, not a movie, not a gift, not even a compliment.

   —From Trussoni, *Falling Through the Earth*

first person	or	second person	or	third person
personal	or	impersonal		
informal	or	formal		

3. Food availability has increased dramatically over the past four decades. The average person in the developing world has experienced a 40 percent increase in available calories. Likewise, the proportion of malnourished has dropped from 50 percent to less than 17 percent.

   —From Lomborg, *Cool It*

first person	or	second person	or	third person
personal	or	impersonal		
informal	or	formal		

4. Lots of people want to ride with you in the limo, but what you want is someone who will take the bus with you when the limo breaks down.

   —Oprah quoted without attribution in Price, *The Best Advice Ever Given*

first person	or	second person	or	third person
personal	or	impersonal		
informal	or	formal		

Interaction 10-4. Distinguishing Point of View from Tone

Read the two passages and answer the questions that follow. Both people are writing about the Toyota Prius. Both write subjectively, so for the questions about tone, give a more specific word that describes the writer's emotion.

1. The gas mileage is not what I thought it would be. The stickers say 51 mpg on the highway and 60 in town. I assumed I would average somewhere in the middle. But in fact, I average 44 mpg. This is not bad, but not what I paid for!

    —http://www.epinions.com/2007_Toyota_Prius/sec_~opinion_list/display_~reviews/
    sort_~date/sort_dir_~des/pp_~1/pa_~1#list (accessed 7/28/07)

   A. What is the author's purpose? _____

   B. What is the author's point of view? _____

   C. What is the tone of this passage? _____

2. I love the car. My commute is 40 miles each direction, a mixture of surface streets and southern California freeway, through the hills of Ventura County (including up and down the steep Conejo Grade on the 101 Freeway). Average mileage over the past year and a half when I drive like I usually do . . . 75–80 mph (when traffic allows) . . . is 47 mpg. If I behave and set the cruise control on the freeway to 65 mph, my mileage averages from 52 to 54 mpg.

    —http://www.epinions.com/content_350201286276

   A. What is the author's purpose? _____

   B. What is the author's point of view? _____

   C. What is the tone of this passage? _____

Positive, Neutral, and Negative Tones

If you heard someone described as *bizarre,* what kinds of actions or characteristics would you picture? What if they were called *exotic*—does that word bring the same, or different characteristics to mind? How about just plain old *strange? Weird?* How about *grotesque?* (If you don't know the meanings of these words, look them up in a dictionary.)

In Chapter 3, you learned that some words have positive connotations (emotional tones), some words have negative connotations, and some words are neutral. Neutral words have no connotative tone, only the denotative, "dictionary" meaning. The following words all have connotations. They each indicate something strange. However, the attraction a person might feel toward the thing being described decreases from left to right.

| (Most attractive) | exotic | bizarre | grotesque | (Least attractive) |

More denotative, neutral words to describe the same basic idea as these three words are *strange* and *unusual*.

Understanding the connotations of words helps you describe the author's tone. If you read, "The *exotic* animals must have come from a place very different from here," you might consider the author fascinated by their strangeness. If, however, you read "The *grotesque* animals must have come from a place very different from here," suddenly the author seems to be saying that there is something wrong with those animals and that place. There is a tone of disgust or extreme dislike.

When the author uses words that mostly do not have connotations at all, you might say the tone is unbiased, objective, or even-handed. Since connotations suggest the author's emotional stance, the lack of such words suggests an attempt to be objective rather than subjective.

Interaction 10-5. Identifying Tone through Connotation and Denotation

Underline words that have connotations, and on the line write a neutral word that has the same denotation. Use a dictionary as needed. Then circle the word that best describes the author's tone.

1. He blathered on for hours and hours.

    Neutral word: _____   Author's tone: patient or impatient

2. My spirit soared as the horse galloped faster and faster.

    Neutral word: _____   Author's tone: happy or depressed

3. The politician's glib explanation infuriated me.

    Two neutral words: _____   Author's tone: joyful or angry

4. You weasel!

    Neutral word: _____   Author's tone: affectionate or cold

5. They flaunt their wealth.

    Neutral word: _____   Author's tone: approving or disapproving

Interaction 10-6. Finding the Tone of a Longer Passage

Determine the tone of the following passages.

1. School Regulations, Japanese Style

- Boys' hair should not touch the eyebrows, the ears, or the top of the collar.
- No one should have a permanent wave, or dye his or her hair. Girls should not wear ribbons or accessories in their hair. Hair dryers should not be used.
- School uniform skirts should be ___ centimeters above the ground, no more and no less (differs by school and region).
- Keep your uniform clean and pressed at all times. Girls' middy blouses should have two buttons on the back collar. Boys' pant cuffs should be of the prescribed width. No more than 12 eyelets should be on shoes. The number of buttons on a shirt and tucks in a shirt are also prescribed.
- Wear your school badge at all times. It should be positioned exactly.
- Going to school in the morning, wear your book bag strap on the right shoulder; in the afternoon on the way home, wear it on the left shoulder. Your book case thickness, filled and unfilled, is also prescribed.
- Girls should wear only regulation white underpants of 100% cotton.
- When you raise your hand to be called on, your arm should extend forward and up at the angle prescribed in your handbook.
- Your own route to and from school is marked in your student rule handbook; carefully observe which side of each street you are to use on the way to and from school.
- After school you are to go directly home, unless your parent has written a note permitting you to go to another location. Permission will not be granted by the school unless this other location is a suitable one. You must not go to coffee shops. You must be home by ___ o'clock.
- It is not permitted to drive or ride a motorcycle, or to have a license to drive one.
- Before and after school, no matter where you are, you represent our school, so you should behave in ways we can all be proud of.

—Duiker/Spielvogel, *World History,* 5th Edition

A. What is the author's purpose? _____

B. What is the author's point of view? _____

C. Are the words used mostly denotative (and thus neutral) or connotative (emotional)? _____

D. What is the tone of this passage? _____

_____

_____

2. India's decision to allow Pepsi Foods Ltd. to open 60 restaurants in India—30 each of Pizza Hut and Kentucky Fried Chicken—marks the first entry of multinational, meat-based junk-food chains into India. If this is allowed to happen, at least a dozen other similar chains will very quickly arrive, including the infamous McDonald's.

The implications of allowing junk-food chains into India are quite stark. As the name denotes, the foods served at Kentucky Fried Chicken (KFC) are chicken-based and fried. This is the worst combination possible for the body and can create a host of health problems, including obesity, high cholesterol, heart ailments, and many kinds of cancer. Pizza Hut products are a combination of white flour, cheese, and meat—again, a combination likely to cause disease. . . .

Then there is the issue of the environmental impact of junk-food chains. Modern meat production involves misuse of crops, water, energy, and grazing areas. In addition, animal agriculture produces surprisingly large amounts of air and water pollution.

KFC and Pizza Hut insist that their chickens be fed corn and soybeans. Consider the diversion of grain for this purpose. As the outlets of KFC and Pizza Hut increase in number, the poultry industry will buy up more and more corn to feed the chickens, which means that the corn will quickly disappear from the villages, and its increased price will place it out of reach for the common man. Turning corn into junk chicken is like turning gold into mud. . .

It is already shameful that, in a country plagued by famine and flood, we divert 37 percent of our arable land to growing animal fodder. Were all of that grain to be consumed directly by humans, it would nourish five times as many people as it does after being converted into meat, milk, and eggs. . . .

Of course, it is not just the KFC and Pizza Hut chains of Pepsi Foods Ltd. that will cause all of this damage. Once we open India up by allowing these chains, dozens more will be eagerly waiting to come in. Each city in America has an average of 5,000 junk-food restaurants. Is that what we want for India?

—Gandhi, "Say No To McDonald's and KFC!"

A. What is the author's purpose? _____

B. What is the author's point of view? _____

C. Are the words used mostly denotative (and thus neutral) or connotative (emotional)?

_____

D. What is the tone of this passage? _____

More Specific Tone Words

It is helpful to become familiar with a range of words you can use to describe an author's tone. If you want to be able to talk in class about an author's ideas, or write about them for a college assignment, you will probably need to use words like these to describe the author's tone. Here are some possibilities.

Words to Describe an Author's Tone

alarmed	cruel	indignant	reticent
ambivalent	cynical	ironic	righteous
ambitious	direct	irreverent	sarcastic
amused	disapproving	loving	sensational
angry	elated	mocking	serious
annoyed	excited	nostalgic	sincere
apathetic	evasive	optimistic	skeptical
appalled	fearful	outraged	thoughtful
arrogant	flippant	outspoken	urgent
bitter	frustrated	pessimistic	wry
bored	humorous	respectful	
celebratory	hyperbolic		

◉ Interaction 10-7. Using Specific Tone Words

Circle the best tone word for each item. Use a dictionary as needed.

1. "I remember when my father used to get home from work," sighed Lori Price. "We would all run outside to meet him on the side porch. Today, my own children barely look up from their computers when Bruce or I walk in."

    evasive   loving   nostalgic

2. Sure, you'll help me. Right over the edge of a cliff, you'll help me.

    cynical   desperate   mocking

3. "Yes, sir, General Motors, you want to close these factories and move them to Mexico? No problem! How can we help you? You say you don't want to pay your corporate taxes? No problem! You don't have to pay *any*! So you want five of us workers to do the exact same job it used to take ten workers to do? Happy to oblige! No, we don't mind working seven days a week! Why give jobs to the unemployed when we can just work longer ourselves! We don't need to see our kids!"

    —Moore, *Downsize This!*

    cruel   reticent   sarcastic

4. "I'd much rather be a woman than a man. Women can cry, they can wear cute clothes, and they are the first to be rescued off of sinking ships."

—Gilda Radner

humorous   outspoken   sincere

5. "Any fine morning, a power saw can fell a tree that took a thousand years to grow."

—Edwin Way Teale

skeptical   serious   respectful

Interaction 10-8. Identifying Tone in a Longer Passage

Read the passage, and answer the questions that follow.

Cancer

Celine knows that she inherited her mother's brown eyes and buoyant sense of humor. She wonders whether she's also inherited "the bad gene"—the cancer-causing one that killed her grandmother and her great-grandmother. Celine's mother was 42 years old when she learned that she, too, had cancer. She died two years later, leaving behind eight sisters. Within the next decade, six had developed breast or ovarian cancer.

Unlike most college students, Celine never thinks of cancer as something that affects only people much older than she. Three of her five sisters have tested positive for what is called "the breast cancer gene." Celine is struggling to decide whether she too will undergo testing.

An estimated 10 percent of cancers are hereditary, but no one is immune from the threat of cancer or other serious diseases.

Cancer has overtaken heart disease as the number-one killer of Americans under age 85. Yet many of the almost 500, 000 deaths caused by cancer each year could be prevented. A third of cancers are related to smoking; another third, to obesity, poor diet, and lack of exercise.

—Hales, *An Invitation to Health*, 12th Edition

A. What is the author's purpose? _____

B. What is the author's point of view? _____

C. Are the words used denotative (dictionary) or connotative (emotional connection)?

_____

D. What is the tone of this passage? _____

Figurative versus Literal Language

- "I'm so hungry I could eat a horse." This statement is a figure of speech (more specifically, it is hyperbole—an intentional exaggeration).

- "I am hungry." This statement is literal.

Figurative language is like connotation: it reveals the author's emotions about whatever he or she is describing. Extreme uses of figurative language are sometimes called "flowery language" or "purple prose." Literal language is linked to denotation. Literal language often appears in the form of facts, and it has a matter-of-fact tone.

Sometimes a description could be figurative in one context and literal in another. For example, you could say that you "waited for hours." You could mean it literally—that is, that you *did* wait for hours (maybe you were stuck in an airport or rush hour traffic). Or you could use it figuratively to emphasize that you waited a long time, even though it wasn't actually hours. (Maybe you got impatient waiting for your date, who was twenty-five minutes late.)

Poets and novelists frequently use figurative language in their literature. We will discuss four common figures of speech—simile, metaphor, personification, and hyperbole—and share some poems that use them.

A Simile Is Like a Metaphor, but a Metaphor Is Not a Simile.

Simile. An indirect comparison of two things using the words "like" or "as" (A is like B).

Metaphor. A direct comparison of two things **without** using the words "like" or "as" (A is B).

Here are some examples:

> Simile: The sun is *like* a big yellow ball bouncing from horizon to horizon.
> Metaphor: The sun *is* a big yellow ball bouncing from horizon to horizon.
> Simile: He is *like* a cat waiting to pounce on its prey.
> Metaphor: He *is* a cat waiting to pounce on its prey.

Read the following poem by Margaret Atwood. Before you read the poem, look at the title and predict what this poem will be about. Do you think the tone will be positive, negative, or neutral?

You Fit into Me

You fit into me
like a hook into an eye

a fish hook
an open eye

Were you surprised? The title seems to suggest that two people are perfect for each other. A "hook and eye" is a fastener for clothing, usually women's clothing. So the first hook and eye in the poem suggests "clasping together" by way of a simile. Then you get the shocker: a fish hook, an open eye! Ouch! This poem points out the power of similes to affect readers' emotions.

Personification

Personification is the act of giving an inanimate object (something that isn't alive or can't move) characteristics of an animate being (something that is alive or can move):

The *words* (inanimate) *leaped* (animate) from the page.

Think of cartoons. These are inanimate objects that are animated. Get it? Animation!

Impress your instructor and get out of trouble by using personification: "I'm sorry I couldn't finish my homework. My bed kept distracting me; it was screaming my name!" Or wiggle out of a sticky situation by explaining to your wife, husband, mom, dad, brother, sister, friend, or second cousin why you ate the last cookie: "Hey, I had no choice. The cookie pushed itself into my mouth with a force greater than my own resistance." Do you see what personification is? A bed does not literally "scream" names, but when you are tired, it sure is hard to resist lying down. Cookies do not have wills of their own. It is our own lack of will power that gets us into trouble.

Look for examples of personification in this poem by Carl Sandburg:

Summer Grass

Summer grass aches and whispers
It wants something: it calls and sings; it pours
out wishes to the overhead stars.
The rain hears; the rain answers; the rain is slow
coming; the rain wets the face of the grass.

(1928)

This short poem personifies both the grass and the rain. The summer grass aches, whispers, wants, calls, sings, and pours out wishes—all actions of a living being. Sandburg uses the phrase "face of the grass," which also suggests a person or animal. And he says the rain hears, and answers, and is "slow coming."

Hyperbole

"If I've told you once, I've told you a thousand times!" If your parent or significant other ever hurled these words at you, their point was to make you realize you haven't been paying close enough attention to their wishes. Hyperbole is intentional exaggeration to make or emphasize a point. Hyperbole is not meant to be taken literally but figuratively.

Interaction 10-9. Creating Hyperbole

w/ class

Write two hyperboles in each category. Don't worry, they can be silly.

Family

_____

_____

Homework

_____

_____

Insects

_____

_____

Physical appearance

_____

_____

Emotions

_____

_____

● Interaction 10-10. Identifying Figures of Speech

Read the following poems. Underline any examples of metaphor, simile, personification, or hyperbole. In the margin, write which figure of speech you find. Then consider what effect they have on the author's tone.

Oh, My Love Is Like a Red, Red Rose
Robert Burns

Oh, my love is like a red, red rose
That's newly sprung in June;
My love is like the melody
That's sweetly played in tune.

So fair art thou, my bonny lass,
So deep in love am I;
And I will love thee still, my dear,
Till a' [all] the seas gang [go] dry.

Till a' [all] the seas gang [go] dry, my dear
And rocks melt wi' the sun;
And I will love thee still, my dear,
While the suns o' life shall run.

And fare thee weel, my only love!
And fare thee weel awhile!
And I will come again my love
Though it were ten thousand miles.

(1796)

What words would you use to describe the poet's tone? _____

_____

My Father as a Guitar
Martin Espada

The cardiologist prescribed
a new medication
and lectured my father
that he had to stop working.
And my father said: *I can't.*
The landlord won't let me.

The heart pills are dice in my father's hand,
gambler who needs cash
by the first of the month.

On the night his mother died
in far away Puerto Rico,
my father lurched upright in bed,
heart hammering
like the fist of a man at the door
with an eviction notice.
Minutes later,
the telephone sputtered
with news of the dead.

Sometimes I dream
my father is a guitar,
with a hole in his chest
where the music throbs
between my fingers.

What words would you use to describe the poet's tone? _____

Harlem

Langston Hughes

What happens to a dream deferred?
Does it dry up
like a raisin in the sun?
Or fester like a sore—
And then run!
Does it stink like rotten meat?
Or crust and sugar over—
like a syrupy sweet?

Maybe it just sags
like a heavy load.

Or does it explode?

What words would you use to describe the author's tone? _____

Understanding Irony

"Better slow down before the police start chasing us," your friend says as you sit in stalled traffic. "But I just love the feeling of the wind in my hair," you reply. These statements are ironic. *Irony* is the use of words or images to express the opposite of what is said. To understand irony, you need to understand what would be the expected response or action in a given situation.

For instance, if you were reading a review of a singer's new CD, for what qualities would you expect the CD to be praised?

> Pop superstar Madonna has once again wowed music critics and consumers alike with her latest offering, *Hard Candy*, an album that has garnered unanimous praise for the ease with which it can be exchanged for money.
>
> —"New Madonna Album Hailed as Available for Purchase,"
> *The Onion*, May 20, 2008; www.theonion.com

You probably would not expect the CD to be praised for being for sale!

Interaction 10-11. Identifying Irony

Identify the irony in the following passages.

1. A doctor was sued for $17 million by an angry patient after the doctor removed the wrong kidney. Asked what might have prevented the lawsuit, the patient replied, "An apology."

What is ironic about this? _____

2. **Mislaid Plans, by Monica Ware**

> A rash of new bills came that morning. The letter from their insurance company announced the cancellation of their policies.
>
> She sighed and rose wearily to tell her husband. The kitchen smelled of gas. On his desk she found the note.
>
> ". . . the money from my life insurance will be enough for you and the children."

What is ironic about this? _____

_____

3. The story *The Gift of the Magi*, by O. Henry, is about a couple too poor to afford Christmas presents for each other. The husband wants to buy combs for his wife, who has long beautiful hair. The wife wants to buy a chain for her husband's antique pocket watch. The wife cuts and sells her hair to buy the watch chain; the husband sells his watch to buy the combs.

What is ironic about this? _____

_____

4. Dogs are rescued from a dog-fighting ring. However, ultimately, the dogs that were saved are put to sleep because they are deemed too dangerous.

What is ironic about this?_____

As you have learned, the author's tone is not a single aspect of a book or article. Instead, it is formed from the interactions between the author's purpose, point of view, and use of denotation, connotation, and figurative language. Irony may also add a twist.

Chapter Summary Activity

This chapter has discussed how to determine the author's tone by using purpose, point of view, denotation and connotation, and figurative language. Construct a Reading Guide below by completing each idea on the left with information from the chapter on the right. You can use this guide anytime you need to figure out an author's tone.

Reading Guide to Analyzing Tone

Complete this idea	with information from the chapter.
The author's tone might also be called the author's ____ toward the subject.	1.
To figure out an author's tone, consider at least these four elements.	2. 3. 4. 5.
The three general purposes people have for writing are	6. 7. 8.
A tone that focuses on giving facts and not the author's feelings is called	9.
In contrast, when the writing does reveal the author's emotional stance, the tone may be called	10.

The two purposes most likely to use a subjective tone are	11. _____ 12. _____
The author may create a focus on his or her own impressions by using this point of view:	13. _____
Or the author might choose to draw the reader into conversation by use of this point of view:	14. _____
Or the author might describe people and events as though neither the readers nor the author are involved in them. This point of view is called	15. _____
When an author uses few or no words that have connotations, the tone might be called	16. _____
The connotations of words can tell you whether the tone is generally	17. _____ 18. _____
Noticing what comparisons the author makes helps a reader figure out the author's meaning and tone. Two types of comparison are	19. _____ 20. _____
The author may choose to make it seem as if objects are living beings in order to set up a certain tone and meaning. This is known as	21. _____
Or an author might choose to exaggerate something to create a certain effect, which is called	22. _____
Collectively, the answers to 19–22 are known as	23. _____
The author can even use words or images to express the opposite meaning of what he or she is saying. This use is called	24. _____
If a reader thinks about all of these factors as they relate to one another and to the subject the author is writing about, the reader can figure out the author's	25. _____

Test Taking Tips
Analyzing the Author's Tone

As you have learned in this chapter, the tone of a reading selection depends on many factors such as the author's purpose and point of view, the positive or negative connotations that certain words have, the meaning of any figurative language the author has used, and even whether the author is writing sincerely or ironically. Examine as many of these factors as you can when you find a tone question on a reading test.

Here is a system you can try:

1. Decide what point of view the author is using, and whether that makes the selection seem more personal or impersonal, and more formal or informal.
2. Look for subjective words (some reading tests call such words "biased") that indicate that the author's attitude or opinion about the topic. In other words, look for words with positive or negative connotations. If there are several, think about what attitude they all add up to. If you don't find any, think about whether the author is being objective.
3. Look for any suggestions that the author is being ironic. Do the words seem appropriate for the situation?
4. Ask yourself, "How does the passage make me feel?" The author chooses a tone to make a certain impression on readers. So take that impression into account.

Some questions about the author's attitude, bias, or tone also ask you to dig deeper and think about what else the author probably believes or assumes. Here is an example:

Sample Reading Selection and Test Questions

. . . Only Ross's vote was needed to obtain the thirty-six votes necessary to convict the President. But not a single person in the room knew how this young Kansan would vote. Unable to conceal the suspense and emotion in his voice, the Chief Justice put the question to him: "Mr. Senator Ross, how say you? Is the respondent Andrew Jackson guilty or not guilty of a high misdemeanor as charged in this Article?" . . .

As Ross himself later described it, his "powers of hearing and seeing seemed developed in an abnormal degree."

> Every individual in that great audience seemed distinctly visible, some with lips apart and bending forward in anxious expectancy, others with hand uplifted as if to ward off an apprehended blow . . . and each peering with an intensity that was almost tragic upon the face of him who was about to cast the fateful vote . . . Every fan was folded, not a foot moved,

not the rustle of a garment, not a whisper was heard . . . It was a tremendous responsibility, and it was not strange that he upon whom it had been imposed by a fateful combination of conditions should have sought to avoid it, to put it away from him as one shuns, or tries to fight off, a nightmare . . . I almost literally looked down into my open grave. Friendships, position, fortune, everything that makes life desirable to an ambitious man were about to be swept away by the breath of my mouth, perhaps forever. . . .

—Kennedy, *Profiles in Courage*

1. What is Ross's tone in the paragraph in which he describes the moments before he casts his vote?

    a. full of dread

    b. excited

    c. indecisive

    d. thoughtful

2. Would Ross agree or disagree with this statement: "Politicians have to ensure their political survival first and foremost—after all, if I do not get re-elected, what good am I to the people of Kansas"?

    a. agree

    b. disagree

The answer to the first question is A. Ross, a young senator from Kansas, has to vote on whether or not the president is guilty. Everyone is looking at him; no one know what he will say. He says he practically looks "into [his] open grave" because he knows that what is he about to say may ruin all that he cares about the most. He wants to put off casting his vote because he dreads the consequences.

Regarding question 2, the answer is B. Ross would disagree with the statement. As he has just said at the end of paragraph 1, he knows that his vote may take away his friends, his position, and his fortune. Yet there is no suggestion that he will change his vote in order to save them.

Common Tone Stems

When you see items on reading tests that use the following language, your task is to figure out the tone of the selection and then, at times, to use that knowledge to decide what else the author might believe.

    ✔ The following words best describe the tone . . .
    ✔ The tone of the passage is . . .
    ✔ The author would agree with the following . . .
    ✔ The author believes . . .
    ✔ The passage suggests that the author's attitude/point of view is . . .
    ✔ The passage affects the reader . . .

Reading 10-1 . . . . **Essay**

● Pre-Reading the Selection

"Why I Want a Wife" is a classic essay by Judy (Syfers) Brady. The essay first appeared in *Ms. Magazine*, a feminist magazine, in 1971.

Guessing the Purpose

Judging from the title of the essay, what do you suppose is the purpose of the selection?

_____

Surveying the Reading

Based on the purpose(s) you chose, as well as some words or phrases that stand out as you survey this reading, what do you think will be the tone of this passage? _____

Predicting the Content

Predict three things this selection will discuss.

- _____

- _____

- _____

Activating Your Knowledge

List several details you know about the role of women in modern families.

- _____

- _____

- _____

Reading with Pen in Hand

Now read the selection. As you read, mark any ideas that seem important, and respond to the questions and vocabulary items in the margin. Monitor your comprehension by putting a ✔ next to a paragraph when you understand most of it. Place an ✘ next to a paragraph when you don't understand most of it.

Visit www.cengage.com/devenglish/doleconnect and select Chapter 10 to hear vocabulary words from this selection and view a video about this topic.

◆ *Reading Journal*

◆What does the phrase "As I thought about him while I was ironing one evening" probably indicate about the author?

◆What reasons does the author give for wanting a wife?

nurturing Based on the examples given, what is *nurturing*?

tolerate Use the context of the whole sentence to figure out the meaning.

mended What does *mended* mean?

◆What reasons does the author give for wanting a wife?

Why I Want a Wife
Judy Brady

1   I belong to that classification of people known as wives. I am a Wife. And, not altogether incidentally, I am a mother. Not too long ago a male friend of mine appeared on the scene from the Midwest fresh from a recent divorce. He had one child, who is, of course, with his ex-wife. He is obviously looking for another wife. As I thought about him while I was ironing one evening, it suddenly occurred to me that I, too, would like to have a wife.

Why do I want a wife?

2   I would like to go back to school, so that I can become economically independent, support myself, and, if need be, support those dependent upon me. I want a wife who will work and send me to school. And while I am going to school I want a wife to take care of my children. I want a wife to keep track of the children's doctor and dentist appointments. And to keep track of mine, too. I want a wife to make sure my children eat properly and are kept clean. I want a wife who will wash the children's clothes and keep them mended. I want a wife who is a good **nurturing** attendant to my children, arranges for their schooling, makes sure that they have an adequate social life with their peers, takes them to the park, the zoo, etc. I want a wife who takes care of the children when they are sick, a wife who arranges to be around when the children need special care, because, of course, I cannot miss classes at school. My wife must arrange to lose time at work and not lose the job. It may mean a small cut in my wife's income from time to time, but I guess I can **tolerate** that. Needless to say, my wife will arrange and pay for the care of the children while my wife is working.

3   I want a wife who will take care of my physical needs. I want a wife who will keep my house clean. A wife who will pick up after my children, a wife who will pick up after me. I want a wife who will keep my clothes clean, ironed, **mended**, replaced when need be, and who will see to it that my personal things are kept in their proper place so that I can find what I need the minute I need it. I want a wife who cooks the meals, a wife who is a good cook. I want a wife who will plan the menus, do the necessary grocery shopping, prepare the

meals, serve them pleasantly, and then do the cleaning up while I do my studying. I want a wife who will care for me when I am sick and sympathize with my pain and loss of time from school. I want a wife to go along when our family takes a vacation so that someone can continue to care for me and my children when I need a rest and a change of scene.

4   I want a wife who will take care of the details of my social life. When my wife and I are invited out by my friends, I want a wife who will take care of the baby-sitting arrangements. When I meet people at school that I like and want to entertain, I want a wife who will have the house clean, will prepare a special meal, serve it to me and my friends, and not interrupt when I talk about the things that interest me and my friends. I want a wife who will have arranged that the children are fed and ready for bed before my guests arrive so that the children do not bother us. I want a wife who takes care of the needs of my guests so that they feel comfortable, who makes sure that they have an ashtray, that they are passed the hors d'oeuvres, that they are offered a second helping of the food, that their wine glasses are **replenished** when necessary, that their coffee is served to them as they like it. And I want a wife who knows that sometimes I need a night out by myself.

5   I want a wife who is sensitive to my sexual needs, a wife who makes love passionately and eagerly when I feel like it, a wife who makes sure that I am satisfied. And, of course, I want a wife who will not demand sexual attention when I am not in the mood for it. I want a wife who assumes the complete responsibility for birth control, because I do not want more children. I want a wife who will remain sexually faithful to me so that I do not have to clutter up my intellectual life with jealousies. And I want a wife who understands that my sexual needs may entail more than strict **adherence** to monogamy. I must, after all, be able to relate to people as fully as possible.

6   If, by chance, I find another person more suitable as a wife than the wife I already have, I want the liberty to replace my present wife with another one. Naturally, I will expect a fresh, new life; my wife will take the children and be solely responsible for them so that I am left free. When I am through with school and have acquired a job, I want my wife to quit working and remain at home so that my wife can more fully and completely take care of a wife's duties.

7   My God, who *wouldn't* want a wife?

◆What reasons does the author give for wanting a wife?

replenished Think about the series of tasks the wife is doing to help you guess at this word's meaning.

◆What reasons does the author give for wanting a wife?

adherence This and the next sentence give clues to the meaning of *adherence.*

◆What two reasons for why the author wants a wife are mentioned?

⬤ Comprehension Questions

Write the letter of the answer on the line. Then explain your thinking.

Main Idea

_____ 1. Which of the following sentences best states the main idea of this reading passage?

    a. I want my wife to quit working and remain at home so that my wife can more fully and completely take care of a wife's duties.

    b. I want a wife who will take care of details of my social life.

    c. As I thought about him while I was ironing one evening, it suddenly occurred to me that I, too, would like to have a wife.

    d. I want a wife to take care of my children.

WHY? What information in the selection leads you to give that answer? _____

_____

_____

_____ 2. What is the main idea of paragraph 5?

    a. I want a wife who will take care of my physical needs.

    b. I want a wife who will keep my house clean.

    c. I want a wife who will keep my clothes clean, ironed, mended, replaced when need be, and who will see to it that my personal things are kept in their proper place so that I can find what I need the minute I need it.

    d. I want a wife who will care for me when I am sick and sympathize with my pain and loss of time from school.

WHY? What information in the selection leads you to give that answer?_____

_____

_____

Supporting Details

_____ 3. Which of the following is *not* a reason the author gives for wanting a wife?

    a. I want a wife who puts my needs above hers.

    b. I want a wife who is open to polygamy.

    c. I want a wife who understands my needs.

    d. I want a wife who will take care of all the household duties.

WHY? What information in the selection leads you to give that answer? _____

_____

_____

_____ 4. According to the passage, which of the following is a privilege the author reserves?

a. entertaining guests

b. infidelity

c. helping clean up after meals

d. giving the wife a night out from time to time

WHY? What information in the selection leads you to give that answer? _____

_____

_____

Author's Purpose

_____ 5. What is the overall purpose of this passage?

a. to inform

b. to entertain

c. to persuade

d. to entertain and persuade

WHY? What information in the selection leads you to give that answer? _____

_____

_____

_____ 6. What is the overall tone of this passage?

a. sincere

b. sarcastic

c. objective

d. descriptive

WHY? What information in the selection leads you to give that answer? _____

_____

_____

Relationships

_____ 7. What is the overall pattern of organization of this passage?

   a. time order

   b. listing

   c. comparison and contrast

   d. cause-and-effect

WHY? What information in the selection leads you to give that answer? _____

_____

_____

_____ 8. What is the main relationship found in this sentence:
   I want a wife who will have arranged that the children are fed and ready for bed before my guests arrive?

   a. time order

   b. comparison and contrast

   c. cause-and-effect

   d. listing

WHY? What leads you to give that answer? _____

_____

_____

Fact, Opinion, and Inference

_____ 9. How would you categorize this sentence:
   It suddenly occurred to me that I, too, would like a wife.

   a. an opinion

   b. a fact

   c. both fact and opinion

   d. an expert opinion

WHY? What leads you to give that answer? _____

_____

_____

____ 10. Which of the following is a valid conclusion you could draw from reading this passage?

a. Everyone should have a wife.

b. The author's husband is a jerk and she should divorce him.

c. The author uses hyperbole to make her point.

d. The Wife in this essay is meant to be a personification of a goddess.

WHY? What information in the selection leads you to give that answer? _____

_____

_____

● Critical Thinking Questions

CRITICAL THINKING LEVEL 1 REMEMBER

Throughout the essay, the words "I want a wife" are repeated time after time. Have you ever heard someone repeating the same phrase over and over like this? What was the effect? _____

_____

_____

CRITICAL THINKING LEVEL 2 UNDERSTAND

Summarize the topic and main idea of this reading.

About: _____

Point: _____

_____

CRITICAL THINKING LEVEL 3 APPLY

Use Brady's tone and style to write a paragraph about something you want. This desire might stem from an unequal relationship like Brady's does, but it doesn't have to. It could be about a person, a thing, an event, or anything else. Use repetition and a lot of details to explain your desire. If you want, after you write the paragraph you can change it into a song. Consider using a refrain (repeated lines) after each stanza (group of lines) to get across the feeling of repetitiveness.

> **CRITICAL THINKING LEVEL 4 ANALYZE**

Examine the reasons that the author gives for wanting a wife. Consider what kinds of reasons she does *not* give that you might expect someone to want in a spouse. Discuss your ideas with your classmates. _____

_____

> **CRITICAL THINKING LEVEL 5 EVALUATE**

Read this pamphlet on being a good wife.

The Good Wife's Guide

- Have dinner ready. Plan ahead, even the night before, to have a delicious meal ready on time for his return. This is a way of letting him know that you have been thinking about him and are concerned about his needs. Most men are hungry when they get home and the prospect of a good meal is part of the warm welcome needed.
- Prepare yourself. Take 15 minutes to rest so you'll be refreshed when he arrives. Touch up your make-up, put a ribbon in your hair and be fresh-looking. He has just been with a lot of work-weary people.
- Be a little gay and a little more interesting for him. His boring day may need a lift and one of your duties is to provide it.
- Clear away the clutter. Make one last trip through the main part of the house just before your husband arrives. Run a dust cloth over the tables.

Image courtesy of The Advertising Archives

- During the cooler months of the year you should prepare and light a fire for him to unwind by. Your husband will feel he has reached a haven of rest and order, and it will give you a lift too. After all, catering to his comfort will provide you with immense personal satisfaction.
- Minimize all noise. At the time of his arrival, eliminate all noise of the washer, dryer or vacuum. Encourage the children to be quiet.
- Be happy to see him.
- Greet him with a warm smile and show sincerity in your desire to please him.
- Listen to him. You may have a dozen important things to tell him, but the moment of his arrival is not the time. Let him talk first—remember, his topics of conversation are more important than yours.
- Don't greet him with complaints and problems.
- Don't complain if he's late for dinner or even if he stays out all night. Count this as minor compared to what he might have gone through at work.
- Make him comfortable. Have him lean back in a comfortable chair or lie him down in the bedroom. Have a cool or warm drink ready for him.
- Arrange his pillow and offer to take off his shoes. Speak in a low, soothing and pleasant voice.
- Don't ask him questions about his actions or question his judgment or integrity. Remember, he is the master of the house and as such will always exercise his will with fairness and truthfulness. You have no right to question him.
- A good wife always knows her place.

What do you think of this list? _____

_____

What is the author's tone? _____

_____

_____

When would you guess this was written? _____

_____

What is the author's purpose in writing this? _____

CRITICAL THINKING LEVEL 6 CREATE

"I Want a Wife" was written in the early 1970s. Single parent households were much less common than they are today. Today, single parent families and other nontraditional families are about equal in number to families that have a husband and a wife. Think about how the changes in culture would affect this essay if it were written today. *Write* an updated version of this essay reflecting your thoughts.

● Vocabulary in Context

The following words, or forms of them, were used in "Why I Want a Wife." Select the best word to complete the meaning of each sentence.

nurture	tolerate	mend	replenish	adherence

1. Parents should _____ their children.

2. Expecting _____ to their rules is not unreasonable, but they should be patient and _____ misbehavior when it occurs (as it will).

3. In addition, parents should plan to _____ their children's clothing and _____ their plates and cups at mealtime, as needed.

Reading 10-2 . . . . Essay

● Pre-Reading the Selection

This reading also examines the role a woman plays in the family. Kristin van Ogtrop writes about how she struggles to balance her work life with her home life.

Guessing the Purpose

Judging from a quick scan of the reading selection and its title, what do you suppose the purpose is of this reading selection? _____

Surveying the Reading

Survey the title and first sentences of each paragraph. What do you think is the topic of the reading selection? _____

Predicting the Content

Predict three things this selection will discuss.

- _____

- _____

- _____

Activating Your Knowledge

Take a moment to write out what you think is the life of a professional woman who has a traditional family life. Use someone you know as inspiration if you can.

_____

_____

_____

Common Knowledge

Attila (*title*) Attila the Hun was the ruler of the Huns, who were horse-riding nomads in Central Asia, from AD 433–453. He is often referred to as a fierce, cruel, and bloodthirsty ruler.

Mr. Rogers (*paragraph 5*) Fred Rogers was the host of a popular children's television show called *Mister Rogers' Neighborhood* from 1968 to 2001. He is an icon in children's entertainment, known for being calm and gentle.

Eye of the storm (*paragraph 10*) This refers to the middle, calm part of a hurricane or tornado.

Reading with Pen in Hand

Now read the selection. As you read, mark any ideas that seem important, and respond to the questions and vocabulary items in the margin. Monitor your comprehension by putting a ✔ next to a paragraph when you understand most of it. Place an ✘ next to a paragraph when you don't understand most of it.

Visit **www.cengage.com/devenglish/doleconnect** and select Chapter 10 to hear vocabulary words from this selection and view a video about this topic.

Attila the Honey I'm Home

Kristin van Ogtrop

It's a Typical Night

◆ *Reading Journal*

1   I arrive home from work, after first stopping to pick up my two boys from my friend Gabrielle's house, where my nanny has left them on a play date. It's seven thirty. No one has had a bath. Foolishly, I have promised that we will make milkshakes. The boys have eaten

◆Why was it "foolish" for the author to promise milkshakes?

dinner. I haven't. My husband is at a basketball game and won't be home until ten.

2   Owen, who is six, tosses a bouquet of flowers—a gift from Gabrielle's garden—into the grass as we get out of the car. Three-year-old Hugo sees the moon. I mention that the sun is out, too; he runs from one end of the front walk to the other, trying to find it, getting closer to the street with each lap. Owen says he wants the milkshake *now*. I unlock the front door and step in. George the cat meows and rubs against my legs, begging to be fed.

◆Why does the author describe herself as an "optimist?"

3   I walk back outside to pick up the flowers, the wet towel (swimming lessons), and my own two bags from work (contents: three unread newspapers, two magazines, a birthday party invitation for Owen, a present for the party, and a folder of work that, ever the optimist, I'm hoping to do tonight). Back into the house with flowers, towel, bags. I put my keys in the bowl next to the front door (small attempt at order). I knock over a framed picture beside it. The glass in the frame shatters. Hugo calls, insistent, for me to come back outside.

insistent Does the word itself give you any clues about its meaning? Think about who is calling. What might Hugo's tone be?

4   Owen hovers behind me, barefoot. He wants to how why, when you combine chocolate and vanilla, does the ice cream turn brown instead of white? I maneuver Owen around the broken glass and ask him to get the Dustbuster as I begin to pick up the shards. He disappears into the kitchen for what seems like ten minutes. I glance out for Hugo, whose voice is fainter but *definitely* still audible. George stands on his hind legs, clawing holes in the screen. Owen reappears with the Dustbuster, revving the motor. He wants to know exactly how long until we make the milk shake, and are we sure we even have chocolate ice cream?

shards Use your logic and the context. What are *shards*?

5   I am talking in my Mr. Rogers voice as my desperation rises. Any minute now my head is going to blast off my body, burst through the screen door, and buzz around my little town, eventually losing steam before landing with a thud somewhere near the train station, where it will be run over by one of my smiling neighbors being picked up by what I imagine are calm spouses who will drive them calmly home to houses calm and collected where the children are already bathed and ready for bed. As for me, it's time to start yelling.

◆What figurative language is used in this paragraph?

The Next Day

6   I get up at 5:30 to leave the house at 6:00, to be driven to the TV studio for hair and makeup at 6:45, to go on the air, live, at 7:40. I'm the executive editor of an enormously popular women's magazine

and am appearing as an "expert" on a local morning show to discuss "what your wallet says about you." I have a hairstylist I've never met and he makes the back of my head look ridiculous, like a ski jump. At 7:25 the segment producer hands me the anchor's script; it contains five questions that weren't part of yesterday's pre-interview. I make up answers that sound informed-clever-peppy enough for morning TV with two minutes to spare. Total airtime: ninety seconds.

7   By the time I get to the office at 8:30 I have six voice mail messages (boss, nanny, human resources manager, unhappy writer, underling editor wanting guidance, my mother), twenty-seven e-mails, and, on my chair, a 4,000-word article I need to edit by the end of the day. I run to the cafeteria to get something to eat, then call boss and nanny and answer most of the e-mails before my 9:30 meeting. At 10:45 two fact-checkers come into my office to describe the problems of a recent story, which kept them at work until 4:00 A.M. the night before. Are fact-checkers or editor to blame? Editor, I decide, and call her in. She is flustered and defensive, and starts to cry. My tissue box is empty, so I hand her a napkin. We talk (well, I talk; she nods) about the fact that she's made similar mistakes in the past, and perhaps this isn't the job for her. After she leaves I call the human resources manager to discuss the problematic editor, a looming legal problem, and staff salaries.

8   I have lunch at my desk and a second cup of coffee while I edit the piece, until two editors visit to complain about coworkers. A third tells me she is overloaded. A fourth confesses her marital problems and starts to cry; now I'm out of napkins, too. I give her the number of a counseling service and suggest she use it. Someone calls to ask about the presentation I'm giving tomorrow; I haven't even begun to think about it, which probably should worry me but somehow doesn't. I finish the edit and drop it in my out box. Before leaving the office at 5:30 I pick up all the paper that blankets my desk and divide it into four discrete piles for the morning. I very well might forget to look through the piles and something will get overlooked, but when I return to work, the neat stacks will make me feel organized and calm. And at work, I usually am.

9   Here are a few things people have said about me at the office:
"You're unflappable."
"Are you ever in a bad mood?"
"You command respect as soon as you walk into a room."
"Your straightforward, no-nonsense style gets things done."

◆Based on the details in paragraphs 6, 7, and 8, describe the type of person the author is at work.

flustered Notice that *flustered* probably refers to an emotional state. Which emotion would fit this situation? How would you feel?

finessing Look at the cause and effect relationship: what does *finessing* result in? What does this mean?

◆ Why is the author "a better mother at work than I am at home?"

◆ What answer does the author give for the question she asks?

"You're good at finessing situations so people don't boil over." Here are things people—OK, the members of my family—have said about me at home:

"Mommy is always grumpy."

"Why are you so tense?"

"You just need to relax."

"You don't need to yell!"

"You're too mean to live in this house and I want you to go back to work for the rest of your life!"

10   That last one is my favorite. It's also the saddest, because it captures such a painful truth: too often I'm a better mother at work than I am at home. Of course, at work, no one shouts at me for five minutes straight in what parents universally refer to as an "outside voice." No one charges into my office, hands outstretched, to smear peanut butter all over my skirt or Vaseline all over my favorite needlepoint rug. At work, when someone is demanding something of me, I can say, "I'll call you back" or "Let's talk about that in the next meeting." When people don't listen to me, they do so after they've left my office, not right in front of me. Yet even if shouting and random acts of destruction were to become the norm at work, I probably would not respond with the angry tantrums that punctuate so many nights at home. We have our own form of chaos in the office, after all. I work with creative people—temperamental, flaky, "difficult"— but my job is to be the eye of the storm.

11   So why this angel-in-the-office, horror-at-home division? Shouldn't the skills that serve me so well at work help me at the end of the day? My friend Chrissie, heroic stay-at-home mother of four, has one explanation: My behavior simply reproduces, in the adult world, the perfect-at-school/demon-at-home phenomenon that is acted out daily among children throughout America. I am on my best behavior at work, just as Owen is on his best behavior at school, but at home we have to ask him seven times to put on his shoes and by the seventh time it's no longer a request but a shouted, boot-camp command. And I am on my worst behavior at home because that's where I can "unwind" after spending eight (or ten, or fourteen) hours at the office keeping my cool.

12   Arlie Russell Hochschild has other ideas about this apparently widespread condition. In her 1997 book *Time Bind: When Work Becomes Home and Home Becomes Work,* she writes, "In this new model of family and work life, a tired parent flees a world of unresolved quarrels and unwashed laundry for the reliable orderliness,

harmony, and managed cheer of work." At the office, I do manage, in all senses of the word. I am paid to be bossy—a trait that, for better and worse, has always been a predominant part of my personality. But at home, that bossiness yields unpleasant dividends, both from two boys who are now officially Grade A backtalkers and from a husband who frequently lets me know he's not someone I need to supervise. Still, the impulse isn't likely to go away, as long as I remain the only one in our household who knows where the library books/soccer cleats/car keys have gone—and what to do with them. At home I am wife, mother, baby-sitting and housekeeping manager, cook, social secretary, gardener, tutor, chauffeur, interior decorator, general contractor, and laundress. That many roles is exhausting, especially at those times when my mind is still in work mode. The other night I said to Hugo, "Do you want to put on your PJs in Owen's office?" It's a messy juggling act, and when a ball drops, I'm never laughing.

13   Last Friday I picked up the cheery note that Owen's kindergarten teacher, Ms. Stenstrom, sends at the end of every week. "We had an exciting morning!" it began. "We finished our touch unit by guessing what was in all the bags—thanks for sending in SUCH mysterious objects!" I had forgotten that Owen was supposed to have taken something interesting to touch in a brown paper bag to school that day. Standing alone in the kitchen, I started to cry. I read the note again, feeling miserable for Owen, miserable for me, miserable for lovely, infinitely patient Ms. Stenstrom. Then I climbed the stairs, cornered Dean, and cried some more. Is that appropriate? To cry for an hour and then have a long, tedious, completely unproductive discussion with an equally sleep deprived husband about All The Things We're Doing Wrong? How did I turn into this?

predominant Use the context to determine the meaning here.

◆What problems have arisen at home because of the author's "bossiness"?

◆Why did the author start crying when she read Ms. Stenstrom's "cheery note?"

● Comprehension Questions

Write the letter of the answer on the line. Then explain your thinking.

Main Idea

_____ 1. What is the main idea of the section entitled "It's a Typical Night"?

    a. Owen is more interested in a chocolate milkshake than in helping his mom clean up the broken glass.

    b. As a harried housewife, the author struggles to keep up with two energetic boys and a cat.

    c. A working mom discusses strategies for balancing home and the office.

    d. A professional mom gives a representative description of her hectic weekday evenings.

WHY? What information in the selection leads you to give that answer? _____

_____

_____

_____ 2. Which sentence best summarizes the main idea of paragraphs 9 and 10?

    a. That last one is my favorite.

    b. It's also the saddest, because it captures such a painful truth: too often I'm a better mother at work than I am at home.

    c. Of course, at work, no one shouts at me for five minutes straight in what parents universally refer to as an "outside voice."

    d. No one charges into my office, hands outstretched, to smear peanut butter all over my skirt or Vaseline all over my favorite needlepoint rug.

WHY? What information in the selection leads you to give that answer? _____

_____

_____

Supporting Details

_____ 3. Which of the following helps the author feel organized at work?

    a. bossiness

    b. arranging papers into piles

    c. coming in to the office early

    d. being an executive editor

WHY? What information in the selection leads you to give that answer? _____

_____

_____ 4. Which of the following is not true about the author's children?

   a. Owen is six.

   b. Hugo is a back-talker.

   c. George is three.

   d. Owen is in kindergarten.

WHY? What information in the selection leads you to give that answer? _____

_____

Author's Purpose

_____ 5. What is the purpose of "such" being in all caps in this sentence in paragraph 13?
   "We finished our touch unit by guessing what was in all the bags—thanks for
   sending in SUCH mysterious objects!"?

   a. The mother had sent in some very mysterious objects.

   b. The teacher was indicating her enthusiasm.

   c. The teacher was yelling at the mother because she had her priorities wrong.

   d. The objects the mother sent in were not mysterious.

WHY? What information in the selection leads you to give that answer? _____

_____

_____ 6. What is the tone of this sentence:
   *I run to the cafeteria to get something to eat, then call boss and nanny and
   answer most of the e-mails before my 9:30 meeting?*

   a. factual

   b. disorganized

   c. objective

   d. hurried

WHY? What leads you to give that answer? _____

_____

Relationships

_____ 7. Identify all the patterns of organization found in the following sentence:
I am on my best behavior at work, just as Owen is on his best behavior at school, but at home we have to ask him seven times to put on his shoes and by the seventh time it's no longer a request but a shouted, boot-camp command.

   a. time order, listing, description

   b. listing, cause-and-effect

   c. comparison, contrast, and time order

   d. cause-and-effect, classification, and comparison and contrast

WHY? What leads you to give that answer? _____

_____

_____

_____ 8. What is the pattern of organization of the section entitled "It's a Typical Night"?

   a. chronological

   b. comparison and contrast

   c. cause-and-effect

   d. listing

WHY? What information in the selection leads you to give that answer? _____

_____

Fact, Opinion, and Inference

_____ 9. Which of the following statements combines fact and opinion?

   a. I have promised that we will make milkshakes.

   b. George the cat meows and rubs against my legs, begging to be fed.

   c. I make up answers that sound informed-clever-peppy enough for morning TV with two minutes to spare.

   d. I have lunch at my desk and a second cup of coffee while I edit the piece, until two editors visit to complain about coworkers.

WHY? What leads you to give that answer? _____

_____

_____ 10. Which of the following can be inferred from the final paragraph?

    a. Ms. Stenstrom does not like Owen's mom.

    b. Though frustrated at times, the author is satisfied with her professional position.

    c. The author is annoyed about her husband's lack of participation in their kids' lives.

    d. The author expects that she can keep track of every single detail at home and work.

WHY? What information in the selection leads you to give that answer? _____

_____

● Critical Thinking Questions

CRITICAL THINKING LEVEL 1 REMEMBER

State the effect "bossiness" has had on the author's work life versus her home life. __

_____

_____

_____

CRITICAL THINKING LEVEL 2 UNDERSTAND

Summarize this reading using a MAPP.

    Mark: Make sure you review your annotations to help you fill out the following:

    About: _____

      Point: _____

        _____

        Proof:

            1. At work:

              _____

              _____

              _____

              _____

              _____

2. At home:

_____

_____

_____

_____

_____

CRITICAL THINKING LEVEL 3 APPLY

A. Find the following figures of speech in the reading and write them here. Note which paragraph they are in.

Hyperbole: _____

Simile: _____

Metaphor: _____

B. Is the following sentence meant figuratively or literally?

"At home we have to ask him seven times to put on his shoes . . ." (paragraph 11)

_____

Give support for your answer. _____

_____

CRITICAL THINKING LEVEL 4 ANALYZE

Analyze the tone of the reading by filling in the following information.

Point of view: _____

Objective or subjective: _____

Positive, neutral, or negative tone: _____

List a few words that have connotations that suggest why you gave that answer. _____

_____

What specific tone word from the list on page 487 describes this author's tone?

_____

CRITICAL THINKING LEVEL 5 EVALUATE

Is this author's need to balance work and home life typical or atypical of contemporary U.S. life? Support your answer with a few pieces of evidence.

Typical   or   atypical?

- _____

- _____

- _____

CRITICAL THINKING LEVEL 6 CREATE

How often does your life seem out of balance? Do you have trouble balancing work, school, and home? Create a schedule that helps you find balance in your schedule. Share your thoughts with a classmate.

_____

_____

_____

● Vocabulary in Context

The following words were used in "Attila the Honey I'm Home." Select the best word to complete the meaning of each sentence.

insistent	shards	flustered	finessing	predominant

1. The teacher was _____ that the students complete their homework on time.

2. After the inexperienced pianist made a mistake in front of the audience, he became _____, and his performance went downhill from there.

3. The _____ opinion in the courtroom was that the judge's ruling had been unfair.

4. The woman was more concerned that she had broken her great-grandmother's heirloom vase than she was with the _____ of glass that littered the floor.

5. Getting children to eat food they do not like may take a good deal of _____.

© Photo Create/Shutterstock

chapter 11

Evaluating the Author's Reasoning and Evidence

> ❝ *I can win an argument against any opponent. People know this, and steer clear of me at parties. Often, as a sign of their great respect, they don't even invite me.* ❞
>
> —Dave Barry

What can you infer from the quotation about Dave Barry's definition of an argument?

Share Your Prior Knowledge

What are some other popular ways to think about argument?

Survey the Chapter

Look ahead at some of the topics in this chapter. What is needed to effectively understand and evaluate an author's reasoning and evidence?

www.cengage.com/devenglish/doleconnect

Videos Related to Readings

Vocab Words on Audio

Prep Readings on Demand

Prep Reading . . . . Newspaper Article

The following reading is from the *New York Times*. It discusses the topic of immigration. As you read this article, think about your views of immigration, and be prepared to discuss them in light of this article after you have read it.

Visit www.cengage.com/devenglish/doleconnect and select Chapter 11 to hear a reading of this selection and view a video about this topic.

Immigrants Work on as Bill Dies

Randal C. Archibold

shantytown Skim paragraph 5 to see what houses are made out of in a shantytown. What is a shantytown?

1 San Diego, June 29—Ediberto Perez pedaled his bicycle out of a canyon **shantytown** in this border city's northern outskirts where he and other migrant workers **scratch out a living**. "So I won't get papers?" he asked at dawn on Friday, more curious than deflated about the defeat in the Senate of an overhaul to immigration law. "Well, I am just going to keep working. What more can I do?"

scratch out a living Think about who is *scratching out a living* as well as the meanings of the words in the phrase. What does it mean?

2 John Ladd, a rancher in southern Arizona, emerged at daybreak, too, to inspect a fence that illegal crossers routinely damage. Once, he called in a civilian patrol group to help deter illegal traffic but now he contemplated the **inevitable**. "Until they dry up the jobs, they're never going to secure the border," Mr. Ladd said.

inevitable Use the context of the paragraph to decide what this word means.

3 The day after the Senate failed to move on a proposal for the broadest change in immigration law in two decades, it was a time to take stock of a debate that played out something like a neutron bomb: blasts of rhetoric, of speeches, marches and convulsing in Congress and on talk radio and television that has left everything pretty much standing as is.

4 And Mr. Perez pedaled off to work, as the daily churn of immigration across the nation carried on. Farm work. Landscaping. Construction. Day jobs. It is all here in northern San Diego, where the stirrings of immigration largely reflect the national debate. With the first light of day, they trickle out of canyons and hills here, mostly men from the Mexican state of Oaxaca, their chattering in Spanish and Mixteco, an Indian language, filling the air. "I was in an apartment downtown when the agents came and took us all to Tijuana," said Margarito Brito, describing his **apprehension** in March by Immigration and Customs Enforcement. "But I came back in April. There is always work here. I have been coming for 20 years."

apprehension The previous sentence describes this word's meaning.

5   A crush of migrant workers and day laborers crowd street corners and parking lots and, with a dearth of affordable apartments and farm-worker housing in the area, they drag tarps, crates and spare wood into the hills and canyons for makeshift housing. At night they can see the glitter of million-dollar homes that brush against tomato fields and hills and ravines less than a mile away, at a closeness that has made some residents of those homes uncomfortable.

dearth Base your guess about the meaning of *dearth* on the meaning of the sentence.

6   The migrant camps have been vandalized. Anti-immigration groups have protested the migrant workers' presence. But men like Mr. Brito keep coming, filling a demand for cheap, convenient labor. He said he never thought legalization would happen for him or his companions, but it is just as well. "I have my wife and four children in Mexico," Mr. Brito said, sitting on a roadside crate, waiting for work. "It would be good to be legal, but I am not, and I am still working."

🔘 Interaction 11-1. Talking about Reading

Respond in writing to the questions below and then discuss your answers with your classmates.

1. What do you think it would be like living in a shantytown? Have you ever known anyone who has? _____

_____

2. Explain what you think John Ladd's view of illegal immigration is. _____

_____

3. Is there an immigration problem? If so, what is it? Do you have any ideas about how to solve it? _____

_____

4. What is your view on illegal immigration? Support your claim with at least three details. _____

_____

The Author's Reasoning

Throughout this book we have been discussing how important it is while reading to analyze and evaluate the author's words and ideas. That need is especially critical when an author is trying to persuade readers to believe something different from what they already believe, or to act in a way they've never before acted—in other words, when the author is making an argument. When an author sets out to influence you in a particular direction, you should carefully evaluate the claim, the reasoning, and the evidence being used.

Some New Terms and Their Connection to MAPPS

You should be familiar by now with the terms **about, point**, and **proof**, what they stand for, and how to find them.

About = topic

Point = main idea

Proof = supporting detail

In argument, the terminology changes, but the concepts are essentially the same.

An argument is "about" an **issue**, that is, a topic that people disagree about.

The "point" in an argument is called the **claim**.

The "proof" is **reasons supported by facts and other forms of evidence.**

When you read an argument, it's a good idea to *mark* the claim, reasons, and evidence because it's the relationships between these things that you'll need to think about. The skill of **summary** will come in handy when you need to respond in conversation or in writing to the argument of an author you have read. Often you will need to share the author's line of argument in order to tell readers or listeners how your opinion is the same and how it is different.

Interaction 11-2. Identifying Issues and Claims

Just as you did in previous chapters for the topic and the main idea, in each sentence bracket the issue and underline the author's claim. Then write a different claim that could be made about each issue. (You don't have to believe the claims.)

1. The drinking age should not be lowered to eighteen.

Different claim about same issue: _____

_____

2. The rights of an unborn child are more important than the rights of the mother.

    Different claim about same issue: _____

    _____

3. Gay marriage should be legalized so that gay people will have a legal means to express their lifelong commitment to each other.

    Different claim about same issue: _____

    _____

4. Children are negatively affected when they see violence on television.

    Different claim about same issue: _____

    _____

5. No scientist should be permitted to experiment on animals.

    Different claim about same issue: _____

    _____

Interaction 11-3. Finding the Claim

As a quick review of how general the topic sentence or thesis statement is compared to the specifics of the evidence, put a C next to the sentence that is the claim for each group and E for the sentences that provide evidence (reasons or facts).

1. ___ The cost of living in the Dallas area is among the most affordable in the United States.

    ___ Dallas has a solid economy.

    ___ The housing market in Dallas is the strongest in the nation.

    ___ The unemployment rate is the lowest in the country.

2. ___ The behavior of the audience at last night's lecture was disrespectful.

    ___ Before the talk even began, there was an atmosphere in the room of people waiting in ambush.

___ Until a student stood up to insist that audience members be quiet, people were booing and laughing at inappropriate moments during the talk.

___ Instead of waiting for the question-and-answer session that was to take place after the lecture, some people shouted out challenges to the lecturer's points as he spoke, causing him to lose track of his ideas.

3. ___ Alcohol causes problems with the cerebellum, which controls coordination, balance, and reflexes.

___ Drinking too much can even limit brain signals to your body for essentials like breathing.

___ People should not drink to excess because alcohol affects your brain.

___ Alcohol slows down brain activity.

4. ___ The United States is the most technologically and economically advanced nation in the world.

___ Almost every home has indoor plumbing and at least one television.

___ Most Americans sleep in a warm bed and wake up to enough to eat.

___ The infrastructure is well constructed and regularly maintained.

> —Adapted from Segal/Gerdes/Steiner, *An Introduction to the Profession of Social Work*, 2nd Edition

5. ___ After Katrina, one insurance company found that the five hundred damaged locations that had implemented all the hurricane-loss prevention methods experienced only one-eighth the losses of those that had not done so.

___ Often, simple structural measures, like bracing and securing roof trusses and walls using straps, clips, or adhesives, can yield big benefits.

___ For example, Hurricane Katrina did so much damage in New Orleans because of bad planning, poorly maintained levees, and environmental degradation of the city's protective wetlands.

___ Policies that address social change will help prevent many more deaths than policies that restrict carbon emissions.

> —Adapted from Lomborg, *Cool It*

The Relevance of the Evidence to the Claim

Relevance refers to how directly related the evidence is to the claim. Imagine that you are watching the Olympics. An athlete who won a silver medal is contesting the gold medal decision, saying that the winner does not deserve the gold. Here are the three reasons given. Which one is the most relevant to the silver medalist's claim?

1. It's not fair.

2. I trained more hours than the other athlete did.

3. The other athlete used performance-enhancing drugs.

As you can see, numbers 1 and 2 are emotional appeals with no relevancy. However, if number 3 proved to be true, then it would be relevant. The gold medalist would be disqualified, giving the silver medalist a chance to trade up for the gold.

● Interaction 11-4. Thinking about Relevance

1. What are some relevant skills and attitudes for being a successful student?

_____

_____

2. What are some relevant skills and attitudes for being a good parent?

_____

_____

3. Which skills that you have listed are relevant both to being a successful student and a good parent? _____

_____

Relevance in Reading

Figuring out how relevant each piece of evidence is to the author's claim when reading is similar. The evidence can't just relate to the general issue, it must be about the claim itself. Suppose you read the following claim:

> Being a successful student takes a lot of hard work.

For evidence to be relevant, it can't simply be about "being a successful student"—that is the issue. Instead, the evidence must relate to the idea that being a successful student "takes a lot of hard work." Even within this claim, there are actually two claims—"a lot" and "hard." Some relevant evidence might be the following:

To support the claim "Being a successful student takes a lot of work":

–Most students spend three hours outside of class for every hour in class.

–When I asked the students in my management class how long they had spent on a recent, typical assignment, more than half of them said fifteen to thirty hours.

–Most of the classes in my major require between 75 and 150 pages of reading per week.

To support the claim "Being a successful students takes hard work":

–Professor Dubert said that students who get A's in her class usually revise their research papers three times, while students who get C's revise them only once.

–The Learning Center tutor told me that most of the Psychology 301 students he has tutored had to study a single textbook chapter alone, in a study group, and with the help of a tutor before they thought they truly understood it.

–Many students now download podcasts of instructors' lectures so they can listen to them a second time to make sure they fully grasp the important points.

The following statements would be irrelevant:

–At my school, you get free passes to the local ski resort if you are a straight-A student. (This sentence has to do with one effect of being a successful student, not the causes.)

–Successful students know how to suck up to their instructors. (This sentence suggests that being a successful student is more a matter of pandering to teachers than working hard.)

Even though these statements are about the issue, they are not about the claim; and thus, they are irrelevant to the claim.

⊙ Interaction 11-5. Choosing between Relevant and Irrelevant Evidence

Put a *C* next to the claim and an *R* next to the relevant evidence. Leave the blank empty if the evidence is not relevant.

1. ___   Make sure you identify the person first and then the disability.

   ___   When writing about a person with a disability, you should use language that accurately reflects the person's life circumstances and does not label the person in pejorative ways.

   ___   If a person has visual impairment, use *partial vision* or *sight* rather than *blind*, which refers to total blindness.

   ___   If you find an error in your report, please mark through it with black ink.

   —Adapted from Summers, *Fundamentals of Case Management* Practice, 2ⁿᵈ Edition

2. ___ One myth is "No pain, no gain."

   ___ Another is that a gym is the only good place to work out.

   ___ When working out, be careful to listen to what your body is telling you.

   ___ When working out, it is smart to avoid some common myths about exercise.
   —Adapted from Hales, *An Invitation To Health*, 12th Edition

3. ___ Most orientations take about an hour, and they can give you the confidence you need to complete your research assignments.

   ___ If you are new to library research or are unfamiliar with the library, you should schedule a tour.

   ___ A library orientation may sound silly or boring, but it can save you hours of wandering around a facility you do not understand.

   ___ Librarians can be an excellent resource.
   —Adapted from Griffin, *Invitation to Public Speaking*, 2nd Edition

4. ___ Interviewers should use structured interviews to be sure they ask standard questions of all applicants.

   ___ Some are situational questions, which ask how an applicant might respond to a hypothetical situation.

   ___ Applicants should be prepared for the interview process both mentally and emotionally.

   ___ Others might include behavioral questions, which ask the applicant what they did in previous positions.
   —Adapted from Williams, *MGMT 2008 Edition*

5. ___ Studies show that, generally, women commit less crime than men.

   ___ One important area of crime research is the relationship between class, crime, and race.

   ___ Arrest statistics show that the poor are more likely to be arrested for crimes.

   ___ Sociologists have demonstrated a strong correlation between unemployment, poverty, and crime.
   —Adapted from Andersen/Taylor, *Sociology*, 4th Edition

⚫ Interaction 11-6. Identifying Irrelevant Evidence in a Paragraph

Underline the claim in the paragraph. Then evaluate each piece of evidence for relevance. Cross out any irrelevant evidence.

1. Danica Patrick is the most popular IndyCar Series racer today. Her teammates, some of whom have won more races than Patrick, like the attention she gets. Teammate Marco Andretti says, "She's a rock star." Fans line up to buy Patrick souvenirs like sweatshirts and baseball caps with Danica's name on them. Her competitors are glad that she draws people to the sport of open-wheel racing. Patrick says, "I'm pretty girly outside the car." She wants to race for another ten years.

> —Excerpted and adapted from Caldwell, "The Brickyard Is Patrick's Backyard," *New York Times*, May 25, 2008.

2. College students should give permission for their parents to be contacted if they are experiencing difficulties. Except in certain emergencies, colleges may not contact students' parents regarding medical, psychological, or academic problems without the student's permission. Because of his violent writings, the shooter at Virginia Tech, for instance, had worried both fellow students and English faculty members, who shared their concerns with the administration. But the administration could not legally contact his parents to gain insight into Cho Seung Hui's problems. Colleges may not send report cards, even for students receiving A's and B's, to parents; they must send them to the students themselves. Students who binge drink, who are depressed, and who are having trouble socially can't get help from their families if their parents don't know they are having trouble.

3. Amy Sutherland wrote an article called "What Shamu Taught Me about a Happy Marriage." In the article she describes how she used the techniques she learned from animal trainers to get her husband to change his habits. The technique called "approximations" was especially helpful. The trainer rewards an animal for each small step it takes toward doing the behavior the trainer wants. When her husband mimics a northern Vermont accent, Sunderland can't help but laugh. Sunderland would thank her husband for throwing a shirt in the hamper, and kiss him for putting in two. Sunderland used smaller approximations whenever she couldn't get Scott to take bigger steps. After two years, she felt she had been successful. Her marriage was smoother and her floor was cleaner.

The Types of Evidence

Authors may draw on several different kinds of evidence as support. Some kinds of evidence usually seem more credible or authoritative than others, but you should ask questions about every kind as you read.

Expert Authority

As we discussed in Chapter 9 (page 445–446), people who are experts in their field have great authority when speaking about that field. When you are evaluating the evidence of an expert authority, ask yourself the following questions:

- What credentials—schooling, books they wrote, employment position—does this person have?
- What biases might the expert have?

Here is an example from a *Newsweek* article in which a scientist is complaining that the war in Iraq is eating up the funds that might have been given to scientists for research into the disease of autism:

> The Iraq war has siphoned off much federal money. "It's like a forest fire running through science and it burns a lot of trees down," says Dan Geschwind, a UCLA neurogeneticist.
>
> —Kantrowitz/Scelfo, "What Happens When They
> Grow Up," *Newsweek*, November 27, 2006

Dan Geschwind is a scientist, and he is commenting on science, so in that sense, his expert opinion should be given authority. But if you stop to think about what a scientist would care more about—funding for science or funding for war—you can see that his position naturally creates a bias. That doesn't mean that you should discount his opinion, but you should understand the larger context.

Facts

Facts carry great weight, just as expert authorities do. That is true by definition, since a fact is a verifiable, objective piece of information. When evaluating facts, ask yourself these questions:

- First of all, is this really true? Is it a fact?
- What use is the author making of the fact?
- Does the fact apply under these conditions?
- What facts are not being stated?

To get a sense of the complicated questions that even facts can raise, consider the following paragraph from the book *How to Watch the TV News*, by Neil Postman and Steve Powers:

> Every news story is a reflection of the reporter who tells the story. The reporter's previous assumptions about what is "out there" edit what he or she thinks is there. For example, many journalists believe that what is called "the intifada" is newsworthy. Let us suppose that a fourteen-year-old Palestinian boy hurls a Molotov cocktail at two eighteen-year-old Israeli soldiers. The explosion knocks one of the soldiers down and damages his left eye. The other soldier, terrified, fires a shot at the Palestinian that kills

him instantly. The injured soldier eventually loses the sight of his eye. What details should be included in reporting this event? Is the age of the Palestinian relevant? Are the ages of the Israeli soldiers relevant? Was the act of the Palestinian provoked by the mere presence of Israeli soldiers? Was the act therefore justified? Is the shooting justified? Is the state of mind of the shooter relevant?

Remember that facts are selected by a person who has a particular point of view.

Statistics

Statistics are numerical data. People tend to believe statistics, but they can be used to misrepresent facts just like words can. Remember, too, that statistics are often represented in graphics (see Chapter 8). Ask yourself:

- How accurate are these numbers?
- How were they gathered, and who analyzed them?
- What use is the author making of them?

The following passage from an article in the *New York Times* offers statistics from experts, a strong combination of evidence.

> Little more than one-third of the 16- to 19-year-olds in the United States are likely to be employed this summer, the smallest share since the government began tracking teenage work in 1948, according to a research paper published by the Center for Labor Market Studies at Northeastern University in Boston. That is a sharp drop from the 45 percent level of teenage employment reached in 2000.
>
> —Goodman, "Toughest Summer Job This Year Is
> Finding One," *New York Times*, May 25, 2008

So far, so good. But if an author tried to use these same statistics to support her argument that no high school students should even bother looking for a job, you should question her motivation and even her logic.

Examples

Examples are used to explain ideas. (See Chapter 5, pages 230–232, for more on examples.) Examples can be persuasive, but they do not have the same level of credibility as expert authority, facts, and statistics, especially if they alone are used to support an idea. Ask yourself:

- Are the examples true? Are they relevant?
- Are the examples representative of most of the instances of an event of this kind?
- What other forms of evidence might the author use—if there is any other evidence?

Read the following paragraph. Examine the claim and the examples used as evidence.

Too many people these days are using the Internet as a way to meet potential partners. My friend Alex met a woman on a chat site last year, and before they even met they had decided to get married! Another friend, Josie, posted her profile on several singles sites over the weekend. She has already received twenty responses from men who would like to get to know her better. My sister Cara flirts in writing with someone she met through a blog. Why aren't people interested in meeting in person anymore?

The examples of three friends can't by themselves prove many claims. However, this particular claim would be difficult to prove at all. Who gets to define how many is "too many"? When you read a paragraph like this, realize that you are reading someone's opinion. In this case, this writer has overgeneralized from too few examples.

Personal Experiences

When an author gives personal experiences as evidence for an argument, think carefully about the same issues you would consider reading any example. Realize that like everyone else's, the author's experiences are colored by his or her own history, culture, beliefs, and so on. Ask yourself:

- Would another person in this situation have a similar experience? In other words, is the experience representative?
- How relevant to others is the author's experience?
- Does the author present any other kinds of evidence along with personal experience?

Consider the opening of an article from *Philadelphia* magazine:

Dear Sirs:

I'm writing to complain about Penn President Amy Gutmann's recent Halloween photos, in which she posed with a young woman dressed as a sexy cat. Every year, cat sex results in millions of unwanted kittens. Why does Miss Gutmann want cats to starve? Should an Ivy League school have a cat starver as president? Won't somebody please THINK OF THE KITTENS!

That's the first draft of a letter I plan to send to the administration of the University of Pennsylvania, because apparently it is now in vogue to complain about absolutely anything.

—Levison, "Worst Amendment," *Philadelphia*, February 2007

The author goes on to give numerous examples of his claim, and this use of a letter is meant to point out the ridiculous nature of some complaints. But if he had stopped here, it would be smart for readers to wonder why he would base a claim on such a far-fetched personal experience.

◖ Interaction 11-7. Identifying the Evidence

For each group of sentences a topic sentence is given. Bracket the issue and underline the claim in each one. Then identify the type of evidence in the other sentences, selecting from the list below. You can use an item more than once. Finally, evaluate each piece of evidence to decide which one is irrelevant to the claim, and cross it out.

opinion	expert authority	facts
examples	statistics	experience (author's personal experience)

1. Topic sentence   Buying a home is a good investment.

   _____   Homes average a 3 to 6% increase in value yearly.

   _____   You receive hefty tax benefits each year for owning a home.

   _____   Owning a home makes one feel like a productive member of society.

2. Topic sentence   Guns should have safety locks on them.

   _____   Children are naturally curious, and if a gun is in the house, then they are going to pick it up and play with it and probably end up killing themselves or a friend by accident.

   _____   The U.S. Centers for Disease Control and Prevention released a report showing that 2,827 children and teens died as a result of gun violence in 2003. This number from one year is higher than the number of American fighting men and women killed in Iraq from 2003 to April 2006.

   _____   National research shows that 40 percent of families with children also have a gun, and one out of four keep their guns loaded.

3. Topic sentence   The death penalty is expensive and all too often used on the wrong people. It should be abolished.

   _____   Carrying out the death penalty costs two to five times more than keeping a person in prison for a life term.

_____ DNA testing has shown that a dozen innocent men and women have been put to death.

_____ Since the death penalty was reinstated in the United States in 1976, more than 1,000 people have been executed.

4.   Topic sentence   You should exercise your muscles to keep them healthy.

_____ Dr. Robert H. Fitts, an exercise physiologist at Marquette University, says that both endurance and strength are important to develop.

_____ William J. Kraemer, a professor of kinesiology at the University of Connecticut, says that many people increase their endurance by walking, but few develop their strength by lifting weights, and when they do lift weights, they often do so incorrectly.

_____ Your muscles will atrophy if you don't use them.

_____ When I started lifting weights again after a five year hiatus, I felt great.

5.   claim   Older people who want to stay in their homes should consider having remote monitors installed so that their children in other cities can track their well-being.

_____ Each morning, Lynn Pitet checks her computer when she wakes up to see if her mother is following her normal routine.

_____ Motion sensors can tell a remotely located relative whether a parent has gotten out of bed, taken medications, and is moving around the house.

_____ Only wealthier people will be able to take advantage of such a system.

_____ Because such sensors are relatively new, insurance may or may not cover the cost of installing them.

◉ Interaction 11-8. Determining Claim, Evidence, Relevance, and Strength

In each passage, underline the claim (which may be in one sentence or two sentences). Number the pieces of supporting evidence. Discuss the relevance and strength of the evidence in supporting the claim.

1. Extending Medicare

Extending Medicare to cover all Americans would strengthen America's economy in three ways. It would reduce administrative expenses, replace costly emergency room visits for those now lacking insurance with more cost-effective preventive care, and improve the global competitiveness of American manufacturers, who now bear much higher health care costs than do their foreign rivals.

— Professor Gregory M. Saltzman, Ann Arbor, Mich., Sept. 7, 2007,
letter to the editor in the *New York Times*

A. Is the evidence relevant? Why or why not? _____

B. Is the evidence strong? Why or why not? _____

_____

_____

2. A Virus among Honeybees

Last week, scientists reported having found a possible—emphasis on *possible*—cause of the collapse of honeybee populations reported in the past year. What is interesting isn't just the virus, called *Israeli acute paralysis virus*, but the use of new methods of genetic screening to determine what pathogens the bees in collapsed colonies had been exposed to. Researchers were able to quickly screen the DNA from all the organisms present in the bees and compare them with the DNA in genomic libraries, a catalog of known organisms. Bees from collapsed hives had the virus. Healthy bees did not.

Two other factors may also have played a role in this die-off. One is drought, which in some areas has affected the plants that bees draw nectar and pollen from. The other—still unproved—may be the commercial trucking of bees from crop to crop for pollination, a potential source of stress. These may have made bees more vulnerable to the effects of this virus.

In some ways, this newly reported research seems all the more important given all the speculation about what has been killing off the honeybees. These hive losses have inspired a kind of myth-making or magical thinking about their possible environmental origins. The suspected culprits include genetically modified crops and cell phones, to name only two.

—Editorial in the *New York Times*, Sept. 11, 2007

A. Is the evidence relevant? Why or why not? _____

_____

B. Is the evidence strong? Why or why not? _____

_____

_____

_____

_____

3. **Off the Charts: Double Warning That a Recession May Be on the Way**

The employment statistics and the bond market are combining to send out a warning that has been heard only rarely in the past two decades: A recession is coming in the United States.

The two charts show the double warning. Both charts warned of an economic downturn before the 1990 and 2001 recessions, and they are doing so again.

While each has arguably registered false warnings, they have never done so together.

The first chart shows the difference between the yield on two-year Treasuries and the Federal Reserve's target rate for federal funds—the rate on loans between banks. In normal times, the Treasury rate is usually higher.

In bond market jargon, the opposite condition is an inverted yield curve. And when it is very inverted, the recession warning is sent.

At the widest spread this week, on Monday, the yield on two-year Treasuries was down to 3.854 percent, while the fed funds target rate was 5.25 percent. That difference, of 1.396 percentage points, is the largest since early January 2001.

It was also in January 2001 that the Fed surprised the market with a 50-basis-point—or half a percentage point—reduction in the target rate for fed funds. That move briefly cheered the stock market, but did not prevent the recession that began in March.

The second chart shows the six-month changes in the number of people with jobs, as reported by the Labor Department's household survey. In a growing economy, with the labor age population rising, the number of jobs almost always increases.

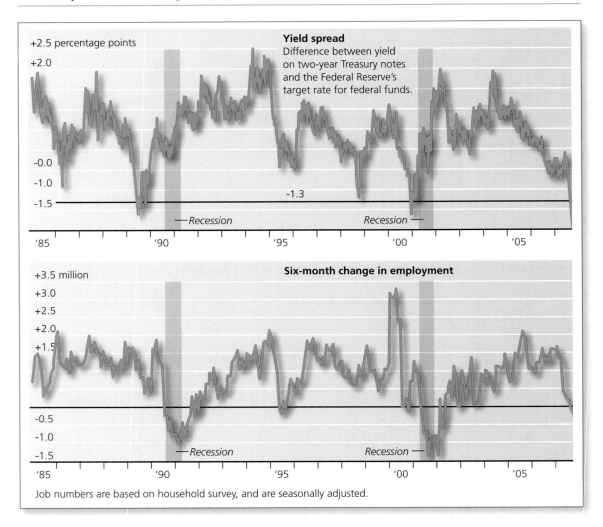

+2.5 percentage points

+2.0

Yield spread
Difference between yield
on two-year Treasury notes
and the Federal Reserve's
target rate for federal funds.

-0.0

-1.0

-1.5 ————————————————— -1.3

— Recession   Recession —

'85   '90   '95   '00   '05

+3.5 million   **Six-month change in employment**

+3.0

+2.5

+2.0

+1.5

-0.5

-1.0

-1.5

— Recession   Recession —

'85   '90   '95   '00   '05

Job numbers are based on household survey, and are seasonally adjusted.

But not now. The August employment figures, reported last week, showed 145,794,000 people with jobs, or 125,000 fewer than in February. When that number goes into negative territory, it is a warning of a slowdown.

As can be seen from the chart, the job warning was sent out in July 1990, the month in which the recession began. A warning of the 2001 recession arrived in July 2000, but few took it seriously.

To be sure, there have been just two recessions in two decades, which is not enough to validate any set of forecast tools. But if one arrives, there will be criticism that the Federal Reserve was too slow to cut interest rates as it ignored the threat of an inverted yield curve, and that it focused on inflation for too long.

"With the core inflation rate comfortably close to 2 percent, and the Treasury market begging for ease for over a year, if it turns out to be a recession, it will also be a policy error," said Robert Barbera, chief economist of ITG.

As the charts show, sometimes one indicator or the other has seemed weak when no recession followed. The job number looked bad in 1995, but there was no confirmation from the interest rate indicator.

Similarly, in 1998 the interest rate indicator came close to sounding a warning amid the fears brought on by the rescue of a large hedge fund, Long-Term Capital Management.

But the difference between the rates never quite reached 1.3 percentage points, and in any case the employment figures remained strong.

Now both look weak. That is no guarantee of a recession, but it may help to explain why the Fed is expected to change course and reduce the federal funds rate next week.

–Floyd Norris, *New York Times*, Sept.15, 2007

A. Is the evidence relevant? Why or why not? _____

_____

B. Is the evidence strong? Why or why not? _____

_____

_____

_____

_____

An Author's Assumptions

We all make assumptions, and authors are no exception. A dictionary typically defines an assumption as something that is believed to be true but has not been proven. This definition usually works for everyday life. You see someone behind the wheel of a car, and you assume it is his or her car. You don't ask to see the name on the title! A wedding ring or lack of one leads to certain assumptions. Styles of clothing, hair color and length, weight, age, and countless other things lead to assumptions in everyday life.

This definition needs to be added to for reading purposes. When an author assumes something, it usually means that he or she accepts certain things as fact and so does not feel the need to support or defend them. An author's religious, cultural, ethnic, and economic background affects his or her assumptions, just as elements of your background affect yours.

Authors may assume that readers share their assumptions. For example, an article entitled "How to Turn the Tides of Global Warming" assumes that global warming exists. Every aspect of an article, book, or other reading material—from its title, to its details, to things left unsaid—can provide clues to an author's assumptions.

Let's look at a puzzle to illustrate a possible assumption on your part:

> A father and son are in a terrible accident. The father dies and the son, in critical condition, is rushed to the hospital for surgery. The surgeon walks in, takes one look at the boy and says, "I can't operate on this boy. He is my son." How is this possible?

It is important to look at what you are reading as objectively as possible. Imagine you are having a conversation with the author and you have to understand where they are coming from in order to understand what they are saying, whether it is clearly stated, implied, or assumed.

◉ Interaction 11-9. Identifying Assumptions

Identify the assumptions in each item.

1. How bizarre that a book on punctuation would be a bestseller in England and America!

   Assumption about punctuation: _____

2. Never go to a doctor whose office plants have died.
   —Erma Bombeck

   Assumption about doctors: _____

3. When a man comes to me for advice, I find out that kind of advice he wants, and I give it to him.

   –Josh Billings

   Assumption: _____

4. More than a dozen countries have liberalized their abortion laws in recent years, including South Africa, Switzerland, Cambodia and Chad. In a handful of others, including Russia and the United States (or parts of it), the movement has been toward criminalizing more and different types of abortions. In South Dakota, the governor recently signed the most restrictive abortion bill since the Supreme Court ruled in 1973, in *Roe v. Wade*, that state laws prohibiting abortion were unconstitutional. The South Dakota law, which its backers acknowledge is designed to test *Roe v. Wade* in the courts, forbids abortion, including those cases in which the pregnancy is a result of rape or incest. Only if an abortion is necessary to save the life of the mother is the procedure permitted. A similar though less restrictive bill is now making its way through the Mississippi Legislature.

   –Hitt, "Pro-Life Nation," *New York Times Magazine*, April 9, 2006

Assumption of the lawmakers in countries that have liberalized their abortion laws:

_____

Assumption of the governor of South Dakota:

_____

5. My biological parents put me up for adoption before I was even one year old. For the rest of my childhood (until I was 18 and legal), I was passed around from family to foster family. One time, when I was 10, I had stayed with one family for almost two years before they told me I had to go. I begged with them to let me stay, but I was still sent away. I do not know why they did not love me enough to keep me (I often ask myself why my biological parents did not love me enough to keep me as well). I think it was at this point that I determined never to be hurt again. I am so fearful of being abandoned again that I do not allow myself to get close to others because then that person will leave me. I am an adult now but still feel like a scared little kid.

List this writer's assumptions about himself. _____

_____

Chapter Summary Activity

This chapter has discussed how to evaluate an author's reasoning. Construct a Reading Guide below by completing each idea on the left with information from the chapter on the right. You can use this guide whenever you read arguments.

Reading Guide to Evaluating the Author's Reasoning

Complete this idea	with information from the chapter.
The terms used to label the parts of an argument have the same essential meanings as the APP in MAPPS. What an argument is about is called the	1.
The main idea that the author will attempt to convince readers of is called the	2.
The proof the author will use as support is called	3.
In an argument, the support consists of	4.

In an argument, the claim is more general than the	5. _____
To analyze the author's reasoning, the reader should consider the relevance of the evidence to the claim. "Relevance" refers to	6. _____
To be relevant, a piece of evidence has to relate to the	7. _____
Another aspect of an argument to analyze is the author's use of different kinds of	8. _____
Two types of evidence that are generally considered very authoritative are	9. _____ 10. _____
Two types of evidence that are not usually convincing when used by themselves are	11. _____ 12. _____
A fact that is given in numbers is called a	13. _____
The one type of evidence that you don't need to analyze and evaluate is	14. _____
Two items to consider when reading an expert's opinion or judgment are	15. _____ 16. _____
Suppose for a moment that you read a fact and you already know that it's true. What are two items to consider about the fact?	17. _____ 18. _____
Suppose you read a statistic. Two questions to ask in order to decide how much weight to give it as evidence are	19. _____ 20. _____
Three questions to ask about examples and personal experiences to decide how much weight to give them as evidence are	21. _____ 22. _____ 23. _____
In reading material, an assumption is	24. _____
The assumption behind asking students to complete these Chapter Summary Activities is that	25. _____

Test-Taking Tips
Evaluating the Author's Reasoning

When you are evaluating an author's reasoning on a reading test, you will want to take into account the suggestions given throughout the chapter. You should start by identifying the claim, and then decide whether the evidence that the author is offering is actually relevant to that claim. To decide how strong the argument is, you can then think about each type of evidence the author includes. As we've noted, expert authority, facts, and statistics are strong sources of support if well used, while personal experience and examples are less so. Finally, sometimes you can identify assumptions that the author doesn't feel the need to support, perhaps believing that everyone already agrees on them. And when values are held in common, the author may be right that assumptions don't need to be supported. For instance, who wouldn't agree with the assumption that "education is valuable"?

Tone can also be an important force in an argument. It can help you decide whether the author seems to be a reasonable, thoughtful person whose evidence you can probably trust. The particular words that author uses can help you identify the author's bias, or subjective stance toward the main idea. Remember that every person has a subjective stance, and there is nothing wrong with having a personal viewpoint. But what if you read a sentence like this one?

The sleazy transient hotels house some of the nation's most pathetic losers.

This author is clearly biased in a negative direction toward the place and the people being described using words such as *sleazy* and *pathetic losers*. Go on alert when you see such negatively connotative words. The author is probably so biased about that particular topic that you should be even more careful than usual in evaluating what he or she has to say.

Reading 11-1 . . . . **History Textbook**

⬤ Pre-Reading the Selection

The following selection, "New Immigration," comes from an American history textbook.

Guessing the Purpose

Judging from the source and title of the article, what do you suppose is the purpose of the selection? _____

Surveying the Reading

Based on the purpose you chose, as well as some words or phrases that stand out as you survey this reading, what do you think will be the tone of this passage? _____

Predicting the Content

Predict three things this selection will discuss.

- _____
- _____
- _____

Activating Your Knowledge

List several details you know about immigration. One detail could be the history of your family's immigration.

- _____
- _____
- _____

Common Knowledge

Fidel Castro (*paragraph 4*) The president of Cuba from 1959 to 2008.

GOP (*paragraph 9*) The Republican party, whose nickname "GOP" means "Grand Old Party."

investment capital (*paragraph 10*) "Capital" refers to money. This term means how much money one has to invest.

Golden Gate State (*paragraph 12*) California is named the "Golden Gate State" because of the Golden Gate Bridge, which was built in the 1930s.

© Stas Volik/Shutterstock

Reading with Pen in Hand

Now read the selection. As you read, mark any ideas that seem important, and respond to the questions and vocabulary items in the margin. Monitor your comprehension by putting a ✔ next to a paragraph when you understand most of it. Place an ✗ next to a paragraph when you don't understand most of it.

Visit **www.cengage.com/devenglish/doleconnect** and select Chapter 11 to hear vocabulary words from this selection and view a video about this topic.

New Immigration

John M. Murrin et al.

1   A dramatic increase in immigration from countries mostly to the south and west of the United States accounted for much of the U.S. population growth, particularly in the southern and western parts of the country. The vast **bulk** of post-1970 immigration came from Asia, Oceania, Latin America, and Africa rather than from Europe, the primary source of immigrants from the 1790s to 1924. In 2000, roughly 12 percent of the U.S. population had been born outside of the United States, compared to the all-time high of 15 percent in 1890.

2   The largest number of non-European immigrants came from Mexico. Responding to labor shortages in the United States and poor economic prospects at home, both legal and undocumented immigration from Mexico rose substantially during the last 30 years of the 20th century. Many immigrants from Mexico arrived as seasonal agricultural workers or temporary laborers, but most soon formed permanent communities. According to the 2000 census, 90 percent of all Mexican Americans lived in the Southwest, primarily Texas and California.

3   Most immigrants from Puerto Rico settled around New York City, but sizable Puerto Rican communities developed in Chicago and in cities in New England and Ohio as well. Economic problems on the mainland during the 1970s prompted some to return to the island, but the flow reversed again after about 1980. By 2000, the Puerto Rican population on the U.S. mainland totaled about 3 million, compared to slightly less than 4 million in Puerto Rico.

4   Cubans had begun immigrating in large numbers in response to Fidel Castro's revolution. After the U.S. Congress, in 1962, designated people fleeing from Castro's Cuba as "refugees" eligible for admittance, more than 800,000 Cubans from every stratum of society came to the United States during the next 20 years. They gradually moved northward into many major American cities, but the greatest impact came in south Florida. An agreement with Castro in 1995 brought the first U.S. restrictions on the flow of immigrants from Cuba. In 2000, however, about half of all the people residing in Miami were of Cuban descent.

◆ *Reading Journal*

◆Where did most of the post-1970 immigration population come from?

bulk Look at the examples that follow the word to guess what *bulk* means.

◆What are the reasons Mexicans came to the United States?

◆List the locations where Puerto Ricans settled.

◆Why did Cubans begin immigrating to the United States?

◆What is significant about the Spanish-speaking population in the United States?

◆What unintended effects did the Immigration Act of 1965 have?

abolished Notice how this small sentence is wedged in between two longer ones. How does it connect them? Notice the word *instead* that starts the next sentence, and ask yourself what *these* refers to.

◆What impact did the Vietnam War have on immigration?

overt The antonym (opposite) of *overt* is *covert*. What does *overt* mean?

◆How was the Refugee Act of 1980 interpreted by U.S. officials?

5   By the early 21st century, the number of Spanish-speaking people in the United States totaled more than in all but four countries of Latin America. Los Angeles became the second largest "Mexican city" in the world, trailing only Mexico City, and L.A.'s Salvadoran population just about equaled that of San Salvador. More Puerto Ricans lived in New York City than in San Juan, and the Big Apple's Dominican population rivaled that of Santo Domingo.

6   Changes in immigration patterns began with the landmark Immigration Act of 1965, which spurred not only population growth but diversity as well. Since the 1920s, the nature of immigration to the United States had been determined by quotas based on national origins. The 1965 act **abolished** these. Instead, it placed a ceiling of 20,000 immigrants for every country, gave preference to those with close family ties in the United States, and accorded priority to people with special skills and those classified as refugees. Although largely unforeseen at the time, this legislation laid the basis not only for a resumption of high-volume immigration but also for a substantial shift in the countries of origin.

7   International events also affected U.S. immigration policy. In the aftermath of the Vietnam War, for example, U.S. officials facilitated the admittance of many Vietnamese, Cambodians, Laotians, and Hmong (an ethnically distinct people who inhabited lands extending across the borders of these three Asian countries). The goal was to resettle people who had allied with the United Stales during the war and whose families were consequently in peril.

8   In response to the growing number of people seeking admission to the United States, Congress later passed the Refugee Act of 1980. It specified that political refugees, "those fleeing **overt** persecution," could be admitted more easily but that people seeking simply to improve their economic circumstances could not. In practice, U.S. officials interpreted the terms "political" and "economic" so that they generally admitted people leaving communist regimes but not those fleeing right-wing dictatorships. For example, Cubans and Soviet Jews invariably qualified under the Refugee Act, but Haitians often did not. (The number of undocumented Haitians entering the United States, however, rose rapidly.) Many Guatemalans and Salvadorans, hoping to escape repressive military governments backed by the United States during the 1980s, stood little chance of being admitted as legal immigrants. Thousands of undocumented immigrants from all over Central America, however, entered the United States to look for work.

9   Immigration soon began generating political controversy. As proponents and opponents of restrictions offered conflicting perspectives on how new immigrants, both legal and undocumented, were affecting domestic life, **partisan** differences emerged. In general, Democrats favored less restrictive policies than their GOP counterparts. Although many congressional Republicans hoped President Ronald Reagan would weigh in on their side, he played a minimal role in the passage of the Immigration Reform and Control Act of 1986. This measure, at first glance, looked fairly restrictive. It granted full residency status to recent immigrants who could prove that they had been living in the United States since 1982, but it included stricter penalties on businesses employing undocumented workers. Lacking effective means of enforcing its penalties on employers, however, the new law did little to halt the flow of immigrants, especially during a time when jobs in the United States remained plentiful.

> **partisan** Look at the examples given in the next two sentences.

> ◆What impact did the Immigration Reform and Control Act of 1986 have?

10   As a result, the debate over immigration grew more acrimonious and increasingly polarized. Another congressional act, in 1990, raised the number of immigrants who could legally be admitted on the basis of special job skills or the investment capital they could bring to the United States. A 1996 report, by a special congressional Commission on Immigration Reform, called for lowering the total of official immigration slots and for tightening restrictions against undocumented workers, but a wide range of political and social movements opposing such changes blocked such a response by Congress.

> ◆Why did Congress not lower the total number of official immigration slots or tighten restrictions against undocumented workers?

11   Conflicting demands and contradictory claims about the economic impact of immigrant workers helped stalemate further change in policy. Most business interests favored relatively open immigration policies and opposed strict enforcement of rules against hiring undocumented workers. They supported the claim that immigrants, both the highly educated and the skilled, along with those at the entry level, filled job slots that would otherwise remain open. Opponents, on the other hand, cited figures that suggested immigrants were assuming jobs formerly held by U.S. citizens, especially ones with minimal education and job training, and driving down wage rates. Data to sustain any claim about the precise impact of immigration remained thin and highly contested. Moreover, political debate generally turned on reciting emotionally charged, largely anecdotal evidence rather than on closely analyzing available economic numbers.

> ◆What were the contradictory claims about the economic impact of immigrant workers?

12   The new immigration likely changed California more than any other state. (States along the southwestern border of the United States also felt the impact of immigration from Mexico but never experienced

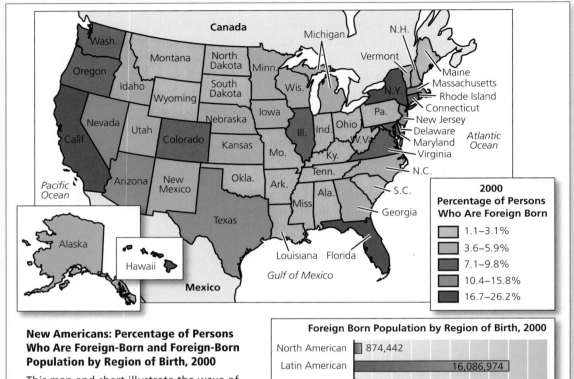

2000 Percentage of Persons Who Are Foreign Born

	1.1–3.1%
	3.6–5.9%
	7.1–9.8%
	10.4–15.8%
	16.7–26.2%

New Americans: Percentage of Persons Who Are Foreign-Born and Foreign-Born Population by Region of Birth, 2000

This map and chart illustrate the wave of new immigration into the United States. Which regions of the world contributed the most immigrants? Which states received the most, and the least, immigration?

Source: U.S. Census Bureau, Census 2000 Summary File 3, Matrix P21; U.S. Census Bureau, Census 2000 American Indian and Alaska Native Summary File, Matrices PCT43, PCT46, PCT48.

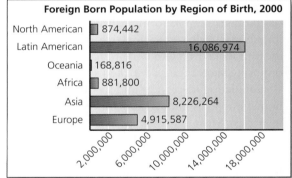

Foreign Born Population by Region of Birth, 2000

Region	Population
North American	874,442
Latin American	16,086,974
Oceania	168,816
Africa	881,800
Asia	8,226,264
Europe	4,915,587

microcosms Los Angeles and Orange counties are compared to the world. What does this suggest about the word *microcosm*? What does the prefix in the word suggest?

◆What effects did immigration have on California?

the same high level of Asian immigration as did California.) In the Golden Gate State, the counties of Los Angeles and Orange seemed microcosms of world culture. By 2000, fewer than half of schoolchildren in L.A. could claim proficiency in English, and no single ethnic group comprised a majority of the city's population. As with the earlier surges of immigration, the wave that began during the 1970s produced not only problems and ethnic-based rivalries but also cooperation and hopes for the benefits of multiculturalism.

● Comprehension Questions

Write the letter of the answer on the line. Then explain your thinking.

Main Idea

____ 1. Which of the following sentences best states the main idea of paragraph 8?

a. In response to the growing number of people seeking admission to the United States, Congress later passed the Refugee Act of 1980.

b. It specified that political refugees, "those fleeing overt persecution," could be admitted more easily but that people seeking simply to improve their economic circumstances could not.

c. In practice, U.S. officials interpreted the terms "political" and "economic" so that they generally admitted people leaving communist regimes but not those fleeing right-wing dictatorships.

d. Thousands of undocumented immigrants from all over Central America, however, entered the United States to look for work.

WHY? What information in the selection leads you to give that answer? _____

_____

____ 2. What of the following best summarizes the main idea of this passage?

a. New Immigration was a long time in coming, and while it faced many setbacks from bipartisan resistance, refugee immigrants are now able to escape despot leaders and establish homes for their families.

b. There have been many patterns of immigration in America, the largest of which was the Latin American immigration of the twentieth century. The second largest was the arrival of refugees from Vietnam, Hmong, and Croatia.

c. The Immigration Reform and Control Act of 1986 had the greatest impact on immigration that the United States had ever seen. It changed the pattern of immigration.

d. Changes in immigration patterns began with the landmark Immigration Act of 1965, which spurred not only population growth but diversity as well.

WHY? What information in the selection leads you to give that answer? _____

_____

Supporting Details

____ 3. According to the passage, when did immigration begin causing serious political debate?

a. in the early 1970s

b. as early as 1790

c. in the 1980s

d. There has always been serious political debate surrounding immigration.

WHY? What information in the selection leads you to give that answer? _____

_____

____ 4. According to the passage, which best supports the claim against immigration?

a. Fewer than half of schoolchildren in L.A. could claim proficiency in English.

b. Haitians were not allowed to enter the United States according to the Refugee Act of 1980.

c. Immigrants were assuming jobs formerly held by U.S. citizens.

d. The United States placed restrictions on the flow of immigrants from Cuba.

WHY? What information in the selection leads you to give that answer? _____

_____

_____

Author's Purpose

____ 5. What is the overall purpose of this passage?

a. to inform

b. to entertain or express

c. to persuade

d. to entertain and persuade

WHY? What information in the selection leads you to give that answer? _____

_____

_____ 6. What is the purpose of the map at the end of the passage?

    a. to illustrate the percentage of the foreign-born population in America in 2000 and the regions they were born in

    b. to illustrate why the foreign-born population in America in 2000 should not be allowed to increase

    c. to illustrate how in 2000, the foreign-born population in America outnumbered the native-born

    d. to illustrate the changes of the foreign-born population in America since 2000

WHY? What information in the selection leads you to give that answer? _____

_____

Relationships

_____ 7. What is the overall pattern of organization of paragraph 4?

    a. time order

    b. listing

    c. comparison contrast

    d. cause and effect

WHY? What information in the selection leads you to give that answer? _____

_____

_____ 8. What is the main relationship found in paragraph 9?

    a. time order

    b. comparison and contrast

    c. cause and effect

    d. listing

WHY? What information in the selection leads you to give that answer? _____

_____

_____

Fact, Opinion, and Inference

____ 9. What inference can be made about the author's point of view toward the political debate over immigration?

    a. The debate is essential to relevant immigration reform.

    b. The author favors the arguments presented by the GOP instead of the Democrats.

    c. The political debate had broken down to biases and was not focused on the objective facts.

    d. The author's point of view suggests a bias against immigrants.

WHY? What information in the selection leads you to give that answer? _____

_____

_____

____ 10. Which of the following is an opinion?

    a. Cubans gradually moved northward into many major American cities, but the greatest impact came in south Florida.

    b. Data to sustain any claim about the precise impact of immigration remained thin.

    c. By the early twenty-first century, the number of Spanish-speaking people in the United States totaled more than all but four countries of Latin America.

    d. The vast bulk of post-1970 immigration came from Asia, Oceania, Latin America, and Africa rather than from Europe, the primary source of immigrants from the 1790s to 1924.

WHY? What leads you to give that answer? _____

_____

_____

● Critical Thinking Questions

CRITICAL THINKING LEVEL 1 REMEMBER

Describe the effects of the Immigration Act of 1965. _____

_____

_____

_____

_____

CRITICAL THINKING LEVEL 2 UNDERSTAND

Summarize this reading using your Marking of the APP.

About: _____

   Point: _____

_____

_____

     Proof: To organize the proof, summarize the main idea of each paragraph.

- _____

- _____
  _____
  _____

- _____
  _____

- _____

- _____

- _____
- _____
- _____
  _____

- _____
  _____

- _____
- _____

CRITICAL THINKING LEVEL 3 APPLY

Apply the knowledge you gained from reading the Prep Reading and the chapter-end readings and any of the videos you watched to write a paragraph about some of the problems immigrants encounter. Use a separate sheet of paper.

CRITICAL THINKING LEVEL 4 ANALYZE

Refer to the map and graph on page 548.

Which regions of the world contributed the most, and the least, immigrants to the United States as a whole? _____

Which states have the highest percentages of foreign-born people? _____

_____

Give at least one reason why these states have high percentages of foreign-born people.

_____

_____

CRITICAL THINKING LEVEL 5 EVALUATE

On the Internet or in the library, find two persuasive articles. One should be pro-immigration, and the other should be anti-immigration. (Each article should be at least five paragraphs in length.) Annotate them as you read. Summarize the claim and support of each article on a separate sheet of paper. Determine whether the claims are well supported by relevant evidence. Decide which kinds of evidence are used and if the evidence is convincing. When you finish, write a paragraph about which one did a better job of convincing you of its claim, and why.

CRITICAL THINKING LEVEL 6 CREATE

Take some time to talk to your parents or grandparents (or whoever else in your family may know) about the history of your family's immigration. Write a short, informal history (one-half to one page in length) to share with your class.

● Vocabulary in Context

The following words were used in the reading selection "New Immigration." Select the best word to complete the meaning of each sentence.

bulk	abolished	overt	partisan	microcosm

Most of us would claim we are _____ of equality. In fact, many people believe that slavery was _____ at the end of the Civil War, even if equality hasn't quite been achieved. And because many Americans don't think much about slavery in other countries, many may believe that the _____ of the problem is in the past. Each modern country is probably a _____ of the world consciousness concerning this belief about slavery. However, while slavery is not as _____ as it once was, there are more slaves in the world today than at any other time in history.

Reading 11-2 . . . . .Editorial

⬤ Pre-Reading the Selection

The following article comes from the editorial section of the *New York Times*. It is written by Kenneth Davis, who is the author of *Don't Know Much About History: Everything You Need to Know About American History but Never Learned*. It discusses how the immigration issue may not be as new as you thought.

Guessing the Purpose

Judging from the title of the article and the fact that it is an editorial, what do you suppose is the purpose of the selection? _____

Surveying the Reading

Based on the purpose you chose, as well as some words or phrases that stand out as you survey this reading, what do you think the tone of this passage will be? _____

_____

Predicting the Content

Predict three things this selection will discuss.

- _____

- _____

- _____

Activating Your Knowledge

List several details you know about the founding immigrants.

- _____

- _____

- _____

Common Knowledge

indentured servant (*paragraph 2*) A person who agrees to work for an employer for a number of years to pay off their "debt of passage".

naturalization (*paragraph 5*) The process of granting full citizenship to an immigrant.

Ku Klux Klan (*paragraph 6*) Best known as a group established to demand white supremacy after the South lost the Civil War, the KKK has used violent means to spread hatred of other minority groups during different times in American history, such as after World War I.

Reading with Pen in Hand

Now read the selection. As you read, mark any ideas that seem important, and respond to the questions and vocabulary items in the margin. Monitor your comprehension by putting a ✔ next to a paragraph when you understand most of it. Place an ✘ next to a paragraph when you don't understand most of it.

Visit www.cengage.com/devenglish/doleconnect and select Chapter 11 to hear vocabulary words from this selection and view a video about this topic.

◆ *Reading Journal*

precarious Reread the previous sentences and guess at the meaning of *precarious*.

◆What was Benjamin Franklin's chief concern?

◆What is ironic about Henry Muhlenberg's view of German immigrants?

The Founding Immigrants

Kenneth C. Davis

1   A prominent American once said, about immigrants, "Few of their children in the country learn English.... The signs in our streets have inscriptions in both languages.... Unless the stream of their importation could be turned they will soon so outnumber us that all the advantages we have will not be able to preserve our language, and even our government will become **precarious**." This sentiment did not emerge from the rancorous debate over the immigration bill defeated last week in the Senate. It was not the lament of some guest of Lou Dobbs or a Republican candidate intent on wooing bedrock conservative votes. Guess again. Voicing this grievance was Benjamin Franklin. And the language so vexing to him was the German spoken by new arrivals to Pennsylvania in the 1750s, a wave of immigrants whom Franklin viewed as the "most stupid of their nation."

2   About the same time, a Lutheran minister named Henry Muhlenberg, himself a recent arrival from Germany, worried that "the whole country is being flooded with ordinary, extraordinary and unprecedented wickedness and crimes.... Oh, what a fearful thing it is to have so many thousands of unruly and brazen sinners

come into this free air and unfenced country." These German masses yearning to breathe free were not the only targets of colonial fear and **loathing**. Echoing the opinions of colonial editors and legislators, Ben Franklin was also troubled by the British practice of dumping its felons on America. With typical Franklin wit, he proposed sending rattlesnakes to Britain in return. (This did not, however, preclude numerous colonists from purchasing these convicts as indentured servants.)

loathing Look at the quotation by Henry Muhlenberg and think about what word seems to be paired naturally with "fear."

3   And still earlier in Pennsylvania, the Scotch-Irish had bred discontent, as their penchant for squatting on choice real estate ran headlong against the colony's founders, the Penn family, and their genteel notions about who should own what. Often, the **disdain** for the foreign was inflamed by religion. Boston's Puritans hanged several Friends after a Bay Colony ban on Quakerism. In Virginia, the Anglicans arrested Baptists.

◆What are two reasons Americans didn't want foreigners to immigrate?

disdain Look at the last sentence to see what happens to the foreigners. What emotion might be in play?

4   But the greatest scorn was generally reserved for Catholics—usually meaning Irish, French, Spanish and Italians. Generations of white American Protestants resented newly arriving "Papists," and even in colonial Maryland, a supposed **haven** for them, Roman Catholics were nonetheless forbidden to vote and hold public office. Once independent, the new nation began to carve its views on immigrants into law. In considering New York's Constitution, for instance, John Jay—later to become the first chief justice of the Supreme Court—suggested erecting "a wall of brass around the country for the exclusion of Catholics."

◆Why were Catholics scorned?

haven Look at the word *supposed* that appears before *haven*. What is Maryland "supposed to be"? Yet what is still happening to Catholics? So what does *haven* mean?

5   By 1790, with the United States Constitution firmly in place, the first federal citizenship law restricted naturalization to "free white persons" who had been in the country for two years. That requirement was later pushed back to five years and, in 1798, to 14 years. Then, as now, politics was key. Federalists feared that too many immigrants were joining the opposition. Under the 1798 Alien Act—with the threat of war in the air over French attacks on American shipping—President John Adams had license to deport anyone he considered "dangerous." Although his secretary of state favored mass deportations, Adams never actually put anybody on a boat. Back then, the French warranted the most suspicion, but there were other worrisome "aliens." A wave of "wild Irish" refugees was thought to harbor dangerous radicals. Harsh "anti-coolie" laws later singled out the Chinese. And, of course, the millions of "involuntary" immigrants from Africa and their offspring were regarded merely as persons "held to service."

◆How was politics important to the first law restricting naturalization?

◆Why does the author say "Disdain for what is foreign is, sad to say, as American as apple pie, slavery and lynching"?

epithets Why would *epithets* be unmentionable? What are they?

◆What does this paragraph suggest about the author's view of the fence along the Mexican border that was being contemplated?

6   Scratch the surface of the current immigration debate and beneath the posturing lies a dirty secret. Anti-immigrant sentiment is older than America itself. Born before the nation, this abiding fear of the "huddled masses" emerged in the early republic and gathered steam into the 19th and 20th centuries, when nativist political parties, exclusionary laws and the Ku Klux Klan swept the land.

7   As we celebrate another Fourth of July, this picture of American intolerance clashes sharply with tidy schoolbook images of the great melting pot. Why has the land of "all men are created equal" forged countless ghettoes and intricate networks of social exclusion? Why the signs reading "No Irish Need Apply"? And why has each new generation of immigrants had to face down a rich glossary of now unmentionable **epithets**? Disdain for what is foreign is, sad to say, as American as apple pie, slavery and lynching.

8   That fence along the Mexican border now being contemplated by Congress is just the latest vestige of a venerable tradition, at least as old as John Jay's "wall of brass." "Don't fence me in" might be America's unofficial anthem of unfettered freedom, but too often the subtext is, "Fence everyone else out."

● Comprehension Questions

Write the letter of the answer on the line. Then explain your thinking.

Main Idea

_____ 1. Which of the following sentences best states the main idea of this selection?

a. As we celebrate another Fourth of July, this picture of American intolerance clashes sharply with tidy schoolbook images of the great melting pot.

b. Once independent, the new nation began to carve its views on immigrants into law.

c. Anti-immigrant sentiment is older than America itself.

d. Often, the disdain for the foreign was inflamed by religion.

WHY? What information in the selection leads you to give that answer? _____

_____ 2. What is the main idea of paragraph 2?

    a. Henry Muhlenberg worried that the country was being flooded with crimes and sinners.

    b. These German masses yearning to breathe free were not the only targets of colonial fear and loathing.

    c. Ben Franklin was also troubled by the British practice of dumping its felons on America.

    d. (This did not, however, preclude numerous colonists from purchasing these convicts as indentured servants.)

WHY? What information in the selection leads you to give that answer? _____

_____

Supporting Details

_____ 3. Who said, "Few of their children in the country learn English. . . ."?

    a. Henry Muhlenberg

    b. Benjamin Franklin

    c. John Jay

    d. Lou Dobbs

WHY? What information in the selection leads you to give that answer? _____

_____

_____ 4. How many years did it take for the residency requirement for the naturalization process to extend to fourteen years?

    a. eight years

    b. ten years

    c. two years

    d. five years

WHY? What information in the selection leads you to give that answer? _____

_____

Author's Purpose

____ 5. What is the overall purpose of this passage?

    a. to inform

    b. to entertain

    c. to persuade

    d. to persuade and inform

WHY? What information in the selection leads you to give that answer? _____

_____

_____

____ 6. What is the tone of paragraph 7?

    a. sincere

    b. pained

    c. humorous

    d. ironic

WHY? What information in the selection leads you to give that answer? _____

_____

Relationships

____ 7. Identify the pattern of this sentence:
Echoing the opinions of colonial editors and legislators, Ben Franklin was also troubled by the British practice of dumping its felons on America.

    a. time order

    b. listing

    c. comparison contrast

    d. cause and effect

WHY? What leads you to give that answer? _____

_____ 8. What relationships are found in the following sentence:

As we celebrate another Fourth of July, this picture of American intolerance clashes sharply with tidy schoolbook images of the great melting pot?

a. narration and contrast

b. comparison and contrast and listing

c. cause and effect and narration

d. listing and classification

WHY? What leads you to give that answer? _____

_____

Fact, Opinion, and Inference

_____ 9. What does the author mean by "the millions of 'involuntary' immigrants from Africa"?

a. The immigrants were "involuntary" because they were slaves.

b. The "involuntary" refers to the children of the immigrants who did not want to leave their friends and schools.

c. Africa was a harsh place to live but it was home. The immigrants were "involuntary" because they did not want to leave but knew America offered a better life.

d. "Involuntary" refers to the views and opinions of the settlers who were already in America and suspicious of any new immigrants.

WHY? What information leads you to give that answer? _____

_____

_____ 10. Which of the following sentence from this passage is an opinion?

a. Once independent, the new nation began to carve its views on immigrants into law.

b. Voicing this grievance was Benjamin Franklin.

c. Oh, what a fearful thing it is to have so many thousands of unruly and brazen sinners come into this free air and unfenced country.

d. John Jay—later to become the first chief justice of the Supreme Court—suggested erecting "a wall of brass around the country for the exclusion of Catholics."

WHY? What leads you to give that answer? _____

_____

Critical Thinking Questions

CRITICAL THINKING LEVEL 1 REMEMBER

Fill in the blanks in this chart, which will summarize the attitudes and actions of certain groups and people toward various immigrants.

This person or group, referring to . . .	this immigrant group . . .	gives this opinion or commits this action.
Benjamin Franklin	Germans	
Henry Muhlenberg	Germans	
	Scotch-Irish	
		hanged
		arrested
Protestants		resented
	Catholics	against (wanted to build a wall to keep them out)
	Everyone not included in "free white persons," i.e., "wild Irish" refugees, the Chinese, and, of course, the millions of "involuntary" immigrants from Africa	against
Those in favor of a border fence		

CRITICAL THINKING LEVEL 2 UNDERSTAND

Summarize this reading using your Marking of the APP.

About: _____

Point: _____

_____

Proof: Summarize the main point of each paragraph except for the last, concluding paragraph.

- _____
  _____
- _____
  _____
- _____
- _____
- _____
- _____
- _____
  _____

CRITICAL THINKING LEVEL 3 APPLY

Refer back to question #4 in Interaction 11-1. Would you change your answer now? If so, *update* your answer as necessary. If not, why not? Double check that you have supported your view with relevant, valid evidence.

CRITICAL THINKING LEVEL 4 ANALYZE

Read this passage and answer the questions that follow.

Talking Points: Readers Respond to "The Terrible, Horrible, Urgent National Disaster That Immigration Isn't"

I agree with those who think immigration into America is horrible. Let's get rid of anyone who wasn't here first! First, get rid of all those white Europeans! Who invited those bozos? Then get rid of the descendants of black slaves. It's not their fault they're here, but they belong in Africa. Ship 'em back! The Asians belong in Asia. Easy do. How about those Indians? They started the mess by migrating across the Bering Strait. That leaves . . . hey! Where'd everybody go?

What is the tone of this paragraph? _____

What is the purpose of the paragraph? _____

What is the author's claim? _____

What support is given? _____

This entire argument could be characterized as which figure of speech? _____

CRITICAL THINKING LEVEL 5 EVALUATE

Evaluate the effect on you as a reader of the previous author's use of the words *horrible, bozos, 'em, easy do, mess,* and *hey!* What do you think of this author? Does using these informal words serve the author's purpose well? Why or why not? _____

_____

_____

CRITICAL THINKING LEVEL 6 CREATE

The class should divide into two groups based on people's responses to the question in Critical Thinking Level 3. Form a group with classmates who had the same overall answer you did. Make a master list of all your reasons. Then have a panel discussion with the other group. Talk objectively about your views. Make sure you listen to your classmates' views, and ask questions to clarify your understanding. Do not criticize their views, simply listen to them. While you are listening, evaluate the validity of the support of their view. Once you have exchanged views, work together on an immigration solution on which you can both agree.

Vocabulary in Context

The following words were used in the reading selection "The Founding Immigrants." Select the best word to complete the meaning of each sentence.

precarious	disdain	loathing	haven	epithets

Unlike the _____ where most of us live, Yau faces a harsh life. Every day is _____ for her. She is met with _____ by others simply because of the way she looks—dirty and unkempt. She can't help being an orphan—both of her parents died from AIDS. Even her relatives treat her with _____, blaming her for her parents' deaths. Every time she sees family members on the streets, they mutter _____ about her under their breath as they quickly walk by.

© Red Circle Images/Fotosearch

casebook

Applying Your Critical Reading Skills to Arguments

www.cengage.com/devenglish/doleconnect

Videos Related to Readings

Vocab Words on Audio

Prep Readings on Demand

The purpose of this casebook is to take a "hot" topic—global warming—and use it as the backdrop for you to practice the reading and thinking skills you have been developing. While thinking critically has been a part of every chapter in this book, the last few chapters have emphasized the concepts of analysis, synthesis, and evaluation. When you deal with fact and opinion, author's tone, and author's reasoning, you are using some major brain cells! And you should be proud of yourself for doing so!

Pre-Reading

Take out a sheet of paper. Jot down your thoughts on the following questions:

- What prior knowledge do you have about global warming?

- Which parts of your prior knowledge are facts, and which are opinions?

Reading

The three readings that follow all take different approaches to global warming: What causes global warming? Is this a significant problem? Is it the world's most important problem? Your job will be to read each selection critically: read to understand what the author is saying, and read to evaluate the strength of the argument.

It would be a good idea to annotate as you read. Since you are dealing with an argument, you should identify the following aspects of each reading selection:

- the author's claim

- the author's evidence (its relevance and strength)

- the author's assumptions

You will be asked to discuss the information in each article, so read actively.

Casebook Reading 1

Al Gore is a former vice president of the United States who served with President Bill Clinton. He has written two books on the environment, including the best-selling book *Earth in the Balance: Ecology and the Human Spirit* (1992). The following reading selection consists of excerpts from different parts of *An Inconvenient Truth*, his book about global warming. The book was made into a documentary film of the same title; it won two Academy Awards. Gore and the Intergovernmental Panel on Climate Change (IPCC) jointly won a Nobel Peace Prize in 2007 for their work on climate change.

For some additional sources of information on global warming, visit www.cengage .com/devenglish/doleconnect and select Casebook.

◆*Reading Journal*

◆As you read, be sure to change title and headings into questions and then look for the answers.

Excerpts from *An Inconvenient Truth*

Al Gore

1   Many people today still assume—mistakenly—that the Earth is so big that we human beings cannot possibly have any major impact on the way our planet's ecological system operates. That assertion may have been true at one time, but it's not the case anymore. We have

grown so numerous and our technologies have become so powerful that we are now capable of having a significant influence on many parts of the Earth's environment. The most vulnerable part of the Earth's ecological system is the atmosphere. It's vulnerable because it's so thin. My friend, the late Carl Sagan, used to say, "If you had a globe covered with a coat of varnish, the thickness of that varnish would be about the same as the thickness of the Earth's atmosphere compared to the Earth itself."

◆ Summarize paragraphs 1 and 2 in a sentence to make sure you understand the argument so far.

2   The atmosphere is thin enough that we are capable of changing its composition. Indeed, the Earth's atmosphere is so thin that we have the capacity to dramatically alter the concentration of some of its basic molecular components. In particular, we have vastly increased the amount of carbon dioxide—the most important of the so-called greenhouse gases.

3   These images illustrate the basic science of global warming.

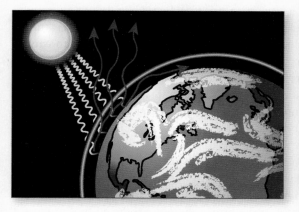 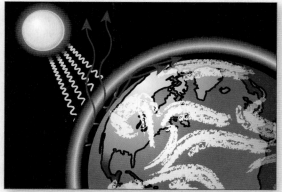

4   The Sun's energy enters the atmosphere in the form of light waves and heats up the Earth. Some of that energy warms the Earth and then is re-radiated back into space in the form of infrared waves. Under normal conditions, a portion of the outgoing infrared radiation is naturally trapped by the atmosphere—and that is a good thing, because it keeps the temperature on Earth within comfortable bounds. The greenhouse gases on Venus are so thick that its temperatures are far too hot for humans. The greenhouse gases surrounding Mars are almost nonexistent, so the temperature there is far too cold. That's why the Earth is sometimes referred to as the "Goldilocks planet"—the temperatures here have been just right.

◆ What is the purpose of the images and paragraphs 4–6? How does the tone influence credibility?

5   The problem we now face is that this thin layer of atmosphere is being thickened by huge quantities of human-caused carbon dioxide

and other greenhouse gases. And as it thickens, it traps a lot of the infrared radiation that would otherwise escape the atmosphere and continue out to the universe. As a result, the temperature of the Earth's atmosphere—and oceans—is getting dangerously warmer.

6   That's what the climate crisis is all about.

What Exactly Are Greenhouse Gases?

7   When we talk about greenhouse gases and climate change, carbon dioxide usually gets the most attention. But there are also some others, although CO_2 is the most important by far.

8   What all greenhouse gases have in common is that they allow light from the sun to come into the atmosphere, but trap a portion of the outward-bound infrared radiation and warm up the air.

9   Having some amount of greenhouse gases is beneficial. Without them, the average temperature of the Earth's surface would be right around 0° F—not a very nice place to live. Greenhouse gases help keep the Earth's surface at a much more hospitable temperature—almost 59° F. But due to increasing concentrations of human-caused greenhouse gases in modern times, we are raising the planet's average temperature and creating the dangerous changes in climate we see all around us. CO_2 usually gets top billing in this because it accounts for 80% of total greenhouse gas emissions. When we burn fossil fuels (oil, natural gas, and coal) in our homes, cars, factories, and power plants, or when we cut or burn down forests, or when we produce cement, we release CO_2 into the atmosphere.

10   Like CO_2, methane and nitrous oxide both predate our presence on the Earth but have gotten huge boosts from us. Sixty percent of the methane currently in the atmosphere is produced by humans; it comes from landfills, livestock farming, fossil-fuel burning, wastewater treatment, and other industry. In large-scale livestock farming, liquid manure is stored in massive tanks that emit methane. Dry manure, left on fields, by contrast, does not. Nitrous oxide (N_2)—another greenhouse culprit—also occurs naturally, though we have added 17% more of it to the atmosphere just in the course of our industrial age, from fertilizers, fossil fuels, and the burning of forests and crop residues.

11   Sulfur hexafluoride (SF_6), PFCs, and HFCs are all greenhouse gases that are produced exclusively by human activity. Not surprisingly, emissions of those gases are on the rise, too. HFCs are used as substitutes for CFCs—which were banned because their emissions in

◆Make sure you are noticing the pattern of organization to get the key evidence the author is presenting to support his claim. You might underline the evidence.

refrigeration systems and elsewhere were destroying the ozone layer. CFCs were also very potent greenhouse gases. PFCs and SF_6 are released into the atmosphere by industrial activities like aluminum smelting and semiconductor manufacturing, as well as the electricity grid that lights up our cities.

12   And finally, water vapor is a natural greenhouse gas that increases in volume with warmer temperatures, thereby magnifying the impact of all artificial greenhouse gases.

Ice Core Samples from the Glaciers

13   Scientist Lonnie Thompson takes his team to the tops of glaciers all over the world. They dig core drills down into the ice, extracting long cylinders filled with ice that was formed year by year over many centuries. Lonnie and his team of experts then examine the tiny bubbles of air trapped in the snow in the year that it fell. They can measure how much CO_2 was in the Earth's atmosphere in the past, year by year. They can also measure the exact temperature of the atmosphere each year by calculating the ratio of different isotopes of oxygen (oxygen-16 and oxygen-18), which provides an ingenious and highly accurate thermometer.

14   The team can count backward in time year by year—the same way an experienced forester can "read" tree rings— by simply observing the clear line of demarcation that separates each year from the one preceding it, as seen in this unique frozen record.

15   The thermometer to the right measures temperatures in the Northern Hemisphere over the past 1,000 years.

16   The blue is cold and the red is hot. The bottom of the graph marks 1,000 years and the current era is at the top.

17   The correlation between temperature and CO_2 concentrations over the last 1,000 years—as measured in the ice core record by Thompson's team—is striking. Nonetheless, the so-called global-warming skeptics often say that global warming is really an illusion reflecting nature's cyclical fluctuations. To support their view, they frequently refer to the Medieval Warm Period. But as Dr. Thompson's thermometer shows, the vaunted Medieval Warm Period (the third little blip from the left, next) was tiny compared to the enormous increases in temperature of the last half-century (the red peaks at the right of the chart).

◆What is the importance of ice core samples to the author's argument?

◆What is the purpose of this graph?

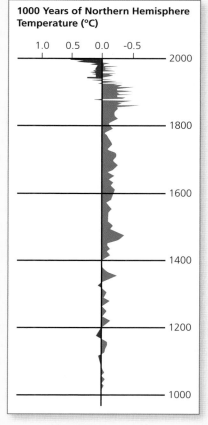

1000 Years of Northern Hemisphere Temperature (°C)

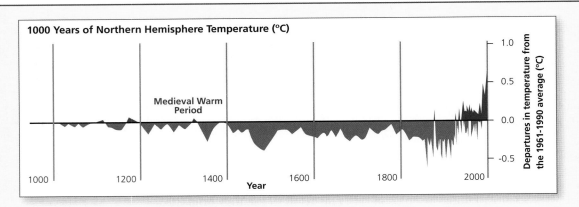

1000 Years of Northern Hemisphere Temperature (°C)

Medieval Warm Period

Departures in temperature from the 1961-1990 average (°C)

Year

◆What is the purpose of this graph? Hint: Notice how it differs from the previous graph.

18   These global-warming skeptics—a group diminishing almost as rapidly as the mountain glaciers—launched a fierce attack against another measurement of the 1,000-year correlation between CO_2 known as the "hockey stick," a graphic image representing the research of climate scientist Michael Mann and his colleagues. But in fact, scientists have confirmed the same basic conclusions in multiple ways—with Thompson's ice core record as one of the most definitive.

◆What is the author doing in paragraphs 17–18? How does this affect the argument's credibility?

CO_2 in Antarctica

19   In Antarctica, measurements of CO_2 concentrations and temperatures go back 650,000 years. The blue line below charts CO_2 concentrations over this period.

20   The top right side of the blue line represents the present era, and that first dip down as you move from right to left is the last ice age. Then, continuing to the left, you can see the second most recent ice age, the third and fourth most recent ice ages, and so on. In between them are periods of warming. At no point in the last 650,000 years before the preindustrial era did the CO_2 concentration go above 300 part per million.

21   The gray line shows the world's temperature over the same 650,000 years. It's a complicated relationship, but the most important part of it is this: When there is more CO_2 in the atmosphere, the temperature increases because more heat from the Sun is trapped inside.

21   There is not a single part of this graph—no fact, date, or number— that is controversial in any way or in dispute by anybody.

◆Did you pay attention to the significance of the statement in paragraph 21?

22   To the extent that there is a controversy at all, it is that a few people in some of the less responsible coal, oil, and utility companies say, "So what? That's not going to cause any problem."

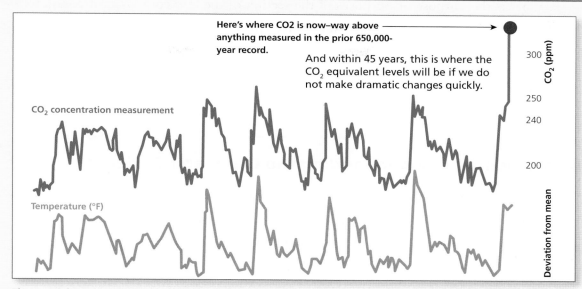

Here's where CO2 is now–way above anything measured in the prior 650,000-year record.

And within 45 years, this is where the CO_2 equivalent levels will be if we do not make dramatic changes quickly.

CO_2 concentration measurement

Temperature (°F)

300

250

240

200

CO_2 (ppm)

Deviation from mean

The top right point of this gray line shows current global temperatures. And the bottom right point marks the depth of the last ice age. That short distance—about an inch in the graph—represents the difference, in Chicago, between a nice day and a mile of ice over your head. Imagine what three times that much on the warm side would mean.

23   But if we allow this [rise in CO_2 levels] to happen, it would be deeply and unforgivably immoral. It would condemn coming generations to a catastrophically diminished future.

24   And that is what is at stake. Our ability to live on planet Earth—to have a future as a civilization.

◆What do paragraphs 21–24 do? What is their purpose and tone?

Interacting with Gore's Argument

Answer the following questions based on your annotations. If you find you need to improve your annotations, please do so.

Interaction A. Establishing the Author's Purpose

1. What is the author's purpose in paragraph 1? _____

_____

2. What do you think the author is trying to achieve when he calls Carl Sagan "my friend"? (If you don't know who Carl Sagan is, visit **www.carlsagan.com** and select "Carl Sagan." Read several paragraphs of his biography.) _____

_____

3. What is the purpose or purposes of the section of the text composed of paragraphs 3–6 and the box titled "What Exactly Are Greenhouse Gases?" _____

_____

_____

4. What is the author's overall purpose? _____

_____

Interaction B. Understanding the Claim and Evidence

1. What does Gore claim is the reason for global warming? Remember that a claim is controversial. You may want to consider the opposing arguments that Gore addresses in order to understand his claim completely. _____

_____

_____

2. What evidence does Gore use to support his claim? Hint: Each group of paragraphs below supports one main idea. Summarize each idea here. Doing this will show Gore's main supporting points.

- Summary of paragraphs 1–2: _____

_____

- Summary of paragraphs 3–6: _____

_____

- Summary of paragraphs 7–12: _____

_____

- Summary of paragraphs 13–18: _____

_____

- Summary of paragraphs 19–24: _____

_____

_____

3. Is the support relevant? _____

4. Reread the paragraphs in which Gore responds to people who don't agree with various parts of his argument. Tell how Gore responds to their viewpoints.

- Paragraph 1 _____

  _____

- Paragraph 17 _____

  _____

  _____

- Paragraph 18 _____

  _____

  _____

  _____

- Paragraph 22 _____

  _____

  _____

Interaction C. Considering Fact, Opinion, and Authority

1. Carl Sagan in paragraph 1

   A. Is the Carl Sagan quotation a fact or an opinion? Explain. _____

   _____

   B. Is Carl Sagan an expert source, an informed source, or a person on the street? Explain. _____

   C. Reread Sagan's words carefully. Evaluate how well they support the point that Gore is making. _____

   _____

2. Al Gore in paragraph 9

   A. Reread paragraph 9. Is the first sentence fact or opinion? Explain. _____

   _____

   B. Is Al Gore an expert source, an informed source, or a person on the street? Explain. _____

   _____

    C. Which of the following statements from paragraph 9 are facts? Put a check
       mark beside each fact.

- The second sentence, which begins "Without them . . ." _____
- The fourth sentence, which begins "But due to increased . . ." _____
- The last sentence, which begins "When we burn fossil fuels . . ." _____

3. Al Gore in paragraph 21

    A. List all the absolute qualifiers in this paragraph. _____

    _____

    B. If you had to argue that this was fact or opinion, what would you say,
       and why? _____

    _____

    _____

    C. Suppose that Gore is correct when he states that all the facts, dates, and
       numbers in this graph are accurate and undisputed. Look back at the
       graph, and give at least two examples of how the graph might still be inac-
       curate. You will have to think about the author's purpose and the author's
       assumptions.

- _____
- _____

    _____

● Interaction D. Identifying the Author's Tone

1. What is the overall tone of this reading? Hint: You may need to use more than one
   adjective. _____

2. Identify the tone in the first sentence of paragraph 18. Give two pieces of evidence
   from the sentence to support your argument about the tone, and explain how they
   contribute to the tone. Tone: _____

    Two pieces of evidence and explanations:

- _____

    _____

    _____

- _____

⟐ Interaction E. Evaluating the Argument

1. Is the author credible? Support your answer. _____

_____

_____

2. Is the argument strong? Why or why not? _____

_____

_____

3. Give the argument an overall evaluation; state your opinion of how convincing it is and back up your opinion with information from Gore's argument. Are parts of it strong and others weak? If so, discuss which parts, and why. Write a paragraph in which your purpose is to inform others of your opinion and give your reasons.

Casebook Reading 2

S. Michael Craven is the president of the Center for Christ and Culture. His weekly syndicated commentaries in Christian publications reach four and a half million readers a week. A frequent guest host of the nationally syndicated radio program, *Point of View*, Craven has also appeared on Fox News, CNN, ABC, and NBC. Craven assumed a full-time ministry in 2001.

For some additional sources of information on global warming, visit www.cengage. com/devenglish/doleconnect and select Casebook.

Are Man-Made Carbon Emissions Driving Climate Change?

S. Michael Craven

◆ *Reading Journal*

1   A recent report in Canada's *National Post* reads "The polar ice cap is shrinking, laying bare deep gullies in the landscape and the climate is the warmest it has been in decades or perhaps centuries." Sounds scary, doesn't it? Well, it is if you're a Martian! According to NASA, data collected from the Mars Odyssey mission reveals that Mars is also experiencing "global warming." NASA scientist William Feldman said, "In some low-latitude areas, the ice has already dissipated." Following a recent analysis of the first twelve months of

◆What is the author doing to establish his credibility?

data collected from Mars, scientists are accumulating evidence that climatic changes similar to Earth's are also occurring on the only other planet in the solar system where climate is now being studied.

2   Now, the obvious question is "How can Mars experience global warming if global warming is caused by an increase in carbon dioxide produced by human industry?"

◆What purpose do the questions in paragraphs 2 and 3 serve?

3   According to the proponents of "man-made" global warming, carbon dioxide emissions are the culprit in climate change. So what is the role of carbon dioxide, if any, and are there other, more plausible explanations for the half-degree centigrade temperature increase that is believed to have occurred over the last century?

4   Astrophysicist Nir Shaviv, one of Israel's top scientists, was once a proponent of the theory that man-made carbon emissions are driving climate change. In an interview with Lawrence Solomon, columnist for the *National Post*, Dr. Shaviv "described the logic that led him— and most everyone else—to conclude that SUVs, coal plants and other things man-made cause global warming." Dr. Shaviv points out that "scientists for decades have postulated that increases in carbon dioxide and other gases could lead to a greenhouse effect." Then, as if on cue, "the temperature rose over the course of the twentieth century while greenhouse gases proliferated due to human activities" and since "no other mechanism explains the warming . . . greenhouse gases necessarily became the cause."

◆What is the purpose of paragraphs 4 and 5?

5   Recently however, he has recanted, saying: "Like many others, I was personally sure that CO_2 is the bad culprit in the story of global warming. But after carefully digging into the evidence, I realized that things are far more complicated than the story sold to us by many climate scientists or the stories regurgitated by the media." As Dr. Shaviv began to dig into the issue he was surprised to discover "there is no concrete evidence—only speculation—that man-made greenhouse gases cause global warming."

6   Solomon points out, "Even research from the Intergovernmental Panel on Climate Change (IPCC)—the United Nations agency that heads the worldwide effort to combat global warming—is bereft of anything here inspiring confidence. In fact, according to the IPCC's own findings, 'man's role is so uncertain that there is a strong possibility that we have been cooling, not warming, the Earth. Unfortunately, our tools are too crude to reveal what man's effect has been in the past, let alone predict how much warming or cooling we might cause in the future.'"

◆Did you recognize the significance of the quotation from the IPCC in paragraph 6?

7   In the wake of mounting scientific evidence, Dr. Shaviv and many others now believe that solar activity offers a much more plausible explanation for global warming than man-made carbon emissions, particularly because of the evidence that has been accumulating over the past decade of the strong relationship that cosmic-ray flux has on our atmosphere.

8   Scientists have learned that the sun's magnetic field deflects some of the cosmic rays that penetrate the Earth's atmosphere, and in so doing it also limits the immense amounts of ions and free electrons that the cosmic rays produce. But something changed in the 20th century: The sun's magnetic field more than doubled in strength, deflecting an extraordinary number of rays. A magnetically active sun boosts the number of sunspots, indicating that vast amounts of energy are being released from deep within. Typically, sunspots flare up and settle down in cycles of about 11 years. "In the last 50 years, we haven't been living in typical times: If you look back into the sun's past, you find that we live in a period of abnormally high solar activity," according to Dr. Nigel Weiss, Professor Emeritus at the Department of Applied Mathematics and Theoretical Physics at the University of Cambridge. Conversely, in the 17th century, sunspots almost completely disappeared for 70 years during what was the coldest interval of the Little Ice Age, when New York Harbor froze, allowing walkers to journey from Manhattan to Staten Island.

9   It is believed that the recent diminution of cosmic rays has limited the formation of clouds, making the Earth warmer. Low-altitude clouds are particularly significant because they especially shield the Earth from the sun to keep us cool. Low cloud cover can vary by 2% in five years, affecting the Earth's surface by as much as 1.2 watts per square meter during that same period. "That figure can be compared with about 1.4 watts per square meter estimated by the IPCC for the greenhouse effect of all the increase in carbon dioxide in the air since the Industrial Revolution," according to Henrik Svensmark, director of the Centre for Sun-Climate Research at the Danish Space Research Institute.

◆It might be helpful to make a drawing of the cosmic ray phenomenon the author is describing.

10   Until recently the relationship between cosmic rays and cloud formation was merely a theory. That is until Dr. Svensmark and his team undertook an elaborate laboratory experiment in a reaction chamber the size of a small room. Reporting on these events Lawrence Solomon writes:

11   The team duplicated the chemistry of the lower atmosphere by injecting the gases found there in the same proportions, and

◆How do the results of the experiment relate to the author's argument?

adding ultraviolet rays to mimic the actions of the sun. What they found left them agape: A vast number of floating microscopic droplets soon filled the reaction chamber. These were ultra-small clusters of sulphuric acid and water molecules—the building blocks for cloud condensation nuclei—that had been catalyzed by the electrons released by cosmic rays. "We were amazed by the speed and efficiency with which the electrons do their work," Dr. Svensmark remarked. For the first time ever, researchers had experimentally identified a causal mechanism by which cosmic rays can facilitate the production of clouds in Earth's atmosphere. "This is a completely new result within climate science."

(*National Post*, Feb 2, 2007)

◆What impact does this last question have on the author's overall purpose and tone?

12   Is it ridiculous to suggest that the largest source of heat energy in the solar system may be the cause of our present warming trend? It is certainly not the politically correct view. . . .

● Interacting with Craven's Argument

Answer the following questions based upon your annotations. If you find you need to improve your annotations, please do so.

● Interaction F. Establishing the Author's Purpose

1. What is the author's overall purpose? _____

_____

2. What is the purpose of paragraphs 1–6? _____

_____

3. What is the purpose of paragraphs 8–11? _____

_____

4. In paragraph 12, why does the author ask a question rather than make a statement: "Is it ridiculous to suggest that the largest source of heat energy in the solar system may be the cause of our present warming trend?" _____

_____

_____

_____

● Interaction G. Understanding the Claim and Evidence

1. What does Craven claim is the reason for global warming? _____

_____

_____

2. What evidence does Craven use to support his claim? Hint: Each group of paragraphs below supports one main idea. Summarize each idea here. Doing so will show
Craven's main supporting points.

- Summary of paragraphs 1–3: _____

_____

- Summary of paragraphs 4–5: _____

_____

_____

- Summary of paragraph 6: _____

_____

- Summary of paragraph 7: _____

_____

- Summary of paragraph 8: _____

_____

- Summary of paragraph 9: _____

_____

- Summary of paragraphs 10–11: _____

_____

- Summary of paragraph 12: _____

_____

3. Is the support relevant? _____

● Interaction H. Considering Fact, Opinion, and Authority

1. William Feldman in paragraph 1

   A. Is the William Feldman quotation a fact or an opinion? Explain. _____

_____

_____

B. Is William Feldman an expert source, an informed source, or a person on the street? Explain. _____

_____

C. Read Feldman's words carefully. Do they directly relate to an argument about the cause of global warming on Earth? _____

_____

2. S. Michael Craven in paragraphs 1, 2, 3, and 12

A. Craven mostly asks questions instead of making statements in these paragraphs. What impact does this have on our ability to determine whether he seems like an author to trust? _____

B. Is Craven an expert source, an informed source, or a person on the street? Explain. _____

_____

_____

_____

_____

3. Nir Shaviv

Identify the following statements as fact (F) or opinion (O) or both (F/O). Explain your answer.

A. "Astrophysicist Nir Shaviv, one of Israel's top scientists, was once a proponent of the theory that man-made carbon emissions are driving climate change." _____

_____

B. Dr. Shaviv says "there is no concrete evidence—only speculation—that man-made greenhouse gases cause global warming." _____

_____

_____

_____

C. "In the wake of mounting scientific evidence, Dr. Shaviv and many others now believe that solar activity offers a much more plausible explanation for global warming than man-made carbon emissions." _____

_____

_____

_____

● Interaction I. Identifying the Author's Tone

1. What tone does the author create in paragraph 1 by discussing the shrinking polar ice cap and then revealing he is referring to Mars? _____

2. For each statement about the author's tone below, give one supporting quotation from the article.

   A. The author's tone is subjective. _____

   _____

   B. The author's tone is objective. _____

   _____

   C. The author uses the second person point of view. _____

   _____

● Interaction J. Evaluating the Argument

1. Does Craven respond to any counterarguments from people who don't agree with his argument? How does this affect his credibility? _____

   _____

2. Is this author credible? Support your answer. _____

   _____

   _____

   _____

3. Is the author's argument strong? Why or why not? _____

   _____

   _____

4. Give the argument an overall evaluation; state your opinion of how convincing it is, and back up your opinion with information from Craven's argument. Are parts of it strong and others weak? If so, discuss which parts, and why. Write a paragraph in which your purpose is to inform others of your opinion and give your reasons.

Group Interaction: Comparing the Claims and Evidence

With a group of classmates, create a visual chart or graph that compares and contrasts the claims and major evidence in the arguments by Gore and Craven. For an idea about how to set up the chart, see page 232. After your group has created your chart, compare it to the chart another group created. Discuss any differences you find.

Casebook Reading 3

Bjorn Lomborg is the author of two books, *The Skeptical Environmentalist* and the book from which the following excerpt is taken, *Cool It: The Skeptical Environmentalist's Guide to Global Warming*. A former director of the Denmark Environmental Assessment Institute, in 2004 Lomborg also started the Copenhagen Consensus Center, in which economists from around the world meet to find the best solutions to the world's biggest challenges. Lomborg was named one of the 100 most influential people in the world by *Time* magazine in 2004, and in 2008 the U.K. *Guardian* called him one of the "50 people who could save the planet." Lomborg is an adjunct professor at the Copenhagen Business School.

For some additional sources of information on global warming, visit www.cengage.com/devenglish/doleconnect and select Casebook.

◆*Reading Journal*

◆What does this title suggest about the author's purpose? Note: If you do not understand the reference in the title to "canaries in a coal mine," then you should try searching online for an explanation.

Polar Bears: Today's Canaries in the Coal Mine?

Bjorn Lomborg

1   Countless politicians proclaim that global warming has emerged as the preeminent issue of our era. The European Union calls it "one of the most threatening issues that we are facing today." Former prime minister Tony Blair of the United Kingdom sees it as "the single most important issue." German chancellor Angela Merkel has vowed to make climate change the top priority within both the G8 and the European Union in 2007, and Italy's Romano Prodi sees climate change as the real threat to global peace. Presidential contenders from John McCain to Hillary Clinton express real concern over the issue. Several coalitions of states have set up regional climate-change initiatives, and in California Republican Governor Arnold Schwarzenegger has helped push through legislation saying that global warming should be a top priority for the state. And of course, Al Gore has presented this message urgently in his lectures

as well as in the book and Oscar-winning movie *An Inconvenient Truth*.

2   In March 2007, while I waited to give evidence to a congressional hearing on climate change, I watched Gore put his case to the politicians. It was obvious to me that Gore is sincerely worried about the world's future. And he's not alone in worrying. A raft of book titles warn that we've reached a *Boiling Point* and will experience a *Climate Crash*. One is even telling us we will be the *Last Generation* because "nature will take her revenge for climate change." Pundits aiming to surpass one another even suggest that we face medieval-style impoverishment and societal collapse in just forty years if we don't make massive and draconian changes to the way we live.

◆How does the first sentence of paragraph 2 impact the author's credibility?

3   Likewise, the media pound us with increasingly dramatic stories of our ever worsening climate. In 2006, *Time* did a special report on global warming, with the cover spelling out the scare story with repetitive austerity: "Be worried. Be very worried." The magazine told us that the climate is crashing, affecting us both globally by playing havoc with the biosphere and individually through such health effects as heatstrokes, asthma, and infectious diseases. The heartbreaking image on the cover was of a lone polar bear on a melting ice floe, searching in vain for the next piece of ice to jump to. *Time* told us that due to global warming bears "are starting to turn up drowned" and that at some point they will become extinct.

◆For what purpose does the author use the first three paragraphs?

4   Padding across the ice, polar bears are beautiful animals. To Greenland—part of my own nation, Denmark—they are a symbol of pride. The loss of this animal would be a tragedy. But the real story of the polar bear is instructive. In many ways, this tale encapsulates the broader problem with the climate-change concern: once you look closely at the supporting data, the narrative falls apart.

◆What effect does Lomborg's saying that Greenland is part of his own nation have?

5   Al Gore shows a picture similar to *Time*'s and tells us "a new scientific study shows that, for the first time, polar bears have been drowning in significant numbers." The World Wildlife Fund actually warns that polar bears might stop reproducing by 2012 and thus become functionally extinct in less than a decade. In their pithy statement, "polar bears will be consigned to history, something that our grandchildren can only read about in books." *The Independent* tells us that temperature increases "mean polar bears are wiped out in their Arctic homeland. The only place they can be seen is in a zoo."

6   Over the past few years, this story has cropped up many times, based first on a World Wildlife Fund report in 2002 and later on the Arctic Climate Impact Assessment from 2004. Both relied extensively

on research published in 2001 by the Polar Bear Specialist Group of the World Conservation Union.

7   But what this group really told us was that of the twenty distinct sub-populations of polar bears, one or possibly two were declining in Baffin Bay; more than half were known to be stable; and two sub-populations were actually *increasing* around the Beaufort Sea. Moreover, it is reported that the global polar-bear population has *increased* dramatically over the past decades, from about five thousand members in the 1960s to twenty-five thousand today, through stricter hunting regulation. Contrary to what you might expect— and what was not pointed out in any of the recent stories—the two populations in decline come from areas where it has actually been getting colder over the past fifty years, whereas the two increasing populations reside in areas where it is getting warmer. Likewise, Al Gore's comment on drowning bears suggests an ongoing process getting ever worse. Actually, there was a single sighting of four dead bears the day after "an abrupt windstorm" in an area housing one of the increasing bear populations.

8   The best-studied polar-bear population lives on the western coast of Hudson Bay. That its population has declined 17 percent, from 1,200 in 1987 to under 950 in 2004, has gotten much press. Not mentioned, though, is that since 1981 the population had soared from just 500, thus eradicating any claim of a decline. Moreover, nowhere in the news coverage is it mentioned that 300 to 500 bears are shot each year, with 49 shot on average on the west coast of Hudson Bay. Even if we take the story of decline at face value, it means we have lost about 15 bears to global warming each year, whereas we have lost 49 each year to hunting.

◆What do paragraphs 7–9 offer to the strength and relevancy of the author's claim?

9   In 2006, a polar-bear biologist from the Canadian government summed up the discrepancy between the data and the PR: "It is just silly to predict the demise of polar bears in 25 years based on media-assisted hysteria." With Canada home to two-thirds of the world's polar bears, global warming will affect them, but "really, there is no need to panic. Of the 13 populations of polar bears in Canada, 11 are stable or increasing in number. They are not going extinct, or even appear to be affected at present."

10 The polar-bear story teaches us three things. First, we hear **vastly exaggerated and emotional claims** that are simply not supported by data. Yes, it is likely that disappearing ice will make it harder for polar bears to continue their traditional foraging patterns and that they will increasingly take up a lifestyle similar to that of brown

bears, from which they evolved. They may eventually decline, though dramatic declines seem unlikely. But over the past forty years, the population has increased dramatically and the populations are now stable. The ones going down are in areas that are getting colder. Yet we are told that global warming will make polar bears extinct, possibly within ten years, and that future kids will have to read about them in storybooks.

11   Second, polar bears are **not the only story.** While we hear only about the troubled species, it is also a fact that many species will do better with climate change. In general the Arctic Climate Impact Assessment projects that the Arctic will experience increasing species richness and higher ecosystem productivity. It will have less polar desert and more forest. The assessment actually finds that higher temperatures mean more nesting birds and more butterflies. This doesn't make up for the polar bears, but we need to hear both parts of the story.

12   The third point is that **our worry makes us focus on the wrong solutions.** We are being told that the plight of the polar bear shows "the need for stricter curbs on greenhouse gas emissions linked to global warming." Even if we accept the flawed idea of using the 1987 population of polar bears around Hudson Bay as a baseline, so that we lose 15 bears each year, what can we do? If we try helping them by cutting greenhouse gases, we can at the very best avoid 15 bears dying. We will later see that realistically we can do not even close to that much good—probably we can save about 0.06 bears per year. But 49 bears from the same population are getting shot each year, and this we can easily do something about. Thus, if we really want a stable population of polar bears, dealing first with the 49 shot ones might be both a smarter and a more viable strategy. Yet it is not the one we end up hearing about. In the debate over the climate, we often don't hear the proposals that will do the most good but only the ones that involve cutting greenhouse-gas emissions. This is fine if our goal is just to cut those gases, but presumably we want to improve human conditions and environmental quality. Sometimes greenhouse-gas cuts might be the best way to get this, but often they won't be. We must ask ourselves if it makes more sense to help 49 bears swiftly and easily or 0.06 bears slowly and expensively.

13   The argument in this book is simple.

◆What is the purpose of paragraphs 10–12?

1. **Global warming is real and man-made.** It will have a serious impact on humans and the environment toward the end of this century.

2. **Statements about the strong, ominous, and immediate consequences of global warming are often wildly exaggerated,** and this is unlikely to result in good policy.

3. **We need simpler, smarter, and more efficient solutions for global warming** rather than excessive if well-intentioned efforts. Large and very expensive CO_2 cuts made now will have only a rather small and insignificant impact far into the future.

4. **Many other issues are much more important than global warming.** We need to get our perspective back. There are many more pressing problems in the world, such as hunger, poverty, and disease. By addressing them, we can help more people, at lower cost, with a much higher chance of success than by pursuing drastic climate policies at a cost of trillions of dollars.

14   These four points will rile a lot of people. We have become so accustomed to the standard story: climate change is not only real but will lead to unimaginable catastrophes, while doing something about it is not only cheap but morally right. We perhaps understandably expect that anyone questioning this line of reasoning must have evil intentions. Yet I think—with the best of intentions—it is necessary that we at least allow ourselves to examine our logic before we embark on the biggest public investment in history.

◆What do paragraphs 13–16 do?

15   **We need to remind ourselves that our ultimate goal is not to reduce greenhouse gases or global warming per se but to improve the quality of life and the environment.** We all want to leave the planet in decent shape for our kids. Radically reducing greenhouse gas emissions is not necessarily the best way to achieve that. As we go through the data, we will see that it actually is one of the least helpful ways of serving humanity or the environment.

16   I hope that this book can help us to better understand global warming, be smarter about solutions to it, and also regain our perspective on the most effective ways to make the world a better place, a desire we all share.

● Interacting with Lomborg's Argument

Answer the following questions based upon your annotations. If you find you need to improve your annotations, please do so.

● Interaction K. Establishing the Author's Purpose

1. How is this author's purpose different from Gore's and Craven's? _____

_____

_____

2. What is the purpose of the first six paragraphs? _____

_____

3. What purpose does the author serve by putting paragraphs 7–9 right after 5–6?

_____

_____

4. What is the author's purpose in ending this part of the book with the phrase "a desire we all share"? _____

● Interaction L. Understanding the Claim and Evidence

1. Paraphrase the author's claim in your own words. _____

_____

2. In which paragraph does the author start to give evidence to support his claim?

_____

3. Put a checkmark next to the one statement below that is a major supporting detail rather than a minor supporting detail.

> A. "Both relied extensively on research published in 2001 by the Polar Bear Specialist Group of the World Conservation Union." (para. 6) _____

> B. "Contrary to what you might expect . . . the two populations in decline come from areas where it has actually been getting colder over the last fifty years." (para. 7) _____

> C. "Nowhere in the news coverage is it mentioned that 300 to 500 bears are shot each year." (para. 8) _____

4. Based on the author's argument, do polar bears perform the same function as the "canaries in coal mines" mentioned in the title? _____

_____

◉ Interaction M. Considering Fact, Opinion, and Authority

1. Identify the following statements from the reading as fact (F) or opinion (O) or both (F/O). Give a reason for your evaluation.

    A. "It was obvious to me that Gore is sincerely worried about the world's future." _____

    B. "Of the 13 populations of polar bears in Canada, 11 are stable or increasing in number." _____

    C. "... our worry makes us focus on the wrong solutions." _____

    D. "We need to remind ourselves that our ultimate goal is not to reduce greenhouse gases or global warming per se but to improve the quality of life and the environment." _____

2. What did the author do to check whether the opinions of world leaders and the media were founded on actual facts? _____ Name the organization whose opinions about polar bears were not verified by Lomborg's research. __

3. How did Lomborg find out that this organization was misrepresenting the facts?

4. Is the person who made this statement an expert source, an informed source, or a person in the street? "It is just silly to predict the demise of polar bears in 25 years." (para. 9) _____

◉ Interaction N. Identifying the Author's Tone

1. What is the tone of the following sentence? What words demonstrate the tone? *The media pound us with increasingly dramatic stories of our ever worsening climate?* _____

2. What insight does this sentence give us into the author's general tone?

This doesn't make up for the polar bears, but we need to hear both parts of the story.

3. What is the overall tone of this passage? _____

◆ Interaction O. Evaluating the Argument

1. Is the author credible? Support your answer. _____

_____

_____

2. Is the argument strong? Why or why not? _____

_____

3. Do you find the author's support of his argument relevant? Why or why not? _____

_____

Group or Individual Interaction: Creating a Summary Slide Show

Create a summary of one of the articles on global warming using PowerPoint or Keynote slides. Give your presentation to the class, who will grade you on whether your presentation accurately summarizes the information from the article.

Group or Individual Interaction: Write and Make a Persuasive Speech

Based on the reading selections as well as any other information you have about global warming, write your own claim to answer the question "Is human activity causing global warming?" Then take whatever information from all the readings that you find important in supporting your claim, and prepare a brief speech to support your claim. Try to convince your classmates that your claim is true. Then the class can vote on who made the best argument.

Group or Individual Interaction: Read Some More about Global Warming

Find an article on global warming in a newspaper or magazine, and read it. As you read, note the claim, major supporting evidence, the author's purpose, tone, and point of view, and facts and opinions used. Finally, evaluate the strength and relevancy of the author's argument. Note this information on a separate sheet of paper. Then exchange articles with a partner. Take the same kind of notes on this second article. Then compare your responses with your partner's responses on both articles. Were they similar? Why or why not?

For some additional sources of information on global warming, visit **www.cengage .com/devenglish/doleconnect** and select Casebook.

chapter 12

Applying Your Critical Reading Skills Online

© Chris Marion/Big Stock Photo

If you use the Internet, do you think Tolkien's comment is applicable to your experience? Why?

Share Your Prior Knowledge

Talk about your Internet use. Is it something you do often . . . or something you avoid? What types of sites do you visit? What do you spend most of your online time doing?

Survey the Chapter

Take two minutes to skim Reading 12-2, "Evaluating Internet Research Sources," on pages 627–630 to find some ways in which you should evaluate the information you are reading online. See if they are the same or different from your prior knowledge.

www.cengage.com/devenglish/doleconnect

Videos Related to Readings

Vocab Words on Audio

Prep Readings on Demand

Prep Reading . . . . Research Findings

The following is an excerpt from "The Internet Goes to College," a survey conducted by the Pew Internet & American Life Project. The study focused on college students' use of the Internet. The section reprinted here discusses how the Internet is affecting student research.

Visit **www.cengage.com/devenglish/doleconnect** and select Chapter 12 to hear a reading of this selection and view a video about this topic.

Study Habits

1   The convenience of the Internet may be taking some of the trouble out of working on class projects for college students, but some educators and librarians are concerned it may also be creating poor research habits.

queries This word means the same thing as another word that starts with the same two letters.

2   Data from the Association of Research Libraries shows that reference **queries** at university libraries have greatly decreased during and since the late 1990s. The convenience of the Internet is likely tempting students to rely very heavily on it when searching for academic resources. In our own research, an overwhelming number of college students reported that the Internet, rather than the library, is the primary site of their information searches. Nearly three-quarters (73%) of college students said they use the Internet more than the library, while only 9% said they use the library more than the Internet for information searching. In response to a general question about overall library use, 80% of college students reported using the library less than three hours each week.

3   Traditionally, and ideally, the library has been a place where students go to study and collect materials used for papers, presentations, and reports. Of course, people often socialize at the library, too. Nowadays, the Internet has changed the way students use the library. Students tend to use the Internet prior to going to the library to find information. During direct observations of college students' use of the Internet in a library and in campus computer labs, it was noted that the majority of students' time was not spent using the library resources online. Rather, email use, instant messaging and Web-surfing **dominated** students' computer activity in the library. Almost every student who was observed checked his or her email while in the computer labs, but very few were observed surfing university-based or library Web sites. Those students who were using

dominated Use the contrast the author makes to figure out the meaning.

the computer lab to do academic-related work made use of commercial search engines rather than university and library Web sites.

4   Many students are likely to use information found on search engines and various Web sites as research material. **Plagiarism** from online sources has become a major issue on many campuses, and faculty often report concerns about the number of URLs included in research paper bibliographies and the decrease in **citations** from traditional scholarly sources. A great challenge for today's colleges is how to teach students search techniques that will get them to the information they want and how to evaluate it.

5   University libraries have tried to adapt to the information resources that the Internet offers by wiring themselves for students' demands. For example, computers are scattered throughout libraries to allow students to search for resources easily. When students visit the library, it is our observation that they use electronic resources more than paper resources. Students often wait in line to use computers at peak times during the semester. We frequently found that libraries **designate** different computers for research, for checking email, or for public access. Although academic resources are offered online, it may be that students have not been taught, or have not yet figured out, how to locate these resources. Students in computer labs and classrooms were heard by observers to say that it is easier to find resources using the Internet, an observation echoed by educators and librarians who worry that students are less adept at recognizing credible, academic sources when conducting research. While few universities require college students to take courses on information seeking, many include a session on it during freshman orientation meetings. College students seem to rely on information seeking habits formed prior to arriving at college. In Teenage Life Online, a Pew Internet & American Life Project report published in June 2001 (**http://www.pewinternet.org/reports/toc.asp?Report=36**), it was found that 94% of online teens have used the Internet for school research, and 71% used it as a major source for a recent school project.

plagiarism Use your dictionary to find the definition of plagiarism.

citations Use the context and your prior knowledge to define *citations* (or use a dictionary).

designate The context provides the clue here.

Use Internet more than library	73%
Use Internet and library about the same amount	16%
Use Internet less than library	9%
Don't know	2%

Table 12.1 Comparing Online Information Searching to Library Use

Source: Pew Internet & American Life Project College Students Survey, n=1032. Margin of error is ±3.5%.

Interaction 12-1. Talking about Reading

Respond in writing to the questions below and then discuss your answers with your classmates.

1. What problem is the Internet causing on college research projects? _____

   _____

2. This study mentions that "nearly three-quarters (73%) of college students said they use the Internet more than the library, while only 9% said they use the library more than the Internet for information searching . . . 80% of college students reported using the library less than three hours each week." How does your class compare on Internet versus library use? Poll the class to find out. _____

   _____

3. What sites do you use when you have to do research? _____

   _____

4. How do you evaluate online information to know if it is valid? _____

   _____

Purposes for Reading Online

Although the Internet started out as a way for scientists to share their data, its use has expanded greatly, and today millions of people go online daily to read the news, check the weather, make travel arrangements, get driving directions, shop for everything from groceries to investments, do research, talk to others from around the world, find dates, make donations to charity, do their banking, and pay their bills.

The most likely reason you will go online for your college courses is to find information, and even outside of school, finding information is one of the major purposes people have for using the Internet. According to research studies conducted by the Pew Internet & American Life Project over the past several years, here are five of the main information-seeking reasons people go online:

84 percent of Internet users search for specific information via a search engine.

76 percent look for information about a specific interest or hobby.

66 percent search for medical or health information.

66 percent are looking for information from a government Web site.

51 percent research information related to their jobs.

You can see from this list that any time you spend learning how to find information efficiently online will pay off handsomely when you need to gather the information you will need for personal and professional reasons.

◉ Interaction 12-2. Surveying Class Members' Experience Online

Use the list of the types of information people seek online to find out how your classmates have used the Internet to find information. What information were they trying to find? What did they find?

The Internet and Internet Addresses

The Internet is a vast network of computer networks all over the world that people can access using their computers. The material that is transferred from computer to computer using a format called "http" (HyperText Transfer Protocol) forms the World Wide Web, which is the most widely used part of the Internet. To access the World Wide Web, computers must have Web browser software, such as Netscape Navigator, Internet Explorer, Safari, Firefox, Google Chrome, or another. Having a Web browser allows you to type an Internet address into a search box and then view the material that is stored on someone else's computer at that Internet address.

An Internet address is called the URL—Uniform Resource Locator. Examine the URLs for these organizations:

Chicago *Sun-Times* (a newspaper): **http://www.suntimes.com**

Miami Dade College: **http://www.mdc.edu**

Texas Department of Public Safety: **http://www.txdps.state.tx.us**

New York Public Library: **http://www.nypl.org**

Notice that each URL begins with *http://*. This is the method by which your browser accesses the Web. The rest of the URLs shown here is called the domain name. You can see that the domain includes *www* for "World Wide Web"; identifies the organization that sponsors the Web site, such as mdc for Miami Dade College; and ends with a two- or three-letter extension, such as *.com*, *.edu*, or *.us*, that provides more information about what kind of organization sponsors the site, or at times, where it is located. **Table 12.2** includes a list of the most commonly used extensions.

Table 12.2 URL Extensions and Web Site Purposes

Extension	Type of Sponsoring Organization	Web Site's General Purpose
.com	commercial: businesses, but others, such as individuals, can also use this extension, which is the most-used one	typically, to persuade readers to make purchases
.edu	educational: schools, colleges, universities	to provide students and others with information about the school, such as how to enroll
.gov	governmental: federal, state, local, tribal governments in the United States	to provide information
.org	organizational: often used by non-profit organizations	to promote the interests of the organization
.net	various, but often used by Internet-related service providers	varies, but often to provide commercial Internet services
.us	United States; can be used by anyone in the United States, but is often used by state governments as the final part of the domain name. For example, notice the *state.tx.us* part of the Texas Department of Public Safety site in the URL on the previous page.	varies widely
.ca, .uk, .de, .jp, .cn	can be used by individuals and companies in the respective country: Canada, United Kingdom, Germany, Japan, China, and so on	varies widely

When you are reading online, you need to remain aware of whose domain you are in. This knowledge will help you decide how to evaluate the information you find.

Finding Information

Two main ways to find information online are by using search engines and by using databases. Even though students tend to know more about using search engines than they do about using databases, information found through databases is often preferred in college. So you should learn how to use the databases at your library.

Using Subscription Databases

A database is a collection of information designed for researchers to be able to locate and read it. For example, InfoTrac OneFile is a database that includes the full text of millions of newspaper and periodical articles. (A periodical is a magazine, newspaper, academic journal, or any publication that is published regularly—for example, a periodical could be published six times a year, every other month, every week, or at another interval.)

Some databases, such as PsycINFO in the field of psychology, provide only abstracts (summaries) of articles rather than the full text. You then have to locate the journal in which the full article is printed in order to read it. Your instructors may prefer that you find information through these databases instead of search engines since databases only collect information from sources that have been edited and are considered reliable.

Your college library probably subscribes to a number of databases that you can access through your library's Web site. You will likely need to have your student ID or library account number handy to use them. Ask your reference librarian how to find out which databases are available, and whether the library or learning center runs information sessions on how to use them. If they do, sign up. The hour or two this will take at the beginning of the semester can save you dozens of hours later.

To use a database, you type in search terms, get a list of "hits," which are the names of and links to articles on a topic, and then figure out which ones are useful for your purpose. Following is a sample result from a keyword search on Expanded Academic ASAP. Every database may display its results somewhat differently, but this will give you an idea of the types of information you will read.

Sample Result from an Academic Search Premier Search: *Causes Iraq War*

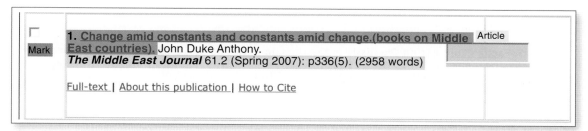

Link to the article, with author's name following.

Name of the journal where the article is published, with volume number, issue number, and publication date. Page number on which the article begins. In parentheses, the number of pages. In the second parentheses, the number of words.

You can scan an entire list of results and mark the ones you want to look at later.

Type of published work. This could be an article, an abstract (a summary of an article), the cover story of a magazine, a biography, and so on.

Interaction 12-3. Reading a Subscription Database's Search Results Page

Suppose you are taking a business management course and become interested in how you might develop your creativity as a manager. So you do a keyword search on Academic Search ASAP using the search phrase *manager's creativity*. Read this excerpt from the results list and then answer the questions that follow.

Academic Journals	Magazines	Reference	News	Multimedia	

	Expand/Limit	Sort by: Publication Date ▼

Mark All | ◄ Previous **Results** 1 **- 20 of 20** GO Next ►

☐ Mark

3. The hypercompetitive global marketplace: the importance of intuition and creativity in expatriate managers.(human resource management research). Michael Harvey and Milorad M. Novicevic.
Journal of World Business 37.2 (Summer 2002): p127(12). (8804 words)

Citation | About this publication | How to Cite

Article

☐ Mark

4. Management Mistakes Squelch Employee Innovation.(Brief Article). Kate Sweetman.
MIT Sloan Management Review 42.4 (Summer 2001): p9. (541 words)

Full-text | 2 PDF pages | About this publication | How to Cite

Brief Article

☐ Mark

5. Factors Influencing Creativity in the Domain of Managerial Decision Making. Cameron M. Ford and Dennis A. Gioia.
Journal of Management 26.4 (July-August 2000): p705. (11940 words)

Full-text with graphics | 28 PDF pages | About this publication | How to Cite

Article

☐ Mark

6. Creativity and Innovation for Managers.(Review).
The Futurist 34.1 (Jan 2000): p59. (50 words)

Full-text with graphics | 1 PDF page | About this publication | How to Cite

Book Review

□ Mark	**11. 'Wish Program' for major innovations. (Exxon Chemical Co.'s management program).** Leonard Berkowitz. *Research-Technology Management* v39.n3 (May-June 1996): pp11(3). Abstract | About this publication | How to Cite	Article
□ Mark	**14. Tapping creativity in others.** Anthony J. DeLellis. *Training & Development* v45.n11 (Nov 1991): pp48(5). (2576 words) Full-text | 5 PDF pages | About this publication | How to Cite	Article
□ Mark	**17. Coaching trainers on winning writing skills. (includes list of information sources).** Stephen D. Gladis. *Training & Development* v45.n6 (June 1991): pp31(3). (1140 words) Full-text | 3 PDF pages | About this publication | How to Cite	Article
□ Mark	**18. Innovations: Creativity Techniques for Hospitality Managers.** Mary L. Tanke. *Cornell Hotel & Restaurant Administration Quarterly* v31.n4 (Feb 1991): pp119(1). Citation | About this publication | How to Cite	Book Review
□ Mark	**20. Imagination to go; can you be taught creativity? Many managers are investing company money to find out.** Berkeley Rice. *Psychology Today* v18.(May 1984): pp48(8). Citation | About this publication | How to Cite	Article

Comprehension Questions

1. What kinds of publications does this results page list? _____

2. How are the results sorted? _____

3. Which articles seem to be about employees' creativity rather than managers'? _____

4. Which articles seem to be about managers' creativity in a specific type of business?

_____

5. Suppose you are not interested in those particular types of businesses. Which articles seem to respond most directly to your search question? List the number of each result. _____

Critical Thinking Questions

6. Which journals may not deal directly with business issues? _____

_____

7. Which are the three most current sources listed? _____

8. What synonym for "creativity" do these sources suggest you may want to use in further searches on this topic? _____

9. Of the three results that respond directly to the search question, which one could you read right now that would give you the most directly relevant, comprehensive, and up-to-date information? Explain your answer. _____

_____

_____

_____

10. Which result refers to a source that you could go to for more detailed information? Explain your answer. _____

As you have just seen, searching through the results list is a process of elimination. You figure out which entries are not likely to be useful by reading each "hit" for clues that you can use to decide not to refer to that source.

Subscription database services will lead you to journal articles, magazine and newspaper articles, reference works, and even multimedia resources. For the most part, when you are reading these sources you will be able to use the same strategies as if you were reading the article in a magazine or newspaper that you were physically holding in your hands.

Using Search Engines

A search engine is a software program designed to find and display the results of Web searches. Several of the most popular search engines are these:

Google   **www.google.com**

Yahoo!   **www.yahoo.com**

Ask	**www.ask.com**
MSN	**www.msn.com**
Dogpile	**www.dogpile.com**

You can type search terms into a search engine, get a list of hits, and figure out which ones are useful for your purpose.

A typical problem in searching is to get so many hits you couldn't possibly examine them all. So you should narrow your topic as much as you can. Suppose you have read in your health textbook that writing in a journal helps control stress. You'd like to find out if there are other benefits to writing in a journal. If you search for the word *journal* alone, you will get all kinds of hits that have nothing to do with your specific question, including many publications that have the word *journal* in them, such as **E-journals.org**. However, if you use all three words—*benefits journal writing*—you'll still get a large number of hits, but most of them will include information directly related to your question.

Here is a sample result from a Google search using the search phrase *immigration debate,* annotated to show the different parts you should notice as you try to determine which Web sites to eliminate and which to visit.

Sample Result from a Google Search: *Immigration debate*

Conservatives Split in **Debate** on Curbing Illegal **Immigration ...**
The **immigration debate** pits one core GOP constituency (law-and-order conservatives) against another (business interests that rely on immigrant labor). ...
www.washingtonpost.com/wp-dyn/articles/A64179-2005Mar24.html - Similar pages

---

The name of the specific Web page or article is shown. In this case, you can see that the page will talk about the different viewpoints conservatives have on how best to stop illegal immigration.

The boldfaced terms show how your search terms are used on the Web page. The content of this partial sentence tells you that the two conservative groups who disagree over what to do are the "law-and-order conservative" and "business interests that rely on immigrant labor."

The domain is a newspaper, *The Washington Post.* The article is from the online version of the newspaper. In the parts of the URL that follow the domain name, notice that you can tell the date of this article: March 24, 2005.

Depending on your particular purpose, this result may or may not be useful—but you can tell a lot about a Web page before you ever visit it if you read the entry carefully, and thus, you can save yourself some time and effort when conducting research online.

Interaction 12-4. Reading a Search Engine's Results Page

Suppose for a political science course you want to investigate the causes of the Iraq War. You use the search phrase *causes Iraq War* on Google. Read the following excerpt from the first page of results, noticing whatever you can about the domains and reading the brief description given for each hit for further clues about the Web site. Then answer the questions that follow.

Our **War** Against **Iraq**

Our **War** Against **Iraq**: **Causes** & Cure. Text of an address. by Most Rev. Dr. Robert M. Bowman, Lt. Col., USAF (retired). President, Institute for Space and ...
www.rmbowman.com/isss/**iraq**sp.htm - 13k - Cached - Similar pages

To Hunt Down the **Causes** of the **Iraq War** is Folly. Consider ...

To Hunt Down the **Causes** of the **Iraq War** is Folly. Consider, Instead, US Hegemony and British Collusion and Look No Further ...
www.commondreams.org/views04/0311-04.htm - 17k - Cached - Similar pages

The History Guy: The Third Persian Gulf **War** (2003)

CAUSES OF CONFLICT:. There are several basic reasons for the second major **war** between a United States-led coalition and **Iraq**. First, there was the lingering ...
www.historyguy.com/Gulf**War**2.html - 106k - Cached - Similar pages

Amazon.com: The **Iraq War**: **Causes** And Consequences (Middle East in ...

Amazon.com: The **Iraq War**: **Causes** And Consequences (Middle East in the International System): Books: Rick Fawn,Raymond A. Hinnebusch by Rick Fawn,Raymond A. ...
www.amazon.com/**Iraq-War-Causes**-Consequences-International/dp/1588264386 - 152k - Jul 27, 2007 - Cached - Similar pages

Ray McGovern: How the 9/11 Report Soft-Pedaled Root **Causes**

The **Iraq War** and Israel. How 9/11 Report Soft-Pedaled Root **Causes**. By RAY McGOVERN Former CIA analyst. The 567-page final report released Thursday by the ...
www.counterpunch.org/mcgovern07282004.html - 78k - Cached - Similar pages

Biased media coverage **causes** misconception of **Iraq war** - Opinion

Biased media coverage **causes** misconception of **Iraq war**,
www.thebatt.com/news/2003/11/05/Opinion/Biased.Media.Coverage.**Causes**.Misconception.Of.**Iraq.War**-548880.shtml - 44k - Cached - Similar pages

---

Comprehension Questions

1. Which two organizations are represented in this list? Assume that their names are the same as their domain names. _____

2. Which .com site seems to be in use by an individual? _____
   _____

3. Which site lists books on this topic? _____

4. Which site may have an informative purpose, despite its .com domain? _____
_____

5. Which site published an article in 2003 that focused on the media coverage of the causes of the Iraq War? _____

Critical Thinking Questions

6. Which two results include words that demonstrate a distinct attitude toward figuring out the causes of the Iraq war? What are the words, and what do they mean? If necessary, look up the meanings in a dictionary.

    • First few words of result: _____

    Tone word and meaning: _____

    • First few words of result: _____

    Tone word and meaning: _____

7. Which entry includes a word that seems to imply the Iraq War is an illness? What is the word?

    First few words of entry: _____

    Word: _____

8. Which two authors seem to have held government positions in the United States? What positions did they hold?

    • _____

    • _____

9. Suppose you are looking purely for information with as little political bias as possible. Which Web site might you visit first to find your answer quickly? Why? _____
_____
_____
_____

10. Of the four Web sites whose URLs are listed on page 595, which two might you visit to find more information about causes of the Iraq War? Why these?

    • _____

    • _____

Search engines use different methods for deciding what hits you will get. When you go to use a search engine for the first time, take the time to read the Help file so that you can determine the most efficient way to search using that engine.

Once you type in a URL or click on a link and your browser opens in the corresponding Web site, you'll need to know how to navigate a Web site.

Navigating Web Sites

Sites on the World Wide Web may include text, images, audio, and video. On a Web site, you can visit the pages in any order you choose. Each page acts as a module, that is, a self-contained unit of information. These are sometimes called *nodes*. Four ways you can move around from page to page within a Web site are making selections from menus, clicking links that are embedded in text, following bread crumb trails, and taking advantage of the file structure in URLs.

Menus to Select from

A Web site normally has a home page that acts almost like the table of contents in a book. The list of contents on a Web site, however, is called a menu. Often, the home page includes a main menu to help you decide where to go first. On page 605 is an example of a home page that includes two different kinds of main menus. The menu across the top of the page includes five different types of resources the Library of Congress has— for example, Global Gateway, which includes resources in different languages about world cultures. The menu that appears on the left is directed to different groups of users, such as families, librarians, publishers, and researchers.

Links Embedded in Text

Another method of navigating Web pages is via hyperlinks placed on words in the text. If you click on text that is linked, you will jump to another Web page. Links are sometimes indicated by underlining, by text that is a different color from the rest, or both. The links on some sites change color after you visit them. Here is an example of an excerpt from a *New York Times* article online that includes links shown in blue. In *Times* articles, link color doesn't change when you have visited an embedded link.

Obesity can spread from person to person, much like a virus, researchers are reporting today. When one person gains weight, close friends tend to gain weight, too.

Their study, published in The New England Journal of Medicine, involved a detailed analysis of a large social network of 12,067 people who had been closely followed for 32 years, from 1971 to 2003.

—From Kolata, "Find Yourself Packing It On? Blame Friends," *New York Times*, July 26, 2007

Figure 12-1 Two menus on the Library of Congress home page: www.loc.gov.
The Library of Congress is the largest library in the world. To use its Web site requires making selections from menus, sub-menus, and even sub-sub-menus.

Some embedded links lead to other pages from the same Web site, and others lead off the current Web site to a different site. You can track which site you are visiting by reading the domain name in the URL in the address bar at the top of the computer screen.

Bread Crumb Trails

Some Web sites make it easy to see exactly where the page you are visiting fits within the site's structure by showing a "bread crumb trail" at the top of the page. Here is an example from the Yahoo! Directory.

Directory > Society and Culture > Issues and Causes > Employment and Workplace Issues > **Minimum Wage**

Save to My Web

The boldfaced term at the end of the trail is the current page. Yahoo! is a search engine, so this is a page of results that summarizes various sources of information on the minimum wage. Each of the other "bread crumbs" in the trail is a link that you can use to jump back to a different page. Each step backward is one level up in the file hierarchy, until you are back at the directory home page. If you were at the minimum wage page and wanted to get back to the main directory, you could click directly on *Directory* instead of backing up through each individual level of the hierarchy.

File Structure in URLs

You can examine the URL in the address bar at the top of your computer screen to get an idea of how the file (the Web page) you are visiting fits into the Web site's structure. You can also use this information to jump back to the home page. Here is an example from a community college Web site.

http://www.dcccd.edu/Current+Students/Libraries/Research+a+Topic/Databases.htm

Read the URL from right to left. The person visiting this page wants to use a database to research a topic. The library subscribes to the database, which only currently enrolled students can access. The college system is the Dallas County Community College system.

Interaction 12-5. Identifying Navigational Aids

Look at the Web page below (**Figure 12.2**). Circle all the different navigational aids offered on the page, and name each type below.

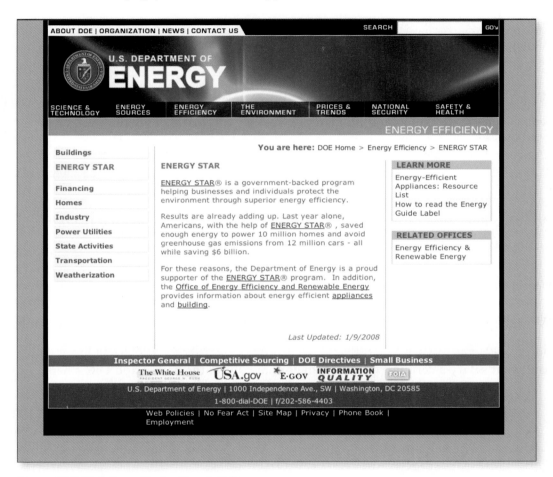

Figure 12.2 Web Page Navigational Aids

- _____
- _____
- _____
- _____

Interaction 12-6. Finding Information on a Web Site

If you have not previously used the Internet, team up with a partner who has. Using the sites mentioned, find the following information online.

1. Go to the Omega Institute Web site at **http://www.eomega.org** to find a statement of Omega's mission. Write it here. _____

   _____

2. Visit the Web site of Greenpeace USA at **http://www.greenpeace.org/usa/** to find out what issues the organization is currently working on. List them here. _____

   _____

   _____

   _____

3. Visit the Republican Party Web site at **http://www.gop.com** to find out the different actions you can take as a volunteer, and list them here. _____

   _____

   _____

4. Visit the Internet Public Library at **www.ipl.org** to find out what guides are available for help with searching for employment. Which two resources might you use to figure out what salary a certain type of job might pay? Write the names and URLs here.

   • _____

   • _____

Evaluating Web Sites

When you are reading information on a Web site, you should decide whether or not you think it is accurate. Two basic questions can help you make such decisions:

• Is the author's work credible (that is, worthy of consideration)?
• Is the information reliable (that is, worthy of trust)?

The third issue that you should always keep in mind is whose domain you are in. A domain that belongs to a chemical company may not offer entirely reliable information on toxic dumps. A domain that belongs to a conservative may not offer a fair discussion of the Green Party's ideas. You may still be able to get some use from sites that have their own agenda on an issue, but you need to realize that the information they provide will probably be biased toward their own interests.

The Author's Credibility

Materials posted to Web sites are widely different in terms of who wrote them and how credible they are. For example, if you read material online that was also published in a major newspaper such as the *Los Angeles Times,* the *Washington Post,* or the *Wall Street Journal,* you can be fairly sure that the journalists and editors at the newspaper have checked the facts and offer the best information they have available.

If, however, you are reading a page from an organization called Ranters.org and you see a passage like the following, you should beware.

> The piggish Bush spends every minute 24/7 gobling up smaller cuntries in an effort to become the first U. S. king.

This sentence demonstrates several of the elements that should cause a red flag to go up as you read.

1. **The thought is extreme and not well-supported by evidence by other sources.** One thought here is that the president wants to be the first king of the United States. The writer also states that Bush is taking over small countries. Really? In order to support such exaggerated statements, the writer would need to provide an enormous amount of evidence—perhaps a whole book's worth—and marshal the argument carefully. If the author gives just one or two brief reasons, you'd do best to ignore this source for college research.

2. **The tone is not suited to the argument.** The author uses casual or even slang words— "piggish," "24/7," and "gobbling up"—to introduce a very serious argument. The choice of words, especially the first one, undercuts the author's message. A more reasonable tone would work better to convince readers that the writer knows what he or she is talking about.

3. **The words don't follow the basic rules of usage and spelling.** Two words are spelled incorrectly: "gobbling" and "country." The author hasn't even bothered to use a basic spell check so that readers can have confidence in the writer.

Remember, too, the basic injunction to always know whose domain you are in. The very name of the Web site—**Ranters.org**—suggests that the site's sponsors are providing writers with a forum where they can sound off on their pet peeves, without expecting readers to take them too seriously.

In contrast, here is a statement from a writer who seems to have more credibility.

Skip Snow, a federal biologist in Everglades National Park, . . . has been spending ever more time studying the remains of the park's birds and animals, extracted from the stomachs of captured or road-killed Burmese pythons, the latest—and most spectacular—addition to Florida's growing list of biological interlopers.

—From Revkin, "A Moveable Beast: Asian Pythons Thrive
in Florida," *New York Times,* July 24, 2007

Some of the clues that suggest this author is credible are the following:

1. **The person being discussed is an expert in the same area that is being discussed.** Skip Snow is a biologist employed by the federal government, and the statement about Burmese pythons is directly related to his area of expertise. If, on the other hand, Snow were discussing the problems faced by runaway teenagers in Los Angeles, we would not accept the information without further proof, because that is not the field he is trained in.

2. **The tone is reasonable, and the description is detailed enough to seem realistic.** The only tone word that is used—"spectacular"—makes sense given the context: pythons from the Asian country of Burma who are now living in the Everglades, eating the native birds and animals. And while not every credible writer needs to use formal language, the words this author uses to describe the action are accurate and appropriate to the context: "extracted," "biological interlopers."

3. **The sentence is well written, usage is standard, and words are spelled correctly.** The sentence demonstrates that the writer can put together a rather complicated set of actions that occur at different times into a well-crafted sentence that is easy to follow.

Finally, the domain is that of the *New York Times,* a nationally respected newspaper, which is another reason to find the author credible.

Interaction 12-7. Evaluating an Author's Credibility

Decide whether each statement is credible, and discuss your reasoning.

1. "Family planning has far-reaching benefits for women and their families. Women who can plan the number and timing of their births enjoy improved health, experience fewer unwanted pregnancies and births, and have lower rates of induced, and often unsafe, abortion." From "Women and Societies Benefit When Childbearing Is Planned," An Issue in Brief from the Guttmacher Institute, a non-profit organization that seeks to advance sexual and reproductive health.

_____

_____

2. "I know it sounds like a pain, but the Web is, in fact, the easiest way to sell stuff. And the marketplace is showing no signs of slowing down—according to Pew Internet Research, about one in six Americans has already used the Web to sell things. A good place to try is i-soldit.com, the site for eBay drop-off stores." From Carmen Wong Ulrich, the author of *Generation Debt: Take Control of Your Money,* writing on **Latina.com.**

_____

_____

_____

3. "Question: Why is abortion sacrosanct to the left? Why have Democrats chosen this as their hill to die on? Why is evolution so important to liberals?

"Answer: Because they basically want to depopulate the world of human beings, hence their love of abortion and their commitment to a belief system that does not distinguish men from lower beasts." From an interview with Ann Coulter, printed August 2, 2006, in her column titled "What I Did on My Summer Vacation," at **Townhall.com.** whose motto is, "Where your opinion counts." Coulter is a conservative political commentator who has written several books, among them *Godless: The Church of Liberalism.*

_____

_____

_____

The Reliability of Information

There is no fast and easy way to tell if a piece of information you read on a Web site is reliable. A few points to consider have already been mentioned:

- If you find the information through a database to which your library subscribes, that source is considered to be generally reliable. The editor of the journal or other periodical has checked the material, for instance. However, this doesn't mean that every single piece of information is accurate.
- If the author seems credible (for example, if the author is an expert in the field), the information will naturally seem more reliable, although that doesn't mean every single piece of information is necessarily accurate.
- If the organization that sponsors a Web site has a financial stake in the information it is providing, the information is quite likely to be biased in the organization's favor.

If you really need to know whether a specific piece of information is reliable—say, because you are writing a research paper for a college course—the best way is to check the information against the information given in other sources—particularly reliable ones, like encyclopedias, government Web sites, and academic journals.

Suppose you read the following in an article titled "Giving Hope, Opportunity" in the online edition of the student newspaper *Viewpoints*, published at Riverside Community College in California:

> The CalWORKs Program is for students who have minor children, work at least 20 hours per week, and attend school.
>
> They can receive support services that include resume assistance, job search, priority registration, case management, counseling, and child care workshops.
>
> CalWORKs is only available to those receiving Temporary Assistance for Needy Families, or TANF.
>
> —From Rollins, "Giving Hope, Opportunity," May 24, 2007

Let's say you need to find out whether the description of eligibility for the CalWORKs Program is accurate. The most direct route to this information is to find materials published online by the program itself. When we did a keyword search for *calworks* we immediately found the site that includes the entire handbook for the program, including a section called "Eligibility Requirements." We were able to confirm many of the details in the article, although not the twenty-hour-per-week work requirement. We visited the TANF Web site to see if the twenty hour requirement came from that program, found a Fact Sheet on TANF Work Activities, and were able to confirm that that fact was also correct. Since these two sources were published by the agencies in charge of the programs in question, we can consider these facts in the article reliable.

How do you determine who is an authority on a topic to check a fact for reliability?

- Is there a relevant government agency? If you aren't sure, check **www.fedstats.gov/agencies.**
- Is there a professor at your college or a nearby college who could give you the name of an authoritative Web site or print source? Check to see if there's a department at your school that seems relevant.
- Check with a reference librarian at your campus library.

Interaction 12-8. Evaluating the Reliability of Information

Work with a partner to decide how you could check the following information. Then go ahead and perform the check. What did you find? Is the information reliable?

> Additionally, drinks are often a significant source of nutritionally empty calories. For example, a large cola (32 ounces) has 310 calories.
>
> —from HelpGuide.org.

1. Who (person, organization, government agency) might be an authority in this area?

   _____

   _____

2. How would you search for the calorie information? _____

   _____

   _____

3. Sites you checked (or phone calls you made): _____

   _____

   _____

   _____

   _____

   _____

   _____

4. Was the information accurate? _____

   _____

Chapter Summary Activity

This chapter has discussed why people read online, how to read search results, and how to find and evaluate material you read online. Construct a Reading Guide below by completing each idea on the left with information from the chapter on the right.

Reading Guide to Reading Online

Complete this idea	with information from the chapter.
The main reason for going online in college is to	1. _____
An Internet address is called the	2. _____
Aside from the http:// part of the Internet address, the rest of the address is the	3. _____

What do each of the following domain extensions mean, briefly?	4. .com: _____ 5. .edu: _____ 6. .org: _____ 7. .gov: _____
Of those four different domains, which two are most likely to be objective?	8. _____ 9. _____
Which two have mostly persuasive purposes?	10. _____ 11. _____
Two different ways to find information online, for example, for research projects, are via	12. _____ 13. _____
Deciding which results to visit is a matter of reading the list of hits to figure out	14. _____
Four navigational aids that you can use to find your way around a Web site are	15. _____ 16. _____ 17. _____ 18. _____
To decide whether to trust the information you find on a Web site, take into account three considerations:	19. _____ 20. _____ 21. _____
Examine the text for three clues to decide whether the author seems worth considering:	22. _____ 23. _____ 24. _____
The main strategy for checking a fact to find out if it seems trustworthy is to	25. _____

Test Taking Tips
How to Take Tests Online

Many colleges and universities have students take reading tests online. If yours is one of them, read the following tips to make sure you do as well as you can on the exam.

● **Before the Test**

✔ Know the access dates and times. They are often flexible, but make sure you do not miss the cut-off date. Instructors are not inclined to allow make-ups when they have usually given ample time to take the test.

✔ Find out as much as you can about the testing format and structure of the test from your instructor before you take the test.

✔ Know the amount of time the instructor has given to take the test. Give yourself enough time, so you are not putting yourself in a situation where you have to rush and increase your chances of making simple mistakes.

✔ Some online sites have a time limit. For example, Blackboard, as used on the Dallas County Community College District campuses, will time you out after three hours. So make sure you log out and log back in just before you start a test so you do not get logged out in the middle of a test.

● **During the Test**

✔ Take the test in a quiet environment so you are not distracted. Turn cell phones, TV, music, and conversations off!

✔ If you have to take the test in a testing center or lab, then wear earplugs. Someone will always be in the room with you making annoying noises.

✔ As with all tests, pay attention to the directions. Read them carefully.

✔ Know whether you will be able to go back and examine an earlier question or if you can only see it before you submit your answer.

✔ Do not close the window of the test before you have completed it for any reason. This will end your test, which is bad, especially since you weren't done.

✔ Double-check your answer choice to ensure you clicked the answer choice you intended.

✔ If you need glasses for computer work, make sure you wear them!

● **After the Test**

✔ If you are taking the test in an online course, e-mail your instructor immediately if something goes wrong. Be specific in your explanation of the problem.

Reading 12-1 . . . . Web Article

● Pre-Reading the Selection

The reading that follows, "Google Zooms In Too Close for Some," is from the online version of the *New York Times*.

Guessing the Purpose

Based on the title, what do you suppose is the general purpose of this article? _____

_____

Surveying the Reading

Survey the reading. In one sentence, summarize the main idea.

_____

_____

_____

Predicting the Content

Predict three things this selection will discuss.

- _____
- _____
- _____

Activating Your Knowledge

How private should your residence address be? What information about you should be available to total strangers? Write a few sentences that include your reasons for answering the way you did.

_____

_____

_____

Common Knowledge

blog (*paragraph 4*) Short name for "Weblog," a Web site where entries are written in chronological (time) order and then viewed in the opposite order, so that readers first see the most recent entry

domestic violence (*paragraph 6*) Violence committed in the home, typically by men toward their wives or girlfriends

First Amendment rights (*paragraph 10*) Part of the Bill of Rights, they establish the right to exercise one's religion, the freedom of the press, the freedom of speech, and the right to assemble peaceably

Reading with Pen in Hand

Now read the selection. As you read, mark any ideas that seem important, and respond to the questions and vocabulary items in the margin. Monitor your comprehension by putting a ✔ next to a paragraph when you understand most of it. Place an ✘ next to a paragraph when you don't understand most of it.

Visit **www.cengage.com/devenglish/doleconnect** and select Chapter 12 to hear vocabulary words from this selection and view a video about this topic.

Google Zooms In Too Close for Some

Miguel Helft

◆ *Reading Journal*

June 1, 2007; Oakland, Calif., May 31—

1   For Mary Kalin-Casey, it was never about her cat.

2   Ms. Kalin-Casey, who manages an apartment building here with her husband, John Casey, was a bit shaken when she tried a new feature in Google's map service called Street View. She typed in her address and the screen showed a street-level view of her building. As she zoomed in, she could see Monty, her cat, sitting on a perch in the living room window of her second-floor apartment.

◆ How did Ms. Kalin-Casey find the image of her cat online?

3   "The issue that I have ultimately is about where you draw the line between taking public photos and zooming in on people's lives," Ms. Kalin-Casey said in an interview Thursday on the front steps of the building. "The next step might be seeing books on my shelf. If the government was doing this, people would be outraged." Her husband quickly added, "It's like peeping."

◆ Why does Ms. Kalin-Casey mention the government?

4   Ms. Kalin-Casey first shared her concerns about the service in an e-mail message to the **blog** Boing Boing on Wednesday. Since then, the Web has been buzzing about the privacy implications of Street View—with varying degrees of seriousness. Several sites have been asking users to submit interesting images captured by the Google service, which offers panoramic views of miles of streets around San Francisco, New York, Las Vegas, Miami, and Denver. On a *Wired* magazine blog, for instance, readers can vote on the "Best Urban Images" that others find in Street View. On Thursday afternoon, a picture of two young women sunbathing in their bikinis on the Stanford campus in Palo Alto, Calif., ranked near the top. Another showed a man scaling the front gate of an apartment building in San Francisco. The caption read, "Is he breaking in or has he just locked himself out?"

What can you figure out from the context about a **blog**?

◆ How have others online responded to the privacy concern?

implications The verb related to this noun is *imply*. What does the noun mean?

◆ What comparison did Google make to respond to the concern about privacy?

◆ What example is given to show how Google worked with organizations as they developed Street View?

◆ Do people have a right not to be photographed when they're out in public?

principal You know what this word means in a school, so what would it mean in this context?

fodder Related to the word *food*, *fodder* can be used as a more general term. Based on that information and the examples given in this paragraph, define *fodder*.

◆ What response to the new service does this paragraph discuss?

5   Google said in a statement that it takes privacy seriously and considered the privacy implications of its service before it was introduced on Tuesday. "Street View only features imagery taken on public property," the company said. "This imagery is no different from what any person can readily capture or see walking down the street."

6   Google said that it had consulted with public service organizations and considered their feedback in developing the service, which allows users to request that a photo be removed for privacy reasons. A Google spokeswoman said the company had received few such requests. For instance, Google worked with the Safety Net Project at the National Network to End Domestic Violence, which represents shelters for victims of domestic violence nationwide, to remove pictures of those shelters. "They reached out in advance to us so we could reach out to our network," said Cindy Southworth, founder and director of the organization.

7   Not everyone believes the service raises serious privacy concerns. "You don't have a right to 'privacy' over what can be seen while driving the speed limit past your house," wrote a Boing Boing reader, identified as Rich Gibson, in response to Ms. Kalin-Casey's complaint. Others dismissed her as a crazy cat lady. Edward A. Jurkevics, a principal at Chesapeake Analytics, a consulting firm specializing in mapping and imagery, said that courts have consistently ruled that people in public spaces can be photographed. "In terms of privacy, I doubt if there is much of a problem," Mr. Jurkevics said.

8   Still, the issues raised by the service, thorny or merely funny, were perfect blog fodder. The hunt was on for quirky or potentially embarrassing images that could be found by wandering the virtual streets of the service. There was the picture of a clearly identifiable man standing in front of an establishment offering lap dances and other entertainment in San Francisco. The site LaudonTech.com showed an image of a man entering a pornographic bookstore in Oakland, but his face was not visible. Others pointed to pictures of cars whose license plates were clearly readable. One pointed to images captured inside the Brooklyn Battery Tunnel, a controversial location for photography in this high-security era. On Lombard Street in San Francisco, various tourists who had come to photograph the famously curvy street were photographed themselves.

9   Google said that the images had been captured by vehicles equipped with special cameras. The company took some of the pho-

tographs itself and purchased others from Immersive Media, a data provider.

10   "I think that this product illustrates a tension between our First Amendment right to document public spaces around us, and the privacy interests people have as they go about their day," said Kevin Bankston, a staff lawyer at the Electronic Frontier Foundation, a digital rights group. Mr. Bankston said Google could have avoided privacy concerns by blurring people's faces.

◆ What does Kevin Bankston suggest is one solution to the privacy issue?

11   Back at her apartment, Ms. Kalin-Casey acknowledged that plenty of information about her—that she manages an apartment complex, that she was an editor at the film site Reel.com—is already easily accessible through Google and other search engines. "People's jobs are pretty public," she said. "But that doesn't mean they want a shot of their sofa on Google." She has asked Google to remove the image of her building, which was still online as of Thursday evening.

acknowledged Thinking about Kalin-Casey's overall opinion and the information in this sentence, what synonym would have the same meaning as *acknowledged* here?

◆ Why does the writer begin and end the article by talking about the cat?

12   When a reporter first arrived to interview her, Monty the cat was visible in the window.

● Comprehension Questions

Write the letter of the answer on the line. Then explain your thinking.

Main Idea

_____   1. Which statement best describes the main idea of this passage?

a. Despite privacy concerns raised by Mary Kalin-Casey and others, Google's Street View is no more intrusive than a pedestrian with a camera.

b. Bloggers couldn't stop talking about the images they saw online from Street View, Google's new map service.

c. The right to take pictures in public is guaranteed by the First Amendment, and therefore Google's Street View is perfectly legal.

d. Despite privacy concerns raised by Mary Kalin-Casey and others, Google's Street View is no more intrusive than a pedestrian with a camera, and it enjoys the same legal rights.

WHY? What information in the selection leads you to give that answer? _____

_____ 2. What is the main idea of paragraph 7?

    a. Not everyone believes the service raises serious privacy concerns.

    b. "You don't have a right to 'privacy' over what can be seen while driving the speed limit past your house."

    c. Others dismissed her as a crazy cat lady.

    d. Edward A. Jurkevics, a principal at Chesapeake Analytics, a consulting firm specializing in mapping and imagery, said that courts have consistently ruled that people in public spaces can be photographed.

WHY? What information in the selection leads you to give that answer? _____

_____

_____

Supporting Details

_____ 3. Which sentence from paragraph 4 is a major supporting detail?

    a. On a _Wired_ magazine blog, for instance, readers can vote on the "Best Urban Images" that others find in Street View.

    b. On Thursday afternoon, a picture of two young women sunbathing in their bikinis on the Stanford campus in Palo Alto, Calif., ranked near the top.

    c. Another showed a man scaling the front gate of an apartment building in San Francisco.

    d. The caption read, "Is he breaking in or has he just locked himself out?"

WHY? What information in the selection leads you to give that answer? _____

_____

_____ 4. The main idea of paragraph 8 is in the second sentence. How many major supporting details for it are in the paragraph?

    a. two

    b. three

    c. four

    d. five

WHY? What information in the selection leads you to give that answer? _____

_____

_____

Relationships

_____ 5. In paragraph 11, what relationship exists between the two parts of the quotation?

a. effect

b. process

c. contrast

d. example

WHY? What information in the selection leads you to give that answer? _____

_____

_____ 6. What pattern of organization provides structure for the supporting details in paragraph 2?

a. cause and effect

b. comparison

c. narration (time order)

d. process

WHY? What information in the selection leads you to give that answer? _____

_____

Author's Purpose

_____ 7. What is the author's general purpose in this passage?

a. to entertain readers

b. to inform readers

c. to persuade readers

d. to move readers to action

WHY? What information in the selection leads you to give that answer? _____

_____

_____

____ 8. Why did the writer include the quotations from Jurkevics in paragraph 7 and Bankston in paragraph 10?

    a. to give at least two different sides to the story

    b. to support the information with expert opinion

    c. to prove Rich Gibson is wrong

    d. to convince readers that Google should have done more to protect people's privacy

WHY? What information in the selection leads you to give that answer? _____

_____

_____

_____

Fact, Opinion, and Inference

____ 9. Read the statement and choose the word that best describes it:
A Google spokesperson said the company had received few . . . requests [for photos to be removed from Street View for privacy reasons].

    a. fact

    b. opinion

    c. expert opinion

    d. inference

WHY? What leads you to give that answer? _____

_____

____ 10. Choose the most logical inference about the sample sentence in question 9, in the context of the article overall.

    a. A lot of Google's e-mail has been going astray, and their phone systems have been down for more than a week.

    b. On Street View, it is easy to find the form on which to request that a photo be removed.

    c. Few people have privacy concerns about what they have seen on Street View.

    d. Few people use Street View.

WHY? What leads you to give that answer? _____

_____

● Critical Thinking Questions

CRITICAL THINKING LEVEL 1 REMEMBER

Describe Street View, giving as much information about *who, what, why, when,* and *how* as possible. _____

_____

_____

CRITICAL THINKING LEVEL 2 UNDERSTAND

Summarize the positions the following people take on the question of whether Street View interferes with people's privacy by placing their names on the continuum: Mary Kalin-Casey, Rich Gibson, Edward A. Jurkevics, Kevin Bankston. Put each person's name beneath the line under their position.

Continuum of Opinion about Street View

It invades
people's privacy.

The needs for
privacy and
public rights
need to be
balanced.

It does not
invade people's
privacy.

_____   _____   _____

                                                   _____

CRITICAL THINKING LEVEL 3 APPLY

Interview a classmate using the following questions, and take notes on his or her responses. Then switch roles and be interviewed.

Would you feel that your privacy had been invaded if you saw on Street View . . .

- the front of your home? Why or why not?

- the inside of your living room? Why or why not?

- the inside of your bedroom? Why or why not?

Compare the responses you got with the rest of the class or your group.

CRITICAL THINKING LEVEL 4 ANALYZE

Explain how the examples given in paragraph 8 can be used to support the idea that Street View does, indeed, interfere unjustly with people's privacy.

_____

_____

_____

_____

_____

_____

_____

_____

_____

CRITICAL THINKING LEVEL 5 EVALUATE

Kalin-Casey says that people would be outraged if government officials spied on their homes the way Google's Street View does. *Consider the following rule* of law, as stated on **Nolo.com**: "Police officers do not need a warrant to search and seize contraband or evidence that is 'in plain view' if the officer has a right to be where the evidence or contraband is first spotted." Suppose that a police officer uses Street View and, using the zoom function, is able to spot a marijuana plant growing in the corner of someone's bedroom. Should the officer be required to get a warrant to search the home, or not? Argue for your position in a few sentences on a separate piece of paper. If you want, you can visit **Nolo.com**, a legal information Web site, to gather more information about the laws regarding search warrants.

CRITICAL THINKING LEVEL 6 CREATE

Working with a small group, *create* a set of rules that Google should follow to ensure that they maintain their right to provide photographs of public places and that also protects individuals from having their privacy invaded unnecessarily or unfairly. For each rule, discuss why it is needed and how it will preserve both sets of rights.

● Vocabulary in Context

The following words were used in "Google Zooms In Too Close for Some." Fill in the blank in each sentence with the word that best completes it meaning.

blog	implications	principal	fodder	acknowledged

1. The Recording Industry Association of America (RIAA) has sued individuals around the country for illegally sharing copyright-protected music files, saying their _____ aim is simply to protect the copyrights of the companies they represent.

2. One student at Cornell University _____ that she had been caught downloading 359 music files; many of the people whom the RIAA sued in 2003 had shared a thousand music files each.

3. The _____ Boing Boing included a link to the August 23, 2007, story in the *Cornell Daily Sun,* the campus newspaper, which reported that the anonymous sophomore and another Cornell student had made lump-sum payments to RIAA to avoid going to court over the allegations.

4. In December 2003, a court in Washington, DC, had ruled that the method RIAA was using to track down file sharers was itself illegal, even though they acknowledged that the file sharing has negative _____ for the music publishing business.

5. The story of Tanya Andersen, a person against whom RIAA brought a lawsuit but then later dropped, is _____ for the arguments people make online about how RIAA is simply trying to squeeze money out of as many people as they can before they become obsolete.

Reading 12-2 . . . . **Web Article**

● Pre-Reading the Selection

Robert Harris is a writer and educator with more than twenty-five years of teaching experience at the college level. The next selection is an excerpt from an online paper he has written explaining some good strategies for evaluating Internet research sources.

Guessing the Purpose

Judging from the title of this article (p. 627), what do you suppose is the purpose for writing it? _____

Surveying the Reading

Survey the title of the selection and the first sentence of each paragraph. What is the general topic of the reading selection?

_____

_____

Predicting the Content

Predict three things this selection will discuss.

- _____
- _____
- _____

Activating Your Knowledge

What do you already know about analyzing information for validity and reliability?

- _____
- _____
- _____

Common Knowledge

supermarket tabloid (*paragraph 1*) A magazine published weekly, often sold in the check-out aisle of grocery stores. Tabloids tend to focus on gossip about celebrities or political and religious figures, often with doubtful "facts." Some tabloids have been known to make up a story and sensationalize it to sell more copies. Some of the more popular tabloids in America are *The National Enquirer, The Sun,* and *Star.*

Reading with Pen in Hand

Now read the selection. As you read, mark any ideas that seem important, and respond to the questions and vocabulary items in the margin. Monitor your comprehension by putting a ✔ next to a paragraph when you understand most of it. Place an ✘ next to a paragraph when you don't understand most of it.

Evaluating Internet Research Sources

Robert Harris

"The central work of life is interpretation."—Proverb

◆ *Reading Journal*

Introduction: The Diversity of Information

Information Is a Commodity Available in Many Flavors

1   Think about the magazine section in your local grocery store. If you reach out with your eyes closed and grab the first magazine you touch, you are about as likely to get a supermarket tabloid as you are a respected journal (actually more likely, since many respected journals don't fare well in grocery stores). Now imagine that your grocer is so accommodating that he lets anyone in town print up a magazine and put it in the magazine section. Now if you reach out blindly, you might get the *Elvis Lives with Aliens Gazette* just as easily as *Atlantic Monthly* or *Time*.

◆ What point does the author make?

accommodating What is the grocer willing to do?

2   Welcome to the Internet. As I hope my analogy makes clear, there is an extremely wide variety of material on the Internet, ranging in its accuracy, reliability, and value. Unlike most traditional information media (books, magazines, organizational documents), no one has to approve the content before it is made public. It's your job as a searcher, then, to evaluate what you locate, in order to determine whether it suits your needs.

◆Why does one need to be cautious about information from the Internet?

Information Exists on a **Continuum** of Reliability and Quality

3   Information is everywhere on the Internet, existing in large quantities and continuously being created and revised. This information exists in a large variety of kinds (facts, opinions, stories, interpretations, statistics) and is created for many purposes (to inform, to persuade, to sell, to present a viewpoint, and to create or change an attitude or belief). For each of these various kinds and purposes, information exists on many levels of quality or reliability. It ranges from very good to very bad and includes every shade in between.

continuum This word is found in the title but explained in the paragraph. Look especially at the last sentence.

◆In what ways does the information on the Internet vary?

Getting Started: Screening Information

Pre-evaluation

◆What is the first stage of evaluating your sources?

4   The first stage of evaluating your sources takes place before you do any searching. Take a minute to ask yourself what exactly you are looking for. Do you want facts, opinions (authoritative or just anyone's), reasoned arguments, statistics, narratives, eyewitness reports, descriptions? Is the purpose of your research to get new ideas, to find either factual or reasoned support for a position, to survey opinion, or something else? Once you decide on this, you will be able to **screen** sources much more quickly by testing them against your research goal. If, for example, you are writing a research paper, and if you are looking for both facts and well-argued opinions to support or challenge a position, you will know which sources can be quickly passed by and which deserve a second look, simply by asking whether each source appears to offer facts and well-argued opinions, or just unsupported claims.

screen Use the definition the sentence gives.

Select Sources Likely to be Reliable

proficient Notice that the author says that being *proficient* requires experience. What does *proficient* mean?

◆What question are you supposed to ask yourself when looking for reliable information?

5   Becoming **proficient** at selecting sources will require experience, of course, but even a beginning researcher can take a few minutes to ask, "What source or what kind of source would be the most credible for providing information in this particular case?" Which sources are likely to be fair, objective, lacking hidden motives, showing quality control? It is important to keep these considerations in mind, so that you will not simply take the opinion of the first source or two you can locate. By thinking about these issues while searching, you will be able to identify suspicious or questionable sources more readily. With so many sources to choose from in a typical search, there is no reason to settle for unreliable material.

Source Selection Tip

6   Try to select sources that offer as much of the following information as possible:

1. author's name
2. author's title or position
3. author's organizational affiliation
4. date of page creation or version
5. author's contact information
6. some of the indicators of information quality (listed on next page)

Evaluating Information: The Tests of Information Quality

Reliable Information Is Power

7   You may have heard that "knowledge is power," or that information, the raw material of knowledge, is power. But the truth is that only some information is power: reliable information. Information serves as the basis for beliefs, decisions, choices, and understanding our world. If we make a decision based on wrong or unreliable information, we do not have power—we have defeat. If we eat something harmful that we believe to be safe, we can become ill; if we avoid something good that we believe to be harmful, we have needlessly restricted the enjoyment of our lives. The same thing applies to every decision to travel, purchase, or act, and every attempt to understand.

◆What is the point of paragraph 7?

Source Evaluation Is an Art

8   Source evaluation—the determination of information quality—is something of an art. That is, there is no single perfect indicator of reliability, truthfulness, or value. Instead, you must make an inference from a collection of clues or indicators, based on the use you plan to make of your source. If, for example, what you need is a reasoned argument, then a source with a clear, well-argued position can stand on its own, without the need for a prestigious author to support it. On the other hand, if you need a judgment to support (or rebut) some position, then that judgment will be strengthened if it comes from a respected source. If you want reliable facts, then using facts from a source that meets certain criteria of quality will help assure the probability that those facts are indeed reliable.

indicator The author is talking about evaluating sources for quality. Use the first three sentences to help you.

◆What point does the author make about source evaluation?

The CARS Checklist

9   The CARS Checklist (credibility, accuracy, reasonableness, support) is designed for ease of learning and use. Few sources will meet every criterion in the list, and even those that do may not possess the highest level of quality possible. But if you learn to use the criteria in this list, you will be much more likely to separate the high quality information from the poor quality information.

◆What does CARS stand for?

Summary of The CARS Checklist for Research Source Evaluation

Credibility	trustworthy source, author's credentials, evidence of quality control, known or respected authority, organizational support. Goal: an authoritative source, a source that supplies some good evidence that allows you to trust it
Accuracy	up-to-date, factual, detailed, exact, comprehensive, audience and purpose reflect intentions of completeness and accuracy. Goal: a source that is correct today (not yesterday), a source that gives the whole truth
Reasonableness	fair, balanced, objective, reasoned, no conflict of interest, absence of fallacies or slanted tone. Goal: a source that engages the subject thoughtfully and reasonably, concerned with the truth
Support	listed sources, contact information, available corroboration, claims supported, documentation supplied. Goal: a source that provides convincing evidence for the claims made, a source you can triangulate (find at least two other sources that support it)

● Comprehension Questions

Write the letter of the answer on the line. Then explain your thinking.

Main Idea

_____ 1. Which of the following is the topic sentence of paragraph 3?

a. Information is everywhere on the Internet, existing in large quantities and continuously being created and revised.

b. This information exists in a large variety of kinds (facts, opinions, stories, interpretations, statistics) and is created for many purposes (to inform, to persuade, to sell, to present a viewpoint, and to create or change an attitude or belief).

c. For each of these various kinds and purposes, information exists on many levels of quality or reliability.

d. It ranges from very good to very bad and includes every shade in between.

WHY? What information in the selection leads you to give that answer? _____

_____

_____

____   2. Which of the following is the topic sentence of paragraph 7?

a. You may have heard that "knowledge is power," or that information, the raw material of knowledge, is power.

b. But the truth is that only some information is power: reliable information.

c. Information serves as the basis for beliefs, decisions, choices, and understanding our world.

d. If we make a decision based on wrong or unreliable information, we do not have power—we have defeat.

WHY? What information in the selection leads you to give that answer? _____

_____

Supporting Details

____   3. According to the passage, which of the following is the first thing one should do when evaluating information?

a. Make sure you know what you are looking for.

b. Use the CARS list.

c. Avoid magazines in supermarkets.

d. Go to your campus library.

WHY? What information in the selection leads you to give that answer? _____

_____

_____

____   4. Based on the reading selection, which of the following is not part of the CARS list?

a. credibility

b. accuracy

c. reasonableness

d. source

WHY? What information in the selection leads you to give that answer? _____

_____

Author's Purpose

_____ 5. What is the purpose of the passage?

   a. to persuade readers to avoid Internet research until they become more proficient at it

   b. to inform the reader of some effective Internet research strategies

   c. to entertain with anecdotal analogies of the problems with finding good Internet sources

   d. to inform the reader that the Internet is increasing in popularity as an academic research tool

WHY? What information in the selection leads you to give that answer? _____

_____

_____ 6. Why does the author open with an analogy of supermarket tabloids?

   a. To illustrate the effective monitoring of Internet sources

   b. To show how many authors and managers are accommodating to their readers and customers

   c. To demonstrate the need to evaluate Internet sources.

   d. To exemplify how supermarkets do not offer quality reading in their magazine aisles.

WHY? What information in the selection leads you to give that answer? _____

_____

_____

Relationships

_____ 7. What is the pattern of organization of the following sentences?
   That is, there is no single perfect indicator of reliability, truthfulness, or value. Instead, you must make an inference from a collection of clues or indicators, based on the use you plan to make of your source.

   a. comparison and/or contrast

   b. cause-and-effect

   c. time order

   d. process

WHY? What leads you to give that answer? _____

_____

____ 8. What organizational pattern do you find in paragraph 4?
  a. cause-and-effect
  b. classification
  c. process
  d. time order

WHY? What information in the selection leads you to give that answer? _____

_____

Fact, Opinion, and Inference

____ 9. Which of the following statements is an opinion?
  a. If you want reliable facts, then using facts from a source that meets certain criteria of quality will help assure the probability that those facts are indeed reliable.
  b. As I hope my analogy makes clear, there is an extremely wide variety of material on the Internet, ranging in its accuracy, reliability, and value.
  c. If we eat something harmful that we believe to be safe, we can become ill.
  d. Source evaluation—the determination of information quality—is something of an art.

WHY? What leads you to give that answer? _____

_____

____ 10. With which of the following inferences would the author be likely to agree?
  a. Learning to evaluate Internet sources can be fun and easy.
  b. It is the responsibility of the Internet content providers to ensure that their information is accurate.
  c. Elvis is still alive and well as proven by information found in reliable sources.
  d. Do not jump to a conclusion or come to a decision too quickly.

WHY? What information in the selection leads you to give that answer? _____

_____

_____

Critical Thinking Questions

CRITICAL THINKING LEVEL 1 REMEMBER

Identify a synonym for each element on the CARS Checklist.

Credibility _____

Accuracy _____

Reasonableness _____

Support _____

CRITICAL THINKING LEVEL 2 UNDERSTAND

Go to the database InfoTrac College Edition using your school or library Web site. Do a keyword search for "Abraham Lincoln's death." You can refine the search as needed. Click on the Academic Journals tab at the top of the page. Find one article that deals with eyewitness accounts of Lincoln's assassination. E-mail it to yourself using the "Tool" box found within each article on the top right side of the page. Bring the article to class to discuss.

CRITICAL THINKING LEVEL 3 APPLY

Identify ways in which the article you chose in Critical Thinking Level 2 shows credibility, accuracy, reasonableness, and support.

Title: _____

Credibility: _____

Accuracy: _____

Reasonableness: _____

Support: _____

CRITICAL THINKING LEVEL 4 ANALYZE

Analyze which of the following people would be considered credible because of their expertise in the fields they are matched with. You will need to go online or to the library to collect information about each person. Give two or three reasons why you think they are or are not expert in that field.

Person	Expertise	Yes or No	Why or Why not
Dr. Kenneth Cooper	brain surgery		1. 2. 3.
Michael Pollan	writing and environmental issues		1. 2. 3.
Linda Chavez	social issues such as labor, civil and human rights, and immigration		1. 2. 3.
Mia Hamm	violinist		1. 2. 3.
Stanley Kubrick	director and producer		1. 2. 3. 4.

CRITICAL THINKING LEVEL 5 EVALUATE

In Reading 12-2, the author says that "reliable information is power." Evaluate the accuracy of the following information by finding a reliable Web source (based on information learned in this chapter) that confirms or refutes the information.

1. "JUST A REMINDER . . . In a few weeks, cell phone numbers are being released to telemarketing companies and you will start to receive sales calls. YOU WILL BE CHARGED FOR THESE CALLS. . . . To prevent this, call the following number from your cell phone: 888/382-1222. It is the National DO NOT CALL list. It will only take a minute of your time. It blocks your number for five (5) years. PASS THIS ON TO ALL YOUR FRIENDS. . . ."

2. The artificial sweetener aspartame has been linked to cancer, Alzheimer's, and several other diseases.

3. Meet Molly—a horse with an artificial leg.

4. Barack Obama is a radical Muslim.

5. There is a Web site you can go to increase your vocabulary and donate food to the hungry at the same time.

CRITICAL THINKING LEVEL 6 CREATE

With a partner *create* a biography (life story) that a person might have in order to be a credible source for some subject that you are interested in. For example, if I am interested in scuba diving, what education, experience, knowledge, and so forth would a person need to have with scuba diving for me to take them seriously? Together with your partner, pick an interesting subject and then create the biography of your expert.

● Vocabulary in Context

The following words were used in "Evaluating Internet Research Sources." Select the best word to complete the meaning of each sentence.

accommodating	continuum	screen	proficient	indicator

Many parents _____ their daughters' suitors. They will want to see how you present yourself or what type of car you own as an _____ of your upbringing and social status. Once you become _____ at understanding how to reassure parents, you might find they can be quite _____. However, it may not always be easy to endear yourself to the parents of the girl you are interested in because, as with most people, their personalities are on a _____.

appendix

A Guide to Reading Novels

"Beginnings are usually scary and endings are usually sad, but it's everything in between that makes it all worth living."

—Sandra Bullock as Birdee Pruitt in
Hope Floats

Reading novels is different from reading nonfiction, as you have been doing throughout this book. Novels are fiction. A novel represents truths about life through character, plot, setting, theme, and symbolism, among other means. Reading a novel is sometimes less straightforward than reading nonfiction, especially nonfiction that is designed to inform readers. Novels have an expressive purpose, so even if readers do wind up feeling they have learned something from a novel, the author's main purpose is to tell a story. Stories are often about how a character or characters change because of their experiences.

The reader's role, however, is similar in reading both fiction and nonfiction. As Angela Carter, a novelist and short story writer, puts it: "Reading a book is like re-writing it for yourself. You bring to a novel anything you read, all your experience of the world. You bring your history and you read it in your own terms." Your prior knowledge matters just as much in reading a novel as it does in reading nonfiction.

Your instructor may assign a particular novel for you to read and give you particular instructions for how to read it. If so, be sure to follow those directions. If not, you may want to use the following brief guide. After the guide you will find a list of novels that reading students around the country often read in their classes. Finally, a list of books that have been made into movies appears, along with a few suggestions for how to think about a work when it appears in two mediums.

Build Some Prior Knowledge

As Angela Carter notes, you bring your prior knowledge to reading a novel—the experiences you have had in the world and the knowledge you gained by living those experiences. Another kind of prior knowledge—knowledge of the different elements that literary authors use to develop a character and a story—is also helpful in reading fiction. In other words, knowledge of these elements will help you build a schema for reading novels.

Be Aware of Literary Elements

- **Characters: Fictional people.** When you read novels, notice what the characters say, what other characters say about them, how the characters look, and how the characters act. At least one of the major characters usually changes over the course of the story, usually in response to emotional or physical challenges or crises.

- **Point of View.** The narrator of a novel is the person who tells the story. The narrator is not the author. The author creates the narrator, and the narrator may not believe, think, or feel what the author does.

  The narrator can tell the story from two different points of view: first person or third person (see pages 480–481). A first person narrator is often a major character (but not always). First person narrators can be reliable or unreliable (just like real people!).

A third person narrator tells the story from a different perspective. Some are omniscient: they know everything, including what each character thinks. Some are limited; these focus on what a single character knows. Other narrators tell the story from a greater distance. Even though they know everything that happens between characters, they can't see into characters' minds. These are called objective narrators.

- **Plot.** The plot is the pattern of events in the story. The author reveals the plot by what characters say to each other and how they interact, by how the different events that occur are arranged, and by cause and effect relationships. The plot doesn't always happen in time order. Sometimes there are flashbacks (scenes from the past).

  The plot usually includes a section called the *exposition* in which the author sets up the background for the story. It includes *complications* that arise as the characters interact, which lead to one or more small *crises*—moments of tension in which important decisions are made. These lead up to a major crisis—the *climax*. The main character(s) changes significantly because of the crisis. After the major crisis is over, the *denoument* ties up some of the plot's loose ends.

- **Setting.** The setting is the place and time of the story. Important elements of the setting may be the physical circumstances, the historical time period, and the country or region in which the plot takes place.

- **Symbolism.** A symbol is a person or thing or action that has two layers of meaning: a literal layer and a figurative layer. (You read about figures of speech in Chapter 10.) At the literal level, the thing is exactly what is seems to be. At the figurative level, it has a more complex meaning; it stands for something more abstract or more general.

- **Author's Style and Tone.** The style and tone are based the some of the same aspects that you think about when reading nonfiction (see Chapter 10). How the author uses words and sentence structures creates a certain feeling. So do the figures of speech such as metaphor, simile, personification, and hyperbole. How the author uses symbols is part of the style, also. The author's tone toward the characters and the story might be optimistic, cynical, humorous, ironic (see pages 483–484), or any of the tones listed on page 487.

- **Theme.** Theme is the central idea or point that the novel makes about life. Think about theme as an implied main idea (see Chapter 6). The author never states the theme, but it is there for readers who think about the novel and let it affect them deeply. The theme is different from the plot. The plot is what happens; the theme is what must be true for the plot to happen. The theme is also not the subject; it's a larger point. If the subject of a story is a particular person, for example, the theme is about what that person' actions reveal about people.

To Survey a Novel or Not to Survey

If your instructor gives you particular directions for surveying a novel, follow them. Otherwise, you might think about the following:

1. **Don't survey.** You can't use the same surveying techniques on a novel that you would on a piece of nonfiction. You would not get an overview of the important points, for example, by reading only the first sentences of paragraphs. Instead, consider immersing yourself in the novel in the order in which the novelist presents it: starting on page 1.

2. **Survey the "edges" of the book.** Reading any copy there may be on the inside and outside of the book covers (called "cover copy") may give you some insight into the main plot, reveal interesting details about the author, or reprint comments made by other authors who read the book. This is more like surveying around the book than surveying the book itself, but doing this survey does give you more of a context for starting to read.

3. **Survey the table of contents.** Sometimes novels include tables of contents. If the table of contents includes chapter titles, reading them may give you a sense of the author's tone, the settings in which the plot will unfold, or the characters' names. If you preview the table of contents, notice what predictions your mind makes out of the titles, or the movement from one chapter title to the next.

4. **Read the first paragraph of a chapter.** If you are reading a novel for class, consider reading the first paragraph of the assigned chapter as a survey. Linger over it. Squeeze out any impressions you can from the name of the character, the description of the setting, or the movement of the plot. What tone is the author setting up? Consider why the author wanted to use the beginning of the chapter—an important spot—for this particular scene. Make a prediction about the chapter. You might list all the ideas you get from the first paragraph before you read the chapter. When you finish the chapter, go back to your list and see if any of your ideas were borne out.

Entering the World of the Novel

If your instructor gives you particular directions for reading a novel, follow them. Otherwise, you might think about the following:

1. **Enter the world of the novel as a believer.** While it is the author's job to write the novel in such a way that you do believe in it, as the reader you can choose to enter

this world as a believer or as a doubter. If you are going to read the novel twice, you can read it the first time as a believer, and the second time as a doubter. (Reading as a doubter is good when you need to write an analysis of the novel.) But if you are going to read it just once, then read as a believer—enter the author's world as a whole-hearted participant.

2. **Read faster and then slower.** If you are reading a novel for class, you'll need to apply some strategies to make sure you understand it well enough to talk about it in terms of the elements of literature listed on pages 640–642. A strong strategy in this situation is to read the assigned section once through at your own pace with the purpose of enjoying the novel and seeing what happens to the characters. Then read the same material more slowly, pausing often to think about what the author is doing. You can assume that the author has a reason for putting each scene and each description right where it is. Ask yourself questions that you make up from the list of literary elements. For example, you can ask yourself "Who are the major characters? Why are they doing what they are doing? Why does the author describe them in the way that he or she does?" and so on. You can make up questions from each one of the elements and think about the possible answers.

3. **Write in the margins and write on separate paper.** Using a pencil, write brief comments in the margin of the novel. Especially write comments that deal with "how" and "why" the author is doing something. On separate paper, write out your fuller responses. You might want to respond to the characters, or to the plot, or to the symbols, tone, or setting.

4. **Write a paragraph (or more) in response to any of the following questions.** They ask you to investigate your personal responses to the novel.
   - Which character do you care about the most? Why?
   - Which character do you dislike the most? Why?
   - What is the most confusing part? What makes it confusing?
   - What is the most interesting scene? What makes it interesting?
   - What is the most important scene? What makes it important?
   - What is the most important symbol? What makes it important?

Reflecting on the Novel

Once you have read the whole novel, it's a good time to take stock of what you read. Your instructor may ask you to complete certain activities to help you sum up the book. Consider these activities as well:

1. **Trace the main character's development.** Using the information from the literary elements list under "character" and "plot," write a timeline or description of the major events that the main character went through and how each one changed the character.

2. **Describe the main conflict.** What is the central conflict in the novel? Who is involved? How do you know this is the main conflict and not just one of the more minor crises?

3. **Write a statement of the novel's theme.** Review the information under "theme" on page 641–642. See if you can write out a statement of the theme. What is the author saying about the world, or about life, or about how people act in general under certain conditions?

4. **Talk about the novel.** In addition to, or instead of writing in response to the first three activities, talk about them with a small group of classmates. Go around the circle of people, allowing each person to start off with the reactions they had as individuals. As each person listens to the others, his or her ideas will probably start changing and deepening. Keep going around the circle until no one has anything left to say about the topic.

Some Novels That People Are Reading

The following is a list of novels that students from around the country are reading. To find out more about any of these novels, go to Amazon (**http://www.amazon.com**) and type in the title. Scroll down until you see the customer reviews or editorial reviews if you want to read an overview of the plot. Be careful! You may find out what happens later in the book.

You can also just get a sense of some novels by using the "Search Inside" feature. Scroll back up to the top of the page and look above the image of the book cover. If it says "search inside," you can click on that. Then click on "front cover," "table of contents," "excerpt," "back cover," or "surprise me!" The excerpt will be the first page or two of the novel.

Alias Grace, by Margaret Atwood

The Alchemist, by Paulo Coelho

Angels and Demons, by Dan Brown

Bastard Out of Carolina, by Dorothy Allison

Beloved, by Toni Morrison

The Book Thief, by Markus Zusak

Call of the Wild, by Jack London

Catch Me If You Can, by Frank Abagnale

The Cell, by Stephen King

The Color of Water, by James McBride

The Count of Monte Cristo, by Alexandre Dumas

The Curious Incident of the Dog in the Night-Time, by Mark Haddon

Disgrace, by J. M. Coetzee

The Five People You Meet in Heaven, by Mitch Albom

Frankenstein, by Mary Shelly

Fried Green Tomatoes at the Whistle Stop Café, by Fannie Flagg

The Golden Compass, by Philip Pullman

The Great Gatsby, by F. Scot Fitzgerald

Harry Potter (series), by J. K. Rowling

Hole in My Life, by Jack Gantos

Holes, by Louis Sachar

The House on Mango Street, by Sandra Cisneros

The Hunt for Red October, by Tom Clancy

The Joy Luck Club, by Amy Tan

Kindred, by Octavia Butler

A Lesson Before Dying, by Ernest Gaines

The Lion, the Witch, and the Wardrobe, by C. S. Lewis

Lord of the Flies, by William Golding

The Lovely Bones, Alice Sebold

The Nanny Diaries, by Emma Mclaughlin and Nicola Kraus

The Notebook, by Nicholas Sparks

The Pearl, by John Steinbeck

Point of Impact, by Stephen Hunter

The Rapture of Canaan, by Sheri Reynolds

The Reader, by Bernhard Schlink

The Secret Life of Bees, by Sue Monk Kidd

The Small Room, by May Sarton

To Kill a Mockingbird, by Harper Lee

A Thousand Splendid Suns, by Khaled Hosseini

A Time to Kill, by John Grisham

The Time Traveler's Wife, by Audrey Niffenegger

Tuesdays with Morrie, by Mitch Albom

Twilight (series), by Stephenie Meyer

A Walk to Remember, by Nicholas Sparks

What Looks Like Crazy on an Ordinary Day, by Pearl Cleage

Women of the Silk, by Gail Tsukiyama

A Sampling of Novels That Have Been Made into Movies

The book: *Of Mice and Men,* by John Steinbeck

The movie: *Of Mice and Men,* starring Gary Sinise and John Malkovich

The book: *Where the Heart Is,* by Billie Letts

The movie: *Where the Heart Is,* starring Natalie Portman and Ashley Judd

The book: *Like Water for Chocolate,* by Laura Esquivel

The movie: *Como Agua Para Chocolate,* starring Lumi Cavazos and Marco Leonardi

The book: *Bringing Down the House,* by Ben Mezrich

The movie: *21,* starring Jim Sturgess, Kevin Spacey, Laurence Fishburne, and Kate Bosworth

The book: *Prince Caspian: The Return to Narnia,* by C. S. Lewis

The movie: *Chronicles of Narnia: Prince Caspian,* starring Ben Barnes, Georgie Henley, Skandar Keynes, William Moseley, Anna Popplewell

The book: *Atonement,* by Ian McEwan

The movie: *Atonement,* starring James McAvoy and Keira Knightley

The book: *Harry Potter and the Order of the Phoenix,* by J. K. Rowling

The movie: *Harry Potter and the Order of the Phoenix,* starring Daniel Radcliffe, Rupert Grint and Emma Watson

The book: *Casino Royale,* by Ian Fleming

The movie: *Casino Royale,* starring Daniel Craig and Eva Green

The book: *The Da Vinci Code,* by Dan Brown

The movie: *The Da Vinci Code,* starring Tom Hanks and Audrey Tautou

The book: *The Devil Wears Prada,* by Lauren Weisberger

The movie: *The Devil Wears Prada,* starring Meryl Streep and Anne Hathaway

The book: *Memoirs of a Geisha,* by Arthur Golden

The movie: *Memoirs of a Geisha,* starring Ziyi Zhang, Suzuka Ohgo, and Ken Watanabe

The book: *Sahara,* by Clive Cussler

The movie: *Sahara,* starring Matthew McConaughey, Steve Zahn, and Penelope Cruz

The book: *Sisterhood of the Traveling Pants,* by Ann Brashares

The movie: *Sisterhood of the Traveling Pants,* starring Amber Tamblyn, Alexis Bledel, America Ferrera, and Blake Lively

The book: *The Mist,* by Stephen King

The movie: *The Mist,* starring Thomas Jane, Marcia Gay Harden, Laurie Holden, and Andre Braugher

The book: *The Kite Runner,* by Kaled Hosseini

The movie: *The Kite Runner,* starring Khalid Abdalla, Homayon Ershadi, Shaun Toub, Atossa Leoni, Said Tashimaoui

To find more books that have been made into movies, you can visit the following site: **http://www.bookreporter.com/features/books2movies.asp**

A Few Tips for Reading the Book and Seeing the Movie

If your instructor gives you particular directions for reading a novel and seeing the movie, follow them. Otherwise, you might think about the following:

1. **Which comes first . . . the book or the movie?** This question has caused a great debate. Some people feel strongly that you should watch the movie first. This way, you will not be disappointed because the movie did not live up to the expectations you had for it. For example, this happened with the movie *Eragon.* Many fans of the book did not like the movie because they felt it was not as good as the book. Another reason given is that by watching the movie first, you will be better able to understand the plot and character interactions in the book. Others swear by reading the book first. They say that you then have a better perspective of the story while you are watching the movie. Sometimes a movie gives a book more depth or adds another dimension to it. You may have more insight into the story and you can enjoy the director's interpretations of a story you enjoyed.

   We think either one is okay. While it is more often the case that the book is better than the movie (because you are using your imagination), both media can be helpful whether you are reading for pleasure or for insight in order to write a report. Reading and viewing are both fun!

2. **Compare and contrast the book and the movie.** Whether you read the book first or watched the movie, a great way to approach the second media choice is by looking for similarities or differences between it and the first. For example, how are the characters, point of view, plot, setting, symbolism, style and tone, and theme of the author and director similar or different?

3. **Compare and contrast your interpretation of the book versus the director's interpretation.** This is similar to the previous suggestion, except you approach it from your point of view. How is the director's vision of the film different or similar from your interpretation of the characters, point of view, plot, setting, symbolism, style and tone, and theme? If you had been the director, what would you have kept the same or done differently?

4. **Pause and take notes.** Whether you are reading first and watching second or vice-versa, stop and take notes of the similarities or differences you want to emphasize while you are in the process of reading or watching. It is much easier to take a moment and stop reading or hit pause and write down your thoughts than it is to go back and try to remember everything from beginning to end.

Good luck and enjoy!

Credits

Chapter 1

p. 9: "'Three Little Words' on Good Morning America (But Not 'Where is Charlie?'" by Brian Stelter, New York Times, Oct. 26, 2007. Copyright ©2007 New York Times. All rights reserved. Reprinted by permission.

p. 16: From "Olympian Ambitions" by Mark Starr, Newsweek, Dec. 31, 2007, p. 56. Copyright ©2007 Newsweek, Inc. All rights reserved. Reprinted by permission.

pp. 27–32: "Amid War, Passion for TV Chefs, Soaps and Idols" by Barry Bearak, New York Times, August 1, 2007. Copyright ©2007 by New York Times. All rights reserved. Reprinted by permission.

pp. 40–43: From *Sociology: The Essentials* 4th ed., by Margaret L. Andersen and Howard F. Taylor, Cengage Learning, p. 52–53. Copyright © Wadsworth, a part of Cengage Learning, Inc. Reprinted by permission. www.cengage.com/permissions.

Chapter 2

p. 50: From T.B. Kashdan, P. Rose, and F.D. Fincham, "Curiosity and exploration: facilitating positive subjective experiences and personal growth opportunities," *Journal of Personality Assessment* 82, 291–305. Reprinted by permission of Taylor & Francis Ltd.

pp. 51–52: "Cultivating Curiosity" by Elizabeth Svoboda, *Psychology Today*, Sept.–Oct. 2006, p. 57–58. Copyright ©2006 Sussex Publishers, LLC. Reprinted by permission.

pp. 52–53: How to Flex Your Curiosity Muscle from "Incitements to Inquiry" by Elizabeth Svoboda, *Psychology Today*, Sept.–Oct. 2006, p. 58. Copyright © 2006 Sussex Publishers LLC. Reprinted by permission.

pp. 62–63: From *Sociology: Your Compass for a New World*, 3rd ed., by Robert J. Brym and John Lie, Cengage Learning, pp. 20–23. Copyright ©2007 Wadsworth, a part of Cengage Learning, Inc. Reprinted by permission. www.cengage.com/permissions.

pp. 66–68: From *Sociology: Your Compass for a New World*, 3rd ed., by Robert J. Brym and John Lie, Cengage Learning, pp. 20–23. Copyright ©2007 Wadsworth, a part of Cengage Learning, Inc. Reprinted by permission. www.cengage.com/permissions.

pp. 75–78: "Trained by Inmates, New Best Friends for Disabled Veterans," by Stephanie Strom, New York Times, Oct. 31, 2006. Copyright ©2006 New York Times. All rights reserved. Reprinted by permission.

pp. 84–88: Adapted from "Language and the orangutan: The old 'person' of the forest," in P. Cavalieri and P. Singer, eds., *The Great Ape Project,* pp. 45–50. Reprinted by permission of St. Martin's Press.

Chapter 3

p. 120 (Fig. 3.4): "Prefixes" table from *Teaching Phonics and Word Study in the Intermediate Grades by Wiley Blevins,* Scholastic Professional Books, p. 206. Copyright ©2001 by Wiley Blevins. Reprinted by permission of Scholastic, Inc.

p. 121 (Fig. 3.5): "Suffixes" table from *Teaching Phonics and Word Study in the Intermediate Grades* by Wiley Blevins, Scholastic Professional Books, p. 206. Copyright ©2001 by Wiley Blevins. Reprinted by permission of Scholastic, Inc.

p. 121: "Reticent" definition from Dictionary.com, retrieved April 5, 2007. Based on the Random House Unabridged Dictionary, Copyright ©2006 Random House, Inc.

pp. 130–132: "Vocabulary—A Treasure Chest for Success" by Ken Olan, from *American Chronicle,* Sept. 20, 2006. Reprinted by permission of the author.

pp. 140–141: From *Sociology: The Essentials* 4th ed., by Margaret L. Andersen and Howard F. Taylor, Cengage Learning, pp. 59–60. Copyright © Wadsworth, a part of Cengage Learning, Inc. Reprinted by permission. www.cengage.com/permissions.

Chapter 4

pp. 150–151: "The Passion of Vision" from *First Things First to Live, To Love, To Learn,* by Stephen Covey, A. Roger Merrill, and Rebecca R. Merrill, pp. 103–104. Reprinted by permission of Franklin Covey Co.

pp. 187–189: From *American Government and Politics Today,* 2007–2008 edition, by Schmidt, Shelley and Bardus, Cengage Learning, pp. 153–154. Copyright ©2007 Wadsworth, a part of Cengage Learning, Inc. Reprinted by permission. www.cengage.com/permissions.

pp. 198–201: "Wiping out TB and Aids" by Michael Satchell, *U.S. News & World Report,* Oct. 31, 2005. Copyright ©2005 U.S. News & World Report. Reprinted by permission.

Chapter 5

pp. 210–212: From "Before Models Can Turn Around, Knockoffs Fly," by Eric Wilson, *New York Times*, Sept. 4, 2007. Copyright ©2007 New York Times. All rights reserved. Reprinted by permission.

p. 225: From *Backpacker* magazine, October 2006, p. 32. Reprinted by permission of the author.

p. 228: "Heart-Healthy Diets," adapted from "Heart Healthy Eating," WomensHealth.gov, U.S. Dept. of Health and Human Services.

pp. 242–244: "Salmon, Shirts, and the Meaning of Low Prices," from *The Wal-Mart Effect*, by Charles Fishman, pp. 183–187. Copyright ©2006 by Charles Fishman. Reprinted by permission of The Penguin Press, a division of Penguin Group (USA) Inc.

pp. 254–257: From *Sociology: Your Compass for a New World*, Brief edition, by Robert J. Brym and John Lie, Cengage Learning, pp. 204–206. Copyright ©2007 Wadsworth, a part of Cengage Learning, Inc. Reprinted by permission. www.cengage.com/permissions.

Chapter 6

p. 266: "Seduced by Snacks? No, Not You" by Kim Severson, *New York Times*, Oct. 11, 2006. Copyright ©2006 New York Times. All rights reserved. Reprinted by permission.

p. 290: "Portion Control: Change Your Thinking or Your Plate?" by Karen Collins, R.D., American Institute for Cancer Research. Reprinted with permission from the American Institute for Cancer Research, www.aicr.org.

p. 297 (Table 6.2): Missouri Diabetes Prevention and Control Program http://www.dhss.mo.gov/diabetes/portionsizeguidelines.pdf.

p. 300: From *An Invitation to Health*, 12th ed. by Hales, Cengage Learning, pp. 176–178. Copyright ©2007 Brooks/Cole, a part of Cengage Learning, Inc. Reprinted by permission. www.cengage.com/permissions.

Chapter 7

p. 320: From *Sociology: Your Compass for a New World*, Brief edition, by Robert J. Brym and John Lie, Cengage Learning. Copyright ©2007 Wadsworth, a part of Cengage Learning, Inc. Reprinted by permission. www.cengage.com/permissions.

p. 353: From Weiten, *Psychology: Themes and Variations* 7th ed., Cengage Learning, pp. 408–411. Copyright ©2007 Wadsworth, a part of Cengage Learning, Inc. Reprinted by permission. www.cengage.com/permissions.

p. 358 (Fig. 7.4): Reproduced from "Martial Status and Happiness," by David G. Myers, Figure 19.1, in *Well-Being, The Foundations of Hedonic Psychology,* edited by Daniel Kahneman, Ed Diener, and Norbert Schwarz. Copyright ©1999 Russell Sage Foundation, 112 East 64th Street, New York, NY 10021. Reprinted with permission.

Chapter 8

p. 375: Used by permission of Cagle Cartoons, Inc.

p. 387 (Fig. 8.4): From Popenoe, David and Barbara Dafoe Whitehead, *State of Our Union: The Social Health of Marriage in America* 2005, Figure 1. Copyright ©2005 by the National Marriage Project at Rutgers University. Reprinted by permission of the National Marriage Project.

p. 389 (Fig. 8.5): From Popenoe, David and Barbara Dafoe Whitehead, *State of Our Union: The Social Health of Marriage in America* 2005, Figure 7. Copyright ©2005 by the National Marriage Project at Rutgers University. Reprinted by permission of the National Marriage Project.

p. 399: From *Sociology: Your Compass for a New World,* 3rd ed., by Robert J. Brym and John Lie, Cengage Learning, pp. 322–324. Copyright ©2007 Wadsworth, a part of Cengage Learning, Inc. Reprinted by permission. www.cengage.com/permissions.

p. 402 (Fig. 8.9): From "The 1997 Body Image Study Results" by David M. Garner, *Psychology Today,* Vol. 30, No. 1, pp. 30–44. Reprinted with permission from Psychology Today Magazine, copyright ©1997 Sussex Publishers, LLC.

p. 411: From Weiten, *Psychology: Themes and Variations* 7th ed., Cengage Learning, pp. 168–169. Copyright ©2007 Wadsworth, a part of Cengage Learning, Inc. Reprinted by permission. www.cengage.com/permissions.

p. 413 (Fig. 8.11): From Joseph Alber, *Interaction of Color.* Copyright ©1963 and reprinted by permission of the publisher, Yale University Press.

Chapter 9

p. 430: "Britney to Rent, Lease or Buy" by David Pogue, *New York Times,* August 7, 2005, p. 2-1. Copyright ©2005 New York Times. All rights reserved. Reprinted by permission.

Chapter 10

Chapter 11

pp. 522–523: "Immigrants Work on as Bill Dies" by Randal C. Archibold, *New York Times*, June 30, 2007. Copyright ©2007 New York Times. All rights reserved. Reprinted by permission.

pp. 536–537: "A Virus Among Honeybees," *New York Times*, Sept. 11, 2007. Copyright ©2007 New York Times. All rights reserved. Reprinted by permission.

pp. 537–539: "Off the Charts: Double Warning that a Recession May Be on the Way" by Floyd Norris, *New York Times*, Sept. 15, 2007. Copyright ©2007 New York Times. All rights reserved. Reprinted by permission.

pp. 545–548: From Murrin et al., *Liberty, Equality, Power* 5th ed, Cengage Learning, pp. 976–978. Copyright ©2008 Wadsworth, a part of Cengage Learning, Inc. Reprinted by permission. www.cengage.com/permissions.

pp. 556–558: "The Founding Immigrants" by Kenneth Davis, *New York Times* opinion, July 3, 2007. Copyright ©2007 New York Times. All rights reserved. Reprinted by permission.

Chapter 11 Casebook

pp. 556–571: From *An Inconvenient Truth* by Al Gore. Copyright ©2006 by Al Gore. Reprinted by permission from Rodale, Inc., Emmaus, PA 18098.

pp. 575–578: ©2007 by S. Michael Craven, Responding to 'Green Politics' - Part V July 2, 2007, accessed at http://www.battlefortruth.org. Reprinted by permission of the author.

pp. 582–586: From *Cool It: The Skeptical Environmentalist's Guide to Global Warming*, by Bjorn Lomborg, pp. 3–9. Copyright ©2007 by Bjorn Lomborg. Reprinted by permission of Alfred A. Knopf, a division of Random House, Inc.

Chapter 12

pp. 617–619: "Google Zooms in Too Close for Some" by Miguel Helft, *New York Times*, June 1, 2007. Copyright ©2007 New York Times. All rights reserved. Reprinted by permission.

pp. 627–630: "Evaluating Internet Research Sources" by Robert Harris, June 15, 2007, accessed at http://www.virtualsalt.com/evalu8it.htm. Reprinted by permission of the author.

Index